ACCULTURATION IN SEVEN AMERICAN INDIAN TRIBES

ACCULTURATION

IN SEVEN AMERICAN INDIAN TRIBES

EDITED BY

RALPH LINTON

Professor of Anthropology
Columbia University

GLOUCESTER, MASS.

PETER SMITH

1963

PREFACE

The primary purpose of this book is to make available information on the acculturation process as it has gone on and still is going on in certain American Indian tribes. A second purpose is to take stock of what is now known about acculturation in general and to present certain conclusions which appear to be justified in the present state of our knowledge. It is hoped that these conclusions may serve as a basis for further investigation in the acculturation field.

All the reports of tribal acculturation which have been included in the present volume are the results of original field work on the part of their authors. In addition to the information on acculturation, they all include a considerable amount of new and hitherto unpublished ethnological material. The field work in question was financed in part by grants made to the Department of Anthropology by the Social Science Research Council of Columbia University in connection with a project for the study of Acculturation which continued from 1930 to 1937. Further field work in the Summer of 1937 was financed partly with budgetary research funds of the Department of Anthropology of Columbia University, partly with the assistance of the Federal Works Progress Administration. Thanks are due to all these agencies and especially to Dr. Edward Kennard, Director of this Writers' Project. Further thanks are due to the Social Science Research Council for a grant, given in connection with the activities of their Committee on Personality and Culture, which has defrayed the expenses of preparing this volume for publication. Thanks are also due the Council for the opportunity given the editor to serve with Drs. Redfield and Herskovits on a subcommittee on acculturation. It was this work which provided the main stimulus for the production of the present book.

R. L.

INTRODUCTION

Recent years have witnessed a steady increase of interest in the phenomena which result when groups of different cultures are brought into contact. Under current conditions the understanding of these phenomena is of great practical importance. Contact situations always entail a certain amount of friction and of conflict in interest. As White world dominance declines, the direct and forceful methods which Europeans have hitherto employed in their dealings with other groups become less effective and more dangerous to their users. There is an obvious need for new techniques and for exact knowledge upon which the development of these techniques can be based. Here in America the problems present themselves in somewhat different forms. The phenomena of contact between groups of different culture has been with us since the first Whites landed, but in the rich new land they did not cause much trouble to the dominant group. Prior to the World War it was assumed that the absorption of minority groups into the American population required nothing more than time and not a great deal of that. European immigrants of all nationalities would be fused in the melting-pot. Indians would die out, with the few survivors losing themselves in the White population. The Negro problem would take care of itself somehow although meanwhile they must be kept in their place. None of these comfortable assumptions have been borne out in practice. Although many of the European immigrant groups have been completely assimilated, others show a strong tendency to survive and encyst themselves in the body politic. Far from dying out, the Indians have become the only racial element in our population with a birth-rate above that required for replacement and have postponed their transformation into Whites indefinitely. Lastly, the rise of racial consciousness and pride among the Negroes and the increasing bitterness of economic competition has widened the gap and made even their final assimilation into the White population somewhat improbable. The need for intelligent handling of all these situations is obvious and it is equally obvious that the first step toward successful planning must be to ascertain the general factors present in all contact situations and how they operate. Only when this has been done can we hope to control and direct the forces at work..

One of the results of the increasing interest in phenomena associated with group and culture contact was the appointment by the Social Science Research Council of a sub-committee on Acculturation, operating under their general committee on Personality and Culture. This sub-committee, consisting of Dr. R. Redfield, Dr. M. J. Herskovits, and myself, with Dr. Redfield as chairman, functioned from 1935 to 1938. In the course of this work it became evident that, although there was a surprising amount of literature already available on the subject of acculturation, much of it did not lend itself readily to the use of the comparative method. Although many of the accounts of acculturation situations were excellent in themselves, they differed widely in techniques of presentation and in their authors' selection of particular aspects of the total situations for purposes of intensive description. It was felt that a series of studies all of which had been prepared in accordance with a single plan or outline would be extremely useful for the testing of certain hypotheses. It is the aim of the present volume to provide such a series of studies together with brief preliminary analyses and a discussion of acculturation phenomena.

The development of a satisfactory outline for the presentation of material already collected by field-workers did not appear difficult in the abstract. The previously mentioned sub-committee on acculturation had already prepared and published "A Memorandum for the Study of Acculturation" (*American Anthropologist, Volume XXXVIII*, pp. 149–152). This proved extremely useful, but unfortunately much of the material upon which the reports had to be based had been collected before the memorandum appeared. There was the further difficulty that the material obtainable with regard to various aspects of the acculturation process differed considerably from one tribe to another. Thus in some cases the early contacts with Whites and their results were well documented; in others there was almost no information. Again, it was plain that certain tribes had been profoundly influenced by their contacts with other aboriginal groups while in other cases such influences could not be traced. The authors of this book were, therefore, confronted with two alternatives. They could present their material according to an outline which would fall within the limits of the information available for all the tribes studied, or they could present it according to an ideal outline of the information which acculturation studies should contain, leaving gaps in those places where the desired information was not available. If the first of these methods had been followed, a great deal of useful and pertinent material with respect to particular tribes would have had to be ruled out. Actually, the material has been organized, as far as possible, according to the following outline:

OUTLINE FOR REPORT ON ACCULTURATION IN ANY GIVEN TRIBE

1. The Aboriginal Community
  A. Size and Density of Population
  B. Economics (Resources, Technology, Trade, etc.)
  C. Social Organization
    1. Families and Kin Groups
    2. Other Social Groupings (Classes, Societies, etc.)
    3. Patterns of Social Dominance
  D. Political Organization
    1. Formal Organization
    2. Powers of Central Authority
    3. Techniques for Control of Individual
  E. Supernaturalism
    1. Concepts
    2. Practices
    3. Functions
  F. Mores
    1. Property Attitudes
    2. Sex Attitudes
    3. Respect Attitudes
  G. Foci of Interest in Culture (Value System)
  H. Integration and Contemporary Rate of Culture Change
2. Influences from Other Aboriginal Groups

In the general discussion of acculturation which concludes this volume, the editor has not confined himself strictly to conclusions drawn from a comparative study of the cases here presented. Although it might have been better to do so from the point of view of formal methodology, such an approach would have left the discussion incomplete at several points. Thus, as far as this report is concerned, the case of the Fox is unique and no general conclusions can be based upon it. None of the other Indian communities described have made an adaptation of a similar sort or become, as it were, encysted within the local White society. An extension of the comparative horizon shows that this situation is a fairly common outcome of close cultural contact, and enables us to draw certain conclusions as to the factors which may produce it. Again, the tribes described in the present volume show a relatively low incidence of nativistic movements, although we know that such movements are a rather common accompaniment of situations of dominance and submission and although many of such movements have been described elsewhere. The editor has, therefore, drawn freely on earlier reports of acculturation situations and on the theoretical discussions of the acculturation process which have already been published. Among the workers in this field, his heaviest debt is to Melville J. Herskovits and to Robert Redfield with both of whom many of the conclusions presented in this book have been discussed.

CONTENTS

ACCULTURATION IN SEVEN AMERICAN INDIAN TRIBES

· I ·

THE PUYALLUP OF WASHINGTON
by Marian W. Smith

The Indians of the southern end of Puget Sound [1] entered into treaty with the government of the United States on Christmas Eve, 1854. The treaty was consummated near a creek known as *tᵘdádab,* a name of ill omen derived from the word for sorcerer or shaman. Since that day it has been unanimously called the Treaty of Medicine Creek. It embraced the Puyallup, the Nisqually, Steilacoom, Squakson and others of the small bands of Coast Salish living on the Puget Sound inlets; it was superintended by the newly arrived Governor of Washington Territory, Isaac Stevens, and signed among others by the ethnographer, George Gibbs. Three reservations were set aside for the use of the Indians, the Squakson, on the island of that name, the Nisqually, on the middle Nisqually River, and the Puyallup, at the mouth of the Puyallup River. The treaty followed the first White settlement in the region by a period of only twenty-two years and it immediately precipitated the local Indian war of 1855–56. Today the Squakson reservation is almost uninhabited, the Nisqually is shrunk to a percentage of its former extent and the Puyallup has been opened up to make way for the busy city of Tacoma, Washington. Because of the peculiarity of the latter situation the discussion which follows has been oriented around the Indians of the Puyallup, a name which is applied throughout to several aboriginal groups all of which took up their residence on the Puyallup Reservation.

[1] For further discussion of the life lived by the Indians before the coming of the Whites see the author's "Puyallup-Nisqually," *Columbia University Contributions to Anthropology, Volume 32* (in press). The material for that work and for the present paper was obtained in the field under the auspices of the Columbia University Council for Research in the Social Sciences.

In aboriginal times the Puyallup commanded the water entrance to the southern Sound. Their villages were placed either on small streams which tumbled down to the Sound from the high lands of the Kitsap Peninsula, or along the river system which drained the west slope of Mt. Rainier and the country lying between the mountain and Commencement Bay. The waters of these streams flowed in a radial network, all of them pointing eventually toward a hub located at or around the mouth of the Puyallup River, the present site of Tacoma, just south of which the Sound narrowed forming a bottle-neck entrance to its upper reaches. The Indians' river canoes plied the Puyallup and its tributaries even when the water was most shallow in midsummer and the bolder sailors of the villages near the Sound made long trips in seaworthy canoes which braved all but the most violent of winter storms.

It was a land with a heavy rainfall, a temperate land of swamps, extensive tide flats, damp, overgrown gullies and sudden floods. The bed of a stream might shift fifty feet in a single year only to return to its old channel the following spring. Salmon were plentiful and could be caught in the Sound at any time of year, but the great catches were made at large fish traps set across streams and operated when the salmon came up into fresh water to spawn, especially during the runs in spring and fall. At these times the fish were cut and smoked, and prepared to keep indefinitely in storage for winter and emergency use. Various kinds of berries and roots were also gathered in quantities for storage and hundreds of clams were smoked each year. Seal and porpoise abounded in the Sound. Black bear fed in the swamp land and deer came down to the shelter of the heavy timber when the weather in the higher foot-hills became severe. Vegetation was so thick that the hunter kept to deadfalls raised well above the underbrush to be able to see any distance at all, and great cedars with twelve-foot buttes fought for space to spread their dark, pendent branches. It was a land which offered food for the taking, a land in which people were said to be starving if their winter diet of smoked and dried food was not varied daily by the addition of fresh fish or meat. But it was a lowering, dank land hemming its inhabitants between walls of thrusting growth.

Open country was apt to be only along water courses swept by tide and flood, and each village was set at the mouth of a stream above the tide flats where it entered the Sound or, in the case of tributaries, at its junction with another stream. The houses were built solidly of split cedar planks, the ridge-pole of the rather high gable roofs following the length of the building. Doorways were placed at each end on a line with the roof peak and, as every house paralleled the bank of a stream above its outlet, one door faced up-stream toward a narrowing vista of water and clear bank and the other faced the wider expanse where two waters met. These really served as back door and front door. With the exception of the village at the mouth of the Puyallup River and that at the junction of the Puyallup and the Carbon, each village was built on its own small stream. No people lived above it on that stream. Traffic passed along the Sound or the main channel of the Puyallup system reducing the directions to "up-Sound" and "down-Sound" or "up-stream" and "down-stream." Canoes approaching in either direction became visible from the front door facing the water artery.

The term "village" suggests a cluster of small houses. But the typical Puyallup village consisted of a single large communal dwelling. It was occupied by most of its inhabitants over a good portion of the year and was seldom left completely alone. The small stream furnished the village with salmon, wood was obtained along its upper reaches and floated or carried back to the house site, hunting followed its course, and berry-pickers found the easiest path to their berry patches lay along its shores. Chance encounters were well nigh impossible in this region; each village supplied its own needs from its own stream and in the matter of raw material there was little to choose between them. For supplies which were not available near the home stream families took longer trips. Famous hunters sometimes went to the mountains for elk, and hunters and harpooners might be gone several days in search of bear or seal. Exceptionally good root or berry patches, clamming grounds and places where the materials for basketry grew most plentifully were often visited at certain seasons of the year by several families from one village. On these longer expeditions away from the village they might expect to encounter other families bent upon the same errand and the meetings were turned into occasions of holiday. Everyone worked, it is true, but the spirit of social relaxation was at its height. Except for these meetings and for the more formal visiting which took place during the winter months, the Indians preferred to stick pretty closely to the familiar neighborhood of their local stream beds.

The house itself was divided into four or six sections, depending upon its length, each of which served as the living quarters of a single family group. Down the length of the house from doorway to doorway ran a sort of passageway which was kept relatively free at all times. The house sections were at either side, one in each corner and, in larger houses, two facing each other in the center of the building. There were no partitions nor any indication that the goods of the family were so arranged as to delimit floor space, but each had its own portion of the bed platform which ran around the walls of the house, of the storage platforms above, and of the drying racks which extended as high as the roof peak. More important than floor space or sleeping or storage space was the fact that family groups maintained their own cooking fires built on stones let down into the dirt floor or directly on the hardened dirt itself. They were laid along the center passageway in pairs. Occasionally several feet separated the fires of each pair so that a lane lay between the fires from end to end of the house. In narrower buildings the fires were built against a log which served as an effective guard, throwing the heat of each fire toward the house section to which it belonged. During fair weather most of the day's activities were carried on out-of-doors, but in storms and early on winter evenings the people gathered in the house. The central passage was open to the use of all and was the site of common recreations such as story-telling and the playing of organized children's games. However, persons kept fairly strictly to their own quarters. The sense of family privacy was strong, centering around the cooking activities which were done quite independently at each fire. As will be brought out more clearly later, nothing could be further from the situation generally associated with communal or the dormitory type of living.

Since the country provided such an adequate food supply, it is not possible to estimate the population before the coming of the

Whites without referring to these living conditions. Although the village at Quartermaster Harbor was not located on a creek, the number of villages was almost exactly determined by the number of permanent streams. The village sites, the streams along which the houses were built, and the people who lived at the sites and habitually made use of the areas surrounding the streams were all called by the same names. There was no physical reason why village sites could not support more than one communal house. But, for reasons which will appear more fully later, the entire southern Sound region with the possible exception of the Squakson boasted only one village which maintained two communal houses for any length of time. That one was at the point where Clark's Creek entered the Puyallup. Very important shamans had their own houses generally across the stream from the other house of the village. They were of the same construction built on a somewhat larger scale, but, nevertheless, they housed only the shaman's own family group. It is safe to say that there would not have been more than one such famous shaman to every six villages.

The author's estimate of the aboriginal populations given in the table on pages 8–11 is based upon an average family group of five, determined from data on ten families who lived in three communal Indian houses about sixty years ago. The estimate also assumes that each village contained one house with six fires, i. e., space for six family groups, giving the average village a population of about thirty. Five is a conservative figure for family groups under aboriginal conditions for they included the unmarried, the widows and widowers. Yet it is probably not far off. Smaller houses had four fires instead of six but it is felt that the discrepancy this would cause is balanced by the fact that occasional villages had additional houses. The number of the villages themselves remained constant. The estimated number of the Squakson is the only one which does not fit in with known data. These people associated closely with the Twana and information was not received from them direct. The figure for them is low, either because there were additional villages or because villages normally had more than one house, or for both of these reasons. Despite the startling correspondence between the total population estimated and that of several of the printed census figures listed, the estimate was made *before* those figures had been brought together for the purposes of this paper. Since there were thirty-four autonomous villages in the Treaty of Medicine Creek, with no fixed relations between them, it is small wonder that "tribal" population figures vary considerably. According to the estimate the eighteen villages which later took up residence upon the Puyallup reservation would have numbered about 540 persons.

POPULATION TABLE

Date	Authority	Name	Description	Population
Estimate (aboriginal conditions)		Nisqually (7 villages)	Nisqually River and vicinity	210
		Squakson (2 villages)	North Bay	60
		Sahehwamish (6 villages)	South Bay, Budd Inlet, Eld Inlet, Totten Inlet and Shelton Inlet	180
		Puyallup [2] (11 villages, one of which was not later on this reservation)	Streams emptying into Commencement Bay and their tributaries	330
		Shomamish [2] (3 villages)	Gig Harbor, Wollochet Bay and Quartermaster Harbor	90
		Shotlemamish [2] (3 villages)	Carr Inlet	90
		Steilacoom [2] (2 villages)	Steilacoom	60
			Total	1020
			Puyallup [2]	540
1844	W. F. Tolmie	(Stak-ta-mish) [3]		(207) [3]
		Squak-s'na-mish		135
		Se-heh-ma-mish		92
		Squalli-a-mish		471

[2] Groups which took up allotments on the Puyallup Reservation.

[3] Chehalis and upper Cowlitz, "upper" or "back people" according to Puyallup terminology, not included in Medicine Creek Treaty nor in this reckoning.

Date	Authority	Name	Description	Population
		Pu-yal-up-a-mish [2]		207
		S'ho-ma-mish [2]		118
			Total	1023
			Puyallup [2]	325
1849	J. Lane	Homamish [2]	from the narrows	500
		Hottunamish [2]	along western	
		Iquahsinawmish	shore of Puget	
		Sáyhaynamish	Sound	
		Stitchafsamish		
		Squallyamish	about the Nis-	550
		Puallip [2]	qually, Puallip	
		Sineramish	and Sineramish	
			Rivers	
			Total	1050
			Puyallup [2]	350(?)
1852	E. A. Starling	Stitcheo-saw-mish	Budd's Inlet and	30
			South Bay, vicin-	
			ity of Olympia	
		Squally-ah-mish	Nisqually Bay and	100
			vicinity	
		Pualli-paw-mish [2]	Puallis River, bay	200
		or Puallis	and vicinity	
		Sho-mam-ish [2]	Vashon's Island	40
		Sroo-tle-mam-ish [2]	Cases Inlet	60
		Quack-ena-mish	Cases Inlet	100
		Say-hay-ma-mish	Totten Inlet	35
			Total	565
			Puyallup [2]	300
1854	I. Stevens	Quak-s'n-a-mish	Cases Inlet	40
		S'Hotla-ma-mish [2]	Carr's Inlet	27
		Sa-heh-wa-mish	Hammersley's Inlet	23
		Sa-wa-mish	Totten's Inlet	3
		Squai-aitl	Eld's Inlet	45
		Steh-cha-sa-mish	Budd's Inlet	20
		Noo-seh-chatl	South Bay	12
		Squalli-ah-mish	Nisqually River	184
		(6 bands)	and vicinity	

[2] Groups which took up allotments on the Puyallup Reservation.

Date	Authority	Name	Description	Population
		Steila-coom-a mish	Steilacoom Creek and vicinity	25
		Puyallup-a-mish [2]	Mouth of Puyallup River	50
		T'qua-qua-mish [2]	Heads of ditto	50
		(Su-qua-mish) [4]	(Peninsula between Hoods Canal and Admiralty Inlet) [4]	(485) [4]
		S'ho-ma-mish [2]	Vashon's Island	33
			Total	512
			Puyallup [2]	160
1858	M. T. Simmons	Nisqually Puyallup Squaksin Squeit-letch Stetch-as Chit-hutbands		1020
			Total	1020
1880	R. H. Milroy	Puyallup [2]	Reservation	539
		Nisqually	"	105
		Squaksin	"	91
		Olympia band	Off reservation	12
		South Bay band	" "	15
		Mud Bay band	" "	26
		Gig Harbor band [2]	" "	8
			Total	796
			Puyallup [2]	547
1884	Puyallup Commission		*Puyallup* [2]	565

The population table should be used with certain facts in mind. Joseph Lane, M. T. Simmons and R. H. Milroy were capable men, trusted by their Indian neighbors, with whom they were closely associated over a period of years and by whom they are still mentioned. Considerable confidence may be placed in their figures, although Lane's estimates on other parts of the Sound country are less reliable.

Starling was located as Indian agent at Fort Steilacoom apparently

[2] Groups which took up allotments on the Puyallup Reservation.
[4] Not included in Medicine Creek Treaty nor in this reckoning.

for about a year and we are told that shortly after his arrival Indians poured in to see him for "curiosity and expectation of presents; and all extremely desirous to learn the intentions of the government in regard to purchasing their lands." There is little doubt that the visitors would be mainly those on friendly terms with the Indians of the Steilacoom village at the site of which the fort had been erected. Steilacoom had its most important contacts with the Puyallup River, the lower Nisqually and the Squakson, and it is probable that Starling's figures are fairly accurate for these groups. The main Nisqually River groups and some of the villages of the upper Puyallup River seem not to have been included at all. The figures for the inlets are certainly too low, such numbers as thirty-five and forty evidently indicating single house groups.

According to every other census the Steven population figures are 50 per cent short. They are included partly because of their historical significance and partly because their discrepancy with other figures is so consistent. It will be noted that adding the Su-qua-mish to his list brought its total up to that of other estimates. His figure for this group is at least 400 per cent too high.

The most significant functioning economic unit in this population was the group of people living in the communal house. Family groups assumed responsibility for their own subsistence. But the importance of the house group lay in the fact that within it activities were coördinated by an efficient economic specialization. If a man was especially fond of mountain huckleberries his was generally the only family group which took the long trip inland to procure a large supply of that berry for drying. Other families went for clams, wapato, etc. Frequently specialization of this sort even broke up the family unit. While a man went hunting, accompanied by his wife and young children who helped dry the meat he was able to procure, an older girl might prefer to go with another family bound for clamming grounds in the opposite direction, and if she became expert at the smoking and curing of clams that fact would determine in part the expeditions taken by her family group after she married. Family specialization did not interfere with the more usual routine of fishing. But in a few fields special skills were raised to the rank of professions. Although a woman who was an expert basket-maker had the usual woman's chores to perform, unless there were slaves or helpers who could be trusted with them, the man who was a skilled wood-worker, who made canoes and paddles and carefully shaped tools and ceremonial objects, devoted almost his entire time to that alone. Hunting and harpooning were also professions. They required not only skills in connection with the actual pursuit of game but also particular paraphernalia which were made, repaired and constantly conditioned.

In addition to these professions the Puyallup held the qualifications for two other positions in mind—the leader and the warrior. The leader was the more important, the "chief," according to popular phrasing. According to Puyallup terminology, "he came first." Through his energies the family activities were coördinated, he was far-seeing, objective, just. He was an expert in human relations, a master diplomat and conciliator, who accomplished his ends quietly without obvious effort. He was never boastful nor aggressive.

The warrior, on the other hand, specialized in aggression. He met every situation belligerently. What he wanted he demanded, and it was usually handed over to him without question. Under normal conditions one of the leader's main concerns was to settle difficulties which the behavior of the warrior precipitated. But when the village was threatened by aggression from without, when defense or retaliation was needed, the leader stepped aside and the warrior, as an expert in war, took matters into his own hands. The bulwark of his protection might be necessary at any time for the safety of the group, and without him it could not long have functioned as an economic unit.

The ideal village contained a professional, a leader *and* a warrior. However, few groups of house community size could boast so much. Actually, leadership was invested in men who showed combinations of these traits. Each house had a leader, its most outstanding man of any one of the three types. Really important men, whose reputations spread beyond the confines of their own village and whose word, consequently, carried authority in wider circles, excelled in some special skill, were aggressive when occasion demanded, but had the self-control to constrain that aggression under ordinary circumstances. The relative importance of villages varied considerably over a period of years according to the character of their leaders. Without important men a group was self-sufficient but its standard of living was appreciably lower. Famous men spread their influence over such villages and there was a tendency for contiguous villages to establish common judgments by which leaders and laymen recognized a hierarchy of ability among their members. This was especially true of the villages in close proximity to one another on the lower Puyallup River. This hierarchy was solely in terms of prestige and operated only upon the comparatively rare occasions when the groups came together. It never served to form any formal organization of a political nature and organization of such a variety remained completely foreign to Puyallup standards.

A leader was said to "own" the house in which he "came first." Frequently it had been built under his supervision and repairs were suggested or approved by him, although it might happen that he supplied neither material nor labor. He could not evict members of the cohering family groups, however, without extreme loss of prestige and he had no right of disposal. It amounted to the fact that all ownership was phrased in purely individualistic terms. The house, as a symbol of group unity, was not really felt to constitute property. Staple foods, likewise, although they were gathered by individual effort, were not denied to those who needed them. Starvation for one family was inconceivable so long as food was available to any, although the sort of living which could be obtained by complete dependence upon other members of the group was subsistence in its most meager form. Within the house group different families had dissimilar standards of living. Both men and women "owned" the things which they produced, and it is clear that there must have been considerable exchange of service and property within the family as well as within the house community. An informant said, "If a man tanned some skin his wife had to sew it for him and it was his; if she made a basket and traded it for a piece of buckskin and made it up, it was hers; but if she sewed on her own material and did not do his he could make trouble." Beyond such statements it is not possible today to learn anything of the give and take which undoubtedly existed.

Different kinds of property, however, may still be distinguished. Certain things, such as ornaments, clothing, tools, etc., which were constantly used by an individual, became identified with his or her personality. The right of disposal of these objects lay completely and absolutely in the hands of the individual. What was in his possession at death was laid away with him. The use of such articles by other individuals was inconceivable under any circumstances and for that reason their loss did not constitute an economic loss to the community. A second class included those which were difficult to procure or to manufacture or which were necessary to the continued maintenance of the family group. Objects made of stone, large canoes and slaves always belonged to this class. They were inherited within the kin group, the most aggressive brother or son often laying claim to and obtaining them. There were no fixed rules of inheritance, and serious quarrels frequently arose over property of this type. A third class lay between these two: objects such as dentalium strings, coiled or twined baskets in good condition, unused clothing, stored food supplies, blankets and, in later days, the white man's money. These were clearly items of wealth accumulated for purposes of wealth display. During the individual's life he or she disposed of such articles in ways best fitted to enhance prestige. They were constantly employed in ceremonial exchange. At the death of the individual they were distributed among the persons who attended the funeral and served, as during their owner's life, to enhance his prestige and enrich his memory. Finally, therefore, they were redistributed for economic manipulation to a number of scattered persons of different communities.

Trade and ceremonial exchange have already been suggested as means of attaining the fluidity of economic goods. The latter was understood in terms of a more widespread practice, that of gift-giving. Gifts expressed friendly relations between the donor and the recipient. It was by gift that the impoverished were maintained and it was on the basis of gift-giving that the economic unit of the family and the house group functioned. Some gifts arose from pure friendliness, others again with a certain calculation of effect. Important also were those given as an assurance of good will by A to B when A himself was conscious of some act on his part that might be interpreted by B as antagonistic. Gifts of this type cleared away suspicion of ill will and laid the foundation for continued friendship. They were not fines in any sense of the word. In all cases the size of the gift depended upon the economic status of the giver, and the amount did not influence the intention even though persons who were known to be financially able to give considerable amounts had higher prestige.

The importance of gift-giving among the Puyallup as an assurance of friendship can be fully appreciated only against the background of their religious convictions. In accordance with these convictions every individual was thought to have a supernatural power, an effective entity, procured around the age of puberty and from that time until death intimately identified with his or her personality. This power was quite apart from the soul, which lent, after all, only the rather indiscriminate quality of humanity. Every one of a man's individual characteristics, his appearance, his skills, his abilities, was dependent upon the nature of the supernatural he had obtained. The concept is today often expressed in English by the idea of a "partnership." The relationship between man and the objects of his everyday world, and that between man and his fellow men, also depended in the last analysis upon these powers. Accidents were ruled out. Things which happened for a man's good happened because of the influence of his own supernatural partners. Mischances were due to the malicious influence of the powers of other people. If a dead branch fell in a hunter's path, if a man stumbled at the doorway as he entered the house in which he lived, if his seine floated off on the crest of an unusually high wave, it was due to interference by the power of some one other person—the relative walking behind him, the acquaintance staring at him from the far corner, or the enemy he had made in the village across the Sound. Ill will and revenge motivated such action only in part. Powers often acted without the conscious direction of their human allies. And the most frequent single motive was a simple test of prowess to determine the relative strength of individuals. It is impossible to exaggerate the state of constant suspicion and surveillance that these beliefs placed the Indian in as a necessary accompaniment to all human relationships.

Shamans differed from other persons only because of the greater strength of their power. The shaman was able to send his power to attack that of some one else, and a battle between the two was waged within the victim's body. When the shaman's power was the stronger, as it generally was, the victim became ill and eventually died unless the foreign power could be withdrawn by another shaman. Curing and killing both were thus in the hands of the shamans and both were aspects of the same supernatural entities. Actually, shamans tended to lean toward one or the other facet of their calling, gaining reputations either as doctors or as sorcerers, but both were given the same name. In ceremonial practice the two were never quite separate, and fame in either was enhanced by success in the other. This did not imply that there was no place in Puyallup ideology for death by natural causes, but it did mean that every case of illness, however slight, and every death was open to the suspicion of sorcery. The shamans themselves were the only diagnosticians. There was no hocus pocus, no magical technique, which had to be performed and by which the culprit could be recognized or intercepted in his work. Frequently, as has been said, the deed was performed without his volition. Even shamans could not tell the identity of the guilty party until the curing ceremony had been performed and they had finally in their hands the power which had caused the trouble and which was now visible to them. Laymen were seldom able to see powers, and that withdrawn by the doctor was never seen by them in any form. The ultimate test of guilt occurred only upon the death-bed of the victim. The power spoke through its victim's voice so that all might hear, calling out, "I am so and so. No one was strong enough to get *me* out. *I* killed him because I am so strong."

Boasting of this kind even under less dramatic circumstances was a characteristic displayed by shamans. They often openly hinted that it was their power that had caused such and such an illness or death. The way to meet their boasting was by a similar show of aggression, to "brave them down." The best person to accomplish this end was another shaman. It was, therefore, to the advantage of a village to number a shaman among its members. Just as the aggressive attitude of the warrior warned outsiders that they would encounter difficulties if they attempted to coerce anyone in his presence, so the shaman also served as a protection to the village in which he lived. Without his power the village was more open to attacks by the powers of others, more liable to sickness and the loss of its members.

Famous shamans sometimes fought with one another in an attempt to demonstrate their superiority. This was done by a sort of shamanistic power duel. A, a shaman, sent his power out against the power of B, a second shaman. While their powers ranged against each other the shamans themselves were safe in their respective villages which might be many miles apart. If A proved stronger, one of the members of B's village was taken with a sudden illness and unless B, or a third shaman called in later, could effect a cure, the person died. If B proved stronger, A's power returned and lodged in one of the members of his own village who, in turn, was taken ill. This attack, however, was not apt to be serious so long as A was willing to take his power from the patient and the practice was not looked upon with great disfavor by A's fellow villagers because it showed that he was strong enough to engage in the duel, the end point of shamanism. Yet it was on this account that a famous shaman usually had his house at some distance from the main communal house of the village. If his power boomeranged it would be more apt to lodge in one of his own family group. Because of the duels, also, it was said that the children of shamans seldom grew to adulthood. Shamans were not averse to trying out their powers upon their relatives but if they fell into disrepute with the members of their village they were always subject to the death penalty for their activities. In the last analysis sorcery was reprehensible and no direct reprisal for the murder of a proven "killing" shaman was possible. Nevertheless, if his village favored a shaman his murder was unlikely because of the ill will the act would occasion.

The members of a village were a relatively amicable group. Despite the disparity in economic status between families within the communal house, a poor family in a well-to-do village was better off than one in a poorly organized and uncoöperative house group. The standard of living depended upon the ability of the leader, and the economic position of each family reflected directly upon his prestige. Whether warrior or harpooner, or true leader, the man who "came first" in the household was generous with other members of the group. Individual differences in ability were clearly recognized but they were thought of as largely qualitative, detracting from interest in a quantitative comparison along a fixed scale of value. Economic specialization developed to the point where each individual had a definite rôle which he or she played without let or hindrance. When a specialist grew elderly he gradually handed over his knowledge to a younger member of the group who showed a willingness or aptitude for training. If he died in his prime, however, the group was deprived of just so much until a younger man or woman grew to take his place or until another specialist in the same field could be brought in by marriage. The alternative was the production of more items by other specialists in order to fill the deficiency in the economy of their own families by trade with persons of neighboring villages. But the village aimed as closely as possible at self-reliance and economic self-sufficiency.

The stratum of suspicion underlying human contacts penetrated every phase of social life. Husband-wife, parent-child, sibling, and in-law relationships were subject to it. Close contacts afforded increased social irritation and intensified suspicion. Mutual trust between individuals, especially between mates, was not too rare an occurrence, but it had to be carefully nurtured. Within the family group, i. e., the related persons who used a single cooking fire, suspicion was at a minimum. The only accepted rule of inheritance had to do with the stability of this group. Since the family was bilateral and residence either matrilocal or patrilocal, its original personnel changed considerably with time, losing and gaining members through marriage. A newly married couple did not ordinarily set up as a separate unit until after the birth of one or more children and, if house sections were not readily available and the family remained congenial, the separation was indefinitely postponed, the efficient maximum of the group being seven or eight individuals of varying ages. The house section "belonged" to the couple that set to housekeeping in it and remained in the possession of the family so long as the continuity of the group was maintained. Thus, the position of responsibility was assumed by the most capable son or son-in-law residing in the group at the death of the father. The family continued unchanged except that its nucleus shifted from one generation to the next. The house section, with sole rights of occupancy, belonged to the group or to any adult who survived its other members. It was not uncommon, therefore, to find one whole section of a communal house occupied by an old man or woman who worked, cooked, ate and lived alone while the next section was sadly over-crowded. Every effort was made to retain the coöperative efficiency of the family; internal irritations became unendurable and were solved whenever possible by splitting the disruptive factions.

Within the house community suspicion ran rampant. But it is necessary to remember that that suspicion had little or nothing to do with economic function. Ordinary power activities never touched an economic level. The financial success of a man was due to his own power and was beyond the reach of the malicious influence of other powers. The constant property exchange between members of the group not only served to establish the show of friendship under circumstances which might otherwise have developed into open antagonism but it was also the expression of a certain degree of amicability, an amicability grounded in the fact that each individual had his own niche which did not conflict with that of his neighbor. There was no rivalry between members of the same village. The prestige of each person reflected the prestige of others of the group and was bolstered by their backing. But it was quite impossible for the village to stand the strain of a situation which involved two men competing for prestige in the same field. It could never hold two warriors, two leaders, or two of any other specialty. So long as the addition of new houses did not interfere with the equilibrium of the social set-up the community could be expanded to include them. This was the case with the so-called "potlatch house" in which the shaman lived alone with his family. Separate communal houses, on the other hand, implied separate leaders and the addition of a new house would have developed almost automatically into a self-destructive antagonism. Despite grudges, suspicions and personal feuds, outwardly competitive situations occurred only between villages. Thus, gamblers practised constantly, but gambling with another member of the home village was inconceivable; and the prestige of only one man in each village depended upon his worth as a wrestler and bets were not placed unless the opponents were from different villages.

In practice, peace could not always be maintained. Families which did meet in summer were those most able to get along together. But winter meetings between whole villages always threatened violence which could generally be avoided only because (1) the success of gambling and ceremonial depended upon both participants and on-lookers ridding their minds of ill will; (2) the prestige of leaders involved the skill with which they kept their adherents under control on such occasions; and (3) the distribution of property at the ceremony and the exchange of gifts established temporary friendliness. Whether the meeting were large or small, it was expected that the malicious activity of shaman and other powers would be stimulated, carefully covered as always by a show of kindly feeling. Peace in the home village was also transient. Any crisis might transform toleration into antagonism, adequate excuse being ever possible on the accusation of adultery or of sorcery. Normally, however, self-interest held A's suspicion of B in a nice balance with B's suspicion of A.

The equilibrium of specialists within the house group was largely attributable to house exogamy. Marriages were always arranged between individuals of different house groups, in effect, therefore, between different villages. This process scattered the kin group over a wide area. It was usual, but not necessary, for members of house groups to be related. The prime factors determining membership were those already discussed, only slightly influenced by the kinship system. Succession was never fixed. If a man had gained importance as a warrior and one of his elder sons showed signs of following in his steps, it was immediately evident that the situation would become intolerable so soon as the boy reached an age at which he might assert his own personality. In choosing a wife he might best serve all interests if she came from a village without a warrior, in which he could take up residence and develop his capacities. Only if the son who took after his father chanced to be a younger son, so that he would reach maturity as his father's powers began to fail, would the marriage be patrilocal with chances of succession. Brothers seldom succeeded in living amicably together unless their traits were totally dissimilar. By placing them in separate villages their rivalry was erased from every day affairs; each made his reputation; and, in case of rivalry from a third source, they could join forces. The main function of the extended kin group was that of hospitality and safe conduct; it did not deter power activities, however disastrous, nor did it prevent assassinations for adultery or sorcery. But just as the individual's prestige was bolstered by that of other members of his house group, so also illustrious kinfolk lent him a sort of reflected glory. The best way to placate an enemy was to maneuver a marriage between his family and yours, and marriages were consistently cited by informants as parallel to the white man's treaties.

The Puyallup had tied themselves by exogamous marriages to scattered villages as far north as the Skagit, south to the Cowlitz and Lower Chehalis and westward to the Coast. Beyond these limits lay enemy peoples known only by hearsay or because of their raids into local territory. Actual contacts, on however slender a basis, since they affected only the kin groups immediately involved, were established and reaffirmed by marriage. These villages lay along the drainage west of the Cascade Range. The area east of the same mountains was inhabited by Sahaptin-speaking peoples who lived roughly the same type of village life but who had the reputation of being more closely organized than the Puyallup and Salish. Mainly because of this they were held in some fear and were collectively known as *tóbcadad,* or band of warriors. In accordance with the accepted manner of dealing with such situations, the Puyallup groups nearer the foot-hills had instigated and accepted marital ties with the Sahaptins until considerable intermingling had taken place. One peculiar factor greatly influenced the results of intermarriage, however. Women went east with their Sahaptin husbands, but men from the Sound country flatly refused to take up permanent residence east of the mountains. Although visiting was fairly frequent, there is not one case on record where a man moved into Sahaptin territory. Even today their objection to it is summed up by, "It's too dry. And there's no wood!" But both men and women filtered west across the mountain passes and settled in the homes of their affinal relatives. The infiltration of Sahaptins into the Puyallup and neighboring valleys thus greatly outnumbered the corresponding eastern movement of Salish, and while, east of the mountains, villages tended to retain their original character, those near the western foot-hills became bilingual.

By the period of White contact the westward seepage had extended about midway on the rivers. Very little, if any, pure Sahaptin blood was to be found on the shores of the Sound itself. The newcomers were taller on an average, and the population of the up-river Salish groups showed a definite tendency toward a height greater than that of groups without this new hereditary strain. Although they were most tenacious of their language, there can be little doubt that other phases of life as well as the linguistic were also influenced. Much work remains to be done among the Sahaptins and the exact effect of their culture upon the local Salish one is difficult to trace. But it is clear that the two cultures differed radically on very few scores and that these were rather readily absorbed.

The coming of the horse brought about a more spectacular change in culture. Although it is difficult to ascertain a positive date, it is nevertheless probable that the introduction of the horse to the southern Sound antedated the heavy infiltration of Sahaptins. The early type of trapping, noticeably the stirrup, was of a wooden construction similar in design to other Salish objects and quite unlike the leather ones adopted later from Sahaptin horsemen. The Cowlitz and Chehalis prairie sent a tongue north to the Nisqually River, back of Steilacoom and on almost to the Puyallup, which afforded a more likely entry than any across the difficult trails of the Cascades. The horse or equine culture of the Sound occurred along the path of the prairie; at no time was it synonymous with groups dominated by Sahaptin influence. Along the Nisqually the bilingual villages coincided roughly with those which possessed horses. But the prairie touched the Puyallup River below its upper reaches and the single village of the Puyallup peoples, which depended in any sense upon the horse, had relatively slight contacts east of the mountains. The upper, bilingual Puyallup villages had few or no horses. In view of these facts, it seems more probable that the presence of the horse on both sides of the Cascades later stimulated contacts than that the horse owed its position in Sound country to those contacts.

Whatever the period of introduction and the direction its influence took, the horse definitely affected the life of the peoples whose villages bordered the prairie pasture lands. It became usual to speak as though there were two types of Indian: the "horse" and the "canoe" Indian. Although only four villages were actually near good pasture, persons of contiguous groups claimed that they were "horse" Indians despite the fact that they owned no horses or, if they did, that the animals died regularly each winter due to the lack of feed in the heavily forested regions. The greater mobility made possible by the use of horse transportation for cross-country travel was raised to the level of a class distinction. The "horse" Indian, irrespective of whether he rode or walked, left the river systems and struck across country for hunting, etc., as his neighbors never did. In his village he could hardly be distinguished from them but he spent less time there. The majority of the population retained its intense devotion to one locality, its local stream bed, and was correspondingly scorned. The class differentiation was not recognized as such by this majority among the "canoe" Indians, but was strong enough in the small group affected to somewhat retard exogamous marriage between the two types. Thus, the prairie village on the Puyallup was the single southern Sound site which maintained two communal houses. They had endured for at least three generations, and intermarriage between them was the rule rather than the exception, house and close kin exogamy being, of course, retained. In other respects, especially in so far as the purposes of this paper are concerned, the culture of the "horse" Indians hardly differed from their Salish neighbors and relatives.

This gives, in brief, a picture of the Indians of the Treaty of Medicine Creek at the advent of the White man. The first recorded White contact occurred when Vancouver sent a ship's boat under the command of Puget and Menzies nosing south of the Narrows in the year 1792. The boat was challenged by a small company of Puyallup under the leadership of a warrior, and farther south it encountered a few bold family groups in canoes and one temporary encampment. Basing his conclusion upon this apparent lack of living inhabitants and upon the neglected air of certain sections bordering the shore, which were given over to the disposal of the dead, Vancouver supposed the Sound population to have been recently decimated by plague. Smallpox journeyed well in advance of its White carriers and quite possibly had hit the Sound before the end of the eighteenth century. Nevertheless, the communal houses of the southern inlets were so situated as not to have been visible from the Sound, and the "graveyards" of the Puyallup were never tended, so that these facts alone indicate only that the people were following their usual tactics of keeping out of harm's way. To their minds the Puyallup had successfully intimidated the invaders, for were not they and their villages intact? News of this feat undoubtedly reached the mouth of the Nisqually before canoes ventured out. But, in any case, a large part of the population, however numerous, would have preferred to play safe.

Early in the nineteenth century Whites penetrated across the continent to the Columbia River, and vessels from the trading posts of the northern coast reached its mouth. The trade controversy between the Hudson's Bay Company and the Astoria Fur Company centered along the Columbia, and by 1818 had arrived at a compromise, the so-called policy of joint occupancy, by which both English and American nationals were given rights of Indian trade. Although the posts lay considerably south of their territory the Indians of the Medicine Creek Treaty undoubtedly benefited indirectly by this trade, through the Chehalis.

The first direct contact occurred some years later, in 1832, when the Hudson's Bay Company set up a subsidiary, the Puget Sound Agricultural Company, with headquarters at Nisqually House on Nisqually Bay. As its name would indicate, the post was not intended primarily for trade but was the center of a permanent agricultural settlement on the Nisqually and Cowlitz prairies. The prairie land was well suited to cultivation and was homesteaded by retiring employees of the Hudson's Bay Company who planned to spend the rest of their lives there as farmers and land-owners. Nisqually House prospered. Captain Wilkes made it the base of the exploring expedition he conducted for the United States government in 1841. By 1845 settlement had spread to Tumwater near the site of Olympia, present state capital. The post was the only one along the coast between the Columbia and what is now British Columbia and, although the treaty accepting the forty-ninth parallel as boundary between the United States and Great Britain was made in 1846, the Puget Sound Agricultural Company held its properties until 1869.

In 1849 occurred two events of importance to the newly settled Sound region: the Wallace incident and the California gold rush. The former involved the Snoqualmie Indians who lived on the river of that name. Under their warrior-leader, Patkenim, they had several times successfully raided the Nisqually. Another raid now centered upon Nisqually House and one man, Wallace, was killed. According to report, Patkenim's avowed purpose was to rid the country of the Whites. Probably, also, he identified Whites who settled in Nisqually territory as Nisqually themselves and was disgruntled at the continued influx of goods which the new village had brought to his enemies. The episode resulted in the precipitate removal of the main body of the post from the Nisqually River northward to Fort Steilacoom where a contingent of troops was stationed thereafter. This move brought White trade to the doorstep of the Puyallup. The California gold rush accentuated the contact. The suddenly increased population to the south demanded supplies and more supplies. The Columbia River and Puget Sound were convenient, compared to eastern ports, and both were in a position to ship lumber and food. Settlers buzzed toward the Northwest to supply the demand. Mills produced shingles and building materials, brick kilns were set up and there was a lively trade in oysters. Seattle, first settled in 1851, jumped to a population of three hundred in four years and the whole region felt the impact of White industry.

The problem of some sort of land agreement with the Indians became pressing. Agents had already been sent out, and at the end of 1854 the first treaty, that of Medicine Creek, was signed, and ratified almost immediately. The Indians of the southern Sound resigned ownership of their lands except for three reservations, the Nisqually, Squakson and Puyallup. The headquarters was placed on Squakson Island and arrangements were included for a school, an acting physician, and a farmer-in-charge. The island is an hour and a half from Tumwater by motor launch and the original treaty plan was eventually to segregate the Indians upon it. But the plan did not reckon with the "horse" Indians. Whether or not they signed the treaty seems still undecided,[5] but it is certain that the reserved lands covered no pasturage except for a small strip on the Nisqually Reservation quite inadequate for herds which had greatly increased during the recent boom. There had never been a village site on the island for it had no salmon stream; it was heav-

5 E. S. Curtis, *The North American Indian*, Harvard University Press, Cambridge, Mass., 1913, *Volume 9*, pp. 16–19.

ily wooded almost to the shore line, and it served only as a summer clamming ground for a few groups of strictly salt-water Indians. No self-respecting "horse" Indian would have been caught dead on Squakson Island. Writing some time later, George Gibbs was most insistent upon a distinction between the two Indian types which had not been taken into account in the treaty itself. The period happened to coincide with a general Indian unrest to the east and south and, egged on by their Sahaptin relatives, the Sound Indians engaged in the hostilities labeled the War of 1855-56.

Several White families were massacred, apparently by the warriors who, on the same night, warned other settlers and carried their children to safety. There were considerable movements of federal troops and volunteers, intermittent sniping activities and finally a concerted attack upon Seattle. With the exception of this attack the warfare was an unorganized affair of personal grudges. The greater part of the Indians showed their good faith by giving themselves up to the authorities and were subsequently gathered on Squakson Island. The Snoqualmie warrior, Patkenim, was enlisted to bring in the head of his enemy Leschi, the Nisqually ringleader. Excitement ran high. Leschi was betrayed by one of his close relatives, brought in to Olympia and sentenced to be hung by the civil authorities. The army and a number of civilians protested the decision without effect. The affair dragged on until in August, 1856, Governor Stevens called a council of Indians on Fox Island "to inquire into the causes of discontent and finding that the Nisqually and Puyallup were dissatisfied with the extent of their reservations, not without a show of reason, he agreed to recommend an enlargement, and a re-survey was ordered. . . ." [6] The war had accomplished its purpose; the unsuitability of Squakson Island as agency headquarters became increasingly apparent; and in 1861 the center shifted to the Puyallup Reservation.

From the time of first White contact, no permanent missionary efforts had been carried on among the Puyallup. In 1838 two French priests followed the Hudson's Bay Company into the Northwest, and the following year missions were held at Cowlitz

[6] H. H. Bancroft, *History of Washington 1845-89*, The History Company, San Francisco, Calif., 1890, *Volume 31*, p. 170.

and Nisqually. Father de Smet visited the region in 1842, and two years later brought with him priests, lay brothers and six sisters of Notre Dame de Namur. By 1847 there was a religious colony of twenty-two persons on the Columbia River and the next spring an oblate father opened a mission on Budd Inlet. But religious teaching of the Puyallup was still only intermittent. Father de Smet had come out in answer to the famous Flathead delegation which journeyed to St. Louis in its search for missions, and the same appeal reached Methodist missionaries, one of whom fixed a mission at Nisqually in 1840 which was abandoned after a little under two years. Not until 1876 was the agency allotted to the Presbyterian Board of Domestic Missions and the Reverend M. G. Mann took up his residence on the Puyallup Reservation. In a year he had a church of 130 members and had also taken over the direction of the school which had been established in 1871. That year the agency employees were temporarily dismissed because of insufficient funds for the Indian Service of the Territory, but Mann stayed on as pastor at his own and the Indians' request. By 1881 there were two churches, a Catholic one of fifty members and the Presbyterian with 200 under the same Reverend Mann, an unusually tolerant and intelligent person who continued his work with the Indians for many years. Before this, however, the education and training in White ways available to the Puyallup was not so haphazard as the brief review of the formal opportunities might suggest.

From the beginning the Whites who came into the Puget Sound area intended to stay; they were settlers on the fertile prairie lands and men who put capital and labor into mills and kilns. There was no introductory period when contact was only through traders. Money was to be made but it was made by hard work. It was still no country for White women. As late as 1857 canoes filled with warriors came from the north, raided the Snohomish, and continued up Sound as far as Steilacoom from whence they were escorted by a revenue cutter. In October of the next year the *Puget Sound Herald*, published at Steilacoom, ran an editorial commenting that "there is probably no community in the Union of a like number of inhabitants, in which so large a proportion are bachelors. We have no spinsters." Some years later A. S. Mercer conceived the idea of importing Civil War widows to make up the deficiency and two consignments of "Mercer's Girls" actually arrived on the Sound. The same situation had existed before the population was swelled by the stimulation of the gold rush. The early British and Americans found that the Indian women made industrious, faithful and pleasant companions. The Indians accepted affinal relatives from outside their own group without question. They were already accustomed to receiving infiltrations of strangers in the same fashion. The women adapted themselves quickly to White ways. Many of them had been brought up to expect a complete change of environment at marriage, and they became excellent housekeepers.

The land law of 1850 allowed a quarter section to a bachelor and a whole section to a married man. Many of the marriages with Indian women became legal. The process of intermarriage was stimulated and, to the credit of both, a great proportion remained stable. The result was to set up a series of pioneer households in which the woman's children by previous marriages and the half-breed youngsters grew up as fully acquainted with White ways as might any pioneer children. In 1880 when the Indian school at Forest Grove was opened, it went begging for children well enough equipped for its curriculum. It serviced the entire coast and its first class consisted of eighteen students, four of them girls and all of them Puyallup.

The first settlers found the Indians willing and ready to work with them. The men had no bias against manual labor, they were good woodsmen, they knew the country and they took easily to the use of White men's tools. A means of communication was available in the Chinook Jargon, that simple trade language so important in the development of the Northwest. If later pioneers confused the Jargon with the true Indian language and looked down upon the race for the simplicity of their speech and the ideas it could convey, this difficulty did not bother the early settlers who knew the Indians more intimately. Whites and Indians worked side by side and the former were "scrupulously careful to prevent any difficulties with the natives by a custom of uniform prices for labor and goods, and perfect equity in dealing with them." [7] In-

[7] *Ibid.*, p. 25.

dian boys who grew up in this atmosphere competed on equal terms in the mills and in the lumber camps. There was no organized tribal life to be disrupted. The economic specialization of the old life made it possible for the house group to expand its activities. Fishing and berry picking continued. The Puyallup Valley had not yet been cleared sufficiently to tempt too great an emphasis upon agriculture by agency employees. In 1858 it was impossible to cut a road to the farming lands, which were three to four miles from the agency and could consequently be reached only in canoes, by an hour and thirty minute paddle each way when the tide was up. Farming, periods of work in the mills which tended to be seasonal, blacksmithing, all could be fitted as specialties into an economy which did not demand coöperation for production but rather a pooling of results.

There was also a certain give and take between the communal house and the pioneer homestead. Old pioneers still have a nostalgia for Indian smoked salmon, and fishing remained the Indians' forte. Much of the fresh meat and the berries consumed by Whites were brought in by Indians in exchange for flour, etc. Herb remedies were freely exchanged. Indians received first aid and the Whites developed an awed respect for the dominating figure of the curing shaman. The Indians accepted the fact that Whites could not be reached by sorcery; they had powers of their own, obviously, which were different from the Indians' and to which their talents could be credited, but they were impervious to the malicious workings of other powers.

The idyl could not last. The back wash of civilization always manages to be in the forefront of its pioneering. The urban centers, Olympia and Seattle, Nisqually, Fort Steilacoom, were not all populated by steady settlers. Liquor came in. Assimilation by marriage was impossible with the numbers of Whites increasing every year. The spring prior to the treaty and the War of 1855-56, one James Burt murdered an Indian near Olympia, was tried and acquitted and fled the country. The civil authorities were new to the ways of the earlier settlement period. Public opinion as expressed in the Olympia newspaper condemned the acquittal and voiced apprehension of the consequences. The later hostilities centered where population was thickest. Still the Puyallup Valley remained a rural community beyond the pressure of city conditions. Not until 1868 did Tacoma get under way as an urban development.

The Indians had already made two major adjustments. The first phase of their culture attacked by White mores was the communal house. Army officials and, probably also, the missionaries openly opposed communal living. Agency employees consistently urged the building of private homes for each family group. The Indians were not loath to comply. The bilateral family was already the unit in which suspicion was least marked. The strain of social contacts was no longer necessary to uphold the economic structure. The introduction of a medium of exchange meant that the appearance of friendliness which had been tied to barter had ceased to be essential. A man received money for his labor or the products of his labor, he purchased what he wanted from a White storekeeper and, if he had no influence over the man's life, at least the man, in turn, could not affect his. Families could still be supported by economic specialization but the need for watchfulness was at an end and the Indian drew a sigh of relief. At first, family groups transferred intact to private houses. Then, it became clear that the continuity of those groups had lost its significance and they broke up into the simple segments of the husband-wife-child relationship. The last shreds of the old basis of unity disappeared under the inducement furnished by the system of private land allotments. In 1874 the "tribal" lands were surveyed at the request of the Indians and broken into individually owned plots.

The second adjustment concerned their religious convictions. Christians introduced a new power, the power of Christ, which healed the sick and made the blind to see—a power completely comprehensible in the Indian's own terms. In a region where trachoma was prevalent, full respect would be accorded any shaman who cured blindness. The amazing feature of the new power was the fact that it could be obtained by certain ways of life. A person had or he did not have the old types of power and that was the end of it. But the tie between the supernatural and ethics, presented to the Indians for the first time, offered an opportunity by which *anyone* could obtain curing power. The first demonstration proving beyond doubt that such power would lodge in an Indian occurred on the Squakson reservation. This was the beginning of the Shaker cult now active and wide-spread among the Indians of the Northwest. It has changed considerably in transmittal. The ceremonials held by these groups in which the cult originated aped shaman cures so exactly that they involved killing as well as healing by power. Shakers, however, were not sorcerers. They consciously rid themselves of malicious and aggressive behavior. The true shamans complained bitterly and still feel resentful, "Every one called in those Shakers. The old way wasn't any good any more." The influence of the shaman was sapped.

After 1868 the Puyallup were in the heart of the mushroom growth of the Northwest. Tacoma flourished. In 1872 the Indians of the Medicine Creek Treaty asked in council that their lands be surveyed into lots and divided in severalty. They still sought release from the tension of necessary social contact. Few of them bothered to collect their annuities which amounted to less than a day's wages. They were self-supporting, all of them speaking some English and a few having absolutely no language difficulty. They dressed and lived like Whites. The allotments were made in 1874. Three years later a railroad branch was constructed by Indian labor through the reservation to an inland coal deposit. Eighteen of the younger generation went to Forest Grove to school and one of the full-bloods who had been a pupil of the Reverend Mann and had assisted in the Puyallup school, Peter Stanup, studied under the Presbytery and was licensed to preach the gospel. Between 1880 and 1886 the population of Washington increased by almost 300 per cent. By the latter date all the patents had been issued for the Puyallup lands, and the following year the General Allotment Plan, which provided that patent-holding allottees should be subject to the State or Territory in which they resided, became law. A bridge was to be built across the Puyallup River at a cost of 3,000 dollars—1,500 dollars from the county, 500 dollars from the Whites in the vicinity and 1,000 dollars from the Puyallup Indians, a sum which they raised without difficulty. The agent wrote in his annual report: "the reservation Indians belonging to this agency are no longer wards of the government, but free-born sovereigns of their native land. With them the Indian problem has been solved." The enthusiasm was premature. The Puyallup were free to come and go as they pleased, they could buy what they wished with money they earned, including liquor. But their lands remained inalienable, reserved to their exclusive use.

At this period the United States was in the throes of a magnificent dream. The railroad was going west! Rail by rail it crept across 3,000 miles of continent. It asked permission of the Indians and it went across their reserves, ever west. Tacoma was chosen as western terminus and doubled its population in two years. The future of the Puget Sound region was assured. But the Puyallup Reservation lay in direct line between Tacoma and Seattle, and in 1889 the Indians refused consent to the Puyallup Valley Railroad Company to cross their lands. In 1890 an appropriation of 10,000 dollars sent a commission of three men from Washington, D.C., to examine the situation and decide whether the restrictions on alienation be removed in whole or part. In 1892 a bill was before the Senate providing that the consent of Congress be given to the State of Washington for removal of the restrictions upon alienation of a portion of the lands embraced in the Puyallup Indian Reservation. The bill was not passed. But legislation was incorporated in the Appropriation Act of March 3, 1893, to the effect that a commission should be appointed by the president to select and appraise portions of the allotted lands and to sell them at public auction. Two years later the sale began.

The commission had no easy task on its hands. In 1896 it reported: "we found that the minds of the Indians had been prejudiced against us, and instead of being ready to have their lands sold according to the provisions of the law, as we had expected, we found them almost to a man bitterly opposed to it." [8] In cases where the original allottee was dead, the matter of determining heirs was almost impossible. Most of the relatives wanted the money, the kin group was widely extended and the people had never had any interest in tracing blood lines. Their kinship terminology used the same term for siblings and for cousins however remote. A financial depression had hit the area and the lands were not selling as well as had been expected. The reservation adjoined the city limits and, since some of it would probably be absorbed,

[8] *Rep. of the Com. of Ind. Affairs*, 1896, p. 35.

it had to be re-divided into city lots. Appraisal was difficult. Nevertheless, by August 1899, 1,884 acres had been sold for 98,859 dollars of which 36,364 dollars was in cash and, minus 10 per cent for the cost of the sale, had been turned over to the allottees.

Despite intermarriage with Whites and Indians from other sections and a certain acceleration in the death rate due to the White man's diseases, a good proportion of the allottees were actually Puyallup. For some reason, perhaps because at the time there had been few shamans among them with any influence or because the agent employees who lived so near were antagonistic to it, the Shaker cult had never greatly affected them. In 1879 an old warrior had publicly killed a Skokomish, resident upon the reservation, because his nephew had mentioned the other's name on his death-bed. Belief in the complete justification of the murder was so strong that no punishment was meted out to the old man. He was kept awhile in jail, which was so cold that he was allowed to sit by the fire in the school-room when school was in session, and then sent home. There had been nothing in their early financial success to destroy the Indian's convictions on individual powers. The professional had as great an advantage as under aboriginal conditions and it was still the man with ability who was most successful. Suddenly, however, money was coming in in large sums. No-account persons shared equally in it. The lands of some of the most able had not been sold at all. Meetings were called again and again but they could not help the Puyallup adjust himself to this new concept of value. Swindlers and real estate sharks swarmed in, plying their prospective clients with liquor, pretending friendship, maneuvering law suits. At the best, people were called to hearings to testify in cases of uncertain heredity. Suspicion flared up again like a rocket.

Suspicion flared up and it had no check. Communal living and the necessity for friendliness had disappeared. With it had gone the transient weight of the leader's word. White authorities stood firmly against revenge killings. The railroad had been built and with it came an alibi which would hold in any White court—the idea of accident. What easier than to stun or kill a man and place him on the tracks for the next train? If the Indians suspected who was guilty, their suspicions could not be proved in court. The matter dropped or it gave rise to another "accident." Up to this time drunkenness had isolated its victim or kept him within the confines of his own family. Now it was encouraged by the land-greedy who played prospect against prospect, and it brought to the surface suspicions and hates long forgotten. Peter Stanup was found dead in the river. The thing had no end. Today informants freely admit that the Puyallup did much to kill themselves off.

In 1936 there were a few scattered Puyallup, and sixteen or twenty families were on lands once included in the reservation. Indians and "old timers" among the Whites agree that this sudden drop in the size of the Puyallup coincided with the opening up of the reservation despite the fact that the influx at that time of heirs from the extended kin kept the apparent population figures stable for another decade. The 1936 remnant truly represented the old Puyallup group. Since the earliest White contact was in 1832, the whole period of acculturation has been almost exactly one hundred years. The process has been telescoped into five generations. The first accepted the material traits of the White man, his instruments, his metals, his clothing. It took eagerly to the cultivation of the potato. But the fields were planted, abandoned, revisited at harvest time. The agriculture had no effect on the life routine and was treated like any other of the wild root crops. The women of the second generation married White men or came into close contact with White families; the men worked for the Whites and fitted into the economic scheme.

It was the third generation which was educated on a footing with White children and grew up to go to Forest Grove. Four of this generation still live on the land allotted to their families or bought subsequently on reservation property. They are completely acculturated. They are well-to-do by the standards of a rural community, they have comfortable homes furnished in good taste, they have front yards with flowers and shrubs, they set good tables. One of them has a Japanese tenant in the manner of his neighbors and belonged to the local berry coöperative when it was operating. Two of these men are full-bloods. One of them is married to a White woman with two years of college education. Three of them are direct descendants of important leaders and warriors. To the same generation, all now in their seventies, belong several women. Although not so well educated as the men, they live comfortably in their own homes. One receives her wood and a small sum from a local relief organization.

The fourth generation grew up in a spreading White community. They also are acculturated, though not so markedly successful. Their fortunes have paralleled those of their White contemporaries. Some of them are industrious and self-sufficient; others have gone the way of the White trash they associated with. Their children are still young and attend school with the Whites. There is no doubt that their position as a racial minority affects both these generations. Attitudes toward them vary, the few Whites who live in the old pioneer tradition accept them, those who came in during or since the urban boom are apt to discriminate against them. Nevertheless, Tacoma offers adequate economic opportunity. Racial mixture continues and it is at this point that discrimination is strongest. The mates they find among the Whites are definitely inferior.

Only two traits still differentiate the Indians of the section. One is the very fact that they are *not* a group. Families stick closely together; they do not have free social contacts with their White neighbors; and they do not visit each other. Two of the families consider themselves very friendly: they see one another once or twice a year, although they live half a mile apart. There is little or no gossip. Remarks about other people are carefully chosen, seldom of a type which could not be made with perfect equanimity in front of anyone. In addition, there are the households of solitary old people. One man died some time ago after living alone and independently for years. Three old women, one over eighty, maintain separate establishments, cook, chop wood, tend their gardens, knit socks for sale. Life goes on for them after their husbands die. Their children leave home and life still goes on uninterrupted. They feel no peculiarity in this and it seems never to appear strange to their relatives. If one is sick, a niece may walk a mile to stay with her a few hours each day and then return to her own home. Old age does not mean dependence and they retain full rights as a family group much as they would have in the communal house.

None of the Puyallup today consider that the "old Indians" were superstitious. Belief in the individual, supernatural powers never met any real rival. One of the more thoughtful men has worked out a careful parallel between the power concept and the tenets of individual psychology as he understands it and, sometimes, the arguments are not unconvincing.

BIBLIOGRAPHY

Because the historical facts used in this paper are not of a controversial nature, they have not been documented in full. Reference to them may be found in one or all of the following works:

Bancroft, Hubert H., *History of Washington, Idaho, and Montana 1845–89, Volume 31,* The History Company, San Francisco, Calif., 1890.

Commissioner of Indian Affairs, *Annual Reports to the Secretary of the Interior,* Washington, D.C., 1849 to date.

Curtis, Edward S., *The North American Indians,* edited by Frederick W. Hodge, *Volume 9,* Harvard University Press, Cambridge, Mass., 1913.

Harrison, Jonathan B., *Latest Studies on Indian Reservations,* Indian Rights' Association, Philadelphia, Pa., 1887.

Meany, Edmond S., *History of the State of Washington,* The Macmillan Company, New York, 1909.

EDITOR'S SUMMARY

PUYALLUP ACCULTURATION

It would be hard to imagine better conditions for the acculturation of a native people than those which existed during the early part of Puyallup-White contact. The Indians were accepted on terms approaching social equality, with many legal intermarriages and the mutual recognition of relationship claims in both groups. Indians and Whites worked side by side at the same tasks and for the same wages, and the only direct attempts to change the native culture were those connected with the abandonment of the communal houses and the introduction of Christianity. Even the latter seems to have been in the hands of intelligent and sympathetic missionaries. The individualistic patterns of the native culture made it easy for certain Indians to take on White habits without waiting for the rest of their group to assume them. The result of all this was the rapid assimilation of the Indians into the White population, and all distinctions would probably have disappeared if it had not been for certain later developments. Among these, although of minor importance, was the introduction of attitudes of social discrimination by the later settlers. However, this seems to have been of minor importance in comparison with the sale of the Indian lands. The deadly results of this came not from a deprivation of resources but from a sudden influx of wealth which the Indians had no patterns for dealing with. The necessity for regular work was removed, while disputes as to ownership intensified the hostilities latent in the native culture. Dr. Smith has pointed out the sudden access of murders under the new conditions, but it seems questionable whether these, in themselves, would have done much to diminish the Indian population. More important factors were the degeneration which came with idleness and plenty of money for liquor. Certain families whose acculturation had progressed

37

far enough at the time of the windfall have survived in a favorable condition, but the bulk of the Puyallup seem to have been killed by kindness. The complete absorption of the remnant into the White population seems only a question of time.

2

THE WHITE KNIFE SHOSHONI OF NEVADA

by Jack S. Harris

THE ABORIGINAL COMMUNITY [1]

Before the advent of the Whites, the *Tosawi*[hi] Shoshoni ranged over that portion of the Great Basin now included in the northeastern section of the state of Nevada. These Indians were localized during the winter along the Humboldt River and its northern tributaries, as far west as Winnemmucca and east to the Independence Mountains. In the summer, the camps foraged for food as far north as the Snake River and some few went south to Austin and Eureka.

Tosawi[hi], or "White Knives," was the term loosely applied to all Indian camps in this area. It appears, however, that this term was restricted at one time to those camps in the immediate vicinity of Tuscarora and Battle Mountain where white flint for knives and other artifacts is found. The White Knives are not to be considered as having a band organization with the traditional ethnological connotations of restriction and cohesiveness. The term was primarily geographical, designating a shifting membership of Indians who were also known by a number of other names depending upon their temporary location or their principal food supply.

These Shoshoni roamed over a high, semi-arid country, broken by ill-defined mountain ranges and long valleys. To the west, the Sierra Nevadas blocked the moisture-laden air currents from the Pacific. The effect of what precipitation did come was minimized by the extremely dry air and great evaporation. The

[1] These data were obtained by the writer and Martha Harris on the Western Shoshoni Reservation at Owyhee, Nevada, during a period of three and a half months in 1937. The field work was financed by Columbia University.

mountains caught the small amount of rain and supported pine nut trees and a greater variety of edible seeds and roots than could the sage-covered valleys, which yielded little more than sparse patches of brush, grass and sunflower seeds. The Humboldt Valley was somewhat more favorable to plant life than the forbidding wastes to the south or the mountainous sage country to the north, but was far from providing an adequate food supply.

The White Knives practised no agriculture; their rivers yielded no vast quantities of fish; buffalo were too far east to be hunted. In fact, they lacked any dependable or regularly recurring source of food, and were forced to utilize for sustenance every aspect of an unfavorable habitat. Consequently, there were no cycles of plenty and starvation; these hunters and gatherers were constantly on the barest subsistence level.

In the Great Basin no river runs to the sea. The Humboldt, emptying into a shallow lake, did not support salmon or other varieties of fish that could be preserved in quantity for winter use. On the other hand, the Snake River just to the north of the physical boundaries of the Basin has a Pacific outlet which provided seasonal runs of salmon. The fish which the White Knives procured from the Humboldt and the neighboring streams, therefore, could not become as important a source of food as the preservable fish which the Salmon Eaters obtained from the Snake River. The movements of the Salmon Eaters, consequently, were restricted to a narrow area along the banks of the Snake, while the White Knives were forced to cover a much wider range in their foraging for plants, seeds, roots and wild game.

The chief but scanty sources of animal food were the rabbit, antelope, deer and mountain sheep. Food tabus extended to few animals and even these were disregarded during the frequent periods of famine. Insects such as crickets and ants formed a substantial item of diet, but the bulk of the food consisted of numerous roots, seeds, plants and berries.

The summers, hot and short, gave way to long, bitter winters in the mountainous northeast. The nomadic summer life was extended as long as possible, sometimes to seven or eight months, since the sedentary existence during the winter was often a battle against time. The food caches were limited to the small surplus which could be accumulated during the summer, replenished only by rabbit-hunting and sporadic fishing during the winter months. Lacking the horse and any means of transportation other than human, little food could be brought to the winter camp. However, a few caches of jerked meat, dried insects, seeds and roots were stored along the summer routes so that once the snows ceased, the camp groups could venture out with some assurance of food awaiting them.

The division of labor in the food quest was primarily along sexual lines and secondarily dependent upon age. Men hunted, fished and occasionally (with a feeling of guilt) did some gathering. The women gathered seeds, roots, berries, insects, and to a small extent hunted and fished near the camp site. From the point of view of the volume of food procured, it may well be that the women were economically more important, although the Shoshoni themselves felt the division to be equal. Children of both sexes, as soon as they were physically competent, helped the women gather seeds and roots. Girls continued in this activity as they grew older. At the age of eight or ten, boys began to hunt for squirrels, chipmunks and the smaller game; when they reached fifteen years, they had already given up women's work and were ready to hunt deer and antelope.

In practically all manufactures there was sexual division of labor. In addition to procuring and preparing food, women made all the basketry and pottery; men made the fish nets, traps, bows, arrows and flint artifacts. Each sex made its own clothes, and both coöperated to build dwellings and to transport the belongings of the camp. There was but slight specialization. A skilled maker of bows and arrows, for example, might manufacture a few of these and trade them to other men for such artifacts as knives and scrapers, but this type of specialization and trade was not important. The only true specialist was the shaman, and even he could not support himself by his practice.

The technology of food production was on a simple level, and the number of artifacts was limited by the restrictions of human transportation in a highly mobile society. Women used a digging-stick, the sharp end of which had usually been hardened by charring in a fire. Seeds were brushed into a conical carrying basket with a willow-woven seed-beater. At the camp site, a small metate and muller, or mortar and pestle, were utilized in pounding and grinding the seeds and other plant and insect foods. Water was stored in baskets when the groups ventured into arid regions. Men primarily used the bow and arrow in the hunt, in addition to traps, nets and clubs for the smaller animals. Because there were so few animals in their territory, only the fortunate had clothing made of skins. Clothing was generally limited to breech clouts for men and the double apron for women, moccasins for both and the rabbit-skin cloak as blanket and general covering. Their small dogs served as companions and adjuncts in the hunt but never for packing or transportation. In the more sedentary winter community, nets, dams and weirs were used to catch fish. The severity of the environment and the scarcity of food, combined with the simple devices which the White Knives used for procuring, transporting and storing food, bring into focus the ceaseless struggle for existence in this area.

These facts are reflected in the population density. Steward estimates that the more fertile localities had one person to two square miles, while such arid regions as the Great Salt Lake Desert had one person to fifty or sixty square miles.[2] A reasonable figure for the White Knives country would be approximately one person to fifteen or twenty square miles. It is difficult to estimate the total aboriginal population of this area, because not only was the membership shifting, but the historical sources are scanty and conflicting.[3] A rough estimate would put the total population of this region between eight hundred and a thousand individuals.

[2] J. H. Steward, "Linguistic Distributions and Political Groups of the Great Basin Shoshoneans," *American Anthropologist, Volume XXXVIII*, p. 628.

[3] In 1866, the population of the Nevada Shoshoni was estimated at 2,500, Parker, *Report of Commissioner of Indian Affairs, 1866*, p. 114. J. H. Powells and G. W. Ingalls, *Report of C.I.A., 1873*, pp. 41–70, state that the population of all the Western Shoshoni is 1,945. L. A. Gheen, farmer of the area, reports "on close examination" that the population of all the Western Shoshoni is 4,000. *Report of C.I.A., 1876*, pp. 116–118.

These Shoshoni were well aware of the dangers of too large a population and economic necessity forced the retention of only virile, capable elements. The unfit were consistently eliminated. The sick, because of the relentless demands of the nomadic food quest, were left alone with some food either to recover or to die. The aged were frequently abandoned or wandered off by themselves to ease the camp burden. There are authenticated cases of cannibalism induced by starvation which, to a much lesser degree, affected the population.

In addition to the deaths hastened or directly caused by the harsh environment and the struggle for food, population was artificially restricted in a number of ways. Fathers taught their sons to practise withdrawal. This failing, women were familiar with a variety of abortive herbs and preparations, as well as more drastic techniques to prevent birth. Because twins demanded too much time of the economically important mother, one of the twins was either given away to a woman who could care for it, or left to perish. This was also done with other babies that economic circumstances had made unwelcome. These factors tended to restrict the number of children to two or three to each set of parents. To have more than three was regarded as an asocial act. It follows that a barren woman was free of stigma, and in many instances considered most desirable as a wife. The population, therefore, remained stable primarily as a direct reflection of the harsh economic determinants, and secondarily as a result of the social attitudes to which these determinants gave rise.

The various Western Shoshonean groups were primarily known by their food supply. The economic character of the area, rather than land-owning or political groups, gave rise to these native names. Thus, there were the Squirrel Eaters, Pine Nut Eaters, Antelope Eaters, Rabbit Eaters, etc. Nor were these appellations permanent, for with a seasonal shift in residence a camp would be known by another group name. It is probably unnecessary to add that these names were given permanence by the Whites; the Indians themselves recognized them merely as convenient and transitory designations. The borders, if they can be termed such, were wide areas which were not only frequented, but often transgressed. There was free intercourse between these groups, and certain members of one would enter the territory of another group, and remain there permanently if they so desired.

The summer months found the White Knives camp groups ranging over an area which extended from southern Idaho to east central Nevada, roughly 25,000 square miles. Of course, not every camp covered this area, but each group followed a more or less well-defined orbit, ranging from twenty-five to one hundred miles from its winter base. The summer shelters were conical willow wind-breaks, easily erected and abandoned when the camp moved to a new location. In the course of this summer nomadism, the White Knives entered not only upon the territory of other Western Shoshoni groups, such as the Salmon Eaters to the north and the Pine Nut Eaters to the south, but continued their search for food beyond the Santa Rosa Mountains to the west into southeastern Oregon and adjoining Northern Paiute country. Similarly, Paiute camps, without danger of reprisal, crossed the loosely designated tribal boundary near Winnemmucca to enter Shoshoni territory to pursue their foragings for food.

The White Knives confined themselves, during the winter months, to small communities on the banks of the Humboldt River and along neighboring streams and sheltered valleys to the north. The first snows found these camps returning with some roots, seeds and dried deer meat. Each camp group maintained its identity during the winter, camping from an eighth-to a quarter-mile away from the next camp. In this manner, a cluster of from two to ten camp groups, usually bound by some kinship ties, would come together. Other camps denied themselves even this temporary consolidation during the winter, and remained alone in some locality where spring came early. The winter huts were more permanent structures, dome-shaped, and closely woven of willow or tule grass or both.

The members of a camp group followed a familiar range, not necessarily the same one each year, but the choice was definitely limited. This was not because they feared to trespass on other territory, but the economic possibilities of their range were desperately well known, and it would have been foolhardy to venture into territory where the food yield and water sources were unknown factors. One old informant described the various seeds and roots which could be found in each small area within a 150-mile summer range. Another camp group could satisfy its food needs within a twenty-five-mile area.

In this latter example, the twenty-five miles from the Owyhee River to Bull Run were known as no man's land. It was *his*—a concept which all people understood. But it was his only in the sense that everyone knew that this man could be found there during the summer. He had neither the right nor the desire to oust another family if it happened to hunt or gather seeds in this territory. Similarly, the Salmon Eaters of the Snake River set traps and nets in certain portions of the river. This section of the river was known to "belong" to one camp group, but it "belonged" only in the sense just described. No one could be prohibited from fishing in the same section. There were two factors involved here. First, if any two camp groups were in proximity and one was in dire need of food, the other camp group ordinarily shared its food with the needy. This was an economic insurance through reciprocal obligations, and it minimized any protest against encroachment. But the second factor largely prevented the occurrence of this encroachment. That is, each camp group knew full well the food limitations of a restricted area and these were ordinarily exhausted within ten days. Consequently, it would have been unwise to camp where these possibilities were being diminished by the activity of another group.

It is highly improbable that the concept of land ownership with its corollaries of rights and defense of those rights ever occurred to these people. However, the products of land and water obtained through such devices as traps, nets or other efforts, despite the fact that they were sometimes shared with outsiders, were indisputably private property and the rights to these were defended. Theft of food from the caches, or of animals caught in traps, was punished by beatings and sometimes death, but only when the thief was caught in the act. Despite this, thievery seems to have flourished and caused some disruption among camp groups. Since these people did not practise even the primitive irrigation that is reported for the Owens Valley Paiute,[4] there was no question of rights to plants, seeds and roots growing on the land.

Thus, these isolated camp groups moved in an orbit to which they were economically habituated, with little animosity toward other groups which roamed over the region. There is little indication that the White Knives were hostile before White contact. Some of the oldest inhabitants recall one or two raids for women which "strange" Indians made upon their camps, but these raiders were not identified. Unorganized and desperately poor, the White Knives had neither the tradition nor equipment of war, and consciously avoided any incident which might precipitate harsh retaliation. There was infrequent contact with the Bannock, Flathead and Nez Percé, usually for the purpose of peaceful trade. Friendly relations existed with the Paiute to the west, and this relationship was materially strengthened by frequent intermarriage.

Among the various Western Shoshonean groups, relations were even more friendly, for here there was not the barrier of an unintelligible language. It has been established that some White Knives families went north and east to Lemhi and Wyoming territory of the sheep- and buffalo-eating Shoshoni, and often remained permanently with these groups, avowedly because of the richer economic life. Frequently, a Salmon Eater group would move into White Knives territory and *vice versa*. Usually a camp would consolidate its position in new territory by intermarriage. But although there were no social or political limitations on this mobility, movements into strange territories were restricted by the economic habituation to familiar land.

The basic and most important unit of White Knives society was the camp group. This group consisted of related persons of one to three, and seldom more than five, families, and rarely exceeded twenty persons. Marriage often consolidated two camp groups unless the number of individuals was too large to be supported as one economic unit. For this reason, a couple might

[4] J. H. Steward, Ethnography of Owens Valley Paiute, *University of California Publications in American Archaeology & Ethnology, Volume XXXIII*, Berkeley, Calif., 1933, pp. 247–250.

break away from a large group after the birth of children. Many camps consisted of no more than husband, wife and children, with perhaps a married daughter and her husband. Residence was generally matrilocal, but certain variable factors, such as personal desire, size of family, circumstances of food, or the personality of the mother-in-law [5] disrupted this general form, so that even membership in the camp group was unstable, and no winter community was a lineage group. Thus, although a man usually lived at his wife's camp, circumstances might send him to his father's camp, to his brother's camp, or he might even wander off alone.

Within the camp, all the women coöperated in the gathering and usually in the preparation of the food. Plant food was consumed by all the members of the group with little reference to who procured it. All the men of the camp coöperated in hunting the larger animals, as well as in the capture of smaller animals where concerted effort was necessary to drive them into nets. Chipmunks and squirrels were caught in individually set traps, and required the labor of but one man. Although it was recognized that an animal belonged to the man who killed it, this "ownership" was primarily a prestige point and carried no exclusive rights to the disposal of the animal; any catch was distributed among all the families in the camp group. Since buckskin clothing was so highly prized, the individual whose arrow had slain the deer would retain the skin. However, if a man had been so fortunate as to kill several deer while other men had killed none, the surplus hides were given away to the others. In effect, therefore, there was an equitable distribution of food within the camp, as well as coöperation in its production.

This close-knit group is to be seen not only in relation to economic coöperation, but to the close kinship bonds which coexisted. Kinship bonds were not strictly formalized because of the variable conditions of residence; it followed that an individual had his closest ties with those with whom he was constantly in

[5] Interference by the mother-in-law in familial affairs was often resented. A common saying reflects this situation: "No matter how much deer fat you stuff into the mouth of your mother-in-law, she can still talk out of the side of her mouth."

association, and the kin patterns were not consistent. There were rarely any strangers in the camp; the only outsiders were those who had married into it and children usually strengthened those ties. A child had its closest relationships, under ordinary circumstances, with its mother's family. The male child and his maternal grandfather called each other by the same term and enjoyed a warm companionship. It was this grandparent who taught the child its first lessons in hunting and trapping, and instructed him in the manufacture of bows, arrows, traps and nets. Similarly, a female child and her maternal grandmother used this reciprocal terminology and participated in a particularly close relationship. The maternal uncle, however, had no greater rights over the children's behavior or companionship than had the father. Indeed, the father frequently resented any over-riding of his authority by his brother-in-law or by any other affinal relative and might even take this as sufficient reason to withdraw his family from the camp group. This contingency, however, was largely avoided by the fact that a brother-in-law, because of the prevailing mode of residence, was rarely in the same camp. Moreover, a wife's family was careful not to antagonize, and thus remove, an important economic unit. The relationship between grandparent and child of like sex was accepted by all as traditional, harmless and desirable.

The man most familiar with the summer range, and the longest resident of the group directed the movements of the camp. Consequently, age and experience were the chief factors which gave an individual some degree of authority, however feeble, in the camp group. Because most marriages involved matrilocal residence, this individual was usually the wife's father, although the wife's maternal grandfather, if not disqualified by infirmity, might retain this slight prerogative.

During the major portion of the year each camp group ranged by itself over the countryside. Participation in rabbit drives, fishing parties, and attendance at shamanistic ceremonies made for transitory alliances during the winter, as did the various gambling games. However, despite these temporary ties to related camp groups in the winter community, each unit retained its fundamental identity.

Marriage was usually monogamous, although both polygyny and polyandry occurred. The only marriages regarded as incestuous were those of parent and child, siblings, and parallel cousins. Because of the frequently erratic composition of the camp group and winter community, kin groupings were not consistent and lateral extensions of relatives beyond those with whom the individual came into contact were sometimes ignored. Thus, a good many types of marriage could occur, although monogamy, and to a lesser extent, polygyny, were predominant. The scope of potential mates was so wide that no individual had fear of remaining without a spouse, nor had the man to search far for a woman who stood in the proper marriage relationship.

Since the woman's seed-gathering and root-digging contributed an important and fairly consistent part of the food supply, polygyny was not restricted by a husband's inability to provide food for more than one wife. On the other hand, polyandrous unions entailed some economic maladjustment because of the more uncertain results of a man's hunting and fishing activities. Not only was polyandry comparatively rare, therefore, but it was often adjusted to the economic demands. Two men (usually brothers) married to a woman would frequently alternate in hunting away from the camp so that only one husband would be with the wife. Furthermore, this type of marriage was often temporary since one of the husbands usually left the union to contract a monogamous marriage.

The forms of polygyny and polyandry are also to be understood in terms of the function of the levirate and sororate.[6] A woman, upon her husband's death, frequently married the brother of the deceased, and similarly any man a woman married while her first husband was still alive was usually her husband's brother. Thus, polyandry was usually fraternal and rarely included more than two brothers. The sororate was similarly linked to polygyny; a man would take his wife's sister as a second spouse, either before or after his first wife's death. It rarely occurred that plural wives were not sisters, for it was almost axiomatic that sisters could live together harmoniously while non-

[6] This point has been treated by J. H. Steward, "Shoshoni Polyandry," *American Anthropologist, Volume XXXVIII*, p. 562.

sisters could not. Polygyny in this sororal form was further strengthened by the fact of the general matrilocal residence. This form of plural marriage was more frequent and more permanent than polyandry.

Only one case was reported of a polygynous marriage in which the husband had three non-related wives. In this instance, the man spent certain portions of the year with each wife. This type of union was rare, however, and might be merely an example of a temporary stabilization of the excessive philandering in which the Shoshoni indulged. Another type of polygyny recorded was that of a man who lived in marriage with both his wife and her widowed mother. This marriage form, although uncommon, is well within the loose framework of possible marital combinations.

Brother-sister exchange in marriage was frequently practiced and two such couples, with their respective children, would usually combine to form a distinct camp group. There was a marked desire to keep children in the same camp after marriage both because of strong kinship bonds and of the advantage in retaining members who were familiar with the food possibilities of the camp range. This was accomplished by cross-cousin marriage. This marital arrangement was often preferred, even when potential mates of this category were not in the same camp group, for they were commonly represented in the larger winter community.[7]

The girl's parents commonly took the initiative in the marriage arrangement. At any one of the infrequent convergences of the camp groups, the mother of the girl would invite an eligible young man—a good hunter—to sleep with her daughter. Sexual

[7] Some informants claimed, however, that cross-cousin marriage had never been sanctioned. Others insisted that it had flourished in the past and had even been practiced recently, although it was considered on the incest fringe. This transitional or attenuated stage at the time of White contact was reflected in the kinship terminology. Parallel cousins were equated with siblings and thus were automatically eliminated from the marriage possibility. The term for cross-cousin of opposite sex, however, was "breast sibling." This meant that the cross-cousin was to be regarded as a sibling only from the navel up. Below the navel, the individual was no longer a sibling so that sexual intercourse was possible with no fear of incest. It is to be further noted in this connection that the breasts had no significance in sexual play.

intercourse usually occurred during the first ten days (the period when a maiden traditionally overcame her shyness). The parents were gratified since this validated the marriage, and a young man had been added to the family who could materially contribute to its economic welfare.[8] A marriage, however, was not considered stabilized until a child had been born to the young couple.

If the trial period was unsuccessful, the temporary marriage relationship usually dissolved. There was no burden placed upon the man to continue in the relationship if the trial situation was distasteful to him. If the girl, however, refused to have sexual relations with the guest, she was bitterly scolded by her mother. The girl's objections were not considered very seriously; it was generally assumed that any woman could become "used to" a man after some time of living together.

Marital unions were often temporary, easily contracted and dissolved. It was the husband who usually initiated divorce by the simple method of leaving his spouse. A man who frequently changed wives, however, might find himself without a mate as he grew old and increasingly undesirable. This was well recognized by the White Knives, and philandering young men were warned of this possibility. Under such circumstances, a man might remain without a wife, or he might contract a marriage with a young female child belonging to some camp group which was willing to relinquish her while she was still an economic liability. In this sort of child marriage, the husband might stay with the camp group; more often, he would wander off with his child wife, impelled by the fear that some of the young bucks in the camp might take advantage of his age to win his wife away from him, as indeed they usually would.

The informality of marriage was further reflected in the absence of bride-price, presents or ceremonies, and the lack of obligations between the families of the bride and groom. As has been noted, however, the camps might combine.

There were no clans, age-classes, societies, or other groupings to complicate the social structure. An individual, consequently,

---

[8] This was reflected in the saying "more fat" when a female was born. Deer fat was highly prized as a delicacy and this was anticipated at the birth of a female since she, at marriage, would bring a hunter of deer into the family.

could not inherit status nor could he achieve it by membership in some organization. Largely restricted to his own camp group and small winter community, a man could attain a slight degree of status by becoming an outstanding hunter, a powerful shaman, or a skilled maker of bows, arrows, nets or traps. A woman could also become a shaman or be proficient in the manufacture of baskets or the crude, untempered pottery; above all, she had to be industrious. To such individuals, some measure of respect was accorded. The lazy, irresponsible person was denounced. This attitude reached its logical conclusion during periods of famine when the lazy individual was the first to be eaten because he was not only economically obnoxious but usually meatier than the others.

It is apparent that the opportunities for social dominance were restricted. There were occasions, however, when certain individuals had somewhat more authority than others. These opportunities were few and vague. Only under exceptional circumstances would the leadership of one man be recognized in the cluster of camps which made up the winter community. This could occur when an individual had wisdom of age, superior skill in hunting, and close kinship ties to the informal leaders of the individual camp groups. But these were unique conditions, rarely realized in a setting of shifting camp groups of irregular composition. The more common pattern, by far, was that of a winter village where each camp maintained its fundamental social, economic and political autonomy.

The authority of the curing shaman was significant only in definite situations. His instructions during the treatment of a patient were strictly obeyed, lest the cure be ineffective, but what other authority a shaman might have was directly dependent upon his other capabilities. Although he commanded a certain degree of respect at all times in recognition of his supernatural healing powers, these bestowed no political dominance. In like manner, no other individual with supernatural power had authority to go beyond the limits of that power. An antelope shaman, for example, was respected and obeyed when he exercised control over the antelope drive, but he could not utilize this limited power as a springboard to wider authority.

There was no period during the year when all the White Knives came together. However, during the spring and sometimes in the fall or summer, from one to 300 people gathered for seasonal dances, games and prayers. All the camp groups in the vicinity would converge for these six days, including those members of other groups who happened to be near enough to accept the invitation to attend. It was recognized that the food supply would allow for no longer than these five and a half days (camp broke on noon of the sixth day). During this time, the economic routine of the people was regulated by a leader, the *Gwini tegwani*,[9] but with the end of the meeting, his authority dissolved and the people resumed their foraging for food as individual camp units. This six-day gathering had as its primary function, fertility prayers and rites. The camps were arranged in a semicircle with the open end toward the east. In the center of the circle, a green willow pole, which symbolized the verdure of the earth, was erected, and about this pole the dances were performed.

Just before sunrise, the leader would stand in the center of the camp half-circle, face the east and pray to the sun. He would ask for rain; that the earth bring forth berries, seeds, plants; that the hills be covered with green and growing things; that the streams be stocked with fish; that the valleys and ranges abound with deer, antelope and mountain sheep. In the evening, between performances of the round dance, he would admonish the people to be industrious, the men to provide abundant game and fish, the women to gather seeds and roots. At the conclusion of the dance each individual clapped his hands over his body, from the ankles, over the legs, at the sides, on the breast, over the head, symbolically brushing and shaking off the evil, filth and disease.

The *Gwini tegwani* was always a man, although theoretically a woman could hold this position. His authority was received from a supernatural power, and this non-hereditary position was usually validated later by supernatural sanction. There were at least three of these ceremony leaders among the White Knives

---

[9] The capitalized "G" is intermediate between "g" and "k." All native terms in this paper are accented on the first syllable.

at one time. During the rest of the year, they worked as would any other individual in a camp group, and little prestige seems to have been accorded them.

It was during this six-day period that these Shoshoni experienced their nearest approach to a band organization. It should be emphasized, however, that a ceremony rarely had the same attendance of camp groups as had the preceding one called by the same ceremony leader. The *Gwini tegwani* sent out his call for the meeting whenever he felt it was necessary, within the general range of a season. Although approximately a week was allowed for the camps to converge, the composition of the attendance depended upon those camps that happened to be in the immediate area at the time. A White Knives camp, consequently, might even meet with Salmon Eaters groups one season, or with Pine Nut Eaters another season, and with varying White Knives camps at others. Thus, even this limited authority was variable and could not be exerted consecutively over the same groups.

Though the group coming together for these ceremonies was small, even fewer gathered together for the pine nut harvest. The pine nut was not an important source of food for the White Knives, and only a comparatively few families went south to the pine nut areas in the fall. Despite the erratic yield the harvest was sufficient to supply the same small groups year after year.[10]

During the pine nut harvest, no man or group was in authority. In rabbit drives, the most capable person, regardless of supernatural sanction, acted as director, or "rabbit boss." During the antelope drive, a shaman with supernatural power to lure the antelope into a corral, officiated. Neither position was hereditary. The rabbit drives were usually held during the winter, with all members of a winter community participating. Antelope hunts were held in the spring and fall, sometimes during the summer, whenever a herd of antelope was in evidence and the services of an antelope shaman could be secured. All neighboring camp

[10] Steward in "Linguistic Distributions and Political Groups of the Great Basin Shoshoneans," *American Anthropologist, Volume XXXVIII*, p. 629, states that the pine nut harvest was the most important factor in bringing the Shoshoni together. This was true south of the Humboldt River, but the White Knives country had comparatively few pine nut trees and the harvest could not function as an important occasion for social life.

groups were invited for the drive. Neither the leader of the rabbit hunt nor the antelope shaman wielded authority outside of their specific tasks in the drive.

Political authority therefore was at a minimum. The basic political, economic and social unit was the camp group, a practically self-sufficient entity with shifting and temporary ties to other camp groups. Techniques for control of the individual were both vague and informal, and usually exercised within the camp itself. The simple social and political structure provided only incipient mechanisms for social or political dominance; the inexorable demands of the economic life practically forbade such possibility.

There were no important property rights, no wars, no land-owning groups with bitterly defended boundaries, not even a marked ethnocentricism to separate one group from the rest and keep it intact. Moreover, these people were not fear-ridden by a dread of supernatural powers, malignantly exerted by an outside group, and any available shaman of another group or even of another tribe, was called in to doctor when needed.

However, these camp groups were not entirely independent units functioning in isolation. Communal hunts and ceremonies, reciprocal economic obligations, seasonal group residence, intermarriage and transient membership of both camp and winter communities wove a loose net of linkages which spread throughout Western Shoshonean society.

The foregoing outline of White Knives social and political life and their grim struggle for existence gives no indication of the wealth of supernatural concepts, beliefs and practices which penetrate every aspect of the culture. The creation of the Shoshoni themselves, their customs and relations to the outside world are laid directly at the door of Coyote, the trickster hero. His unique exploits in the beginning of things make explicable their own character, attitudes and behavior. That this behavior is not always commendable they willingly admit; they add, however, that after all, they are children of Coyote and cannot act otherwise.

More important than Coyote, however, is the concept of an animistic universe charged with extraordinary power. At the apex is *apö*,[11] the fountain-head of supernatural power. *Apö* is identified with the sun. How clear this identification was in the aboriginal society it is now difficult to say. The importance of the concept is clear, however, for all prayers were directed to *apö* (i. e., to the sun, or by way of the sun), not only the individual morning prayers of the adults, but the ceremonial prayers of the *Gwini tegwani*. The ceremonial, shamanistic and secular alignments toward the east, the rising sun, underline this concept. Furthermore, there is some evidence that it was *apö* who guided the guardian spirits to the individuals. Practically all informants concurred in the opinion that *apö* had the power to bring rain, make plants grow, stock the earth with game and the streams with fish, and to preserve the well-being of the people. But it would be erroneous to conceive of *apö* as a supreme deity who guided and controlled the movements of the universe and its inhabitants. This power was too remote and amorphous to exercise immediate control over the lives of the people.[12]

Certainly the richest religious expression of Shoshonean life is to be found in the concept of *Buha*[13]—supernatural power—and its embodiment in shamanistic practice.[14] Merely in order to live every person must possess the bird-like *Buha*, the life-

[11] The Shoshoni term for father.

[12] I am aware that this identification of *apö* and the sun as the prime-generator may be a crystallization of monotheism precipitated by White concepts. However, Col. A. G. Brackett, writing of the Northern Shoshoni in 1879, says: "The Indians have not much of an idea of God, although they believe in Tamapah, or Sun-Father, who is the Father of the Day and Father of us all, and lives in the sun." *The Shoshone or Snake Indians, their Religion, Superstitions and Manners*, pp. 328–333. M. K. Opler, *Acculturation of Southern Ute*, has found the sun-deity operative among the Southern Ute, as has W. Z. Park among the Paviotso, although in somewhat attentuated form, *Shamanism in Western North America*, p. 14. R. H. Lowie, *The Northern Shoshone*, p. 226, refers to *Apö* as the supernatural Father, but does not identify him with the sun. H. H. Bancroft, *History of Nevada*, p. 50, quotes manuscript (1841) of Shoshoni, who upon receiving a gift, "immediately turned toward the sun and commenced a long and eloquent harangue." None of the following sources on the Great Basin mention the sun in this connection: I. T. Kelly, *Surprise Valley Paiute:* J. H. Steward, *Owens Valley Paiute:* R. H. Lowie, *Notes on Shoshonean Ethnography*.

[13] The capital "B" is intermediate between "b" and "p."

[14] For an excellent account of shamanism among the neighboring Paviotso, as well as for a general Great Basin study, see W. Z. Park, *Shamanism in Western North America*.

principle. But beyond this essential minimum, supernatural power was accorded each individual in varying degrees. The most prevalent form was the power to cure illness, and this ranged from the specialized power of one person to cure a specific illness, like that caused by snake-bite, to the all-inclusive curing powers of the real *Buhagant*—the power-possessor.

A shaman who could cure only the lesser disorders was known by the qualifying title, *tümagüni Buhagant*, and was restricted to praying and chiropractic techniques. The sweat-house shaman, for example, was in this category. Only the powerful *Buhagant*, with no terminological qualifications, could employ the sucking technique to remove the intrusive substance which had entered the body of the patient to obstruct his normal functioning.

Although both men and women were shamans, powerful *Buhagants* were not numerous in the aboriginal society. Throughout the summer nomadism, camps would constantly recheck the location of shamans so that they could be called immediately in the event of illness befalling one of the camp group. Despite these precautions, many individuals died because of lack of treatment. No shaman, however, could refuse the request to heal a patient. To do so caused the frustrated *Buha* to turn upon its carrier and inflict severe illness or death.

Power was obtained through two principal sources, involuntarily through dreams, or by solicitation in specified places. Unsolicited power through dreams frequently was thought of as inherited from some relative of like sex, known or unknown, through either lineage. These dreams were experienced repeatedly by an individual who would know by certain signs when the power was sufficiently strong within him to utilize it in doctoring. If the recipient refused to exercise this power, as he might, because of the responsibility and tabus inherent in its possession, the power frequently turned upon the possessor to weaken him or actually to cause his death.

Power which was deliberately sought was considered stronger than that received via the involuntary route of dreams. Contrary to Plains pattern, visions were never induced by fasting, torture, or long withdrawal from camp life. The *Buha* was obtained in localities recognized as reservoirs for specific powers—caves, mountain passes or hidden valleys. The suppliant remained here overnight; if the "powers," or *apö*, desired that he receive *Buha*, he experienced the proper vision. If not, the individual was prevented from sleeping or was frightened away by ogres or mountain dwarfs. If allowed to dream, he was directed by an unseen force, or, as in one case, by a "huge, handsome Indian whose face I couldn't see," to follow certain instructions. The suppliant's ability in fulfilling these requirements often determined the strength but not the type of *Buha* received. Each locality conferred but one kind of power so that no confusion could result. Upon awakening, the individual would find certain paraphernalia; an eagle feather, a weasel skin, etc., which he used or displayed thereafter in curing or in exercise of the power.[15]

Informants were divided on the question whether the *Buha* came directly from such tutelaries as birds, animals and naturalistic phenomena, or whether it stemmed primarily from *apö*, who passed it on through these guardian spirits.[16] The *Buhagant*, when curing, would call upon weasel to travel through the body of the patient to determine the nature of the illness. When this had been ascertained, the shaman called for that "power" which could best cure the diagnosed disease. Other informants stated that the *Buhagant* went into a trance and thus became an intermediary between *apö* and the patient. It would be *apö* who sent down, through the medicine doctor, the "powers" best suited to cure. Thus, otter power was good for curing fever since the otter can break through ice; similarly, rain was effective as a cooling medium; the woodpecker ate poison out of the body as it eats worms in ordinary life. The power within the shaman sucked out the disease. If successful, the shaman would display the disease in the form of dirt, "quicksilver," or a "jelly-like some-

[15] The loss of this paraphernalia might cause loss of power and illness. As related by an informant: "Old Man X went to the Pendleton round-up and rode in the parade all dressed up. He put his medicine eagle feather in his horse's tail. Some white man who was always collecting souvenirs took this out of the horse's tail. Old Man X didn't know this until the end of the parade. Then he got real mad and scared and said he couldn't cure any more because he couldn't have the tail feather which showed he had power. That's maybe why he died so soon after that."

[16] This may be another indication of Christian influence.

thing." The disease, cupped in the palm of the *Buhagant's* hand, was then blown away toward the east.

A curing ceremony was an important affair in Shoshonean life. Not only did the health or fate of a loved one depend upon the doctoring rites, but the ceremony itself provided a welcome diversion from the humdrum routine of the daily round. The news of a curing ritual speedily traveled to neighboring camp groups and served for a temporary group gathering in an existence which ordinarily forbade such meetings.

The lack of shamanistic authority, other than that bestowed by specific supernatural power, has been noted in a previous paragraph. We need only add here that a shaman ideally was a poor and humble person. Although he was paid at each doctoring performance, the payment was directly dependent upon the instructions he received in trance. To violate these instructions was to invite supernatural displeasure and consequent disaster. Often the payment asked was an economically worthless object, such as the skin of a humming-bird. If the payment took the form of some prized article like buckskin, the shaman, as often as not, gave it away to some person in his camp group. Thus the *Buhagant* not only lacked secular authority, but he was usually poverty-stricken as well—a situation which stands in marked contrast to that of surrounding areas.[17]

Finally, in this brief consideration of *Buha*, it remains to summarize its extensions to activities of Shoshonean life other than that of curing. It has already been pointed out that the *tegwani* of the important *Gwini* ceremony had both initial and continuing supernatural sanction to function as leader.

The antelope shaman received his "charming" power supernaturally through vision. His ability to "hypnotize" the antelope leader and thus force it to bring a herd of antelope into a corral where they could be slaughtered was a most important factor in augmenting the meagre food supply.

The *Badsai* medicine men had power to control the weather

---

[17] Compare, for example, A. H. Gayton, *Yokuts-Mono Chiefs and Shamans*, especially pp. 398–401. See also P. Radin, *Primitive Religion*, pp. 40–58, for a stimulating discussion of the problem of the political and economic importance of shamans in primitive societies.

and especially to curtail the winter seasons which, if they lingered, prevented the camp group from starting on its nomadic search for food until after the caches were empty. An individual with this power went out in a blizzard in early morning, his nude body painted red, and prayed toward the east. That evening, the Chinook (South Wind) came and melted the snow. Or he employed the technique of sympathetic magic by mixing some snow with mustard seed, and blowing smoke from his pipe upon this mixture until it had all melted. This was done to induce the wind to come and the clouds to roll so that a torrent of rain would melt the snow.

In addition to the foregoing *Buha* possessors, whose activities affected the group as a whole, many individuals had guardian spirits that bestowed unique capabilities upon the recipients. Thus, a man with wolf power was cunning in the hunt; the eagle, antelope, fox or cloud gave *Buha* to run fast; the bear gave fighting *Buha,* i. e.: "If one man steals another's wife, and the husband catches up with them, the man who has the bear *Buha* can win the fight." Power gotten from the dwarf men, *nünümBi,* gave its possessor singular luck in finding game. An informant stated:

In a dream a man who has this power will hear the *nünümBi* directing him to a certain place in a mountain where he can find a deer. When the man wakes up, he goes to this place and he will find a deer which has been freshly killed by the *nünümBi*. There is no wound on the outside of the deer. It has been killed from within.

Power gotten from the water babies gave its recipients long life since these creatures were strong and could not be killed.

Although every individual felt a vague identification with cunning, unscrupulous, lascivious Coyote, there were those who had these characteristics intensified by direct supernatural relation to Coyote. One who had Coyote power could break the common tabus since he, like Coyote, was recognized as a licentious, lawless being. Thus, a man with this power could enter his wife's menstrual hut, or violate the incest tabus, secure in the knowledge that he was safe from any supernatural punishment. This is not to say, however, that he was therefore immune from the harsh, earthly wrath of his fellows. Minor violations might be forgiven an individual with Coyote *Buha,* but major infractions often led to death.

Charms and magical techniques, as well as *Buha,* were utilized to transcend a world of matter-of-fact cause and effect. Practically all charms involved the attainment of desired results through techniques of analogy; that is, through sympathetic magic. As might be expected, there were numerous hunting and fishing charms which automatically brought good fortune in these pursuits without personal appeal to supernatural will. It was enough that the individual knew the formulaic expression, the proper composition and use of a charm; these had power *per se,* and the desired effect could not help but follow.

A close second in importance to these economic aids were those charms and magical techniques which had to do with success of the other two consuming passions of Shoshonean culture—gambling and sex.

Within the camp group, and at all occasions when a few camps came together, both forms of recreation were pursued. Gambling, of course, was indulged in openly; there were many gambling games, but the favorite, by far, was the hand game. Stakes were never high, but this in no way dulled the keen competition. The charms were numerous, and although some types were generally recognized as efficacious, many individuals had their favorite gambling charms whose manufacture was divulged to none. One common charm was a mixture of dried bull frog and red paint. This was rubbed on the wrist of the gambler. Whenever he functioned as guesser in the hand game, his mouth would draw over toward the side where the white bone was concealed, and he would make the croaking sounds of a bull frog. Extreme caution had to be taken with this, as with other gambling charms. Any violation of the formula invited danger. The presence of a menstruating woman, for example, not only rendered the charm void, but might react harmfully upon the user.

Not only were love charms secretly manufactured, but their results had to be concealed from those who might feel a keen sense of loss or rage because of their operation.

There also were various omens of ill fortune which were disregarded only by the most foolhardy. A man who felt a twitching of his arm, leg or eye muscles was convinced that he should post-pone whatever task he had set for himself that day lest mis-fortune befall him. A hunter, for example, would not venture out on the day he experienced these muscular movements.

Muscle twitching was linked with the infrequent sorcery of aboriginal life. *DijiBo*, this power for evil, was acquired through a series of "bad" dreams, usually dreams of death, and frequently manifested itself by palpitations in the body of the possessor and possessed. It could be "thrown" into the body of the victim by intense concentration on the part of the sorcerer, who often ac-companied the transfer with some muscular movement.

The most vicious form of sorcery appeared to be that concerned with the transfer of evil from a woman, through the twitching of her vulva, to a man. However, it was recognized that a person might not only possess *DijiBo* unwillingly, but might transfer it to another without intending to do so. Not every woman had complete control of her vulval movements.

As a possible corollary to the foregoing, a woman's genitals were always considered dangerous, and hidden from the eyes of men. Even a husband dared not see them, although he might play with them while engaged in sexual traffic with his wife. If a male happened to catch a glimpse, intentionally or not, he might become ill or blind. No Soshoni woman would sit with her legs carelessly spread apart. The skirt of the female was always cut in strips along the lower edge, so that if she forgot and sat with her legs apart, the strips covered her genitals. She was forci-bly reminded of any carelessness in the sitting posture by the traditional duty of the brother or a male relative to jab a burn-ing stick between her thighs.

The camp group furnished the setting in which the drama of birth, puberty and death was enacted. Each of these life crises was emphasized by the group and marked by ceremonial behavior and beliefs. The term of pregnancy was accurately gauged by the woman, who kept a knotted string which marked the phases of the moon. During the last few weeks, or sometimes at the onset of labor pains, a conical willow shelter was erected by the woman's mother or sister. A shallow pit was dug in which a slow-burning fire was built. This was covered with a layer of dry earth and grass, and upon this insulation the woman stretched herself so that the heat would allow her blood to flow freely to bring about painless birth and easy expulsion of the after-birth. Any woman in the camp group would aid in birth, and although men were usually excluded from the hut, the husband might aid his wife if no woman helper was available.

A pole which had been driven into the ground was grasped by the woman as she squatted in the birth position. If the delivery was difficult, the person aiding her might force the baby out by pressing her knee against the mother's stomach, or by rubbing the stomach with weasel fur. The woman's mother washed the baby's body and then carried it outside the hut. The child was held up toward the east and the grandmother blew upon it, murmuring a wish for its health and fruitful life, as did Coyote when he made the Shoshoni out of clay.

The mother and baby stayed in this hut for a month. If birth occurred during the summer, the woman followed behind the other members of the group during the frequent shifts of residence, until her term of seclusion had expired.[18] Certain dietary restrictions had to be observed at this time. The mother drank only water which had been boiled and could eat no food which had any connection with blood. This excludes at the present time not only meat and fish, but eggs and even milk. Since the food that she could eat—roots, seeds and berries—was the most common and easily procurable through her own efforts, there was no undue burden on the general food problem. The woman could leave the hut and forage for food and even enjoy the companionship of the other women in the group; she could not, however, come into the common camp site or have contact with men.

The husband also observed traditional modes of behavior at the birth of his first son and daughter. Often, a separate enclosure was erected for him with the aid of his mother-in-law, and in this enclosure the man lived for five days observing the same food tabus as his wife. He could neither hunt nor fish, nor eat

---

[18] Some informants stated that the period of seclusion at the birth of the first-born was three months; at the second-born, one and a half months; and one month at all subsequent births. There is no need to weigh one statement against the other; no two camps conformed to an exact standard of behavior.

fatty or heavy foods, lest his blood coagulate and make him lazy and slow of thought.[19] Most important, the father had to keep constantly moving during this period; his nimble actions during the first five days of his child's life determined his own vigor and keenness in later life. As soon as the baby came from the mother's womb, the father rushed to the nearest stream, broke the ice if necessary, washed his penis, and jumped in. Before sunrise every morning, he quickly ran up a steep hill, holding a young twig in his hand. Whenever he stopped to rest, he placed a small bundle of sagebrush under each arm, in each bent elbow, each knee. Upon his return to the camp, he deposited the twig in the branches of a healthy tree. To ignore any of these ritual acts invited a future existence of indolence and misfortune.

Both the mother and father strictly observed other tabus during this crucial period. They scratched their skins only with a stick lest their fingers grow listless and welts mar their bodies; they touched their hair only with a grass brush, otherwise it soon fell out; if they laughed indiscriminately, they were doomed to stupidity.

These birth ceremonies which affected both father and mother were almost identical with those which each had undergone at puberty and may, therefore, be viewed as a formal reaffirmation of the individual's eagerness to make himself adequate to the demands upon him.

At pubescence, each sex conformed to those ritual acts which counteracted the socially stigmatized qualities of stupidity and sluggish behavior. The young man was isolated for five days when his voice cracked and deepened, in much the same way as was his father at his birth. The same dietary and behavior tabus were observed, and for the same reasons. He had to keep a fire constantly burning in this "make-self-over-hut." Every morning, before sunrise, he ran as fast and as far as he could for the load of firewood which was to last until the next morning. On the last of the five (or seven) days, the boy brought water from the

[19] This fear of heavy, sluggish blood as a threat to keenness and industry was prevalent throughout adult life and was counteracted by frequent arm incisions to allow blood to flow out and so become "thin."

creek, washed himself thoroughly, and donned new garments. The first deer he killed could not be eaten by himself or any of his immediate family, but was given to other kin in the camp group. This ensured luck in future hunting.

The first menses marked the puberty ceremony for the maiden. The familiar tabus were strictly observed. The girl was secluded from the men in the camp during this first period until five days after the appearance of the second menses. At each subsequent menstrual period she retired for five days, the flow usually being completed by that time. She wore only her oldest and dirtiest garments, and these were carefully put away until the next period of menstrual seclusion. Since none could eat the seeds or roots which a woman gathered during this time, a surplus was sometimes produced which was set aside for the next period. Famine broke down this tabu as it did others, and even this dangerous menstrual food reserve was eaten by others during periods of starvation.

The White Knives felt that menstrual blood was always dangerous. Not only did entrance to the menstrual hut cause a man's illness by nosebleed or the vomiting of his own blood, but if a woman in this condition crossed a hunter's path, he would suffer misfortune for some time. The White Knives themselves declared that it was precisely to safeguard the hunter's ability that women retreated to the menstrual hut at this time. The dangers extended to other activities—a gambler would suffer reverses if his wife was menstruating; the presence of such a woman at a shamanistic performance would nullify the cure; no antelope would enter the corral if it smelled such blood.

Birth and puberty, biological phenomena, involved ceremonial behavior. Marriage, a social phenomenon, did not. Death had a minimum of formal rites, although the beliefs associated with it were numerous. To understand the behavior of the White Knives when death occurred, we must turn to their concepts of soul, ghost and afterworld.

The soul or spirit, *muguwa*,[20] was inevitably acquired at birth, nebulous in form, and localized somewhere in the head. The *muguwa's* development was completed with the closing of the

[20] The *muguwa* was identified with the bird-like *Buha,* or life-principle.

fontanel suture. It was always dangerous to touch the soft part of the child's head, for this would allow the *muguwa* to escape, and cause the child's death. Even in adulthood, the *muguwa* might be ejected from the body by a hard fall or a sharp blow. It was then necessary to call a shaman who would attempt to recall the spirit before it had decided to remain in the afterworld.

The afterworld was hazily visualized, somewhere to the west near a large body of water, a pleasant place with much green grass and shade, dancing, gambling and abundant food. Versions of the spirit world differ somewhat, since a number of individuals whose *muguwa* had traveled there and returned contributed constant variations to the concept. Relatives there would plead with the spirit to remain. Indeed, in so pleasant a setting, it was often loathe to return, so that the shaman who sent his own *muguwa* after it to persuade it to come back, had a difficult task. In fact, shamans often endangered their own lives, since their own *muguwa* were reluctant to return after such an excursion.

But it is *tsoap*, the ghost, who impinged on everyday life, for when an individual died his soul was gone forever but his ghost often returned to the spot where its human counterpart had perished to plague those in the vicinity.[21] It was dangerous even to speak the name of the deceased lest its *tsoap* appear. The ghost returned in the form of dust whirlwinds or of coyote, or it took no tangible form but its presence was sensed. To meet a *tsoap* often presaged misfortune or death.

Since the *muguwa* automatically went to the afterworld at death, no ceremonies were necessary to direct or speed its departure. A sick person, often left behind as the camp moved on, frequently succumbed in the small willow enclosure which the group had built for him. Otherwise the corpse, its face toward the east, was laid out flat and covered with sagebrush and the rocks which had been displaced to make the shallow grave. Sometimes the deceased was left in his hut, and the hut smashed down over the body. Burial occurred the same day as death and the

---

[21] Informants were vague and conflicting on the question of whether the soul and ghost were two distinct entities. Some claimed that the soul was transformed into the ghost at death.

camp immediately shifted its residence, impelled both by the fear of *tsoap* and the demands of the food quest. The immediate vicinity where death had occurred was avoided in the future by the camp group.

This fear of *tsoap* extended to all the possessions of the deceased, so that his few pieces of clothing, his bow, arrows and flint artifacts were either burned, cast away or buried with him. Even the hut in which the dead person had lived was demolished. This, however, worked no hardship in the summer and little in the winter since shelters were quickly and easily erected.

There was no specific period for the duration of mourning, although it was usually a month before grief abated. Immediate kin cut off their hair in irregular chunks, gashed their arms, legs and ear lobes, and remained unwashed for some time so that their tear-stained faces were outward manifestations of grief. A wife or mother mourned before sunrise since, at this time, the deceased could hear the wailing. An adult male rarely cried, although he might give vent to his grief when he was away from others.

Suicides were rare, but occasionally they did occur. The prime motive was frustration in love. Two parallel cousins in love and forbidden to marry because of the incest tabus, might take their own lives. A suitor rejected by a girl's coldness, or by her family's refusal, might commit suicide if he were unable to overcome these objections by forceful capture or elopement. A suicide received the customary burial and mourning. It was thought, however, that its *muguwa* was denied the sanctuary of the afterworld, and hovered about wailing at night and annoying people.

Sex behavior was both relatively unformalized and realistic. The rôle of the sexes in reproduction was clearly recognized. Marital fidelity was an ideal to which lip service was given, but only the rare and the very simple conformed. Outside of the narrow tabu circle, any woman, married or not, was a challenge to a man's prowess as a lover. If a man and a woman talked and laughed together or even walked together, it was tacitly assumed that they were having sexual relations. Since intimacy or any of its outward signs could not be openly flouted for fear of arousing recrimination from those who felt deprived by such relations, philandering was driven undercover. Whenever a few camps met, sex intrigue and clandestine affairs usually followed.

An outraged husband might do a number of things, depending upon his anger. He might kill both his wife and her lover if he found them in *flagrante delicto,* or he might kill either; usually, he killed neither, but resorted to beating the one he thought most to blame. He might banish his wife, but if he loved her sufficiently, he would forgive her trespasses. A wife, however, expected her husband to philander somewhat, although she might beat her rival and rip her skirt, expose her genitals and shame her by spitting on them.

Under certain circumstances, however, pre- or extra-marital relations enjoyed *sub-rosa* tolerance. Because cross-cousins were potential mates, they engaged in a particularly warm joking relationship, often to the extent of coitus. Before the marriage of either cross-cousin, this relationship continued with only mild rebuke. After marriage to other mates, however, if this state of affairs persisted, caution had to be observed not to incur the wrath of the respective husband or wife. The relationship between a man and his wife's sisters, or a woman and her husband's brothers, was also of this same type, and enjoyed its *sub-rosa* sanction through recognition of the lien each held on the other through the potential functioning of the sororate and levirate. Any sexual pleasures which were enjoyed before the actual operation of these institutions were regarded as good sport by all except the resentful spouse.

This relationship was given even heartier social sanction at certain times. During the final few months of pregnancy and often until the child was weaned or could crawl about, a husband abstained from sexual relations with his wife. He could fill this interim, however, by sleeping with his wife's sister, if she was available and willing. The wife might protest, but social opinion upheld the man at this time more strongly than at others.

In this atmosphere of philandering, it was inevitable, despite techniques of birth control, that there should be a number of illegitimate children. Since each child was born into a camp group of close kin, its relations were assured. The attitude toward it, however, had nothing to do with the fact of illegitimacy—this had no social stigma—but depended largely upon whether the resources of the group could support a child. If not, it was abandoned. But if the camp could take care of it, the baby was accepted and cherished as was any other. Furthermore, the marital opportunities of the mother were in no way handicapped by this consequence of former philandering.

There were no behavior restrictions which were strong enough to justify the term "avoidance." To prevent the possibility of incest, however, a brother and sister were enjoined from sex play and salacious conversation. These "respect" attitudes were observed by parallel cousins and those others between whom sexual relations were forbidden. Although a man and his mother-in-law did not stand in this strict incest relationship, his attitude toward her was usually one of respect. However, if the mother-in-law was fairly young and desirable, sexual desire, regardless of respect, might triumph.

Respect for age and kinship accorded in any camp with respect for persons with superior skill, supernatural or mundane, to procure food or to protect those who could procure it. It is difficult to disentangle the two.

Property concepts were relatively simple. Production and use were the determining criteria of ownership. Except small children's, clothing was made by each individual for his own use, and was indisputably personal property. Basketry and pottery made by women, and clubs, bows, arrows and flint artifacts made by men were used by each exclusively or nearly so, and these also fell into the category of private property. The instruments of production, such as the large nets used in hunting and fishing, were usually made and used by the coöperative activity of a number of individuals in a camp group, and were jointly owned. If but one individual had manufactured a net, he was accorded certain privileges, but he could not refuse its use to other members of the group. Thus, although one man's net was used in a fish catch, the fish were equally divided. The maker of the net, however, had first claim in the division and so obtained the choicest fish, but because of the continued reciprocal obligations in the camp group, it was to his interests not to be greedy.

As has been noted, land and other natural resources were neither individually nor jointly owned. It was used by various groups and no efforts were expended upon it to increase its production.

The problem of inheritance, perplexing and fraught with hostility in so many primitive societies, was neatly resolved among the White Knives. There simply was no inheritance. The strong fear of evoking the ghost of the dead automatically prevented any individual from appropriating what few personal articles the deceased had possessed. If he had had a predominant share in the manufacture or use of jointly operated instruments of production, they were also destroyed; otherwise it was felt that the participation of the others outweighed the danger of ghostly recrimination. Moreover, those articles which constituted personal property were necessarily few in number, for an accumulation would have hindered the necessary camp movements. The amount of property was strictly limited by the sparse yield of the environment, the demands of a high mobility, and inadequate transportation facilities.[22]

There was no individual ownership of such incorporeal property as songs or dances. Supernatural power, of course, was individually owned because only the possessor could utilize it. Although this power could be inherited from some dead relative, it could not be bequeathed to a specific individual; the powers themselves selected the recipient.

In this framework of loose and limited ownership, with so few articles to be owned, the concept of wealth (and the lack of any defense of, or desire to increase that wealth) was one of the many factors which converged to make for the remarkably low level of antagonism.

The foregoing sketch of White Knives culture throws into relief the harsh economic life and the adjustment of the culture to its demands. This bare subsistence level, and the activities of these Shoshoni to maintain it, is the focal point about which the rest of the culture is integrated. The size of the camp group it-

---

[22] A few skin tipis obtained in trade from the Bannock or Nez Percé were cut up into moccasins and clothing precisely because of lack of transportation facilities.

self was limited by the exigencies of the habitat and the techniques of production. Circumstances of food supply and poor transportation facilities prevented the occurrence of large or frequent group gatherings over an extended period of time, and true band organization was impossible. The camp group, therefore, was practically a complete ethnic unit, a microcosm of almost the total White Knives culture.

This fundamental independence of the camp group is extremely important in understanding the informal, amorphous character of the culture. Of course, the isolation was not complete, but it precluded any consistent or significant control from outside the camp itself, or uniform conformity to more than the broadest outlines of the culture pattern. There was a certain latitude, within limits, allowed these small camp groups in working out the constellations of behavior, not to be found in a more stabilized society where the constant interaction of a large number of individuals could result in a high degree of integration and cultural conformity.

It is difficult to estimate the length of time that the White Knives have had this type of culture. As with so many other primitive groups, their pre-White history is now buried in a forgotten past. The few archaeological excavations in the Great Basin demonstrate that simple hunting and gathering peoples have been in this area for a very long period.[23] The rate of culture change must have been very slow. Indeed, these Shoshoni evinced but few more cultural elements than those commonly assumed for the Asiatic immigrants when they first came to the American continent, some ten thousand years ago.[24] Denied the horse complex which transformed the Plains cultures in the seventeenth to nineteenth centuries, or the agriculture practiced in the Southwest, or any improvement in economy which could make for an economic or social surplus, the White Knives retained their crude level of existence. However, with the impact

[23] M. R. Harrington, *Gypsum Cave, Nevada;* L. L. Loud and M. R. Harrington, *Lovelock Cave;* J. H. Steward, *Ancient Caves of the Great Salt Lake Region.*

[24] For example, the hypothetical picture which Kroeber gives for these immigrants is, in essence, a summary of White Knives culture. A. L. Kroeber, *Anthropology,* p. 349.

of the Whites, cultural elements were introduced to engender a ferment which has not yet been resolved.

THE CONTACT CONTINUUM

The Great Basin was the last portion of the United States to be explored. The early sixteenth century expeditions of the Spaniards touched only the southern and eastern fringes of the Basin. It was not until the second quarter of the nineteenth century that the first Whites penetrated this region. The record of the first contact comes from the reports of the Hudson's Bay Company's fur-trapping expeditions in the years 1825–29. Peter Skeene Ogden's party, working down from the base in Vancouver, followed the Owyhee River south and dropped down to the Humboldt, the first Whites to enter this area. During the same summer of 1825, American trappers from the St. Louis frontier, working west, met Ogden's party in northeastern Nevada.[25]

There followed about ten years of desultory trapping of beaver and other fur-bearing animals in a region which had never been rich in this respect. The barren nature of the country and the lack of water away from the Humboldt and its tributaries effectively limited the number of trapping parties, so that it never reached the proportions of those in other parts of the West.

This initial contact had but slight influence on the aboriginal life. A contemporary account furnishes vivid evidence of the desolate country, the straggling, poverty-stricken "naked wretches."[26] Zenas Leonard, a member of the Bonneville-Walker party which moved along the Humboldt River in 1833–34, emphasizes the simple camp organization, the starvation economy:

They are . . . small and cowardly, and travel in small groups of from four to five families—this they are compelled to do in order to keep

[25] *The Peter Ogden Journals,* T. C. Elliott, editor. Also H. H. Bancroft, *History of Nevada, Colorado and Wyoming, 1540–1888, Volume 25,* pp. 36–45. The History Company, San Francisco, Calif., 1890.

[26] "Journal of John Work's Snake Country Expedition of 1830–31," *Oregon Historical Society Quarterly, Volume XIV,* pp. 280–314, 1913. See also Washington Irving, *Adventures of Captain Bonneville,* for a contemporary account (1833–34) of the "Root Diggers," pp. 259–261.

from starvation. They are always roving from plain to plain, and from valley to valley—never remaining in one place longer than till game gets scarce.[27]

Leonard also recorded another significant fact, that the horse had not yet come to these Shoshoni, and expressed indignation upon noting that the women carried "a load of perhaps a hundred weight a whole day, without manifesting the least fatigue or complaint." Furthermore, he also records the non-hostility of these people, with, however, the regretful reservation that a few of his traps had been stolen.[28]

By 1840, the Whites found it no longer profitable to trap in this territory; even the meagre resources of game had dwindled. But a fresh impetus to westward penetration immediately followed. From 1840 to 1848, parties of emigrants intent upon securing fertile lands for cultivation pushed on to Oregon and California over the Oregon Trail. Some of these wagon trains branched off at Fort Hall to follow the Humboldt Valley route to the Sierra Nevadas. The official exploring expeditions of Fremont in the Great Basin (1843–45) were given wide publicity in the East. Over 100,000 copies of his report were circulated free throughout the states, and this was a potent factor in stimulating emigration to the West.[29]

Not until the accounts of some twenty years later, when the geography of the region and its inhabitants were better known, can we determine the natives referred to with any degree of accuracy. These references are rendered more ambiguous when we recall the high mobility of these Indians, nor are we aided by the generic designations of "Digger," "Shoshone" or "Shoshokoe." Not only is there doubt as to the group of Western Shoshoni referred to, but the descriptions may well apply to the Gosiutes on the east or the Paiute and Paviotso on the west.

Nevertheless, there are various records of the first encounters with the natives of this area, and some of these must have been White Knives. The first clash between the Whites and the In-

[27] Quaife, M. M., editor, *Narrative of the Adventures of Zenas Leonard*, The Lakeside Press, R. R. Donnelly and Sons, Chicago, Ill., 1934, pp. 78–79.
[28] *Ibid.*, p. 79. For a similar experience, see Work, *op. cit.*, p. 300.
[29] John Charles Fremont, *Report of Exploring Expedition*, also *Memoirs*.

dians is recorded by Leonard. The natives stole the traps which had been set by the party all along the Humboldt River. Some of the men gave vent to their annoyance by killing several Indians they happened to meet. However, a more drastic massacre occurred a few weeks later at Humboldt Sink when this same party killed thirty-nine natives, probably Paiutes, merely on suspicion of hostility.[30] One of the first emigrant parties to use the Humboldt Valley route to California (1845) left this note: "None of our company was killed by the Indians; but John Greenwood, son of the pilot, shot down an Indian by the roadside, and afterward boasted of it." [31]

Lacking horses or firearms, the Indians were at the mercy of these first Whites. Although the Whites knew nothing of the Great Basin, they were well acquainted with the Indian wars on the Plains and were quick to interpret smoke or advances as evidence of battle, and equally quick to kill. Among the White Knives, at least, resentment against these deaths without cause must have stimulated retaliation. Of probably greater importance, the Whites passed through with cattle, horses and other food which the Shoshoni were eager to obtain.[32] Such depredations, however, were not important until traffic along the Humboldt Valley reached its third stage.

In 1848, gold was discovered in southern California. The treaty with Mexico a few weeks later made Nevada a part of the United States. In 1849, gold was found in Nevada itself, at Gold Canyon on the Carson River. The great army which streamed westward, once over the divide into the Great Basin, had the choice of two routes, each of which led over northeastern Nevada. The journey through Nevada was dreaded because of the intense heat, the sterile wastes, the appalling toll of animal and human life.

Clashes between the natives and the emigrants increased. Although some of these occurred along the eastern Humboldt, the greater number were in Paiute country to the west. Here the somewhat more settled life of the Paiute suffered greater threat,

[30] Z. Leonard, *op. cit.*, p. 165.

[31] Quoted from a manuscript of the Grigsby-Ide party, H. H. Bancroft, p. 60.

[32] See E. M. Mack, *History of Nevada*, pp. 113–114, for one of the first recorded raids for livestock, in 1846.

and offered, through existing band organization, a better means of retaliation.[33] Nevertheless, the Shoshoni also suffered, not only through death at the hands of those who felt a prestige-gain with every Indian killed, but through the ecological disturbances which the California migrations caused.[34] The hundreds of trains and the accompanying herds of stock seriously drained the meagre economic resources of the area. Impelled by the lack of food and the desire for revenge, the Indians stole from the emigrants. As a further complication, former fur-trappers of several nationalities had married into Indian groups. These "squawmen" precipitated native attacks on emigrant trains so that stock could be driven off, and the Whites were forced to repurchase their stock at exorbitant prices.[35]

By 1852, theft and murder were so prevalent that an Indian agent was sent out to this territory to stop depredations. His efforts were unsuccessful; his recommendation to the Shoshoni was that they retire to the hills during the travel season, away from the highways of traffic. The agent reported to the Commissioner of Indian Affairs that relations with the Indians in Humboldt Valley "remain in a very unsettled and precarious condition, arising out of the constant and unavoidable encroachment upon their territory by the Whites and no provision being made for indemnifying and placing them beyond the reach of the injuries inflicted." [36] Shortly thereafter, troops of soldiers were sent to this area to patrol the emigrant routes.

Even during this late period of 1850, it seems that the White Knives did not yet have horses. Mules and horses were stolen, it was true, but they were not used for transportation, but to supplement the meagre food supply which had already been diminished by the activity of the fur-trappers during the initial stage of contact and intensified by the passing of the emigrant trains. Humfreville describes what this food meant to them:

[33] H. H. Bancroft, op. cit., pp. 205–217.
[34] Report of Agent Wilson, 1850, Senate Executive Documents, No. 18, 31st Congress, First Session, IX, pp. 97–98.
[35] E. M. Mack, op. cit., p. 291.
[36] Report of Agent Holeman, Senate Executive Documents, No. 1, 33rd Congress, First Session, pp. 259–260.

Their voracity when they could procure a supply of food was almost incredible. Five or six of them would sit around the carcass of a horse or mule and remain there until nothing but the bones were left. Unlike their Indian neighbors, they stole horses and mules, not to ride but to slaughter for food.[37]

In 1854, it was noted that the utility of the horse as a pack animal had outweighed in some cases its importance as mere food supply.[38] It was during this time, from 1850 to 1860, that the Shoshoni of the Humboldt Valley were intent upon getting horses from the emigrant trains. It is doubtful whether many horses were obtained from the surrounding Indian groups, though Bonneville noted that some of the Shoshoni north of the Snake River had received horses in trade from the lower Nez Percé.[39] Salmon Eaters informants stated that although a few horses were traded from the Bannock and Nez Percé, these were very few until after both the Bannock and Nez Percé uprisings in the latter 1870's. The White Knives themselves claimed that the only horses they obtained in pre-reservation days were those stolen from the Whites, and that many families had none until they were received from the government itself.

Far more important than the question of where these Shoshoni obtained their horses, is the consideration of what they did with them. For, by the year 1856, the Indian agent for Utah territory met a party of about fifty White Knives "well supplied with guns and horses."[40] The emigrant trains that year complained repeatedly that they had been fired upon and their property stolen in the White Knives territory.[41] By 1859, Agent Forney could speak of seven bands which roamed throughout the valleys of the Humboldt, and that each band had one principal chief and at least one sub-chief.[42]

[37] J. Lee Humfreville, *Twenty Years Among Our Hostile Indians*, Hunter and Company, New York, N. Y., 1899, p. 214.

[38] This record marks a transition in the use of the horse. At least in this one case, the horse was used as a pack animal. Lieut. E. G. Beckwith, *Report of Explorations for a Route for the Pacific Railroad of the Line of the Forty-First Parallel of North Latitude*, p. 31.

[39] W. Irving, *op. cit.*, p. 263.

[40] Agent Garland Hurt, *Report of C.I.A.*, 1856, p. 779.

[41] *Ibid.*, p. 781.

[42] Agent Forney, *Report of C.I.A.*, 1859, p. 362.

Thus, within the short span of approximately ten years, a most significant change in White Knives society had occurred. The factors which had been lacking for numerous centuries had now sharply converged to weld these Shoshoni into a band-like organization. There now was a common bond of resentment toward the Whites and a desire to obtain their property through warfare. But by far the most important factor was the introduction of the horse. Not only could this facilitate raids, but the horse could be used to overcome the former economic necessity of scattering the people over a vast territory; it was now possible to transport food to a central point where a larger population could assemble, and even to allow larger groups to move as units. Furthermore, the horse was used as a means of wider communication and coöperation so that the camp groups enjoyed a measure of consolidation formerly denied them.[43]

Probably the most important band of this short period was that which had Timoak as its leader and Ruby Valley as its nucleus, a territory south and east of White Knives territory. Attempts to determine whether Timoak had formerly been a shaman or ceremony leader have been fruitless. The information points to the fact that he had been only a local headman who had gathered a number of camps about him. This concentration was duplicated in five or six smaller bands along the Humboldt; at least two of these were composed of White Knives. The White Knives "chiefs," Captain Sam and Captain Charlie, had no shamanistic power; they rose in authority through a combination of shrewdness and force of personality. Captain George Washington, however, was a ceremony leader later on the reservation and might have functioned in this capacity before that time.[44] Their positions (and titles) were solidified by the White soldiers and officials who, after experience with Plains band organizations and the need to deal with a group through its representative, selected these men as spokesmen. By so doing, they enhanced the prestige

[43] J. H. Steward, *Linguistic Distributions and Political Groups of the Great Basin Shoshoneans*, pp. 630–632.

[44] Among the neighboring Paviotso, the relationship between supernatural power and chieftainship seems to have been stronger. Such outstanding chiefs as the Winnemuccas and Captain Dave were also famous for their curative powers. See W. Z. Park, *op. cit.*, pp. 66–67.

and authority of these "captains" among their followers. This band development took place only in the immediate vicinity of the Humboldt Valley where the racial impact was most severe. North of the valley, the camp groups still continued as autonomous units much as in aboriginal times.

However, these bands were never clearly developed. The camp groups, although now operating in a larger framework, still maintained their entity and often broke off to resume individual foraging for food.[45] Authority was significant only at times of raid or dealings with the Whites; at all times the camps functioned independently. This band organization had no opportunity to develop to such proportions as it assumed among the Southern Utes who, although starting from a cultural base similar to thàt of the White Knives, evolved an almost Plains-like pattern of organization in the two centuries of possession of the horse-complex.[46] The White Knives had not sufficient time to develop such consequences of band and war organization as societies, war honors, spies or the host of other traits which characterize neighboring horse tribes. Yet there were certain discernible beginnings of this type of structure. In accordance with the familiar Bannock and Wyoming Shoshoni war pattern, peace and war chiefs arose among the White Knives, although in attenuated form. The peace chief was the former camp headman who now had extended authority over a larger group of camps. The war chief was the bravest in battle and led the attack. The authority of the war chief was obtained just as any White Knives in aboriginal times had received power—supernaturally, through dream. Captain Buck dreamed that in times of battle his body was like fog and that bullets could pass through without hurting him. Thereafter, this *Buha* made him invulnerable in battle. It is significant that other men were now interpreting as war power the power of the wolf, which formerly gave cunning in the hunt.

But this embryonic band organization was short-lived. The

[45] Agent Forney, *op. cit.*, p. 362: "These bands frequently subdivide into many small squads to clean thoroughly the country, through which they roam, of everything containing a life-sustaining principle."

[46] See M. K. Opler, *op. cit.*, for the cultural consequences of the horse-complex among the Southern Ute.

fabulous Comstock lode discovered in 1857 attracted a stream of miners and gave rise to numerous boom towns throughout Nevada. By this time, also, thousands of settlers had come in to establish themselves in the fertile valleys. Indian raids were now a more serious threat. Aroused by Paiute and Shoshoni depredations in Nevada, the government first sent soldiers into the area to quell uprisings, and later attempted to preserve a measure of peace with some presents of blankets and various kinds of clothing. In 1863, a number of treaties were signed between the government and the Great Basin groups. The Ruby Valley Treaty was signed by Timoak and eleven other Western Shoshonean headmen. The government promised to establish a reservation in the territory and to pay the Indians 5,000 dollars annually for a term of twenty years. The Shoshoni, as their part of the agreement, promised that hostilities would cease, that the mail and telegraph lines would operate free of interference and that their territory could be mined and explored, ranches established and a railroad constructed.[47]

However, even before the treaty was signed, the embryonic band organization had begun to disintegrate. There had never been many horses.[48] Severe winters combined with lack of food and increasing White protection against the pilfering raids forced many of the camps to scatter and seek sustenance again by hunting and gathering; some groups were even clothed and fed by White settlers and the mining camps.[49] With a treaty signed and hope for a reservation of their own, this band organization, which never had any great cohesion, fell apart and depredations practically ceased.[50] A few renegades continued to operate, but even the Shoshoni themselves coöperated with the Whites in attempting to stop these last thieving raids.

[47] Treaty reprinted in *Survey of Conditions of the Indians in the United States,* 72nd Congress, First Session, Part 28, 1934, pp. 15843–44.
[48] Agent Mann, *Report of C.I.A.,* 1862, p. 204.
[49] Agent Hatch, *Report of C.I.A.,* 1862, p. 207.
[50] Commissioner Dole, *Report of C.I.A.,* 1864, p. 15: "The Shoshonees (Nevada) have been entirely peaceable since the treaty of friendship made with them." J. H. Simpson reports in 1869 that although the White Knives had been very treacherous, they have proved very friendly in late years. *The*

Despite the good faith of the Indians and their increasing poverty, no reservation was established for fourteen years. It was during these years that the Shoshoni suffered their most drastic adjustment to White culture. Although the incipient band organization existed for only a brief period, its repercussions persisted in later years. The leaders still retained their importance in the eyes of the Whites, and some of this prestige was reflected in the attitude of the natives themselves, so that these men continued to exert some loose authority.

It was not impossible to return completely to the old mode of life. Most of the animals had been killed off the lowlands; herds of antelope and deer were wiped out; dams and the fishing of the Whites were depleting the streams. Always poor in the meat of the larger animals, they were forced now more than ever to live on rats, ants, crickets, grubworms and other insects. The trees that bore the piñon nuts were being cut down and burned in the quartz mills. Dole, in 1864, notes further: ". . . the grass, upon the seeds of which they (Indians) have largely depended is being eaten off by the cattle of the settlers and the valleys where their stock has found pasturage are being occupied by them." [51] One account tells of the Whites Knives washing horse manure for whatever grain and seeds could be salvaged.[52]

The annual payments of 5,000 dollars were practically negligible to the Shoshoni, for out of this amount was deducted the salaries of the farmer agent and a medical officer.[53] There was also suspicion of graft. Furthermore, the freight rates from the New York or Chicago purchasing base were high. The articles which were distributed often had no value to the natives; hair-combs and fish-hooks were thrown away; flour was used as white

Shortest Route to California Illustrated by a History of Explorations of the Great Basin of the Utah, p. 47. Also see G. M. Wheeler, *Preliminary Report upon a Reconnaissance Through Southern and Southeastern Nevada,* p. 36.

[51] Commissioner Dole, *op. cit.,* p. 15. Also Farmer Gheen, *Report of C.I.A.,* 1876, pp. 116–118.

[52] Agent Wasson, *Report of C.I.A.,* 1862, p. 218.

[53] The farmer himself received $1,500 plus $500 for traveling expenses annually, out of this $5,000 allotment. Furthermore, the cost of medical treatment was deducted from the annual payment. *Correspondence of Levi Gheen,* letter dated January 13, 1873.

paint for their faces. A contemporary newspaper account is significant:

The Indian Agent has come and gone and that is all that can be said for him . . . At this place there were some 250 Indians in the circle, and the agent gave them 15 pairs of blankets, 8 coats, and a few dozen shirts and shawls, a bolt or two of blue drilling, combs, beads, fish-hooks, and knives, which competent judges say would not cost to exceed $250 or $300. During this winter we have heard of several Indians dying from exposure consequent to the lack of blankets and clothing.
. . . The generous person who distributed the above got curses, and has spread general discontent. The Indians say, "White man heap cheat"; and I think so too. These Indians are peaceable and generally honest. Who were these blankets for? If the Government has entrusted an agent with blankets and he has not done his duty, it can easily be proven, and the lowest penalty for such conduct should be to hang the agent to a telegraph pole.[54]

As early as 1855 and again in 1859, some Indians, with government aid, attempted to do some farming.[55] However, these first farms were unsuccessful and abandoned; the groups returned to the mountains and rejoined the foraging bands.[56] Later, when some of the Indians were successful in raising crops, the Whites dispossessed them from the fertile land. This was done by due legal process since the Whites established the proper claim for whatever Indian land they saw flourishing, and the natives were ignorant of the mechanism necessary to transfer public domain into private property.[57] In 1875, Farmer Gheen reported:

Some of the Indians who are engaged in farming, are compelled to rent land from the whites, nearly all the tillable land being claimed by the white settlers . . . The whites are rapidly settling this country, and in many cases the Indians are compelled to give up their little farms.[58]

In other cases, the necessary water used by the Indians in irrigating their small patches was diverted from the streams above the

54 *The Elko Independent*, January 18, 1873. Reprinted in *Survey of Conditions of the Indians in the United States, op. cit.*, p. 14868. Also see pages 14856, 14869.
55 Agent Hurt, *Report C.I.A.*, 1856, pp. 779–781. Also Agent Forney, *op. cit.*, p. 369.
56 Agent Davis, *Report C.I.A.*, 1861, p. 129.
57 Superintendent Parker, *Report C.I.A.*, 1866, p. 114. Also *Report C.I.A.*, 1869, p. 103.
58 Farmer Gheen, *Report C.I.A.*, 1875, p. 343. This "rent" of land from Whites was paid in labor. See Gheen, *Report C.I.A.*, 1878, p. 104.

Indian farms by White ranchers, thereby rendering the land valueless.[59] Those Shoshoni who were now working for ranchers complained that the wages of twenty-five cents a day that they received were insufficient.[60]

With such disturbances to their aboriginal food supply, the White Knives could no longer forage as self-sufficient camp units and so resume their former mode of life. Thoroughly discouraged by their failure to compete with the Whites as farmers, disheartened by the exploitation and their distrust of the Whites, many Indians completely gave up the fight to gain their livelihood from the land. Furthermore, they were now dependent upon guns, whiskey, clothing and tools which could only be gotten from the traders. Their solution was to attach themselves in small groups, often under the loose leadership of the recently broken band headman, to mining towns, ranches and railroad towns. Their new attempt at adjustment was to eke out what existence they could by doing wood-cutting, herding, washing clothes, odd jobs, pilfering and begging in the winter, and some hunting and gathering during the summer.[61]

The plight of these Indian settlements in frontier Nevada of the 1870's is most depressing. One report gives us the following picture:

They hang around mining-towns and live partly upon refuse thrown away from the restaurants and boarding houses. In some places they eat meat that is thoroughly rotten, and they are the most degraded beings I ever saw. They are very fond of whiskey and will do almost anything for it. The whiskey sold to them by the White people and Chinese is almost rank poison.[62]

Horses and mules were again being stolen to augment the scanty food supply. The social position of the Indians at this time is sharply reminiscent of that of the Negro at present in some

[59] Farmer Gheen, *Report of C.I.A.*, 1877, p. 151.

[60] *Ibid.*, 1876, pp. 116–118.

[61] W. J. Hoffman, *Miscellaneous Ethnographic Observations on Indians Inhabiting Nevada, California and Arizona*, p. 465. Also Agent Parker in *Report of C.I.A.*, 1866, p. 114, after enumerating the types of labor the White Knives do for the Whites, adds: "They have made little or no progress in morals."

[62] Farmer Gheen, *Report of C.I.A.*, 1877, p. 152. The Chinese referred to were those first brought in as cheap labor for the building of the Central Pacific Railroad in 1868.

Southern communities. The Shoshoni are described as lazy, shiftless, ignorant and thieving. In one instance, at least, the killing of a White man by a drunken Indian resulted in the death of four other Indians by an angry mob that also captured the original murderer from the town officer and lynched him.[63]

Many of the native women had become prostitutes, an easy thing to do in the frontier towns which had a preponderance of such men as soldiers, prospectors and laborers, who lived hard and enjoyed life by every form of diversion these mining and railroad towns offered.[64] The women were certainly motivated by the necessary money which they obtained through this employment. As a concomitant of prostitution, venereal diseases now appeared.[65]

During this period from 1860 to 1877, the White Knives underwent a period of partial adaptation to the demands of the new situation. Living in symbiotic relationship with the Whites and enjoying a somewhat more stable food supply, these scattered communities now had their mobility restricted. The camp groups, however, seem to have suffered little change; they still functioned as kinship and coöperative units. The relative stability and nearness to other Indians now made for greater consolidation, and former band headmen retained some authority without, however, a return to the band organization. Dances and *Gwini* ceremonies enjoyed a larger and more consistent attendance; shamanistic curings attracted more people. Many groups still coöperated in the antelope and rabbit drives, although in the summer a number of communities would again break up into foraging units.

The material culture changed most rapidly in this stage of contact. Bows and arrows coexisted with guns for some time but firearms soon supplanted the primitive weapons. The art of making flint artifacts diminished during this period, and cheap metal knives and other metal tools were substituted. With the be-

[63] Farmer Gheen, *Report of C.I.A.*, 1875, p. 343.

[64] For description of Indians at this time, see report of Special Commissioners Powell and Ingalls: Conditions of . . . Western Shoshones of Nevada, *Report of C.I.A.*, 1873, pp. 41–70.

[65] The introduction of venereal disease is now crystallized in the Shoshoni language. The White Knives term for these diseases, translated, is: "Black clothing sickness." The clothing refers to the navy blue uniform of the cavalry soldiers of this period.

ginnings of farming, new techniques and tools were introduced—hoes, plows, irrigation and the entire agriculture complex. The scanty aboriginal clothing was quickly displaced by the more adequate frontier garb of the settlers; the women soon learned from the actions of the white men that their breasts had sexual significance and now had to be covered. The coming of cattle, pigs and cultivated plants introduced new foods and modes of cooking. With less need for constant movements in the food search, commercial tents and even ramshackle frame structures were now used as dwellings by the more fortunate. A number of Indians had acquired a few English words with the first contact; under this more constant association, some could now speak coherently with the Whites.[66]

Despite these outward material changes, however, the old customs and beliefs flourished. Shamanism, particularly, was as strong as ever and may even have been strengthened by the need to cure the new diseases which had cropped up.[67] The causes of these new illnesses the White Knives, and particularly the shamans, now explained by reference to their own framework of beliefs: the Whites were practicing wholesale witchcraft in an attempt to entirely eliminate the natives.[68] The puberty ceremonies and the couvade-like observances of the father at birth must have persisted for some time, but with the shift from a pure hunting and gathering economy, the need for these observances lessened, and only a few remnants remained by the time of removal to the reservation in 1877. Birth and the menses, biological constants in any society, continued to be explained in the old terms and women still followed the traditional observances. The *Gwini*

[66] The first words were picked up from the bullwhackers of the emigrant trains. The customary greeting from the Indians to the emigrants was: "How do you do—whoa! haw! God damn you!" As an extension, the oxen were called "whoa! haws!" and the Whites, "God damns." E. M. Mack, *op. cit.*, pp. 52–53, quoting Alonzo Delano, *Life on the Plains and at the Diggings*, Auburn, Miller, and Mulligan, 1854.

[67] In addition to the venereal diseases, an outbreak of smallpox occurred in 1871–72. (*Levi Gheen's Correspondence.* Letter dated April 4th, 1872.) The number of deaths is not known. Other factors which increased the disease and death rate are bad whiskey, rotten food, and poor adjustment to strange clothing and shelter.

[68] Farmer Gheen, *Report of C.I.A.*, 1877, p. 152.

ceremonies became more stabilized, and dancing, games and gambling overshadowed the religious and fertility rites; the ceremony itself was now being called a "fandango." However, there is no adequate record of the functioning of these ceremonies and the presence of the old customs at this period. We can follow their development more clearly during the reservation period.

The nativistic movement of 1870 which arose among the Paiutes near the Walker River Reservation may have touched the neighboring White Knives, but in this the record is unclear.[69] Christian missionaries had not yet extended their activities to this area. The Mormons, who missionized many Gosiutes, Bannock and other Fort Hall Shoshoni, exerted some influence over the White Knives at this time. In accordance with the Mormon theory that the Indians were descendants of one of the "ten lost tribes" they were welcomed and even a few baptized. During this period of sharpening conflict between the government and the Mormons, the Shoshoni were exhorted to resist the authority of the government.[70] Although these preachings undoubtedly strengthened the general feeling of resentment toward the officials, it could not result in open clashes or rebellion; the White Knives were now too broken and demoralized.

The attitude toward White acculturation at this time was resentful because of the severe ecological changes which had occurred, the appropriation by the Whites of the choicest land, the failure to carry out the terms of the treaty, the introduction of new diseases, whiskey and prostitution, and the hardships entailed in adjustment to the new economy. Yet at the same time there appeared to be a resignation to change, even an attitude of defeatism. The quick attempt at agriculture and herding, the adoption of White tools and clothing, the acquisition of the English language and even its writing does not argue for a proud

[69] No informant could recall such movement. J. Mooney, *The Ghost Dance Religion*, p. 701, merely notes that the influence was felt among the Bannock and Shoshoni, as well as among all the scattered bands of Paiute.

[70] J. Mooney, *The Ghost Dance Religion*, pp. 703–704. Also letter of May 16, 1877, in which Gheen is quoted as saying: "Bishop Tadlock—Mormon—is preaching to the Indians and doing all in his power to embitter them against the Government of the United States." *Levi Gheen's Correspondence* (1869–1873).

retention of the old mode of life. Indeed, as the White Knives themselves often stated, they lacked pride. After all, they were children of Coyote and were not rich, warlike and powerful like the Bannock, Nez Percé or Flathead; consequently, they had nothing to make them proud, and so little to lose through change. Nevertheless, they were not content to live in this poverty-stricken relationship with Whites who treated them as inferiors. The headmen repeatedly appealed to the authorities asking that the reservation be set aside for them in accordance with the treaty so that they might have their own ranches and live in peace and dignity.[71]

After repeated entreaties and pressure by the Whites themselves to remove the Indians, the government in 1877 finally established a reservation at Duck Valley for the Western Shoshonean groups. The selection of this site alienated Timoak's band, the Ruby Valley Shoshoni. Because of the relative fertility of Ruby Valley, those Shoshoni achieved somewhat greater stability and solidarity both before and after White contact than did the White Knives. At the time the treaty was drawn up, because of Timoak's influence, the boundaries of the Western Shoshoni were delineated as those strictly within the foraging orbits of Timoak's own people, in territory partly overlapping and somewhat to the east and south of that of the White Knives. Within this area, the government had promised to establish the reservation. However, during the few years immediately preceding the selection of the reservation, the government farmer of the area was influenced by Captain Sam, the White Knives leader, who had not even signed the treaty. Captain Sam urged that the reservation be established in country familiar to the White Knives themselves, just north of the boundaries stipulated in the treaty.[72] This was done. Although during the first few years some of the Ruby Valley Shoshoni and contiguous groups went up to the reservation, they later withdrew and returned to live in scattered communities along the Humboldt Valley, as they still do.[73]

[71] *Levi Gheen's Correspondence* (1869–1873). Letter dated April 3rd, 1873.
[72] Gheen, *Report of C.I.A.*, 1877, pp. 151–153.
[73] At the present time (1937) there are approximately 800 Western Shoshoni living outside the reservation. The "Timoak" Indians are agitating for gov-

The acculturation process, therefore, falls into four clearly defined time periods of contact. (1) The first fifteen years of contact (1825–40) brought few trappers into the area and resulted in the beginnings of ecological disturbances and a few clashes; otherwise, there were no significant changes. (2) The following decade (1840–50) saw a number of emigrant trains passing through Nevada on their way to the coast. There were some pilfering raids and the horse was acquired, but only to be eaten. (3) The third period followed on the heels of the gold rush and the discovery of both silver and gold in Nevada itself. The stream of emigrants, miners and settlers now reached major proportions, and were being raided by the White Knives, who had acquired the horse and gun. An incipient band organization arose, and these Shoshoni experienced their greatest degree of consolidation. (4) The fourth period (1860–77) saw the disintegration of the weak band; yet, because of the severe drain on the aboriginal food supply and settlement by the Whites, a return to the former mode of life was impossible. This new phase resulted in a period of breakdown and partial adjustment. Many natives still remain in this fourth phase, living outside of the reservation and attempting, with varied success, to adapt themselves to White culture. But the majority of the White Knives moved to the Western Shoshoni Reservation, where they entered the fifth phase of the acculturation process.

THE RESERVATION

The Western Shoshoni Reservation was not selected until the better parts of Nevada had been claimed by the Whites. Therefore, although the site has some agricultural and herding advantages, it is in one of the least accessible portions of the territory, a hundred miles from the nearest railroad over poor roads. This isolation, until the last few years, worked to the advantage of the Indians since they were now free of the influence of the less desirable White elements.

---

ernment compensation on the grounds that the government did not establish the reservation in the agreed territory. For an account of their arguments and their present conditions, see the testimony and documents in *Survey of Conditions of Indians in the United States, op. cit.,* pp. 14807–14893.

At present, there is a population of 670 Indians living on the reservation. Probably two-thirds of these are White Knives, but there has been so much intermarriage with the Paiutes that an exact statement of the proportion is now impossible. The Paiutes from southeastern Oregon, the Paddy Kap band, came to the reservation in 1886. The ethnology of this latter group is not known in detail, but their aboriginal culture was broadly similar to that of the White Knives. They maintain themselves at the northern end of the reservation and do not participate as actively in agency politics and affairs as do the Shoshoni, since they have strong social and kinship ties with the Paiutes at the Warm Springs Agency in Oregon. Nevertheless, the relations between the two groups on the reservation are thoroughly amicable. This situation is entirely in accordance with the aboriginal pattern of necessary friendliness and sharply differs from the situation on the Wind River Reservation where the richer and more powerful Plains Shoshoni still maintain a strong hostility toward their traditional enemies, the Arapaho. That this feeling of band pride among the Plains Shoshoni was a concomitant of their buffalo economy and consequent band organization seems obvious when we recognize that they once had the same cultural and economic base as had the White Knives.

The Western Shoshoni Reservation contains approximately 400 square miles; the boundary between the states of Nevada and Idaho bisects it midway north and south. The eastern third is mountainous, reaching an elevation of over 7,000 feet. The western third is rocky plateau region and furnishes both spring and fall range for the stock which graze in the higher mountains in midsummer. The middle third contains the valley where the Indians live and where are all the irrigable lands. This valley has an average elevation of about 5,500 feet which makes for a severe climate. The long, bitter winter and the late frosts in the spring and early frosts in the fall effectively shorten the growing season.

The Owyhee River rises about fifty miles south of the reservation and traces its way from its southeast to northwest corner. Although during the first few years of reservation life, the river provided fish and adequate irrigation, it now dries up each summer because so many ranches above the reservation divert its waters into reservoirs for their own irrigation purpose. The Indians have only the gravity flow of the river and flood irrigation in the early spring run-off, so that the lack of water now limits the hay and alfalfa crops and, as a consequence, limits the number of cattle that can be successfully raised.[74]

After long centuries of cultural accommodation to the harsh demands of their environment, White contact operated to disturb the economy and to upset the balance between the culture elements. Customs, beliefs and practices which had been meaningful in relation to the simple hunting and gathering life were now rendered anomalous. Some of the consequences of this changing economic base have already been noted, and it is fruitful from this point of view to observe further the economic developments on the reservation.

During the period between the breakdown of the loose band organization and the establishment of the reservation, most of the Shoshoni had alternated between the aboriginal hunting-gathering life and some of the forms of labor which the Whites introduced. For most of the White Knives, this was farming. For ten years before the reservation was established most of them had worked on farms for wages, so that the agriculture which was encouraged on the reservation was not a strange technique. The government furnished most of the implements and the seed, and driven now by a desire to become self-supporting and independent, most of the natives worked industriously to make the land yield.

The transition from a food-gathering economy to agriculture, and later to herding, was accomplished with relatively little difficulty. Unlike many other primitive groups, the food quest of the White Knives needed no incentive other than the actual desire for food; the urge to work was not socially determined by such institutions as the potlatch, ceremonial feasts, nor by the necessity to maintain a system of affinal exchange. Consequently,

[74] The government, in the summer of 1937, had almost completed the Wild Horse Dam which it intended to make available for use in 1938. It is expected that this dam will increase the irrigable lands from the 5,500 acres at present to 25,000 acres.

these Shoshoni were immune from the danger which other cultures had to face under White impact inasmuch as there was no structure to disintegrate, leaving the natives with little motivation for any activity, let alone a new form of economy.

It was but natural that the organization of the White Knives when they first arrived upon the reservation would have been that to which they had grown accustomed. They settled along the fertile banks of the Owyhee in communities of between ten and twenty families, each community resolving itself into camp units of the same composition as in aboriginal times. This clustering was reminiscent of both the aboriginal winter community and the recent band organization. The first census of the reservation, taken in 1882, shows the population split into two large communities, each under the leadership of a "captain," who was recognized by the agency as the "chief" of the group. These "captains," of course, were the former headmen of the short-lived band.

There were no individual or family land grants. Each community appropriated as much of the land as it was able to cultivate. Under this arrangement, the two aboriginal patterns of production and distribution coexisted. The camps worked cooperatively in the community fields, and each was expected to contribute as much labor as possible. No camp was allowed to suffer by the gain of another, and the products of this communal labor were equitably divided among the entire group, as they had been in the communal antelope drive or rabbit hunt. On the other hand, each camp continued to hunt and gather seeds and roots during short and infrequent portions of the year as individual units, and the products of these efforts were distributed only within the camp itself as in former times. In each case, ownership of property continued to be based on production.

In the face of repeated discouragements and loss of crops through inadequate harvesting equipment, grasshopper and cricket invasions, cattle depredations, weed ravages and, with the years, an increasing lack of water, it is surprising to read the almost monotonous consistency of agency reports attesting to the industry and initiative of the White Knives. Even in the light of their cultural insistence upon these qualities, or their former hardships in maintaining the barest existence level, it might be thought strange that this energy had persisted through the demoralizing years of indolence and resignation which preceded the establishment of the reservation. Indeed, there are two sides to this situation. The industry which the agents remarked was almost wholly that of those who had maintained these qualities through their work on ranches and settlements during the pre-reservation period. Although this group was in the majority, there was also a number of Indians on the reservation that had succumbed to the easier aspects of the frontier situation, and these latter natives now became the trouble-makers and continued to drink and gamble while the others labored.

Furthermore, coöperation between camp groups over the major portion of the year was not consistent with the aboriginal pattern and threatened the self-sufficiency and independence which had marked the camp in former times. Economic coöperation had been primarily a function of the close-knit kin of the camp group, and had been extended outside the camp only at infrequent periods. Furthermore, agriculture now produced a surplus which enabled some to live off the labor of others. Within the camp, this laziness could be handled, but no technique was available to force delinquent individuals of other camps to produce. The recognition of the differential in labor with no consequent distribution based upon this differential created considerable resentment.

In view of this situation, it is to be expected that the communal working and sharing system soon broke down. Four years after the establishment of the reservation, the first protests were voiced:

For the first time I have noticed a feeling against the idlers and loungers on the reservation. A disinclination to divide with those, who, by every way they can, decline to work, arouses inquiries, often made, when the government will give them land in severalty.[75]

Most of the wheat was taken to the agency mill where it was ground into flour. The superintendent attempted to distribute this flour and other supplies in proportion to the labor which he considered each native had put into the land. A number of

---

[75] Agent John How, *Report of C.I.A.*, 1881, pp. 132–134.

White Knives were outraged by this favoritism and attempted an exodus to Fort Hall where they had heard from visiting Shoshoni that it was possible to get enough to eat without working.

This conflict continued and repeated appeals were made to the superintendent to allot a parcel of land to each camp group so that each could enjoy the returns of its own labor. In 1883, each camp, for the first time, cultivated its own plot of ground. This break from the community organization persisted and was finally consolidated by an act in 1910 which awarded each adult forty acres of land. Thus there was a reversion to the economic independence of the immediate kin group.

The basic economy on the reservation slowly shifted during the first ten years from that of agriculture to herding. The vast grazing lands unsuitable for cultivation are well adapted to cattle raising. Truck gardening is profitable only in small patches along the upper portions of the river, and the yield is barely sufficient to feed the families which raise the vegetables. Hunting and gathering slowly diminished with the ecological changes so that now only rare and sporadic hunts are formed, and only the older women gather roots and seeds. The energies of the others are now solely directed toward making their ranches self-sustaining enterprises.

Fortunately for the Indians, there have never been permanent land allotments, so that land sales to the Whites were impossible, and although each adult is entitled to forty acres, he retains the right to this land only while he uses it; the title rests with the tribe. The only Whites on their reservation, therefore, other than agency employees, are the two traders, their families, and laborers on construction jobs. Lack of outside income from leases, land sales or annuities has made the White Knives solely reliant upon their own efforts.

Annuity payments were continued only until 1883, and the last payment took the form of 300 calves. The number of cattle was gradually built up on the reservation until, at the present time, there are 3,300 head. Although the summer range can accommodate approximately 10,000 head, the lack of feed during the winter restricts the cattle to the present optimum number which the Indians own. This discrepancy between summer and winter capacity is resolved by awarding grazing permits to nearby ranches to allow their cattle to forage on reservation grounds during the summer.[76]

The greatest number of cattle belonging to one family is a little over 100 head. The next largest herd is ninety-four head, and this rapidly scales down to fifteen, ten, five and even one head. About 20 per cent of the families on the reservation have no cattle. Disregarding the extremes, we find that the average head of cattle per family is twelve.

The cattle sales each fall constitute the major part of the family income. Lesser sources of income are sales of hay, freighting, relief,[77] agency wages, and wages from various government projects and seasonal labor for neighboring White ranchers. However, only a few families are in the higher income brackets of approximately 1,500 dollars annually, while the majority of the families are on the poverty fringe with an annual income of between 350 dollars and 600 dollars for an average family of six.[78]

Although practically any change from the aboriginal sub-

[76] These grazing permits have been a constant source of resentment to the Indians, although between 4,000 and 7,000 dollars yearly are realized from them. Until a few years ago, this money went to pay for salaries and the general operation of the agency. The natives complain that their land is being overgrazed and that they receive no direct benefit from these permits, although the money now goes into the revolving fund. Furthermore, they resent the payment of twenty-five cents per head of cattle which they must make to their livestock association, protesting that the money from the grazing permits should cover this.

[77] In September, 1937, thirty-seven individuals were receiving monthly checks of between ten dollars and forty dollars for blind assistance, old age pensions and support of dependent children. This cash relief, however, goes only to Indians on the reservation living in Idaho. Although the bulk of the population is concentrated in Nevada, and many of these Indians are also deserving of this type of relief, it is not available to them since cash relief is administered through the state and only Idaho has contributed these funds. Of course, many Nevada residents are resentful since this appears to be official discrimination. However, forty-four families of both states were receiving monthly food and clothing rations. The entire relief roll covers about 170 individuals or 25 per cent of the total population.

[78] These figures represent gross income. The money which actually comes into the household is considerably less. For one thing, the agency deducts from 10 per cent to 25 per cent from all cattle sales, wages, etc., as part payment for the loans which most Indians have contracted from the government. Many Indians bitterly charge that the agency makes these deductions mechanically without any reference to their pressing financial needs.

sistence level would have been for the better, the standard of living is still deplorably low, even though material possessions have increased tremendously. This is not only because the culture contact introduced a host of new necessities or that the freighting charge raises the price of foodstuffs and clothing, but the birthrate has automatically increased with the expanding economy. Therefore, although there is a much greater production, consumption has grown proportionally. The aboriginal methods of birth control are still known, as are new methods of contraception, yet the rigid restrictions which the former economy had demanded are now gone. Because of the somewhat shifting nature of a number of families on the reservation, it is difficult to ascertain the absolute increase in population, but that the birthrate has expanded is obvious.[79]

The aboriginal dwellings are evident now only as temporary summer shelters, and the dome-shaped sweat and menstrual houses have the same basic construction, although most of them are now covered with canvas. The majority of the dwellings at present are log cabins of native construction. Very few families have frame houses because of the exorbitant price of cut lumber. Of a total of 147 residences, twenty-two are commercial tents or makeshift packing box houses, and only eighty-four of the total number of houses have wooden floors. The furnishings, of course, vary, but the minimum is a stove, table, one or two benches and some bedding. A few families have beds or cots, but many sleep either on the wooden floor or on the bare ground protected by commercial or rabbit-skin blankets.

The material culture has been considerably changed and enriched. Metal pots and oil cans have displaced pottery for so long that even the technique of its manufacture is lost. Basketry persists, however, and is made by some of the older women who sell to the younger. It has even been adapted to new forms for

[79] Available material on fifty-two families where the parents are forty years of age or over shows that of these only eight families have less than three children. Of the other forty-four families, eight have three children, thirteen have four children, five have five children, eight have six children, seven have seven children, two have eight, and one family has nine children. These figures refer only to children now living; the mortality rate on the reservation is high.

such uses as clothes baskets and other receptacles. The necessity for making flint artifacts disappeared in pre-reservation days, and at the present time the Indians collect and prize the arrow-heads and knives they find in the hills, no longer as useful articles, but as souvenirs. Although hunting by bow and arrow has ceased, a number of women still dig roots with the metal counterpart of the digging stick—the crowbar.

Attitudes toward property are now more sharply defined. Ownership is no longer vested in the functioning group, but the White pattern of individual ownership of cattle, land and personal possessions has been taken over entirely. Because marriage alliances are still unstable, many women have learned to retain individual title to their forty acres and their own brand on their cattle. With the exception of relatives, among whom a measure of economic coöperation still exists, a Shoshoni demands wages for any work he may do for another Indian.

Although a fear of the dead still persists, this fear no longer extends to the property of the deceased. For the first fifteen years, burial rites on the reservation continued as in aboriginal times. Not only were the clothes and gun of the dead man buried with him, but his horse was killed and laid alongside his grave. His house was burned or demolished and his family erected a new one, and sometimes even moved to a new locality. However, the sharpening realization of the value of property operated to change these customs. Since houses were now permanent dwellings representing considerable labor and money, certain compromises were made. Now a house may be taken down, but this is done carefully and all the parts are saved so that it may be erected on another part of the reservation or the relatives may use this material to construct privies or sheds on their land. In other cases, the dwelling may be abandoned for five or six months while the family camps nearby and returns to it when it feels the danger is over. In practically all cases, however, the bedding used by the deceased is burned. His gun is no longer buried with him although the corpse is dressed in its finest clothes. Horses are no longer killed, but their tails may be cut or ribbons woven through their manes or tails to show that they, too, are in mourning. Thus there are the necessary concessions to custom through convenient rationalization without sacrifice of property.

Since the deceased, at present, usually leaves a number of possessions, inheritance has for the first time become a problem. Land remains in the family if there is someone who has not yet reached maturity and who can claim it within a few years. If not, the agency usually allows the widow to use it until she dies or remarries. However, the disposition of cattle, horses, automobile, and what other property the deceased may have possessed usually creates a dispute among the kin group which has to be resolved at the agency. Since there never have been tribal laws governing inheritance, the agency resorts to state laws and discretion in apportioning these goods and the claimants usually proceed on the assumption that he who "yells the loudest gets the most."

The social organization, at present, has changed slightly from that of the aboriginal camp group. Because the tentative land allotments are individual, the basic unit has become the immediate family. Post-marital residence is still erratic and there is no longer a tendency to matrilocal residence, but the traditional factors of economic expediency and personal preference still govern the choice. The tendency is now toward patrilocal residence since a man usually prefers to bring his wife to his own family where his possessions and land holdings are frequently associated with those of his father. In other cases, a youth may acquire his forty acres upon marriage and combine them with his wife's land to set up a new economic household. The ties to immediate kin are still close, but, although they may aid each other in haying or the round-up, there cannot be the intimate day to day coöperation which marked the aboriginal camp group.

Authority within the family is centered in the parents, although if the grandparents live in the same household they, too, will wield influence over the children, as they did in the camp group. The child is still cherished and rarely beaten. The grandparent-grandchild relationship continues to be very close and although it frequently functions now between paternal grandparents and child, there is still the feeling that the child's warmest ties are with the maternal grandparents.

The new economy places somewhat more emphasis on male labor than did the old. Freed of the time-consuming activity of gathering and digging, women now help in the fields to a small extent, but most of their work is in the home where they raise the children, cook, and do the other household work. This slight shift, however, does not impair the position of women in the society. Although the informal authority of the sexes was about equal in the aboriginal culture, the initial White contact and the present agency administration have formalized the position of the men as spokesmen, but their ideas are frequently influenced and formulated by their wives.

The only form of marriage at present is monogamy. No polyandrous household has been set up since settlement on the reservation, but polygyny persisted for some fifteen years. It had been fostered by the early years of White contact, when all the "captains" felt it in keeping with their prestige to have at least one wife more than the others. The agency, however, consistently ridiculed plural marriage and levied penalties upon it. Familiar with the polygyny of the Mormons, the natives protested for some time that the government was hypocritical in its attitude, allowing it to flourish in one place while it suppressed it in another. Nevertheless it eventually disappeared. Nomadism and the isolation of camp groups have gone. Such forms of marriage as brother-sister exchange, child marriage, levirate, sororate and cross-cousin marriage have lost their sanctions. The economic and social factors which had underlined these marital forms in order to keep the kin group intact and to preserve the marriage contract are no longer operative in the present society where permanent residence provides relatives who are always available to lend their support. A man, for example, no longer feels it incumbent upon himself to marry his sister-in-law after the death of his wife, for he is no longer a necessary unit in the maternal camp group. These marriage forms had never been rigid in the aboriginal society and even though a few marriages on the reservation have followed the levirate-sororate pattern, these resulted from personal preference and not from social pressure.

Although the incest prohibitions had formerly included only a small circle of immediate relatives, even these limits of forbidden marriage have narrowed today. Cross-cousin marriage still flourishes but this is not in response to the old pattern, for marriages between parallel cousins are just as frequent. The older people feel strongly that this latter will result in no good, but beyond gossiping about the sad breakdown in the younger generation, little is done to enforce the old restrictions. The younger people, in order to justify these marriages, state their own criteria of what constitutes an incestuous union: that of a parent and a child and that of persons who have suckled from the same breast.

Marriage arrangements are still informal. Only among those few who ape the Whites will there be a wedding ceremony or feast, or will presents be exchanged. Most unions occur and continue without benefit of clergy or of agency record. There is very good reason for this, other than that of conformity to the aboriginal pattern. A recorded marriage involves court proceedings, distasteful agency disputes, a probable division of property and possibly a jail sentence before the union can be dissolved. Since marital alliances are still very brittle, few men bind themselves to such an unfavorable contract. The women, however, have now learned that it is to their advantage to insist upon it in order to have their interests protected.

There is still a great deal of sexual promiscuity, although this no longer requires even the *sub-rosa* sanction that the aboriginal culture lent to those who stood in a potential marriage relationship. The attitude toward these affairs is reflected in the fact that there have been no killings in recent times because of adultery, although jealousy and outraged feelings still find expression in beatings. A woman, moreover, now has recourse to the native court (under agency supervision) and can win a divorce from an unfaithful husband and force him to pay her or to support their children. Adultery, when brought to the attention of the court, often leads to fines or jail sentences. These legal penalties for extra- and pre-marital relations, combined with the stabilized economy and permanent residence seem to have had a restraining effect on broken marriages and new alliances, for marriages now are less brittle than they had been.[80]

[80] An analysis of 102 marriages on the reservation where both the husband and wife are over thirty-five years of age shows that of these, thirty-one mar-

Illegitimate children are still very common. There is a belief prevalent on the reservation that only continued sexual intercourse with one man will produce a child. In proof of this theory, Indians point out girls whom they know have been conducting affairs with various men for short periods, and have not borne children. Therefore, if a woman gives birth to an illegitimate child, the man who has been with her most constantly is assumed to be the child's father. If a case of illegitimate birth is brought to the attention of the agency, and if the mother insists and the marriage seems feasible, the agent endeavors to force a marriage between the parents. However, if the father of the illegitimate child is a ne'er-do-well, the maternal grandfather is content to accept the child into his own family, give it his surname and rear it as one of his own. This is the usual disposition of such cases. Illegitimacy, as in former times, places no stigma on the mother nor does it impair her opportunities for marriage with other men. Nor is there any stigma attached to the child. As one informant put it: "If you start calling one person a bastard, you'd have to call most of the people on the reservation bastards." This has a broad basis of truth, not only because of promiscuity among the Indians themselves, but because during the period directly preceding reservation days many White laborers, ranchers and soldiers had access to Indian women, sometimes at the point of a gun, and this contact has brought results in the form of numerous half-breeds who are now among the leading men on the reservation.

Political organization, so amorphous and ill-defined under aboriginal conditions, has become somewhat more formalized

---

riages were contracted between mates who had never been married before. There were sixteen marriages where the husband had not been married before, but the wife once; nineteen marriages where the wife had not been married before, but the husband once; fifteen marriages where both the husband and wife had been married once before; seven marriages where the wife had been twice married before, and the husband but once; four marriages where the husband had been married twice before and the wife but once; three marriages where the wife had not been married before but the husband twice; one marriage where both the husband and wife had been married twice before; three marriages where the husband had been married three times before, but the wife only once; two marriages where the wife had been married three times before, but the husband only once; and one marriage where the husband had not been married before, but the wife three times.

under White contact. We have already sketched the rise, short duration and dissolution of the band organization. The authority of the "captain" still continued to be emphasized in dealings with the agency; the agency relied on these "chiefs" to influence their people to obey the Whites, to cultivate the land, to remain at peace. The "chiefs" even served as mouthpieces for the first missionaries, exhorting the people to go to church although they themselves did not attend. The fact that the Indians paid no great attention to these "talking chiefs" whom they now accuse of aiding in their exploitation, probably escaped the attention of the officials who rewarded the "captains" by building houses for them, conferring gifts, and by extending other favors. The rise of these "chiefs" and their limited secular authority which was not even sanctioned through the traditional supernatural vision is well understood by the White Knives. As one informant remarked:

The White people say that Captain Sam was our chief. He was only chief because the White men made him chief, and he was glad to be a chief. He was something like X [a hated agency official]. He talked a lot and pushed himself forward. He wasn't very bright. Captain Sam was told by the White people to keep the Indians from fighting and drinking, that otherwise the army would kill us off. I guess it was easy for Captain Sam to be chief because all the people were in one group on the reservation and they could listen to one man where they couldn't have in the old days. But we didn't pay much attention to him.

One of these Indian "chiefs" is even accused of keeping fifty head of cattle which one superintendent had turned over to him to be redistributed among the Indians.

It is obvious that under these conditions these "captains" were not likely to leave successors as hereditary leaders of the reservation. After these "chiefs" had died, two factions arose on the reservation which, at the present time, are clearly formulated. These factions have no roots in the aboriginal life. One group is led by the "educated, White-talking" Indians and the other group, much larger, is termed the "conservative." This latter faction is not conservative in the sense that it demands a retention of the old culture, which no one really wishes to see preserved, but it insists that it looks after the interests of the Indians while the other group caters to the White officials. For one thing, the members of this group claim to have uncovered a "secret treaty" which the Shoshoni made with the Whites a number of years ago, which would give the Indians a great deal more land and money than they have ever received. So firm are they in this belief, that a lawyer was hired to investigate this claim. On the other hand, they accuse the other group of being in league with the agency to suppress knowledge of this treaty, and to keep the Indians in bondage. The so-called "progressive" group is even accused of receiving patronage in the form of relief money and supplies, liberal loans and other favors from the agency in exchange for this treason.

These charges, of course, are not founded in fact. The prime motivating factor in the split between the Indians is a deep-seated resentment against the Whites, and particularly the agency officials. Ever since the first period of White contact, the Indians have felt themselves to be oppressed and discriminated against. This resentment, often justified, finds some release against the Whites in such forms as malicious gossip, jokes, sullenness and drunken outbursts, but its formalized expression is in factionalism among the Indians themselves. It is significant that the "progressive" group is led by the three principal Indian families on the reservation who are the richest, the best educated, who are "church" Indians and who hold the commanding positions in the native councils, school board and associations. It is precisely because this group is most closely identified with the White pattern that it forms a convenient nucleus toward which the others can direct their resentment.

The "progressive" Indians themselves have no great liking for the agency officials, but because they honestly believe that they are working for the good of the reservation by holding positions in the councils and by working along with the agency officials rather than by maintaining the attitude of sullen resentment or passive resistance which the "conservative" group manifests, the dichotomy became inevitable. Although the councils and boards are selected by popular election, very few of the Indians vote and it is not difficult for this "progressive" group to remain in office. Once, however, the "conservative" group elected their entire slate, but the "progressives" accused them of stirring up so much trouble on the reservation that the council room was barred to them and although they continued to hold their meetings in various places, none of their recommendations or decisions was honored.

The native council meets sporadically and, although it is empowered by their constitution to act as the governing body for the reservation,[81] both the "conservatives" and the council itself accuse the agency superintendent of running affairs as he thinks best. As a member of the council expressed it:

If we decide against X the (superintendent) he shakes his head and we never carry it. The council is afraid to ride over X. I find that it's best to leave things alone, otherwise X will make me and my family suffer by not giving me jobs; and (the clerk) will refuse to give me loans and be hard on the collections.

Other Indians state that if they write to Washington to complain of some maltreatment on the reservation, the situation which they describe may be rectified, but the agent always knows who made the charge and will later discriminate against them.[82]

Although the aboriginal political organization was too informal and amorphous to cope with the reservation situation and a new form had to arise to meet a unique set of conditions, supernaturalism, on the other hand, had a wealth of traditional customs, beliefs and practices upon which to draw. In this population of 670 Indians, there are eight shamans who actively ply their trade. This aspect of Shoshonean culture was the one least dependent upon the economic organization and, consequently, the one least affected by its changing phases.

Curing ceremonies, still very important, attract many individuals and are little changed from those of former times. The same tabus are observed, the sucking technique employed, spectators still paint their faces, and there is the same pipe-lighting ritual. The fire must be lit, as in the old days, and though it may now blaze in a stove instead of on the open ground, this in no way impairs the cure. Power is still received in the traditional manner, through supernatural vision, but it is no longer actively

[81] *Constitution and Bylaws of the Shoshone-Paiute Tribes of the Duck Valley Reservation of Nevada*, pp. 1–5.

[82] There was no opportunity to investigate these charges, but the fact that the natives themselves feel that they are true is significant in this treatment of political organization.

sought; the youngest shamans on the reservation have received their power involuntarily through dreams. The same hierarchy of shamans exists, and even a new type of curing doctor, the eye doctor who treats trachoma, has arisen in answer to new afflictions. The shamanistic paraphernalia continues to be displayed in curing and if, as in one case where the tutelary is represented as the eagle triumphantly clutching an American flag, it may assume somewhat different form, it is still utilized in the traditional manner.

Only a small minority on the reservation doubt the efficacy of shamanistic ability, although a sophisticated few, while conceding the power of the shaman to cure disease, attempt to explain it on the grounds of the deep faith which the Indians themselves have in their medicine doctors. This faith is being constantly reinforced by the numerous cases of illness which the Shoshoni report the shaman has been able to cure after the White doctor had given up the patient as lost.

Shamanism, however, has not completely escaped the taint of the new commercialism. The people protest that, whereas in the old days the shaman was dependent as to type of payment upon the instructions which he received while in the trance state, the Indian doctor now charges a flat rate of three dollars or five dollars for his services. There has also been a case where two men, attracted by the financial returns of shamanism, pretended to have received this supernatural power and actually practiced for a while before they were exposed.

A few natives are torn in their choice between the agency hospital and the Indian doctor, but most of the Shoshoni resolve this conflict by patronizing both. This is in keeping with their tolerant attitude toward any type of treatment which proves effective; many natives even patronize the Chinese herb specialists in the neighboring towns. Practically all cases of broken bones, wounds and external ailments are treated at the hospital, since this requires only ordinary medical skill. Most internal diseases, however, are related to the native's *muguwa,* of which the White doctor knows nothing, and these cases are treated by the native doctor.

Although curing shamanism continues to flourish, other forms could not persist when the need for them had disappeared. The antelope no longer roam in large herds and although the corrals still stand as mute evidence of their one-time importance, there is no shaman left to charm the few remaining antelope. With a stabilized economy and the disappearance of nomadism, the urgent necessity to control the weather is gone.[83] The last sweat-house shaman on the reservation died two years ago and no one has taken his place, for even though sweat-houses still exist, the burden of the cure has shifted from the shaman's prayers to the sweat bath itself. Some individuals, however, now pray to Jesus while taking the sweat bath in order to make the cleansing both physically and spiritually effective.

Individual supernatural power other than for healing is no longer received, for although this type of power once changed from special capability in hunting to that of war in response to the first phases of culture contact, the elasticity of the concept has not extended to the current needs—agriculture or herding power. Only one individual on the reservation claims to have coyote power. This man has exercised the prerogatives given by this power for not only has he had sexual relations with his sister, but he has had two children by his daughter. Other natives insist that this claim of power is a rationalization after the fact. Beyond a mild boycott of this man, however, the Indians do not resort to the more drastic techniques of disapproval such as the harsh beatings which would have been inflicted on this individual in former times.

Charms and magical techniques still continue to be very popular. If love magic has decreased somewhat in recent times, gambling charms certainly have not, for gambling under the present conditions of continued group residence has enjoyed even a stronger popularity than was possible in the past. There have been repeated agency efforts to suppress the hand game, dice games and the various card gambling games which the natives

[83] Weather control shamans in the aboriginal society induced rain in order to melt the snow so that the groups could be freed from their winter confinement. There was no need to cause rain during the summer since the group was not dependent upon agriculture. Under the new economy, however, even though rain is earnestly desired for the crops, no supernatural techniques of weather control have arisen.

eagerly took over from the Whites. Indian police often refuse to coöperate in these drives and once, when a zealous policeman insisted that the game cease and attempted to arrest the participants, his clothes were stripped from him and he was sent back to the agency tied to his horse. The stakes in the hand game often go as high as fifty and seventy-five dollars and although most of the Indians can ill afford to lose their money in gambling, all attempts at suppression have been fruitless.

Omens continue to be observed by many of the older people. The blacksmith, for example, will not continue working on a particular job if he feels any of his muscles twitching. The fear of sorcery, never strong, has practically ceased to exist. Only one case of sorcery was reported on the reservation, and that was over twenty years ago. Even the danger of its possible corollary, the sight of the female genitals, while still strong, is no longer feared as it was.[84] Many of the older people attribute the cases of blindness and defective eyesight (actually caused by trachoma) to the violation of this old tabu.

The old customs which emphasized the life crises are now gone, and no new ceremonies have arisen as a substitute. The White religion on the reservation is so weak that even puberty observances cannot be transferred to confirmation rites as has been accomplished on other reservations. Men and boys no longer feel the need to perform those ritual acts which once gave hunting and fishing ability, and few women observe birth and menstruation in the traditional manner. The older women who insist that these are terrible violations can no longer set an example for the younger girls, since they have now passed the menopause. Most children, within recent years, have been born in the hospital, although some women still retreat to their little hut for a few weeks after they return home. The antagonism toward hospital deliveries, now well broken down, was rooted in the fear of cold water and ice bags which the doctors used, in violation of the old insistence upon keeping the blood warm, thin and

---

[84] The attitude of the natives toward the sight of the female genitals expressed itself in a baby health contest which the hospital conducted a few years ago. Unfortunately, the nurses completely unclothed the female babies, which resulted in such consternation that no contest of this sort has been conducted since.

circulating, and many were outraged by the doctor's method of aiding in birth, since no self-respecting man would look at the genitals and would certainly not touch them. Fear of menstrual blood is not as strong as it had been, although many point out that this disregard of its dangers results in those blood symptoms characterizing tuberculosis, a disease which now accounts for one third of the deaths upon the reservation.

The belief in *muguwa* and the afterworld still persists, although some now divide the afterworld in accordance with Christian dogma; the aboriginal one is reserved for "good" Indians and a new hellish repository has been created for the "bad" or non-Christian Indians. Despite the fact that a majority of the natives profess a disbelief in this dichotomy, yet, to be on the safe side, the minister is called upon to preach at practically all funerals, even though he may be disregarded at other times.

The corpse, still buried with its face toward the east, is now laid away in a coffin made by the agency carpenter, although the more affluent purchase a silk-lined coffin from one of the neighboring towns and even bank it with flowers. Funeral feasts were unknown and impossible in former times because of the lack of surplus food. Today, however, a funeral feast is a necessary part of the death rites. This custom probably came from the Paiutes who, in turn, had been influenced by California Indians with whom they had been in contact. The corpse, which had formerly been buried on the day of death, because of the fear of *tsoap*, now rests in the home for two or three days while the family feasts the visitors with fresh calf meat and canned foods. In accordance with the acquisition of property and the prestige which accrues from its possession, each family's funeral feast is as elaborate as its economic circumstances will allow. Many plunge into debt and kill one of their precious calves for the feast, but this custom has now become so well integrated with the rapidly developing concept of prestige through property accumulation and consumption that the efforts of the agency to stop these feasts have been to no avail.

Missionary activity on the reservation has not been very significant. The first missionaries were Catholics who stayed but a short time and left before their influence could be felt, and since then the church has been in the hands of Presbyterian ministers. At the peak of the church's popularity, ten years ago, it enjoyed an attendance of about seventy individuals or a little less than 10 per cent of the population. The people at that time were attracted by a crusading fundamentalist, "who preached with tears streaming down his face." This minister organized a church orchestra and choir, and was actively solicitous about the welfare of his congregation. The natives reacted sympathetically both to his sincerity and the good performance he offered. His success, even though small, was not duplicated by any of the unpopular ministers that followed, and at the present time there are only three families who attend services. These families are those same three who are leaders of the "progressive" group, and their presence and position as elders operate to keep others from attending. Another contributing factor has been the church's aversion to gambling and perhaps it is not chance that the gambling grounds are directly opposite the church so that the chant from the hand game often mingles with the words of the minister's sermon.

Only those few who have been most affected by the church's teachings now feel it necessary to make some compromise with the aboriginal religious beliefs. Fortunately, the sun deity who was the prime supernatural force in the old days already had some identification with *apö*, or father, and this easily became God. The Christ, however, was not so easily fitted into the aboriginal beliefs and the Indians have taken the minister's word that He was the son of God. The acceptance of Jesus, moreover, in at least two cases, occurred in the traditional mode of revelation—through dreams. The Indians are unwilling to relinquish, even at the present time, their concepts of power through dreams which stood them in such good stead. There is a convenient rationalization of this to adjust it to Christian thinking, and one informant remarked:

In the Bible it says that the old men will dream dreams and the young men will see visions. In the same way, God directed the Shoshoni in the old days. Didn't God give Moses a dream, just like He gives our own *Buhagants* dreams?

It is not surprising to find that nativistic movements had never been important among a people whose lack of hostility had made sorcery even less significant after White contact than before. The only nativistic movement which enjoyed even a brief popularity was the Ghost Dance of 1890, but it lasted for only one season and was easily suppressed by the ridicule which the agency heaped upon it, and the incredulous attitude of the Shoshoni themselves toward its efficacy. The sun dance never reached the reservation, although a few of the natives go to Fort Hall each summer to participate in it. Peyote is just beginning to filter down from the Fort Hall Agency, but it has never reached ceremonial proportions, and is used only individually by a few Indians whenever they feel somewhat ill. One movement to bring peyote in on a large scale was scotched by the "progressive" group who informed the leader that if he attempted to do so, they would see to it, through their positions in the council, that his lucrative freighting contract would be taken away.

The only formal perpetuation of the old ceremonies is the annual Fourth of July "fandango" held on the reservation grounds. This, of course, has developed from the *Gwini* ceremony. When the reservation was first established, and the Shoshoni discovered that they could meet more often without danger of completely exhausting their food supply, the ceremony was held four and five times a year instead of only once or twice as had previously been the case. However, these frequent meetings demanded six days of complete attention to the ceremonies without regard for the demands of their new economic life. That this situation could not continue is evident from the agent's report in 1890:

It is the custom of these people to have four fandangos a year, when all, old and young, move to a common camp, selected for the purpose, where they erect tents and willow wikiups and engage in singing, dancing and gambling until worn out . . . everything goes to destruction while the fandango lasts. No work is done; crops perish for want of water or are destroyed by stock; the few that have milch cows turn them out; the chickens and pigs die. . . .[85]

Shortly thereafter, the agency suggested to the natives that as they were now part of the United States, it would be more fit-

[85] Agent William Plumb, *Report of C.I.A.*, 1890, p. 151.

ting to hold their celebration only once a year on the national holiday, the entire Fourth of July week. This suggestion has been carried out since that time.

The religious and fertility aspects of this ceremony have almost completely disappeared and although the camp half-circle is still open toward the east, a flag pole has taken the place of the green willow pole in the center. After the death of Captain George Washington, no *tegwani* appeared to assume leadership. A few of the older men still ride around and speak to the group when they are congregated for the dances in the evening, exhorting them to be industrious, to drink less whiskey, to be at peace with one another. Many still paint their faces red, although some now use rouge or mercurochrome in place of the old ground rock paint. A number of the natives have adopted the Plains costume and head dress as being more attractive and dignified for this "fandango" than their own scanty garb of former times, or the gaudy cowboy costumes which other White Knives wear during this period.

The round dance is still performed in much the same fashion as it had been in the past and there is the same ceremonial hand-clapping over the body to rid it of disease. In addition to the round dance, however, a number of new dances have been introduced from the Ute, Paiute and other neighboring tribes. Most of these dances have come from Fort Hall where there has been contact with the Bannock and the Northern Shoshoni. One of these, a war dance, requires the proud display of scars obtained in battle, but since the White Knives have led remarkably peaceful lives they have had to substitute red daubs of paint on their arms and legs in keeping with the spirit of the dance. Drums have recently appeared for the first time as necessary accompaniment for these dances.

This six-day period now serves as a complete holiday for the Shoshoni. In addition to the dances, there are various gambling games and extended opportunities for gossip and visiting back and forth. The younger people have introduced new and strange forms of the dance, the fox-trot and waltz, which they learned at boarding-schools. The boys play baseball and other games unknown to their grandfathers. However, even though the White

Knives look forward each year to the celebration, the attendance and popularity of this "fandango" has been declining within the past few years. A few of the Indians are beginning to feel that even this six-day respite from their ranches cannot be afforded, since the celebration comes during the important haying season. Many of the younger Indians go to neighboring Mountain City to participate in the rodeo and the boxing contests during this week and some of their families follow them there.

Mountain City is a small town about eighteen miles southeast of the reservation which, in the past few years, has boomed in response to the activity of the Rio Tinto copper mine. The operations of this mine have ended the protective isolation which the Shoshoni have experienced since the establishment of the reservation. Not only has Mountain City expanded with stores, saloons, new gambling places and a house of prostitution, but the mine built a gravel road through the reservation to connect it with the railroad a hundred miles north. This new road has accelerated the acculturation process within the past few years, for it now provides a three-hour route to the larger cities which formerly took over two days of travel. A number of Indians have invested in automobiles to enable them to travel to these cities, and the type of automobile owned is fast becoming a prestige factor.

The road has also brought in weekly movie films [86] which are exhibited by an itinerant entrepreneur who makes the rounds of the neighboring towns. These films are making the Shoshoni more keenly aware of the customs and habits of the Whites.[87]

[86] Moving pictures are called *tsoap* (ghost) because "They talk and there's nobody there. You see people moving but you can't touch them."

[87] These movies, of course, can be interpreted only in terms of the natives' own background. The "Western" type is thoroughly enjoyed for the Indians understand cowboys, cattle, the roundup and the scenery. Drawing-room dramas, however, are beyond their ken and leave them restless. Love and romantic intrigue are interpreted somewhat more drastically than the director intended. The White Knives feel that if a young man and girl walk together or hold hands it is a brazen indication of intimate relationship. A husband and wife do not display signs of even casual affection in public. Consequently, since most of the movies show the hero displaying these manifestations of "intimate" relationship with many women, many natives naturally assume that the Whites indulge in excessive philandering. Any reproach on the part

Although many of these movies leave them considerably bewildered, they are influencing some of the superficial aspects of
the society. For one thing, many of the women are becoming
conscious of White fashion ideals. A beauty parlor has recently
opened in the rear of a saloon in Mountain City to cater to an
increasing number of women who now feel the need to have their
hair waved, and the trader has had to stock a supply of hair dyes
and red finger-nail polish.

The attitude of the Indians toward the Whites has already
been noted in discussing the rise of factions. There are a number
of grievances upon which this attitude is based. Disregarding
the numerous specific charges which the Indians make concerning
agency administration, and many of these have a valid basis in
fact, there are other accusations which have resulted from a tendency to attribute all misfortune to a general campaign of race
discrimination on the part of the Whites which will slowly result in the extinction of the Indians. Some even insist that the
recurring cricket and grasshopper invasions which visit the reservation in four- or five-year cycles are encouraged by the government. These insects, they claim, are much larger, more numerous and differently shaped than were the insects of aboriginal
times which their grandparents ate. The fact that one of the government projects has actively engaged some of the White Knives
to fight these ravages is explained by them merely as an ineffective sop and, as a further point, "the White men in the neighboring towns working on the same project are paid five dollars
a day while we get only a dollar and a half."

This type of reaction against the Whites, however, coexists
with the aboriginal attitude of resignation. It will be remembered
that the Shoshoni considered themselves as offspring of Coyote
and used this coyote identification to explain in general terms
their poverty, their lack of ceremonialism and social elaboration,
their poor dress—in fact to explain all the circumstances by
which they suffered in comparison with other tribes. It is not
surprising, therefore, to find that today many of the older people
invoke this origin tale as an explanation of their present condi-

---

of the agency in reference to the natives' sexual behavior is interpreted by
many, therefore, as merely another indication of White hypocrisy.

tion, and so justify submission and convenient resignation to poverty. Indeed, their folklore has continued to develop along this general pattern, so that at the present time there are a number of tales which recount Coyote's behavior when he first met the Whites, since these are taken to be determinative of the behavior of the Shoshoni at the present time. Although Coyote, in some instances, proved to be much shrewder than the Whites (the laughter when the Shoshoni recount these stories is obviously a form of release), other tales demonstrate that Coyote chose rather to be lazy while the White man became rich through industry. One of these tales illustrates the general pattern:

Coyote and White man were good friends. They planted wheat together. White man found out that Coyote was lazy. The White man said, "Are you getting tired?" Coyote said, "Yes." Then the White man said, "All right, go to the mountains and eat the currants that you eat this time of year." Then Coyote went to the hills and loafed around and ate currants. That's why we are lazy and don't like to work because we are the children of Coyote. If Coyote had stayed with the White man, we would have good farms too, and we would have become rich.

There is no great discrepancy between the approved personality type of modern time and that of the aboriginal society. There is the same insistence upon the qualities of keenness and industry; the shaman continues to be respected for his skill. The informal authority of the older and more experienced individuals has perhaps not carried over with the same weight, but these people are still respected. With the exception of the small "progressive" group, however, the resentment toward the Whites militates against wholehearted adoption of White standards. The successful person is now the one who has become financially independent through his own efforts, with a minimum of reliance upon agency help. If an individual is suspected of catering to the agency, his prestige in the eyes of the other natives drops proportionately. This attitude presents some difficulty to the younger people who have just returned from the non-reservation boarding-schools and are confronted with the discrepancy in the natives' attitude toward the Whites and that which they have been taught in the schools. But this conflict is not serious and most of the younger people readily fall in with the socially sanctioned attitude of contempt, although perhaps not to the same bitter degree as their parents.

The acculturation process among this Western Shoshonean group has been comparatively free of maladjustments. Perhaps the most important factor is that the aboriginal society was both meagre in content and simple in structure and the impact of a strange civilization, therefore, could not result in such sharp conflict of values or so intricate a confusion of aboriginal and modern beliefs, customs and practices as that which characterizes, for example, the far more socially elaborate Plains Indian group studied by Mead.[88] Furthermore, the White Knives were spared the removal to strange territory or the close association with Whites which have operated as disintegrative factors in other cases of Indian acculturation.

The pattern of White Knives culture which existed before White contact corresponded at crucial points to that which the Whites brought with them. There was the same general type of family structure, for one thing, and the same preoccupation with economic factors. The shift from a hunting-gathering to an agriculture-herding economy was easily effected, primarily because the incentive to work was independent of those cultural institutions which usually break down under White contact. Once the economy had risen above the bare subsistence level, the strict limitations which it had imposed upon the aboriginal culture were lifted and the White Knives enjoyed a period of cultural efflorescence formerly denied them. The expanding economy, moreover, is developing toward the White pattern of prestige gain and ego gratification through property possession and display.

Some adjustments were necessary in the marriage forms, but the deviations from monogamy had never been rigid in the old society and the change worked no great hardship nor did it radically alter the social organization. The phase of Shoshonean society which was very significant in former times is the most virile today and has been spared the need of harsh adaptation, since not only does shamanism and the concept of "powers" lend

[88] M. Mead, *The Changing Culture of an Indian Tribe,* Columbia University Press, New York, N. Y., 1932.

itself readily to Christian dogma, but Christianity itself has made no great effort to penetrate this culture. The amorphous and somewhat flexible nature of the aboriginal culture and the relative unconcern of its participants in its retention further operated to ease this process of acculturation which has resulted in such disastrous breakdown in other instances.

BIBLIOGRAPHY

This bibliography includes only those titles to which actual reference has been made.

Bancroft, Hubert H., *History of Nevada, Colorado, and Wyoming, 1540–1888, Volume 25,* The History Company, San Francisco, Calif., 1890.

Beckwith, Lieut. Edward G., *Report of Explorations for a Route for the Pacific Railroad of the Line of the Forty-First Parallel of North Latitude,* Government Printing Office, Washington, D.C., 1854.

Brackett, Col. A. G., The Shoshone or Snake Indians, their Religion, Superstitions, and Manners, *Annual Report of the Smithsonian Institution,* Washington, D.C., 1879, pp. 328–333.

Commissioner of Indian Affairs, *Annual Reports to the Secretary of the Interior,* Government Printing Office, Washington, D.C., 1850–1909. (Referred to in text as *Report of C.I.A.*)

Fremont, John C., *Memoirs of My Life,* Belford, Clarke, and Company, New York, N.Y., 1887.

—— *Report of the Exploring Expedition to the Rocky Mountains in the Year 1854, and to Oregon and North California in the Years 1843–44,* Gales and Seaton, Washington, D.C., 1845.

Gayton, Anna H., Yokuts-Mono Chiefs and Shamans, *University of California Publications in American Archaeology and Ethnology, Volume 24, No. 8,* Berkeley, Calif., 1930.

Gheen, L. A., *Correspondence 1869–73,* MS., Files of the Western Shoshone Reservation at Owyhee, Nevada.

Harrington, Mark R., Gypsum Cave, Nevada, *Southwest Museum Papers, No. 8,* Los Angeles, Calif., 1933.

Hoffman, W. J., Miscellaneous Ethnographic Observations on Indians Inhabiting Nevada, California, Arizona, *Tenth Annual Report of United States Geological and Geographical Survey of the Territories 1876,* Washington, D.C., 1878.

Humfreville, James L., *Twenty Years Among Our Hostile Indians,* Hunter and Company, New York, N.Y., 1899.

Irving, Washington, *The Adventures of Captain Bonneville, U.S.A. in the Rocky Mountains and the Far West,* G. P. Putnam and Sons, New York, N.Y., 1850.

Kelly, Isabel T., Ethnography of the Surprise Valley Paiute, *University of California Publications in American Archaeology and Ethnology*, Volume *31, No. 3*, Berkeley, Calif., 1932.

Kroeber, Alfred L., *Anthropology*, Harcourt Brace and Company, New York, N.Y., 1923.

Loud, Llewellyn L., and Harrington, Mark R., Lovelock Cave, *University of California Publications in American Archaeology and Ethnology*, Volume *25, No. 1*, Berkeley, Calif., 1929.

Lowie, Robert H., The Northern Shoshone, *Anthropological Papers of the American Museum of Natural History*, Volume 2, Part 2. New York, N.Y., 1909.

—— Notes on Shoshonean Ethnography, *Anthropological Papers of the American Museum of Natural History*, Volume 20, Part 3, New York, N.Y., 1924.

Mack, Effie M., *Nevada, A History of the State from the Earliest Times through the Civil War*, The Arthur H. Clark Company, Glendale, Calif., 1936.

Mead, Margaret, *The Changing Culture of an Indian Tribe*, Columbia University Press, New York, N.Y., 1932.

Mooney, James, The Ghost Dance and the Sioux Outbreak of 1890, *Fourteenth Annual Report of the Bureau of American Ethnology*, Part 2, Smithsonian Institution, Washington, D.C., 1896.

Ogden, Peter Skeene, Journals, edited by T. C. Elliott, *Oregon Historical Society Quarterly*, Volume *11*, pp. 201–222, 1910.

Opler, Marvin K., The Southern Ute of Colorado, in *Acculturation in Seven American Indian Tribes*, edited by Ralph Linton, D. Appleton-Century Company, Inc., New York, N.Y., 1939.

Park, Willard Z., Shamanism in Western North America, *Northwestern University Studies in the Social Sciences, No. 2*, Evanston, Ill., 1938.

Powell, John H. and Ingalls, G. W., Report of Special Commissioners Powell and Ingalls, *Report of the Commissioner of Indian Affairs*, Government Printing Office, Washington, D.C., 1873, pp. 41–74.

Quaife, Milo M., Editor, *Narrative of the Adventures of Zenas Leonard*, The Lakeside Press, R. R. Donnelly and Sons, Chicago, Ill., 1934.

Radin, Paul, *Primitive Religion*, The Viking Press, New York, N.Y., 1937.

Simpson, Brevet Brig.-Gen. James H., *The Shortest Route to California Illustrated by a History of Explorations to the Great Basin of Utah*, J. B. Lippincott Company, Philadelphia, Pa., 1869.

Steward, Julian H., Ancient Caves of the Great Salt Lake Region, *Bulletin 116, Bureau of American Ethnology*, Smithsonian Institution, Washington, D.C., 1937.

—— Ethnography of the Owens Valley Paiute, *University of California Publications in American Archaeology and Ethnology*, Volume *33, No. 3*, Berkeley, Calif., 1933.

—— Linguistic Distributions and Political Groups of the Great Basin

Shoshoneans, *American Anthropologist, New Series, Volume 39*, pp. 625–634, Menasha, Wis., 1937.

Steward, Julian H., Shoshoni Polyandry, *American Anthropologist, New Series, Volume 38*, pp. 561–564, Menasha, Wis., 1936.

United States Congress, *Senate Executive Documents*, 31st Congress, First Session, No. 18, Government Printing Office, Washington, D.C., 1849.

—— *Senate Executive Documents*, 33rd Congress, First Session, No. 1, Government Printing Office, Washington, D.C., 1853.

—— *Senate Survey of the Conditions of the Indians of the United States*, 72nd Congress, First Session, Part 28, Nevada, Government Printing Office, Washington, D.C., 1934.

United States Department of the Interior (Office of Indian Affairs), *Constitution and Bylaws of the Shoshone Paiute Tribes of the Duck Valley Reservation, Nevada*, Government Printing Office, Washington, D.C., 1936.

—— *Corporate Charter of the Shoshone-Paiute Tribes of the Duck Valley Reservation, Idaho and Nevada*, Government Printing Office, Washington, D.C, 1936.

Wheeler, Lieut. George M., *Preliminary Report Concerning Explorations and Surveys Principally to Nevada and Arizona*, Government Printing Office, Washington, D.C., 1872.

—— *Preliminary Report upon a Reconnaissance through Southern and Southeastern Nevada Made in 1869*, Government Printing Office, Washington, D.C., 1875.

Work, John, Journal of John Work's Snake Country Expedition of 1830–31, *Oregon Historical Society Quarterly, Volume 14*, pp. 280–314, 1913.

EDITOR'S SUMMARY

WHITE KNIFE ACCULTURATION

Aboriginal White Knife culture was so simple and amorphous that there was little to be destroyed by European contact. Their economic status was already at a bare subsistence level; their social organization scarcely extended beyond the biological family, while their religion, with the solitary exception of the *Gwini* ceremonies, was informal and highly individualized. For the ordinary individual Ego satisfaction seems to have been derived mainly from the response of the members of his immediate family and from diversified sexual experience, while prestige outside the family group derived from supernatural experience and the consequent ability to heal. None of their basic culture patterns have been seriously inhibited at any period in the contact continuum. Even the *Gwini* ceremonies, with their opportunities for widened individual contacts, have been successfully transformed into Fourth of July celebrations which serve the same purpose.

Prior to the opening up of the mines, White Knife contact with Europeans was sporadic, giving them no opportunity to familiarize themselves with any but the material aspects of White culture. It seems probable that the recognition of their own inferiority which has characterized them in recent times was already present, for they seem to have been willing to borrow at all points, subject only to the limitations imposed by their low economic status. During this period the natural environment was little affected and their old techniques of food getting retained their efficiency. The acceptance of the horse, metal tools, guns, etc., improved their condition and made possible an incipient band organization, but the period was too short for the thorough integration of this with the rest of the culture.

Real difficulties began with the influx of Whites in large numbers and the resulting changes in the environment. With the destruction of the wild food supply, many of the previous techniques no longer sufficed to meet the needs of the group. The White Knives seem to have tried to meet the situation by imitating certain White techniques, i. e., wage-labor and farming, but the attempt was largely unsuccessful. The wage-scale for Indians was too low, while land which they brought under cultivation was repeatedly seized by Europeans. Most of the tribe made the only adaptation which was successful under the circumstances. They became hangers-on of the White communities, dependent on charity, odd jobs, and the prostitution of their women. The preëxisting sex mores made the assumption of the last relatively easy. The failure of the government to keep its promises to them, and the repeated thwartings of individuals who tried to improve their own condition led to the development of attitudes of suspicion and discouragement which have persisted down to the present time.

The first attempts at directed culture change came with the agency period. These were mainly in the form of additions to the culture, with little if any attempt to interfere with aboriginal practices. The abandonment of many of these seems to have been gradual and almost unconscious, with no resulting derangement to the individual. In spite of the suspicion of the government and some actual hardships, there have been no nativistic movements. Apparently the White Knives realize the hardness of aboriginal conditions and have no tendency to glorify the past. The fact that they are increasing in numbers indicates that they have made a successful adaptation in terms of the local conditions, although new difficulties will probably arise whenever there are changes in these. Their present culture is a well-integrated mixture of aboriginal and European elements with the latter on the increase. There seem to be no internal factors which would prevent their complete Europeanization.

3

THE SOUTHERN UTE OF COLORADO

by Marvin K. Opler

INTRODUCTORY STATEMENT

An Indian friend of philosophical bent once concluded a story of aboriginal times with the following remarks:

. . . Then the people moved camp to a new site. Those camps and that life are gone now. Everything moves on and is lost. That is why the Ute say: "It is bad luck to plan ahead." For nothing can stop. Nothing is left of those days but my story and your words. Nothing remains behind.

Surprising as it may seem, the subject of social dynamics on the pre-literate level still remains in the vague Heraclitean formulation of our dramatic story-teller stirred by his nostalgic mood. The history of social science in this regard is still replete with examples of those who blandly accept the transformations of society as facts so patent and familiar that they fail to compel further attention. On the other hand, there are those who prefer to make a frank denial of processes of change in a frantic effort to find solace in the traditional absolutes of given cultures. But social change, whether disregarded as illusion, or accepted as something so elusive as to defy explanation, is nevertheless always with us.

While the history of Indian tribes offers no exception to the rule that cultures grow, change and retrogress, in the past this common knowledge of a simple fact too often provided the impetus either for loose reconstructions of American Indian history or for inadequate a priori declarations concerning the processes underlying social transformation. The other extreme, the *simpliste* formulation of change simply *as change* or historical accident, has helped as little to solve the problems of social dynamics as those grand schemes based on slip-shod historical reconstruction or on erroneous notions of what motivates a changing culture. The failure of these attempts may be attributed not only to the inherent difficulties involved in understanding a changing phenomenon, but also to yawning gaps in our record of pre-literate history. The result, however, is that the field of social dynamics is still virtually unexplored, and few analyses of the processes involved are attempted even in the most limited and specific sense.

For whether one describes acculturation in terms of the re-adaptation of the culture pattern to new features, or the feeble attempts to salvage the older culture from the shifting sands of a changed economy, or even in terms of ruthless extermination, the description loses in theoretic value unless it furnishes an analysis growing out of the facts in the case. The need for basic analysis rather than random description makes it clear that although the field of dynamics is still open for pioneer work, the value of such exploration will depend in large measure on the path we take. We must, therefore, take stock of methodological cautions if we are to prevent waste of effort.

Following the turn of the century, modern anthropology laid its greatest stress upon the variety and variability of cultures the world over. In scarcely four decades, there accumulated a vast body of data on primitive society which illustrated, in disparity of detail, an amazing diversity of customs and institutions among mankind. The anthropologist, however, was not content to record merely the endless facts of human social life as revealed in specific, concrete studies of culture. In contrast to the older comparative method, his view of social life took cognizance of inter-relations within the culture pattern and this involved, not only a more painstaking description of society, but also an emphasis upon the nature of its integration. This approach to the actual functioning of culture viewed as a whole has been called the functional method; its main theoretic corollary on the comparative plane is the relativity of cultural values.

It is widely believed among anthropologists of the present day that any searching analysis of such value systems will reveal that they, in turn, are end-products of a process by which institutions condition social behavior with all the pervasiveness that custom, creed, and tradition can muster. Indeed, the more atomistic the analysis, the more strikingly these patterns recur in custom, myth, and institution. It becomes obvious that the functional method, so employed, has all the advantage not only of broad relativistic perspective in general, but of careful atomistic analysis in particular. It is rooted in no single culture for its conclusions and is yet in a position to draw exhaustively from any for its material.

As an exclusive approach to the problems of social anthropology, however, it is no less obvious that the functional method is static, beginning and ending with the specific culture in a given time and place. As such, it cannot lead to explanations concerning the generality of cultural processes viewed dynamically. To avoid this "solipsism of the present moment," modern anthropology has recourse to a second corollary of considerable significance; namely, that history provides the frame within which the stability and continuity of the culture may best be viewed.

What is needed, apparently, is a type of investigation that includes both historical sweep and a knowledge of the totality of culture at every point within the continuum. An encouraging indication of interest in such analysis is the appearance, in recent years, of studies in acculturation. The study of acculturation processes furnishes excellent material for the student of dynamics insofar as it is based upon accurately checked history and upon deep insight into the functioning culture at significant points within the time span observed. In the degree to which both these conditions are met lies the possibility for a dynamic analysis which neither employs reconstructed history uncritically nor sacrifices the specific local problem in the interests of a much abused comparative method. With such material in hand, moreover, we are in a position to test a major hypothesis of the functional school—namely, that no specific part of culture is basic to the total integration. When one part of culture changes, must other parts change accordingly?

It can be added that no single study of this sort will establish the nature of cultural dynamics except for a single culture. The following pages on the acculturation of the Southern Ute Indians of Colorado will, therefore, have this theoretic limitation. Yet the bearing of such studies upon the deep-seated processes at work in the transformation of cultures is perfectly clear, and it is with the wish to discover something of these processes that the following data are presented.

THE ABORIGINAL COMMUNITY

The Southern Ute Indians of Colorado represent an offshoot of Shoshonean-speaking peoples located to the north and west. How the Ute came to inhabit that entire southwestern portion of Colorado below the Gunnison River and the present town of Denver is a matter which lies obscured in the remote past of this tribe, for archaeology has as yet left unanswered the question of their original provenience. What we do know definitely is that both in language and in custom the closest relatives of the Ute are such various peoples as the Paiute and Shoshoni, the Hopi of Arizona, and certain Californian tribes, all of which still bear traces of an earlier connection in spite of the many cultural differences that have subsequently arisen.

As the following pages will indicate, some light is thrown upon Ute cultural affiliations by a knowledge of the society as it functioned before White contact. While resemblances in artifact content are discernible between Ute and Plains Indian material culture, it is necessary to point out carefully that in its less material aspects this society was certainly a good deal closer in spirit to Paiute and Western Shoshonean patterns than travelers' accounts, following White contact, lead one to suspect. The early travelers and explorers among the Ute wrote of the culture as it appeared to them in their day, rather than as it functioned before the Spaniards made their appearance in the province of New Mexico. From these casual observations has come the traditional view of Ute culture as marginal to the Plains. Inasmuch as the culture area classifications of early American ethnology were based, in the main, on material artifacts, they merely intensified this impressionistic view without due regard to Ute customs and beliefs. Since the Ute have been less studied than practically any other people of the United States, no real attempt could be

made to point out the inter-relation of traits and complexes forming the totality we call Ute, and surely, no effort to follow the
fortunes of this culture in anything like an historical sequence
was at all possible. In short, Ute culture was so little studied,
apart from excellent compilations of mythology, that no delinea-
tion of its characteristics was practicable in terms of ethnology
or history.

The shift to Plains was recent and followed the introduction of
the horse in Ute economic structure at a time when the Ute
bands became increasingly dependent upon the buffalo hunt as a
chief source of food supply. Before the Spaniards arrived in New
Mexico, these people did not possess horses or hold communal
buffalo hunts, and the band itself did not exist as a sharply
delineated political structure. Three centuries ago, the Ute
ranged over the mountains of southwestern Colorado bordering
the Continental Divide, and over the more level land of states
adjoining their rugged base: over southeastern Utah, northeastern Arizona, northern New Mexico, a corner of Oklahoma,
and even as far east, on rare occasions, as the Panhandle of Texas.
This wide expanse of territory is a land of sharp contrasts and
dramatic changes of scenery. In the northern part of the Ute
range lies the heart of the Southern Rockies, a tangled crisscross
of mountain chains, narrow passes, rock-pockets, and swift
streams. Farther south, near the border of New Mexico, are roll-
ing hills that level out in semi-arid mesa and desert country on
the west, and flatten down into dreary plains and prairies on the
southeast.

Surely, one would expect these broad lands of mountains and
plains to be the original home of a large and powerful tribe.
Yet nothing is further from the truth. The Ute were never
strong in numbers. Before the advent of the horse and subsequent consolidation into warlike bands, they were peaceful and
withdrawn—anything but a dominant, predatory people. In
spring, when food was comparatively plentiful, these Indians
moved in small family groups to favorite mountain camps located near the springs and rivers of the sheltered valleys. Here
they found a safe summer's retreat from the depredations of
Plains Indians who surged along the eastern edge of the moun-

tainous stronghold and often ventured deep into Ute country. In winter, however, snows locked the mountain passes and heavy drifts filled the narrow valleys, forcing the Ute late in the fall of each year southward to the level plateaus. By this migration the hunters naturally followed the southward path of large herds of antelope which provided them with a winter supply of meat. In short, the rigors of a hunting and gathering way of life kept the Ute constantly on the move in winter when they foraged to the south, while the danger of enemies forced them back to their mountain fastnesses in the summer of each year. This annual circuit was a function, then, of a severe struggle for existence, of a pressing need for food in winter, and of a desire for protection from alien marauders in the warmer seasons. Each family moved within the circuit according to the dictates of its older, more experienced members whose counsels prevailed in the settlement of any practical problem. The Ute recognized no higher authority than the pronouncements of older relatives—men and women whose advanced years bore witness to their intimate knowledge of the harsh conditions of existence.

Although an inexorable law of survival impelled the Ute upon a circuitous path, their travels were not the aimless wanderings of a people unaccustomed to the resources of their land. The southern winter range, the scene of intensive hunting and gathering was, of necessity, known to the Ute in great detail. The tie that binds a social group to the familiar country it inhabits is one often remarked for primitive people; in some societies this relationship is formalized, while among others the same sentimental attachment, while not institutionalized, exists nevertheless in full force on the emotional level. The aboriginal Ute belong clearly in the latter category of a people who recognized territorial rights, not simply as land valued *per se,* but rather as the habitual hunting and gathering ground of an extended family group. The family hunting territory had no assigned value and no clear demarcations. It had worth rather as the familiar setting within which the drama of life took place. These were the accustomed places where a man hunted, a woman gathered her wild plant foods, and a child played. In other words, the Ute knew certain portions of his country better than others, and here his family pitched camp in the northward-southward circuit throughout band territory. These customary camp sites formed the perpetual reserve for hunting and gathering of any family group. To camp in unfamiliar country, where one neither knew the lay of the land nor its potential resources, was simply to invite disaster. Each family was expected to follow a known circuit according to the season of the year, so that no one challenged its right to a certain hunting ground or berry patch which had been established by seasonal occupancy and long usage. So well were these "addresses" known throughout the band, that it was not difficult to find a certain medicine-man for curing purposes despite the general mobility of population.

The Ute, at this period, entirely lacked techniques of agriculture. Corn, beans, and squash were obtained by direct trade with Pueblo Indians to the south. Since the winter supply of meat and hides was rarely sufficient, the Ute could spare but little of their own possessions and trade lagged. Yet the practice of wintering in the northern part of the Rio Grande Pueblo area, a fact noted by early Spanish observers, did occasionally lead to a barter of meat and hides for agricultural products. In keeping with their peaceful disposition at this period, the Ute rarely resorted to looting or raiding these neighbors though their wants were often critical.

In the absence of any method for exercising control over their food supply, the Ute scattered out thinly over the land in order to assure each family sufficient territory for an adequate supply of food and other necessities procurable within the limits of this type of economy. The total lack of any emphasis upon property in land coupled with the rigors of a hunting and gathering economy undoubtedly account for this scattering of population. When to these factors we add that hunting was rarely accomplished by setting individual trap lines, it becomes clear at once that trespass as a concept was unthinkable to the Ute. There was nothing in the social structure to prevent families from convening in larger local units. Actually, the scattered families did convene for a limited period of time in the spring of every year when the annual bear dance ushered in a brief period of social contacts, courtship, amusements, and dances. Except for this brief consolidation of the band group, the Ute scattered out in family units because of the restrictions of the food supply in any traversable area.

The total population of the Southern Ute at no time following White contact greatly exceeded one thousand people. Since the amount of food and raw materials greatly increased with initial contact, we are justified in assuming that aboriginal methods of exploiting the territory did not support a larger population and most likely supported a smaller one. At any rate, there is no good evidence, either in historical documents or ethnological data, to suggest a larger population at any period in Ute history. When one considers that territorial occupation of this whole vast country was by widely separated family groups, the relative density of population may be estimated at an extremely low figure.

The Utes who ranged below the Gunnison River are called the Southern Ute. For while there are no marked cultural differences between these people and those who live farther to the north, the Continental Divide which cuts across Colorado below the Gunnison served to separate the northern and southern divisions of the tribe. This geographic barrier has always hindered the expression of cultural and linguistic homogeneity among the Ute. A central political structure for the entire tribe has always been absent. While the Southern Ute fully realizes that his northern neighbor speaks the same language and "thinks as he does," nevertheless he sees no need for greater tribal solidarity than is expressed in the term applied to all his tribesmen—*nutc,* or "The People." Formerly, as now, there was no closer bond of unity nor any greater identity of interests beyond this general feeling of cultural similarity. The tribe, as a political unit, has never existed in any real or significant way for the Southern Ute.

Before White contact, tribal subdivisions, or bands, existed in a rather formal and abstract sense. Like the northern and southern divisions of the tribe, the band groupings were largely delimited by geographic position. West of the Divide below the Gunnison, and down as far as the Navajo country on the south, lived the Weminutc, a band who pitched their summer camps in the La Plata and San Miguel ranges, or less often, on the western slopes of the San Juan mountains around Pagosa Springs. To the east of them, on the other side of the Divide, lived the Kapota, occupying the region around the Sangre de Cristo and San Juan ranges in the warmer seasons. Still farther to the east lived the Mowatsi, who occupied the territory between the Sangre de Cristo and Culebra ranges on the west over as far east as the present sites of Denver, Colorado Springs, Pueblo, Raton, and Trinidad. These three groups, bound together by geographic proximity and occasional intermarriage, are known as the Southern Ute bands.

Each band, as we have seen, had its definite range marked off by mountain barriers. The Weminutc, separated from the other two bands by the Divide, were at all times the most isolated. The Kapota and Mowatsi, living in closer proximity and facing inroads from warlike eastern enemies, tended toward greater unity in times when destruction threatened at the hands of the Kiowa, Cheyenne, and Arapaho Indians of the Plains. On such occasions, messengers were dispatched to all camps within reach, urging tribesmen to come together for defense and warning them of impending danger. The leadership in such defensive warfare was entirely casual and temporary, and the participants, as often as not, came from two bands rather than one. The Ute, at this period, neither moved together nor camped together in bands, so that defensive warfare was entirely a function of the invaded locality. In brief, the band of this period in Ute history had no political cohesiveness and no centralized authority.

Of cultural differences between any of the bands in aboriginal times, not one can be mentioned. There were no institutionalized mechanisms serving to differentiate one band from another. Because of the limitations of economy, any protracted concentration of population into band camps was impossible. Nevertheless, the Ute felt band solidarity as something more real and important than tribal affiliation. Intra-band contacts were more frequent than inter-band contacts. For although it is true that occasionally members of different bands contracted marriages and consolidated friendships, this was by no means frequent enough to blur the lines of band affiliation. Rather, these contacts averted inter-band conflict so that territorial boundaries were mutually respected. Even after White contact, inter-band warfare never broke out between the groups, although even then real tribal unity was never achieved.

The social groupings described thus far did not loom large in the life of the Ute during the aboriginal period. The tribe was more conceptual than real in any functional sense. Defensive warfare being a function of the invaded locality, it therefore did not involve the band. In fact, the band functioned as a cohesive social unit only for a brief period of festivity in spring, a period ushered in by the bear dance and soon terminated, after much visiting, courtship, and gambling, by the shortage in food. While a few families, usually related by marriage or actual blood ties, sometimes assembled at favorite summer camps near springs and along rivers, these associations also were short-lived and never survived the winter season.

It is apparent by now that the social horizon of the Ute intensified as its scope narrowed. The general rules of hospitality operated in dealing with fellow tribesmen. A member of one's band was known as a participant in the spring bear dance, perhaps as a splendid story-teller, a clever hand at gambling games, a wise medicine-man, or even as a rake for whom women fought openly beside the dance grounds. Yet the major Ute loyalties were directed toward a still smaller association, the extended family group to which one belonged by birth and marriage. Here beneath the loose and relatively unimportant band grouping of the aboriginal community, lay the roots of social life firmly planted in the family structure.

The Ute family was somewhat more inclusive than a group composed only of parents and children. Sometimes, it is true, the family camp included no more than a married couple who called each other by the term *piwan* and who, by mutual consent, preferred to live alone rather than camp with the parents of either spouse. More commonly, however, a young couple lived with the parents of either husband or wife who most needed their aid and with whom their relationship was most congenial. Despite the looseness of these rules governing marital residence, the first household of the married couple was usually matrilocal and was the natural outgrowth of a courtship which had become more intimate, finally culminating in sexual relations. Since women always attended to camp equipment, the girl's female relatives were expected to erect a tipi for the new son-in-law. The emphasis upon matrilocal residence, however, did not extend beyond this point. Sometimes it was mutually agreed by the families of the marrying couple that residence should be patrilocal, especially if the boy's parents needed his help or his wife's. When the affinal relatives on both sides of the newly formed family made no strong bid for aid, then the young couple was perfectly free to fend for itself or to visit back and forth between the two sets of parents-in-law.

This freedom from formal restrictions in residence does not mean that the Ute paid little attention to the kinship bonds recognized in their society. Indeed, the actual situation was quite the opposite. While the extended family group consolidated and dispersed with the constant shifting of family alliances, certain norms of behavior, socially determined, endured in every family camp. Throughout the kinship system, sex and age distinctions are paramount in a society where the division of labor was along sex lines and where age and experience formed the sole basis for authority. To this extent, there existed a general correspondence between social behavior and kinship terminology.

The Ute group all consanguineous relatives of one's own generation—cross cousins, parallel cousins, and siblings—into four categories in which the only distinctions made are between older or younger, male or female relative of the one generation. Sex and age distinctions apply also to uncles and aunts, whom the Ute distinguish according to whether they are related through the mother or the father, are older or younger than the respective parents, and are male or female. Nepotic-avuncular terminology is verbally reciprocal. Great-grandparent and great-grandchild employ a single reciprocal term irrespective of sex. The four grandparental terms, referring to mother's and father's parents, are likewise verbally reciprocal.

While the consanguineous system bears out at almost all points the social importance of age and sex distinctions, the affinal system recognizes only a difference in sex; one term classifies male in-laws and another female affinals.

The careful distinctions of relative age in relationship terminology reflected an important ideal of Ute social behavior. To the native way of thinking, age meant simply the authority of wiser counsels. An elder sibling or cousin knew more of the world and was therefore heeded. A younger sibling listened attentively. When two brothers or two sisters camped together with their descendants, the entire camp showed greater respect for the elder of the two, and this authority of age commonly over-rode even the authority of the parent-child relation. It must not be thought, however, that this gerontocracy (extended to older women also) furnished an utterly inflexible pattern of social or familial dominance. The graybeard who played petty tyrant without rhyme or reason was merely tolerated in actual practice among the Ute, just as the man in his dotage was amiably ignored. In fact, we are constantly reminded by informants that orders were not issued to specific individuals in the aboriginal community. It was enough, when the camp surroundings were exhausted of food products, for an older responsible person to say, "We must go on to the next place. There is no food here." There was no coercion; rather age was tacitly understood to be the wisest sort of guidance. The authority of years was reinforced by countless rules of etiquette, whereby the eldest took the seat of honor opposite the door of the tipi, was the first served, and the first to speak. To drink before an elder, or to light a cigarette from the same firebrand that he used made one old before his time, the Ute said.

In a society where age demanded respect, where brothers commonly camped with brothers, and where the household was rarely complete without some member of the grandparental generation, the parent-child relationship was far less authoritarian than in modern European families. A Ute child was apt to show more respect to a grandparent than to a parent who was constantly showing tacit deference to age and authority. In the main, children were indulged and generously spoiled. Even to this day they are often breast-fed until the age of four or five. As babies, they are fondled and caressed constantly. When older, they are amused with cat's cradles and leaf cut-outs. Children are never punished bodily, and brief reference to mythological ogres said to kidnap the more recalcitrant, is usually sufficient to instil obedience. In this connection, it is noteworthy that the true lip-kiss, rare among primitive peoples generally, is found among the Ute restricted to smaller children as a public display of affection. The small child, left most of the time to the supervision of grandparents or older siblings and checked only now and then by their shrill admonishing cries, spends his youngest years fairly free and unhampered in the family circle, shy and restrained only before strangers. Young children, consequently, are happy, active and impulsive. It is a matter of common observation that the more mischievous often take liberties quite heedlessly, not scrupling to bite or strike adults, parents included. Punishment for such action is always interpreted as needless cruelty on the part of the adult.

Soon life must take on a more sombre aspect. Well before puberty, the Ute child was required to take part in the serious labor of camp life and became absorbed little by little in adult tasks. He has learned previously that certain tasks devolve upon men and others upon women. At the very time when a Ute learns to avoid any great intimacy with relatives of opposite sex, his own energies and interests are channeled in proper occupations of his own. Here the division of labor is equally, but strictly, apportioned between the sexes. However, the process of assuming adult duties is neither jarring nor abrupt for the young Ute.

A child's instruction begins at first at the hands of older siblings of like sex, and is later supervised, more systematically, by his parents, their siblings and grandparents of the same sex. A girl learns that women do the household tasks, gather all vegetable food, and care for camp equipment. Until now, she has crudely imitated her elders in child's play. Around the age of five or six she is given small jugs and cradles as playthings, and adults in all mock seriousness begin to treat her on occasion as a grown-up. About three years later, actual instruction begins in the tasks assigned to women. Gradually she learns how to tan hides; to make baskets, clay pipes, and pitch-lined basketry jugs; to sew and repair clothing; dry meat; haul wood and carry water. Before puberty she usually helps tend a baby sister or younger cousin and watches the making of its cradle. When older and stronger, she helps pitch the tipis and build the brush summer lodges, sew the tipi covers, govern the instruction of younger girls, and make wooden cups and ladles. Girls are taught these techniques as soon as possible. At puberty, around fourteen or fifteen years of age, they are capable of entering into adult economic life to the fullest extent.

At the same time, men instruct boys in the tasks reserved for males. The men in Ute society were expected to spend most of their time in hunting, chiefly by the stalking method; in fishing; in clearing the camp site and gathering tipi poles; in butchering meat; in making rope and building fires; in supplying the family stock of arrows, shields and weapons in general; when alone, even in cooking.

How well the Ute recognized the complex developmental growth of children is profusely illustrated by a vocabulary rich in fine and subtle terms for stages of infancy and childhood. There are terms for new-born infants, small baby, little child, child before puberty, pubescence and maturity. The care with which children were trained and guided by the entire extended family reflects both the cherishing of children felt among the Ute as well as the solidarity of this dominant social unit. By virtue of its economic coöperation and closely knit interests, the aboriginal family made every effort to develop children into industrious and useful members of the group. In this effort, not only parents, but their siblings, grandparents, and the elder siblings of the child, all coöperated more or less equally. Thus it happened that a child was virtually brought up by a father's brother, a mother's father, or any elder who took a keener interest in his welfare than the rest, although all elders comprising the family camp shared somewhat in the child's development, and all, certainly, felt deep concern for his welfare. Although every effort was made to hasten this development, to make the child industrious and helpful in the family circle, child-adult relationships were not without their humor and fun. For example, children were told of the queer tabus incumbent upon them. They were many, but were always announced with a tongue-in-the-cheek air of dry humor. "Don't point at that rainbow, or you'll lose your finger." Any child over six understood this as the best joke in the world, especially designed to twit him.

The solidarity of the extended family group, then, was emphasized by the use of a common camp site, the sharing of food, the equitable apportioning of tasks around the camp, and finally, by the actual isolation of the family itself over long winter months. Each family, therefore, reflected the total culture in the microcosm of its small community. Each person found his place established in the family structure according to age and sex. As might be expected, all ceremonial concerning the life crises centered in the family. The same social unit which supervised the Ute's early training, governed his marital choice, determined his marital residence, protected him and avenged his death, was also the one primarily concerned in guiding him through the crises of life.

Birth, death and puberty assume significance far beyond their natural biologic importance to the Ute Indian. To some extent, of course, the fact of birth is accepted in a strictly biological sense, so that three or four months before childbirth prospective parents observed stringent rules of continence, while after birth intercourse was proscribed for at least a year in order to safeguard the health of the child. Dancing also fell under the ban for pregnant women, and prospective fathers were excluded from gambling games, not only because of the belief that luck failed them at this time but also because they were expected to show greater concern for more serious matters during a wife's pregnancy. Similarly, the theory of conception had its naturalistic aspect; semen, *wana'tcpi*, in a woman's body produced the baby. A woman was believed to have no counterpart of *wana'tcpi* but rather an amniotic sac, *no'gup*, which the male filled sometimes in a single intercourse, sometimes over a protracted period of time. Inferior semen, or *qawi'nat*, was said to explain childlessness or widely separated births. The cessation of menstrual flow marked the beginning of pregnancy.

Yet to state the crude biological conceptions of the Ute in this bald fashion is to miss the wealth of social ideology which gives the event of birth its real significance. This theory of conception furnished the justification for believing that the child belonged not only to the parents who produced it, but to all consanguineous lines where biological relationship could be traced. The child, consequently, was not attached merely to his immediate family, but to the extended family group we have described above. The lines of blood relationship descended from a great-grandparental, a grandparental, and a parental generation on both the mother's and the father's side. Since the duality of parenthood was construed wholly in terms of physical relationship, the way was clear to think of the child as belonging to a consanguineous group of relatives larger than the single unit of parents and children. An illustration of this point occurred recently in an interesting case where a girl had a baby immediately following the death of her husband. The dead man's mother demanded the baby according to the common Ute practice of giving the child to the grandparental generation whenever any grandparent so requested. Naturally, more than this was involved since the paternal grandmother of the child wanted her daughter-in-law to remain with the child at the grandparental camp and contribute to the economic support and comfort of the older generation. The young girl, however, had other plans; she preferred to return to a former paramour now that her husband was gone, and begin life over again. The girl prevented her mother-in-law's seizure of the child simply by saying, "You can't do this. That baby has two fathers. Another man helped make it!" It was obvious then that the child belonged to at least three lineages, one maternal and two paternal, and that a single paternal line had no exclusive right to it. The girl's own mother was dead, but her paramour's mother claimed the child and this settled the question. As a result, the girl was unhindered in her wish to live with the other "father" of the child, and the child's training was henceforth placed in the hands of a second paternal grandmother.

In the same way, a casual consideration of the control of property in the aboriginal community fails to do justice to the cohesiveness of the family structure. While it is certainly true that property—whether personal, technological, or supernatural—was individually owned among the Southern Ute, what this meant in a society where material property was decidedly limited was that each owned the products of his labor. There were important exceptions, however. As we have seen, food, shelter and clothing—the *sine qua non* of biologic survival—were jointly controlled by the extended family group. Clothing was ordinarily made by the women of the camp for any male or female relatives. The essentials of life, therefore, were strictly shared within the family circle.

In accordance with the principle that each person himself produced other necessities, over and above food, shelter and clothing, no Ute was free to dispose of objects not specifically of his manufacture. This age-old concept persists even to this day, as, for example, when a husband cannot dispose of his wife's baskets without her consent. On one occasion, while purchasing artifacts from the wife of the much-esteemed chief, Buckskin Charlie, the latter insisted that I pay less for baskets than his wife saw fit. Despite all his arguments on my behalf, the lady held to her original price with an air of authoritative finality. The baskets represented her effort and both the decision to sell and the price itself were her prerogatives.

Yet it is possible to carry too far the principle of individual autonomy in exercising control over such objects as baskets, jugs and arrows. At this point we must distinguish between property as used and property as inherited among the Ute. The right to use what one made gave the right to dispose of it by gift or by verbal testament before death. With every death, there went a distribution of property to members of the bilateral family. Death also was accompanied by the destruction of personal effects and cherished belongings of the deceased not so willed. Although a verbal will allowed one to bequeath property to anyone at all, and thus save any object from subsequent destruction, the solidarity of the bilateral family usually secured such willed property to consanguineous and affinal kin alike, so that the actual direction of the bequest was either to wife or children or siblings of the same sex. Finally, since bequeathed property entailed the danger of ghost sickness by reminding one too often of the deceased himself, it was usually traded beyond the confines of the family circle for objects of like nature. Later, after the introduction of the horse by the Spaniards, the favorite horse of the deceased was killed at his grave, while additional mounts which had been bequeathed were traded for horses from another band.

But the world was not merely material according to the native way of thinking. The sun which traveled clockwise around a flat earth and the stars which moved in the same direction with the seasons were but moving characters in an animistic universe, alive with supernatural power and filled with human purpose. Cosmological notions bear the stamp of a thorough anthropomorphism. The Milky Way, used to get one's bearings when on the move, is the backbone of the earth or the strewn ashes of a mythical camp-fire. The Big Dipper was *qam,* the jack-rabbit, or else the prototype of the familiar wooden ladle seen around the camp. The Pleiades became understandable in a myth wherein Sunav, the wolf, breaks the Indian rule proscribing sexual relations with one's daughter; the largest star, Eta or Alcyone of the Pleiades, is no other than the enraged wife of Sunav, surrounded by her children.

Naturalistic adjustments to man and nature as outlined in our sketch of social organization and economics were inter-penetrated and complicated by a world view heavily charged with religious concepts and practices. Once within the supernatural domain, actual relationships and realistic techniques for mastering the outer world counted for very little. While this characterization does not distinguish Ute religion from any other, it defines this strange and bizarre domain of belief and practice in its broadest aspect. My own introduction to Ute religion came when an informant described cyclones as follows:

If the Ute saw a cyclone coming, they were afraid. It meant something evil was coming in that cloud. Maybe it was someone's bad power or someone's bad wish. Well, the Ute waved a black obsidian knife at that cyclone. That would fix it so it couldn't strike, so it would turn to one side.

We had been discussing cosmology, and, as he told me later, the picture of the world was not complete without these "religious things."

Yet for all the strange supernatural relationships that stud Ute religious beliefs, these conceptions are on the whole somewhat more social in their significance than the mere view of religion as illusion allows. It is true that Ute religion rested on an animistic premise of a universe charged with supernatural power. The Ute are consistent theologians in this respect, for virtually nothing is beyond the scope of religion. Anthropomorphic values are injected into a universe which responds warmly to the good wish or the bad. Here is a complete system for obtaining *rapport* with the universe, for indulging to the hilt the omnipotence of thought. But on the other hand, Ute religion is a form of social regulation. Not only do their shamans fight black magic, but they identify sorcerers in the diagnosis. Death from sorcery opened the way for vengeance on the part of near kin and a fourth cousin was expected to respond with passion to any outrage committed on a classificatory brother. Inter-family feuds were traceable to murder, whether real or imagined.

Furthermore, the ceremonies contingent upon birth and death greatly intensified the solidarity of the extended domestic family. When a woman was about to give birth, the family camp was moved far from neighboring tipis. This removal was said to protect unrelated men and sick individuals from the mother's blood which like menstrual blood caused illness. The prospective father then called one or two old women to act as midwives. Although women ordinarily hauled wood and fetched water, on this occasion the husband himself took over these functions. Before the birth, the husband and midwife dug two pits on either side of the fireplace the length of a man's body and a foot and a half deep. When the fire burned down, they put hot ashes in the holes, placed cedar bark over the ashes, and laid green brush on top as insulation. A sheepskin or rawhide covering made this so-called "hot bed" ready for occupancy. For thirty days after birth, the mother remained on this bed; for four days the father also remained in his "hot bed." At the time of birth and for thirty days afterwards, a mother drank only warm water said to clean out the bad blood which had accumulated in her body since the moment of conception. Cold water was said to coagulate this blood inside the body. For thirty days there were strict tabus against a mother's eating meat or fish lest she spoil her husband's luck in hunting or fishing from that time on. For four days the father likewise observed the tabus against eating meat and fish. The old woman who acted as midwife was required to remake the "hot beds" every evening before supper was given to her at the camp of the parents. Both parents used scratching sticks throughout the period of confinement and they were strictly forbidden to use their nails lest they leave welts on the skin. Throughout the period of these proscriptions a heavy pall lay over the *towaoqan,* or baby-camp. Actually, the fact of birth signalized an event important beyond the thirty days accouchement, an event of serious consequence to the entire family concerned. It was thought that if the parents scratched their ears at this time, they would become deaf. Nor could they laugh, for their faces would become old and wrinkled if they did. If they were forgetful at this time, they would henceforth be forgetful. All relatives went seriously about their business with quiet solemnity and serious demeanor, for the future of the family line was at stake during these crucial days. The behavior of the parents at the birth of each child was strictly determinative of their future character and success in life.

After the father's four days of ceremonial lying-in, or couvade, meat was cooked for him at the baby-camp. A grandparent of the child appeared and cooked this meat for the father. If the child's grandparents were not living, an older couple standing in the relationship of brother or sister, real or classificatory, to the grandparents, appeared at this time. In presenting the food the grandfather said, "After you eat, you can be like me and live long to an old age and be strong. You can be a good hunter. Take care of this wife and child. Shoot plenty of game. Let us teach this child the right way to do everything and bring him up the right way. Now you can laugh and talk and eat this meat. But your wife is not out yet. When she comes out, we will return and tell her the right ways. My wife will tell her."

At this time the infant was named and the father exchanged clothes with the old man in order to obtain long life. Later, when the mother was given a similar blessing by the old woman, she too exchanged clothes with the older relative. The meat for the feast which accompanied the naming ceremony was provided by the old man as a token of the hunting prowess he bestowed upon his younger relative at this time. Before the father ate, the old man painted his face with a mixture of deer grease and red ochre while he prayed for his young friend's future welfare. The entire ceremony was directed toward obtaining long life and skill in hunting for the young man since it was thought that the fortunes of the entire family, and of the newborn infant as well, depended entirely upon this precondition.

After the feast was over, the father went alone on a ceremonial hunt, during which he imitated in grossly exaggerated form the actions of a most sedulous and exemplary hunter. Though nothing really was killed, he ran anxiously up-hill and down, breaking twigs from trees to mark his path and keeping ever alert for deer tracks and antelope trails. This feverish activity, from which he returned exhausted often several days later, insured him of future speed and endurance, of watchfulness for hostile Indians, of ability to catch deer and track antelope. Only through this ceremonial mechanism could he become a good provider for the camp. Failure to observe this custom foredoomed him to a life of laziness, improvidence, and dishonor; for the entire family concerned, it spelled crushing misfortune.

In the meantime, the child was tenderly moulded by its grandmother, the nose pulled gently, the face rounded, the ears pressed in while the old lady chanted, "You will be handsome and grow straight up—that is my desire." Of a handsome youth or pretty girl, the Ute say, "The old one who moulded that person as a baby did it well."

Equally social in their significance were the beliefs surrounding the menstruation of women. At first menstruation, a girl was taken an eighth or a quarter of a mile from the family camp and segregated in a brush wickiup. Her grandmother or the older female relative who accompanied her made a cedar bark wickiup in cold winter weather. There she was instructed in sexual affairs and told of the dangerous potency of menstrual blood to things masculine. She was warned that contact with menstrual blood cut the wind of a good runner or induced fevers, chills and backache in a man. She was instructed to leave the family camp during menstruation and hereafter to make her own brush wickiup by placing willows in a circle and tying them at the top. Unless she obeyed these rules, she would become old before her time, her back bent, and her teeth prematurely decayed. Besides protecting her own health and the health of close male relatives by this act of seclusion, a woman observed certain food tabus in the menstrual lodge which were said to protect the family larder. If she ate fish during menstruation, she ruined forever her male relatives' skill in fishing. Similarly, to eat meat at this time spoiled the hunting ability of male kin. A good hunter or fisherman contaminated by menstrual blood met the same fate. After the horse was introduced among the Ute, the ill effects of menstrual blood were extended to riding mounts around the camp. A woman rode an old mare to the blood camp, but never a colt or a stallion. After her first seclusion, a girl was ceremonially bathed by her attendant, who prayed for her long life, health, and happy future.

A pubescent boy underwent a comparable ceremony. He was taken on a hunt by an older relative who killed a large game animal before his eyes and then rubbed the blood over the boy's body. By this act the boy obtained attributes of the animal killed in his presence; if a deer, he became a tireless hunter; if a coyote, he was henceforth crafty and clever; if a mountain lion, powerful and stout, a cunning stalker of game. Then the first time a boy hunted alone, he brought back the game and presented it to the older male relative who gave him instruction in hunting. The older person then ceremonially bathed him, praying that he be a good hunter from that time on. In much the same manner, a girl who picked berries or sunflower seeds for the first time presented them to an older female relative who received the gift and then bathed and blessed her.

However, religious life among the Ute usually antedates puberty or the time of the first hunting or gathering. At seven or eight years of age a child may begin to notice that he dreams of strange and wonderful things. The ordinary dream embodying the commonplace event is taken simply as a dream among these people. But the unusual dream, the dream of animals talking, of birds living like humans, of buffalo, moose or eagle, the sun, the moon, and the stars—these things mean nothing less than a nocturnal visitation of supernatural power.

Now supernatural power among the Ute is a matter of immense importance. Not only do religious ideas figure prominently in explanations of the most commonplace events, but even the supernatural realm itself reflects the needs and exigencies of the everyday world. As we have seen, the central purpose of crisis ceremonialism at birth and puberty is to obtain such benefits as long life, good health, and economic skills. Since illness threatened the delicate economic balance of the aboriginal community, narrowing the margin between survival and extinction of the entire family group, it is not surprising to find that the great majority of ceremonials were curing rites again designed to safeguard the health and vigor of an essentially mobile population.

Accordingly, the key figure of religious life is the shaman, or as the Ute call him, the Indian doctor or *pö'rat*. His power to cure, his songs, his ritual rules and ceremonial possessions are unique endowments offered to him alone in dream encounters between himself and the supernatural. The Ute shaman prides himself on the peculiar individuality of his power. He calls it his secret way and will divulge no more of its nature than is actually necessary in ceremonial practice. For supernatural power is not something trivial to be bandied about, nor is it easy to obtain. The Ute constantly stress that this possession is dangerous to hold, and is entrusted in the first place only to those who have proven their serious intent and faultless character. Power will not, therefore, be given to one easily angered or prone to despair. Power is primarily to "do good."

The fountain-head of supernatural power is variously conceived as a supreme god called Creator-of-Humans; as Sunavawi, the Wolf, a culture-hero part benefactor and part trickster; and as the Sun. To these deities the Ute address their most fervent prayers and present their most pressing wants. But beneath this concept of potent creative powers, there operate a host of lesser supernatural agencies, animals, plants and natural phenomena which transmit the high voltage of supernatural power to more humble human practitioners or doctors. Chief among these reservoirs of power are the moon and stars, eagle, elk, antelope, buffalo, lightning, cyclone and wind. This power is usually transmitted during puberty or even before and with it come the rules and paraphernalia governing its use. To rid oneself of the insistent dreams of a power which one fears to accept requires the help of another shaman whose strength is greater. Merely to disregard repeated dreams of this nature, or to allow them to prey on one's mind leads to illness. To accept, however, entails future responsibility.

The doctor whose abilities became known was expected to answer any call for help, no matter how far distant. The relative of the sick person who approached him was advised in advance of the proper procedure for the summons. Some doctors required a formal presentation of eagle feathers, a painted stick or some other symbol of their office. Some required a gift in advance or a token of what was later to come. After the horse was adopted by the Ute, it became the almost standard payment for ceremonial services. To promise a gift and later refuse it often led to a supernatural attack either on the medicine-man, or on the cured individual whose formal sign of gratitude was still forthcoming.

The doctor who practised publicly (and many performed only within the family confines) was known by certain insignia of his occupation—downy eagle feathers, a black obsidian knife, a painted stick, or a medicine bundle uniquely designed for him by his power. His tipi was often decorated with weird designs and his buckskin shirt with pictures of the animal which worked through him. In actual curing practice, he was often stripped to the waist while he dramatized, by sleight of hand, dancing feathers, or the swallowing of hot coals, his violent and courageous assault upon the illness and its originator. While actual techniques for curing varied tremendously, the dramatic element, the singing, praying, sucking out and swallowing down of evil was never absent. The vivid appeal of a sing, so-called, was always heightened for the observer when the shaman called upon the kin of the sick person to join in his songs and help him fight the evil. Here, as with the payment for shamanistic services, the solidarity of the extended family was again evinced.

The constant swallowing down of illness on the part of sha-mans is conceptually clear when once we realize that most sha-mans have inside of themselves a small manikin, called *pöwa'a*. This tiny being directs the use of power and is the one to swallow the sickness. Recently, when a shaman was conducting his rite in the government hospital, he produced a wad of dirt as the disease and proceeded to swallow it. The nurse objected on the grounds that there were germs in the wad, whereupon the shaman proudly announced that not he, but his power, swallowed that sickness. The theory of *pöwa'a* also conforms to the dual nature of power in Ute religious ideology. For besides power for good, there is its counterpart, *iwïpö'warat*, or power for evil. It is thought that if *pöwa'a* is angered or unskillfully directed, he may kill rather than cure. If one promised a shaman a certain payment and then gave another, *pöwa'a* fell into a rage and the power took a victim. Once *pöwa'a* has killed in anger, he keeps calling for blood. The shaman can plead with his power, but to no avail. His power has become *iwïpö'warat*, and he is now a sorcerer whose rôle is to cause illness and misfortune. When death from witchcraft was estab-lished by the diagnosis of another medicine-man, the Ute family angrily wiped out its loss by murdering the sorcerer. There was no other way to stop the misdeeds of an evil *pöwa'a*. Either the sorcerer must die and *pöwa'a* cease working through him, or witchcraft would continue.

Also interesting in terms of psychology is the belief that medi-cine power can wreak vengeance on members of the shaman's own family. A power may become so weakened by long years of curing that it retaliates by attacking its human embodiment, the shaman who uses it. Should a shaman ward off the personal at-tack successfully, his *pöwa'a* strikes at his younger relatives, par-ticularly children. Thus the Ute feel that a power should not be used when once it shows signs of weakening. A power is always rested if not abandoned at the loss of a patient. If approached at this time, a doctor said, "*Pö'rat* (curing power) has left me for a while," or "The medicine isn't strong just now." This concept of power not only accounts for the death of great shamans, but by a neat rationalization, it allows younger relatives to express indirectly, in supernatural terms, their suppressed resentment against the authority of age which certainly exists within the family circle. To this day, the older shaman is feared by his close relatives, and the ostensible reason offered is that his much-taxed power represents a potent source of danger to themselves.

The close connection of supernatural power and the dream experience gives *pöwa'a* yet another function. In terms sharply reminiscent of Tylor's ingenious theory of the origin of religion, the Ute say that the unusual dream is a visitation of the tiny manikin. The power may travel far in this medicine-body while the actual man is sleeping. Thus it happens that in dreams one goes far afield and does strange things. Should one dream repeatedly of buffalo attacking, this means simply that someone with buffalo power is visiting in troubled sleep. If illness results, a shaman is called in to exorcize the evil. For this reason, a good deal of Ute curing consists in the recounting of strange dreams and their interpretation by the practitioner. How close we approach here to a primitive version of psychoanalytic dream analysis is a moot question, especially since it must be borne in mind that personal names are largely animal names, while dreams of animals are, as we have seen, the most significant in supernatural terms. It is possible that the animal serves as a surrogate in dream experience for the person so named.

The most interesting facet of the Ute theory of the dream is the arresting idea of the ghost. One informant, in discussing the ghosts of the departed, said:

Relatives can give dreams. If you dream of a dead mother as if she were alive, that means that she wants to take you back to the future life with her. You dream of them; they are trying every way to take you in death. If I'm very sick and getting worse, then to have these *ini'putc* (ghost) dreams means I'm going very fast.

Can the medicine-man drive them away? Sometimes the ghosts are shaped like buffalo, owl or snake. Sometimes they come like real persons. The medicine-man asks the sick person, "Have you been dreaming of *ini'putc?*" If not, you are getting better. When the medicine-man puts his head down to the patient, he can find that evil and draw it out.

The *ini'putc* put evil in the body in those dreams. Often the ghosts have tiny arrows that they shoot into their live relative. This makes the sharp pain. The doctor can drive these out.

When my wife dies, suppose I'm sick with sorrow. I call the doctor and he sings. He might say: "Your wife is *ini'putc* to you and she is coming back in another ghost-body. You are thinking too much about her. You think, well, your good wife is gone. You want her back. Her power has entered your body. I shall take it away." He draws it off. Then he says, "Your wife wanted you. She loved to be with you. She made *ini'putc* kind of love. Don't think about her any more."

The Ute call it *ini'puvawaqwi*, to be possessed with love for a dead person when they come back. If I sleep with a woman once and forget about her, I can get sick when she comes back to make love to me. The doctor might ask, "Did you ever sleep with that woman?" Well, you can't lie so you admit it. Then he drives this old lover out.

An old woman I knew was like this for her husband. She told my brother who was giving her treatment about this. "My husband is in my dreams," she said. He told her, "Not by thinking about your good husband will you get well. He is dead. Forget about him."

Usually the Ute get *ini'putc* sickness from an older person. A small child or a baby who died was too young to make *ini'putc*. But older people are dangerous. If you keep their things around camp after they die, they want them and come around.

Thus the ghosts, particularly those of older relatives, haunted the living in dreams. Their visitations caused illness and even led to death.

Closely connected with the idea of the ghost were concepts and customs concerning death itself. When a person died, the Ute said that his heart left his body. The medicine-man, confronted with a slowly sinking patient, sang his most powerful songs to restore the weakening heart. He sent a light feather after the heart, and pleaded with his power, "That heart cannot move away fast. Make it catch on trees or rocks!" Men rushed from the tipi to call the heart back. If the doctor was successful, he blew on his feather and returned the breath to the sick man. For it was believed that *sua'pun,* or breath, left the body in extreme illness and could be recalled by the medicine-man as *sua'pits,* returned breath. This constituted a cure and the patient then received a new name and perhaps some food tabus. But when death came, the medicine-man often said, "I tried my best; there were too many *ini'putc* near to get that man. They were laughing at me. I could do nothing against so many." Then the dead person was quickly buried under rocks or burned on a pyre. With all haste the camp was moved and the family took care never to return to that spot. All close relatives cut their hair, the immediate family donned old clothes and for four days quiet reigned and there was no singing or laughter. The entire family, throughout this period, lived in the very shadow of death, since other dead relatives came close to their camp to take the newly dead back with them. While not all the dead were said to become *inï'putc*, there were always some to meet the deceased at the moment when life ended. Birth, puberty and death completed a cycle in which the supernatural was always present, whether in the form of the creator to whom the pious wish was uttered, or the animal power whose transient appearance either killed or cured.

Sex attitudes among the Ute, aside from ideas connected with birth and menstruation, are preëminently realistic. Here the religious element is almost completely excluded. Even the menstrual camp itself became the scene of surreptitious courtship despite the insistent warnings to youths that the odor of menstrual blood was enough to induce illness. A boy usually approached the menstrual lodge in order to be close enough to speak privately with the girl who caught his fancy. There were no puritanical attitudes to check the natural expression of sex interest in young people past puberty and no double standards by which to define the virtuous life of either male or female.

Before puberty, however, sex play and sex interest were sternly discouraged. There was good reason for this. In the first place, the family camp was isolated throughout the winter months and young children were kept at home in the company of siblings and cousins. As children grew up, they were taught to avoid physical intimacy with siblings and cousins of opposite sex. Even a fourth cousin belonged in the same category as brother or sister. There was no brother-sister avoidance except in relation to sexual matters. As soon as children learned to dress themselves, years before puberty, they were taught to don the G-string. Immature boys and girls were openly warned against sexual intimacy even with non-relatives on the grounds that illness resulted from premature sexual relations. In the immediate family circle, a brother was careful not to uncover before a classificatory sister and she before him. Parents and children of opposite sex observed the same rule, which applied also to uncles, aunts and grandparents. Between relatives of the same sex, however, a great deal of good-natured salacious banter occurred, usually directed toward younger relatives in conformity with the one-way respect attitudes of the Ute. The interest in sex as a topic for joking was further intensified by a mythology unsparing in the humorous sexual angle. Such stories were frequently told to young and old alike and mixed company offered no curb to the unabashed story-teller. The only rule observed in relation to sexual jokes of an obscene sort was that the older relative moved out of earshot when a younger, mature relative of opposite sex was also present.

At puberty, the latent vicarious concern with sex was translated into action. At this time, young people began to leave the camp on lone hunting or gathering expeditions and family control of sex activity was considerably lessened. Although parents continued to uphold the ideal of continence, followed by a marriage prearranged by themselves alone, adolescents preferred to spend their first years of freedom in sexual experimentation with mates of their own choosing. Only the very shy or particularly repulsive youth actually conformed to the ideal of pre-marital chastity. Actually, the rule was a vigorous hetero-sexuality in which considerable emphasis was placed on superior sex technique. In this setting, the transvestite was more often physically aberrant than functionally disordered; in the latter event, the person was universally regarded as demented, and in either case, occupied a disgraceful position in society. Such people were avoided and kept hard at work at tasks reserved for women. There was no supernatural outlet open to them in shamanism. So general was the horror of homosexuality, frigidity, or impotence that children were never allowed to change sex in playing or in fantasy and adults were never permitted to wear clothing of the opposite sex on pain of someday giving life to such a child.

The normal procedure for a boy was to court his girl by frequenting the neighborhood of her blood camp, by waiting for her near the river when she came to fetch water, and by haunting her camp with the four-holed flageolet. The flageolet serenade usually furnished the best introduction. It was fashioned to fit the boy's voice; if high, he pitched his instrument high; if a bass, he pitched it low. The phrasing of the music indicated the word accompaniment. There were certain recurrent themes like, "——— (Girl's name), she is wearing my belt." Girls were laughingly rebuked for sitting idly around camp puzzling out the word content of these musical messages. A more curious girl soon tried to discover who was playing. Sometimes the boy included his own name in the song. On rare occasions parental restraint was exercised over a too zealous flageolet player when the boy was not welcome in the neighborhood. After the flageolet was used for a while, the boy's parents themselves warned him to fill it with pebbles and throw it in the river under penalty, otherwise, of falling ill. He was told, further, that illness fell to the lot of one who used the same flageolet for more than one girl. Actually, the instrument was used only for philandering, so that by its use one was really encouraged to spread favors widely at first, and to withhold more serious advances until after a series of such romantic affairs. Philandering nevertheless served to preclude early marriages among younger and less experienced people.

There were other methods of courtship. The bear dance, as we have said, ushered in a spring season of social dancing and festivity. For a brief period the people of the band camped close together and the choice of paramours was less unrestricted. In public dances, the women took the initiative in choosing partners and in this way indicated their preference. A more serious advance, an invitation to visit her at her camp that night, was made by throwing something, a stick or a stone, into the lap of a man. In such clandestine visits, a man was either concealed in the tipi before the older people came home or else told to wait outside until the rest of the camp had fallen asleep. Men and boys were dressed to kill when on these *naqwi'tpaqwi*, or "girl-hunting" expeditions even though it was never quite clear which sex really did the hunting. At all seasons of the year the creeping lover at night was a more or less permanent institution.

The creeping lover, however, was a risky method of courtship. When boys were caught *in flagrante delicto*, they were either asked to marry the girl, or in case a boy was not favorably regarded as a future son-in-law, told to leave the camp and never be seen in the vicinity again. A rebuff, where the intentions were entirely and mutually serious, normally led to an elopement.

Elopements, however, were not socially approved because they conflicted with parental authority in the arrangement of marriages. Although there was no punishment for such drastic action, usually a boy followed the social rule of sending a go-between— an older male relative, sibling or uncle—to the girl's parents to plead the case for matrimony before resorting to any such extreme measures.

Marriage as a rule did not directly follow sexual intimacy. After a few years of philandering, during which parents protested feebly on occasion, two compatible individuals began to settle down in what, to all intents and purposes, was trial-marriage. The two called each other by the term *piwan'na"pun,* meaning sweetheart, and were, in the eyes of the world, really engaged. At this time, they were not closely watched and sexual relations commonly occurred. Such loose, informal unions led to marriage in most instances, especially when a child was born to the couple. Less frequently, the relationship continued indefinitely. As with more fragile unions, the *piwan'na"pun* trial-marriage relation was instigated by the missile-throwing of an interested girl in reply to the attentions of an ardent lover. This steady relationship was approved by the older generation as a method of testing a future mate.

In addition to the trial-marriage period, there was another method of determining compatibility and this method constituted the marriage ceremony. A couple who had proved their serious intentions was often asked by prospective parents-in-law to undergo a smoke-test ordeal designed to test patience and endurance. They were confined in a tipi filled with smoke and just enough air to prevent suffocation. After hours of this confinement, they were allowed to emerge as man and wife provided their conversation had been pleasant and amiable during the confinement. To faint, to argue, to complain at this time presaged future weakness and incompatibility. Such failure was taken to mean that separation should follow.

Because marriages occurred late and were preceded by a protracted period of active sexuality, illegitimate births were by no means unknown. Yet they were much less frequent than one would expect not only because of the late puberty and low birth rate of these people, but also because withdrawal was practised as a method of birth control. When girls became pregnant despite this precaution, the fate of the unborn child depended upon the attitude of the family. Girls sometimes secretly attempted abortion by violent means,—jumping, falling, striking, and rough massage—but secrecy was not always necessary. If the child was not wanted, older female relatives often instructed the girl in effective methods of abortion. On the other hand, grandparents might offer to take the child, and ask the girl to bear it for them. There was no stigma attached to illegitimacy *per se,* since each child had relatives by virtue of a known ancestry. The worst situation occurred when the former paramour had already married another while the girl's relatives found the child an inconvenient burden to themselves. Otherwise, the way was paved for normal marriage.

The behavior patterns toward affinals did not differ markedly from the general pattern of age and authority we observed for consanguineous kin. The authority of parents and older relatives was occasionally transferred to parents-in-law and older affinals with no break in continuity. It must be remembered, however, that the young couple normally visited back and forth between the two sets of parents-in-law and usually lingered the greater length of time with the older family which proved the most congenial. If neither camp provided pleasant company, they were free to camp alone or with some sibling or cousin where relationships were more amicable. In any camp, youth obeyed the wishes of age so that there was nothing new in this for the newly married. Nevertheless, the marital status carried with it the option of camping alone and thereby weakening the control of older affinal relatives.

In keeping with this picture of shifting family alliances is the total lack of affinal control outside of the age-authority pattern. There were no gift exchanges, no avoidances, no joking relationships or post-marital rights of affinals. The Southern Ute have always regarded the complex affinal behavior of their Jicarilla Apache neighbors either with hearty amusement or quizzical astonishment. Their own marriages are not marked by elaborate gift-giving, and the economic interdependence of affinals breaks off with a change in residence or ceases entirely with divorce. Although each first marriage was approached with cautious preliminaries and none of the naïvete of a repressed and puritanical people, the looseness of economic ties between affinal relatives accounts for the brittle character of Ute marriages. Divorces were effected simply by returning alone to the camp of one's parents. A further encouragement to brittle unions was the practice of turning children over to older relatives after they were weaned, a custom which freed active young people for complete absorption in the economic tasks of hunting and gathering, but at the same time destroyed a powerful bond of mutual interest.

The levirate and sororate both functioned at the death of a spouse in cases where a son-in-law or daughter-in-law was so well-liked, usually by reason of his hunting prowess or her industry at women's tasks, that the parents-in-law sought to keep them close to their camp. If remarriage to an affinal were not effected some time after the death of a spouse, however, the affinal ties dissolved completely. So it happened that often when a hunter had proved his ability to support more than one wife, a sister or a cousin of his wife was given him in marriage in order to bind him more firmly to the affinal kin whose fortunes already were linked to his own. The other form of polygamy, where the wives were totally unrelated and occupied separate tipis, was always less stable than the sororal form, not merely because of the jealousy between wives related only by marriage, but because of the difficulty of pleasing all affinals at once. In general, polygamy was rare because of the limitations of economy, and polyandry, except of the adulterous variety, was out of question.

In case of female adultery or discordant relations between wives of a polygamous household, the right to the man was settled openly by an unarmed struggle between the women. The scuffle was always recommended on the grounds that the woman who really cared would never admit defeat and that the stronger made the best wife anyway. A woman who didn't care or a wife whose ideals were dashed by a knowledge of adultery on the part of her husband retaliated by destroying some possession of her rival—a dress, her winter cape, her baskets or her jugs. The destruction of property was accompanied by the taunt, "That man is yours now; you can keep him." On the other hand, property was sometimes taken as a fair exchange. A husband overcome by jealousy often killed his rival if he wanted to retain his wife. When less attached, he too might claim property as fair exchange. After the introduction of the horse, the standard method of retaliation short of murder was for a man to kill or take possession of the favorite riding horse of the detested rival. A less courageous method was to complain pettishly to the parents of the girl. But a man who was seen going to the camp of his parents-in-law either to complain of infidelity or to fetch home a dissatisfied wife was always the subject of social disdain. "He is going to marry her younger sister," the Ute say as an amusing inversion of the actual situation. There are humorous myths of the husband who is forever calling on his wife's father. Women never killed the adulteress; when thoroughly outraged the utmost they could do was to cut the rival's hair and this, too, was called payment.

The constant break-up of marriages accounts for still another polygamous form among the Ute. In marrying a woman who had a mature daughter, the husband often took his stepdaughter as a second wife providing she was in no way related to himself. Of all the relatively rare forms of polygamy, the sororate and mother-stepdaughter marriage were the most common.

So much for the aboriginal community. What we have done in the foregoing pages is to sketch, in bare outline, the main features of the pre-literate culture before White contact. The sparse population, the hunting and gathering economy, the scattered family organization, the shamanistic religion, and the preoccupation of a nomadic people with health and economic skills, all give an impression of functional integration in a pattern harmoniously adapted to economic structure and social values. But this pattern, despite its cohesive symmetry, was not immutable. Ute culture has changed since aboriginal times and is today changing according to a process which now claims our attention.

THE CONTACT CONTINUUM: THE FIRST AND FINAL PHASES OF ACCULTURATION

In a stimulating recent volume on *The History of Ethnological Theory*, Robert Lowie states that "the time factor is not a thing adventitiously linked with culture." [1] The picture just presented of aboriginal Ute society before the introduction of the horse is not, in any sense, a timeless picture. Dated before the appearance of the Spaniards in the province of New Mexico, the traditional account crystallizes at a given point in time the culture of a people who still speak of customs and activities long since vanished but vividly remembered. What imparts a genuine ring of truth to these remembrances of things past or only partially surviving is not merely the consonance of functioning components in the aboriginal community nor even the care with which the historically minded Ute preserve their manifold traditions, but rather the clear relationship of older Ute society to other Great Basin Shoshonean cultures which did not possess the horse.

Recent investigations throughout the Basin area have demonstrated conclusively that Shoshonean-speaking peoples possess a common central core of similar religious conceptions, social organization, mythology and beliefs; and, with the gradual accumulation of field data it becomes more certain that the Ute represent a southeastern offshoot of a pattern focally centered to the north and west. Today the linguistic similarity pointing to this conclusion is strongly corroborated by a consideration of Ute culture as it functioned before the horse, before the buffalo hunt, before the band camp, and before the warlike raiding complex turned the Southern Ute in a new and somewhat unexpected direction. To bring the aboriginal community into sharp focus, one has only to mention the concept of supernatural power as emanating from a limited number of natural reservoirs and offered in dreams to likely recipients; the birth ceremonies, menstrual tabus, and methods of courtship; withdrawal and abortion as birth-control techniques; the initial matrilocal residence followed by shifting family alliances; the seasonal circuit of family

[1] R. H. Lowie, *op. cit.*, Farrar and Rinehart, New York, N.Y., 1937, p. 287.

groups within a known orbit; the loose patterns of authority by virtue of age and experience reflected with varying emphasis in kinship terminology; the sun-deity; the solely territorial nature of early band grouping, with occasional communal gatherings for winter rabbit hunts and fall antelope drives; and even such minor arrangements as the position of the transvestite in society. These features, seen both in their complexity and in their cultural context, give an impression of a unity of pattern typically Shoshonean.

Having noted these functional cultural affiliations, one could go further and observe the striking parallelism of development that marks Great Basin Shoshonean cultures following the introduction of the horse. Throughout the Humboldt River valley, band organization and war-chieftainship followed close upon the introduction of horses around the middle of the nineteenth century, since the horse allowed for concentration of population by making possible for the first time the transporting of food to central camp sites. As Dr. Julian Steward has noted for this area, "It is an empirical fact that the western limit of the horse also was the western limit of true bands."[2]

Yet even a more striking confirmation of Ute-Great Basin connection is furnished, strangely enough, by the divergences of Southern Ute society from the Western Shoshonean. The common Shoshonean pattern of winter consolidation into villages and summer scattering of population was seasonally reversed among the Southern Ute prior to band camp organization. As we have seen, the Ute scattered out in winter, meeting as a band unit only for a brief period in spring. This seasonal reversal of population movement from the expected pattern is best understood as a result of a unique ecology, the pressure of Plains invasions in the summer and the difficulty of wintering in the mountains. As Colonel R. I. Dodge aptly put it in the '8o's, "the Utes are the Switzers of America and though the whole force of mountain bands numbers but little over four hundred men, all the powerful Plains tribes, though holding them in utter contempt on the Plains have absolute terror of them in the moun-

[2] "Linguistic Distributions and Political Groups of the Great Basin Shoshoneans," *American Anthropologist,* Volume 39, No. 4, 1937, p. 632.

tains."[3] Yet these "Switzers of America" were quite unable to consolidate in winter villages among mountains ridged by the high peaks of the Continental Divide. For not only did deep drifts fill the narrow valleys and close the passes, but the antelope, in autumn, congregated in great herds on the southern foothills, luring the Ute south for fall antelope drives in order to lay in a winter supply of meat.[4] The southern winter range in northern New Mexico and adjoining states was the scene of only occasional consolidations between extended family groups for communal rabbit hunts or trading expeditions to the pueblos, since here again the danger of Plains enemies was an ever-present reality which the Ute met with a widely dispersed and mobile population not easily subject to attack. Thus, geographical position even in the aboriginal community required a shift from Shoshonean patterns of consolidation.

Or, one could remark the relative lack among the Ute of fertility ceremonies characteristic of, say, the Western Shoshoni. But there is a connection which, although worn thin among the Southern Ute, is nevertheless still traceable. For one thing the Ute regard the sun as a prime generator, the source of all power and life. The bulk of prayers are addressed to the sun and each household head is expected to begin the day with invocations to this central deity. More conclusive than this Shoshonean resemblance is the record of a dance formerly held among the Ute in honor of the sun and for the purpose of obtaining an increased food supply. This dance, the *tasu'tcinqap* or deer-hoof rattle dance, is today reported only by informants over eighty and was actually witnessed by only two Utes of my acquaintance, both of whom were over ninety years of age. Willows three feet long were cut, covered with buckskin, and deer-hoof rattles were attached at the top. These sticks were then handed to men and women present who ranged themselves in parallel lines, each man side by side with a woman, and each holding a staff in the right hand. In single files they faced the east. An eagle feather or some brightly colored bird feather was tied to the top of the staff

[3] *Our Wild Indians*, A. B. Worthington, Hartford, Conn., 1882, p. 442.
[4] See G. F. Ruxton, *Adventures in Mexico and the Rocky Mountains*, 1847, p. 277. Compare R. I. Dodge, *The Plains of the Great West*, 1877, p. 201.

which was then stamped on the ground rhythmically in time to the songs. The singer who knew the proper songs to the sun sat apart and likewise pounded the earth with a similar staff. The dancers just shook their bodies in place. Their faces were painted symbolically as personal power individually directed them; in addition, their hair was streaked with red and yellow paint to represent the sundown. Both the songs of the leader and the prayers of the dancers called for the regeneration of the sun since the dance occurred late in the afternoon after the sun had passed far beyond its zenith and when its reappearance the following morning was urgently requested. Finally, they prayed to the sun, facing its eastern home with an implicit faith in the powers of their appeal for the multiplication of plant and animal life, for food, health, and vigor. There is some evidence, then, that the Ute also formerly held fertility ceremonies in connection with sun-worship.

However, this relatively peaceful period of family organization in which the main concerns of life were food and health and supernatural *rapport* with the world gave way to a period of band organization in which considerable emphasis was placed on war and raiding. From small family groupings in which authority rested with the older and more experienced relatives in the camp, the Ute consolidated into large band camps dominated by powerful war leaders. In place of the family hunting and foraging unit, a new coöperative group emerged in the band where food, again, was shared, and where the buffalo hunt as a communal enterprise gradually overshadowed the earlier impermanent consolidations for antelope drives and rabbit surrounds. The rare expeditions on foot of these small family groups to the level plains in quest of buffalo disappeared completely from the picture, and were replaced by the equestrian hunting party, a function of the band. In short, Ute culture changed fundamentally within historic times. It is to these changes, following initial White contact, that we now turn.

The Spanish Governor Otermin was the first to enter into treaties with the Ute. This was around the year 1675.[5] Yet it

[5] R. E. Twitchell, *Leading Facts of New Mexico History, Volume I*, 1911, p. 349.

is well known that the Ute by this time already were equestrian, powerfully organized into band camps with camp leaders.
Throughout this early period, the Ute together with the Apache
are reported in the Spanish chronicles as being in close contact
with the Spanish frontier. The Ute, however, in contradistinction
to the Apache, lived to the north of Spanish settlements and were
in no way inclined to regard the centers of Spanish influence as
encroachments upon their own territorial rights. Because of this,
early Ute relations with the Spaniards were as prevailingly peaceful as contacts with the Pueblos had been previously. The trading
across the frontier, which flourished throughout the eighteenth
century, doubtlessly occurred in the latter half of the preceding
century as well. Onate's settlements are still remembered among
the Ute, who regard the region around Santa Fé, the southern
limit of their former winter range, as the place of first White
contact. According to Ute tradition, the horse was borrowed
from the Spaniards. Their own equestrian accoutrements, the
saddle, quirt, and trappings are all primitive replicas of early
Spanish models, obviously borrowed, probably around 1640.[6]

The Spanish records of this trade are by no means full enough
to provide the complete story of this borrowing of the horse
complex. Fortunately, the Ute have preserved their own record
of this trade and the subsequent cultural changes it entailed in a
formidable body of traditional tales. These stories bear a resemblance to mythological tales only in the uniformity with
which they are transmitted from generation to generation and in
the identity of versions throughout the three bands. Nevertheless, they are in no sense myths, either in form or in the attitude
the Ute take toward them. These stories are devoid of impossible episodes, do not occur in any mythical period, and lack the
dubious elements of supernaturalism. Rather, they offer as good
a source of ethnological information as might result from any of
the more conventional avenues of approach. The Ute themselves insist that these accounts are of actual, historical events
and that they furnish true, functional pictures of aboriginal life.
Where it is possible to check more recent happenings with his-

[6] Compare Francis Haines, "Where Did the Plains Indians Get their Horses?"
American Anthropologist, Volume 40, No. 1, p. 112.

torical documents from English and Spanish sources, these traditions are found to be accurate in the smallest details. They check also with formal ethnological information, and in addition name specifically the persons and places associated with the described events. Thus it is possible to identify a former Ute chief, Maiyoar, as a tall, slim man, to relate in detail certain outstanding events connected with his life, and to trace his genealogy back through the great-grandfather of a middle-aged Ute now living. Or one could tell the story of Yoa, a Kapota chief who lived at a time when the Ute were still under Mexican jurisdiction. His story begins:

Santa Fé was the oldest town. From there a group of Mexicans started west to buy up Indian children. They wanted these children to be like their own and herd sheep. First they went to the Paiute at Monticello. There they captured some children. When the old Paiutes found this out, they followed the Mexicans. The Kapota were around Tierra Amarilla then, and their chief at that time was Yoa. The Paiutes came to Yoa and asked him to help them get their children back. . . .

However, it is not the purpose of this study to present these traditional accounts in any of their original detail. It must suffice to state that they are markedly different from the body of mythology dealing with animal characters who lived contemporaneously with the culture-hero, Wolf, in times when all the beasts were like Utes in language and behavior. In contrast to these myths, the true stories of the Ute contain countless concrete instances of war and feud, cures and courtship and the like. They tell, with amazing accuracy, of such things as treaty negotiations with Abraham Lincoln in Washington, or even of such more remote matters as the first Mexican mining operations in Ute country. As such, they provide the ethnographer with historical insights of an exactitude not always characteristic of traditional history.

According to these remarkable traditions, the nature of initial contact in the latter half of the seventeenth century was peaceful trade somewhat reminiscent of the barter that the Ute carried on in the early 1700's and not very different from earlier trade relations with the Rio Grande Pueblos. In general, the Ute supplied meat and hides in exchange for agricultural products. However, a new item of trade was the horse. For not only did

the Ute find the horse an invaluable aid in reaching the plains
for buffalo, but it furnished a convenient means of evading Plains
Indians who over-ran Ute country constantly. In the initial period of Spanish trade, therefore, the Ute regarded the horse as a
most welcome addition to their economy.

At the same time, the Spanish frontiersmen demanded a price
for their horses. To the Ute, whose economy hardly provided
more than the bare essentials of subsistence, the price in meat
and hides was often prohibitive. For this reason, another form of
payment was sought during the period of early contact, a payment in Ute children. The Ute explain this practice by saying
that without a mount, an individual was left behind the camp at
the mercy of Plains invaders. Yet this grotesque form of barter
also found some justification in the older custom of giving children to the grandparental generation so that the parental couple
could maintain the mobility and freedom from restrictions demanded by the exigencies of hunting and gathering. While the
giving away of children to non-relatives outside the band was
not characteristic of the early family organization, it was not
unthinkable in terms of adoption customs, and was, indeed,
formerly resorted to in the case of twins. One child from any pair
of twins was always adopted by an unrelated family from a different locality. Unclaimed children born of pre-marital relationships often met the same fate. The reason for this separation of
twins, for the adoption of unclaimed children outside the band,
or for the transfer of children to the grandparental household
was always the same; namely, the difficulty of feeding more than
one child at a time and the need for preserving the mobility of
the active, mature Utes of child-bearing age. Sometimes the replacing of still-born children was effected by the same system of
adoption. By the same line of reasoning, the Ute rationalized
their method of obtaining horses from the Spaniards.

How well this strange form of barter met the needs of Spanish
frontiersmen becomes clear when we remember that the early
settlements relied chiefly on cattle and sheep-raising. The Ute
child, thus obtained, normally took over the tasks of shepherd
and cowherd. This practice has persisted into relatively recent
times; even such a noted Ute as Ouray was adopted by Mexican

settlers and spent his early years employed as a shepherd. In the earlier period, when Spanish settlements were precariously situated on the borderlands of unknown Indian country, the presence of Indian youths must have helped to bridge the gap between Ute and frontiersmen. The peaceful Ute were sought, in 1675, as allies against the traditionally hostile Apache; in the years following, they were used to quell recurring Pueblo disorders. Still later, the Ute served the same function as allies in Spanish wars against the Comanche. That peaceful barter paved the way for these alliances cannot be doubted.

Throughout this early period of contact, however, the peaceful institutions of the Ute underwent rapid transformation. As trading in horses flourished, the large band camps under the authority of war leaders sprang into existence. While formerly foot expeditions to the plains for buffalo rarely drew the family group into the adjoining states of Kansas, Oklahoma, and Texas, now the buffalo hunt, under the authority of a band leader, preceded by two scouts and cautiously directed, came to be the common pattern for fall hunting. While actual band range was not greatly extended, the effective utilization of these broad lands was tremendously increased. Now the Ute did not linger long in the foot-hills of the Rockies for fall antelope drives. With great haste they filled their caches and pressed on for bigger game in the plains country. There they found their chief economic mainstay in the buffalo which provided tipi covers and buffalo robes, sinew-thread, bowstrings, horn-glue, skin bags, moccasins, and meat in greater abundance than the Ute had ever known. Consequently, throughout this period of early contact, the Ute pressed more insistently upon the borders of their former winter range. The horse, which allowed them to transport supplies back to central camp sites, and at the same time, provided the means for hasty withdrawals from dangerous enemy territory, was mainly responsible for this change in economic base and for the cultural transformations entailed.

Before discussing the changes occasioned by the introduction of the horse, it is necessary to consider the changing aspects of Ute contact. For not only did the horse allow for band consolidation under centralized leadership, but this entire process was intensified around the turn of the century [7] by the appearance of the Comanche in the region around West Texas. While this is not the place to dispute the claim that a Ute alliance brought the Comanche to the northern frontier of New Mexico,[8] it must be stated that their appearance here was anything but welcome, not only to the Spanish settlers, but to the Ute as well. The traditional friendship of the Spaniards and Ute as well as the raiding propensities of the Comanche entirely account for this attitude.

As a result of the Comanche migration, a new incentive drew the Ute to the plains country. The Comanche were rich in horses. Now, with band mobility among the Ute increased by the introduction of the horse, the supply of horses could be renewed by less painful methods than child-barter. The horse, which allowed the Ute to live in band camps, was now sought in enemy territory. When camps of the Comanche, Kiowa, Cheyenne, or Southern Arapaho were sighted, Utes were dispatched to cut away the fast, picketed mounts from the center of enemy villages and to drive off as many of these as possible. Once in the plains country, a hunting party might easily be turned into a war party or a raiding expedition. In all three types of expedition, central authority was required of the group leader and two scouts warily preceded the men.

After 1706, the Ute, together with the Apache, Navajo, and Comanche, turned against the Spanish frontier in raids for livestock and horses. The Ute, however, are less identified with the depredations of this period than any of their neighbors. In their own version of this brief period of hostility, the Ute claim that they rarely fell upon the Spanish settlements and then only for food and horses. There is reason to believe that the elaborate accounts of Utes stealing Spanish horses are not always correct, especially when one finds the Spanish soldiers themselves uncertain whether the raiders were Ute or Comanche.[9] In 1719, the Spanish governor included the Ute in a declaration of war upon the Comanche solely on the basis of reports from Taos and

[7] A. B. Thomas, *After Coronado*, 1935, p. 3. Also R. N. Richardson, *The Comanche Barrier to South Plains Settlement*, 1933, p. 15.

[8] A. B. Thomas, *op. cit.*, p. 26 ff.

[9] For the typical testimony of a Spanish soldier, Captain Sebastian Martin, see A. B. Thomas, *op. cit.*, p. 103.

Cochiti that Utes had participated in hostilities there. This declaration of war closed a long chapter of prevailingly peaceful relations which would have been impossible had the Ute allied themselves with the hostile Comanche during the preceding years.

The warlike activities of the Ute at this period are not, therefore, the result of Spanish-Ute relations alone. Nor are they the result of a Comanche-Ute alliance. Rather, it would seem, the Comanche movement into the southern plains at the beginning of the eighteenth century also played a rôle in the resulting conflicts. Throughout the years 1727–1786, Comanche and Ute fought constantly. The Jicarilla, to the southeast, moved westward at this time and no longer formed a barrier between these hostile tribes. Warfare flared on the southern plains as hunting and raiding progressed. Throughout the period of the Comanche wars, the Spanish-Ute alliance was again solidified and Utes became the scouts of Spanish punitive expeditions against their enemy. Of all the Plains Indians, the Comanche provided the most convenient target for Ute depredation. There, in Comanche country, the buffalo were fattest in fall and most accessible; there the enemy was evenly matched. Buffalo hunting invariably led to fights over buffalo grounds. The Ute, who were poorer in horses than the Comanche, frequently raided their neighbor's supply in order to replenish their own. The Ute, in contrast with the Comanche, did not make a practice of breeding horses.

Warfare, then, was more the result of horse raiding and buffalo hunting than any desire on the part of the Ute to win prestige by rash displays of valor. There were no war honors institutionalized in the culture. The choice between taking a scalp, capturing a horse, or stripping an enemy of his possessions was settled solely in terms of expediency. So greatly were the Ute opposed to any foolhardy shedding of blood, that a war leader who proved his incompetence by severe loss of men risked a flogging at the hands of resentful warriors. In fact, standing fights were avoided whenever possible.

The Ute capture of the Kiowa sun-dance doll was entirely of this order. In brief, the Ute met a party of Kiowa and Comanche. The leaders of the groups parleyed together and the Utes proclaimed their peaceful intentions. Their enemies threatened, and in reply, the Ute, sensing impending disaster, scattered out, quickly fleeing in small groups to divide the enemy forces. In the ensuing skirmish, one Kiowa was caught alone at the head of an arroyo. The Utes who shot and stripped him discovered the sundance doll bundle on his person. In their haste to get away, they carried the doll along and only later, when they were back again in safe territory, did they stop to examine it. Upon investigation, it was thought to be a dangerous object, and was then thrown into a gopher hole. In short, the headlong flight of the Ute on this occasion accounts for the capture of the doll which caused so much dismay among the Kiowa. The Ute were a Great Basin culture. For them, war honors played no formalized rôle and bravery was not valued for its own sake.

In order to understand Ute culture in pre-reservation days, it is necessary to enter the relatively recent band camp and survey the main features of community life. In contrast to the earlier picture of population movement, the band now moves as a mobile unit directed in its seasonal migrations by a few camp leaders. The individual family camps are now spread out for half a mile along a stream or river bank. In camp life, there is the same activity and mobility which formerly characterized the scattered family camps. But now, the social life of the band, the games, dances and visiting that once marked the brief period of early spring is a year-long interest made possible by a centralized population. Organized buffalo hunting expeditions and raids for horses from enemy camps are in full swing, since now the centralized population requires a uniform food supply and the horses which make a steady supply of buffalo meat possible. The clearing-house of all these matter-of-fact economic operations is the tipi of the camp leader, slightly larger than the rest to accommodate the council meetings of the older, more experienced men of the camp. From this center of activity a band leader announces each morning to his followers the order of the day. If he is aged, or his voice weak, the news is broadcast through a camp crier. The chiefs themselves are variously called by such titles as *ni'mwi ta'wav* (band chief), *ta'wats* (*the* man), *tava'namum* leader or head man in the camp), and *nago'tu ta'wats* (man of

war, or war leader). Only such respected camp leaders are qualified to call out for organized buffalo hunts or raids. They are
men who have proven their worth as daring scouts and wise
counselors, who have been publicly chosen for such office by
previous incumbents, whose leadership requires the sanction of
their followers before it can be effective, and whose authority
holds only so long as they lead wisely and well.

Because of the economic gains involved in raiding, the most
popular camp leaders were those who called out most often that
tonight they danced and tomorrow raided. Then those who were
anxious to return a gift to a friend or to provide a relative with
a horse eagerly volunteered to join the expedition. Important
prerogatives of leadership were thus won in part through outstanding service in war. Only the war leaders were entrusted with
dangerous expeditions. Only a camp leader wore the eagle tail
bonnet decorated with the feathered streamer down the back.
In every camp there were usually as many as three or four outstanding leaders of this sort.

In addition, such leaders were respected equally for their initiative in camp activity of every peaceful sort. While not supplant-
ing the authority of older relatives within the family circle, the
camp leaders mobilized communal activity by calling out daily
orders for organized hunts, camp movements or dances. Now,
with band mobility greatly increased by the horse, there was a
tendency for the women of the band to gather wild plant products in communal excursions while the men left camp in groups
to hunt together. The authority of camp leaders extended beyond
military pursuits to communal economic activities, and the aboriginal pattern of the initiative of older relatives persisted in
the achieved status of band chiefs. The functions of band leadership merely reflected the new need for the organization of military and economic structure along band lines. Chiefs won their
laurels outside of the more narrow confines of family organization.

In warfare, no matter how high the feelings of hostility flared,
the main interest of the Southern Ute band centered in loot.
For one thing, the most common war stratagem consisted simply

in dismounting the enemy and making off with their horses. The Ute trained their mounts to respond to the knee movements of their riders so that commonly bridles were unnecessary. In this way, the hands were freed to unhorse enemy riders. Or else the Ute rode to cover with the enemy in hot pursuit and dismounted at positions suitable for ambush; scouts were then sent behind the enemy position to drive their horses off, a maneuver which had the effect both of cutting off the enemy retreat, and of insuring the Ute retreat with plenty of additional mounts.

Then, too, loot did not end with the capture of horses. Just as the Ute hunter was expected to divide fresh meat with those who needed it in the band camp, so the warrior, upon his return to camp, was met by friends and relatives in quest of a share in the spoils. The Ute generally equate the hunt and the raid in their own descriptive accounts; the typical statement is the following:

After a raid, the Ute gave away the horses they didn't need. The warriors gave them away to people who wanted them. But if a man was poor, he could trade those horses for something he needed—buckskin or meat. They gave away buffalo meat the same way when they came back from the hunt. Anyone could send a child over for fresh meat. The child came over to the camp when they brought the meat in, and just sat there, waiting. Never say a word. Everyone knew what the child was sent for. In the band camp, you were expected to give a present when it was needed. Some day the other family would help you out. Captured horses were the same. A man would be wanted for chief if he gave away horses to all those poor people.

A returning war party was always preceded by scouts who rode ahead to notify the camp of success or failure. Then any person who wished to welcome the warriors back from their raids, rode out of camp singing the praises of the more fortunate members of the expedition. The men thus honored were expected to reciprocate by handing out presents of loot on the end of a stick. At a subsequent scalp dance more speeches or praise were uttered and further presents were publicly bestowed. A warrior already rich according to the standards of the Ute honorably retained only the scalps he had taken when others stood in need. If the spoils of war were not generously divided at the public scalp dance, a third mechanism of distribution was still possible. It was customary for poor people to go in a body to the tipis of returned warriors to dance there and to honor them with a view to more presents.

Through these mechanisms of distribution, warfare became a means of enriching the entire band. War, which previously had been mere localized defense of one's kin in widely scattered family camps, now became a means of strengthening band solidarity. Unless one wished to be stigmatized as stingy, gift led to return gift and the benefits of every raid, in horses, enemy clothing, pipes, arrows, bows, and camp equipment generally, were spread evenly throughout the band. The mobility afforded the Ute band by the introduction of the horse led to a type of warfare motivated socially by a desire for loot. How true this is, may be seen also in the function of Ute women in warfare.

During raids in enemy country, the women packed the camp equipment, keeping all in readiness for a speedy departure in the event of a retaliatory raid of the hostile tribe. However, when standing fights in Ute country could not be averted, the older women of the band frequently followed the men into battle. Armed and wearing headdresses, their function was to scalp and strip the dead enemy. Comanche clothing, or any loot obtained in this manner, was likewise given away at victory celebrations. Only scalps were saved as private property to be sewn on the shirts of male relatives who had slain the enemy. Far from embodying a feeling of disdain for these enemy possessions, the women's function of securing loot gave them an added position of importance. Women who participated in raids had a counterpart of the war dance in full regalia; this dance symbolized in its peculiar lame step the difficulty of carrying back to camp the heavy burden of loot. These women also were qualified to take part in the ostentatious parades around the band camp, preceded by the noted warriors on horseback.

Besides providing a group sufficiently large to undertake successful raids, the band also guaranteed greater safety for one's kin than was possible in the scattered family camps of former days. Among the developments making for band solidarity was the organization of protective mechanisms for guarding the band camp. When the band moved, scouts reconnoitred far in advance of the main body; when camp was pitched, the chief appointed scouts to post themselves on high hills or look-outs in order to keep watch for the enemy. Most often, the scouts were younger men chosen by chiefs to work in close collaboration with themselves, or younger relatives of leaders being trained for future leadership. With a small parfleche of dried meat and a tiny jug of water, these men sat motionless until relieved and then returned to camp for further orders. If enemies were sighted, they ran their horses back and forth, constantly watching the movements of the enemy and never leaving their posts unless recalled.

Working in close coöperation with the scouts, though not formally associated, was a camp society of young men including recruits, orphans of war and unadopted child captives. This company, the *sari'dzka,* or Dogs, lived a short distance from the main camp and constituted the military training society of the Ute band. While training for hunting by the stalking method was still a family function, instruction in organized buffalo hunt techniques and preparation for warfare were band concerns, supervised by a few older leaders who controlled the Dog Company. With this group lived one older woman, called *Bi'a* (mother) honorifically by the boys. It was *Bi'a* who cooked for the Dogs and acted as their go-between with people in the main camp. The entire group served as camp watchmen, and to this end climbed into the hills every morning and evening to scan the surrounding countryside. When the camp moved, the Dog Company was stationed as rear-guard off to one side in hills above the main body. There they maintained the strictest vigilance for hostile invaders. Their name, *sari'dzka,* corresponded to their "watchdog function" and also to the peculiar way in which they notified the main camp of enemy marauders; for, when hostile Indians were seen in the vicinity, the woman in the company ran ahead on foot and the *sari'dzka* trotted after her, "just as male dogs run behind the female dog." Otherwise, their only peculiar mark of distinction was a necklace of slit wolfskin. When no danger was imminent, the Dog Company serenaded the camp from the surrounding hillsides, or entered camp in the daytime to organize dances.

At the same time, the Dog Company offers an excellent illustration of the growing solidarity of the band in this warlike period of Ute history. Though not an age group, the company comprised the active, unmarried men and boys of the band. As long as they were members, the boys were said to be without families, and familial obligations, where they did exist, were entirely inoperative throughout the training period. Membership continued as long as one wished, or until matrimony intervened. On occasion, the company ate stews of dog meat said to impart the alertness and agility necessary for successful membership; but boys who had been out with girls from the band camp the night before were forbidden to partake of the feast. In this way, the tender-minded lover was discovered and severely lectured for his disloyal yielding to romantic impulses. But far from suppressing sexual desires, the Dog Company sought to channelize them in terms of its own harsh patterns of institutionalized philandering and outright rape. For when the Dogs entered camp, women and girls were forbidden to laugh at them despite their most provocative antics. If a woman laughed, the Dogs were then free to spirit the offender off to their separate hillside camp, where she was held for a time, in contradistinction to the strictly untouchable *Bi'a* for purposes of sexual diversion. This institutionalized rape befell older women also when they failed to withhold their mirth in the presence of the Dogs. Thus age-respect patterns broke down completely at this point.

Membership in this society was either voluntary or according to a kidnap method of recruiting. There were times when the *sari'dzka* entered camp to capture a pubescent boy who had just undergone the puberty hunting ceremonies. The novice was stripped and bluntly told that he must now become a hardened fighter. If the newcomer cried out, he was whipped. The entire aim of the Dog Company was to furnish the band with future protectors and valiant raiders, and in so doing it brooked no interference from the camp youth. No concessions were made to the former pattern of the romantic adolescent. This point of conflict was simply solved by *Bi'a* serving as messenger between the isolated boys and eligible young girls who were approached in this way for their consent to act as dancing partners in the social dances or as sexual mates in secret assignations. A strictly watched or bashful girl refused, but any woman found out of camp alone was fair game, relatives and those under menstrual tabus forming the only exceptions.

It would not be difficult to find other examples of the correlation between the horse-complex, the buffalo hunt, and the warlike band of more recent Ute society. Certainly the band, because of these associated interests, bade fair to become the predominant unit in Southern Ute society. In economic organization, in warfare, and in child training this was demonstrably the case, as we have seen. Yet these activities are precisely those most closely associated with the horse raiding and buffalo hunting complex of the period just discussed. In other connections, where changes in social organization were not required, the older customs and institutions fitted unaltered into the newer setting.

To illustrate this point, one might examine Ute punishment of crime. Thievery within the band, while it rarely occurred, was solely a family affair. One simply complained to an elder relative of the culprit, the object was returned, and the thief whipped by his own relatives. With economic sharing and gift-giving forming the foundation of coöperation within the band, gangs of boys and girls were often good-naturedly allowed to rifle unguarded stores of buffalo meat for private feasts. In all affairs regarding individuals, however, the family group remained the social unit to which one first appealed and where justice was meted out according to the older patterns. In case of adultery, the aggrieved husband seized the horse of his rival while the aggrieved wife fought her rival or robbed her of personal possessions. In more heinous crimes, like witchcraft and murder, the aboriginal methods of settlement continued unabated; the family was, again, the protecting and avenging unit. Chiefly authority stopped at the tipi door of every family camp and chiefs were powerless to control feuds or to interfere in marital disputes. Since the authority of chieftains did not extend beyond communal economic and social activities, individual family groups were perfectly free to leave camp at will or to form renegade camps under new leaders. Thus the autonomy and practical independence of the family unit found its reflection neatly mirrored in legal concepts. It was not that the family ceased to function with the gradual emergence of band organization, but simply that new patterns of authority and formal organization arose to cope with new problems resulting from the buffalo hunt, the horse raid and the band camp.

As the Southern Ute became equestrian, the raid and the buffalo hunt carried them more frequently into the southern periphery of their former range and sometimes far beyond these rough boundaries. The Jicarilla, directly to the south, continued to remain friendly with the Ute; they intermarried, had access to each others' range and even camped together. The Mowatsi band of the Ute commonly joined with the Jicarilla for raids on Plains enemies even to the exclusion of other Ute bands. Similarly, the Weminutc band called upon the Jicarilla in war with the Navajo. In recent times, the Weminutc ranged into southeastern Utah, northeastern Arizona, and northern New Mexico, while all three bands followed a southeasterly path to Texas and Oklahoma to strike at the settlements of Plains Indians. Such was the golden period of Ute expansion, a period which glorified the victorious Ute in the person of the warrior. It was a period marked by generally peaceful contacts with White traders and White settlers during which great impetus was given the changing culture by the introduction of the horse.

The eighteenth century had been, for the Utes, a period of territorial expansion. The century that followed brought with it the full impact of White civilization, ushering in long years of defeat, of territorial loss, of utter disillusion. These severe reverses in fortune were not without effect upon Ute culture. Naturally, the shrinkage of range was accompanied by changes in density of population, in band mobility, in the effective utilization of economic resources and even in natural environment. Indeed, the shrinkage of range runs like a major theme throughout recent Ute history even down to the present, underlying the gradual defeat of these people and determining their attitude toward White culture as well. It is necessary, therefore, before considering the social and economic results of later contact, to summarize briefly the main features of the historical continuum.

Before the middle of the seventeenth century, territorial occupation had been by extended family groups. From Bandelier we learn that the Ute ravaged the neighborhood of Pecos even before Coronado's journey of 1540.[10] Yet, as we have seen, attacks on the Rio Grande Pueblos were only occasional interruptions of lengthy periods of trade. Elsewhere Bandelier notes that "the Yutahs traded at Taos." [11] The Ute themselves insist upon early trade relations with the Rio Grande Pueblos in days before the Spanish conquest. Taos, Picuris, and San Juan figure prominently in Ute accounts of trade, and informants report as a common practice following the introduction of the horse, the sending of pack trains from Tewa and Tiwa Pueblos north to Ute country. Dr. Elsie Clews Parsons has called attention to Ute visits at Taos.[12] Despite the occasional barter of meat for agricultural products, the recent friendly contacts and intermarriages,[13] Ute culture has borrowed but few Pueblo traits.

The opposite is true of Spanish contact. The entire horse-complex which proved such a source of enrichment and advance for this nomadic people was borrowed directly, around 1640, on the Spanish frontier. From the same source came the Spanish game, Canute, a number of Spanish folk-tales revised in terms of animal characters, water-spirits, and ogres, and perhaps even the central deity, Creator-of-Humans. The first period of peaceful Spanish contact from around 1630–1706 was disturbed, in the eighteenth century, by the northward movement of frontier settlements. By this time, the Ute had already been organized for over half a century in band camps and were impelled upon a path of plunder and raid by the need for horses and the aggression of Comanches to the southeast. At a time when the Ute themselves were beginning to expand to the south and east, they found themselves hemmed in because of great population movements set in motion far beyond the boundaries of their range. Comanche, Kiowa, Cheyenne and Arapaho—all swept along their eastern boundary. Consequently, when the Spanish settlers

[10] A. F. Bandelier, "Ruins in the Valley of the Rio Pecos," *Volume I*, 1883, *Archaeological Institute of America*, p. 111.

[11] A. F. Bandelier, *Final Report on Investigations among the Indians of the Southwestern United States*, 1890, p. 164.

[12] E. C. Parsons, Taos Pueblo, *General Series in Anthropology*, No. 2, 1936, pp. 13, 60.

[13] A. F. Bandelier, *Final Report on Investigations among the Indians of the Southwestern United States*, 1890, p. 258.

moved north into Ute territory, this intrusion was by no means viewed with equanimity. As Bandelier writes, "Although the Yutes and Comanches in the 18th Century greatly harassed the settlers of San Pedro de Chama (the district around Chamita) . . . the number of Spanish inhabitants considerably increased." [14] From the Ute standpoint, naturally, this process was reversed; the Spaniards flocked into their territory and would not be driven out. From a footnote to the above quotation we learn that the settlement of this district was in the nature of a pressure movement, directed north by Spanish colonial policy. Bandelier adds:

A list nearly complete of the murders committed by the roaming Indians in the Chamita (Chama) district is contained in the Libro de Entierros de Santa Clara. In 1748, the people of Chamita applied for permission to abandon their homes owing to these hostilities. . . . This was refused.

Bandelier also records

that the Yutas occasionally impinged upon the northern sections of New Mexico. . . . In the first half of the past century (1700–1750), the Yutas troubled the settlers of Abiquiu greatly. They even caused its temporary abandonment. [15]

Naturally, this movement north from Santa Fé was bitterly opposed by the Ute at this time, when simultaneously, their eastern boundary was being threatened. Moreover, the region around Chamita and Abiquiu had always been considered southern winter range.

The complaints against Utes for killing livestock during this period [16] are easily matched by the records of Spanish outrages against the natives. Both the capture of Ute women and the theft of Ute horses are mentioned in these accounts. In 1748, the bond of Pablo Salazar was issued for the return of a fugitive Ute woman, who he claimed belonged to him. [17] In 1762, proceedings were begun against Juan de la Cruz Valdez for stealing a horse

14 A. F. Bandelier, op. cit., p. 62.
15 A. F. Bandelier, op. cit., p. 174.
16 R. E. Twitchell, Spanish Archives of New Mexico, Volume II, 1914, pp. 188, 208.
17 Ibid., p. 227.

belonging to the Ute.[18] Border incidents, when they did occur, were by no means one-sided. In 1778, a *bando* was finally issued from Chihuahua "prohibiting settlers and allied Indians from visiting the Utes for purposes of trade and barter." [19] In the years following, illegal trade continued [20] and provoking border incidents occurred. Only the Spanish-Ute military alliance against the Comanche prevented the Ute from breaking off peaceful relations completely. In the war upon the Comanche (1786), the Ute allies showed a characteristic lack of interest in conquest, which was the Spanish motive. Having captured horses after crossing the Arkansas, "almost all the Ute suddenly and unceremoniously deserted without so much as a farewell" [21] although the military campaign was then at its height. Careful perusal of Spanish documents from this period indicates that although the Ute were nominally allies in the Spanish conquest, their real interests did not actually coincide with those of the Spaniards. The Ute were interested in raiding for horses and in the preservation of tribal boundaries, not in political hegemony or in a war to extermination. To the Comanche threat of unceasing warfare, the Ute replied with the Spanish alliance. The beginning of the nineteenth century again found the Ute allied with the Jicarilla against the Kiowa and Comanche, and once more at peace with the Spanish frontier.[22]

In the eighteenth century the Ute had begun to pay in territory for their Spanish alliance. In the century following, this process went on apace, forcing the three bands back to the mountains of New Mexico and Colorado. Cowed by the overwhelming strength of Spanish military power and wearied by a century of futile opposition, no sustained effort was made to protest the Spanish influx. On the cultural level, however, Spanish influence was strongly resisted. As Antonio de Bonilla had noted previously, the Ute "do not consider being converted." [23] At the time

[18] *Ibid.*, p. 237.
[19] *Ibid.*, p. 263.
[20] *Ibid.*, pp. 291, 297, 384, 430.
[21] A. B. Thomas, *Forgotten Frontiers*, 1932, pp. 68, 137.
[22] R. E. Twitchell, *op. cit.*, p. 550; Richardson, R.N., *op. cit.*, p. 49.
[23] A. B. Thomas, *Antonio De Bonilla's Spanish Plans for the Defense of New Mexico, New Spain, and the Anglo-American West.* Contributions to H. E. Bolton, *Volume I, New Spain*, George Hammond, New York, 1932, p. 202.

of Pike's explorations in 1805–1807, the Ute were still a warlike, roving people, though now more definitely under Spanish control. In *The Expeditions of Zebulon M. Pike,* the following description is given:

> The Utahs wander at the sources of the Rio del Norte . . . , are armed in the same manner and pursue the same game as the Kyoways. They are, however, a little more civilized, from having more connection with the Spaniards, with whom they . . . were then at peace, and waging war with the Tetaus (Comanche).[24]
>
> A battle was fought between them and the Tetaus in September, 1806, near the village of Tons (Taos). There were about 400 combatants on each side, but they were separated by a Spanish alcalde riding out to the field of battle. . . The Utahs gave all the horses taken to the Spaniards. This shows the influence the Spaniards have over those Indians.[25]
>
> Maguire's remarks seem to me to be judicious. . . In the early days of the settlement of the country, the Mosca (across the Sangre de Cristo range) was well travelled by the Southern Utes on their journeys to the Plains, and their hieroglyphics of which Pike speaks, were to be seen out in the bark of the aspen trees.[26]
>
> . . . A trail which ran north . . . through Cochetope Pass to the Gunnison and Grande rivers . . . was formerly much used by the Utes en route to Santa Fé and was no doubt in existence in 1807.[27]

A similar impression of Ute life is given in *The Journal of Jacob Fowler* [28] by the entry of March 7, 1822, which describes an event that happened near the south fork of the Rio Grande: [29]

> the then moved off from our Camp and We Came In—Wheare We found taylor—tho the Indeans Had Stolen two Buffelow Roabs Some lead and two knives—and Ware of the Utaws nation Which Roame about and live In the mountains without Haveing any Settled Home and live alltogether on the Chase Raising no grain.

Later in the same year, Fowler mentions the Utes stealing horses.[30] G. F. Ruxton, a member of the British Ethnological So-

24 Edited by E. Coues, New York, N.Y., Harper and Brothers, 1895, *Volume II,* pp. 744, 492 (footnote) and 596 (footnote).

25 *Idem.*

26 *Idem.*

27 *Idem.*

28 Edited by E. Coues, Harper and Brothers, New York, N.Y., 1898, pp. 122, 137.

29 *Idem.*

30 *Idem.*

ciety, describes the last New Mexican settlement at Rio Colorado where about fifty people settled with a few Ute Indians. According to his account, the Indians got a supply of corn and cattle without recourse to raids on Santa Fé or Taos; the Utes allow the people of Rio Colorado to remain and "tolerate their presence in their country for the sole purpose of having at their command a stock of grain and a herd of mules and horses, which they make no scruple of helping themselves to, whenever they require a remount or a supply of farinaceous food." [31] At the same time, Ruxton reports that the Ute and Arapaho frequent the Colorado mountains and are traditional enemies. [32]

The American conquest of New Mexico did not, at first, involve any change in the peaceful disposition of the Ute toward their White neighbors. A report that the Ute were combining with the Pueblos and New Mexicans to oppose Doniphan's march of 1846 proved utterly false. [33] When Major Gilpin returned to Abiquiu, he noticed the "utmost tranquillity amongst the Mexicans, Pueblos, and Yutas." [34] That this peaceful attitude on the part of the Ute was more the result of inferior military strength than any desire on their part to welcome White domination is seen in the following statement of Josiah Gregg: [35]

The habits of the tribe are altogether itinerant. A band of about a thousand spend their winters mostly in the mountain valleys northward of Taos, and the summer seasons generally in the prairie plains to the east, hunting buffalo. . . . Although these Indians are nominally at peace with the New Mexican government, they do not hesitate to lay the hunters and traders who happen to fall in with their scouring parties under severe contributions; and on some occasions they have been known to proceed even to personal violence. A prominent Mexican officer (Don Juan Andres Archuleta) was scourged not long ago by a party of Yutas. . . .

Gregg indicates that the same veiled hostility existed in Ute dealings with eastern Indian neighbors. He writes: [36]

[31] G. F. Ruxton, *Adventures in Mexico and the Rocky Mountains*, John Murray, London, 1847, pp. 208–209.
[32] *Idem*, p. 225.
[33] J. T. Hughes, *Doniphan's Expedition*, 1848, p. 29.
[34] *Idem.*, p. 67.
[35] Josiah Gregg, *Commerce of the Prairies*, J. W. Moore, Philadelphia, Pa., 1850, p. 300.
[36] *Ibid.*, p. 301.

In the summer of 1837, a small band of but five or six Shawnees fell in with a large party of Yutas near the eastern borders of the Rocky Mountains, south of the Arkansas river. At first they were received with every demonstration of friendship; but the Yutas, emboldened . . . by the small number of their visitors, very soon concluded to relieve them of whatever surplus property they might be possessed of. . . .

The same was true of dealings with the Whites.[37]

The sporadic resistance to White rule was soon curtailed by the treaties and troops of the United States government. In a letter of Bent to Medill, dated November, 1846, the Ute are characterized as a "hardy, warlike people, subsisting by the chase, and several bands of them have been carrying on a predatory war with the New Mexicans. . . . Since General Kearney's arrival, these Indians have sued for peace." [38] At the close of the Mexican campaign, therefore, the United States government negotiated a treaty with the Ute at Abiquiu, December 30th, 1849, through Indian Agent James S. Calhoun. According to Calhoun's letter of January 1st, 1850, "these Indians, since last September, have frequently manifested a disposition to enter into treaty stipulations with the United States. . . . The influence of traders and perhaps the three Navajo chiefs prevented their coming in on the 29th of December." [39] Calhoun's letter of January 31st, 1850, gives an interesting sidelight on Ute relations at this time: [40]

My letter of the 17th of this month informed you that a Ute had been killed and subsequently, seven Mexicans, near Abiquiu, and several herds of stock were driven off. . . . The Indians were less to blame (if blameable at all), than the Mexicans. It is an ascertained fact, the Ute was first killed by the Mexicans. . . . Abiquiu has long been the Head Quarters of a very mischievous band of traders with the Navajos and Utes; and anything like order and quiet will have an injurious effect upon their vicious practices with these Indians, and that they caused the outbreak mentioned, I entertain not the slightest doubt.

By this time, the nomadic and predatory life of the Ute band was definitely on the decline. The invention of more effective

---

37 Josiah Gregg, *Commerce of the Prairies*, pp. 302–303.

38 *The Official Correspondence of James S. Calhoun, While Indian Agent at Santa Fé*, 1915, edited by A. H. Abel, Washington, Government Print, p. 7.

39 *Ibid.*, p. 96.

40 *Ibid.*, p. 125. In Calhoun's letter of June 12, 1850, it is stated that the Ute asked for a government trading post because they feared the disappearance of their hunting supply of game. *Vide*, p. 208.

firearms, the dollar-a-hide slaughter of the buffalo herds, and the arming of Plains Indian enemies [41] brought the Ute under the heel of White domination. In 1851–53, John Greiner was stationed at Taos, and in 1853–59, Kit Carson had charge of this agency.[42] A last feeble stand was taken by the Ute in 1853 when they joined forces with the Jicarilla against Governor Merriwether. The final defeat was administered by Colonel Fauntleroy in 1855.[43] Of this period, Twitchell writes: [44]

The Jicarilla country was properly east of the Rio Grande, and the Mohuache Utes also claimed this section as their home, the agency for both tribes being at Taos, and later at Cimarron, on the ranch of Lucien B. Maxwell. The Ute country was west of the river, stretching northwest into Colorado and Utah . . . and the agency for most of those Utes who roamed in Northwestern New Mexico was situated at Abiquiu. The Utes and Jicarillas were in a way related by marriage and were naturally averse to restraint of any kind. The Utes were brave ./ . . bold in the assertion of their rights to the broad tract over which they ranged, wholly opposed to farming and reservation life, they were willing to be friendly . . . if liberally supplied with food. Their ideal was to retain their hunting grounds, periodically visiting the agency to receive their gifts, which must not be less than other tribes received—and having free access to the settlements, where whiskey could be procured.

The other side of this picture is furnished by the *Report to the Commissioner of Indian Affairs* for 1854. Again we are told that the Ute are warlike, but the following is added: [45]

The latter Indians (Cheyenne and Arapaho), having been supplied with arms and ammunition, have proved more than a match for the former, and consequently the Utahs dare not visit the buffalo regions in search of food. Hence, they rob and roam about under petty chiefs.

Occasionally, parties of them come into the settlements for a short time and labor for the citizens particularly threshing out the grain, which

[41] According to the *Reports to the Commissioner of Indian Affairs*, 1857–1868, the Ute received firearms later and in less quantity than their Plains Indian neighbors. In all probability, this was true as far back as 1768 during the Comanche wars. A. B. Thomas, in *Forgotten Frontiers*, p. 61, quotes Mendinueta to the effect that the Comanche received seventeen loads of guns and ammunition by way of English trade.

[42] H. H. Bancroft, *History of Arizona and New Mexico*, p. 668.

[43] R. E. Twitchell, *Leading Facts of New Mexico History, Volume II*, The Torch Press, Cedar Rapids, Iowa, 1911, p. 299.

[44] *Ibid.*, p. 300.

[45] P. 169.

they are enabled to do with their own mules and horses; they then leave and nothing more is heard of them for months.

Yet this period was not without definite attempts by the Ute to make adjustments to White civilization. In 1856, Governor Merriwether reported to the Commissioner of Indian Affairs that "both the Capote and Mohuache bands of this tribe have remained peaceful . . . professing a willingness to commence farming next spring, provided permanent homes are assigned to them." The year following, Kit Carson, then agent at Abiquiu, stated in glowing terms the case for the Mowatsi.[46] Vices, prostitution and drunkenness, he says, are unknown among them; they hunt, but the supply of game is so depleted in the southern winter range that the government must provide for them in the winter season. In view of their needs, Carson then suggests that they be removed from White settlements and furnished with farmers and mechanics. Otherwise, it is stated, the tribe must live by robbery and raids on surrounding settlements.

The complaints against neighboring Whites at this time are reminiscent of the strained relations noted previously in relation to Spanish domination. In the report just cited, Carson relates that a Mexican killed an Indian man and woman, and the Ute, "knowing no other law than that of restitution, demanded payment for the Indians murdered. I could not comply with their demand. They stole some fifteen head of horses and mules from the settlements of Rio Colorado and Culibra."[47] In December, 1862, a more revolting outrage is reported:[48]

An Indian of the Utah tribe was in Taos recently where certain parties are said to have gotten him drunk, then to have saturated his clothing

[46] *Report to the Commissioner of Indian Affairs*, 1857, p. 279.

[47] *Idem.*, p. 279.

[48] R. E. Twitchell, *Leading Facts of New Mexico History, Volume III*, 1911, p. 419. The threat of vengeance in this case, as in similar outrages, was never carried out. To quote R. E. Twitchell, *op. cit., Volume III*, p. 534: "For the protection of the northwestern portions of the Territory, and those of the regions now composing the southern tier of counties of the state of Colorado, a military force was maintained at Abiquiu and another at Cantonment Burgwin near Taos during the military occupation of New Mexico, 1846–1850. This disposition of troops was continued after New Mexico became a territory, during which time several treaties were made with the Utes and Apaches." In other words, organized resistance would have been futile.

with turpentine and set fire to the clothing. . . . From the effects of this burning the Indian is said to have died. The Utah tribe to which he belonged is . . . very much incensed at this inhuman outrage and threaten to be avenged. . . .

Events of this sort were so frequent that the agency center finally was removed to Maxwell's ranch. Indian Superintendent Collins explained this removal to the Commissioner of Indian Affairs in his report of 1861: [49]

The agency for the Mohuaches has been removed to the neighborhood of Maxwell's ranch on the east side of the mountains; this change was found necessary on account of the whiskey dealers who live in Taos.

Collins, like Carson before him, blames the nearness of settlements and the lack of reservation land for the recurring troubles with the Ute. Carson, in his Report to the Commissioner in 1859 had suggested farming and reservation life for the tribe; concerning their plight, he had added, "So far as regards their numerical strength, they are on the decline and the causes of this decrease in population are disease and frequent conflicts with other warlike tribes." William Arny, who succeeded Carson, stated that despite their resentment toward the Whites, the Motwatsi Ute protected them from nearby Indians.[50] Undoubtedly an important factor in this relationship was the yearly presentation of gifts to the Ute at Abiquiu.[51] Collins, in 1861, summarized the Ute contribution to this symbiotic connection when he wrote: [52]

In gratifying contrast with the position assumed by the Apaches and Navajoes may be mentioned the Pueblos and Mohuache Utes, with whom our relations are as satisfactory as at any former period. . . . The Mohuache are enterprizing, loyal, and intelligent to that degree that they have tendered their services for the protection of white settlers against the assaults of rebels as well as savage foes.

In all of this, however, it is apparent that native interests were steadily becoming more subservient to those of neighboring

---

[49] P. 126.
[50] *Idem.*, p. 126.
[51] *Ibid.*, 1857, p. 279.
[52] *Ibid.*, 1861.

Whites and that native culture was recoiling before the on-
slaught of increasing White domination.

At the same time, Plains Indians continued their assaults on
the Ute in the Cimarron Valley and at the Conejos Agency.[53]
In one of these battles, twelve Utes fought off about three
hundred Plains warriors "until nine of the Utahs were killed,
one wounded, and two remained unhurt. The two seized the
wounded chief, Sesareva, and the dead chief, Benita, and dragged
them to some bushes where they fought the . . . whole of the
Indians until they retreated." [54] In 1863, similarly, a large band
of Arapaho descended upon the Cimarron Agency to wipe out
the Utes located there. The Indian Agent at the time, L. J.
Keithly, concluded his account of the battle with a statement
showing clearly the lack of support extended to the Ute; he said,
"It is the nature of the Indian [i. e., the Ute] to view with suspicion and jealousy any favors extended to his adversary by the
Whites." [55] In the same year, it was reported from Tierra Amarilla that the Kapota and Weminutc bands located there were
being used to protect the American citizens of the territory.[56] It
is no wonder, then, that part of the Mowatsi band broke into
open hostility in 1866, or that Chavves, a renegade Kapota, led
some sixty-one rebels from his band in 1868.[57] The agency centers of this period offered little protection and served no purpose
other than dominance of a people already defeated and now
definitely at bay.

The war of suppression, begun by White troops and traders
and effectively continued by the assaults of Plains enemies, was
furthered, in the years following, by the treaties of the United
States government. It is not necessary here to dwell in detail on
the familiar story of broken treaties, lavish promises to pay "as
long as grass grows and the rivers flow," and ceded lands. It must
suffice to state that land was relinquished by the Ute and that
their economic independence, as hunters and gatherers, was increasingly impaired. As early as 1868, a Report to the Commis-

[53] *Ibid.*, 1861 and 1862.
[54] *Ibid.*, 1862, p. 245.
[55] *Ibid.*, 1863, by Jose A. Mausinares and L. J. Keithly.
[56] *Ibid.*, Jose Mausinares.
[57] *Ibid.*, 1868, by W. F. Arny. See also Carson's 1866 report.

sioner of Indian Affairs stated that the Mowatsi Ute and Jicarilla of the Cimarron Agency were fed by White soldiers, produced nothing and were unable to live by hunting alone. Concurrently, the Kapota and Weminutc of Abiquiu were asking to be located at a reservation in the San Juan Valley in order to pursue the old life in less restricted quarters. However, the treaty of March 2, 1868 created a reservation located wholly in western Colorado and various reserves established previously were ordered vacated and sold. More land was lost by the treaty of 1873, whereby a portion of the new reservation containing the San Juan mining region was ceded to the United States for a money equivalent. This treaty left merely a strip about fifteen miles wide and roughly one hundred miles long as the Southern Ute Reservation.[58] By the treaty of November 9, 1878, the Southern Ute ceded their right to the Confederated Ute territory "except such lands . . . as might be allotted to them in severalty." In 1880, the Southern Ute agreed to settle the unoccupied agricultural lands bordering the La Plata River in Colorado, and in 1895, allotting of farms finally took place along the Pine, Animas and Piedras Rivers.

The reservation which resulted from these negotiations was long and narrow, so that Indian stock grazed out of bounds while White stock broke into the reservation lands. In August, 1886, the Indian Agent, Stollsteimer, reported to the Commissioner of Indian Affairs:

Most of the chiefs and head men of the bands comprising the tribe interviewed me in reference to a removal to a more desirable reservation.

This removal never took place, but instead the allotting of farms to the Ute was followed by a lengthy period of land sales, during which the natives were actively encouraged to part with land for cash payment. Money benefits were, in turn, exchanged for inferior horses and trade goods which the White settlers in the vicinity eagerly unloaded on the Indian population. As a result, disillusionment followed and was accompanied by much general resentment against the Whites. The Ute began to dislike the

[58] *United States Statutes-at-Large, Volume 18, Part 3,* p. 36.

idea of farming. They feared their lands would disappear in competition with the White homesteaders. They had seen the collusion between their White neighbors and the agency superintendent. The land sales had resulted in the ceding of some of the best farm lands in Colorado to White homesteaders.

The decrease in population, in band mobility, in land and economic resources, noted above, form the background for the final chapter in Ute history. The period of land sales led inevitably to a split between the Weminutc band, now at the Towaoc subagency, and the Mowatsi and Kapota, who now live near the main agency center at Ignacio. The cultural dichotomy of these two groups is obvious to any naïve observer and is usually phrased in terms of the backward, unprogressive nature of the Towaoc Ute. This explanation, while refreshingly simple, hardly does justice to the unfortunate history of the Towaoc Ute or to the similar cultural background of all three bands. The naïve observer is apt to forget that the split in the Confederated Ute Reservation dates back to a time when excellent farm lands in Colorado were taken from the Weminutc in exchange for the arid region around Towaoc, their present location. The unsavory manner in which this transfer was effected and the subsequent impoverishment of the Towaoc group now claim our attention.

At the Ignacio, or eastern end, of the Consolidated Ute Reservation are located two bands of the Southern Ute, the Mowatsi and Kapota, under a single reservation chieftain. At Towaoc, over to the west, is located the Weminutc band under separate leadership. At Ignacio, the land is allotted; at Towaoc, it is not. This fact alone, as we shall see, has affected differentially the culture of each group. Yet the history of the transfer of the Weminutc band to Towaoc lies at the root of the cultural differences existing today. The Towaoc and Ignacio groups have diverged since their separation in 1895. Before this date, all three bands were culturally the same. Actually, men of the Weminutc band were the first to farm in this region and among the first to relinquish land for cash payment. The shrinkage of the reservation by treaty and land sale played a greater rôle in alienating the Weminutc from "White ways" and farming than any alleged cultural conservatism.

The present-day cultural conservatism of the Towaoc group is, therefore, a result, not a cause, of recent events in reservation history. Yet cultural factors also operated in the splitting of the modern reservation. By far the best clue to the understanding of this split is the influence of chieftainship in band politics. How true this is may be seen by reference to the rôles played by the chiefs, respectively of Towaoc and Ignacio, during this crucial time. It was largely due to the attitude taken by Buckskin Charlie of Ignacio that the Mowatsi and Kapota seriously became interested in farming and education. His reaction to the shrinkage of Ute tribal lands differed markedly from that of the Towaoc band leader, for to him, the disappearance of the old economic base in hunting and gathering indicated a need for Indian farming. Accordingly, he was one of the first men of Ignacio to raise crops and to insist upon the education of his children. The reaction of the Weminutc chief to land shrinkage was quite different. Resentment against White ways, imperfectly understood, impressed itself upon his mind, and he was able to lead the exodus of his entire band to Towaoc. The Ute band leader is still one who, in the familiar phrase, "talks with his people."

The Weminutc exodus to Towaoc brought this band to an unallotted reserve thoroughly unsuited for farming. There the hostility to Whites has grown in isolation. At first, the Weminutc leaders, in their opposition to farming, were easily persuaded to locate at Towaoc, where they were assured, agriculture was impossible and the land remote and arid enough to forestall White occupation. The occasion for this withdrawal was the allotment negotiations of 1895, at which time the Weminutc refused allotted lands (under pressure of interested Whites) and withdrew to the sub-agency now known as the Ute Mountain Reservation with headquarters at Towaoc. The lands thus vacated were returned to public domain only to be reclaimed by the White homesteaders and transformed rapidly into lucrative farms. As a result, the Southern Ute of Ignacio now live on individual holdings scattered among White farms, while the Ute Mountain band of Towaoc has for years wandered over a closed reservation thirteen miles from the nearest town.

The acculturation process was, in its first phase of expansion, a process of cultural elaboration. The introduction of the horse allowed Ute bands to consolidate, to establish political leadership, to develop society organization and social mechanisms for the cohesive functioning of the band, and finally, to embark upon a career of raid and military glory. The second phase of acculturation cancelled these gains and dislocated the culture at important points. The Dog Company, no longer useful as a protective and military organization, soon degenerated into a singing society and then passed out of existence entirely. There was little choice in this, for to the Ute a custom had no value apart from its function. The war songs of raiding prowess likewise were forgotten; better so, since now they no longer served a useful purpose. Rather, as reminders of the dead past, war songs had only an unhealthy emphasis. Similarly, the horse parades and old dances became the mere mementos of better days, now reënacted as showy spectacles at Mexican fiestas. The stories of the great exploits of notable chiefs, formerly told at public gatherings, were left unsaid. To meet the new life, the Ute invented new dances and borrowed others from neighboring tribes. Revivalism, inherent in the ghost dance and peyote cult, was seized upon eagerly. The organization of military power was effectively broken by White contact. In the latest period in which we can trace the development of the raiding complex among the Ute, we find the band steadily retreating before the superior strength of White troops. The war leaders lost their function as supreme military strategists. Today, the function of band chiefs and tribal elders has become wholly civilian and has retained none of the meaning and content of former days.

THE MODERN COMMUNITY

The final phase of acculturation had brought to a close a period of defeat and destruction. It had laid the basis for a bitter reaction against White civilization, and it had provided little to take the place of a glorious past. Yet the Ute, throughout this period of sweeping change, still sought a basis of social integration.

For almost forty years, the Southern Ute of Ignacio have occupied farms adjoining those of White neighbors. Following the example of their chief, Buckskin Charlie, they have raised crops by the same methods and sold them in the same market as the Whites. They have built barns, houses, fences and corrals to improve their holdings, and familial property is inherited and divided in a legalistic manner. Yet in spite of this partial adjustment to White civilization, in spite of tribal councils and their business meetings, the Ignacio Ute have attempted to retain the aboriginal ideology in many important respects. Even in more superficial aspects like clothing, the preference for old ways is still to be seen; the older men wear long hair braids and the older women still retain the long, full calico dress as something peculiarly Indian.

In sharp contrast to the Ignacio farmers the Weminutc band at Towaoc still live a nomadic existence. Unwilling to farm, lacking houses, and buying almost exclusively from licensed traders, the Towaoc Ute wander with movable tents and flocks of sheep, following seasonal pasturage. The Weminutc, in their travels, accumulate little of material value. Their contacts with the Whites are much rarer than those of the Ignacio Utes. To a still greater extent, they rebel against a too insistent supervision of their affairs and regard the intrusion of White ideas with unconcealed resentment. In superficial aspects, like clothing and manners, the Towaoc Ute has maintained a more strictly Indian appearance than his eastern tribesman. His bear dance, for example, is closer to the aboriginal standards. In mental outlook, in economic status, and in the present mode of living, the gap between Ignacio and Towaoc is deep and wide.

An important factor in explaining this cultural differential, and one which throws much light on the mental outlook of the Towaoc Ute, is the rationing system which obtained upon this reservation until 1931. Up to this time, it was possible for every Ute—man, woman, and child—to receive dispensations of cash, clothing and food from the government entirely without labor. At Ignacio, the natural result of the rationing system was lessened by the farming already in practice there and by the progressive counsels of the reservation chief. But at Towaoc, where poverty and disillusion assumed their most bitter form, rations, cash, and

clothing became the sole support, and a proud and predatory people, unable to live independently, tried to recapture the past
with cultural weapons. At Towaoc, White labor and White enterprise became anathema. At Towaoc, the last battle for cultural
autonomy was fought with the battle-cry: We have been wronged;
the government must provide for us; we will live like Utes, not
like White farmers!

There is good reason, then, for the resistance of the Towaoc
Ute to White ways and agency supervision. While no Weminutc
openly admits that he was duped into leaving pleasant farmlands
at Ignacio for the arid waste he now inhabits, no one will dispute
the fact that Towaoc land is semi-arid and the water-supply
poor. Disease is rampant at Towaoc. The native's constant complaint of poverty and disease is abundantly founded in fact. Attempts have been made upon the lives of at least two agency officials. The organized opposition is manifested in the refusal of
these people to accept a tribal constitution similar to that of the
Ignacio Ute, or to function through a tribal council other than
a most informal gathering of prominent elders and shamans under the leadership of a conservative chief. In the meantime, disease takes its toll among the Weminutc with syphilis claiming a
quarter of the population, and gonorrheal arthritis, together with
trachoma, assuming epidemic proportions. In one family alone,
five deaths occurred from tuberculosis within a three-year period.
In short, the situation at Towaoc is far from healthful, either in
a literal or figurative sense.

Both the organized opposition and the influence of the aboriginal pattern have resulted in placing social control in the
hands of the most conservative elements at Towaoc. The background of this cultural conservatism is the undisputed authority
of the family elders. Family relationship is still reckoned to the
fourth cousin, and within the kinship constellation thus defined,
the elder sibling, cousin, uncle or aunt is still the brighter star.
Here where property in land cannot exist, the young own next
to nothing in their own right. Since the social sanctions of the
aboriginal community favored the authority of the elders, their
control of family policies by virtue of age is free to continue unabated. The band chieftainship, a chronologically later develop-

ment than gerontocratic family organization, likewise functions to the same end of glorifying the pattern of age and authority as something peculiarly Indian.

In such a setting as this, adjustments to White civilization are difficult. Of a total population of 450, only half a dozen Towaoc Utes speak English and even less than this number have had the benefits of a secondary school education. The community farm, located on Mancos Creek, is still run by Navajo farmers. Hospitalization and medication are sternly disapproved. The young people, thus isolated from White civilization, and unable to participate fully in a disintegrating native culture, have no real stake in any coherent social background. The lack of activity at Towaoc is largely responsible for the colossal waste of time in gambling there. Gambling is definitely an economic activity of the younger generation. On Sunday afternoons, the games cease only when the sun has set, at which time the traders' stores are promptly opened. Then those who had good luck buy with cash, while those less fortunate buy with credit. In bewailing the modern turn of events, an educated young Weminutc said characteristically, "The old people had better brains. We youngsters have nothing and we do nothing."

At Ignacio, on the other hand, the rule of age has for some time been challenged by the economic independence of the younger generation. Of the 72,508 acres originally allotted in 1895, 33,202 acres were sold to Whites during the period of land sales. Nevertheless, through inheritance of the remaining lands, almost all mature Utes at Ignacio have come into possession of farms and homes, while the number of dependent, landless people has dwindled with the passage of time to an insignificant and steadily diminishing few. In 1931, the stoppage of rations brought agriculture more definitely to the fore as an economic mainstay and the reliance of older people on younger relatives was greatly increased. Knowledge of how to repair a wagon wheel became of more immediate importance than being steeped in the traditional lore of the past. Schooling replaced the myth-telling and moral precepts of the older culture. The law of the Ignacio Ute became the decision of lawfully elected tribal councilmen, young and middle-aged men chosen for their practical abilities and natural qualities of leadership. Here it is the older generation which, in certain cases, comprises the maladjusted few. At open council meetings a patriarch will sometimes oppose a vote, holding that decision is best reached through oratory, the former method in chiefly councils. Since all discussion is conducted in Ute, the young are at a disadvantage. They lack the dramatic note of older orators, grope for Ute words, and usually fumble their case verbally. Etiquette demands that they listen attentively to their elders, do not interrupt them, or speak at too great length after the elders have spoken. When by the sheer weight of numbers or the intercession of some older progressive elements, the young win out, the conservative clique leaves in a huff. The conflict between generations at Ignacio, while not sharp, is always precipitated by the economic independence of the younger generation and their real stake in current policies made possible by a brand new mode of living.

On the Ute Mountain Reservation, where such conflict is not implemented by similar property considerations, it is almost non-existent. Yet the authority of age is so meaningless in the modern setting that conflict between generations is not suppressed in every instance. In one case, for example, a young girl of sixteen became pregnant and attempted to separate her paramour completely from his first wife and family. The man's mother opposed the separation and widely broadcast her insistence upon the *status quo*. As a result, the girl brutishly beat her mother-in-law on two occasions, and so little was the son affected by this drastic action that the separation is now a definite possibility.

In view of this gradual weakening of the aboriginal cultural norms and the long history of defeat suffered by these people, it is not surprising to find revivalistic movements flourishing among them. First among these was the ghost dance, epitomized by Lesser in the following terms: [59]

The Ghost Dance was not merely a religious revival movement. Its roots lie deep in the gradual cultural destruction which preceded it. Its doctrine and the activities it demanded infused new life into the culture,

[59] Alexander Lesser, "The Cultural Significance of the Ghost Dance," *American Anthropologist, Volume 35, No. 1,* 1933, p. 115.

and constituted instrumentalities for the actual renaissance of the forms of old culture.

For the Ute, this doctrine of hope and cultural rebirth was accepted eagerly at first. As far back as fifty years ago, dances were introduced by a Weminutc who had traveled to the west among the Paiute. Through Paiute contacts, he received songs and supernatural power. His messages to the Southern Ute uniformly prophesied the spiritual return of the dead as well as the urgent necessity for the living to prepare themselves for this visitation by more rigid adherence to aboriginal custom. At his death, Jack Wilson, a Paiute prophet of the new cult, sent Yunitckwo'ov as his personal emissary to teach the Ghost Dance Religion to the Utes. Hitherto, the return of the dead had been construed to mean nothing more than their spiritual guidance in the whole-hearted return of the living to older cultural forms. Now Yunitckwo'ov disabused the Ute of this false conception; the Ute ancestors would come from the west in bodily form, there would be a huge whirlwind and the Whites would perish. Rashly, Yunitckwo'ov set the time within the next year. The Ute waited, torn between fear of the actual ghostly visitations (which, according to their own beliefs spelled death for the living) and doubt that such an event could ever happen. A year passed and the *sunavawi owitwi,* or ghost dance prophet was discredited. Immediately, the *sunavinkap,* or ghost dance ceased.

To the extent to which the ghost dance provided a means of cultural revival, it has been accepted. In the actual dance, as practised by the Ute, the musicians stamped their feet and the men and women danced clockwise in a circle, crossing the right foot in front and dragging the left in back. A man or woman fell down in the center of the circle in a trance. Then the man who had called the dance shouted, "She's in the land of the dead. Soon she will come back with a message." In Ute conception, the trance was wholly voluntary. The dead did not come to the living to claim them in death; rather, the living made the visitation and returned with moral injunctions to live well, to follow Ute ways. The entire emphasis was on the living, not the dead. Even the name, *momövinkap* or "ancestor dance," was rarely used. The common name of *sunavinkap,* with more of the meaning of "spirit dance," was applied to this rite, wherein the living played the dominant rôle, and dead souls were the passive onlookers.

Such was the ghost dance introduced by the Weminutc. The actual visitation by the dead was carefully excluded. The clue to this elimination of Paiute cultural elements must be sought in the aboriginal ideology of Ute culture according to which the ghost can claim a relative in death. Even today, the pictures of the dead are destroyed. At Towaoc, the tent and property of the deceased are either destroyed or else sold or traded. Rationalizing their fear of ghostly reminders, some older people refuse to have their pictures taken because "this makes a person die quickly." Alone at night, one can actually see ghosts with the eyes. There are haunted spots where ghosts lurk, the *ïnupi'arat tubuts.* Whistling at night is not allowed, so others may not be afraid, thinking *inï'putc,* the ghost, appears. The screech-owl, *Otus asio,* is still feared as an omen of death.

In view of this fear of the ghost, it is interesting to note what became of the ghost dance following the rash promises of Yunitckwo'ov. Once the Paiute prophet had been discredited, the ghost dance became the culturally sanctioned butt of a joke. A new dance arose to parody the old, and it was named derisively "Dance for Making Medicine in Daytime on a Sick Person" or *tomu'gunikap.* Again, the musicians stamped their feet, the participants forming a ring to dance. After each song, the performers fell into the center of the circle pell-mell, one on top of another. Then the dance-leader called out, "That woman who fell wants someone to lie on top of her." The joke was greeted with much hilarity. This new version of the Paiute dance provided an amusing outlet for the suppressed shame and embarrassment occasioned by the unhappy outcome of the Ute Ghost Dance Religion.[60]

Equally instructive as an attempt at cultural integration on the religious level is the study of the peyote cult among the Ute,

[60] For a strict parallel to the Southern Ute *tomu'gunikap,* see Dr. R. H. Lowie's reference to the Northern Ute *tomu'gwenikapi* in "Dances and Societies of the Plains Shoshone," Anthropological Papers of the American Museum of Natural History, *Volume XI, Part X,* 1915, p. 832.

and the varying emphasis laid upon this rite at Towaoc and Ignacio. At Towaoc, so long as the supply of peyote lasts, the meetings continue regularly on successive Saturday nights. There the leading shamans have joined forces in a peyote-eating society with curative functions and the cult receives active support from all members of the community. At Ignacio, on the other hand, a similar society struggles for existence with only a handful of unwavering stalwarts behind the movement, faced by the vigorous opposition of both the agency officials and a powerful faction of leading medicine-men. Before discussing this interesting cultural differential, however, it is necessary, first of all, to consider the effective appeal of peyote among those who really support its use.

At Towaoc, there are two White missions, a Roman Catholic and a Protestant. At Ignacio, there are no missions, but rather town churches. The few Ignacio Utes who have become regular church-goers frequent the Mexican Catholic where their presence is entirely voluntary. Very few of the Ute to this day consider being converted. Instead, they exult in the power of their shamans to cure, hold tenaciously to old ceremonialism, and oppose their own Indian religion to White doctrines. At Towaoc, where band interests are still more cohesively organized under the leadership of a conservative faction, peyote has become a bulwark of faith in things Indian, a defense against the onrushing tide of White medicine and missionary influence. A young Weminutc repeated to me the following conversation with a missionary:

He said to me, "What is the good of this peyote? It only makes you rave." So I told him it was the Indian way. I said, "You hold your Book. We hold the cane and the rattle. You sing a hymn. We sing our Indian songs. For us it is a good way—the straight peyote way. It is an Indian road, and we are Indian. We wear braids like the horns of a bull. We sing! We eat peyote!" He could not answer when I said this was our own religious way. No answer. . . .

All Southern Utes find intense satisfaction in the belief that Indian religion is an inviolable retreat where White interference cannot enter. At Towaoc, peyote has provided a stronger rallying point for ceremonial life than individualistic shamanistic performances. There every tent is provided with a peyote gourd rattle of the Kiowa type and canes and drumsticks are everywhere to be seen.

Peyote was first introduced among the Southern Ute by Sam Loganberry, or Cactus Pete as he is sometimes called. The desideratum has always been an organized Peyote Church of the Oklahoma type, but one in which the Christianized version of the cult, common among Plains tribes, is carefully excluded. So opposed are the Towaoc natives to this version that they today disclaim Cactus Pete as their first teacher. "His way was crooked," said one Weminutc, "instead of the straight Indian way. Not he, but John Peehart, was our first teacher." The Ignacio Ute, in keeping with their more complete acculturation, accept Sam Loganberry as the first real proselytizer and incorporate slightly more Christian symbology into their rite. Yet, on both sides of the reservation, the peyote cult remains a definitely Ute ceremony in which shamans pool their powers to cure a patient. This ceremony is of relatively late introduction and its spread among the Ute coincides neatly with the recent establishment of missions for these people and their final banishment to reservation lands.

The pooling of shamanistic powers is not something entirely new in Ute ceremonialism. With the gradual emergence of the band camp and the growing solidarity of the warlike Ute band, a ritualistic form of round dance arose to combat the spread of disease. The Round Dance Ceremony, or *mawö'qwipani,* was danced to the accompaniment of curing songs; no drums were used. The men, women, and children who participated danced sideways in a circle, moving clockwise. The medicine-men stood in the center, singing and fanning the people as they passed with an eagle tail-feather wand. The left side and then the right side of the dancer was fanned from head to foot. Characteristically, the people were called upon to join in the singing. Between songs, a shaman told of the approaching illness and of his efforts to drive it away. The fanning was designed to combat sickness, to bring health and vigor to those who danced.

With the introduction of the peyote cult, the ideology of the round dance was transferred to the new ceremonial. The prayers to an animistic world of nature; the coöperation of those quali-

fied to cure the ill; the entrance into the peyote tent in a clockwise direction; the rule that when a peyote leader takes his position at the west point of the tipi, the others shall pass around
before him to take their places in the semi-circle; the use of
eagle-tail feather wands to pass out the peyote; and finally, the
ritual fanning of the patient and the sucking out of illness—all
these features of the new rite are strongly reminiscent of the
older ceremonialism. The cane passed clockwise as each cult
member sings curative songs represents the cane of Christ when
"He walked on this earth." The twelve feathers represent his
twelve disciples. Yet these features are familiar adjuncts of
shamanistic paraphernalia used in former curing ceremonies,
while Christ himself is here interpreted as the Great Healer, the
creator of humans who used power always to "do good." Nor is
the use of the narcotic, peyote, surprising in view of the widespread utilization of herbs, roots and specifics formerly employed
in Ute shamanistic rites. The half-moon mound of earth fashioned in the wet clay of the tipi-floor before peyote meetings
represents an old and potent source of supernatural power to the
Ute. The facing of the tipi itself to the east in order that the
patient may rise with the sun is an old conception rooted in the
fertility magic at all times associated with the sun, the source of
vigor and life. In short, the peyote cult has crystallized a number
of older Ute conceptions and welded them into a church-like organization able to compete with mission influence for the spiritual welfare of a rising generation. In its main emphasis, however, peyote remains a Ute curing ceremony with just enough
of Christian symbology to bridge the gap between older religious
values and a modern American environment.

At Ignacio, as we have noted, the new cult encounters great
difficulties. In the first place, the Southern Ute of Ignacio are
subject, by constitution, to the state laws of Colorado. Peyote is
illegal, therefore, and ritual paraphernalia have occasionally been
discovered and confiscated. The peyote stalwarts have failed in
attempts to lease a town church and thereby obtain the semblance of legality. A native farming population, already money-
minded, has objected to the five-dollar grocery bill required of
every cult member for each peyote feast. The donations expected

of members for the drug itself are often considered needless expenditure. In 1917, when peyote was introduced at Ignacio, farming already was in progress and the appeal of old custom was on the wane. Peyote today fights for mere existence at Ignacio, while the same rite flourishes at Towaoc in the rich soil of cultural reaction.

Another factor hindering the growth of the peyote cult at Ignacio is the active resistance of medicine-men to the joint ceremonial. Here band cohesiveness is passing away with the breakdown of the old pattern. Individual shamanism is fighting for its very life. Within the last year, four *pö'rat* gave up public practice. A peyote cult follower sardonically said of this: "They are out of work now; they are *unemployed.*" But the *pö'rat* themselves see the handwriting on the wall. A few years ago, the most respected shaman of Ignacio offered his services to the government hospital at Ignacio for $400 a year in order "to help the White doctor stop sickness." Last year, the same man told me of the modern difficulties of shamanism in the following terms:

Today, the Indian doctors are not so good because they live in houses. They forget the old ways. The young people go to the White hospital, thinking that the White doctor can cure Indian sickness. In the old days, everyone knew that the Indian doctor alone could cure Indian sickness and they believed him. They helped singing in the tipi when the *pö'rat* sang his strongest songs. They took him in a serious way. Today they laugh when they see him. The *pö'rat* forgets.

Yet the remaining shamans of Ignacio still believe that the *pö'rat* best understands Indian ailments, while the White doctor knows only White diseases. Their natural interest in shamanistic fees predisposes them all the more to regard the hospital, along with the peyote cult, as unwelcome infringements upon their curative duties. The growing appeal of hospitalization at Ignacio as well as the peyote curing society have left the *pö'rat* almost without function. Today, the respect that the shamans enjoin upon a conservative clique is more than counterbalanced by the disregard of an independent younger generation. More than that, the peyote cult of Ignacio is a joint venture led by less conservative elements with slight leanings toward Christianity. Such is the threat to the social security of the shaman. With the

peyote cult vying for the small practice he still retains, the shaman feels his songs will die with him, his ceremony go unheeded,
and his abilities fall into disrepute. Stories are circulated by the
faction behind the shaman to the effect that peyote is ruinous
and that cult activities destroy the virtue of young girls. But the
battle is a losing one. Both the peyote cult and shamanism are in
retreat at Ignacio before the growing awareness of a germ theory
of disease.

At Towaoc, not only does the peyote cult flourish, but much of
the older ceremonialism is still extant. The Weminutc know
nothing of disease and its causes. As sickness spreads, so does the
influence of Ute supernaturalism. The Whites, according to one
belief, send those ailments with their bad wishes. Hospitalization
is a fraud and a delusion. Consequently, up to 1931, there was
only one confinement in the Towaoc Hospital; the hot bed and
couvade ceremonial held full sway. In the seventy hospital con-
finements since 1931, it was difficult to make the mothers drink
cold water or have ice-bags on the abdomen following birth.
When a birth was whispered through the hospital, the men inside, fearing contamination from the "bad blood," rose from
their sick-beds and rushed outside no matter what the weather.
Similarly, deaths occurring in the hospital made the institution
unfit for habitation in the Ute mind. Naturally, deaths are frequent since the people employ medicine-men, and only as a last
resort, when there is little hope, use medication.

The native birth ceremony is rarely catastrophic because of
the apparent immunity of Ute women to puerperal fever. Babies
are healthy despite the lack of sanitation around the camp, probably because of the late weaning among the Ute; it is still possible to see a child of three or four nursing. The practice of
making a child learn to walk by passing a bow between its legs is
still in evidence; the old explanation that the sinew bow-string
makes the child a fleet runner is still heard. At the death of a
relative, the Towaoc Ute open the eyes of the corpse and stand
before it, weeping as a last farewell; this show of grief, no matter
how fervent, is construed to exhibit one's sorrow to the ghost still
lurking near the dead body and it is meant as a token that the
ghost should not return to the living and cause them to grieve.

Just as the ghost is today feared at Towaoc, so the sorcerer is publicly accused for his complicity in causing death. Recently, a Northern Ute in residence at Towaoc was charged with the death of two chiefs and other people as well. He fled for his life, but the Utes, insisting upon an eye for an eye, appealed to the agency to have him returned for punishment. The Northern Ute's downfall they dated at a time when his power received the wrong horse in payment for a cure, whereupon his *pöwa'a* called out to be fed with the blood of victims "like a dog." At Towaoc, one occasionally sees the medicine bundle of a shaman or happens upon a camp when a curing-ceremony is in progress. The shamanistic medicine bundles themselves are symbolic, as it were, of the older cultural values in their newer setting. Bright cloth wrappings for ostentation often encase the buckskin, feather, bone, and stone objects used by the shaman to perform his marvelous cures; occasionally today, strange objects—glass cylinders for thunderbolts, brass balls for stars—have intruded. Yet the Towaoc people are still aboriginal in psychology and point of view.

The Ignacio situation, in respect to specific customs of this sort, is markedly different. Only to a slight extent is the ghost still feared. At death, the deceased is buried in his personal finery. But other property—horses, homes, and valuable possessions—is never destroyed. While the name of the deceased is rarely mentioned before his close relatives, this avoidance is today phrased as politeness, as a desire not to hurt the bereaved persons needlessly. One informant explained this as follows:

> I lost a cousin, and he has a daughter, ———, living. We won't speak his name. We get around it by doing this: we say, "That man who got on his horse and rode away not long ago." We are polite to each other with those thoughts. That is why children are never given the names of dead people. The Ute don't like to worry about *ini'putc*.

After the death of a noted Ignacio chief not long ago, his name was still heard widely and there was no evidence of the elaborate circumlocutions noticed at Towaoc. Only among the closest relatives were teknonomy and metaphor invoked, and even here relatives would use the name in the absence of other related persons.

At Towaoc, much of the old life is left. The navel cord of an infant is still saved and placed in an ant-hill. This age-old practice is to protect the health of the child, since ants are always active and busy. To throw the navel cord away or to forget to place it either in the ant-hill or in a buckskin bag tied to the infant's cradle resulted in the child becoming foolish when he grew up. Similarly, the Towaoc Ute cuts his finger and toe-nails only at night and offers them to a benevolent being called *inu'sakats* with the prayer: "Give me long life and help me, Inusakats!" This, too, is an old practice.

But at Ignacio, no such careful persistence in the old customs is at all apparent. Instead, one finds such shifts to White civilization as hospital confinement, property inheritance, and Christian burial. The tea dance of Ignacio, or *tinqap*, was nothing more than a slavish imitation of a White social gathering at which tea was served and the young people danced together. Here the guests sat in a circle and tea was passed out clockwise to the company. After this, the women chose their partners. The dancers then circled around the fire to the music of old social dance songs accompanied by a drum. They joined hands, each woman next to her male partner.

The whole tenor of this shift toward White norms of conduct at Ignacio is illustrated in the reported conversation of a young father with his more conservative parent:

My father came to see me after the boy was born in the Government Hospital. He asked me, "Did you go off alone and run after your baby was born?" I had to tell him I just took the day off resting around home. He told me I'd be lazy because I didn't run. He said they always did this in the old days when a baby came. I'd do it just to please him, but the others would laugh at me. Besides I have too much work on the ranch now and that tires me out.

As with the birth ceremony, so with other ceremonies at Ignacio. The two annual ceremonies among the Ute are the bear dance, formerly held early in spring, and the sun dance of midsummer. At Towaoc, both ceremonies are still held according to the old seasonal calendar. But at Ignacio they are held months later at times when they do not interfere with farming operations. At Towaoc, the bear dance is still the occasion for great festivity; at Ignacio, many Utes do not even bother to attend. In the observation of the sun dance, used as a method of obtaining supernatural power, one notes the same differential in effect. During the past year only five men danced in the sun dance at Ignacio, and the sun dance leader, in charge of the ceremony, publicly announced his decision to retire. At Towaoc, this number of performers was almost trebled, while the actual observance of the rite was accurate in detail and accompanied by much social excitement throughout the band. At the root of this shift toward White norms among the Ute of Ignacio is the increased reliance upon an individualistic economy inherent in farming, competitively organized. This change in economic organization has effectively destroyed band solidarity and has replaced a coherent aboriginal system of values with new interests. It has left little time for the observance of old dances and has wrought havoc with the tribal mores.

In one respect only can the new integration at Towaoc and Ignacio be said to be parallel. In reference to sexual behavior, the old patterns of brittle marriages and shifting family alliances still obtain. At Towaoc, the flageolet serenade is heard throughout the summer, marking the girl-hunting expeditions. The bear dance, today as formerly, is still the occasion for courtship at both ends of the reservation. Illegitimate births are fairly common, yet even today no stigma is attached to illegitimacy. Divorce is of frequent occurrence, while the uncertainties of marriage account for the widespread preference to marry "the Indian way" without benefit of seal or clergy. The disparity between the ages of mates allows for the continuance of marriage to a woman and her daughter by a former marriage. At Ignacio, in many of the cases where this polygamous form of marriage has occurred, property considerations have entered into the bargain; many a young man has married an older propertied woman legally and thereby acquired the right to her lands and holdings in cases where the real love affair developed between the husband and his older wife's mature daughter. As long as no blood relationship is traceable between a man and his stepdaughter, such a marriage is sanctioned by the native community and finds repercussions in the older pattern of "mother-stepdaughter" marriage.

But even at Ignacio, property considerations have not led uniformly to the stability of the marriage bond. For it must be remembered that almost all mature Utes of Ignacio today hold property in land or expect to inherit it. While economic ambitions sometimes prompt marriages to older mates, the general pattern of shifting family alliances is the rule. A typical divorce case occurred recently when an Ignacio Ute was married by the local judge for three dollars and not long afterwards brought the judge six dollars to effect a speedy divorce. The Ute was surprised to learn that divorce proceedings would be a trifle more complicated. He had thought that by doubling the price of a marriage, a divorce could be obtained. Most Ignacio Utes are aware of the difficulty of divorce proceedings, and, for this reason, many prefer not to marry legally. In addition, the three dollar marriage fee has served as an effective barrier to marriage "the White way."

The money-mindedness of the Ignacio Ute has not, however, broken down patterns of familial solidarity. The young help older relatives about their farms, and property is still strictly shared within the family circle. Since the average money income per family scarcely exceeds a few hundred dollars a year, such coöperation is an urgent necessity. Similarly, the average family displays a good deal of coöperation in agricultural labor; where the holdings of parents and children are separate, a son or younger affinal relative will often work two farms simultaneously.

At Towaoc, the same solidarity is exhibited between relatives in economic matters. In one case a sister spent an inheritance of 1,200 dollars in annuity funds within a short period to purchase the proper food for a tubercular brother. Since the economic level at Towaoc is even lower than that at Ignacio, relatives often find it expedient to descend upon the camp of a relation in slightly better circumstances for an extended visit. The easy movability of the camps, the lack of any stationary property, and the feeling of solidarity between relatives by blood or marriage—all serve to make such extended visits possible. At Ignacio, however, only the landless few are free to live at the expense of relatives, while the great majority of families are rooted to the farms which require so much constant care. Here the landless few are rarely parasitical; to live with a relative entails working for one's keep, for only the aged are exempt from active labor on the busy farms.

At Towaoc, a new cultural element has been accepted within the last few years, the source of the complex being the Paiute settlement around Blanding, Utah. As we have noted previously, in discussing the aboriginal community, the Ute have never associated things sexual with ideas of supernatural punishment. (Specific female functions, like birth and menstruation have been singled out for special emphasis, and form the only exceptions to this rule.) Consequently, the lack of supernatural danger in the normal functioning of sexual desire has led to the use of a strange new love magic at Towaoc. Using parts of dead bodies, exhumed, dried and powdered, one seeks to attract the desired girl. The body parts used are sexual organs, male and female, and the tips of tongues, fingers, lips and toes. Contact with the medicine is said to result in unbridled sexual desire. The dead body, being the mere shell of the living person, never arouses fear. In the absence of an active social life with frequent dances and opportunities for courtship, the love medicine is accepted as a substitute. In the many affairs of every youth it figures as an indispensable asset. Yet the emphasis upon this form of secret courtship is not altogether healthy even according to Ute standards. It is felt that the careless use of the medicine may result in the illness of the boy, his sweetheart, or both. Its use is therefore secret and has led, on occasion, to charges of sorcery and violent arguments. Today, marriages occur as early among the Weminutc as formerly, but with less of the protracted romance that once attended the event.

A final word may be said concerning the approved personality types at Towaoc and at Ignacio. As one would expect, the cultural differential between the two groups operates in defining the good life and the good man. At Ignacio, the virtues of sobriety and industry are valued highly. The tribal councilmen, elected by the Utes in residence, are without exception successful farmers, progressive leaders, and men whose interests are serious and intelligent. While the shaman is still respected in some quarters, he is respected only for his serious effort to preserve life, not because of his close connection with the aboriginal values. At Ignacio, one finds vigorous farmers over sixty insisting upon the virtues of White medicine, White morality, and even White law.

In this setting of vastly changed values, the conservative clique and the hold of shamanism are rapidly passing by the board.

At Towaoc, however, the band leadership regards the agency center as an unwelcome and dictatorial authority. Generosity and loyalty to aboriginal standards of behavior make the good life. The Towaoc Ute believes in sharing for use, not hoarding for the future. His leaders are the shamans and tribal elders steeped in the traditional lore of the past. It is still possible for an irate shaman to enter the hospital and by his exhortations prevail upon the patients to leave. A tribal chief, recently deceased, publicly opposed the use of government medical facilities while privately repairing to the hospital for treatment of chronic kidney trouble. In countless cases, the government doctor cures a patient, whereupon the native medicine-man easily convinces the patient that his songs were actually responsible for the cure. Wherever it is a choice between the doctor's and the shaman's ability, the Towaoc Ute insists upon the superiority of shamanism. He still feels that the shaman is one who comes to the patient's camp and remains until the sick man is cured or the case becomes hopeless. The shaman is one who, in the familiar phrase "understands Indian illness." As with White medicine, so with White law and White morality. The approved leaders of Towaoc sentiment still oppose the intrusion of such ideas and practices. Even the girl who cuts her clothes according to the scant and economical White pattern is taunted with the accusation of wishing to become "a White lady."

Ute culture, it would seem, has found new bases for integration after long years of trial and error. The process of adjusting to White civilization has met with varying success at Towaoc and at Ignacio. In the former case, a reactive impulse is largely responsible for the rigid adherence to old beliefs and practices, for the feverish quest after old cultural values in the peyote cult and in the ghost dance, and for the backward-looking emphasis in the total adjustment. At Ignacio, the old values have been powerfully challenged by a new economy, and there Ute culture steadily approaches its final resolution in complete assimilation. The process of acculturation among these people, fortuitous, unplanned, impelled by harsh economic determinants, and guided only by an aboriginal system of values was not without its toll in the health and happiness of some 800 Southern Utes now located upon the Consolidated Ute Reservation of Colorado.

BIBLIOGRAPHY

Abel, Annie H., *The Official Correspondence of James S. Calhoun, While Indian Agent at Santa Fé, New Mexico,* Government Printing Office, Washington, D.C., 1915.

Bancroft, Hubert H., *History of Arizona and New Mexico, 1530–1888,* The History Company, San Francisco, Calif., 1899.

Bandelier, Alfred F., Report on a Visit to the Aboriginal Ruins of Rio Pecos, *Papers of the Archaeological Institute of America, American Series, Volume 1, Part 2,* Cupples, Upham, Boston, Mass., 1883.

────── *Final Report on Investigation among the Indians of the Southwestern United States,* J. Wilson and Son, Cambridge, Mass., 1890.

Commissioner of Indian Affairs, *Reports to the Secretary of the Interior, 1857, 1861–63, 1868,* Government Printing Office, Washington, D.C.

Dodge, Richard I., *Our Wild Indians,* A. B. Worthington, Hartford, Conn., 1882.

────── *The Plains of the Great West,* G. P. Putnam and Sons, New York, N.Y., 1877.

Fowler, Jacob, *Journal,* edited by Elliott Coues, F. P. Harper, New York, N.Y., 1898.

Gregg, Josiah, *Commerce of the Prairies,* 4th edition, J. W. Moore, Philadelphia, Pa., 1850.

Haines, Francis, "Where Did the Indians Get their Horses?," *American Anthropologist,* New Series, *Volume 40, No. 1,* 1938.

Hughes, John T., *Doniphan's Expedition,* J. A. and U. P. James, Cincinnati, Ohio, 1848.

Lesser, Alexander, "Cultural Significance of the Ghost Dance," *American Anthropologist,* New Series, *Volume 35, No. 1,* 1933.

Lowie, Robert H., Dances and Societies of the Plains Shoshone, *Anthropological Papers of the American Museum of Natural History, Volume 11, Part 10,* New York, N.Y., 1915.

────── *History of Ethnological Theory,* Farrar and Rinehart, New York, N.Y., 1937.

Parsons, Elsie C., "Toas Pueblo," *General Series in Anthropology, No. 2,* George Banta Publishing Company, Menasha, Wis., 1936.

Pike, Zebulon M., *Expedition of, to the Headwaters of the Mississippi River, etc., 1805–07,* edited by Elliott Coues, *Volume 2,* F. P. Harper, New York, N.Y., 1895.

Richardson, Rupert N., *The Comanche Barrier to South Plains Settlement,* The Arthur H. Clark Company, Glendale, Calif., 1933.

Ruxton, George F., *Adventures in New Mexico and the Rocky Mountains,* John Murray, London, England, 1847.

Steward, Julian, "Linguistic Distribution and Political Groups of the Great Basin Shoshoneans," *American Anthropologist, Volume 39, No. 1,* Menasha, Wis., 1937.

Thomas, Alfred B., *After Coronado,* University of Oklahoma Press, Norman, Okla., 1935.

—— *Antonio de Bonilla's Spanish Plans for Defense of New Mexico, New Spain and the Anglo-American West,* Contributions to H. E. Bolton, *Volume 1, New Spain,* pp. 183–209, Private Printing, Los Angeles, 1932.

—— *Forgotten Frontiers,* University of Oklahoma Press, Norman, Okla., 1932.

Twitchell, Ralph E., *Leading Facts of New Mexico History, Volume 1,* The Torch Press, Cedar Rapids, Iowa, 1911–17.

—— *Spanish Archives of New Mexico, Volume 2,* The Torch Press, Cedar Rapids, Iowa, 1914.

United States Laws, Statutes-at-Large, Volume 18, Part 3, Government Printing Office, Washington, D.C., 1873–75.

EDITOR'S SUMMARY

The contrast between the acculturation process among the Utes and among the White Knife Shoshoni, described in the previous chapter, is of particular interest because the two peoples are closely related and originally had cultures of very much the same sort. However, the cultures which were called upon to meet the impact of White domination in each case were markedly different. While the Shoshoni faced the Whites from the archaic level of scanty subsistence economy and family hunting group organization, the Utes faced them with well organized bands, developed war patterns and a considerable economic surplus. This difference must be seen as primarily a result of accidents of time and geographic location. The Utes, because of their more southern position, received horses first and were able to revolutionize certain aspects of their life before White pressure became serious. The Shoshoni, on the other hand, received the horse late. Cultural modifications of the sort it produced among the Utes seem to have been under way but were still so poorly integrated with the rest of the culture that they were soon swept away. In Ute acculturation there was thus an important stage which was missing for the Shoshoni.

The results of the acceptance of the horse by the Utes are of particular interest as showing the speed with which important changes can be consummated in aboriginal cultures. Wide areas of native life were transformed within three or four generations. The horse and the equipment immediately connected with its use were, of course, borrowed, but it is impossible to say how far the changes which followed in its train were influenced by borrowing or how far they were adaptations and amplifications which arose directly out of the preëxisting culture. The rise of band patterns can certainly be accounted for on the latter basis. The nucleus was already present in pre-horse days in the recogni tion of units larger than the family hunting group and their periodic assembly. The war patterns may have been borrowed in part, but it is significant that if this was the case most of the honorary accompaniments of warfare among the Plains tribes were lost in the process. Ute war was not a game for individual prestige but an efficient business, a valuable addition to the subsistence economy. The curious Dog Society of this period, while faintly reminiscent of the Plains warrior societies has so many distinctive features that only the initial impetus toward its development could have been received from them. The whole transformation of the Utes into horse nomads shows how readily a culture can adapt itself to new elements in the absence of complicating external factors.

Lacking this period of horse .nomadism, the Utes would probably have submitted to the Whites as readily as the Shoshoni did and accepted the new conditions with the same sly sullenness. As it was, they had to be subjugated by force of arms. Their eager acceptance of the ghost dance, as contrasted with the relative indifference of the Shoshoni, reflects the fact that they had fallen from a higher estate and had really had good old times to which they wished to return. This difference is also reflected in their differing response to White ill treatment. While the Shoshoni seem to have remained throughout willing to accept any elements of White culture which would function under actual conditions, one division of the Utes has idealized the earlier culture and has attempted to maintain it at all points.

The present existence among the Utes of progressive and conservative groups is also important as indicating the rôle which particular personalities may play in the acculturation process. Both evolved from a common level of cultural inadequacy and discontent, but their subsequent course seems to have been determined by the personalities of their band chiefs. The leader of the Weminutc band, now located at Towaoc, reacted to the situation by leading his people into a region where the very poverty of the resources afforded some shield from White aggression. Buckskin Charlie, the Ignacio chief, took a more realistic view of the situation and persuaded his followers that they would have to meet the Whites on their own terms. He encouraged farming and education and the trends which he established have resulted in a fairly good adaptation for his band. Although this group still have a strong feeling of solidarity and attach high emotional value to certain aspects of their old culture, it seems probable that the acculturation process has already gone so far that it will move on to its end in assimilation. It is hard to imagine them developing into an encysted social and cultural unit like the Fox. The Towaoc Ute, on the other hand, have resisted acculturation to an unusual degree, although they have been able to do so only with the aid of government rations. The ultimate result of the increasing disharmony between their aboriginal culture and the external realities will probably be a complete collapse of both the culture and the society, leaving the latter's component individuals to adjust as best they can.

· 4 ·

THE NORTHERN ARAPAHO OF WYOMING

by Henry Elkin

PART ONE

I

When tribes from surrounding areas acquired the horse and entered the Great Plains, among them were five groups who spoke variations of one form of the Algonquin languages. Three of these became known as the Northern Arapaho, the Southern Arapaho and the Gros Ventre. The others became assimilated to the Northern and Southern Arapaho, and thus lost their separate identities.[1]

Of their life before they secured the horse, we know little. According to their traditions, the Northern Arapaho had lived in settled communities where they practised both agriculture and hunting, and the earliest people with whom they were in contact were the Arikara, a tribe that continued to live in this manner until modern times.

At the beginning of our historic record, the Northern Arapaho had lost all direct traces of settled agricultural life. With the use of the horse they took on a completely nomadic existence based on hunting the buffalo, and roamed the high plains of Wyoming, southern Montana and northern Colorado, from the Black Hills in the east to the Rocky Mountains in the west.

On their southern border, they were often in contact with the Southern Arapaho, of similar culture and language. Both tribes felt themselves closely identified, and they often intermarried. The Northern Arapaho also had close and friendly relations with the Cheyenne and the Dakota, whom they met in their own ter-

[1] A. L. Kroeber, The Arapaho, *American Museum of Natural History, Bulletin 18,* 1902.

ritory. With the Crow, who lived for the most part to the north, and with the Wind River Shoshoni and the Ute to the south and east, they were in an almost constant state of war.

The buffalo was the mainstay of their economy; elk, antelope and deer followed in importance. The meat and hides of these animals supplied the basic needs of food, clothing and shelter. Smaller game, and young dogs which they raised, were eaten to vary the fare. During the summer season, various wild roots and berries were gathered which, when mixed with meat, formed an important part of their diet. They planted tobacco in the spring and returned to harvest it in the fall.

The possession of the horse was the basis of their way of life. Its importance can be gauged by the fact that special names existed categorizing horses in terms of their suitability for warfare, packing and hunting. Horses were generally obtained through warfare, and to a lesser extent through the taming of wild stock, and trade. Four or five horses were the indispensable minimum for a man and wife; two for riding and the rest for packing. The average household had about ten head. The possession of twenty or more was an indication of wealth.

The technology and material products of the Arapaho, though extremely simple, made efficient use of their limited range of resources, and provided for the necessities of nomadic existence. Their tipis of buffalo hide, stretched on a framework of long straight poles, could be put up and taken down quickly and easily. Inside the tipis were beds of willow frames covered with piles of skins. Both men and women wore robes of buffalo skins and tailored clothing of tanned elk and antelope hides. Food was preserved by drying in the sun. Rawhide containers, filled with hot stones and water, were used for boiling meat. Rawhide was used further for parfleches, which were packed on horseback when traveling, for bridles, and when cut into strips, for cord. Wood was used for saddles, bows and lances. Porcupine quills later superseded by colored beads, and clay paints, served as decorative materials.

In their economic life, there was simple division of labor. The men hunted game, captured, tamed and cared for the horses, made saddles, weapons and ceremonial objects. The women occupied themselves with domestic duties and manufactures and often aided and protected by men too old to hunt gathered roots and berries. They cooked, worked hides, constructed tipis, and made and decorated their clothing and other leather products.

Inter-tribal trade was small and relatively unimportant. Their own resources supplied practically all their needs. They did, however, exchange for horses, which were more abundant among the Southern Arapaho, tipi poles and antelope teeth, easily procurable in their own territory. With the more northerly tribes, there was only a very minor trade, largely confined to decorative objects such as beaded shirts and feather headdresses.

II

The Northern Arapaho, numbering over two thousand, were divided into four bands. The "Quick Tempered," about 800 in all, was the largest of these and constituted the focal center for the tribal organization. Then came the "Antelope," some 600, and two smaller groups, the "Greasy Faced" of about 400, and the "Middle People" of about 250.[2]

The band system allowed the Arapaho to meet effectively the seasonal fluctuations in the game supply with corresponding changes in their social grouping. During the summer, buffalo were found in large herds and were generally hunted in tribal surrounds. All the bands joined in a single line of march and camped together in a tribal circle. Though each band tended to occupy a distinct part of the circle, about half the members of the tribe generally put up their tipis with relatives in other than their own bands. During the rest of the year, when game ran only singly or in small groups, the tribe as a whole was too large and unwieldy to function as a unit. The bands separated and most of the hunting was carried on by small groups of men.

Even then, however, the bands did not live completely apart. They generally remained fairly close together and informed the "Quick Tempered" band, which contained the Sacred Pipe and most of the tribal chiefs, of their movements. For the winter camp, a spot was usually chosen in the wooded foot-hills of the

[2] Estimates from Arapaho informants.

mountains where two or more streams came together and game was known to be present. The bands would locate along the streams about five to thirty miles from one another, to form an enclosed game-preserve between them. The winter season was quiet and restful. They lived on the food they had stored during the summer and on the buffalo that gathered in the vicinity. While the horses fattened on bark, members of different bands visited, played games and told stories.

When spring arrived, they left their winter quarters and followed the streams down to the plains. This was the hardest season. Their winter stocks were depleted and buffalo were thin and scarce. Their chief dependence now was on antelope, and even these were hard to find. The bands moved separately, though more or less parallel with one another as in the fall. Messengers were sent back and forth telling of the location of game.

The band system was thus primarily a form of economic organization. Although the bands joked and competed with one another, individual band solidarity and communal spirit was limited. Band membership had no relation to marriage restrictions. The four groups were thoroughly intertwined by bonds of kinship as well as by those of the age-societies. Individuals often went to live with relatives in other bands, where they sometimes permanently remained.

III

The social groupings, organized on the basis of kinship, were of great importance in governing behavior in all phases of social life. Serving a broad range of the individual's interests throughout his entire life, membership in the kin grouping was characterized by even stronger and more pervasive bonds than membership in the tribe itself.

The nucleus of the kin grouping was a man, his one or more wives and their children, living together in a tipi. The relation between the husband and wife was defined in terms of the manifold complementary functions of the two sexes. The husband supplied the raw materials, the wife took care of the household duties and manufactures, and each owned the property they individually made or used.[3] They formed a unit as well in many phases of the social and religious life, in which the status and rôle of the wife were primarily determined by that of her husband. Together they were the primary agency for passing on the cultural heritage to the next generation, the father training the sons, and the mother, the daughters.

This simple family group, however, did not function in isolation. In all its activities, it was joined by kin on both sides. Almost invariably during the winter, and often at other times of the year, it camped with the husband's or more usually with the wife's parents. Thus an older couple, their married children and their families, their younger children, and possibly one or two stray relatives, formed an extended household, hunting and gathering food together, cooking from the same fire, eating together, and taking care of each other's children.

The Arapaho applied the same kinship terms to relatives in the direct linear line, those collaterally related through a common grandparental ancestor, and some related only through marriage. In the parental generation, "father" covered one's own father, his brothers and male cousins and the husbands of the mother's sisters and female cousins. "Mother" covered one's own mother, her sisters and female cousins, and the wives of the father's brothers and male cousins. "Mother's brother" was applied to the brothers and male cousins of the "mothers" and to the husbands of the "father's" sisters and female cousins. "Father's sister" covered the sisters and female cousins of the "fathers" and the wives of the "mothers' brothers." Special terms were used for the father-in-law, and the mother-in-law.[4]

In one's own generation, the four terms for older and younger "brother" and "sister" covered the children of all those to whom one applied relationship terms in the ascending generation. "Brother-in-law" covered both the wife's "brothers" and the "sisters'" husbands. "Sister-in-law" covered the wife's "sisters" and the "brothers'" wives. In the first descending generation, the children of relatives of one's own sex were "sons and daughters"

---

[3] F. Eggan, *Social Anthropology of North American Tribes*, University of Chicago Press, Chicago, Ill., 1937, p. 52.

[4] A. L. Kroeber, *op. cit.*, p. 9. F. Eggan, *op. cit.*, pp. 43-45.

and of the opposite sex, "nephews and nieces." All relatives at a distance of two generations were "grandparents" or "grandchildren."

One's attitude and behavior patterns towards relatives addressed by the same term, were similar in quality. However, as would be expected in view of the functioning household groupings, they varied greatly in intensity according to circumstances and to distance or relationship from the direct linear line. Qualified by this all important factor of degree, we find that "parents" took care of their "children;" they were respected, obeyed, and, in old age, were in turn taken care of by them. "Fathers' sisters" and "mothers' brothers" were affectionate and gave gifts to their "nephews and nieces." Between brothers and between sisters there existed as close a bond as between parents and children. They worked and played together and helped each other at all times, the older advising the younger. Although brother and sister were limited by a pattern of semi-avoidance, they helped one another and were greatly concerned with each other's welfare.[5]

In-laws helped and looked out for one another's interests. There was a marked difference, however, between those of different generations. Brothers- and sisters-in-law had complete liberties and joked roughly with one another. Children-in-law respected and obeyed parents-in-law of the same sex, and strictly avoided all direct social intercourse with those of the opposite sex.

Marriage could take place between all who did not have a common grandparent. When a young man desired to marry a particular girl, he mentioned his wish to his family. If his mother and sisters were pleased, one of them went to the girl's family and requested her hand. The decision rested less upon the girl herself than upon the members of her family, particularly her brother. If agreed upon, the ceremony soon occurred at a feast given by the family of the bride to the family of the groom. Here the inter-familial gift exchange took place which validated the new relationship, and was often accompanied by the supernatural blessing of an old medicine-man.[6] The wife's family sup-

[5] F. Eggan, *op. cit.*, pp. 49–58.
[6] A. L. Kroeber, *op. cit.*, p. 12. F. Eggan, *op. cit.*, pp. 58–60.

plied the couple with a tipi, and relatives on both sides saw that they were provided with sufficient goods to run a household.

If any of the relatives were dissatisfied with the proposed marriage, the young couple would very likely elope to another band or to the Southern Arapaho. Usually and soon afterwards, the two families would legitimatize the relationship by an exchange of gifts.

If the husband was a good provider and well-liked by his parents-in-law, they would probably give him another of their daughters as a second wife. When one of the parties in a marriage died, the relationship between the two families generally continued through the levirate or sororate.

Divorce, arising from incompatibility or the wife's infidelity, was frequent. Where infidelity was the cause, divorce was apt to occasion sadness among the kin. If the relatives could not by censure or advice adjust a difficulty arising from incompatibility, the separation would not greatly distress them.

IV

In addition to the kin and band organization, Arapaho society was further differentiated internally into age-graded associations or "societies." These groupings constituted a series covering the entire period from youth to old age. Each was composed of a group of men, of approximately the same age, who, as a body, mounted the rungs in the series.[7] Although there was one women's association, a woman's social position was determined more by her husband's society membership than by her own.

Testifying to the pervading character of social stratification along age-lines was the fact that even children were members of well defined age-groupings. From the time they left their mother's care to play in groups, they were "Blackbirds." At about ten, they became "Wild Rose Bushes," "thorny," given to fighting and teasing. At puberty when they began to prepare themselves for the activities of manhood, they became "Calves." Although these

[7] A. L. Kroeber, The Arapaho, *American Museum of Natural History, Bulletin 18,* 1904.

groupings were not formalized to the degree of the men's societies, boys were referred to by the name of their particular group, and excluded older or younger boys from their activities.

The system of men's societies and the approximate ages at which a man entered,[8] are as follows:

1. *Kit-Fox* 17
2. *Star* 21
3. *Tomahawk* 25
4. *Bi⁰tahenɛnɔ* 30
5. *Crazy* 35
6. *Dog* 45
7. *Hinañahenɛnɔ* 60
8. *Water-Sprinkling-
     Old-Men* 70

A men's society, or company, began when all the young men in the tribe of about seventeen years of age organized themselves as a Kit-Fox Society. Their principal task was to get five or six of the bravest and best-liked members of the Tomahawk as their "older brothers" who thenceforth controlled the activities of the younger group throughout life. An institutionalized attitude required these prospective "older brothers" to show reluctance, so that they had to be captured, though in good-natured spirit. After being chosen, the "older brothers" arbitrarily divided the company into two equal parts, the "Tall Men" and the "Short Men." These sub-groupings sat opposite each other during meetings and ceremonies and had no function other than competition in the various activities of the organization. When the group changed from one society to another, the "older brothers" redivided the members into these same sections.

The four societies, Tomahawk, Bi⁰tahenɛnɔ, Crazy and Dog, were essentially similar to one another in structure. They were differentiated from the two younger societies in that they were associated with particular "lodge-dance" ceremonies. To gain admittance to each of these societies, a company had to perform the "lodge-dance" ceremony connected with it. Each dancer had to choose an older man of the second group above his own to instruct him in the ritual and to prepare his regalia. The dancer and

---

[8] A. L. Kroeber, The Arapaho, *American Museum of Natural History, Bulletin 18*, 1904.

instructor were henceforth "grandfather" and "grandson" to each other. On the first evening of the lodge dances, the "older brothers" assembled the participating company and gave a fixed number of "honor degrees" to the bravest and most able. When degrees were given to an even number of men, they were divided equally between the "Tall Men" and the "Short Men." [9]

The structure of the two oldest societies, the Hinañahenɛnɔ and the Water-Sprinkling-Old-Men, differed considerably from that of the younger societies, in that the former were not organized on the basis of age alone. The possession of supernatural power was an added requirement, and participation therefore was restricted to a small number of old men. Their wives also had a form of membership; they played important rôles in the ceremonies, shared their husband's religious power, and were called "Hinanáseenɔ" and "Water-Sprinkling-Old-Women."

V

Warfare was one of the major activities in Arapaho life. Throughout the summer, and at other times of the year, Arapaho war parties went out to fight the Crow, the Shoshoni and the Ute, and the tribe was constantly aware of the necessity of defending itself against enemy raids.

The capture of enemy horses, the most valuable form of property, was the material incentive for participation. Warfare, however, was surrounded by institutional elaborations of status and prestige to so marked a degree that the material incentive often manifested itself only incidentally. Men acquired distinction within the framework of an intricate system of graded military deeds. These deeds were not ranked according to the criteria of effectiveness in defeating the enemy, or of stealing horses, but solely on the basis of bravery and of the degree of risk entailed. For example, merely to strike a living enemy gave far more prestige than to kill him. All men kept strict count of their deeds and formally enumerated them at gatherings. The age-societies competed against one another in special games that involved recounting their feats. Men who had performed out-

[9] *Ibid.*

standing exploits were sought after to give children names and to perform particular rites in tribal ceremonies.

Warfare was organized largely within the structure of the age-graded system. Whenever an individual wanted to go on a war party, he discussed it with his company. The "older brothers" would inquire after the plans of the other "companies" and would then advise the group whether to join with another company, to welcome other individuals in the party, or to go out secretly alone. When more than one company took part, each generally started out separately, joining at a short distance beyond camp. The ablest of the "older brothers" were usually the leaders of the party.

The inter-relationship between warfare and the age-graded system is manifested clearly in the lodge-dances of the Tomahawk, Biˈˈtahenenɔ, Crazy and Dog Societies. In ceremonies of the first three of these groups, the dancers carried clubs, bows, swords and lances as part of their insignia. Immediately after all four of the ceremonies, the dancers were obliged to set out on a war party, and those holding "honor degrees" had to strike the enemy with the weapons that were a part of their regalia.[10] If unsuccessful, they had to resume this attempt on following war parties.

The Kit-Fox and the Star were not enjoined to participate in warfare by such ceremonial obligation. Nevertheless, they were expected to do so more often than any of the other groups. The Crazy, and particularly the Dog Society scarcely went to war *en masse* except as a ritual necessity. The Tomahawk and Biˈˈtahenenɔ fought more frequently. The Kit-Fox and Star, however, were almost constantly setting off on the war path. Warfare was by far their chief interest. Throughout the winter months, when they were prevented from actively engaging, they competed with one another in the recitation of exploits. In the accumulation of war honors, they sometimes went to extremes not countenanced by the society at large. If a captive woman was to be sent home to her own people, she had to leave secretly at night for fear a Kit-Fox or Star man would overtake her and falsely claim her scalp as taken from an enemy.

[10] A. L. Kroeber, The Arapaho, *American Museum of Natural History, Bulletin 18,* 1904, p. 157.

VI

Arapaho religion was based on the belief in a vague, all-pervading, mysterious and divine force that exerted a controlling influence on human destiny. The welfare of both the individual and the tribe as a whole was dependent on it, and, in various religious practices, The Arapaho sought to acquire this supernatural power or blessing. These practices were of three kinds—those associated with the Sacred Pipe, the series of "bayaawu," or lodge-dance ceremonies, and the vision quest.

The Sacred Pipe was the object of extreme veneration. While belonging to the tribe as a whole, it was in the special custodianship of the Sacred Pipe Owner and his wife. They had received it from either his or her parents along with the instructions in its ritual, care, and the personal tabus which accompanied their rôle. By virtue of their position, they supervised the ceremony of "covering the pipe," in which individuals added gifts to the pipe bundle, bringing supernatural blessings on both themselves and the tribe.

The Sacred Pipe was essentially a symbol of the whole tribe, and served to keep intact the bonds of communal solidarity. The Arapaho themselves were cognizant of this. They said, "Without the pipe there would be no Arapaho," and "It is the pipe that holds us together." If the pipe were not properly cared for, the well-being of the tribe would suffer.

The practices orientated about the pipe clearly demonstrate its function in the social organization. The tipi of the Sacred Pipe Owner had a special place in the center of the camp circle. The pipe was always at the head of the line of march and the tribe or band had to halt when the pipe halted, starting again when the pipe started. When spring came, the other bands had to wait until the band with the pipe broke camp before they could follow suit.

The "bayaawu" or lodge-dance ceremonies were the sun dance, the dances of the various men's associations, and that of the single women's society. These were performed in the center of the camp circle, during the summer when the whole tribe was together. The ceremonies were all arranged for by individuals who had vowed to do so to enlist supernatural aid when they themselves, or a close relative, were in grave danger.

The sun dance, the most elaborate of all the ceremonies, was held nearly every summer. In contrast to the other lodge dances which were organized by the individual societies, the sun dance was a tribal ceremony par excellence; in its preparation and ritual all the companies took part or were represented.[11]

The more advanced the society in the series, the greater the supernatural power given by its dance to the participants. Thus an individual acquired more and more power as he grew older. If he joined the two oldest societies, the Hinanaheneno and particularly the Water-Sprinkling-Old-Men, he acquired the greatest degree of supernatural power in the tribe. Often accompanied by his wife, he prevented disease, cured the sick, made love medicine, gave divine support to the war parties and hunting expeditions, and foretold the future. Together with other old medicinemen, he supervised all the lodge-dance ceremonies.[12]

Membership in these two oldest societies conferred a marked degree of priestly status. In most of their religious activities, the old men acted as intermediaries with the supernatural on behalf of the tribe. They were asked to intercede with the divine power in all situations endangering the well-being of the group. Their power served the communal welfare, except when they used it for sorcery, of which they were capable. Following this misuse, the supernatural worked harm on both themselves and the tribe.

The vision quest had a more limited rôle among the Arapaho than among most Plains tribes. Few went on such a quest, and those who did usually went long after puberty. The religious power acquired in the quest, and in dreams, was latent until sanctioned in the more thoroughly organized spheres of religious practice. When a man received power in a vision, he kept it secret until he had arrived at about the age of Dog Society membership. Then he informed the Sacred Pipe Owner of his power and

11 A. L. Kroeber, The Arapaho, *American Museum of Natural History, Bulletin 18,* New York, 1902, pp. 279–308. G. Dorsey, The Arapaho Sun Dance. *Field Museum Publications, Volume IV,* 1903.

12 A. L. Kroeber, *op. cit.,* pp. 3–4.

of his desire to use it. If he tried to use it earlier, it would not be effective, and would be lost to the possessor forever. The Arapaho vision quest thus supplemented the society structure as a means of conferring supernatural power, and primarily served as a preparation for membership in the two oldest groups.

The extent to which religious beliefs and practices fitted in with the social organization is demonstrated by their function as mechanisms of social control. If a wife was beaten by her husband, or if an adulterer or murderer were afraid of being killed, refuge was immediately sought in the tipi of the Sacred Pipe Owner. They remained there briefly, and could not be harmed afterwards.

To settle a case of adultery, the guilty one sought out the "ceremonial grandfather" of the aggrieved party; gave him four horses to present to his injured grandson along with the pipe offering, which the latter was obliged to accept by divine command. A similar adjustment had to be made with the victim's family in case of murder. Here a strong religious sanction was involved over and above that obtaining in cases of adultery. The murderer had to go through a rite of purification before he could resume his rightful place in the community. An old medicine-man covered him thoroughly with white clay to remove the "sin" which enveloped him. In this state, he left the tribe to wander off alone until "game looked at him once more," that is, until he found himself in a position to effect a kill.

VII

Arapaho government was more complex than is general in societies of equally simple social differentiation. The conditions of Plains life subjected the Arapaho to quick changes in the availability of food supply, and to sudden and unexpected attacks from enemy raiding parties. To meet the precariousness imposed by these circumstances, they were faced with the necessity of planning the tribal movements and activities, and of enforcing the regulations to insure the execution of these plans. Moreover, the process of deciding and planning required a flexibility adequate to correlate the frequently diverging interests of the different bands and age-groupings, and merge them into the framework of communal interests.

To meet these demands, the tribal government operated as a function of the age-society organization and the institution of chieftainship, itself a function of the associational structure. The system of age-graded associations, including all men of the tribe, represented the entire community, and through it, the function of government acquired a simple democratic form. The institution of chieftainship on the other hand, provided centralized control and concentrated responsibility in the most adept hands.

All formalized leadership, except in the sphere of religion, was covered by various categories of chieftainship. Outstanding Kit-Fox and Star men were "little chiefs"; they had meagre authority but were expected to rise to higher ranks. The Tomahawk and Biꞌᵗahenɛnɔ who were chosen as "older brothers" became "brother chiefs," while others became "company chiefs." At the top of the chieftainship scale were four "tribal chiefs" who were formally and ceremonially inducted to their positions. When two of the four died, or, more frequently, retired with old age, the remaining chiefs chose the most capable men to replace them from among the Dog or perhaps the Crazy Society. There were also several "chiefs' helpers," likewise middle-aged, who had often as much effective prestige and voice in the tribal affairs as the tribal chiefs themselves.

When problems arose concerning the welfare or activities of the tribe, such as plans for the protection of the camp, the proper time to seek tipi poles, or choice of the winter location, the tribal chiefs first met privately for counsel among themselves. If they deemed the matter required little discussion, they called a general meeting of all the societies. One of them stated the problem and asked the assembled crowd for its opinion. A few of the lesser chiefs and older men spoke, and only then were the tribal chiefs asked to voice their opinions, which in most cases were but summations of what had been previously stated. General agreement was usually quickly arrived at, and the meeting was closed. If, however, the matter required more thorough consideration, or if there was considerable disagreement in the general meeting, the tribal chiefs asked the societies to discuss it in their separate groupings. In this case, the rule that "grandfathers" and "grandsons" should never disagree, prevented discussion by all the societies. The "grandfather societies" requested the "grandson societies" to make the decision, or vice-versa. If religious practices were primarily concerned, the two oldest societies decided the matter. The Tomahawk and Biʲ'taheneᴐ usually dealt with matters chiefly concerning warfare. In most cases, however, both the older and younger groups remained silent and left the decision to the Crazy and Dog Societies.[13]

Beyond the formulation of policy, the function of government included the enforcement of rules pertaining to a number of tribal activities, such as hunting, the line of march, the breaking and formation of the camp circle, and the maintenance of order within camp.

Although the tribal chiefs were ultimately concerned with these regulatory and disciplinary powers and duties, they themselves did not directly perform them, but gave over the responsibility for their execution to the "soldier-police" companies, the first four in the series, the Kit-Fox, Star, Tomahawk and Biʲ'taheneᴐ. The tribal chiefs shifted control from one to another of these groups at indefinite times, and in no definite order, and gave the "older brothers" of the acting police complete authority for carrying out the plans.

When they broke camp, the soldier-police saw that everybody packed and formed the line of march. They distributed themselves on all sides as guards, and allowed no one to straggle from the main body. Immediately behind the front detail of soldier-police, escorting the Sacred Pipe, rode the "older brothers" with the chiefs and the old medicine-men. At noon, the police gathered in front and prepared their own meal. Later in the day, if the tribe was in no hurry and had not marched far into the evening, a camp circle was formed. The line slowed down while the Sacred Pipe Owner went ahead to choose a place for the pipe bundle. When this was done, the police spread out in such fashion as to delineate the circle in relation to this fixed point. The

[13] See R. M. MacIver, *Society*. Discussion of "integrated" type of group agreement, pp. 241-243.

tribe then moved in and set up their tipis along the line formed by the mounted police.

In the control of the hunt, the soldier-police showed the greatest extent of their power. Availability of game was always considerably dependent on chance. When it was abundant and there was no longer need for storage, regulations were unnecessary, and individuals or small groups hunted as they saw fit. When game was scarce, however, or was required in large quantities, the latter procedure jeopardized the general welfare. Communal coöperation was needed to make the most of the available resources, and it was the duty of the soldier-police to organize such coöperation. Their first step was to forbid anyone to hunt alone for fear of scaring away the game. The tribal chiefs sent out a number of scouts in all directions who were gone often for several days at a time. As soon as a herd was reported, the tribe made off to overtake it. When about to give chase, all lined up as in a race. The police took positions at intervals along the line, and the "older brothers" supervised at each end. When everything was in order, and the line perfectly straight, they gave the signal to begin.

In winter, the men were forbidden to hunt or even to cross the "preserve," the area surrounded by the bands on two or three of its sides. At given intervals, the police rounded up a herd of the required size in a given spot so as not to disturb the other game, and one or more bands joined in a communal hunt.

The disciplinary powers of the police were practically unlimited. The general attitude was that the police could properly go to any extreme to enforce their rules and discipline offenders. If someone refused to move his camp, didn't pack up hurriedly enough, or otherwise proceeded without regard for the rules, the police shot the offender's dogs in warning. If the individual persisted in his behavior, the next move was to destroy his tipi and belongings or to kill his horses. If an individual were discovered hunting when it was forbidden to do so, the police took away his kill and destroyed his belongings. When on a communal hunt, a man tried to inch himself ahead of the line or start before the signal, the police took his bow and held his horse until the others had begun the chase. The police, themselves inconvenienced by their duties, were given meat by those who were most successful in the hunt. If an offender attacked the police, he was promptly shot. Whenever this occurred, the police had to dispose of his body. The dead man's kin stayed away for fear they might become enraged at the police, even if they voiced approval of their action.

The police powers, significantly, were less effective in regulating warfare than other activities. War parties were forbidden at certain times, as during preparations for ceremonies or the gathering of tipi poles. The Kit-Fox and Star Societies frequently attempted to set out secretly. If the police discovered their plans, they all received beatings. If they succeeded in sneaking away, nothing further was done. A successful raid on the enemy made the evasion all the more a lark. If they suffered defeat, no revenge party was formed. People said "they had only themselves to blame."

VIII

The qualities of personal behavior most prized by the Arapaho were bravery, good judgment, kindness and generosity. Fathers tried to imbue their sons with these qualities. From early manhood, they were judged by their possession of these virtues, and their status and prestige in the society varied with the degree to which they demonstrated them.

In Arapaho society, accumulation of property for the exclusive aim of personal possession beyond that required for sustenance, was relatively non-existent. With their simple material way of life, based on a few necessities, such as horses, weapons, food, clothing and shelter, and with the primitive state of their technology, there was little objective possibility for differentiation in their material condition. Some individuals might have more desirable houses, better tipis and more finely decorated clothing, but the range of variation did not go beyond this.

The primary stimulus for economic activity beyond supplying oneself with an adequate number of good horses and ample meats and hides, was the ambition to give it away, thus improving one's standing in the community. As long as there was some meat in the tribe, no one went hungry. If a man's horses were stolen by the enemy, he was soon reëquipped by his kin or by others who had an ample supply.

The possession of wealth, other than that it permitted one to gain a reputation for liberality, was thus not in itself a criterion for the ascription of prestige. The horse, however, under proper circumstances, might have allowed for social stratification on a property basis. Unlike other forms of property, it was the essential means of procuring a livelihood; was differentiated into relative values, and deteriorated slowly. Nevertheless, any development along this line was precluded by constant warfare. The frequency with which whole herds were won or lost, served to prevent property ownership from becoming permanently concentrated. The spoils of a successful raid, moreover, were equally divided among all participants, though those who acted most effectively received first choice.

It is, however, significant that the horse served as capital, bringing a return in interest. Good hunting horses were keenly valued and were often borrowed. In return for the use of a horse, the hunter was expected to give half the kill to the owner. This interest was hardly of a contractual kind, since it varied with the personal qualities of the lender and borrower. If the owner had less need of the meat than did the hunter, he did not accept his share. If a boy borrowed the horse to kill for sport, the owner took all the catch. But old, sick or crippled men, widows and semi-berdaches, who possessed good horses but who could not hunt, often gained their livelihood in this way.

The sexual mores of the Arapaho involved separate standards of conduct for the two sexes. Whereas men had complete freedom of behavior, women were bound to chastity and fidelity, and generally lost prestige whenever they infringed upon these ideals. When confined to the unmarried, the mores worked out rather harmoniously. The girls were strictly chaperoned by their mothers, wore chastity belts at night, and were conditioned to shy away from males. Young men in turn engaged in devious though acceptable methods of courting, and kept their successes more or less secret so as not to harm the girl's reputation.[14]

---

[14] Much of Arapaho humor, told only among the men and often for the purpose of genial ribbing, revolved about the unusual and unexpected in the

Among the married, however, the sexual code resulted in more conflict than any other phase of life, because men often turned their attention to the wives of others with frequently disastrous results. A contributory element and aggravation of the situation was the fact that highly respected old men often married young women.

Thus nearly all cases of murder were the result of fights between husbands and paramours. The society tried to prevent such occurrences by virtue of the institutionalized practice of the pipe offering with the payment of four horses, and by greatly respecting a betrayed husband if he showed no desire for revenge, took the whole matter stoically and gave away the horses that he had received in payment. Following a peaceful settlement of adultery a marriage seldom lasted because it was understood that the husband would be tempted to beat his wife. After he smoked the pipe, he usually told her to leave. She packed up her belongings and, if agreed, went to live as the wife of her extra-marital partner, or if not, with one of her relatives.

IX

The principal means of attaining high status in Arapaho society was through outstanding activity in warfare, government and religion. In warfare, every man was rated according to his bravery, and those who showed themselves to be outstanding were praised on all sides. To be selected for chieftainship, one had to show, above all, good judgment and generosity. Bravery too was important, but was not as necessary as these other qualities. There were men with outstanding military reputations who never became chiefs. To have an important place in religion, the necessary personal qualities, besides the possession of supernatural power, were less conventionalized, though one generally had to have led a successful life.

It is of fundamental significance that in the tribal life of the Arapaho the individual engaged in these various activities at

---

love quest. It frequently relates to sodomy, in non-human form, and masturbation, in which young men seem to have engaged rather often, in a spirit of good-natured sport.

different times in his life. A young man, as a member of the Kit-Fox and Star Societies, was primarily concerned in the accumulation of war honors, his only sphere of distinction. As he grew older, he aspired to chieftainship, and whether he was successful or not, gained more and more voice in the tribal government. Finally, when old enough, he could become a medicine-man. Thus, although status in the tribe was of the achieved rather than of the ascribed variety, the individual's sphere of achievement was limited at all points of his life. He had always to demonstrate his abilities in the particular activities expected of his age-group.

This differentiation or rôle among the members of the various age-groups functioned above all as a force making for greater harmony and cohesiveness in the society at large. Since men of the different age-levels participated in different complexes of activities, they were less apt to compete with one another. All competition took place between men of about the same age-levels who pursued the same activities. The Kit-Fox and Star, the Tomahawk and Bi¹'taheneno, etc., and the sub-groupings within the companies, the "Tall Men" and the "Short Men," competed with one another in both the more serious and the convivial undertakings. In this society where intense pursuit of glory and distinction might have led to a condition of thorough-going and uncontrollable rivalry, the age-society structure cast it into a formalized mold which directed it along conventional and socially desirable lines.[15]

The more the individual advanced in age, the more differentiated was his social rôle from that of his age-mates. As a young man, he participated in warfare with all his society companions, and outstanding achievement on his part was given little formal recognition. In mounting the age-society scale, chieftainship and governmental function allowed further differentiation of the individual rôle both in behavior and in formal standing. Finally, among the old men, there was the broad distinction between the intelligentsia, who belonged to the two highest societies and those who did not. Hence, the age-society organization served as a sieve, a kind of selecting process in which individualization was in large part a function of age advancement.

[15] Compare with the Crow. R. H. Lowie, *The Crow Indians*, Farrar and Rinehart, New York, N.Y., 1935.

Testifying to the manner in which the society intensively fostered the desire of high status, and at the same time rigidly directed behavior along socially desirable lines, is the fact that men with high standing were required to demonstrate great modesty and reserve in all except the conventionalized pattern of reciting their record of military prowess. When men were to be selected as "older brothers," they were required to show reluctance. In the tribal meetings, the chiefs never offered their own opinions first but waited to be asked. This ideal of the modest personality which, though possessing great prestige and high status, showed no marked dominance in his personal relations with others, is possibly correlated with the Arapaho ideal of manly beauty, in which a greater than average height was as little desirable as was smallness in stature.

*   *   *   *   *

Before contact with White civilization, Arapaho life can be said to have followed a fairly harmonious course. The society had achieved a fairly high degree of balance and stability both in its adjustment to external conditions, and in its inner organization. It effectively met the precariousness contingent upon its very mode of existence with a highly developed form of communal responsibility. Within its limits the society gave opportunity for the full and satisfactory organization of individual lives. Its members generally identified themselves with the expectations made of them, and offered little opposition to the existing rules and institutions.

PART TWO

I

From the 1830's onward, the Arapaho, on the southern limits of their wanderings, met with Mexicans and occasional American explorers. No disruption arose from this first contact; the Mexicans were few in number, and were able to supply knives and various other utensils that were welcome to the Indians.

Until the 1850's there was neither frequent nor prolonged contact with the Whites, nor any great change in the Arapaho way of life. However, great numbers of Whites were beginning to move west over the routes that became known as the Overland and Oregon Trails, and military posts were established to protect the immigrant caravans from desultory Indian raids. In 1851, all the tribes of the western plains were called together at Fort Laramie to sign a treaty with the government to prevent such disturbances. The various tribes were given rights over demarcated territory, the Northern Arapaho within the confines of their traditional hunting grounds, and were pledged not to molest the Whites. The latter, in turn, were to keep to their fixed trails and not venture into Indian territory. Following the agreement, the government was to distribute annuity goods to the tribes from the military posts in the region.

This treaty was a complete failure. In the years that followed, the situation of the Indians and their relations with the Whites grew worse and worse. The influx of new immigration drove the buffalo from their usual feeding grounds and the herds became smaller and harder to find every year. The 1860's were years of calamity. Gold was discovered north of the area and soon long wagon trains branched off from the east-west routes and followed the Bozeman Trail, which ran through the center of the Indian territory.[16] The Cheyenne, Dakota and probably some Arapaho, enraged at this final threat to their well-being, attacked the Whites. To protect the trails, the government sent a number of military expeditions into the area to build forts and drive off the tribes. A number of bloody battles followed.

During this period an outstanding figure among the Arapaho was one "Friday." His life has since become surrounded by fiction so that it is no longer easy to ascertain the facts. It seems certain, however, that about 1840, an investigator of a fur company came upon an Arapaho boy who had become separated from his tribe. He named the boy "Friday" and sent him to his home in St. Louis. After remaining among the Whites for several years, Friday wandered west and rejoined his own people.[17] During this period of great stress he had a decisive influence on the tribe and repre-

---

[16] *Report of the Commission of Indian Affairs,* 1863, p. 259.
[17] L. R. Hafen, and W. J. Ghent, *Broken Hand,* Old West Publishing Company, Denver, Colorado, 1931.

sented them in all their dealings with the Whites. He continually counseled his people not to join the other tribes, pleading that they were powerless against the unlimited resources of the invaders. Conflict arose within the tribe between those who agreed with Friday and those who wished to fight with the Cheyenne and Dakota. In certain cases, the tribe split, some of the bands under Friday's influence going off by themselves.

Throughout these years, the Arapaho, wretched and confused, wandered from one hunting ground to another and gathered at the military posts to get their rations. Racked by smallpox and other diseases, long periods of starvation, and the whiskey sold to them by the low order of frontiersman who settled in the region, they were fast becoming demoralized.[18] Men gave the use of their female kin in trade for whiskey. The chiefs were often unheeded and the governmental authority weakened. After a number of drunken brawls, the soldier-police forbade drinking and severely punished offenders, but this rule could not be enforced and had to be lifted.

In 1868, they were offered a place with the Southern Arapaho in the Indian territory to the south.[19] They refused the offer and instead loosely attached themselves to an agency in Montana.[20] They wandered off every year along the Big Horn Mountains to the foot-hills of the Rockies, where game was still to be found. Here they attacked and stole horses from the Wind River Shoshoni, who already lived on their reservation, and clashed with the Whites who had come to mine gold to the south. A joint expedition of Shoshoni and United States troops punished them severely.

The government thereupon offered to settle them on a portion of the Wind River Reservation alongside the Shoshoni, who had been living there for several years. Harried and worn, and with buffalo hardly to be found, they relinquished all hope of ever continuing their old life. They listened to the Whites tell of the many advantages which settled agricultural life would bring them, and realized they had no choice but to accept.

In 1877, the Northern Arapaho, reduced to 938 individuals,

---

18 *Report of the Commission of Indian Affairs,* 1862, p. 131.
19 *Ibid.,* 1869, p. 35.
20 *Ibid.,* 1873, p. 6.

of whom there were only 198 men, possessing 2,000 horses, moved in on the southeastern portion of the reservation. The agent reported, "They are in such indigent circumstances as to be wholly unable, without generous assistance from the government, to speedily emerge from their present state of mendicity." [21]

The entry of the Indians on the reservation completely changed the attitude of the government. While roaming the country in search of game and enemy horses, they were a constant threat to the Whites. Now that they were under direct supervision, and the Whites could follow their activities undisturbed, there was scarcely an "Indian Problem" any longer. It was held that the reservation system would not only benefit the Whites but the Indians as well. It would serve to raise them from their state of savagery to civilization. This process was viewed as a simple one; under the tutelage of the government, and with the instruction of the Church, the Indians would be civilized in a few years. That is to say, each family would have their prosperous farm on which they would raise their grain and vegetables, live in a house, learn English, go to church, and send their children to school. In short, they would become farmers, no whit different from Whites.

II

The Wind River Reservation lies in the heart of an attractive and rich country to the east of the Continental Divide in western Wyoming. The Whites of this region depend on cattle and sheep as the basis of their economy. In more recent years, large-scale irrigation projects have been started in certain sections, and farming has been carried on, but it has proved profitable only as an adjunct to the livestock industry.[22]

The social milieu conforms to the general pattern of western "cow country." There are large ranches, often far apart. The population is sparse, and composed largely of men who set a tone of culture proportionate to their numerical predominance and to the fact that the occupational and social conditions are of a pronounced masculine character. Extreme looseness of social bonds

[21] *Ibid.*, 1878, pp. 148, 154.
[22] *United States Soil Conservation Service, Wind River Report,* A-1, p. 1.

and great mobility are especially marked among the relatively large employed element. In comparison with older and more populous regions, the social restraints are less rigid and permit more spontaneity in individual behavior.

Lander and Riverton, commercial centers for the surrounding country, each having a population of about 2,000, are from ten to twenty miles from the Arapaho settlements. On their main streets are various stores, saloons, gambling establishments and movie houses. A railway line runs 150 miles to Caspar, a town of 15,000 population, the urban center of the region.

The reservation itself lies in the most favorable spot in the area. Its western part, high in the mountains, is the source of several streams which flow down and across the reservation. The most important of these, the Big Wind and the Little Wind Rivers, divide the reservation into several sections. The Big Wind River separates the southern part of the reservation, comprised of 831,-400 acres, from the "ceded portion" on the north, an area of almost 1,500,000 acres which has scarcely been of use to the Indians.[23] The Little Wind River, south of this, crosses the reservation proper. On its northern side, the land is not irrigated and scarcely inhabited. The Indian population is concentrated on the land to the south of this river.

Three socially distinct groups live here. The Shoshoni inhabit the western half, bordering the mountains, the Arapaho the southeastern part, and, interspersed among these two groups, are a number of White settlers who have purchased or leased Indian allotments.

A period of sixty years of living together has done little to break down the differences between the Arapaho and Shoshoni. The social division between them is as clear cut as is their geographical division. Although reservation life interrupted active hostility, the passive detachment and lack of friendliness between them contrast with the warm feelings both groups extend to Indians from other tribes. Their old fighting days are still remembered, and the Shoshoni still regard their neighbors as interlopers, without proper right to their share of the reservation. The separation extends to all phases of life. There have been only four inter-

<hr/>

[23] *Ibid.*

marriages between them. They belong to different churches, attend different schools, trade at different stores, and sit in separate groups whenever they are together; and the agency must rigidly maintain impartiality toward them in all dealings.[24]

Fort Washakie, the agency headquarters, lies in the center of the inhabited portion of the reservation, and is the focal point for the Shoshoni who live to the west and in its immediate surroundings, and for the Arapaho, whose habitations begin several miles to the east and follow the course of the Little Wind River to the limit of the reservation, about sixteen miles away. At each end of this area are the centers of Arapaho communal life. Ethete, to the west, is the location of the Episcopal mission, St. Michael's. At the eastern end is St. Stephen's, the Jesuit mission, and the settlement of Arapahoe. At each center there is a general store, and a dance hall which serves for all larger gatherings. The Arapaho live scattered along several roads leading to the agency, or clustered in the neighborhood of the missions, which at first glance resemble large manorial houses in the midst of an impoverished peasantry.

The Arapaho population has continued relatively stable since settling on the reservation. In 1895, there were 837; fifty-nine years later, in 1935, they had increased to 1,126. In contrast to the Shoshoni, who are equal in number, and who continually mix with Whites, the Arapaho have remained surprisingly pure. There are 852, or 74 per cent, who are still full-blooded.[25]

III

Although agriculture was far from the most feasible economy for the Arapaho, the government never questioned its policy of making the Indians farmers. With their background of nomadic hunting, the Arapaho undoubtedly could more easily have taken over livestock, ideally suited to the resources of the region. This

[24] *Ibid.*, p. 34. It must be stressed that the separation between the two groups is not primarily associated with hostility, but with the profound feeling that they constitute distinct social unities having little or no communality of interest. Intermarriage, involving familial relations with members of the other group, may perhaps serve as an example. It evokes no particular disapproval; it is merely regarded as unusual.

[25] *United States Soil Conservation Service, Wind River Report*, A-1 p. 1.

course, however, was never considered for a number of reasons; it was held that the Indians could be kept under control only if they stopped roaming about and settled; an agricultural economy, moreover, conformed to the traditional White picture of civilized life; then too, the surrounding Whites could exploit the rich grazing lands on the reservation.

That this policy should prove a failure throughout was to be expected; to learn to till the soil, to build houses, use wagons for transport, learn the use of money and principles of commerce, and to acquire a new language with nothing in the old pattern to serve as a basis upon which to build this new way of life—a more drastic cultural transformation would be hard to envisage. In hunting and war, the Arapaho were accustomed to constant mobility, coöperative endeavor and quick changes in speed of activity. Their prestige values centered about warfare and the giving away of goods. To live in permanent closed dwellings, to engage individually in the steady and plodding routine of farming on land from which one permanently secured a livelihood, and to invest in labor with the expectation that at some future time one would be repaid with products that represented a new and unappreciated form of value, was completely discordant with their ingrained attitudes and habitual patterns of behavior.

Despite all this the Arapaho might have made a better adjustment to agriculture had circumstances been more favorable. But in this region, agriculture presents such inherent difficulties, that even Whites have been unable to develop a suitable existence from it. To begin with, the land had to be irrigated, which required a specialized knowledge over and above that necessary for plowing and reaping. Moreover, large stretches of land were unsuited for crops even if properly irrigated.[26] The growing season was very short, and, as though this were not enough, farm crops did not pay because of a lack of markets.

After their first laborious and infinitely wearisome effort at farming, the Arapaho were baffled and discouraged. Desultory attempts at agriculture continued, however, under the tutelage of government farmers who often themselves knew nothing of irrigation, much less understood the particular problem of teaching

[26] *Ibid.*, p. 4.

the Indians. The tribe continued to eke out its existence largely on the rations which the government supplied; often through fear the famished Indians would kill the Whites' cattle that roamed about.[27] In times of starvation, they were forced to eat the seed that the government allotted for planting.

By 1907, after an extensive irrigation system was completed, the government instituted the allotment system, by which each Arapaho was given a parcel of land on which to settle and make his living. Besides the fact that much of this land was unsuitable for agriculture, the heirship complications that followed this system led to even further barriers to farming. On the death of the owner, each heir was given, not a designated section of land, but a fractional share. Today, an allotment may be owned by from one to eighty heirs, while an individual may hold shares in as many as thirty separate parcels of land inherited from various members of his family. Almost 60 per cent of the Arapaho have no portion of land in their possession which they can suitably farm.[28]

Beset with so many difficulties, agriculture has never succeeded in awakening a strong interest in the tribe or in acquiring a firm set of social values. In most cases, it has simply led to discouragement and despair. After sixty years of effort, an agricultural economy has been established only to a limited degree. Some have sold or leased their land to Whites. Of what remains, much is in wild pasture and lies practically idle. Moreover, the farming that is done is of poor quality; the Arapaho return per acre is appreciably less than that of the Whites.[29]

In their farming practice, the Arapaho have instituted a system of "return help." In reaping and threshing, a group of neighbors join together for the work, start on one farm and go on to others until it is all completed. The same order of mutual help, though not so well organized, prevails in other types of activity. Those who assist others are not paid but are sure of help in return.

Although it was never intended as a basic part of their economy, the Arapaho have had a number of experiences with stock-raising. Soon after entering the reservation, they received a herd of stock

27 *Report of Commissioner of Indian Affairs*, 1885, p. 209.
28 *U.S. Soil Conservation Service, Wind River Report*, C-1.
29 *Ibid., Report* A-1, p. 5.

cattle from the government, probably as a result of a treaty provision.[30] As no attempt was made to explain the purpose of the animals or to guide them in their care, the Arapaho simply took them to be an annuity issue which would be repeated every year. They left them unbranded and the cattle were soon eaten by the Arapaho or gobbled up by White cattlemen. Thus ended the first attempt to introduce livestock.[31]

In 1913 the government purchased 2,000 head of cattle from the tribal funds of the Arapaho and Shoshoni, to be managed as a joint tribal herd. The intention was not to develop a livestock industry, but to furnish a market for the Indian hay, previously supplied by the military units until then stationed at Fort Washakie. The herd became immediately popular with the Indians. They sold their hay to the government, a number of individuals were given employment, the aged and the indigent got ration issues of beef, and, through legal or illegal channels, the tribes as a whole depended on the herd for their meat supply. Until 1920 the herd payed for itself through annual sales. With low cattle prices, the herd was no longer a purely financial asset, and in 1927 the government disposed of it to the great displeasure of the Indians.[32]

A plan then arose by which individual Indians could borrow money from the tribal funds to purchase stock. A number of men began to buy cattle and sheep for the first time. The stock increased and soon supplied both meat and cash. The animals were kept on individual farms, and since the fences were in poor condition, they had much trouble in keeping strange herds, including those of the Whites, off their land. Thus, the more livestock was profitable and was taken up by the Indians, the more it resulted in confusion and dispute.

Finally in 1931, stimulated by the government, the Arapaho and Shoshoni stock owners jointly formed Cattle and Sheep Associations for the coöperative management of the individual herds. Under the control of an elected Board of Directors, the cattle and sheep were taken off the farms for most of the year and driven

[30] *Report of Commissioner of Indian Affairs,* 1880, p. 298; 1884, p. 182.
[31] *Ibid.*
[32] *U.S. Soil Conservation Service, Report,* C-2.

to good grazing lands on distant parts of the reservation. The costs involved were pooled and pro-rated to the individual members according to their number of head.

Although membership is not very large, thirty-one Arapaho belonging to the Cattle Association and thirty-two to the Sheep Association, they are fairly sure to grow and be successful. These organizations enable the small owner to operate under conditions which allow the largest profit on his investment. They afford rational management of the stock, the purchase of pure bulls and rams for breeding purposes, and collective marketing. Previously, the lone Arapaho sold to any buyer who chanced to come to the reservation, and often ignorant of market values, was badly victimized. The associations, however, sort the herds properly and sell by closed bid or by auction. This has resulted in an appreciably higher gain than would otherwise be the case.[33] Aside from the material advantages, moreover, the Arapaho like the irregular and collective activity of gelding, shearing and sorting. They have shown themselves so proficient in this work that it stands alone as a form of labor offered them by individual White employers.[34]

In addition to agriculture and livestock, the chief occupation is in government employment on various building and improvement projects. This constitutes, for all practical purposes, the only opportunity for wage work.

In the early years of the reservation, the only occupation that the Arapaho did not find distasteful was the long periodic freight haul from the railroad, then 150 miles away.[35] Under government supervision, there has always been work on the irrigation projects, building and repairing roads, etc., which gave employment to varying numbers of Arapaho. More recently, there has been a tremendous increase of work on government projects. As many as 90 per cent of the able-bodied men and a considerable number of women have worked on these projects at one time or another.[36] From the beginning, the Arapaho have found this type of work relatively agreeable and whenever they have the opportunity, they

33 *U.S. Soil Conservation Service, Report*, C-2.
34 *Ibid., Report*, C-1.
35 *Ibid., Report*, A-1, p. 5.
36 *Ibid.*

abandon agriculture for it. They like the payment of a fixed amount of money for a fixed amount of work, obtainable directly upon completion of this work. It gives them a greater sense of security and purpose, and requires less reflection and planning than does agriculture. Moreover, they prefer group work to the relative isolation of most agricultural activity.

The marked increase of such work in recent years has noticeably affected Arapaho life. Since they have a greater cash income they can now purchase more artifacts of White culture. The men have acquired a knowledge of machinery and tools.[37] This creates a further break with agriculture, as they tend to lose all feeling for the land and learn none of the traditional skills necessary for putting it to use.

IV

In its material aspect, reservation life shows an extreme diversity, accounted for by a heterogeneous pattern of values derived from an elaboration of their older norms to fit the new conditions of life. That they have never bodily accepted the standards of American civilization is apparent throughout. Whatever they have taken over has either conformed to their aboriginal set of values, or its function has been appreciably transformed.

The reservation is almost completely bereft of public utilities. The roads are so poor as to be frequently impassable. Electricity and illuminating gas are non-existent. Since wells, to be useful, would have to be dug to a depth of from 100 to 200 feet, and since there is no system of supply other than irrigation ditches, the Indians can obtain water only from these ditches, or can haul it from the Little Wind River.

Pride in one's own dwelling, common among Whites, is absent largely except among some younger married couples. In the old days, the tipi provided little more than shelter and a place to sleep. The conception that the abode serves the bare essentials of usage still remains. Most families live in small one-room log houses with single windows and dirt floors without seeming to notice the general uncleanliness and disorder. In the summer they are over-run by flies, though screening could be cheaply and easily obtained. A

[37] *Ibid., Report* C-1.

small "A" tent stands near the house and is often preferred to the log house, especially by the older people. Many families, in fact, have no houses and live permanently in such tents. There is a brush shelter in which the family and friends sit and talk. Close by are often a number of farming tools, a wagon, a discarded auto and a pile of trash. An outhouse may be a short way off. The essential furnishings are one or two cast-iron stoves, shifted during the seasons between the house, tent or outdoors, and several beds on which a number of individuals sleep closely huddled together; others may sleep around the sides of the tent. A number of other objects, purchased second-hand, such as chests, boxes, chairs, blankets, cooking utensils and old sewing-machines, complete the picture.

Despite the fact that there is no longer a material need for their old pattern of mobility, the Arapaho have retained it to a surprising degree. A number of Arapaho are always on visits. They will spend the winter with the Southern Arapaho in Oklahoma, or less often, will visit the Crow or Cheyenne in Montana. In turn, they are visited by members of these tribes.

On the reservation itself, the Arapaho are not bound to their homes in the manner of the Whites. Their strongest tie is to their half of the reservation rather than to their particular property. They visit back and forth, for the duration of a meal or for intervals of weeks or months. It is common practice for one family to stay with relatives until the food is gone, whereupon the hosts will move to another household and eat there. When they do not visit family or friends, men spend hours sitting around the mission stations.

The greatest movement of the population occurs during the seasonal shifts between summer and winter. In winter, the irrigation water is turned off and the roads are often impassable. Many families leave their houses, take their livestock and pitch tents close to the Little Wind River near Ethete or Arapahoe, where wood, water and supplies are available, and the grouping of households afford close conviviality, suggestive of the winter camp of bygone days.

The pattern of mobility, traditionally based on the horse, has made the Arapaho take over the automobile more enthusiastically than any other White trait. As soon as he is able, an Arapaho will buy an automobile, generally second-hand, and often at a poor bargain. In many households, any money above the bare essential goes toward the payment, repair or fuel of the car.[38] The automobile has given the Arapaho his most thorough sense of value and prestige since warfare and the buffalo hunt. Visits and movements both on and away from the reservation have been greatly facilitated. This correspondingly has changed their recreation and buying habits. The rôle of the trader and the mission store has diminished appreciably and the frequent visits to town have given the Arapaho a greater familiarity with White ways.

Besides the automobile, the most prized White manufacture is the non-electric washing-machine. Because it serves a specific and utilitarian purpose, that is, it obviates the use of river and irrigation ditches for washing purposes, it more readily fits into their scheme of life than would other appliances, seemingly less dispensable, whose function would tend to alter more general phases of their existence. Moreover, the Arapaho are more conscious of cleanliness in their personal dress than they are in their households.

White styles in clothing and personal adornment have generally been adopted. The men have taken over the attire of cowhands, and wear overall trousers, colored shirts, riding boots and broad-brimmed hats. Women wear cheap calico dresses (for modesty's sake several sizes too large), shawls, and never hats. The old people continue to wear braids and moccasins. The old men pluck their eyebrows, and around the house often wear leggings of cloth, cut in the pattern of the old hide leggings.

Aboriginal food habits have scarcely changed. Boiled meat is still the staple and favorite food, and is eaten along with fried bread at almost every meal. One frequently sees meat hanging in the sun to dry, after which it lies on the ground for days. Young dogs are still eaten as delicacies. Coffee, rice, and dried prunes are liked, and fresh fruits and vegetables are slowly coming to be eaten. Food is served on light tin plates, and is usually managed with help of pocket knife and fork.

Except for the making of pipes, which is still carried on by one

[38] *U.S. Soil Conservation Service, Report*, C-1.

or two old men, all forms of men's handiwork have long since passed away. A number of old techniques practised by women, however, remain. When wild berries are ripe, women and old men drive out to gather them in an automobile or wagon. The old women then prepare them in the traditional manner, pounding with mortar and pestle and adding them to soup. Leather- and bead-work are still practised along the old forms. Since few hides are obtainable, such work does not attain its desired extent, though every procurable skin is used. The women also make cradle-boards in which they carry their babies strapped to their backs.

The Arapaho consistently suffer from ill health, a result in large part of inadequate housing and an unbalanced diet, and because they are congenitally less resistant to certain diseases than Whites. The death-rate of children is extremely high, and is largely due to bronchial pneumonia and intestinal disorders.[39] Tuberculosis takes an abnormally high toll among the young men and women. Trachoma is fairly widespread in all age groups. Were it not for the high birth-rate, the population would surely decrease.

V

In view of the fundamental changes in the conditions of Arapaho life, the extent to which the traditional social forms have continued to function is striking. The fact, however, that the Arapaho have continued to be a distinct and cohesive ethnic group accounts for what has been, under the circumstances, a minimum of social exchange. Living in face-to-face relations, on a confined area surrounded by Whites and dominated by their authority, the tribal community has remained as coherent and well-knit as in the days when it formed a camp circle and moved in a single line of march. Within the unity of the larger community, however, the modification and decay of group interests have necessarily involved considerable reshifting and conversion of the aboriginal forms.

The kinship organization has changed little. The primary household group of husband, wife and children is as suited to the new life as it was to the old. Only monogamy exists today as

[39] U.S. Soil Conservation Service, Report, C-1.

plural marriages were forbidden by the Whites, though undoubtedly they would have disappeared under the new social conditions. Although at variance with White standards and with the occupational and ownership norms associated with agricultural life, the extended family continues to represent almost as much of a collectivity under present conditions as it did in the past. Married couples either live with their parents or alongside them. The feelings of solidarity and the behavior patterns between kin have hardly weakened.

More marriages occur today by semi-elopement than in the past. The two families frequently come together at a feast, but fewer gifts are exchanged than formerly. A clergyman usually performs the Christian service, often after the couple has lived together, during which time they are considered married by the group. Following the ban on plural marriages, the practices of levirate and sororate became impracticable.

In contrast to the kinship forms, the age-societies have passed out of existence as organized bodies. Since warfare, policing and traditional chieftainship disappeared, and nothing of an associational character came to replace them, the societies were left with no function in reservation life. Few lodge dances have been held beyond the early years. Several years ago after a long interval, a number of young men put on the tomahawk dance, but it had little of the old meaning.

The band structure, on the other hand, went through a marked transformation and survived in the form of neighborhood groupings. When they entered the reservation, the "Quick Tempered" band settled on the western and the "Antelope" on the eastern portion of the area. The smaller bands diffused. Today the two groups constitute the neighborhood groupings of Ethete and Arapaho but are scarcely cognizant of their former band membership. By virtue of the bonds resulting from territorial adjacency, each has its own gathering place, social activities, and its share of representation in all tribal undertakings.

Of all religious phenomena, the attitudes and practices associated with the Sacred Pipe and sun dance have remained most intact. These had a distinct tribal character, and serve, now as then, as symbols of the communal solidarity. The pipe is still "covered," and when in recent years the custodian was suspected of not giving it the proper care, he was held responsible for the unhappy condition of the people. The sun dance is the one great festivity of their life. The tribe camps on the surrounding grounds and engages in quiet merrymaking for the duration of the ceremony.

The disintegration of the age-graded society system has removed the institutionalized framework for the ascription of religious status. Only the old men, who have passed through the first three or four lodge dances in their youth, have marked supernatural power. The death of all remaining "naṅahenɛnɔ" and Water-Sprinkling-Old-Men prevented their joining the two oldest societies. Most of the old men nevertheless have assumed the rôle traditionally conferred on members of these higher bodies. They supervise the sun dance, take part in the sweat-lodge ceremonies, narrate the mythology and sacred lore, concern themselves with the care and ritual of the pipe, and practise curing.

The disappearance of the society lodge dance has confined the younger men to a meagre rôle in the traditional ceremonial life. This has facilitated in the spread of the peyote cult, introduced to the reservation about twenty-five years ago. In contrast to the ghost dance, which never gained a firm place, the "Peyote Brotherhood" has steadily grown and now includes a large number of young and especially middle-aged men. It is a religion of "good thoughts" and mutual help, and has taken over a number of Christian symbols and beliefs. Sessions are held on Saturday nights and, accompanied by drums and the singing of prayers, the participants eat the peyote buttons to induce visions. The ritual ends the next morning with a ceremonial feast prepared by the women. Shoshoni and Arapaho often take part in each other's sessions, and this more than any other feature of reservation life serves as a bond between members of the two groups. A decided break has occurred between the peyote members and the old medicine-men. The latter, having a vested interest in the traditional religious forms, and deriving material gain from their treatment of disease, are antagonistic to the peyote cult, and cast aspersion on the medicinal value of the peyote which, apart from the regular ceremony, is widely eaten as a curing device.

The old medicine-men still have a considerable curing practice, despite the fact that the reservation offers excellent medical facilities free of charge. The general atmosphere of the hospital, the White doctor, and the intricate devices such as operations, administration of ether, etc., tend to inspire fear. Because of this, and the fact that the hospital does not serve enough meat and bread, the Arapaho feel more comfortable when treated by the medicine-man, though his fee is often very high. The Arapaho have no fixed belief in the superiority of the one treatment over the other, and are apt to try either or both, although if the illness is indeterminable or lingering, they are more likely to call in the medicine-man.

VI

The missions are responsible for the Christianity and the formal education of the Arapaho. During the first years a single missionary worked primarily with the Shoshoni, giving little attention to the Arapaho. At the end of the eighties, the Jesuits built St. Stephen's, a large and well-equipped mission at the eastern end of the reservation. This was the first real contact the Arapaho had with White religion. Several years later the Episcopal Church established a mission, now St. Michael's, at Ethete.

Under the influence of the missions, the entire tribe was quickly proselytized, as though they regarded the process as a necessary part of the new order. Moreover, the Arapaho seemed to take to the missions more easily than to any other phase of White culture. The latter were clearly not responsible for their material distress, and spoke to them in terms of instruction and of moral and spiritual precepts, a sphere in which the Arapaho felt at home. The generosity of the missions as demonstrated in gifts of food and clothing, subsidies and loans,[40] corresponded with the Arapaho conception of kindness and consideration, aside from being actually profitable. The women, offered their first opportunity to participate in a realm of religious life equally with the men, took advantage of this new outlet.

The Catholics have continued to enjoy much greater success than the Episcopalians, and the great majority of the Arapaho are Catholics. This can be attributed only in part to the fact that the

[40] *U.S. Soil Conservation Service, Report,* C-1.

Jesuits were there first. Their ritual and ceremony offered the emotional experience which the Indians felt to be the essence of religion, and the sacred pictures and crucifixes accorded with their conception of sacredness embodied in material objects. The Arapaho could not help believing that the Catholics were in closer rapport with the supernatural than were the Protestants, who merely stressed Christian belief and conviction.

The special qualities of the priest, moreover, as contrasted with those of the Protestant minister, were doubly persuasive. The pastor's life and deportment were less different from those of other White men, and the pastors who came to the reservation varied in their policies and in their behavior, further confusing the Indian. As a result, St. Michael's has only a small number of devotees, composed in large part of the least active of those living in the vicinity, who are tempted by the hand-outs and special privileges offered by the mission. St. Stephen's, on the other hand, with communicants all over the reservation, has erected several smaller churches for services in various neighborhoods. The new Episcopal minister has understood the situation clearly. To increase the influence of his establishment, he has added more ritual, instituted the confession, is seen in clerical garb, and has himself addressed as "Father."

Most of the children attend school at St. Stephen's, although a number of Catholic parents sent their children to St. Michael's. Buses take them from their homes on Monday mornings and return them to their families on Friday. The children thus divide their time between two diverse worlds. While at school, they are fed and clothed free of charge, considerably lessening the burden of support for the families.

Their education consists of a simplified public school curriculum together with moral and religious teachings. The older children receive training in handicrafts of various kinds, and the boys take care of stock and agriculture on the mission fields. The fact that most of the children hardly speak a word of English when they begin their schooling, together with the long absences caused by frequent illnesses and general lack of interest, places a severe handicap on instruction. The majority leave between the sixth and eighth grades, at approximately fifteen years of age, the girls often to marry. The few who continue for one or two more years are generally sent to Haskell or other schools for occupational training.

VII

The adjustment to reservation life has affected diversely the life-patterns of different strata within the society. As far as Arapaho women are concerned, the change has been negligible. Their sphere of interests was largely encompassed by the family, which remains intact. The changes that have occurred in the material aspects of rearing children and performing the household duties have scarcely modified individual habit patterns, much less occasioned new forms of social behavior. With few exceptions, girls leave school, soon marry, have children and lead lives little different from those of the older women, toward whom they behave with traditional deference.

The pattern of men's lives, on the other hand, was more complex, and its equilibrium has been shattered by reservation life. The old men, ranging from seventy to eighty-seven years of age, who remember the pre-reservation days and of whom at least one remembers participating in several war parties, seem to have fared best in the process of readjustment. They occupy themselves solely with religion and medicine practice, which brings them deference and respect from the whole community. Their prestige is doubly enhanced by the fact that aboriginal values alone prevail in their sphere of activity, and for this they receive traditional social recognition, which the younger men do not. These old men are the most self-assured, and, except for the children, show more freedom of behavior than any other group on the reservation. They gather together, talk of the past, recount old tales, and complain of the present life and the failings of the young.

The middle-aged men are far more personally disorganized, and have achieved a passive and listless adjustment. Nearly all speak some English. A number have spent some years at school where they learned a trade they were never able to follow. Since they are not old enough to have an important rôle in the religion, they frequently turn to peyote. A few work hard, and are more actively concerned with the future of the reservation. These are less apt to be dominated by the old men and tend to resist them occasionally.

The young men, under thirty, fare the worst. A good part of their lives has been spent in school, and now they have left, there is nothing to turn to. The older people treat them like children. They get drunk frequently and are apt to be involved in auto crashes and fights. The recent expansion of the government work projects, however, has been a great boon for them. In the group life of the camps, they work well and are happy.

VIII

The outsider, observing the Arapaho, is struck by their apparent shyness and reserve, such as we often associate with insecurity. As they themselves express it, they are given to feeling "shame" in direct social intercourse. When they speak they never look at one another, but gaze at the ground or off at a distance. Dark glasses, serving the same psychological purpose, are worn prevalently even indoors. When they visit or meet one another they show no overt sign of heightened interest. Conversation is carried on in low tones. Laughter is restrained. At social dances and gatherings they sit quietly against the wall and sometimes whisper to one another. Should something humorous occur, they titter slyly.

Such behavior, of course, does not have the same meaning for the Arapaho as it does for us. The timidity and self-consciousness is as it should be; it is the expected behavior. One should not hide one's "shame." On the contrary, one is looked at askance if suspected of lacking this quality.

It is true that in the old days, the Arapaho recounted their brave deeds on many occasions. The festivities following a successful war party abounded in joyful conviviality, the praise of valor and the ridicule of cowardice. The age-societies, the "Tall Men" and the "Short Men," and the different bands competed and joked freely with one another. In all these things, it is significant to note that individuals acted within a rigid framework of social groupings and guided their lives by a fixed scheme of values by which social recognition was accorded. In relations between members of different, non-competing societies, and in situations of a less formalized non-group character, the individual had to feel "shame" always; he had to feel insecurity in his own personality. With the disruption of the age-societies, and the acquisition of new activities requiring individually differentiated conduct, the pattern of "shame" behavior has merely spread out and become the norm over a broader area of life.[41] The use of the automobile is an example. Arapaho often go on foot to the agency or general store for as great a distance as twelve miles. Should someone, not closely related, drive by, the driver will neither stop nor will the man on foot ask for a lift. Both would be "ashamed" to act otherwise. In regard to food there is not the slightest hesitation in eating that of others. The possession of an automobile, however, offers a new situation so tied up with individualism and prestige value that it cannot be brought in line with the traditional schemes of behavior.

The character of Arapaho personality creates maladjustment in their relations with Whites. Since they lack the flexibility and freedom of behavior demanded by our society, they are baffled and discouraged in their dealings outside their own community. They regard the White man as too outspoken and aggressive, and become self-conscious and embarrassed when in conversation he looks directly at them or breaks into his free and easy laughter. As they hide their diffidence behind an outward calm, the White man tends to assume, in conformity with his own social usages, that the passivity of the Arapaho denotes their readiness to fall into a submissive rôle in the given situation. This, however, is not the case. Arapaho personalities are molded by social forms that limit ego expression in terms of a surface equality in which even those with the highest formal authority exercise their power almost inconspicuously. The variances between this pattern and the more pronounced dominance-submission polarity of White behavior makes for this basic discord. To be sure, the Arapaho have been forced to behave in a more or less submissive rôle because of the objective power the Whites exert over their well-being.

[41] The writer is aware that this treatment of personality cannot but involve subjective considerations and that the above interpretation has only partial validity in explaining so complex a phenomenon.

Since they have to a large extent acquired the habit of submission, their conflict is all the stronger. Intimidated by the manner of the Whites, and forced to accede to White authority, they retire inwardly and harbor a submerged resentment against this race whom they regard as cruel, overbearing, and without "pity." If a White makes a request they do not like, they find it hard to refuse; they appear acquiescent, and then refrain from acting on it. At the same time they are highly gratified by the few situations in which the Whites appear to show deference, as when the latter ask their opinion regarding certain matters, attend the sun dance, or desire their presence at town celebrations. In like manner, the few young men who have had relations with White women regard it in a fashion indicative of decided ego gratification.

The system of education has significant bearing on this problem of Indian-White relations. Until adulthood their only association with Whites is in the school. The children are immersed in the stereotyped and very special behavior pattern characteristic of the teacher-pupil relationship; complete authority on the one side, and on the other, the necessity of acting along rigidly defined lines imposed from above. In this case, however, the positional rôles become indelibly associated with the ethnic juxtaposition involved. Thus, instead of developing the mental flexibility and initiative required for satisfactory behavior with Whites, the school conditions the Arapaho to reticent subservience from the very start. Since, moreover, the school scarcely succeeds in implanting the basic values of our civilization, it hardly facilitates deeper ties with the children, all of whose emotional attachments are in a sphere entirely apart from their teachers. In this manner, the Indian-White relationship becomes fixed as a purely external one in which the overt submissiveness is a kind of mechanical habit.

IX

The Arapaho's inability in personal relations to regard Whites other than in the light of total dissimilarity is reflected in their lack of feeling any common interests with the world of the Whites, which, in its entirety, remains something wholly apart from their own sphere of life. Their mental outlook is strictly limited to the reservation. Even in the vast area of the west, the scene of the old people's stories, they feel themselves strangers; it is now little more than a land to be traversed in reaching other reservations.

The schooling hardly succeeds in broadening their interests. Most of what is taught them does not fit in with their social experience and either passes over their heads immediately or is acquired by rote and soon forgotten. When they leave they have learned little more than to read, write, and speak the most simple English, which they subsequently use only in their direct dealings with Whites. When they stop school they stop reading. The only printed matter seen on the reservation are a few illustrated papers, comic strips, mail-order catalogues, and religious tracts passed out by the missions. When they visit town, they never enter the public library. The films that catch their fancy are western pictures, the only ones meaningful in terms of their cultural experience.

Once outside the normal world of the reservation, they have no standards to apply to experience, and face life as an unlimited sphere of incalculable possibilities. The most fantastic information concerning the larger world would be as readily believed and evoke no more surprise than would some matter-of-fact news about a nearby town. Experience in the larger world, not organized in a framework of conceptual categories, remains fluid and meaningless. A number of Arapaho have been with traveling shows to New York, Hollywood, and even to London and Paris, but beyond the pleasant recollection of the financial returns gathered, the trips have left no impression other than fortifying their previous realization that the world of the Whites is a vast and infinitely complex one.

Yet the reservation is not entirely cut off from our civilization. In certain phases of their life the Arapaho must act in terms of White norms. They manage to do so successfully in situations involving only interests of a simple, primitive variety, as in taking part in rodeos or in frontier-day celebrations. Otherwise, where behavior rooted on a rational conceptual level of thought is required, they fail miserably. Applying the norms valid in their own society, they often arrive at views of the most pathetic naïveté. The political order, for example, is extremely simple; it is a prime function of the United States government to look after the Arapaho, of whose existence the president down to the last employee is at all times cognizant. When it is perceived that this view does not apply, the political order is then apt to become an impersonal, mysterious power whose machinations are totally unpredictable.[42] In dealings involving money, whose successful manipulation requires the highest degree of rational action, they are similarly at a loss. To be sure, they understand its almost mechanical transferability for the satisfaction of immediate needs, but savings, loans, payments, and the like are grasped very imperfectly. The price for which an Arapaho will be pleased to sell his goods is more often determined by its adequacy for the fulfillment of a particular want than by a conception of value. When tribal claims against the government involving millions of dollars are in question, all evaluative sense is hopelessly gone.

Relations with the larger world, despite their relatively narrow scope, have nevertheless a deep-rooted effect on the inner stability of Arapaho society. The diverse norms of social behavior, that of the outside and that within the tribe, converge primarily in the political life. The tribal council is composed of six Arapaho elected by the group to represent them in all dealings with the government. Its composition is particularly relevant to group values both because of its significance to the general tribal welfare, and because of its intimate connection with the pattern of status and prestige. Membership in the tribal council retains the social meaning and rank of traditional chieftainship, and as such, a councilman should measure up to the traditional criteria of social recognition. Aside from having good judgment, he must be one of the best-liked members of the community, showing kindness, generosity, and consideration to all—a standard, moreover, not without direct meaning in present reservation life. In his position of tribal representative, the councilman is expected to understand best the behavior of Whites and to deal effectively with them. This ability, however, is possessed in most cases by personalities considerably different from the traditional norm. Thus every

---

[42] All pertaining to the national government, as the president, whether McKinley or F. D. Roosevelt, are referred to as *Vash'ton*, i. e., Washington. Compare W. I. Thomas and F. Znaniecki, *The Polish Peasant in Europe and America, Volume I,* pp. 141–143.

choice of a councilman, and indirectly, every evaluation of an individual, involves conflicting standards of recognition, a perplexity inevitably resulting in social malaise.

This anomalous situation is readily conducive to the disorganization of individual personality. To acquire the highest social status demands a kind of ambivalent psychology capable of acting along disparate lines; within the society, one must conform to the traditional pattern of extreme modesty, self-abnegation, and helpfulness, whereas, on the outside, one must feel at home in the larger society and be able to "talk back" to Whites so as to avoid the easily aroused suspicion of "giving in" to them. It is probable that these conflicting norms, in part at least, account for the often domineering, bellicose manner of the Arapaho when drunk, and may well be a factor determining their very desire to drink. The most illuminating though perhaps extreme case of what may be considered personal disorganization is offered by one of the leading councilmen, rather well-known to the writer. Having absorbed White attitudes while away at school and in the East, he would sincerely like to develop his farm so as to enjoy living standards comparable to that of Whites. He is more desirous, however, of the prestige accruing from his position of foremost representative of his people, and must devote the greater part of his energy to tribal affairs, and to all who come to him for help or advice. He lives, accordingly, on the general level of squalor, meanwhile bemoaning his condition. His behavior with Whites is such that, viewed by them, he appears one of the most straightforward and clear-spoken of the Arapaho, though he often discloses a hypersensitive, over-aggressive streak. Among his own people he is outwardly modest and self-effacing, despite the fact that on occasion, when his dominance is challenged, he succumbs to furious rage, evoking suspicious reactions from many of the tribe.

X

It is clear that Arapaho society, despite all effects from contact with the larger world and the variations in individual personality thereby engendered, is yet, in a sense, isolated from the vast complex society within whose sphere it continues to exist. Its structure remains, in modified form, a web of essentially traditional, non-rational social relations, in which individual behavior is chiefly dependent upon immediate social response and recognition. As such, it is still an integral unity, its sanctioned institutions meeting little opposition from its members, whose interests it continues to absorb.

This internal cohesion of Arapaho society, however, is not based on the conscious desires of its members, except possibly for the old men. The great majority, unable to attain within its scope a full and satisfactory organization of their lives, display no conviction in the ultimate value of the cultural forms or real interest in their perpetuation. They elect to the council a half-breed woman, long married to a White, who neither speaks Arapaho nor has any firm connection with the society. Younger men often voice the desire to break away from the reservation and enter the world of the Whites. Older men lament that they had not done so, and want their children to go off to school and obtain positions elsewhere with the Indian Service, the most feasible way of leaving. Yet these desires are seldom if ever materialized. The Arapaho, disorientated in the freedom [43] beyond, cling to the simple order and relative security obtained within the groove of their system of social behavior. Here the widespread character of their frustrations makes them individually less oppressive, and allows the Indians to evade responsibility by blaming their state on the Whites.

It is this condition that accounts for the inability of the Arapaho to reconstruct their society along the lines of White cultural patterns, on a level more efficient in terms of their inner personality organization.[44] For such a development would have to arise from a moral force within the individuals themselves. They would have to acquire positive values from our society that cannot be fulfilled within the old social forms, and a new set of attitudes which would oppose these forms and lead to the establishment of new ones. However, the habits of thought derived from their social experi-

[43] Defined sociologically, in terms of the relative possibility for the individual in a given situation to exercise spontaneous initiative and personal choice. See K. Mannheim, *Mensch und Gesellschaft im Zeitalter des Umbaus*, Leyden, 1935, Footnote, p. 109.

[44] W. I. Thomas, and F. Znaniecki. "The Concept of Social Disorganization," *op. cit., Volume II*, pp. 1127-33.

ence do not permit them to do this. They are able to take over means that are more effective in terms of their own values, such as automobiles or household goods. In the passivity born of desperation, they have adopted whole institutional complexes, such as agriculture, though in an outward, almost mechanical fashion. But they cannot embrace White values themselves. To do so without directly engaging in the everyday social experience of Whites, would require reflective comparison leading them to doubt the correctness of their own views. Of this mental operation, the great majority of the Arapaho are, of course, incapable. Either they hold a view integrally, with utter finality, or it is totally meaningless to them from the start. Thus, although they know that Whites have views different from their own, the contrast provokes no process of thought. Significantly, they readily accept White religion, a phase of our culture which can be appreciated in terms of primitive non-rational values. That they do not perceive it on a higher plane is confirmed by the fact that they see no conflict between Christianity and the aboriginal religion. Hence, when the Arapaho speak of leaving the reservation, or, as some do occasionally, express the desirability of tearing up the society by its roots and scattering its members among the Whites, they show profound insight into the social situation; namely, that to adopt White attitudes and behavior the individual must detach himself completely from his old sphere of social experience.

An effective reorganization of the society might be feasible, however, if, rather than imitating White patterns, the Arapaho allowed the reorganization to grow out of their own social forms. Economic activities, though stemming from our culture, need not necessarily be pursued in their present institutional forms, but may possibly be integrated into the indigenous schemes of behavior. This would be a difficult process if only for the deadweight of years of sluggish passivity and the widespread personality disorganization. Yet the success of the livestock associations attests its practicability.[45] Land ownership could be converted from its individualistic basis, and even agriculture could be carried on in

[45] Since they are so recent and of limited range, the livestock associations cannot be analysed in their full significance. In any case, their effects have not yet measurably altered the general picture.

communal, probably neighborhood form. From a successful re-organization of this kind, new interest should emerge conducive to richer individual lives and a general flourishing of the culture. For the time being, however, Arapaho society, its active vitality blunted by moral inertia, can effect but a clumsy and inept adjustment to the conditions of its existence.

BIBLIOGRAPHY

Benedict, Ruth, *Patterns of Culture,* Houghton Mifflin Company, Boston, Mass., 1934.

Commissioner of Indian Affairs, *Annual Reports to the Secretary of the Interior,* Government Printing Office, Washington, D.C., 1862, 1863, 1878, 1880, 1884, 1885.

Cooley, Charles H., *Social Organization,* Charles Scribner's Sons, New York, N.Y., 1909.

Curtis, Edward S., *The North American Indians,* edited by Frederick Hodge, *Volume 6,* Harvard University Press, Cambridge, Mass., 1911.

Dorsey, George A., The Arapaho Sun Dance, *Anthropological Series, Field Museum of Natural History Publications, Volume 4,* Chicago, Ill., 1902.

Dorsey, George A. and Kroeber, Alfred L., Traditions of the Arapaho, *Anthropological Series, Field Museum of Natural History Publications, Volume 5,* Chicago, Ill., 1903.

Eggan, Frederick, *Social Anthropology of the North American Indians,* University of Chicago Press, Chicago, Ill., 1937.

Grinnell, George B., *The Cheyenne,* 2 volumes, Yale University Press, New Haven, Conn., 1923.

Hafen, LeRoy R. and Ghent, W. J., *Broken Hand,* Old West Publishing Company, Denver, Colorado, 1931.

Herskovits, Melville J., *Acculturation,* J. J. Augustin, New York, N.Y., 1938.

Kroeber, Alfred L., The Arapaho, *Bulletin No. 18, American Museum of Natural History,* New York, N.Y., 1902.

Lesser, Alexander, The Pawnee Ghost-Dance Hand Game, *Columbia University Contributions to Anthropology, Volume 16,* Columbia University Press, New York, N.Y., 1933.

Linton, Ralph, *The Study of Man,* D. Appleton-Century Company, Inc., New York, N.Y., 1936.

Lowie, Robert H., Plains Indians Age-Societies: Historical and Comparative Summary, *Anthropological Papers, American Museum of Natural History, Volume 11, Part 13,* New York, N.Y., 1916.

—— *The Crow,* Farrar and Rinehart, New York, N.Y., 1935.

MacIver, R. M., *Community*, The Macmillan Company, New York, N.Y., 1917.

—— *Society*, Farrar and Rinehart, New York, N.Y., 1937.

MacLeod, W. C., *The American Indian Frontier*, Alfred A. Knopf, New York, N.Y., 1928.

Mannheim, K., *Ideology and Utopia*, Harcourt, Brace and Company, New York, N.Y., 1936.

Maximilian, Prince of Wied, *Travels in the Interior of North America*, Ackermann, London, England, 1843.

Mead, Margaret, *The Changing Culture of an Indian Tribe*, Columbia University Press, New York, N.Y., 1932.

Mekeel, H. Scudder, The Economy of a Modern Teton Dakota Community, *Yale University Publications in Anthropology, No. 6*, New Haven, Conn., 1936.

Michelson, Truman, "Narrative of an Arapaho Woman," *American Anthropologist, New Series, Volume 35*, 1933.

Mooney, James, The Ghost Dance Religion, *Bureau of American Ethnology, Annual Report 14, Part 2*, Smithsonian Institution, Government Printing Office, Washington, D.C., 1896.

Schoolcraft, Henry R., *Information Respecting the History, Condition and Prospects of the Indian Tribes of the United States*, 6 volumes, Lippincott, Grambo, Philadelphia, Pa., 1860.

Scott, Hugh L., "Early History of the Names of the Arapaho," *American Anthropologist, New Series, Volume 9*, pp. 545–60, 1907.

Seger, John H., *Early Days among the Cheyenne and Arapahoe Indians*, edited by Stanley Vestal, University of Oklahoma Press, Norman, Okla., 1934.

Thomas, William I. and Znaniecki, Florian, *The Polish Peasant in Europe and America*, 2 volumes, Alfred A. Knopf, New York, N.Y., 1927.

Weber, W., "Grundriss der Sozialokonomik," *Wirtschaft und Gesellschaft, 3 Abteilung*, Frankfurter societaes-druckerei G. m.b.H., Frankfurt, Germany, 1924.

Reports of Wind River Reservation, United States Soil Conservation Service, Technical Coöperation, Bureau of Indian Affairs.

EDITOR'S SUMMARY

ARAPAHO ACCULTURATION

In comparison with many of the other Indian tribes the Arapaho have not been badly treated by the Whites. Their warfare with the conquerors was less bitter and prolonged than that of many of the other Plains Indians. The part which the semi-legendary Friday played in this affords an example of the influence which particular personalities may exert in crucial situations. The Arapaho also had the advantage of being placed on a reservation within their aboriginal range, a condition which is usually an aid to successful adaptation. However, in this case the destruction of the buffalo by Whites eliminated the most important aboriginal resource of the territory, while the region was poorly suited to the agriculture which the Whites offered them as an economic substitute for hunting. They were reduced at once to a condition of economic dependence upon the Whites and could not have survived without government rations and the small income derived from unskilled labor.

It is impossible to say how far these unfavorable economic conditions are responsible for their present lack of adjustment, but much of the difficulty certainly derives from particular patterns within the aboriginal culture. Their social and political organization seems to have been unusually close and elaborate for a Plains tribe. There was a rigid prescription of statuses and rôles with a concentration of power in the hands of the old, the very group which would be least adapted to coping with new conditions. The only opportunity for individual initiative lay in war, and when this activity was suddenly inhibited the younger men found themselves condemned to long-continued inferiority. A by-product of the rigidity of organization and thorough integration of the individual into his society was the development of certain personality characteristics ably described by Dr. Elkin. The sense of "shame" served to keep the younger generation in their place and to make the highly formalized social system work smoothly. At the same time it unfitted and apparently still unfits the average member of the tribe for participation in White culture. The aggressive patterns of this culture are repugnant to the Arapaho as are those of individual aggrandizement and wealth accumulation. The latter are in direct conflict with the deep-seated aboriginal patterns of generosity and recognition of kinship obligations, and in this conflict the aboriginal patterns seem to have won, preventing even the abler individuals from achieving economic independence.

It seems that the adaptation which the Arapaho have achieved so far is of a very superficial sort. There has been a considerable loss of culture content, such institutions as the age-societies having disappeared without any replacement. Acceptance of White institutions has taken place mainly in two fields, technology and religion. In the former nearly all the old arts and crafts have been replaced by White manufactured goods, while the automobile has replaced the horse. The automobile fitted so perfectly into the aboriginal nomadic patterns that it was accepted enthusiastically. In religion there has been widespread conversion to Christianity with a preference for the more highly ritualized forms, yet this has been a simple addition to the culture, accomplished without the elimination of the older beliefs or many of the aboriginal ceremonies. Another addition to religion has been the peyote cult, borrowed from other tribes. All these superficial changes in culture appear to have left most of the aboriginal values intact. Tribal solidarity seems to have been, if anything, exaggerated by the conditions of White contact, and the social pressure exerted upon individuals who behave in ways differing from the cultural stereotypes is a serious bar to successful individual adaptation. This is the more remarkable in view of the apparent loss of faith in the aboriginal culture. Individuals seem to realize its short-comings but are too timid to risk the loss of the only emotional security they possess, that of the good will of their fellow tribesmen. Dr. Elkin's use of sociological concepts in analysing this situation should be noted as an example of how much certain of these concepts aid in clarifying both cultural and personality problems.

The picture of the Arapaho which emerges from this study is that of a bewildered, frightened group who have lost faith in themselves and are marking time. Their successful adaptation either in terms of acculturation or in those of the development of an independent culture compatible with reality must await a transformation of values and of the personality systems which derive from these.

5

THE FOX OF IOWA

by Natalie F. Joffe

INTRODUCTION

When the problem of the acculturation of the Fox tribe with the White man is viewed over a long time span, one dominant leitmotiv, namely that of vigorous and planned counter-opposition to pressure, is apparent. At no time in their early history were the Fox eager to embrace White culture *in toto;* obviously superior White technology was soon adopted, but beyond this the ways of the White man made no permanent inroads. This attitude of continuous animosity has been aptly phrased by Louise Phelps Kellogg in her book entitled *The French Régime in Wisconsin and the Northwest:*

They (the Fox) were as we shall see, the Wisconsin tribe which longest maintained its primitive independence, and was the last to succumb to French influences and to yield submission to white men. Their courage was greater than that of the other surrounding tribes, as well as their determination to live as their forefathers did, uncontaminated by white contact. To this end they not only fought the French for two generations, but they reared as many children as possible, and trained them for the same fierce resistance to civilization. By far the most fierce, the Outagami (Fox) were certainly the most interesting of the Wisconsin aborigines.[1]

Coupled with such hostility was considerable political skill and foresight, which enabled them through military and pacific means to withstand the impact of White culture that came to them through the channels of exploiting colonial governments and the general westward migration of the last century. Their intense dislike for the French made them amenable to Britain's suggestion

[1] *Op. cit.,* p. 128.

that they block the trade routes that lay to the south and west of Wisconsin, and resulted in their becoming a target for extermination at the hands of the former power.

The long period of unrest and hostility to Whites from the earliest date of contact, including removal into Kansas territory, culminated in the purchase of land by the Fox in Tama, Iowa, in 1854. Acquisition of land by such means is unparalleled in the history of the American Indian. This act is indicative of their resourcefulness, and suggests why in the face of exposure to White contact of the most oppressive nature for over 250 years, Fox culture has remained essentially Indian.

The history of the Fox people is then not only one of determined resistance to persecution, maintained by isolating themselves and thus avoiding certain inevitable conflicts, but also one of realistic adjustment. Since it was not feasible to achieve the desired sanctuary, as was done by many tribes of the North American Southwest, by virtue of geographical position, the next best method was to meet the situation on the terms of the White man. This they accomplished by legal purchase of a tract of land, which gave them status as tax-paying residents of the state of Iowa.

Perhaps the fact that they have successfully fought for the preservation of tribal integrity accounts for their individual and cultural stability. Whenever they received large sums of money (from the sale of lands in Indian Territory, or from the restoration of annuities owing them), these were invested in more tribal land, for Iowa soil was precious to the Fox after experience in Kansas. Unlike the Omaha and Osage, the Fox did not dissipate these cash windfalls. Even the advent of the horse did not prove to be as disruptive to Fox life as it was to their neighbors on the south and west. Whether it was because the Fox never had a surplus of horses, or even enough of them to supply each person with one, or that the Fox did not choose to move into the Plains, they never relied on the buffalo for their existence. Among other tribes, namely the southern Siouian peoples, the effects of the horse were cataclysmic. This fact is especially noteworthy in view of the fact that the Fox [2]

[2] The other Central Algonkian tribes (Sauk and Kickapoo) had substantially the same course of development as did the Fox until removal in the nineteenth century.

and the southern Sioux both started from the same aboriginal base. In pre-horse days both groups subsisted upon hunting and some agriculture, maintained permanent villages where they raised their crops, and went on nomadic hunts therefrom. Possession of the horse made it possible for Woodlands tribes to move into the Plains and to follow the buffalo, and this nomadic mode of life consequently grew at the expense of the sedentary phase, which became minimized or was altogether abandoned. Elaboration of this migratory pattern was contingent upon one ecological factor—the presence of vast herds of bison in the Plains. Food, shelter and clothing were provided by the buffalo, and in order to exploit this resource successfully, conflicts arose with other tribes who were also competing for the animals. These wars gave impetus to military aspects that were already present in the cultures, and led to the growth of the elaborate system of war honors, making the horse indispensable in social and legal arrangements, for possession of this animal made for wealth and prestige. The Fox had only dim reflections of this picture, and therefore when the buffalo were exterminated, they suffered less.

Thus developments among the Fox were not built up on the buffalo as a foundation; rather they grew in a direction that enabled them to survive. Religious ideology was based upon various agricultural and first fruits patterns, and the latter idea was even used to embrace certain aspects of hunting. Whether by accident or perspicacity the Fox arrived at the method which permitted them to continue their old culture after the arrival of the Whites. Attachment to land was something which the White man not only understood, but was valued by him. The Fox hit at the crux of the situation when they acquired land through a channel acceptable to the Whites (by purchase).

The Central Algonkian were notoriously conservative, waging a constant battle against the encroachment of White mores. When the Sauk, Fox and Kickapoo were removed to Kansas, two of them reacted typically. The Sauk, who had never been as strongly hostile to Whites as the Fox, gave in to the press of circumstances and followed the course of development paralleling that of other tribes in Indian Territory, succumbing rapidly to acculturation. The band of Kickapoo, who were unwilling to meet the change, fled to Mexico. On the other hand the Fox chose to purchase land as a way out of their difficulties.

The Fox had become inured to hardships during the many years of conflict. Chief Pemoussa's challenge,[3] boasting of the immortality of his tribe, proved prophetic in the light of subsequent developments. The Fox were cut to pieces not once but many times, yet nevertheless they as an independent nation have outlasted upon this continent their numerous and implacable enemy, the French. Their numbers were at a low point at the time of the return trek from Kansas in the 1850's. The wretched band of 250 who straggled back were less than a tenth of the number ascribed to the Fox by the earliest French chronicles. That these few became the nucleus which set the tribe back on its feet and preserved the traditions of the old culture is to be marveled at, in view of the difficulties they encountered in the first years back "home."

ABORIGINAL CULTURE

The earliest mentioned home of the Fox was in the southern part of the Michigan peninsula. Owing to the push of population from the east, and the collapse of the so-called "empire" of the Winnebago, they along with the Sauk and Potawotami moved into Wisconsin, settling near Green Bay. The Fox were met here by the first French traders, and the first mission, that of St. Marc, was established here for the tribe in 1670. They lived in this vicinity, roaming south and west, until 1735 when, due to fear of the wrath of the French, who had defeated the Fox decisively in 1730, they migrated southward together with the Sauk, who had offered them asylum after this last battle. Until 1830 they ranged through Iowa and Illinois, with sporadic intrusions back into Wisconsin, having headquarters at Rock Island on the confluence of the Rock and Mississippi Rivers.

The Fox are an Algonkian speaking people, most closely allied

[3] In 1712, during the siege of Detroit, Pemoussa taunted the French with the following words: "But I know that the Renard (Fox) is immortal, and that if in defending myself I spill blood, my father cannot reproach me." Louise Phelps Kellogg, "The Fox Indians During the French Régime," *Proceedings of the Wisconsin State Historical Society*, p. 161, Madison, Wisconsin, 1907.

linguistically with the Sauk and Kickapoo. Dependent upon hunting and agriculture for their livelihood, they had a typically Woodlands culture. They had been influenced by some of the more western tribes, notably the Winnebago, which influence persists today.

The first detailed records of Fox culture date from the early 1820's.[4] From these accounts we learn that they were a village people, the tribe numbering about 2,000 persons at this period. The largest village at Rock Island contained thirty-five large summer houses, with two smaller towns lying to the north, and scattered bands dwelling west of the Mississippi as far west as the Missouri River.

Some acculturation had already taken place by this date; both the Fox and the Sauk were using many articles of White manufacture, they had adopted the canoe from their more northern neighbors, and had taken over the horse. They also conducted winter group hunts, in which the community returned together, with Plains methods of policing.

MATERIAL CULTURE

The two principal sources of Fox food were hunting and agriculture. Corn, beans, squash and pumpkins were raised by the women in small garden plots in the permanent village. The bulk of the corn which they raised was dried, put into bark bags and stored in cache pits, save for the five bushels or so which each family took on the winter hunt. Wild vegetable foods were also gathered and eaten. These consisted of maple sugar, wild plum, wild potato, roots, berries and nuts. Some wild rice was obtained from the Menomini and Winnebago. Venison and deer suet bulked large as protein foods in Fox diet. The hunting of the deer as well as of other animals was the main preoccupation of the man. Bear was also a favored meat, but all kinds of small game and birds were

4 Letter to Rev. Dr. Jedidiah Morse, by Major Morrell Marston, U.S.A., November 1820, and Thomas Forsyth, "Account of the Manners and Customs of the Sauk and Fox Nations of Indian Traditions." Both printed in *The Indian Tribes of the Upper Mississippi Valley and Region of the Great Lakes*, edited by Emma Helen Blair, *Volume II*, The Arthur H. Clark Company, Cleveland, 1912.

utilized as food. Fish was eaten only in the summer when other flesh foods were scarce.

In the course of his hunting activities it was the duty of the man to kill enough animals, not only to supply the immediate needs of his family (for food and clothing), but also to barter for trade goods. He also took care of the horses, made the saddles for them, and built and propelled the canoes and flat-boats. The woman, in addition to her planting and gardening activities, took care of the children, cooked, carried wood and water, skinned the game, dressed and tanned the skins, and made the clothing for her family.

Fox life had two distinct phases, a sedentary agricultural aspect in the spring and summer and a nomadic hunting existence in the fall and winter. Living arrangements were different during the two parts of the year. From April to August the people lived in permanent villages. Here they had long rectangular houses covered with elm bark. These buildings were often fifty to sixty feet long and accommodated as many persons. There were openings at either end of the house, and two sleeping benches about three feet high and four wide, ran along the side walls. From September to April they used the small, mat-covered wickiup. This was a round or oval domed structure. It was easy to heat and simple to transport. The mat coverings, made of cat-tails, were rolled up and taken to deck the new frame when the family reached the camping site.

The yearly cycle corresponded with their calendric year. Both began in September, after they had taken the harvest in:

About the middle of September the Sauk and Fox Indians all begin to move from their villages to go towards the country they mean to hunt during the ensuing winter, they generally go westwards in the interior in the headwaters of the Ihoway and DeMoine rivers and some go beyond those rivers quite in the interiour of the country. There are some who have no horses as also many old people who descend the Mississippi in canoes as far as the Ihoway, Scunk and other rivers and ascend those rivers to the different places where they mean to pass the winter a hunting. Those Indians who have a sufficiency of horses to transport their families and baggage go as far westward in their hunting excursions as the Missouri River and sometimes are invited by the Kansez and other Indians to cross the Missouri River and hunt in this country as far westward on the small streams that fall into the Arkansaw River. They generally stop hunting deer when the weather begins to be severe and form (s) themselves into grand encampments to pass the remainder of the winter or severe weather. They are at this time visited by their traders who go and receive their credits and also to trade with them.[5] On the opening of the spring those that have traps go to beaver hunting others to hunt bear and they generally finish their hunt about the 10th of April. They formerly had general hunting parties before the buffalo removed so far westward. "The only instances wherein I have ever known any laws enforced or penalties exacted for a disobedience of them by the Sauks and Foxes, are when they are returning in the spring from their hunting grounds to their village. The village chiefs then advise the war chiefs (?) to declare the martial law to be in force, which is soon proclaimed and the whole authority is placed in the hands of the war chiefs. Their principal object in so doing appears to be to prevent one family from returning before another whereby it might be exposed to an enemy; or by arriving at the village before the others, dig up its neighbours' corn. It is the business of the war chiefs to keep all the canoes together; and on land to regulate the march of those who are mounted or on foot. One of the chiefs goes ahead to pitch upon the encamping ground for each night, where he will set up a painted pole or stake as a signal for them to halt; any Indian going beyond this is punished by having his canoe, and whatever else he may have along with him destroyed. On their arrival sentinels are posted, and no one is allowed to leave his village until everything is put in order; when this is accomplished the martial law ceases to be in force.[6]

SOCIAL ORGANIZATION

The functioning social unit [7] consisted of a man, his wife or wives, children, children-in-law, and grandchildren. All of the proceeds of the hunt and garden were shared by this group. It was the duty of the head of the household to keep them supplied with meat and skins. Polgyny was common, and even encouraged, as was adoption from other tribes, for it augmented the man power of the tribe. From two to five wives was the usual number of plural spouses, and polygyny was preferably sororal as a group of sisters was regarded as being more amicable. The first wife was also the

[5] M. Marston, *op. cit.*, pp. 149–151. "In good seasons the Indians will be able to pay their credits and get blankets, strouding and ammunition, and have a surplus. In 1819–1820, there were five traders, with nine clerks and interpreters for the two nations who bought 10,082 skins worth $58,800.00 (28,680 deer, 13,440 raccoon, and 12,900 muskrat, etc.) also feathers and beeswax."

[6] *Ibid.*, pp. 163–164.

[7] *Ibid.*, p. 176.

head wife, having authority to dispose of her husband's game, and doing all of the purchasing for the family. Also there were slaves. These were people who had been captured in war. Female war captives could be espoused, and their offspring were considered free Fox.

There were several methods open to a young man for obtaining a bride, of which the most common was service for her. He might approach the girl himself, or cultivate the acquaintance of her brother in order to make his intentions known. If his suit was acceptable, he told his parents about it. If the young man concerned were a very good hunter, his family might be unwilling to lose his services and would attempt to proffer gifts to the parents of the girl in lieu of them. In the event that the gifts were refused, the boy would serve for a period of from one to three years, generally until his wife bore a child. During this time all the game that he killed belonged to his affinals. At the termination of the service, or when gifts instead of service had been accepted, the husband might take his wife to live with his parents, remain with her kin, or set up a new household. Elopement was also a course open to a man as a method of securing a wife. A man could persuade a girl to accompany him on a summer hunt. Upon his return, he would present the girl's parents with food, cloth and possibly a horse. It was even likely that a man might serve for his later wives too.

Divorce was usually amicable, with sterility a common cause for it, yet if a woman left her husband he could force her to return to him. A man had the power to kill his wife without fear of retaliation by her relatives, or could punish her for adultery by biting off her nose or cutting off her ears. If the guilty woman's husband were very jealous he could kill the erring pair, but if the paramour escaped death, he got no punishment beyond gossip, and then only if he had used force.[8]

Upon the death of an adult, all his property save for the few objects, i. e., burial garments, etc., buried with him, was given away to those persons who had buried him. The funeral was conducted by some person, generally not related by blood to the deceased, who appointed helpers. These helpers could be affinal relatives of the deceased, members of a gens or society who had

[8] T. Forsyth, op. cit., p. 214.

mutual burying rights with the group of the deceased, or chosen at random. Just before the grave was closed, some old warrior who was no kin to the deceased, would make a speech announcing the number and sexes of those persons the speaker had killed in battle and giving their spirits to the dead one as slaves in the next world. He also bade the deceased farewell for the group. The chief attendant distributed the property of the deceased to his assistants. Included among these goods were valuables which the relatives and friends of the dead man had presented to the bereft family when they came to view the corpse as it lay in state.

The relict, whether male or female, mourned for a period up to four years, dressed in rags, with blackened face, unwashed and uncombed. This period was brought to a close by an adoption feast which was given by the bereaved family. At the feast, a non-relative of the same sex and approximately the same age as the deceased was "adopted" into his family to release the soul of the dead person. (According to Fox belief the soul quits the earth four days after death, but it returns at intervals. If an adoption feast is not held within four years from the date of death, to cut the soul's ties with this world, the soul becomes an owl.) This type of adoption did not involve residence of the adoptee with the sponsoring family. It was a purely formal relationship in which the kinship terms and behavior patterns used by and toward the deceased, were assumed by both the adoptee and sponsoring family. If a man had been killed on the warpath, the adoptee considered himself responsible for the revenge obligations. When he next went to war, he attempted to avenge the death of the deceased by killing an enemy. In order to release a widow or widower from the burden of the mourning proscriptions, the relict was summoned by his affinal relatives, who washed him and clothed him in new garments. He was now free to paint with vermilion (a sign that one was interested in marriage), and to marry again. If the family was fond of the relict, he was urged to marry some relative of the deceased (levirate-sororate), or even the adopted person. Mourning duties sat more heavily upon women than they did on men, for the former generally mourned for a longer period.

There were also well-defined customs governing the birth and education of children. During her pregnancy a woman was supposed not to eat anything with a rind or skin on it, so that the impending delivery might not be impeded, nor any food covered with spines or protuberances, for if she did so, her child would have a pimply skin. When labor came on she retired to a small bark hut, and there was delivered. Often she had no assistance, although sometimes some old woman would come to her aid. If the delivery were particularly difficult, a medicine-man or woman would come and sing around the birth lodge, but would render no actual obstetrical help. She was isolated from twenty to forty days after the birth, and if the child happened to be still-born, both the mother and father were kept in seclusion. During this period the two parents were held especially dangerous to the growth of vegetation. All lochial discharges were considered highly charged with great danger, so that the instrument used to cut the umbilical cord had to be thrown away, and the garments that the woman wore in the birth lodge were not used outside of it.

A child was strapped in a cradle-board, and carried about on its mother's back. Education of any child lay chiefly in the hands of its parents. No favoritism was shown to children until the boys reached the hunting age, and then the oldest child or the one who was the best hunter became his mother's favorite. When a boy was old enough to handle a weapon (six or seven years of age), he left the tutelage of his mother, and his father began to take care of the boy's training. At this age he was given a small bow and arrows and sent to hunt birds. His first kill was made into a feast, regardless of size, and set before someone not of his immediate household. (This is but an instance of the idea of first fruits, which permeates the harvest festivals, etc., of the Fox today.) When he was about twelve, he received a gun and went to hunt small game. In the winter evenings his father would instruct him in the arts of hunting, tracking, and the manufacture and use of hunting magic. If a young boy fell heir to the chieftainship, he was formally introduced to the council, and until old enough to take his seat in that body, he was instructed by the elder male relatives of his father's family.

Paralleling this curriculum, the girl was taught the various domestic arts by her mother. At the age of seven she began to sew clothes for her dolls, at nine or ten years of age she helped to plant and hoe the garden and learned to cook, when she was ten she began to fetch wood and water, and at twelve to make moccasins and house mats. Her mother watched her carefully for signs of approaching puberty. Upon the advent of the menarche, she was isolated in a special bark hut under the care of an old woman, usually her grandmother. The girl had to cook for herself on a separate fire. For ten days she was kept concealed, with a blanket over her head, for her glance would blight the earth. At the end of this period, she was led to a stream and bathed, after which she was pecked all over her body, especially on the back and thighs, with a sharp object. The cutting was done so that the blood would flow profusely, in order that she might not menstruate too freely. She was then conducted back and remained in seclusion for another ten days. At the end of this second period she was bathed again, dressed in new clothes and returned to her home. Her old garments were left in the menstrual hut and were worn during subsequent catamenial periods.

When the girl was fifteen she learned to do fine bead-work and make ribbon appliqué. When she had learned all of these skills she was considered ready for marriage. Constant advice was showered upon her about seemly behavior by her mother and her mother's brothers. The latter were joking relatives, and were the ones shamed if she became promiscuous. She was continuously warned not to giggle, for the giggling girl was considered to be easily accessible.

Social organization was gentile of the Omaha type. In 1827 eight gentes [9] were described, and there appear to have been at least fourteen in the earliest records. These were exogamous units, named after animals, plants, or natural phenomena. In addition to regulating marriage, the gens had certain religious and social functions. Gentile devices were painted on the grave posts, and among the Fox as among the Omaha, the members of the various gentes had distinctive haircuts.[10] The Bear gens was subdivided into three ranked parts, with the tribal chieftainship hereditary in the Black Bear division. The War Chiefs (Fox) gens seems to have

[9] T. Forsyth, op. cit., p. 192.
[10] T. Michelson, American Anthropologist, Volume 40, Pt. 3, p. 487, 1938.

had special duties in inter-tribal alliances. The first name that a child received came from a stock of gentile names, which was bestowed on him at a feast given shortly after his birth.

Cutting across the gentile structure of the tribe were the moieties. These were purely social and ceremonial groups, and had no reference to marriage. The first child was assigned to the moiety of which its father was *not* a member, and the next one to the moiety of its father. Alternation of subsequent children followed so that the tribe was equally divided. The names of the moieties were Kic'ko and To'kan; members of the former painted themselves with white paint, and stood and danced in the south half of a lodge at a ceremony, and members of the latter painted themselves with black and performed in the north sector. The divisions served also as opponents in the playing of games. Each moiety had a leader whose status was not formal; he was a particularly successful warrior, and was called "War Chief" by Marston.[11]

POLITICAL ORGANIZATION

The chief political unit of the Fox was the village. The Fox were governed by a set of civil chiefs who obtained their titles by virtue of descent in a line of males. This power descended to the oldest son of a chief, and if he refused it or was not permitted to accept it, it went to the brothers or nephews of the former chief and so on down the line. It is apparent, although not explicit in the literature, that the village chief was the important officer. The village was the hunting unit, and the recruits for a war party came mainly from the village. It was likely that in emergency situations, calling for war-making units larger than the village, the man (probably a chief, as all Fox men were warriors) who was the best military tactician took the lead. The functions of the chief were executive and judicial. His orders were carried out by the warrior group. When the chiefs sat in secret council, the principal braves planted sentinels outside to guard the council. If these men failed in their duty on any occasion, they were publicly caned by the women. The chief also took charge if the aggrieved parties in a murder could not reach a decision (i. e., compound for the offense,

[11] M. Marston, *op. cit.*, p. 156.

etc.). The two sides would abide by the decision of the chief in such an event. The chief was also assisted by a council. The personnel of this group is not very clear, but it seems probable that it consisted of the principal men and warriors of the tribe or village, in addition to the chiefs. Unanimity was essential in any decision reached by this body. The importance of the council in Fox ideology lies not in the structure and function of any specific body of men, but in the concept of a group of men who met *in council* to decide upon tribal or village matters. The power of the chief was checked by the council. It was men who met *in council* who decided where the winter hunt was to be held. The chief, for all of his imputed authority, was primarily the spokesman for the tribe, and his power was directive, not coercive.

All inter-tribal affairs were settled by the chiefs in council. Inter-tribal alliances, intention of war and all other matters of international policy were treated by means of wampum. Wampum belts were made of beads woven with deer sinew. The design and color of the belts varied with the nature of the content. White beads meant peace, and those colored red with vermilion signified war. These belts were sent as messages, and the greater the size of the belt, the more forceful was the intent conveyed. Wampum was further sanctioned by smoking. The calumet was early described as a mechanism for cementing good faith. Perrot attempted in 1683 to seal a peace between the Fox on one side and the Sioux and Ojibwa on the other, for the year before the Fox had taken captive the daughter of an Ojibwa chief. Her father joined Perrot, taking along gifts for her ransom, although he feared that not only he himself, but also his daughter, might be sacrificed. Perrot persuaded one faction of the Fox to relinquish the girl, and got the recalcitrant leader, who had before refused to smoke, to accept the calumet and a number of gifts, and he thereupon gave up the girl.[12]

The chief and council were aided by a group of three ceremonial runners. These were men who had obtained their power on the vision quest. The spirit who had blessed them made them fleet of foot and good-natured. They went on errands at long distances,

[12] Claude La Potherie, "Savage Allies of New France," in Blair, *op. cit.*, Volume I, pp. 358 *et seq.*

announced deaths to the village, advised the council, and they adjudicated when the chief was unable to reach a decision. They could also conjure for rain and warmth, when they were needed.

Composition for murder (payment for the death with gifts) was in the hands of the families involved, with the chief stepping in if no satisfactory decision could be reached. The murderer also had the alternative of marrying the widow of his victim, so that she might suffer no disadvantages because of his deed. In cases of debt and theft, the old people from both sides handled the settlement if the aggrieved parties could not end the dispute themselves.

For children discipline was maintained by making them fast and by certain other measures. They went without food, with their faces blackened. This was a sign that they were being punished so that no one would feed them. They were also doused with cold water if they had misbehaved, and older boys were made to dive through the ice in the winter as punishment. The chiefs and principal men went to much trouble to stress to the young the importance of correct behavior and duty. In the early morning, they would walk about their villages exhorting and advising on good conduct in very loud voices. The importance of the mother's brother in correcting his wayward niece has been mentioned. However, a girl was more likely than not to have had sex experience before the time of her marriage. This prenuptial intercourse did not lessen the probability of her acquiring a husband. Yet if a woman had lived with a White man, her chances of obtaining a young husband were less good than those of a girl whose affairs had been with Indian men.

SUPERNATURALISM

Religious developments among the Fox grew around the concept of Manitou. Manitou was an impersonal force that pervaded the universe. It was an abstraction, yet it could manifest itself concretely in objects and persons. Manitou could be transmitted by contagion with an object that contained it. A person obtained Manitou power on the vision quest. The supplicant blackened his face and fasted until a spirit appeared and instructed him in that which he sought. In many cases this spirit would give some token to the seeker, which became the basis for a medicine bundle. Both men and women could go on the vision quest. A man began to fast early in adolescence. His father would give him a short willow twig, telling him to burn the end of it and use the charcoal to blacken his face. He should fast until the twig was consumed, which usually took a whole winter. These fasts were not complete abstentions from food, but the faster ate a minimum. This practice was kept up throughout life, for one fasted whenever the need for guidance was felt. The visions could be interpreted by old wise men, who had received the power to counsel through a vision. They would tell the suppliants how to carry out the teachings of a vision. Not all who sought visions would receive them. Also as part of the Manitou concept was belief in sorcery, for Manitou could be either good or evil. Sorcery power came to one through teaching or through the vision quest. A sorcerer caused illness by sending objects into the body of his victim. The patient could be cured by having the objects sucked out.[13]

Every person had two souls, each with a different function. The small soul was equivalent to the life of the individual and was present in the unborn child. When this soul left the body, the person died. The small soul came from Gitche Manitou and could be reborn four times, traveling underground to the west, four days after death. The large soul was the guardian of the small one and originated with Wisaka (the Great Hare), hovering near the unborn child until birth, when it entered the body. This large soul could not be reincarnated, for when the small soul was reborn it was provided with a new guardian. It was the small soul that had to be released from its earthly ties by means of the adoption feast. After its journey to the after-world it would return at intervals to the village where it had lived, and if its connection with the earthly abode were not severed within four years from the time of death, it would become an owl.

The after-world was divided into two parts, in one of which lived those who had been good on earth and in the other the wrong-doers. Originally there were two brothers, Gitche Manitou

---

[13] The discussion of the Manitou concept is taken from William Jones, "The Algonkin Manitou," *Journal of American Folklore, Volume XVII*, pp. 183–190, 1905.

(the Great Spirit) and Machi Manitou (the Evil Spirit). Both of them were good, but the latter died and went to another world, and ever since then he has been evil. Since all who died had to cross a narrow bridge over a swift stream to get to the after-world, only those who had been good were able to cross in safety. The evil-doers fell off the bridge and went to the domain of the evil brother. Children did not have enough sense to get across properly, so the Machi Manitou would deprive them of their brains, in order that when they grew up they would not know enough to leave him. His brother, to circumvent this, would send an eagle [14] to peck a hole in the head of every child as soon as it appeared in the other world, deprive the child of his brain and hide it. When the child was of suitable age, his brains would be restored to him and he could then escape and rejoin his family and friends.[15]

Gitche Manitou was the Great Manitou, impersonal and omnipotent. Wisaka was the culture-hero and the being who transformed the world into its present semblance. There was also a group of numerous mythological beings, mainly animals, who blessed men and provided power; the bear and snake granted medicine power, the deer and humming-bird made one fleet of foot. Experiences with these beings provided the basis for sacred pack rituals that formed the core of Fox ceremonialism. The origin myths of each pack ritual described the events by which the founder of a cult group received instruction for the performance of one of these ceremonies.

The bundle festivals were of both gentile and non-gentile type. The gens and the societies to which the sacred packs belonged were the main cult groups. Position in these groups was achieved by being born into one of them, or by learning the songs and being invited to participate as an attendant at a festival. The dog feast was part of the ritual in both of these types. In addition there

---

[14] This idea took an interesting turn in later years, for instead of regarding the removal of brains as a safeguard, the eagle became an old woman who cracked the skulls of ghosts and dug out a fingerful of brains from each. Hence dying persons requested that a weapon be buried with them. This request was often refused, for the ghosts on return might discover malefactions and injure the living. William Jones, *Mortuary Observances and the Adoption Rites of the Algonkin Foxes of Iowa, International Congress of Americanists*, 1906, pp. 265–266.

[15] M. Marston, *op. cit.*, pp. 174–175.

were several secret societies in which membership was bought. The Midewiwin was the only one of this type described by the early Whites.[16] An older member had to sponsor the initiate, having first obtained the consent of the head of the society. Both men and women could join this cult. There were four levels of membership, and since it was expensive to join the cult and each degree attained required further expenditure, few persons reached the fourth rank. The novice was instructed and prepared for a year prior to his first participation. Each member possessed a sacred bundle. The number of memberships available was limited.

The dead were buried in the ground or placed in trees. The corpse was clothed in his best garments and his jewelry was interred with him. When a child died, a puppy was strangled and buried near him so that his journey might not be lonely. All of the preparations for the funeral were under the direction of some wise old man. The body was placed in a bark or plank casket and borne to the shallow grave on the shoulders of four old women. Women were the principal mourners, and if widowed, mourned for a longer period than did men, although the latter were not exempted from the same obligations. After death a vigil was kept at the grave by the mourners, to divine whether the death was caused by sorcery. The sorcerer was greatly dreaded and exerted much influence because of this fear. One did not want to incur the wrath of a sorcerer, for he could avenge any slight by means of his magical power. In addition to magical cures for illness, disease was treated by the use of herb medicines and the sweat-bath. The Fox doctors were also skilled in simple surgery, such as the setting of fractures and the letting of blood. In order to set a broken limb, first the fracture was reduced and the injured member was bound with basswood bark to keep it rigid until healed.

Except for sorcery and evil magic, the ideas that underlay Fox supernaturalism were set up in terms of common good. The purpose of the gens festivals was to secure the blessings and beneficence of nature for the entire group. One had to share the bounty of the

16 T. Forsyth, op. cit., pp. 223–231. Since this has been written, it has come to the author's attention, that though this is the general Central Algonkian pattern for Midewiwin, it might not specifically apply to the Fox case. Forsyth calls this ranked society "Grand Medicine" which may or may not be synonymous with Midewiwin.

earth, therefore the first fruits of a harvest or the first seasonal fruits gathered, might not be eaten by some member of the household which had produced them, until someone not of the household had partaken. To have done so would have caused ill luck. For the same reason the hosts at a gens festival might not eat. The glance of a widow or widower unreleased from mourning tabus, or of the parents of a still-born child, or of a newly adolescent girl, caused drought to fall upon the land and so endanger the welfare of the entire group. Therefore they had to remain in seclusion and not touch the soil. It was especially dangerous for a widow or widower to touch the ground with bare feet, so moccasins were always worn and it was the duty of the affinal relatives to keep such persons supplied with foot-gear. If a widowed person or pubescent girl sat under a tree, the tree would die from bodily contact. This dangerous state was ceremonially terminated in the adoption feast for the widowed, and the second ritual bath of the neo-menstruant.

WAR

For a man one of the major interests in life was war. One went to war for three reasons: the first was to acquire new hunting territories, or to avenge trespass on already existing ones; the second was to avenge the death of those who had been killed in battle; [17] and the third was for prestige. Sometimes a Fox war party would join forces with one from another tribe, being lured by the promise of land if the enemy were defeated.[18] A boy first went on a war party between the ages of fifteen and eighteen years.

Young Indians are always fond of war, they hear the old warriours boasting of their exploits and it may be said, that the principle of war is instilled into them from their cradles, they therefore embrace the first opportunity to go to war even in company with strange nations so that they may be able to proclaim at the dance, I have killed such a person, etc.[19]

Any individual could raise a war party and lead it. He would blacken his face and fast for a vision. If his dreams were lucky, he would prepare tobacco and wampum in a lodge outside the village,

---

[17] J. B. Patterson, *Autobiography of Black Hawk,* p. 76.
[18] T. Forsyth, *op. cit.,* p. 194.
[19] *Ibid.,* p. 195.

where he was joined by those who wished to accompany him, and who would pledge their aid by means of smoking, wampum, and red cloth. He invoked divine aid to assure the success of his undertaking, or to find out whether it would be wise for him to go to war.

Two or more partizans may join their parties together, and may or may not divide when they near the enemies country. The business of the partizan (leader) is to shew his followers the enemy, and they are to act, the partizan may if he pleases go into the fight. In going to war, the Indians always travel slowly, and stop to hunt occasionally, where they deposit their jerked meat for their return, in going off the partizan leads the party, carrying his Mee-shome or medicine sack on his back, and on leaving the village the village sings the She-go-dem or war song, i. e. the partizan takes up his medicine sack and sings words to the following effect: "We are going to war, we must be brave, as the Great Spirit is with us." The warriors rejoined by singing heugh! heugh! heugh! in quick time dancing around the partizan. Sometimes a certain place distant from the villages is appointed for the party to rendezvous at, in this case, every one as he departs from his residence sings his war song, and on the departure of the whole from the general rendezvous, they sing the She-go-dem or general war song as described above.

The form of a war encampment is this, small forks the size of a mans arm are planted in two rows about five or six feet apart and about four feet out of the ground, on which are laid small poles, these rows extend in length proportionate to the number of warriours, and the rows are about fifteen feet apart, thro the center are other forks set up on which other poles are placed, these forks are about six feet out of the ground, and the poles are stoughter than the side forks and poles. The warriours lay side by side with their guns laying against the side poles if the weather is fair, if wet they place them under their blankets.

The Indian who carries the kettle is the cook for the party and when encamped the warriors must bring him wood and water, furnish meat, etc., the cook divides the vituals, and has the priviledge of keeping the best morsel for himself. The partizan and warriours when preparing for war, are very abstemious from the company of women, after having accepted the wampum or scarlet cloth before spoken of the(y) cease to cohabit with their wives and consider the contrary a sacrilidge. A woman may go to war with her husband, but must cease during the period to have any connection. Before making an attack they send forward some of their smartest young men as spies, the attack is generally made a little before daylight, the great object is to surprise, if defeated, every one makes the best of his way home stopping and taking some of the meat jerked and burried on the way out. If a party is victorious the person who killed the first of the enemy heads the party back, by marching in front, the prisoners in the center and the partizan in the rear. On the arrival of a victorious party of indians at their village they dance around their prisoners by way of triumph after which the prisoners are disposed of: elderly prisoners are generally killed on the way home, and their spirits sent as an atonement to that of their deceased friends.[20]

Although it was accounted honorable to steal horses in war, this practice flourished only on a small scale. There is no mention of coup counts graded about horse taking.

Religion played an important rôle in the Fox war complex. One needed supernatural aid for success in war, and if the prognostications of visions were unfavorable, plans for an attack were abandoned. If a war party comprised more than twenty persons, a great sacred pack was taken along under the care of a special person guarding it. In smaller parties the leader's own medicine bundle provided enough supernatural protection. Cannibalism was practised for magical reasons. Children were fed portions of the eyebrow and heart of an enemy to make them brave in war, and adults partook of these too.

Women might also participate in war honors. Some man who had killed an enemy might have a female relative club the head of the corpse. Once a woman had done this, she was socially equivalent to a man and could function as an attendant at gens festivals, and had certain other duties connected with funerals.

Another prerogative rising out of participation in war was the right to take a new name. A man kept the name bestowed on him at birth until he had gone on a war party. The new name did not necessarily have any relation to the gentile names, but he could adopt the name of an ancestor. Even if a man had gone on only one war party he could change his name as many times as he wished. A woman, on the other hand, could change her name after marriage if she so desired, especially in accordance with a vision she had received. Male slaves, themselves captured in war as children, were encouraged to go to war when they had grown up. If they did this, they might take new names and assume the status of free men. Female war captives were taken as wives, and the children of such unions were regarded as free Fox. (All of the foregoing applies to inter-tribal war. Information as to whether the

[20] T. Forsyth, *op. cit.*, pp. 195–197.

same usages prevailed in warfare with the Whites is not available from the published literature.)

The initial White contact of the Fox was with the French traders, for when Father Allouez arrived in 1669, he found metal tools already in use. Whether this earlier acquaintance was on a large scale is not definitely known, but Nicholas Perrot, the famous voyageur, had encountered the Fox as early as 1665. Perrot acquired a good deal of influence among the tribes around Green Bay, for he was a shrewd individual and because of his courage had won the respect of these Indians. He was a good friend to all the peoples of the Green Bay region, advising them wisely and keeping them out of wars. When Allouez returned in 1670, he founded the mission of St. Marc for the Fox. His work met with little success at first, but slowly he gained the confidence of the Fox, and when he was leaving in 1673, they begged him to return. The faith of the Fox in conversion to Catholicism rested on directly observable, material results. They regarded the cross as potent war medicine for a time, because thirty young warriors had painted the device on their shields and come off successfully from an encounter with the Sioux, with whom they were at war during the last decade of the seventeenth century. Men and women made the sign of the cross at all hours of the day. However, the following year they lost faith in the power of the symbol when a number of their braves were killed. The first conversions were of old men and dying infants, later on a few able-bodied adults, but Christianity never took firm root among these people and was definitely in abeyance at the end of the Fox wars.[21] Yet they did realize that some of the White men were their friends, for by 1701 the Fox sent to Montreal requesting a resident Jesuit, saying that they had no sense since Perrot had left the region in 1695, and that possibly a missionary might do them some good, as Perrot was unable to return.[22]

[21] Louise Phelps Kellogg, "The Fox Indians During the French Régime," *Proceedings of the Wisconsin State Historical Society*, 1907, p. 149.

[22] P. F. X. De Charlevoix, *Histoire de la Nouvelle France, Volume V*, p. 144; E. H. Blair, *op. cit., Appendix A, Volume II*, p. 255.

Hostility to the French was manifest from the earliest date. The Fox's dislike for the French has been ascribed to their distaste for the beards that the White men wore, but it has a more realistic basis in the ill treatment that some of their number had suffered at the hands of the French in Montreal in 1671. For these acts the Fox vowed vengeance.[23] The prices offered by the British [24] for furs were much better than those received from the French. This fact, coupled with the growing animosity to Frenchmen, made the Fox particularly receptive to the suggestion of the British that the French be driven from the territory. England had her eye on the valuable fur trade of the Northwest, and incited the Fox, through her allies the Iroquois, to war upon the French and the latter's Indian allies. The uprising resulted in the Siege of Detroit in 1712. The Fox had planned to burn the fort and thus force the French to abandon the region, but a Christian Fox informed the garrison of the plans of his tribesmen. Because of this treacherous act, the Fox were trapped in their own fort while awaiting the aid of English troops and their Kickapoo allies, and although they were willing to surrender to the French and make over what captives they had taken, amnesty was not granted. The siege was resumed, again the leaders of the two sides parleyed, but once more they reached no armistice. After nineteen days of siege, the Fox escaped under cover of a rain-storm, but were pursued and attacked. The remnants of those who had escaped slaughter, some 150 men, plus women and children, were captured and enslaved.[25]

The Fox were infuriated by the loss at Detroit, and in 1714, alone or aided by the Sioux and Iroquois, they plundered all of the tribes who traded with the French, thus closing trade routes. In 1716 a party of 800 French and their Indian allies, marched against the Fox at Butte des Morts. Some 500 men and 3,000 women and children were in a fort, expecting reinforcements of 300 more warriors, but nevertheless they capitulated. After some

[23] P. F. X. De Charlevoix, *op. cit.*, *Volume III*, p. 185; *Jesuit Relations, Volume LV*, 1670–71, Thwaites edition, pp. 187, 219.
[24] Tailhan, "Commentary on Perrot's Memoir," in E. H. Blair, *op. cit., Volume I*, footnote, p. 259.
[25] P. F. X. De Charlevoix, *op. cit.*, *Volume V*, pp. 257–263.

delay on the part of the French, peace was made by all parties involved under the following conditions: prisoners were to be surrendered to the French in advance; the Fox were to replace all of the members of the French-Indian allied tribes that they had killed with slaves from distant tribes; and the Fox were to pay the expenses entailed in this punitive expedition from the profits of their hunting.[26] As further evidence of good faith, six chieftain-hostages were taken to Montreal. An epidemic of smallpox broke out and three of them died. The French feared that the deaths would be construed as a breach of faith and make the Fox break the treaty, so they sent the remaining chiefs back in 1717 with liberal presents to pay for the dead, and to show that they had taken good care of the hostages. They were received with the calumet, and the Fox promised the French that they would send deputies to Montreal as proof of their good will. (This last they never did.) The Fox had not abided by all the articles of the treaty made in 1716, having only surrendered the prisoners, so in 1719 the French again attempted to induce them to come to terms.[27]

In the meantime the British had not ceased to covet the French sphere of influence, and the latter power feared the danger of a solid alliance stretching from the Iroquois on the east to the Sioux in the west. They realized that such a ring would disrupt trade channels, and determined to exterminate the Fox who were the ringleaders of this entente. The benefits of a trading-post in Sioux territory were obvious, for it would wean these people from their devotion to the British via the Fox, and therefore included in the plans of the French was the idea of setting up such a center.

It was impossible at this time to carry out this policy of complete destruction of the Fox because of the inter-tribal warfare which had broken out. The Fox were at war with the Illinois from 1719 until 1726 in retaliation for a massacre which had occurred on the return from a summer hunt. In 1723 the Fox had concluded an alliance with the Sioux in order to fight the tribe to the west, and the French dared not pursue them into this region. After 1726, when the Fox had made peace with the Illinois, it seemed

[26] *Ibid.*, pp. 305-306.
[27] P. F. X. De Charlevoix, *op. cit., Volume V*, pp. 307-308.

likely that there would be no more trouble with the former, but by the following year the British had once more incited them to drive the French out.

The new outbreak crystallized the determination of the French to get rid of the Fox once and for all, so in the summer of 1728 a party marched against them, comprising 450 Whites and a band of 1,200 Indians. They made no headway, beyond razing the villages, until Indians were sent against the Fox.[28] In 1729 the Fox were severely crippled by an ambush of Winnebago, Ottawa, Menomini and Ojibwa. While the Fox were returning from a long hunt, 377 in twenty flat-boats, were massacred by these 200 Indians.[29] Through this maneuver the fur traffic was disrupted.[30] After an Indian (Winnebago, Ottawa, and Menomini) attack upon a Fox village in the fall of 1729, the French aided the attackers and the war continued into 1730.[31] The Fox were also harried on all sides by other Indians, for they were at war with the Kickapoo, Mascoutens, Hurons, and Christian Iroquois. A fierce six-weeks campaign in the region of Lake Winnebago was fought against the Fox by France and her Indian allies; the Fox were besieged again and once more escaped because of an opportune storm. They attempted to reach asylum in the country of the Iroquois, but the cries of their children betrayed them and terrific carnage ensued. The tribe was dispersed and the French considered that it had been annihilated. About 800 Fox were killed in this battle, the remnants seeking refuge among their neighbors.[32]

This catastrophe aroused the pity of the Sauk and some of the other northern tribes, who permitted the survivors to come and

---

[28] The French Régime in Wisconsin, III, *Wisconsin Historical Collections, Volume XVII*, p. 21.

[29] Report of M. de Beauharnois, May 6, 1730, of an Expedition Made by the Outaouacs, Sauteaux, Folles-Avoines and Puants, *Wisconsin Historical Collections, Volume V*, p. 104.

[30] *Wisconsin Historical Collections, Volume XII*, p. xv (Preface).

[31] The French Régime in Wisconsin, III, *Wisconsin Historical Collection, Volume XVII*, pp. 80 and 90.

[32] The French Régime in Wisconsin, III, *Wisconsin Historical Collection, Volume XVII*, pp. xii–xv (Preface). Messrs de Beauharnois and Hocquart's Letter to the Minister, Nov. 2, 1730, Relating the Defeat of the Foxes, *Ibid.*, p. 107.

live with them. In 1733 the French sent an officer and some soldiers to seek the fugitives for deportation as slaves to the West Indies, but the Sauk refused to relinquish them. The officer who demanded their release threatened them with a show of arms. One of the Sauk shot the son of the officer and the Whites retaliated, the officer being killed in the fracas that followed. The Sauk feared the consequences that would arise from the slaughter of an officer, so they fled south to Iowa and Illinois in 1735. Here they were joined by bands of fugitive Fox who had been held captive among French allies. In the new territory they continued to harass traders and the Illinois, and forced abandonment of the Sioux post. (This had been set up late in the 1720's, dropped as a result of the last Fox war, and reëstablished in 1732.) By 1743 the Sauk and Fox had allied with their one-time enemy, the Sioux, and continued to plague the French settlers in the region.[33]

Unceasing opposition by the Fox to settlement and trade, plus the debilitating effects of the Fox wars were one of the strongest factors in the breakdown of the French empire in the New World. While the Fox were making the territory unsafe for the traders and precluding any possibility of permanent settlements in the region which they roamed, France was unable to extend her holdings. France made no attempt to control the traffic in liquor as she had promised. The British extended credit to the Fox and granted them more liberal prices for their furs, together with cheaper liquor, so it was natural for the Fox to favor the latter power.

After the French and Indian War, in 1760, British domination was established on the territory. England set up trading-posts, and the military took over control. In addition the Spanish began to compete for the favor of the Fox, and amicable relations were established with this power, the Fox going to St. Louis to trade with them. During the Revolutionary War, the Fox sided first with the British, but ultimately pledged allegiance to the United States of America in 1778.[34] In the meantime they had maintained

[33] The French Régime in Wisconsin, IV, Ibid., Volume XVIII, p. xii (Preface). Lyman C. Draper, Historical Notices of DeLouvigny, Perrot, de Lignery, de Beaujeu, Marin, de Buisson, de Villiers, de Noyelle, and St. Ange, Ibid., Volume V, p. 113.

[34] Wisconsin Historical Collections, Volume XV, p. xviii.

a constant state of warfare with other Indians. Their enemies at this time were the Pawnee and various southern Siouian peoples.[35]

The first important treaty with the new government was signed in 1804. One of the tribesmen had killed an American, and was jailed for this offense in St. Louis. Five Sauk and Fox were sent to this place with gifts to compound for the death and to bring the prisoner back. He was released from prison, but was shot in the back as he left the building. In the interim the five chiefs were made drunk and signed a treaty. This agreement ceded lands on both sides of the Mississippi, and received the Sauk and Fox into the protection of the United States. In return for this land, they obtained goods worth 2,234 dollars and fifty cents, and an annuity of 1,000 dollars (600 dollars for the Sauk and 400 dollars for the Fox), which was also to be paid in goods, the value of which were determined by prices prevailing at the place of purchase. The United States promised never to disturb them, or permit Whites to settle within their domain, if the Indians promised not to sell any of their land to Whites. If Whites squatted within the boundaries, the Indians were to complain to the superintendent who would see that they were removed. Native law was to be abandoned, but if complaints were filed, the superintendent would inform the chiefs, who would see that the culprit was brought to trial in the courts of the state or territory, and the Sauk and Fox would be liable to punishment under the same code as were the Whites. If an Indian stole from a White man, compensation would be deducted from the annuities, and if the converse occurred, the United States government would recompense the victim. All traders were to be licensed, and the government promised to establish a trading-house or factory. The Sauk and Fox were to make peace with the Osage. The most important article, however, was the one that was later violated, guaranteeing to the Sauk and Fox their right to remain on their lands as long as they resided there.[36]

The English traders who were in the region to the north still offered the Fox better prices and advanced them credit. When Whites began to poach on the Indians' land, the Fox drove them off, acting on the advice of British friends, and this antagonized

---

[35] Benjamin Drake, *The Life of Black Hawk*, p. 47.
[36] *Ibid.*, pp. 50–58.

the United States government. When the War of 1812 broke out, the Sauk and Fox sent a delegation to Washington requesting permission to participate. The president told them to remain neutral, but a band of 200 fought under the Union Jack under the leadership of Black Hawk.[37] At the end of the war, a treaty was concluded at Portage des Sioux, forgiving the offenders and reaffirming the treaty of 1804.

The land on which the Indians were situated was excellent for farming, and valuable mines (principally lead) were also in the region. By a series of land cessions the Sauk and Fox were gradually pushed to the west. By one of the earlier agreements (that of 1804) a trading-post was to be set up in the territory of these Indians, but in September, 1822, they waived the right to this for 1,000 dollars. In 1824 they ceded more land, this time south of a line in the Missouri Territory, for 1,000 dollars per annum for ten years. Because they had been at war with the Sioux, they made formal peace with them in 1825. These last three treaties were of less importance than the ones which came later. Although the government had guaranteed to keep Indian lands free of White settlers and remove all trespassers, the lead mines proved an irresistible attraction. A temporary agreement about the mines was reached in August, 1828, which permitted Whites to occupy land near the mines, and in 1829 a treaty was made by which the Indians relinquished these lands. The government made restitution of 20,000 dollars for thefts by the Whites, and reassured the Sauk and Fox of territorial sanctity. Under the articles of the new treaty, 8,000,000 acres of land west of the Mississippi, extending from the upper end of Rock Island to the mouth of the Wisconsin River, were ceded.[38]

Owing to the rapidity with which the Whites were coming in, the Indians found on their return from their winter hunt in 1830, that the first sale of the ceded lands had taken place. They were particularly aggrieved when they found out that one of the Rock Island traders, who had been a particular friend of the Indians, had purchased a good deal of it. The agent informed the Indians that they no longer had any right to remain within the region. The president ordered that they be moved peaceably, but when this

37 *Ibid.*, pp. 62–64.
38 *Ibid.*, pp. 66–72.

proved impossible, the cavalry was summoned. On June 7, 1830, they held a parley, but Black Hawk refused to move his village. On the twenty-fifth of June, a band of 1,600 mounted troops reached Rock River and took the Sauk village the next day, only to find that the Indians had quietly decamped during the night. It was abrogation of the treaties and the unfair treatment that part of the Sauk and Fox felt they had received at the hands of the United States that were two of the principal causes of the Black Hawk war.

The Sauk and Fox signed another treaty a month later, which granted them immunity provided they went west, and stipulated that Black Hawk's band, which had supported the British in the War of 1812, was not to cross the Mississippi. The Fox paid little heed to this edict, for in the fall of the year, a band ascended the river to avenge the death of several of their number who had fallen at the hands of the Menomini and Sioux. The Fox attacked a camp of Menomini and killed twenty-eight. The authorities demanded that the killers be given up for trial in accordance with the previous treaties (1804, 1825), and the Fox refused. In the meantime they had sent to the British for aid, and had also received promises of assistance from the Ottawa, Potawotami, Ojibwa, and Winnebago, so that they might fight to retain their land. Black Hawk also solicited help from those bands who were across the Mississippi, which was not granted.

In 1832, in violation of the treaty of the previous year, Black Hawk assembled his people and crossed the river to raise a crop of corn in the territory of the Winnebago. He was twice overtaken and ordered back, but he refused to return. The Winnebago and Potawotami who had so glibly promised their assistance were afraid to antagonize the federal government, and would not help him. The militia was summoned and went out, being met by a truce party from the Black Hawk contingent. The soldiers refused to recognize the white flag, and captured the three emissaries. Later this attempt to parley was repeated, and the Whites killed two of the truce bearers. This maneuver incensed Black Hawk, so he and his band of forty charged the 275 soldiers and put them to rout at the Battle of Sycamore Creek. The success of this foray aroused the confidence of the Winnebago and they joined

Black Hawk. The Potawotami also took advantage of the situation and wiped out a settlement of Whites. Several pitched battles ensued between Whites and Indians, in one of which many women and children were slain as they attempted to gain sanctuary with the bands who were not involved in the war, on the west bank of the Mississippi. After the Battle of Bad Axe (August 25, 1832), Black Hawk and his ally Wabokieshiek [39] were taken and delivered into the custody of the army.

On September 21, 1832, a treaty was signed at Prairie des Chiens, which provided for the cession of Iowa lands. In return for the land cession, the government was to pay off the debts the tribes owed to the traders; to supply them with smiths; and to pay them 20,000 dollars a year for thirty years. The agency at Rock Island was discontinued, and it was not until 1838 that a new agency was set up for the Sauk and Fox. In 1837, another treaty was signed which provided for the payment of the interest instead of the principal of the money accruing from land cessions. Early in 1838 the site for the new agency was chosen on the Des Moines River. There were a farm, two mills and smithies. The agent was subordinate to the governor of Iowa, and not to the army as before. There were three bands of Fox, and it was planned that each of them was to have a model farm near the village. Fences were erected and some ground was broken for plowing. It is likely that plans for rapid acculturation would have succeeded, but illegal settlers came in and the whiskey trade flourished. The agent was powerless to control this traffic as he had no authority and there was no garrison near at hand.

The Indians ran rapidly into debt. Annuities had been paid to the chiefs and not to heads of families. The chiefs favored the American Fur Company, which made other traders angry. The Indians became indolent and refused to farm, they tore down fences and let their ponies into the wheat fields, the chiefs abused their privileges and turned over to the traders even the funds that had been set aside for educational purposes. (This payment to chiefs was a policy which the government had favored since it strengthened the authority of the chiefs.) Things came to such

[39] Wabokieshiek was a half Sauk, half Winnebago Indian who achieved some note as a "prophet."

a pass in 1841 that the governor of Iowa ordered the annuities to be paid directly to the heads of families. The traders were opposed to "civilizing" the Indians, as they would lose their supply of furs and the control they exercised over the Sauk and Fox by supplying them with liquor and extending them credit. In order to control the whiskey traffic, it was proposed that only licensed traders, and only one to a tribe at that, be permitted to live in each area. (With several traders to extend credit the Indian could buy as much liquor as he desired, and buy anything at an exorbitant price on credit.) Yet the abuses continued and illegal settlers and traders became so defiant that a troop of dragoons came to keep order.

On October 11, 1842, the Sauk and Fox met with the governor to consider complete cession of Iowa territory. They were over a quarter of a million dollars in debt, and though they loved their home, the pressure of debt and of Whites coming in was too much for them. They could remain where they were until May 1, 1843, when they were to move west of the White Breast fork of the Des Moines River and then were to leave the state after three years. Since this removal within Iowa was temporary, no effort was made to set up schools or farms. The Indians planted a few acres, but established no villages. Outrages under military jurisdiction were infinitely worse than they had been under civilian control. The soldiers gave liquor to the Indians in the presence of their officers. Health conditions were very bad, and seventy-nine Indians died in one year. The Sauk departed in 1845 for their new home in Kansas, and the Fox followed later, stopping off to visit the Potawotami en route, and arrived in Kansas in 1846.

Although the Fox had officially quit Iowa territory, several groups straggled back to squat there, as they loathed Kansas. General distaste for their new home, plus two other direct causes brought about the purchase of land in Tama.

The sojourn in Kansas was unpleasant. Accustomed to green woods with abundant water, the Fox disliked the flat, treeless prairie. In 1854, while a group of them were on a hunt, they were attacked by a party of Kiowa, Comanche, Cheyenne and Arapaho, whom they put to rout. Fearing the displeasure of the federal government in consequence of this act, they sneaked back to Iowa. Money was raised to purchase the first eighty acres in Tama county through the sale of their ponies. The Sauk in 1858 took advantage of the absence of the Fox, while the latter were on a hunt, to sign a new treaty, which allotted some of the lands in severalty and ceded others. This action incensed the Fox and they protested. The agent deposed the protesting chief. Thereupon the remaining Fox rejoined their tribesmen in Tama, forfeiting the annuities due them.

In 1856 the legislature of Iowa passed a law which permitted the Fox to dwell within the confines of the state. This legal recognition of the right of residence is most significant, in that it made the tribe responsible not only to the federal government but also to the local authorities. The land that they had purchased was held in trust for the tribe by the state governor. In 1867, Congress was persuaded to restore the back annuities due them, and to allow the Fox to remain in Iowa as long as they abided by the laws of the state.

The community of 250 who had returned from Kansas suffered many hardships during their first years back in Iowa. They were desperately poor and eked out a miserable existence by doing a little gardening, hunting, begging and selling trinkets. They lived on their land in the summer and scattered to hunt and trap in the winter months. They received nothing from the government until the spring of 1867, when the first payment of the annuity (5,588 dollars and forty-six cents) was made to them. The agent, who had been appointed the year before, was asked by the Indians to hold 2,000 dollars of this sum to purchase more land for them. The Fox were land hungry and upon the receipt of any considerable sum of money (from the restoration of back annuities, or from the sale of their land in Indian Territory) augmented their holdings. They bitterly opposed schools and Christianity. In 1876, the first school was built for them, but shortly after its opening it was forced to close because the Fox still maintained their old practice of dispersing for the winter, which interfered with school attendance.

Although the Fox were continuously buying land with their moneys, they were still suspicious of the government, and when in 1878 they were requested to give their names for the annuity lists, they refused. They cited religious reasons for this refusal to coöperate. A new agent was appointed and he succeeded in obtaining the names of all but thirty of the Indians for the rolls, yet still the annuities were withheld. The Fox sent a delegation to the governor of the State to inquire about the trouble. He had been informed by the agent that the land had been seized for taxes, and that redemption would expire shortly thereafter, and was requested to report this fact to the Indians. It was finally discovered that the interpreter had been fomenting the opposition to enrollment. The agent could speak Fox and gained the confidence of the people, so they submitted at last to the governmental dictum about the lists. In January, 1882, they received the first payment of the newly restored annuities and redeemed their land.

The Fox still opposed schooling, and the idea of men farming was repugnant to them. The adult Indians told the children that they would be taken away by the soldiers, which acted as an effective deterrent to attendance. School was reopened in May, 1883, with two women teachers from the Ladies Home Missionary Society, but attendance was again small. The Fox complained to Washington in 1887. They refused to be instructed by a farmer, accept agricultural tools, or permit their children to attend school, but were willing to use their funds to support their own agency and physician.

Money began to come in from the sale of the Oklahoma allotments, some of which had been held in the name of the Fox. These funds were again applied to the purchase of land, so that by 1894 they had increased their holdings to 2,800 acres. The tax problem was finally met by renting to Whites two plots which did not impinge on the main tract of their land. The rents accruing from these leases were used to pay the state levies. Such a system is in use today and eliminated the necessity of pro rata or other assessment.

The distaste for Christianity which the Fox had acquired in the years of their early experience with the French was still strong. They had had no permanent contacts with active proselytization from the early period of contact until the decade of the 70's, when the United Presbyterian Church established a mission on the east border of the Fox land. This mission met with little success; nevertheless it attempted to reach the Fox through the school. This institution had a total of ten pupils in 1893. Many Whites felt that the Fox should have an adequate school that would attract more pupils. To achieve that end they formed a body known as The Indian Rights Association of Iowa. This group brought pressure to bear on Congress, which resulted in the appropriation of 35,000 dollars for the construction of an industrial boarding-school. Seventy acres of land, in the township of Toledo three miles from Fox land, were bought for this purpose, and the school was opened in 1897. The pupils attended classes during the week, but were allowed to go home over the week-ends. Students attended from other states as there were not enough Fox to keep the school filled. The school met much opposition at first, but managed to struggle along until 1912, when it was turned into a tuberculosis sanatorium for young people.

The trusteeship of the land passed from the hands of the state governor to those of the Secretary of the Interior in February, 1895. However, the transfer did not become final until 1908 because of the peculiar circumstances surrounding the original purchase of some of the land. The title had been registered for their heirs and assigns in perpetuity, in the names of five men who, acting as agents for the tribe, had actually bought the land. This was construed as possibly meaning the descendants of these five and not of the tribe as a whole.

In 1937 a new constitution was drafted, which has been accepted by the Fox tribe. Under the new system they will be able as a group to borrow money for the purchase of additional land, since more acreage is required if the Fox are ever to become completely self-sustaining.

THE ACCULTURATION PROCESS

The acceptance of new cultural elements has proceeded along the lines of gradual substitution of new traits rather than sudden and complete elimination of old ones. The first wholesale replacement antedates even direct White contact, for when the French first encountered the Fox, metal tools had already supplanted those made of stone. Although the Fox were relatively unclothed when the French came upon them, they rapidly adopted cloth garments. Yet even today moccasins of deerskin, or of commercially tanned leather combined with canvas are frequently worn. In the last century leggings were worn by both sexes. The costume of women consisted of a frilled skirt and yoked blouse made of cotton print or silk with a wrap around skirt of black broadcloth and a corresponding top piece worn for best. The men were garbed in breech clouts and blankets. Now both sexes wear the clothes of the White man, but women continue to wear shawls and to cut many of their garments on the old two-piece pattern. Clothing of Indian design is worn at festivals and at pow-wow. The Fox first began to wear undergarments when the children were made to don them at the boarding-schools.

Face painting has vanished, except for some few artistic souls who paint at pow-wow, and for the adoptee at an adoption feast. Men do not roach their heads any more but wear their hair cropped in White fashion. The women may wear theirs bobbed, even having permanent waves. Those with long hair plait it, let it hang down the back caught with a barette or comb, or put it up in a chignon or coronet. Some women use rouge, powder and lipstick, and it is these cosmetics that serve as face paint when the occasion demands it. The men (when necessary) shave with razors and no longer perform facial epilation with tweezers or with a twist of wire.

Both the horse, which was in use by the middle of the eighteenth century, and the canoe and flat-boat, which were adopted by 1730, extended the Fox range considerably and permitted cultural elaboration. Horses were obtained from tribes west of the Mississippi, who in turn had obtained them from Santa Fé. There is also evidence that the Sauk went directly to that source for their animals.

Pottery was manufactured as late as 1820 and sherds have been found in the Rock Island sites, but even traditional knowledge of the craft has perished. The brass kettle which was brought in by the early traders quickly found favor and is in wide use today. Durability was undoubtedly a factor in the rapid adoption of metal utensils, since they are eminently more suited to transportation than are clay vessels.

Wheat flour and meat are purchased from the stores in town. The former is often made into fried bread, which is cooked in a skillet on the embers, or into biscuits. The use of white flour was already common by the latter half of the nineteenth century. Much of the diet still consists of products raised or gathered at home, and of small game that is trapped. Canning as a technique of food preservation is not much more than ten years old. In addition to this new method, the old techniques of food storage are still used. Corn is shelled and dried, or made into hominy. Beans are also dried, and the squash and pumpkins grown are cut into strips, braided and dried for storage. Cucumbers are eaten raw or made into pickles. Among the other new crops raised are oats, alfalfa, potatoes, beets, onions, tomatoes, and cabbage. Fish is caught in a chicken-wire weir that closely approximates the aboriginal pattern. Corn is no longer pounded in the wooden mortar; instead it is ground in the feed-mill in Tama.

It is in the field of law and politics that the major social changes have occurred. With the signing of the treaty of 1804, the Fox began to abandon the native scheme of internal control and became subject to the jurisdiction of White courts-of-law. The disappearance of warfare weakened the power of the chief, whose principal function had been of an inter-tribal nature. The calumet was apparently superseded by wampum by about 1820, for Forsyth and Marston mention it only in passing, and then as an accessory to wampum which had taken on the same functions. Control by the ceremonial runners lapsed soon after arrival in Tama. With the restriction in range due to land purchase and the disappearance of game from the region, the long, seasonal hunt was abandoned as a group function. As police service rendered by the braves was no longer needed, and there was no field open in which to gain war honors, this group no longer had any *raison d'être*, and as there was no way of augmenting the group (i. e., no war in which to gain prestige), it soon died out. The council is now an elective body and exerts what little internal control it can. Divorces and some property disputes come to the attention of the local White court. Few major crimes are committed, most of these few being either theft, which is infrequently prosecuted, or liquor offenses.

The Fox as a tribe have never embraced Christianity. The small success enjoyed by the French Jesuits in converting some of them to Catholicism was over by the end of the Fox wars. In the 1870's the United Presbyterian Church set up a mission on the threshold of the Fox land, but it has gained hardly more than a foothold since that time. At the turn of the century one young woman who was regarded as a good friend by the Indians brought many into the church, but membership dwindled after she was removed. Some of the young people profess Christianity, but they usually slough it off later in life, or participate in the native ceremonials concurrently. It is the opportunity afforded by the Church as a place for social gathering that gives the Church what little hold it has upon the Fox.

The date when the Algonquin syllabary was introduced is problematical. It was in wide use at the end of the nineteenth century. Many persons who are unable to write in English handle it with utmost ease. It came apparently to the Central Algonkian from some of the more easterly tribes. English is still not spoken by more than one third of the people, but there is no one who does not speak Fox. It is used in the home at all times, and often women who have married into the tribe are forced to learn Fox in self-defense.

It is not difficult to see that the idea of surnames should come easily to a society organized into gentes. American names, with several conspicuous exceptions, have only been in common use for the last forty or fifty years. Two families bear the surnames of White traders or agents who had Indian wives. Several of the names of obvious White origin come from intermarriages with Potawotami, Sauk and Winnebago. A large group of names are direct translations of gens names, the children taking as surname the name of the father. A third group of names consists of Fox names that have been reduced to English characters for ease of transcription. The name is not precisely fixed for there have been name changes during the lifetime of the individual. Nicknames are popular, which represents an aboriginal practice translated into English usage.

Since the dispersion of the village in 1902, the frame house has been widely used, but the bark or mat-covered wickiup is still common and especially popular for summer use. Many men still use the brush-covered arbor, with the plank platform, for sleeping in hot weather. The long summer house is no longer covered with bark but is made of boards. Seven of these structures survive and are used solely for ceremonial purposes, although they were formerly lived in as well. Peyote meetings are held in a canvas tipi, which is set up in the yard of one of the members. The Drum Society meets in an open enclosure on one of the hilltops. The menstrual hut stands at the side or back of the house. It is a small dome-shaped structure covered with bark or tarpaulin, and while women no longer sleep there, they do all of their cooking on a separate fire during their catamenial periods.

The riding horse has been supplanted by draught animals and by automobiles. Now there is some tendency to replace the former by tractors and other motor-driven farm machinery.

In the acceptance of White culture there have been sexual, lineal and factional differences. For women to adapt themselves to new ways, a less drastic readjustment was involved than for men. The rôle of women remained essentially unimpaired with the coming of the Whites, although their tasks were materially lightened. Less time had to be spent in the preparation of food, for they no longer had to pound corn meal, and an iron-bladed hatchet was superior to a stone tool for cutting tough bark. It was infinitely more difficult for the men to adapt themselves to a new technology. Traditionally they regarded farming as women's work, and the men consistently opposed adopting this form of occupation. No appreciable group evinced any interest in agriculture until the last decade of the nineteenth century.

Schism into progressive and conservative factions began with the first White contact. Mention constantly recurs of pro- and anti-White groups. The last chief to be recognized by the government was of the progressive faction and he was among the first to send his children to school. There is a tendency on the part of the descendants of one of the White traders to dissociate themselves from participation in native ceremonial. They are active, however, in the political and economic affairs of the tribe.

On the whole, Fox history has been one of organized opposition to White culture. Ty-ee-ma, one of the Fox chiefs, summed up the attitude of his people to Marston: [40] he believed that the Great Spirit put the Indians on earth to hunt and to gain a living from

<hr>

40 M. Marston, *op. cit.*, p. 155.

nature; he said that when any of his people departed from the ways of their ancestors by attempting to learn to read and write and to live by the ways of the White man, the displeasure of the Great Spirit was incurred, and the offender soon died.

The general refusal to accept schooling, conversion, enrollment by name in the annuity lists even at the price of forfeiting their funds, shows the strong determination to preserve and defend their own way of life since the land purchase. The schism into factions brought about a bitter feud, reaching such a climax that the duly elected member who was a leader of the conservative faction refused to sit on the council.

Peyote and the Drum Society are two religious cults that have been imported from other Indian groups. The first incorporates many elements of Christian doctrine and worship. The main source of the mescal button used in peyote worship is from the Sauk in Oklahoma, but one of the participants also raises the plant in boxes in his home. The leaders of both factions oppose these innovations, yet membership closely follows factional lines. The bulk of the peyote members are drawn from the conservative group, while those who belong to the Drum Society side largely with the progressives.

Aboriginal culture is valued, but the Fox are not blind to certain obvious benefits to be found in White ways. The superior technological knowledge and skill of the Whites was rapidly acknowledged. The Fox do not expect a small child to be interested in the things adults do. Children have to be dragged to ceremonies, and when they attend them, pay little attention. But this is to be expected, for they are only children and no more is demanded of them. White education is appreciated in that it equips the Indian to cope with the White man and the problems that he poses. At first it was the boys who attended school for a longer period than did girls, but at present the obverse is the case. Fewer girls play truant too. Girls are eager to learn domestic science and dressmaking, since such skills enable them to become better housewives.

The skill of White physicians is recognized for what are considered White diseases (e. g., smallpox, venereal diseases, spotted fever, diphtheria, measles, etc.). An outbreak of Rocky Mountain spotted fever occurred in 1937, and more than half of the people submitted to blood tests. When there was a field nurse for this tribe her clinic for the treatment of venereal disease was well attended. The obvious benefits achieved through hospital delivery are realized. It is easier for the government to bear the burden of contamination from parturient and post-parturient women, than it is for a family (and less expensive too).

For the old culture it is impossible to judge the system of economic valuation. Today money is well understood and appreciated. Personal evaluation has not changed. The man who is sober, industrious, faithful and not a gossip, is the one who is respected. He should not lie, nor fawn on the Whites. The girl who is modest, neat and a good worker, is the one who will be a good wife. Although ideally she should be chaste, this standard is more honored in the breach than in observance, but she must not be talked about or bear illegitimate children. One hundred years ago there was much prenuptial sexual activity on the part of girls and that is the case today. Yet when such a girl married, she was expected to be faithful to her husband, and generally lived up to this expectation.[41]

The Fox, unlike many other Indian tribes, are not "historically minded." They have short memories and even their stories do not include many archaic cultural traits. Instead, their mental activities have been utilized for reaching a working adjustment to each new situation, and not preserving the outward formal shell of life when the inner meaning had gone. As each element of their culture lost its use, it was rapidly discarded and not retained for its doubtful antique value. Even the method of butchering bear and buffalo was not remembered in 1910, a scant sixty years since they had actually used these animals.

NON-CULTURAL RESULTS OF CONTACT

One of the earliest changes to come about was the change in tribal name. The Fox call themselves Meskwawki, which means literally Red-Earth People. Their neighbors called them Outagami, the translation of which is "People from the Other Side." When the French first met a band of Fox they asked them their

[41] T. Forsyth, *op. cit.*, p. 215.

names, wishing to ascertain the tribal affiliation. The Indians misunderstood and thought they were seeking gentile affiliation. As the persons the French encountered belonged to the Fox (War Chiefs) gens, they gave this association as the answer. The appellation of Fox has persisted as the tribal name.

None of the earliest accounts gives the Fox more than 3,000 persons as a maximum number. Although it is unlikely that not one of the French chroniclers ever saw the entire tribe together, it is improbable that the top estimate was ever exceeded or even reached. The tribe dwindled in size until the middle of the last century owing to the ravages of decimating wars, epidemics, and liquor. After that time the population increased slowly, owing to better living conditions and through the Sauk, Potawotami and Winnebago who came to live with the Fox. A severe outbreak of smallpox occurred in 1902 which killed off forty-two individuals. Since this epidemic the numbers have been on the increase, so that the Fox now number over 450, representing a net gain of something over 25 per cent in the last thirty years. The birth-rate is very high, and the death-rate relatively low.

The Fox are a healthy people and amazingly free from tuberculosis. Venereal diseases have not yet made great inroads. Trachoma is the most common affliction but wide incidence of the disease seems to be at least 110 years old.[42]

Until the removal to Kansas, the tribe had never lived all together. Now, since all Fox except those who have taken up residence with other tribes or in towns live within the limits of 2,800 acres, population density is greater than at any other time in their recorded history.

The change from a semi-nomadic to a completely sedentary economy has meant a curtailment in range for most of the people. Although in 1880 about half of the people dispersed to hunt in the winter, now there are no longer any village hunts. Since the abandonment of boarding-schools, fewer persons manage to travel very far afield. Some of the men who attended Carlisle have been as

[42] T. Forsyth, op. cit., p. 218. Mention is made of the wide prevalence of "sore eyes" (1827), which the author ascribes to the great amount of irritating smoke present in the lodges of the Sauk and Fox.

far east as New York, and visits to relatives and friends in Oklahoma, Kansas, Nebraska, and Wisconsin are frequent. Many Fox have traveled with rodeos and circuses. Within the confines of the State of Iowa, jaunts are common. The Indians are much in demand at county fairs, demonstrations of the American Legion, and similar affairs. The baseball teams and the brass band play away from home several times during the year. Two men got to France as soldiers in the World War, and one of them to a training camp in Texas. There is little desire to settle away from Tama. All but one of the men who have held jobs in cities have returned and settled with their families. The sole exception is the man who is employed by the State Historical Society in Des Moines, but he visits his relatives often. Several women and one man have married out of the tribe and taken up residence elsewhere. One man is enlisted in the Navy.

The rich lead mines and abundant fur supplies once available to the Fox are of course gone. Although some trapping of small animals is still practised, the large game animals once so important in their economy have long since vanished. The amount of land available to support each individual has been drastically curtailed, but with the change in economy less acreage is needed. Many more manufactured articles are now in use by the Fox, and these have become more plentiful with the passage of time.

THE PRESENT COMMUNITY

There are two crucial incidents that serve to demarcate changes in the mode of Fox life. The first one is of course the purchase of land in 1854. It is the position as tax-paying residents of the State of Iowa that has buttressed the pride of the Fox, and contributed to their great sense of security, which is reflected in their cultural stability. The acquisition of land through acceptable legal channels has fixed their status as tax-paying residents and prevented them from being regarded as interlopers by the Whites. They lived in a village until 1902, when the second critical incident took place. This was a severe epidemic of smallpox, which resulted in the burning of their village at the order of White authorities. As a result of this destruction by the local health officers, they dispersed and took up residence in various parts of the tribally owned land.

Some 450 Fox now live on 2,800 acres of land in Central Iowa. (Figures are as of 1937.) Farming is the economic basis of their lives. All the women cultivate gardens as was done long ago, but it is the men who raise oats, hay, corn, and alfalfa, thus preserving the ancient division of labor, which held the man responsible for securing the White man's goods for his family. Houses are still also conceptually female property, although they are often owned and willed by men. House and garden sites are available to all persons enrolled, but not everyone possesses fields on which to raise cash crops, for certain historical reasons that will be discussed later. Men do the rough work, such as plowing and clearing the gardens, and suffer no loss of caste by performing these and other garden tasks. One of the best gardens is kept by a bachelor who devotes much time and care to his vegetables. Men take the same pride in having good gardens that women do. This fact is all the more striking in view of the unwillingness of Fox men, over a long period of time, to perform what was always regarded as "women's work."

ECONOMIC CONDITIONS

The tribal land holdings consist of some 3,300 acres—one large tract of 2,800 acres where the Fox live, and 520 acres separated from the rest which are leased to Whites. The money from this latter land is used for the payment of taxes. The land is tribally owned with perpetual rights thereof guaranteed to all enrolled and the descendants of males so listed. The tract lies about three miles west of Tama, Iowa, which is the nearest town. Two railroads, which provide an irregular source of casual labor, run across the land. The Iowa River flows through the tract, and the Lincoln Highway traverses it. Several stands for the sale of souvenirs and trinkets have been erected along this artery.

The sanatorium located several miles to the northeast, is the seat of the superintendency, and provides steady employment for about twenty persons, and sporadic work for as many more. Several members of the superintendency personnel are employed in various capacities at the school. In addition two men have contracts to drive the school buses.

The Fox are far from wealthy. In 1936 the average family income for the year was just under five hundred dollars. This figure included not only wages and salaries, money resulting from the sale of farm products and other articles, but all forms of relief and interest on tribal funds. Their land is valuable, being worth 225,-000 dollars. Some tribal funds are on deposit in Washington, which yield about 6,500 dollars a year. Some of this source will be depleted in the near future, as pro rata shares may be withdrawn from the larger part of it by persons on reaching majority. In order to receive this money, the recipient has to show evidence of wanting to use the funds for some definite purpose (i. e., for the building of a house, or the purchase of horses or machinery). The consent of the superintendent is necessary before the application may be submitted to the government.

Because the Fox geared themselves to a money economy early in their history, and depend on trade goods for many necessities, conditions in 1933–37 were crucial. The farming population was hard hit by the drought. These unfavorable conditions which came on in the midst of depressed agricultural prices, plus the decrease in their annuities and the general loss of income through the increasing poverty of the surrounding White farmers, have forced many of the Fox to accept relief. (In 1936, a drought year, seventy-six out of a total of ninety-one families received some form of relief.) The non-farming class, which comprises over half of the families, has been similarly hard hit by these conditions. It has been estimated that ten acres per person are necessary for support in this region, so that even with maximum utilization of all land owned, their acreage would be insufficient for sustenance. With incorporation of the tribe, plans are afoot to borrow money for the purchase of additional acreage in the near future.

There is private property in land in the sense that inalienable title to arable fields is held by individuals. These plots cannot be sold, but may be rented to other Fox for cash or farmed on half shares. Only about one third of the land the tribe owns is tilled; the remainder has never been cleared. Because only half of the families have access to cleared fields, there is dissatisfaction with the present land arrangements. The landed group received title to these lands in the late 90's, when some of the men who had become interested in farming as an occupation, were allotted tracts of land by the council. Although the transactions were never recorded, title is firmly held by the original assignees or their heirs. These lands have never been reallocated.

The soil is extremely fertile, and irrigation is unnecessary for the water table is high in this region. Although subject to periodic drought, the land with proper care yields excellent crops. In 1925 Henry Wallace, now Secretary of Agriculture, inspected the farms of the Fox and reported to the State on their condition. He commented that while the Fox were not the best farmers in Iowa, they were far from the worst.[43] The men take a lively and intelligent interest in farming, subscribing to agricultural journals, and talking over their problems with the government farmer. It is unfortunate that at the time when boys were attending boarding-schools, during the first three decades of this century, little emphasis was placed on instructing them in more efficient methods of agriculture. Instead they learned various trades, which they have had little opportunity to use in later years.

Oats, corn, and hay form the largest cash crops. They are sold to Whites, mainly for feed. Threshing of oats is done in accordance with White methods. The entire pattern of the threshing bee has been adopted, i. e., a group of men take turns at threshing the oats of each member of the party. If a man who has had the services of another for his crop cannot pay in kind when the latter's turn comes, he makes up the deficit in cash. The thresher is rented at a cost of three cents per bushel of oats threshed. Beans, which ripen all summer, are dried for home consumption, canned or sold to the cannery in Marshalltown, which lies twenty miles to the west of Tama.

Recently four men formed a partnership for the purchase of a tractor, with a plow, harrow and discing machine. The owners are responsible for running it and providing the fuel, and have

<hr>

[43] Edgar A. Harlan, The Mesquakie Indians and the Wheeler-Howard Act, quoting from "Wallace's Farmer," September 1925, *Annals of Iowa*, July 1936, p. 381.

arranged to do whatever plowing, etc., is requested of them for hire. In 1937 nineteen men had availed themselves of these services, for a total of 266 acres.

Credit is obtainable from local banks and from the government on short term loans, secured by a lien on crops or chattel mortgages, in order to finance planting, etc.

Although the country is admirably suited to dairy farming and the raising of livestock, the Fox do not like to raise cattle and hogs. To these people a cow is something to be killed as meat and eaten. The trouble involved in feeding and sheltering the animals for the winter makes them prefer to buy meat, milk, and butter from the stores. Nevertheless a few men keep hogs and cattle.

In 1936 forty-three individuals owned a total of 105 horses. These were all work animals. Some horses which have been bred from crosses between ponies and draught animals are used for riding, mainly by the young people. Horses are usually hitched to plows or wagons, while buggies stand idle in the house yards.

About half of the families buy chicks in the spring, via mail-order. They are raised for meat, egg production being incidental. The mortality-rate for these birds is very high as many of them get run over by automobiles. Three families raised ducks for meat in 1936. Dogs are plentiful. The puppies are in great demand for feasts, and often when there is a shortage of them locally, the men make trips to the neighboring farms to buy pups. Cats are less common than dogs but may be found in several homes.

Half of the families own automobiles. Those who do not travel to town on foot, by taxi, or with relatives and friends, frequently buying gasoline for those who drive them in. Most of the shopping is done in Tama. Stores in this town carry plaid shawls, silk neckerchiefs, beads and other articles desired by the Indians. Some buying is done from mail-order houses, especially the small seed beads from which belts and headbands are made. If something is required which the local shops do not offer, a trip may be made to Marshalltown which boasts of being the shopping center of central Iowa. Food is bought in Tama or Toledo, which lies two miles north of Tama. On Wednesdays and Thursdays respectively during the months of July and August, the stores stay open late in the evenings, and band concerts are held, which form an inducement to come into town and shop.

Wide use is made of the resources the country offers. Maple sugar is made in the spring, blackberries and other wild fruits are gathered as they ripen, nuts are collected and used at home or sold. Baskets for sale and home use are woven from black ash, which may still be found growing in the neighborhood but is relatively rare, or the wood may be imported from friends and relatives in Wisconsin. Although the deer and other large game have gone, they make moccasins and other articles of buckskin obtained from Wisconsin and Oklahoma. Deer hair is dyed and plaited into roaches, which the men wear on festive and ceremonial occasions. The small animals that they trap furnish furs for sale. Sometimes the skin of a mink is used for the band of a fancy head-dress. All edible birds are consumed with relish. Fish may be sold to Whites or eaten at home. Herbs are collected and used in curing. Sometimes the Fox doctors blend their potions with commercially prepared drugs to increase the efficacy of the medicine.

The Fox live in small frame houses, with outbuildings clustered about them in the yard. Barns, corn-cribs, chicken-coops and vegetable gardens are near the house. The canvas-covered menstrual hut is off to one side or in the back. Women rarely sleep in them now, but they eat there, and when they do not avail themselves of the hospital facilities, give birth to their babies therein. The houses range in size from one to six rooms. Water is obtained from wells, which may be dug anywhere with certainty of success. They use hand pumps to get the water, but no house has any water piped into it. Sanitary conditions are very poor. There are no toilet facilities in many homes, and when these are present take the form of small privies, frequently roofless. Furniture is scanty, bedsteads and bedding making up the bulk of it. A great deal of the cooking is done out-of-doors over an open fire. The wickiup and arbor with the long wooden sleeping platform is used a great deal. Here it is that the men sit, discussing the affairs of the day, while the children play all around them. The fields may be situated at some distance from the house, due to the changes in residence since the lands were originally assigned, or the desire to build a new house far from the fields.

SOCIAL ORGANIZATION

The biological family is the principal social unit, the members of it forming the core of the residential group. A man, his wife, their children, the children of either of the spouses by a former marriage, and unmarried relatives constitute the household. The unattached persons may be individuals who have not married yet, the widowed and those who are divorced or separated. The household is by and large the economic unit too, but its unity is tenuous, for all persons who live in a house may not be contributors to its expenses, although they usually all share in the labor necessary to keep the house going. The rôle played by small children in the work of the family is solely dependent on the wishes of their parents.

A very slight preference for matrilocal residence obtains, but residence rules are informal and depend largely on mood or economic expediency. Often because they have quarreled with their parents, young people will move in with some relative. Relatives as a rule tend to build houses close to the homes of their kin. No English is spoken in the home, so a child first begins to learn it when he attends school.

During the early years of maturity, marriage is apt to be brittle, some persons of twenty-five having been married as many as six times. Children tend to stabilize marriage. A few couples are married at the United Presbyterian Mission, or by the justice of the peace, but it is more usual, especially for second and later marriages, for the couple merely to live together openly. Marital exchange is less common than it was in former times, but is still kept up by those conservative Fox who can afford it. Where property is involved there may be recourse to legal divorce, but informal amicable separation is more usual.

Ideally young persons of both sexes should be chaste until they are ready for marriage. This actually is not the case today any more than it was in 1820, for both boys and girls have a good deal of sexual experience. Theoretically a promiscuous girl cannot get a young husband. What is really meant by this standard is that illegitimate children are under a great handicap. In the eyes of the Fox no good can ever come of a bastard. Such children are not only looked down upon, but are also pitied. Illegitimate children are more apt to be rude and undisciplined than those born in wedlock. Since social sanction of a birth is arrived at by naming, the biological factor or paternity *per se* is not the important one. Contraceptive measures are employed, one of which consists of a potion which the woman drinks just after having borne a child. This sterility is temporary and may be waived by counter medicine. If it is difficult for a woman to conceive, both she and her husband drink medicine which facilitates conception. Divorced persons are not supposed to speak to each other and certainly not have sexual connection. Whereas prenuptial sex experience is expected of the young, illicit affairs between married and unmarried persons are decidedly *de trop*.

The Fox have the institution of joking relatives. Reciprocal joking obtains between nepotic relatives, and siblings-in-law. Between the latter pairs of relatives, obscene joking is the rule and nepotic joking manifests itself usually in teasing and the playing of pranks. Great reticence is the rule between parents and children, siblings (especially those of opposite sexes), and between parents- and children-in-law.

The immediate blood kin are those involved in affinal and other types of exchange that have been set up along kinship lines. Marital exchange is conducted on a scale less lavish than it was in bygone years, owing to the increasing poverty of the Fox. Adoption, which includes exchange obligations, is universally kept up, although it is no longer possible to do so on the scale that was customary when they had ponies.

Gift exchange is institutionalized in requiring that if an initial gift is of cloth (clothing and dry goods), the return gift should be of food and vice versa. There are three types of exchange between groups of kin—marital, adoptive, and mortuary; and that which is part of the behavior obtaining between certain pairs of joking relatives. This last type can be divided into two categories —joking about food and appropriation of property. Food joking of the reciprocal type obtains between a man and the daughters of his classificatory sisters. The men involved in this give the women or girls meat, and they reciprocate by giving something sweet, like candy, to the men. (They can also give each other fancy garments.)

The second category deals with the behavior of a man and his mother's brother. The former has the privilege of taking anything that belongs to his uncle, without the latter's permission. The man from whom the object has been taken may retaliate in kind, but has no other mode of redress.

Marital exchange seems to have supplanted bride service as a mode of obtaining a wife. The basis of this exchange was present in 1820 in the validation of an elopement by the acceptance of gifts. It is not known whether return gifts were also made, but this custom is present now. The exchange is instituted by the mother and sisters of the groom. It takes place only when the family of the man patently approves of the groom's wife, and is the only marriage ceremony of the Fox. The groom's kinswomen prepare a complete new set of Indian garments for the girl. These are given to her when she comes to the home of her husband, with other gifts of dry goods, household utensils, and in former times possibly a horse. Then she goes back to the home of her parents. She takes off her new clothes, and may give them to her sisters, and returns to her husband's family's house with gifts of food, such as flour, sugar, and coffee. This return gift of store groceries is a substitute for the garden products, which she herself had grown, which she used to give at the end of some months. From time to time sisters-in-law will make gifts to each other. If a woman gives her brother's wife a gift of clothing or dry goods, she in turn will make a return gift of food or of something she had made. This institution reflects the old division of labor in which men supplied the raw material for clothing, or the wherewithal to purchase cloth, from their hunting activities, and the women furnished the manufactured objects and vegetable foods.

When a death occurs, the persons who have been in charge of the food for the funeral, either relatives or non-relatives, although not members of the same household as the deceased, are given gifts of dry goods, in recompense for their services and the food they brought. They are the ones responsible for the preparation of the feast held four days after the death, and do not receive the dry goods until this feast has been made. All persons come to visit the corpse before burial, and if they can afford it bring a gift of food or of dry goods. These form part of the payment of the pall-bearers, as do the possessions of the deceased, which are piled up and distributed at the funeral to the attendants who have served during the burial activities. The persons who do the burying may be the affinal relatives of the deceased, which is a further extension of affinal exchange.

The adoption feast is held at any time from four days to four years after a death. The adoptee is of the same sex as the deceased, but not always of approximately the same age. He is someone who is not a member of the same household as the deceased nor a close blood relative. If the adoptee is about the same age that the deceased was, the kinship terms and behavior patterns that the relatives of the deceased used to him are taken over *in toto,* but if the adoptee is markedly older or younger then the terms and behavior are modified to suit the circumstances. On the day of the adoption feast, the adoptee is summoned to the house where the adoption is to take place. He comes dressed in his own garments. The sponsors give him an entire outfit of new clothes in native design, which he dons, and paint his face with red cosmetics. Dress lengths of dry goods are displayed on a rack and other gifts are placed nearby. The adoptee is handed a number of short invitation sticks, as many as there are pieces of material, and he chooses persons to dance, giving a stick to each one. The dancers are of the same sex as the adoptee and they form a line behind the adoptee and dance around the display of gifts during the ceremony. After they have finished dancing they line up near the cloth. The sponsor gives the pieces of material to the adoptee who presents each dancer with one length of cloth. The invitation sticks are passed out before the feast is served and eaten. Everybody comes to an adoption feast, and all those present are expected to eat, and it is a serious breach of etiquette to refuse to do so. When the feasting has been concluded, the dancing takes place. If the adoptee is married, his spouse also dances in the line. When the gift-giving part of the adoption is over, the adoptee goes home but the guests linger. The adoptee takes all of his gifts home including his new garments, and he may not visit his adopted family until he is ready to bring them a substantial gift of groceries. After this return gift has been made, he is free to come and visit whenever he wishes. The sponsoring household keeps gifts in readiness for him against surprise visits, and he in turn tries to have gifts ready for his adopted relatives in his own house, should they chance to visit him. It is this adoption feast that frees a widow or widower from the handicaps of mourning, under which he has been laboring. (One aspect of avuncular-nepotic exchange stems directly from this release. When a widow has been released by the performance of adoption rites, she carries dry goods to her mother's brother(s), and a widower does the same, carrying the cloth to his sister's daughter(s).) [44]

There are five large functioning gentes—Bear, Thunder, War Chiefs, Wolf, and the Water group. The first two of these comprise nearly half of the tribe, so some endogamy has occurred. Of the remainder of the original number listed, some have become extinct, some are represented only by one or two members, and some, although more numerous, have nevertheless ceased to hold gens festivals.

Gentile affiliation may be achieved in three ways. The first is by "legitimate" birth, in which the child is named from the gens of its father and so placed in it. Naming constitutes the social recognition of paternity by the father and his kin, which establishes legitimacy. (Biological paternity is not important for the father may name as his own child the offspring of his wife by another man. The community regards a child so named as his.) Illegitimacy, i. e., non-recognition of the child by his father, *not* birth out of wedlock, automatically affiliates the child with the gens of its mother, for her family then names it. If there has been a succession of infant deaths in a family, someone not of the father's gens may be requested to name the child and thus avert bad luck. When such a change occurs, association with the naming gens lasts for one generation only, and the child of a man so named will in the normal course of events belong to the gens of its father's father.

Each gens owns one or more great sacred bundles around which ceremonies are performed. The gens festivals are held three times during the year in accordance with the old annual cycle. Rites occur in the spring to correspond with planting; in mid-summer when the crops begin to ripen; and in the winter. The winter cere-

[44] T. Michelson, Miscellaneous Notes on Fox Mortuary Customs, *Annual Reports of the Bureau of American Ethnology, Volume 40*, p. 463.

monials are less elaborate than the other two, for the bundle is not unwrapped. The order in which each gens holds its festivals is fixed, the Bear gens holding its ceremonies first. The other sacred pack organizations share some 'of the characteristics of the gens. They also have sacred bundles. Both the gentes and the societies have mutual burying rights with one another; e. g., the Bear gens and the Wolf gens bury each other, as do the Fish gens and Menstruating society.[45]

The moieties retain the social and ceremonial rôles they had years ago. At an adoption feast, if a game is played (lacrosse and the moccasin game if the deceased was a man, and the double ball game or squaw dice, if a woman), the moiety to which the deceased belonged is permitted to win.

The factional schism between progressive and conservative is sharp. It cuts across gens lines. Marriages can traverse faction lines, and often women will change their factional adherence to those of their husbands. The Fox have had a long history of internal dissension, for one of the earliest references to them describes such a cleavage over the return of a captive Ojibwa girl,[46] and schism was also pronounced during the period of the Fox wars, when there was a pro-French group just as there is a pro-White group today. The pro-American, pro-British split, of which Black Hawk's band fighting for the latter power in the War of 1812 is an example, lasted until at least 1832. The present factions are based on a dispute that dates back to 1881, when the rightful heir to the chieftainship, a son of the former chief was refused office, and the council declared Pushetonequa chief in his stead. Pushetonequa came from a lower division of the Bear gens than did the chiefly line. This act was accepted with good grace by the Fox until fifteen years later when some question arose over the annuities and the problem of the chieftainship flared up. The group of Fox who had conservative tendencies formed a bloc against the proposed changes. The progressive faction now embraces the

---

[45] T. Michelson, Notes, Fox Miscellany, *Bulletins of the Bureau of American Ethnology, Bulletin 114,* p. 65.

[46] La Potherie "Savage Allies of New France," in Blair, *op. cit., Volume I* pp. 358–359.

adherents of Pushetonequa, whose son is their leader (the office of chief being now in abeyance), and their descendants. They have controlled the council and local politics, but under the new elections there has been some factional change, for office-holders are now drawn from both groups. Most of the professing Christians are members of the progressive faction.

POLITICAL ORGANIZATION

The Fox have accepted reorganization under the Wheeler-Howard Act. There are seven officers on the new council including a chief-of-council, a president and a treasurer. This council has the power to act for the tribe in the purchase of further land by the tribe as a body.

As the Fox have inalienable land rights, the parents of children resulting from inter-tribal marriages are eager to have them enrolled as Fox, in order to assure them of a home in the future. Before 1932 any child, one of whose parents was an enrolled Fox, was eligible for enrollment. In that year an election was held, the results of which limited eligibility of enrollment to those whose fathers were enrolled.

In 1916 the last chief appointed a council which was self-perpetuating until 1929, when an election was held. At that time three members from each faction were elected, but a dispute arose and they refused to meet with each other, so that this council never sat. Later on more elections took place for the council, but this body never had any real authority. It did, however, have a great deal of prestige, and vigorous political campaigning went on. The progressive faction were the more astute politicians and had things their way until 1937, when a new council was elected under the new constitution and both sides seemed to be content with the results. Women may and do vote among the Fox.

The legal status of the Fox in White courts is peculiar. Although the Fox are responsible to the state courts for crimes committed against "citizens" of Iowa, the court refused to apply the criminal laws of the state to cases involving the domestic relations of the Indians themselves. (*Peters vs. Millin, III, Federal*

244, 1901.) The state act of February 14, 1896, which transferred the title of their lands to the trust of the federal government and made the Indians liable to rights of eminent domain, taxation and judicial jurisdiction (*Laws of Iowa, 1896, Chapter 110, pp. 114–115*), was to be interpreted as set forth in the foregoing case.

Drunkenness and property disputes are the most common offenses to be prosecuted. The Indians themselves may petition the local courts and bring suits. At pow-wow time the committee sends any intoxicated person to jail. Sporadic cases of bootlegging crop up and are dealt with by the federal grand jury at Cedar Rapids, Iowa. This is particularly true of Indians who purvey liquor, as the sale of any liquor but beer over the counter is a state offense, and no one may purchase intoxicating beverages in this state without a liquor license. Indians are of course by federal statute unable to obtain such permits. Theft among the Fox themselves may be left unprosecuted, as the Indians are reluctant to press charges against one of their own kind. If, however, the matter is haled to court, the authorities are inclined to be lenient. Murder, by direct violence, has not occurred for many years. Rape, which the Fox believe is usually accomplished with the aid of love magic, may be punished by imprisonment or the offender goes free, depending on circumstances.

The Fox are not given to violence among themselves. Men are less apt to be embroiled in fisticuffs than are women. If men are angered, especially over sex matters, they will threaten to club one another. These threats are often carried out. There is an aversion to using knives on an enemy, but hitting one on the head is the accepted mode of attack. If the justification is great, Fox men will even threaten (and carry out these threats) to attack White men, and it is worthy of note that when such a case occurred recently, the attacker was dismissed by the court on the ground that the assault was justified.

RELIGION

The concept of Manitou and belief in the necessity of releasing the souls of the dead, have remained the same. One still gives a feast for the first fruits, and no member of the household which has been instrumental in their production will eat of them until this ceremony has been observed.

Formal worship revolves around the sacred packs which belong to the gentes and societies. While the imported cults (Peyote and the Drum Society) and sacred bundle worship are mutually exclusive in their ideology, active participation in one of these groups does not preclude the possibility of functioning at a gens festival. Factional differences are laid aside in the performance of a gens festival, and even those who profess Christianity attend sacred pack ceremonies.

The sacred bundle cults are both gentile and non-gentile. There are eleven groups of sacred packs, and within each group of bundles there are several major and several minor packs. If a person belongs to any of the major packs of a group, he is a member *ipso facto* of all of the other major packs within this group. One becomes a member of minor packs only by virtue of belonging to specific major packs about which the minor ones cluster. In addition to belonging to a gentile pack by birth, if one is named from another gens, one is automatically affiliated with the bundles of this gens. A person who is a good singer and knows the correct songs may be invited to act as a host at a gens or other bundle ceremonial, and is thereafter a member of that pack. Certain gentes and societies have mutual rights to be waiters and attendants at the festivals. The persons who play the major rôles at the feast of one bundle are more likely than not to have similar rôles in the performance of other bundle festivals. This is especially true of bundles within a group.

In former times when each gens owned a long summer house where the festivals were held, the non-gentile cult groups, e. g., Buffalo packs, had their own houses where all the members of the related cults, i. e., Bear, Wolf, and Thunder Buffalo packs, held their ceremonies. From the above evidence it is not difficult to see that the line demarcating the purely social from the ceremonial functions of the gens cannot be clearly drawn. The gens is primarily a bundle cult group and shares many characteristics with any of the non-gentile religious societies.

Bundle group ceremonies are held in the long summer houses. Each ceremony lasts but one day, from the morning until sunset.

The singers and drummers sit along the platform that stretches the length of the house. In the center of the house is the fire where kettles of food are simmering. The food has been prepared by the hosts, and the waiters, who belong to another gens or society, are at hand to serve it. The main dish (except for the Wolf gens festivals) consists of stewed puppies, that have been ceremonially clubbed to death. There are usually four sets of dances, accompanied by songs for each group. The bundle has been opened and various parts of it are used in the performance of the rites. In some cases love medicines have replaced the war medicines that were present in the bundles (the latter no longer have any *raison d'être*), with corresponding changes in music. The rôle that women play in the ceremonies is that of hummers; they hum while the men sing. These hummers are women who have passed the menopause. Some women dance in some of the ceremonies. These are small girls or older unmarried girls ("virgins"), and in some cases they also hum. Each dance is introduced by the playing of the flute to the cardinal points of the compass or to various objects in the bundle. For the dancing the doors of the house are kept open and those not participating in the ceremony are permitted to watch. Between the dances there are songs and prayers, the doors of the house being kept closed. The feast is eaten between the third and fourth sets of dances. The bones of the dogs that have been consumed are gathered up carefully and destroyed by burning. Both men and women are permitted to participate in the summer ceremonies, but only men at the winter celebration. The dancers are lined up in single file and dance behind the leader around the sacred objects which have been laid out in the center of the house. Men and women dance in very different styles.

The three non-bundle cults are the Singing-Around-Society, Peyote and the Drum Society. The members of the Singing-Around-Society are drawn from all groups and both sexes. A member usually names his successor, but if a member dies intestate, the person who has been ceremonially adopted takes his place. If a person is cured through the efforts of this cult, he often joins it. The society sings during drought or, when epidemics threaten, at the homes of various members or of sick people. This society is of relatively recent origin, but the exact date when it was founded is unknown. It had only nine members in 1923,[47] but in 1934 it had increased its membership to forty-six. It appears to be losing what prestige it had to the peyote cult.[48]

Peyote is regarded as a cure-all. It is open to all persons who care to join, but membership is confined so far mainly to four families. It has been growing in importance in the last thirty years. The doctrines of the peyote cult emphasize the falsity of aboriginal belief, so that it is difficult for the "pagan" Fox to reconcile the two types of religion, yet it is from the conservative group that most of the peyote worshipers come, and some of them still participate in the gens festivals. Peyote meetings are held on Saturday nights in a canvas tipi.

The Drum Society on the other hand draws its members from the progressive faction, which is a striking fact, for it emphasizes the return to the worship of Manitou. This cult is a recent importation from the Wisconsin Potawotami, and corresponds to the "dream dance" (also known as the "religion dance") of the Ojibwa and Sioux. Worship revolves around four drums. The ceremonies are held four times during the year in a circular enclosure on a hilltop. Membership is open to all who show the proper inclination, but leadership in the society is concentrated in the hands of a few families. The headquarters of this cult is in Wisconsin, and the group of Ojibwa there issue orders from time to time as to how the ceremony is to be conducted. In contra-distinction to the Ojibwa, the Tama Fox do not use the cross in their worship [49] nor do they divorce unfaithful wives at the performance of this dance.[50]

Important among the cult activities of the Indians are those bundle ceremonies performed by the Potawotami who live with the Fox in Tama. These ceremonies are held by the Potawotami

[47] T. Michelson, The Singing Around Rite, Ethnological Notes, *Annual Report of the Bureau of American Ethnology, Volume 40*, p. 549.

[48] Sol Tax, *The Social Organization of the Fox Indians*, Chicago, 1937, p. 267.

[49] Cf. Oklahoma Sauk and Fox, A. Skinner, Associations and Ceremonies of the Menomini Indians, *Anthropological Papers, American Museum of Natural History*, XIII, p. 175.

[50] *Ibid.*, p. 30.

and some of the Fox who have Potawotami blood or affiliations. The rites are of the same type as those of the Fox bundle feasts and membership is achieved in the same way.

As soon as a Fox is apprised of a death, it is customary for him to visit the house of the bereaved. If he can afford it he will bring a gift, but even if he is not in a position to make a present he will pay this visit anyway. The body is dressed up and placed in the coffin. Coffins are purchased in town if the family can afford it, or got from the carpenter at the sanatorium. Those who assist with the burial receive the personal possessions of the deceased plus the gifts that the visitors have brought. There are three cemeteries on the Fox land and the Indians tend to bury relatives together. The body is interred on the day of the death if that is possible, or on the day following at the latest. If there is any suspicion of foul play about the death or if the deceased had met a violent end, a vigil is kept to ascertain the cause of the death. For four days the bereaved family mourns and no one does any work around the house. This period is terminated with the ghost feast, which is prepared by the women who have charge of the cooking during this interval.

Sorcery power is achieved in two ways, by the vision quest and by learning. If one seeks out a vision, one may receive malignant power in the course of one's fast. Sorcery in the form of love magic is rather widespread. One can also purchase love medicine or receive it as a gift. If a man possesses love magic, women will talk to him of their own accord, for it is the woman who makes the first overt move in sexual affairs. If a man is reasonably good-looking and a good worker, but is unsuccessful with women, it is because he has none of this magic. On the other hand, men who apparently have nothing to recommend them but who are exceedingly successful owe their success to the love medicine. The same holds true for women. Once a woman has used love medicine on her husband he cannot leave her. Love medicine may not be kept in the house. If the owner of any magic is married, his spouse must share with him the knowledge that he possesses magical power. Love medicine may be used in death sorcery and may be bought for this purpose. If a person loves someone who does not reciprocate, he may by his medicine make him insane, and eventually the victim will commit suicide. The idea that lies behind this behavior is that if a person will not love you, you out of envy and anger will make him undesirable to others. In order to attain this end, hair from the victim's head is tied around the bag containing the love medicine. In time the victim will go mad and kill himself. Even if the death results from apparently natural causes, it is regarded as suicide.

Sorcerers have the power to assume the shape of a bear or snake, and may go about in spirit form, assuming these shapes at will. If one suspects the presence of a witch, one shoots at the place where the sorcerer is presumed to be, and the guilty person will die on the fourth day afterward. Witch dolls were used either singly or in pairs. This usage may be a European trait, for the procedure smacks of the common peasant technique. The doll was pierced with some sharp object, and the victim was wounded in a corresponding spot on his body. It was dangerous to have these dolls around and not use them, because if they were not employed for any length of time the power in them would begin to work of itself and injure some member of the owner's family.

The wind is used to send out sorcery power and the sorcerer is thus able to transfix his victim in a hypnotic fashion. Sorcerers could move objects at will. The sorcerer is not above such simple means as food to send power into his victim. Placing medicine in food is used both as a means of transmitting love magic and to make a victim ill.

In addition to learning the medical techniques, power to cure may be obtained on the vision quest, the tutelary being the snake or the bear. The animal would leave a claw or bone that became the basis for a medicine pack. Parents teach their children the names, appearance, locale, and uses of herbs. The child may be given a description of a plant and sent to fetch it. Only the children who were intelligent would be taught these techniques, and in the case of sorcery, only the child who can be trusted not to talk about it will be selected as a pupil. Both boys and girls learn how to cure, but a woman does not begin to practise until she has passed the menopause.

A successful practitioner enjoys definite economic advantages, for his fees are high. He is paid in dry goods and garments, while in the old days even a horse might be included in his fee. The goods are stacked up in the house, and formerly, if a horse was to be given, the halter was placed on top of the pile. The doctor comes in to see the patient, and incidentally the size of the fee. If enough merchandise is offered he will take the case. The doctor is also given two pints of alcohol for his own use. He performs the cure by singing, dosage with herbs and sucking out objects. The doctor may suck them out directly or through the bone or claw of a snake or bear. If a foreign body is removed in this manner, it is placed in a saucer of alcohol. Herbs are made into decoctions and administered as teas or lotions. Sometimes nothing else may be eaten for four days, or multiples of four, than these herb potions. Although there is reluctance to pay the local White physicians their fee of one dollar, if an Indian is dissatisfied with the treatment he receives from the physician employed by the government, and goes to an Indian doctor, he will pay the native practitioner twenty-five dollars in goods without a murmur. Some of the Indian herb doctors enjoy a good deal of repute in the treatment of arthritic and rheumatic conditions among the local Whites.

Sweat-baths are used as a prophylactic measure and are thought to make one bear the heat of the summer well. They are often set up in the spring for this purpose, although now the practice is less frequent than in former days. Both men and women may use the same sweat-lodge but not at the same time. Sweat-baths are always accompanied by ritual sprinkling of the hot stones with herb liquor and singing.

To treat stiff joints, a steaming method is employed. A hole is dug in the ground to accommodate a small stone, with a shallow trench leading in from one side. The stone is heated red hot and placed in the hole, and the patient lies down with the sore spot directly over the excavation. The afflicted part is then covered, and water poured into the trench. The water flows into the hole and when it comes in contact with the stone, generates steam which eases the stiffness.

SCHOOLS

At six years of age children begin to attend school. The linguistic barrier is great, for they know no English. From 1912 until 1937 there were two day-schools, one of them having the first through the fourth grades, and the other the fifth through the eighth. In 1937 the two day-schools were consolidated. The new school building has a gymnasium and other recreational facilities that were lacking before. It is under the charge of three teachers. The children are taken to and from school in buses, and eat their lunches at school. These are hot meals which are prepared in the school kitchen by Indian women. Those who wish to attend high school, may go to the public high school in Tama. In 1937 only two students went to Haskell from this tribe and none to any of the other boarding-schools. Two persons have attended college, but neither of them completed the course. It is very difficult for the Fox to continue education away from home because of their financial straits. The new governmental policy favoring attendance at local secondary schools rather than at boarding-schools has met with Fox approval.

Excellent library facilities are available at Tama, but not many persons make use of them, and books are loaned out through the school. Many magazines are read, principally of the household or confession variety for women, and pulp-paper adventure ones by boys. Men read newspapers (as do women), subscribing to city journals in addition to local sheets. The newspaper printed in Toledo features a column of Fox news conducted by one of the members of the tribe.

Entertainment available in town is varied. Shopping and the movies are popular sources of amusement. The pool-parlors, in some of which beer may be obtained, are very popular with the men and boys. Carnivals and other celebrations of this type bring out a large Indian attendance, and when the circus comes to Marshalltown everyone makes an effort to see it.

There are many sources of amusement for the Indians within their own group in addition to the outside ones mentioned above. There is a brass band which plays at pow-wow. Several members of this organization play also in the town band concerts during the summer. The men's baseball team plays on Sunday afternoons during the summer months, and often has games away from home. Girls have a softball baseball team, and for the winter of 1937–38 a basketball team was projected. The church holds parties and dances, which the young people attend, and an annual picnic for all the Indians. There are illustrated lectures occasionally at the mission, and of course the services on Sunday. There are several clubs too. One of them is the women's club which meets once a month. One of the school-teachers and the wife of the missionary take an active interest in this organization. There is a great deal of visiting both within and outside of the tribe. In the fall, visits to Wisconsin friends and kin are especially popular because it affords them a chance to hunt. Many visitors come from other states for the pow-wow or to attend an adoption feast. Ceremonies, both the aboriginal bundle feasts and the more recent cult groups, are certainly one of the principal foci of interest.

The more active athletic games of the Fox are played rarely nowadays. The men play lacrosse infrequently, but in 1937 there was a revival of interest in the double ball game played by girls and women. A team of White girls in Tama was organized and the Fox girls taught them how to play, engaging in several matches with them. During the summer there is much swimming in the Iowa River, and in the winter there is ice-skating there.

In the winter months the Fox play several gambling games. The men play the moccasin game. In this game a large steel ball bearing is hidden under one of several squares of cloth, the guesser having to indicate with a stick under which piece of fabric the ball is concealed. Teams may compete with one another and the tallies are kept with short sticks. The women play squaw dice against each other. In this game eight or nine bone pieces are employed. Six or seven of them are flat discs, about half an inch in diameter, plain on one side and colored on the other. The other two discs are in the shape of animals (bears, turtles, or horse's heads). The dice are thrown in a wooden bowl, the score depending on the fall of the dice. A player has only one turn, but if he throws a winning combination, he may take another toss. Two persons are the minimum number that may play this game, and twenty the maximum. The players and spectators place money bets and goods on each throw or player. The well-known hand game is not an old Fox pastime, but they are familiar with it, although it is infrequently played.

Despite the fact that the Fox have many songs, both sacred and secular, and a very rich life, only peyote songs are being composed today. The instruments on which they play these songs and accompany their singing are the flute, rattle, and drum. The last instrument ranges in size from small individual drums to large ones made of a keg or tub that six men play at pow-wow. This large drum has to have its head heated, before it can be beaten. Several persons own battery radio sets.

The ancient decorative arts are still found among the Fox. They embellish their garments and household objects skillfully. The Fox are expert embroiderers and needle-women. The men carve bowls and ladles of wood. Plaited and wicker baskets are made of dyed wood splints. The colors used for these are ordinary commercial dyes, but some knowledge of vegetable colors exists. Beadwork is made, incorporating the angular motifs of Plains art with some naturalistic curvilinear design. Among the most popular ornaments for adoption and other dress costumes are plaited woolen belts and garters, woven of brightly colored yarn.

The most important group interest, both as a financial undertaking and a social event, is the annual pow-wow. This performance was inaugurated in 1913. It is a four-day celebration held in the late summer of each year. Two performances are given daily, one in the afternoon and one at night. There are singing, dancing, games and renditions by the band. Gorgeous costumes are worn by the participants, who go to much trouble to prepare the colorful trappings. Exhibits of antiques, garden products, and handicrafts are featured. Prizes are offered for the best vegetables grown and for some types of handwork. These are donated by merchants and other interested persons. On the afternoon of the last day the climax is reached, for two dance contests are staged, one for small boys and the other for men. Indians from other tribes come to compete in the latter event. The celebration draws a large crowd, both Indian and White. Pow-wow is a considerable source of income, but as the proceeds are pro rated among those participating, the share received by each person is not very large. All work, except the most necessary is given up for the duration of pow-wow. Many Indians pack up their household effects and erect tents or mat-covered wickiups and camp on the pow-wow grounds, as do some Whites. Stands are set up around the grounds where soft drinks, ice-cream and souvenirs are sold. On the last night of pow-wow men and boys beat a drum and sing in front of each stand. Every concessionaire contributes something to this group for the visitors, as it is considered inhospitable to permit them to go home empty-handed.

The relations that the Fox maintain with other tribes and with the Whites vary according to circumstance. With the Sauk who are their closest linguistic affiliates, the ties are most amicable. They visit and correspond with them, and obtain peyote, buckskin and other things from this Oklahoma tribe. The Potawotami they regard as good friends. There are many Potawotami and persons of such descent among the Fox who even have their own sacred pack groups. The Fox visit them frequently in Kansas and Wisconsin, and are in turn visited by them. (The dream dance has headquarters at Whitefish, Wisconsin. Orders concerning changes and additions to the ceremonies performance issue from here.) With the Wisconsin Ojibwa, who live around the headquarters of the Drum Society, there are strong ties. This tribe is regarded as having particularly proficient doctors. In 1937 the Fox received the gift of a dance at pow-wow from a group of Lac de Flambeau Ojibwa who came down for the celebration. This gift was accompanied by presents of tobacco, and the Fox did not dance this dance until the following day when it had actually become Fox property. The Sioux, who are their literary and historic enemies, are regarded by the Fox with the friendliest feelings. Two Sioux women have married into the tribe and are well liked, but it is difficult for them to converse at home as they know no Fox. The Winnebago on the other hand, who have intermarried quite freely with the Fox, and with whom they have been in intimate contact since their earliest recorded history, are a great source of contention. The Fox feel that the Winnebago try to run things on the Fox land, and bitterly resent any persons of Winnebago birth or blood obtaining jobs from the superintendency. They feel that it is unfair competition. Any relief work that is given to the Nebraska

Winnebago, in their own home area, is viewed as rank favoritism on the part of the government. The Fox visit with the Winnebago constantly both in Wisconsin and Nebraska, and depend on them for venison and buckskin, as well as black ash logs for their baskets. Two of the best basket-makers in Tama are Winnebago women who have married in; their skill is recognized but the animosity felt to all Winnebago remains.

To the White man the Fox does not display any feeling of inferiority. He feels that the agency is supported by his funds, and as such the personnel of the Indian Service is as dependent upon the Indian as the Indian is on the White. The farmer's office, which is open three times a week in the summer, is a popular meeting-place. Through this channel, orders and rations are doled out, and waiting for them furnishes an excuse to sit and chat for long periods of time. The average Fox feels no qualms about requesting the assistance that he considers due him from any one of the government employees.

With the non-superintendency Whites, the average Fox maintains only the most amicable of business relations. These on both sides are courteous and respectful. The Fox does not want the affection of the Whites if it has to be bought at the price of his integrity. Persons who have developed servile attitudes of accommodation are looked down upon. Fox life is so full for the average Indian that he does not need to go outside of his own group to achieve satisfaction and prestige. The working adjustment that Fox culture has reached by acculturation is vigorous and living, so strong that the great in-group feeling has been buttressed. There is remarkably little sexual traffic with Whites. It is striking that any Fox-White affairs of serious proportions within recent years have been between Fox men and White women, and not the converse picture which is usual in such cases. Indian and White half-breeds suffer practically the same handicaps as Indian-Negro crosses. There was considerable infiltration of White blood about three generations ago, but it has practically ceased now, and the descendants of such unions regard themselves as Indians. It would be literally impossible for any White woman to come and live as the wife of a Fox man. In the first place she would find it hard to adjust to the intimate living conditions, and the censure to which she would be exposed by her husband's people. She could not understand the language at first and it would be doubly difficult for her to learn it, as few persons would be willing to cooperate in her instruction. The adjustment which other Indian women have to undergo to fit into the scheme of Fox life is slight compared to the drastic one to which a White woman would have to submit. In one case when the family of a White woman offered a Fox man a farm in another state, on which he could live with their daughter, this gift was refused and the man came back to live in Tama.

Fox culture has of course altered considerably in many of its aspects since the advent of the White man. A large number of the changes have been due, either directly or indirectly, to borrowing of traits from Whites or other Indian tribes, but these have not been disruptive to Fox life. The most complete shift has been in the economy of the Fox. The present economic basis of the Fox existence is farming, and their technology is that of the White man. That the Fox have been able to adjust themselves to a completely new method of making a living is in a large measure owing to the lack of conflict between the old institutions which made for personal prestige, and the prestige standards of White culture. In former times the two chief sources of male prestige were war honors and the respect accruing to the man who was a good provider. Inter-tribal warfare slowly diminished in this region after the end of the eighteenth century, and with it went the possibilities of obtaining military honors. For the Fox the elimination of war did not prove to be as disruptive as it was to the Dakota for example. On the Plains the war complex was broken by Federal law, but among the Fox it died of inanition. With the disappearance of war honors as a prestige point, it remained possible for men to achieve respect by taking good care of their families. Therefore when they began to farm, provision of the necessities of life from a new and untraditional source could be set up in terms of the old prestige standards. This is in sharp contrast to the Omaha, whose institutions were so fixed that the chief mechanism for obtaining prestige was phrased in terms of the distribution of property rather than in production for use.

Despite the fact that present day Fox life is based on the White man's technology, the other major cultural foci are Indian. The fundamental social organization is almost intact, and this is even truer of their religion. Although no new bundle cults have arisen in recent years, many of the old ceremonies are tenaciously observed. New bundles based on personal supernatural experiences are not manufactured, but fasting for revelations does take place during critical periods in the life of an individual such as illness and mourning. The medical practitioner also seeks supernatural guidance during the performance of a cure.

Certain aspects of Fox culture have persisted as symbols of tribal solidarity. The survival of religion and language are the most notable examples. The Christian Church has never been able to dislodge the fundamental belief of the Fox in Manitou, nor has peyote or the dream dance, for all of them coexist with the observance of bundle ceremonies. The Fox have clung persistently to speaking their mother tongue. Even those persons who have spent much time with English-speaking peoples, use Fox when they are at home. It is possible that knowledge of the Algonquin syllabary permitted correspondence between those away from home and their relatives. When the absentees returned, they were familiar with the events taking place during the time they were away. Common possession of this syllabary also may have reduced the conflict which often arises between a literate and illiterate group.

The survival of the Fox can be attributed to four major factors, all of which may be understood in terms of a strong in-group feeling and tribal solidarity. First, with great skill the warlike Fox repelled physical domination by the White man. Second, with equal stubbornness they resisted unwanted cultural influences from the same source. Third, such cultural traits of the Whites as seemed valuable to them they took; and these they incorporated expertly into their own traditional, cultural framework. Fourth, unlike most other Indians whose decline correlates with the gradual loss of lands to White encroachers, the Fox, before it was too late, began collectively to purchase land from individual White owners. The last factor may be regarded as crucial, for it enabled the Fox to go on in their own way, yet on terms completely comprehensible to the White man. Those groups of American Indians who have managed to continue their own lives under changed conditions, for example the pueblo and nomadic peoples of the Southwest, share with the Fox one important factor; they have been able to settle on a mode of livelihood that has not altered under changing conditions. Even such tribes as the Ojibwa and Iroquois are a good deal more like their ancestors than are the Omaha and Osage. The Minnesota Ojibwa hunt, make maple sugar and gather wild rice, much as they did two hundred years ago; the Iroquois still are agriculturalists who hold their green corn and false face ceremonies.

When they first began to buy land, the Fox thought they were securing a haven of refuge where life would go on as in the old days. Within forty years, however, despite their old aversion to farming, the men of the tribe had begun to lay out fields. Some did so later and more reluctantly than others, to be sure, yet the whole process demonstrates a recognition that they had to farm or die. Where outside compulsion had failed to make agriculturalists of them, their own voluntary adoption of farming succeeded. At present the Fox are attempting to augment their landholdings and will in all likelihood continue to flourish and increase as they have for the last thirty-five years.

BIBLIOGRAPHY

Barrett, Samuel A., The Dream Dance of the Chippewa and Menomini Indians of Northern Wisconsin, *Bulletin Public Museum of the City of Milwaukee, Volume 1, No. 4, Milwaukee,* Wis., 1911.

Black Hawk, *Life of Black Hawk, His Own Autobiography,* translated by Antoine Le Claire, J. B. Patterson, Rock Island, Ill., 1834. Exact reprint of the original by the Iowa State Historical Society, Iowa City, Iowa, 1932.

Blair, Emma Helen, *Indian Tribes of the Upper Mississippi Valley and Region of the Great Lakes,* Two volumes, The Arthur H. Clark Company, Cleveland, Ohio, 1912.

Busby, Allie B., *Two Summers among the Musquakies,* Herald Book and Job Rooms, Vinton, Iowa, 1886.

Charlevoix, S.J., Pierre F. X. de, *History and General Description of New France,* translated with notes by John G. Shea, Six volumes, J. G. Shea, New York, N.Y., 1866–72.

Cole, Cyrenus, *I am a Man—The Indian Black Hawk,* State Historical Society, Iowa City, Iowa, 1938.

Denig, Edwin Thompson, Indian Tribes of the Upper Missouri, *Bureau of American Ethnology, Annual Report 46,* pp. 375–629, Smithsonian Institution, Government Printing Office, Washington, D.C., 1930.

Dorsey, James Owen, Omaha Sociology, *Bureau of American Ethnology, Annual Report 3,* Smithsonian Institution, Government Printing Office, Washington, D.C., 1882.

——— A Study of Siouan Cults, *Bureau of American Ethnology, Annual Report 11,* Smithsonian Institution, Government Printing Office, Washington, D.C., 1885.

Drake, Benjamin, *The Life and Adventures of Black Hawk,* 7th edition Applegate, Cincinnati, Ohio, 1851.

Ferris, Ida M., The Sauks and Foxes in Osage and Franklin Counties, *Kansas State Historical Collections, Volume 11,* pp. 333–395, 1901.

Forsyth, Thomas, "Account of the Manners and Customs of the Sauk and Fox Nations of Indian Traditions," Blair, *op. cit., Volume 2,* 1912.

Galleher, Ruth A., "Indian Agents in Iowa," *Iowa Journal of History and Politics, Volume 14,* July and October, 1916, pp. 349–393, 577–596.

Harlan, Edgar R., The Mesquakie Indians and the Wheeler-Howard Act, *Annals of Iowa,* July, 1936, Historical, Memorial, and Art Department of Iowa, Des Moines, Iowa, 1936, pp. 381–386.

Harrington, Mark R., Sacred Bundles of the Sac and Fox Indians, *University of Pennsylvania, University Museum, Anthropological Publications, Volume 4, No. 2,* Philadelphia, Pa., 1914.

Herskovits, Melville J., *Acculturation: The Study of Culture Contact,* J. J. Augustin, New York, N.Y., 1938.

Hewitt, John N. B., "Sauk," *Handbook of American Indians, Part 2, Bureau of American Ethnology, Bulletin 30, Volume 1,* Smithsonian Institution, Government Printing Office, Washington, D.C., 1910.

——— Editor, Journal of Rudolph F. Kurz, translated by Myrtis Jarrell, *Bureau of American Ethnology, Bulletin 115,* Smithsonian Institution, Washington, D.C., 1937.

History of the Indian Rights Association of Iowa and the Indian Training School, Toledo, Ohio, 1897.

Hoffman, W. O., The Midewiwin or Grand Medicine Lodge of the Ojibway Indians, *Bureau of American Ethnology, Annual Report 7,* Smithsonian Institution, Washington, D.C., 1886.

Hunt, George Talbot, *Intertribal Relations in the Region of the Great Lakes, 1609–83,* Unpublished Ph.D. Thesis, University of Wisconsin, Madison, Wis., 1936.

Huot, Martha Champion, "Two Fox Peyote Songs," *Transition*, June, 1936, pp. 117–120, New York, N.Y.

Indian Affairs, U.S.A., *Reports of the Commissioner to the Secretary of the Interior, 1857, 1859, 1866, 1872, 1873, 1875, 1877–1884, 1889, 1890, 1892, 1897, 1903–1905, 1907, 1910, 1919,* Government Printing Office, Washington, D.C.

Jones, William, "The Algonkin Manitou," *Journal of American Folklore, Volume 18,* pp. 183–190, 1905. Houghton Mifflin Company, Boston.

—— "Algonquin (Fox)," revised by Truman Michelson, *Handbook of American Indian Languages, Part 1, Bureau of American Ethnology, Bulletin 40,* pp. 735–873, Smithsonian Institution, Washington, D.C., 1911.

—— "An Algonquin Syllabary," *Boas Anniversary Volume,* pp. 88–93, G. E. Stechert, New York, N.Y., 1906.

—— "Episodes in the Culture-Hero Myth of the Sauks and Foxes," *Journal of American Folklore, Volume 14,* pp. 225–239, 1901.

—— Fox Texts, *Publications of the American Ethnological Society, Volume 1,* C. J. Brill, Leyden, Holland, 1907.

—— Mortuary Observances and the Adoption Rites of the Algonquin Foxes of Iowa, *International Congress of Americanists, XV Session,* pp. 263–277, 1907.

—— "Notes on the Fox Indians," *Journal of American Folklore, Volume 24,* pp. 209–237, G. E. Stechert, New York, 1911.

Kellogg, Louise Phelps, The British Régime in Wisconsin and the Northwest, *Wisconsin History Series, Volume 2,* Wisconsin State Historical Society, Madison, Wis., 1927.

—— The Fox Indians during the French Régime, *Wisconsin State Historical Proceedings, 1907,* pp. 142–188, Wisconsin State Historical Society, Madison, Wis., 1908.

—— The French Régime in Wisconsin and the Northwest, *Wisconsin History Series, Volume 1,* Wisconsin State Historical Society, Madison, Wis., 1925.

Landes, Ruth, Ojibwa Sociology, *Columbia University Contributions to Anthropology,* Columbia University Press, New York, N.Y., 1937.

—— *Potawotami Manuscript* (unpublished), Columbia University, 1936.

—— *Santee Sociology* (unpublished manuscript), Columbia University, New York, 1935.

LaPotherie, C., "History of the Savage Allies of New France," in Blair, *op. cit., Volumes 1 and 2.*

Marsh, Cutting, Letter to Rev. David Greene, March 25, 1835, *Wisconsin State Historical Collections, Volume 15,* pp. 104–155, 1900.

Marston, Major Morrell, Letter to Rev. Jedidiah Morse, November 1820, in Blair, *op. cit., Volume 2.*

Maximilian, Prince of Wied, *Travels in the Interior of North America in the Years 1832–34*, Ackermann, London, England, 1842.

Mead, Margaret, The Changing Culture of an Indian Tribe, *Columbia University Contributions to Anthropology*, Columbia University Press, 1932.

Michelson, Truman, The Autobiography of a Fox Indian Woman, *Bureau of American Ethnology, Annual Report 40*, pp. 291–349, 1925.

—— The Buffalo Head Dance of the Thunder Gens of the Fox Indians, *Bureau of American Ethnology, Bulletin 87*, Smithsonian Institution, Washington, D.C., 1928.

—— Contributions to Fox Ethnology, *Bureau of American Ethnology, Bulletin 85*, Smithsonian Institution, Washington, D.C., 1927.

—— Contributions to Fox Ethnology, II, *Bureau of American Ethnology, Bulletin 95*, Smithsonian Institution, Washington, D.C., 1930.

—— Fox Miscellany, *Bureau of American Ethnology, Bulletin 114*, Smithsonian Institution, Washington, D.C., 1937.

—— "Further Remarks on the Origin of the So-Called Dream Dance of the Central Algonkians," *American Anthropologist, New Series, Volume 26, No. 2;* pp. 293–294, 1924.

—— "How Meskwaki Children Should Be Brought Up," *American Indian Life*, edited by Elsie C. Parsons, pp. 81–86, B. W. Huebsch, New York, N.Y., 1922.

—— The Mythical Origin of the White Buffalo Dance of the Fox Indians, *Bureau of American Ethnology, Annual Report 40*, pp. 23–289, Smithsonian Institution, Washington, D.C., 1925.

—— Notes on Fox Mortuary Customs and Beliefs, *Bureau of American Ethnology, Annual Report 40*, pp. 351–496, Smithsonian Institution, Washington, D.C., 1925.

—— Notes on the Fox Society Known as "Those who Worship the Little Spotted Buffalo," *Bureau of American Ethnology, Annual Report 40*, pp. 497–539, Smithsonian Institution, Washington, D.C., 1925.

—— Notes on the Fox Wapanowiweni, *Bureau of American Ethnology, Bulletin 105*, Smithsonian Institution, Washington, D.C., 1932.

—— "Notes on the Social Organization of the Fox Indians," *American Anthropologist, New Series, Volume 15*, pp. 691–693, 1913.

—— "On the Origin of the So-Called Dream Dance of the Central Algonkians," *American Anthropologist, New Series, Volume 25*, pp. 277–278, 1923.

—— The Owl Sacred Pack of the Fox Indians, *Bureau of American Ethnology, Bulletin 72*, Smithsonian Institution, Washington, D.C., 1921.

—— The Traditional Origin of the Fox Society known as the "Singing Around Rite," *Bureau of American Ethnology, Annual Report 40*, pp. 541–611, Smithsonian Institution, Washington, D.C., 1925.

Michelson, Truman, Book Review; "The Oto, by William Whitman," *American Anthropologist, New Series, Volume 40, No. 3,* p. 487, 1938.

Mooney, James and Thomas C., "Foxes," *Handbook of American Indians, Bureau of American Ethnology, Bulletin 30, Part 1,* pp. 472–474, Smithsonian Institution, Washington, D.C., 1907.

Owen, Mary Alicia, Folklore of the Musquakie Indians of North America, *Publications of the Folklore Society, No. 51,* D. Nutt, London, England, 1904.

Radin, Paul, *Crashing Thunder, The Autobiography of an American Indian,* D. Appleton and Company, New York, N.Y., 1928.

Re(o)bok, Horace M., *The Last of the Mus-qua-kies and the Indian Congress,* W. O. Funk, Dayton, Ohio, 1900.

Rideout, Henry M., *William Jones,* Frederick A. Stokes Company, New York, N.Y., 1912.

Scott, Thomas J., *Report of the Government Farmer, Tama, Iowa,* (manuscript), Washington, D.C., 1936.

Skinner, Alanson B., Associations and Ceremonies of the Menomini Indians, *Anthropological Papers of the American Museum of Natural History, Volume 16, Part 2,* New York, N.Y., 1915.

—— "A Further Note on the Origin of the Dream Dance of the Central Algonkian and Southern Siouan Indians," *American Anthropologist, New Series, Volume 25, No. 3,* pp. 427–428, 1923.

—— Observations on the Ethnology of the Sauk Indians, *Bulletin, The Public Museum of the City of Milwaukee, Volume 5, No. 1,* Milwaukee, Wis., 1923.

Snelling, William J., *Tales of the Northwest,* reprinted by the University of Minnesota Press, Minneapolis, Minn., 1936.

Stevens, Frank E., *The Black Hawk War,* F. E. Stevens, Chicago, Ill., 1903.

"Tama," *Tama County News,* Tama, Iowa, September, 1901.

Tax, Sol, The Fox Peyote Cult (unpublished manuscript), University of Chicago, Chicago, Ill., 1935.

—— "The Social Organization of the Fox Indians," *Social Organization of North American Tribes,* edited by F. Eggan, University of Chicago Press, Chicago, Ill., 1937.

Thwaites, Reuben Gold, editor, The French Régime in Wisconsin, *Wisconsin Historical Collections, Volumes 16, 17, 18,* Wisconsin Historical Society, Democratic Printing Company, Madison, Wis., 1902–08.

—— *Jesuit Relations, 1672–3, Volume 51,* The Burrows Bros. Company, Cleveland, Ohio, 1896–1901.

—— *Wisconsin State Historical Society Collections and Proceedings,* especially *Volume 5,* which is a series of letters and documents written by French Colonial officers and voyageurs during the latter days of the French Colonies, 1700–1750, edited by Reuben Gold Thwaites, Madison, Wis., 1890.

Ward, Duren J. H., "Meskwakia," *Iowa Journal of History and Politics, Volume 4*, pp. 179–89, April, 1906, State Historical Society, Iowa City, Iowa.

———— "The Meskwaki People of Today," *Iowa Journal of History and Politics, Volume 4*, pp. 190–219, State Historical Society, Iowa City, Iowa, 1906.

Westwood, Charlotte T., *Memorandum for John Collier (U.S. Commissioner of Indian Affairs)* (manuscript), January, 1937.

Whitman, William, The Oto, *Columbia University Contributions to Anthropology, Volume 28,* Columbia University Press, New York, N.Y., 1937.

Wissler, Clark, General Discussion of Shamanistic and Dancing Societies, *Anthropological Papers of the American Museum of Natural History, Volume 11, Part 12*, New York, N.Y., 1916.

EDITOR'S SUMMARY

FOX ACCULTURATION

Dr. Joffe's excellent summary makes extended comment on this case unnecessary. The Fox present an example of a group which has become encysted within another society and culture. They have achieved a successful adaptation to their White neighbors and there seems to be no prospect of their being absorbed either racially or culturally for several generations to come. Their success in achieving this independence seems to be correlated primarily with a psychological factor, their strong sense of solidarity. However, this in itself would not have sufficed to keep the tribe unbroken. They were fortunate in having a long period of not too close contact with Europeans before the intensive contact which began with the arrival of White settlers in numbers. They were thus given an opportunity to make initial adjustments. Adjustment was also facilitated by their continued residence within the same ecological area, a condition made possible at the last by their acceptance of the European technique of land purchase. In this area the diminution of the natural resources upon which they had relied in aboriginal times was a gradual one. There was no necessity for an abrupt change in subsistence economy like that which came to the Plains tribes with the extinction of the buffalo. They were thus given time to make a transition from one set of economic techniques to another and it is significant that it is in this sector of their culture that they have borrowed most extensively and most willingly from the Whites. At the same time, the integrity of their culture has been maintained by the attachment of symbolic values to those elements of the previous culture which were still able to function under the new conditions. They seem to show little if any resistance to the acceptance of new mechanical appliances, such as the automobile or improved farm machinery, but show a very high resistance to changes in language, religion or social organization.

6

THE ALKATCHO CARRIER OF BRITISH COLUMBIA

by Irving Goldman

The Alkatcho Carrier, an Athabascan speaking people, inhabit a small village on Lake Gatcho on the eastern slope of the Coast Range Mountains in central British Columbia. Situated in mountainous, heavily pine-forested country remote from the usual lanes of travel and commerce, this branch of the Carrier, comprising little over a hundred individuals, has escaped the direct and often disastrous impact of White civilization. Not that Carrier culture has remained untouched; but in circumstances where they have met the White trader and missionary under better than equal conditions, the Carrier have been able to adapt their social forms slowly and consciously in response to the new problems posed by Western civilization. From their comprehension of the achievements of the Whites—particularly in technology—most of the Carrier welcome with eagerness the new opportunities offered them in their contact with the representatives of Western society.

But only about 150 years ago, a century before direct contact with the Whites, Carrier culture had undergone profound change from another source. Approximately at this period the Carrier adopted the social forms of their West Coast neighbors, the Bella Coola. Prior to that time we assume the Alkatcho Carrier had a culture similar to that of the Northeastern Athabascan.

Thus, we can view two phases of Carrier acculturation; and because the time span has been relatively short, it is possible to lay bare in broad outline the dynamic processes of culture change and of cultural integration. Some of the specific aspects of the earlier phase of Northwest Coast acculturation have already been treated elsewhere,[1] and so only a résumé of these problems will be

[1] I. Goldman, *The Alkatcho Carrier: Historical Background of Crest Prerogatives,* Doctoral dissertation in manuscript.

presented here. In many respects the problem of Alkatcho Carrier acculturation represents a continuum, from the period of integration of the potlatch-rank system of the Northwest Coast to the present period of disintegration of this system.

RELATIONS WITH THE COAST TRIBES AND THE ADOPTION OF THE POTLATCH-RANK SYSTEM

Prior to the adoption of the potlatch-rank system from the tribes of the Northwest Coast, Alkatcho Carrier culture must have resembled more or less closely the Northeastern Athabascan type. This may be inferred from present similarities between Alkatcho Carrier and "simple" Athabascan and from the general consideration that wherever any Athabascan group is differentiated from the Northeastern Athabascan type, as exemplified by the Chipewyan, Slave, Dogrib, Yellowknives, etc., the differentiation parallels closely the cultural forms of the neighboring groups. The Tahltan, for example, show definite Tlingit influences, the Sekani and the Upper Carrier tribes have adopted the social forms of the Tsimshian, and the Sarcee are barely distinguishable from the Plains Algonquian.

All Alkatcho Carrier informants are agreed that "in the old days" there were no chiefs. The relatively cohesive social unit was the extended family consisting of a group of siblings, their wives and children. This group known as the *sadeku* recognized the limited authority of a headman—*detsa*, "first one," the first-born of the sibling line. The *detsa* regulated the joint hunting and trapping activities of the group. There seem to have been no sanctions preventing the fragmentation of the *sadeku* into individual families. Members of the same *sadeku* inhabited semi-permanent winter villages, dwelling in the typical semi-underground house of the Plateau, as indicated both by testimony of some of the older natives and archaeological evidence.[2] The presence of a considerable number of these dwellings suggests that a number of family lines lived together in the same winter village.

No evidence is available on aboriginal land property arrangements, but before White contact the *sadeku* utilized a common

[2] Harlan I. Smith, *Fieldnotes on Alkatcho Carrier Material Culture.*

trap-line, each individual setting his traps under the direction of the *detsa,* the headman. The *sadeku* never became a very large group because genealogies were never traced beyond three generations, and because individual families could split from the group and settle elsewhere.

The present kinship structure is not particularly revealing as to aboriginal cultural affiliations, because it resembles the Bella Coola and general Salishan form as much as the Northeastern Athabascan in that all *sadeku* members of the same generation are classified as older and younger sibling. Marriage was, and still is, prohibited within the *sadeku* range. The sororate and levirate are still practised. Residence was optional with some stress upon patrilocality. Bride-service, considering its distribution among Northern Athabascan, was probably an aboriginal practice.

Religious theory and practice still follow the Mackenzie Basin and Plateau forms. Ceremonialism was strikingly undeveloped. Menstruants were regarded as dangerous to the food supply and practised the usual avoidance of contact with hunters, their equipment, the paths hunters followed, etc. Boys and girls underwent a series of puberty rites calculated to develop motor skills, health, and industriousness; and to win a guardian spirit. Shamans acquired power through visions and cured by removing some foreign object or "animal" by the laying on of the palm. Death was attributed to the departure of the "soul" through the top of the head. Mourning practices were particularly severe for the widow, who at the time of cremation was required to slash her face and to fling herself at the burning corpse or to be pushed into the fire and beaten by his *sadeku* relatives. The mourning period lasted two years, the widow during that period keeping her hair cut and face blackened.

Among the Northeastern Athabascans [3] we find substantially the same cultural picture. The basis of social organization was the band consisting of several "families," each band with a recognized leader, usually an elderly man. Social cohesiveness was extremely weak, though each band occupied joint winter quarters, living in caribou-skin-covered lodges. Marriage appears to have been perfectly unrestricted within or without group, band, or

[3] J. Alden Mason, *The Northeastern Athabascan* (manuscripts).

tribe. Bride-service was demanded, and a small feast held at the marriage. Attitudes towards menstruants and girl's puberty were identical with Carrier practice. Boy's puberty, however, went unmarked. The band practised group hunting and the sharing of food within the camp.

A fuller description of a Northeastern Athabascan culture is given by Osgood.[4] The Satudene, culturally akin to the Dogrib, are a nomadic people subsisting mainly upon caribou and fish, living either in crude, easily constructed log and brush shelters or in skin-covered lodges.

The family is the fundamental social unit of the Satudene. The members of a family share the same shelter, have a common larder, and to some degree use the same tools and equipment. Often two closely related families will live in the same tent, and hunting and trapping relationships are generally based upon family affinity.[5]

There seems to be no exercise of authority. Ownership is weakly developed, trap-lines being owned only in the sense that the group using it has a monopoly for their period of use. They have no concept of individual ownership of land.

The Satudene . . . split into groups irregularly, oftentimes families changing from one group to another several times during the course of a single winter—the Satudene groups have no stability, nor are families limited to any large area.[6]

There were no chiefs. The few kinship terms given are not adequate for comparison with the Alkatcho Carrier. Marriage restriction was in the line of consanguinity, and as among the Alkatcho Carrier, bride-service was practised. Girl's puberty and menstrual practices are also typical. Ceremonialism is undeveloped.

If we may interpolate from this brief résumé of Northeastern Athabascan to reinforce suggestions from the Alkatcho Carrier data, it can be assumed that the loose social structure, lack of chieftainship, semi-nomadism, the absence of ceremonialism so characteristic of "simple" Athabascan were also characteristic of the Alkatcho Carrier. With this as a basis we may then analyse the

[4] C. Osgood, *The Ethnography of the Great Bear Lake Indians*, National Museum of Canada, Bulletin 70, 1932, pp. 31–99.

[5] *Ibid.*, p. 70.

[6] *Ibid.*, p. 74.

nature of contact with the Coast cultures and the bearing of that contact upon Alkatcho Carrier Culture.

Offhand, in view of the continuous and direct contact between the Carrier and the Bella Coola of the Coast and the general resemblance between the formal structure of the potlatch-rank complex in both cultures, the source of the Carrier potlatch-rank complex might be definitely attributed to Bella Coola. But before accepting this premise it is necessary to dispose of two other possibilities. The potlatching complex might have been derived directly from the Tsimshian, with whom the Carrier have had some contact, or indirectly from the Tsimshian by way of the Upper Carrier at Hazelton, with whom contact was intermittent though not infrequent, even some intermarriage having taken place. The former possibility is improbable simply on the basis of meagreness of contact. The latter possibility, though, must be considered with some seriousness, particularly since the Alkatcho Carrier use of crests can be derived, as will be seen later, from the clan and phratry system of the Upper Carrier, which in turn had been drawn from the Tsimshian. But an analysis of the historical factors responsible for the particular integration of crest prerogatives at Alkatcho is the very key to the source of the potlatch-rank complex in that culture. This problem has already been considered in some detail.[7] A summary will suffice.

An analysis of one of the social units among the Alkatcho Carrier, referred to by the natives as a *nEtsi,* or crest group, is puzzling because of the contradictory information given by the Indians.

On the one hand the crest group is described as a local group having economic and ceremonial functions in common, and owning the prerogative of displaying the crest animal as a carving on grave posts, house ridge-poles, paintings on house fronts, and on such various other objects as spoons, clothing, etc. Each *nEtsi* has its own songs and dances. None of the crest groups had a legend relating to its origin. It appears that since the ownership and display of a crest must be validated by a distribution of property, membership can be accessible only to the nobility—in Alkatcho Carrier terms, anyone who can potlatch. On the other hand, a genealogical study of crests reveals that a *nEtsi* has no marriage

7 I. Goldman, *op. cit.*

regulatory functions, that it is not a local group, and that membership in the *nEtsi* cross-cuts the basic economic unit in Alkatcho Carrier society, the group of siblings and their descendants living together. It also appears that an individual may own any number of crests, and that in spite of a theory of descent, may in practice dispose of his crest in any manner he chooses.

A comparison of the Alkatcho Carrier *nEtsi* with the phratric forms of the northern Coast tribes, and with the Carrier at Hazeiton leaves no doubt, both on the basis of identities of name and similarities in function, that the *nEtsi* is historically connected with the phratry forms in the north. But the *nEtsi* has functions sharply differentiating it from the phratry, such as the absence of marriage regulatory functions, and admission to membership of nobles only. In these it corresponds to the system of crests at Bella Coola.

Further, Bella Coola influence on Carrier social organization was instrumental in maintaining an emphasis upon bilaterality at Alkatcho, while the Carrier groups to the north had accepted a system of matrilineal descent from their neighboring coast tribes. Thus, just as the social organization of the upper Carrier corresponded to that of their coast neighbors, so the Alkatcho social organization was modeled closely upon the Bella Coola system.

The relations between the Alkatcho Carrier and Bella Coola were effective not only in transforming a phratric group, orienting it as an honorific body primarily, and in maintaining at Alkatcho what must have been an original stress upon bilaterality in descent, but it can be shown that many features of the potlatch-rank complex, if not the entire potlatch ideology, were derived from Bella Coola.

Because of the similarity of potlatching forms in this region it is difficult to trace its diffusion merely on the basis of element list comparisons. Fortunately we need not rely upon this method alone. A study of noble names held by the Carrier leaves no doubt that these come from the Bella Coola. The Carrier themselves are fully aware of this fact, and claim that not only did they get all their honorific names from Bella Coola, but that they sought Bella Coola craftsmen to carve their crests for them. Further, while the Alkatcho Carrier rarely invited the Upper Carrier to their potlatches, they always included the Bella Coola among their guests.

RELATIONS BETWEEN THE ALKATCHO CARRIER AND THE
BELLA COOLA

At what period in their history the Alkatcho Carrier established contact with the Bella Coola we do not know. Alkatcho informants claim that in the "old days" they used to winter at Bella Coola, for two main reasons—first, because they frequently ran short of food during the winter months, and second, because the Bella Coola furnished a market for their furs. They would, therefore, take their pelts to the coast in exchange for dried salmon, olachen grease, implements of White manufacture, and dentalia shells. The Bella Coola welcomed the Carrier, although despising them, because the fur trade was profitable and because it pleased them to have strangers present at their winter ceremonies as awe-stricken guests. This information is verified by the Bella Coola:

In summer they [the Carrier] came down to the river valley to fish or trade for salmon, and in the winter they were forced by cold and starvation to visit Bella Coola, Bella Bella, or Rivers Inlet. They intermarried a great deal with the upper valley inhabitants and so were able to spend the cold months with relatives. The Bella Coola considered them utterly foreign in habits and beliefs. To call a man a "Carrier" is still a great insult. They regarded them with scorn and contempt. The presence of a few . . . Carrier was, however, almost necessary to the correct performance of the winter dances since they were uinitiated spectators whom it was necessary to impress and delude.[8]

It is impossible to date the period of initial contact between the Alkatcho Carrier and the Bella Coola; but regardless of when first contact occurred there is some evidence to suggest that the potlatch-rank complex was not adopted before the beginning or the middle of the nineteenth century. In the first place, Alkatcho Carrier tradition puts the beginnings of potlatching back no more than four or five generations. At that time, they say, they were too poor to potlatch. It is at about this time, too, that the characteristic Plateau semi-underground house gave way, among the Carrier to the rather crude counterpart of the Coast plank house. All potlatches are described in a plank house setting, suggesting that the two formed a linked complex. The phratric system in its particu-

[8] T. F. McIlwraith, *The Bella Coola* (manuscripts).

lar reorientation, which definitely diffused from the Coast, did not reach the Shuswap until 1850 from the Upper Carrier. Other indications of the relatively early age of the potlatch-rank complex among the Alkatcho Carrier are, first, that neither potlatches nor rank concepts appear in the mythology, and, second, that neither genealogies of noble names nor traditions of potlatching go back more than four generations. McKenzie's *Journal* (1789) unfortunately offers no clue as to the presence of Northwest Coast culture elements among the Carrier.

But assuming for the moment on the basis of this sketchy evidence that the potlatch-rank complex diffused to the Alkatcho Carrier no earlier than the beginning of the nineteenth century, we observe a rather striking correlation between the above chronology and the development of an active fur trade on the Northwest Coast.

The fur trade on the southern British Columbia coast did not attain any proportions until after 1786. In that early period the chief fur demanded was that of the sea-otter. As a result of this trade the Coast Indians came into the possession of quantities of manufactured implements which began to find their way inland.

Many of the natives on the coast traded the articles thus obtained from the ships with the adjacent inland tribes, and these with those beyond, so that when the first expeditions crossed the Rocky Mountains going westward they found European articles five hundred and in some instances eight hundred miles from the coast.[9]

As the fur trade expanded, the demand expanded to include all types of furs from the interior, fox, lynx, beaver, marten, etc. But since it was not until the beginnings of the nineteenth century that Hudson's Bay Company posts were established west of the Rockies, trade relations between the coast and interior Indians continued to grow.

Trade between the Alkatcho Carrier and the Bella Coola apparently remained uninterrupted until the very present, although at about 1834 the Hudson's Bay Company had established a post which was destined to be short-lived, at Kluskus. This was intended for the benefit both of Carriers and Chilcotins, and its principal object

[9] H. H. Bancroft, *History of the Northwest Coast*, A. L. Bancroft, San Francisco, Calif., 1884, p. 523.

was to prevent these Indians from disposing of their furs in favor of the free traders on the coast.[10]

By 1850 the post was no longer in existence.

A summary appended to the report of Boas to the British Association for the Advancement of Science on the Indians of the Northwest Coast is further evidence of the trade relations between the Bella Coola and the tribes of the interior.

In connection with the Bilqula (Bella Coola) it is important to note that they, by reason of their position, have held the most important natural pass and trade route through the coast range from the ocean to the interior which exists between the Skeena River and the Fraser, a distance exceeding four hundred miles. This circumstance has rendered their situation peculiarly favorable in some respects. It has induced them to engage in intertribal trade, and evidently affords a clue to some of the peculiarities which Dr. Boas points out. From time immemorial . . . a route has been beaten out by way of the Bella Coola River, thence northward to the Salmon River, and then along the north side of the Blackwater River to the Upper Fraser. This is commonly known to the Tinneh of the Interior as the "grease trail," from the fact that the chief article of value received from the coast was in early times the oil of the olachen, or candlefish, though dentalium shells were also brought in. When trading vessels began to visit the coast, besides the natural products of the sea, iron and various kinds of manufactured goods found their way into the interior by the same route; while the fine furs of the inland region were carried back to the coast and sold to the vessels. It was by this same route, well known to the natives, that Sir Alexander McKenzie was enabled to complete the first traverse of the North American continent from sea to sea and reach the shore of the Pacific in 1793. As a result of this intercommunication between the Bilqula and the Tinneh it is found that houses essentially similar in construction to those of the Coast Indians, though smaller and less skilfully built occur far inland on the upper waters of the Salmon and Blackwater Rivers; while on the other hand the practical identity of some points in the mythology of the Bilqula with that of the Tinneh is a clear instance of reciprocal influence.[11]

Undoubtedly trade between the Bella Coola and the Carrier preceded the active development of coast trade relations with the Whites. But when the White fur trade developed, the Indians

[10] A. G. Morice, *History of the Northern Interior of British Columbia*, Briggs, Toronto, 1905, p. 244.

[11] F. Boas, Report of the Northwestern Indians of Canada, *Reports of the British Association for the Advancement of Science*, 1891, p. 408.

performed the function of middlemen between the Europeans and the natives of the interior. However, at least two considerations point to the probability that not until White trade became important did coast culture make its strong imprint upon the Alkatcho Carrier. The suggestions as to the probable chronology of the potlatch-rank complex integration at Alkatcho and its correlation with the growth of the fur trade have already been indicated. This alone would lend fair credibility to the assumption that the diffusion and adaptation of Bella Coola cultural elements followed not upon aboriginal trade, but upon rapidly expanding White fur trade.

Trade relations alone could hardly account for the acceptance of a system of social stratification, and the potlatch with its consequent economic strain; but intermarriage between the Carrier and Bella Coola, as will be seen, makes inevitable the acceptance of the potlatch-rank complex. But why should the Bella Coola, whose chief concern in negotiating a marriage was to increase the quantity and quality of honorific prerogatives within the family line, seek alliances with the Carrier whom they admittedly despised, and who could offer no such advantages? Further, the Bella Coola, in order to preserve within the ancestral family honorific names and prerogatives, encouraged endogamy to the point where occurred symbolic marriages between a man and one of his limbs. Thus, Bella Coola-Carrier matches could be accounted for on two possible grounds, either the Carrier married only within the commoner families at Bella Coola, or the Carrier had other advantages to offer in compensation for their lack of genealogical distinction. An examination of Bella Coola derived names among the Carrier disposes of the first possibility. These names are derived from noble families mainly.

Once the Alkatcho Carrier became important as a source of wealth, however, they might very well be welcomed within the Bella Coola lineages. For though social status at Bella Coola depended upon genealogical distinction, vertical nobility within the caste structure depended primarily upon wealth. Where honorific names and prerogatives could be derived bilaterally from a number of family lines any individual possessing enough wealth to potlatch could easily assume the titles of nobility. In contrast to the Kwakiutl, who might be regarded as an aristocratic society, the Bella Coola were plutocratic. With the development of the White fur trade on the coast, and with an increasing demand for furs from the interior, the Alkatcho Carrier assumed new significance in Bella Coola economy. In the competition for new sources of wealth that characterized Northwest Coast economy a Carrier son-in-law gave a Bella Coola man a virtual trade monopoly, particularly in view of the Carrier concepts of bride-service.

Thus the increasing importance of trade between the Bella Coola and the Alkatcho Carrier, as a result of the growing White fur trade on the coast of British Columbia at the end of the eighteenth century, must have promoted intermarriage. The types of social relationships involved in marriage resulted inevitably in the integration of the potlatch-rank complex at Alkatcho.

This process of trade, intermarriage, and acculturation was by no means a unique development in British Columbia, but, on the contrary, was characteristic of coast-interior relationships. The Bulkley River Carrier have intermarried with the Gitksan group of the Tsimshian with whom they have always had friendly trade relations. The latter controlled the trade route down the Skeena River. They traded shells and copper with the Carrier for moosehides and furs. Correlated with the trade and marriage relations between the Bulkley Carrier and the Gitksan are similarities of social organization and equation of phratries. The same thing happened with Sekani. To quote Jenness:

When the Sekani were confined to the western side of the Rockies through the hostility of the Cree and the Beaver they impinged upon the Gitksan and Carrier. The Sekani not only fought, traded, and intermarried with them, but assimilated many of their customs, and tried to adopt their divisions into exogamous matrilineal phratries.[12]

The McLeod Lake band farthest from the Gitksan "abandoned the phratry system before it could be well established." [13] The phratry system of the western divisions of the Tahltan were introduced by marriage with the Tlingit; but the Nelson River Indians well over to the east, out of the line of trade, never adopted phratries at all. Trade between the Tahltan and the Tlingit de-

---

[12] D. Jenness, *The Sekani Indians of British Columbia* (manuscripts).
[13] *Ibid.*

veloped only after the establishment of trading-posts by the Russians. The Tlingit became the middlemen for trade between the Indians of the interior and the White fur traders. The Tahltan traded almost exclusively with the Tlingit and with the Kaska.[14]

Bella Coola-Carrier intermarriages were not very common, and for good reasons. Not only did the Bella Coola endogamic tendencies restrict such alliances, but the economic strain upon any Carrier family entering into a series of affinal potlatch exchanges and the necessity of participating in the rivalrous potlatches more or less upon Bella Coola terms was more than most Carrier families could sustain. Therefore, only a few Carrier individuals, the successful hunters, the shrewd and energetic traders, the lucky gamblers, were able to acquire enough wealth to participate upon a basis of relative equality in Bella Coola potlatches. These individuals, having acquired "big names" from the coast, apparently formed the first Carrier aristocracy.

Unfortunately, detailed accounts of marriages and the consequences therefrom are lacking both from the Carrier and the Bella Coola data. But a knowledge of marriage practices of these groups makes possible at least a hypothetical reconstruction of the inter-marriage process. For the Bella Coola no marriage was socially sanctioned unless it had been validated by a series of property exchanges. At the engagement "secret gifts" were given to the bride's parents. Then food and presents were distributed by the family of the groom to the village of the bride. To "open the door" for the bride, the groom's family and friends were required to give presents to the bride's family and to perform a number of menial tasks for them. At the wedding ceremony, after a recitation of the family myths, a name from the lineage of the bride was bestowed upon the groom, to be used by his children. Subsequently, relations between the two families were further cemented by mutual assistance in ceremonies. At intervals after the marriage the bride's family made payments to the groom to "repurchase" the woman, the latter rising in social status with each "repurchase." It is obvious how, once such a marriage had been consummated, the Carrier family would be completely enmeshed in the total fabric of Bella Coola culture. In fact, one individual at present at Alkatcho whose

---

[14] James Teit. Incomplete manuscripts on Tahltan.

mother is a Bella Coola Indian regrets very much his Coast affiliation because of the heavy economic burden it entails, and because of his liability to Bella Coola sorcery should be evade his
responsibilities.

After the birth of children Bella Coola parents attempted to
elevate them in rank through a series of four potlatches. It is not
difficult to see how pressure by the Bella Coola, who were concerned, would force the adoption of this practice by the Carrier.

Most marriages appear to have been between Carrier men and
Bella Coola women. With patrilocal residence recognized by both
groups the women of the Coast were brought to Alkatcho where
they must have inevitably become foci of acculturation.

INTEGRATION OF THE POTLATCH-RANK COMPLEX
AT ALKATCHO

The potlatch complex on the Coast developed under conditions
of economic abundance. In fact, prior to the coming of the White
fur traders and the subsequent enrichment of the Coast peoples,
potlatching was not very common. At Bella Coola, according to
McIlwraith, "until the increase of wealth in recent years the potlatch was rare. . . ." [15] A rivalrous potlatch system demands not
only an economy of abundance, but an expanding economy. On
the Coast, where potlatching involved not only returns with interest but the destruction of considerable property, wealth in cir-
culation at each subsequent potlatch must have grown at a rate
depending upon the amount of interest affixed to each exchange.
Thus, among the Kwakiutl, with the interest rate at 100 per cent,
circulating wealth must, theoretically at least, have increased in a
geometric ratio. The rate of increase was considerably lower at
Bella Coola, where no fixed interest rate was prescribed. Nevertheless, the destruction of property and rivalry in gift exchanges
demanded substantial wealth increases. Among the techniques
evolved on the Northwest Coast for meeting the requirements of
an expanding economy were the following: group coöperation in
the financing of potlatches, and in the production of wealth; rigidly
defined concepts of private property reflecting the general competi-

[15] T. F. McIlwraith, *The Bella Coola* (manuscript).

tion for wealth; utilization of trade with the Whites and the interior Indians as a means of adding to their wealth from outside sources; and war for the purposes of defending property rights and for the capture of slaves to be held for ransom, traded, used as labor or as commodities in potlatches.

On the Coast, in spite of great abundance of sea-food, making possible the accumulation of food surpluses within a relatively short time and permitting much time for the production of other commodities, such as boxes, canoes, dishes, houses, blankets, totem poles, etc., the potlatch-rank complex was a great economic strain.[16] But with the Carrier operating on a subsistence economy, obviously either the potlatch-rank system had to be markedly altered or the social and economic base, or both.

Carrier trade with the coast resulted in increased economic productivity. Not only did the introduction of guns, steel traps, steel axes, and later, in 1870, horses create an expanding food supply, but the spread of trade eastward into the interior opened up new opportunities for acquiring wealth. Just as the Bella Coola were the middlemen between the Alkatcho Carrier and the Whites, so the former were now the middlemen between the Bella Coola and the surrounding Carrier and Chilcotin villages. As the Carrier became wealthy through trade, they were able to adopt the potlatch-rank system. And once they began to potlatch rivalrously their economic activities were all the more stimulated. This increase in wealth, a result largely of technological improvements and the profit derived from trade, though making possible the occasional feasts at which as many as 150 or more people were fed, still left the Alkatcho Carrier poor as compared with their Coast neighbors. No amount of technological improvement could alter the essential ecological differences between the two regions.

The discussion of the potlatch-rank complex as it functioned in Alkatcho Carrier society will be taken up later. At this point it will suffice to consider merely the more general aspects of Northwest Coast, specifically Bella Coola influence. By and large, the general motives behind the potlatch were the same both at Alkatcho and at Bella Coola, though among the latter the potlatch-

---

[16] An analysis of the relationship between potlatching and the necessity for an expanding economy is in preparation as a separate paper. I. G.

lim, "the giving away of goods that might otherwise rot" was given a somewhat religious setting. That is, among the Bella Coola, formally, the potlatch was given in honor of the return of a deceased ancestor to visit the living. Nevertheless the following rites really set the dominant "tone" of the feast:

1. The initiation of young men and women into the *sisaok* secret society. These were usually relatives of the host.
2. The payment by the wife of the donor of the potlatch and her family to repurchase her from her husband in order to maintain the status of the children.
3. The strengthening of the donor's seat; i. e., the firmer establishment of the social status of the donor by each successive property distribution.
4. The strengthening and establishing of new seats for young relatives.

The Carrier potlatch differed in a few respects. No religious motives were involved, and wives were not repurchased. Purchase of membership in the crest groups was the analogue to the secret society initiation. In other formal respects there were no differences.

Quantitative differences were, however, marked. Bella Coola potlatches involved hundreds of blankets, great quantities of food, and lasted sometimes for months. A Carrier potlatch lasted two days, an ordinary exchange involved some ten blankets; and property was never actually destroyed, although symbolically "thrown into the fire." Actual destruction of property occurred at Bella Coola. The Carrier, further, were quite conscious of the differing effects in potlatches between themselves and their Coast neighbors. They thought the latter were crazy for taking potlatching so seriously. And as a comment on cultural relativity it is interesting to note that the Bella Coola viewed the Kwakiutl potlatch in precisely the same way.

The symbolic destruction of property among the Carrier was not only significant of their particular attachment to material goods but represented for them a way out of the continually mounting property exchanges. For even though a gift was returned with only a small increment it was not long before the economic strain was felt. When this occurred, one of the principals, choosing the pretext of an insult "threw property into the fire" by giving his rival some blankets or other commodity which was not to be returned. This formalized the disruption of the rivalry. The rival was temporarily shamed; but at a later date the two might have resumed the rivalry at scratch. The mechanism could hardly have been abused because the recipient of the "thrown into the fire" property, though losing face for the moment, acquired new wealth which he could utilize at another potlatch.

As elsewhere on the Northwest Coast, Carrier potlatching was never an individual enterprise. The Carrier potlatch necessarily had to entail the collective effort of the extended family—the group of siblings, their wives, children, and children's wives. At the head of this unit was the oldest of the sibling group, who when not a noble was called *detsa* "first one." In pre-Coast days, when Carrier social organization approximated that of the Northern Athabascans, the *detsa* was probably the equivalent of a band leader who regulated hunting somewhat, but whose authority was not strong enough to prevent the constant fragmentation of the band. Under the conditions of potlatching and the drive for building social prestige, the extended family became a more cohesive unit. Leadership was strengthened. The sanctions supporting the authority of a chief, who had a fixed rank as a noble and who necessarily had to serve as the spear-head for the collective potlatch, were more concretely developed. In addition, a new sanction revolving around social status—fear of being shamed through the non-performance of the formal obligations attendant upon the maintenance of rank—acted as an effective force in strengthening group unity. The chief could determine his successor, and was instrumental in elevating one of the family-line-descendants to nobility.

Group cohesiveness, however, never developed effectively beyond the extended family. It is probable that in earlier days, as elsewhere on the Coast, village and extended family were synonymous. But where a number of family lines inhabited the same village, village solidarity was expressed in two ways; a common front was presented against invaders of village hunting territory, and the most important noble of the group was recognized as the potlatch chief for the entire village. He built the central potlatch house, and was the center in inter-village potlatches. To the extent that he was respected as a potlatch figure his opinions carried weight. In the final analysis, though, no individual among the Carrier had political authority; and even on the Coast, centralization of authority was not very highly developed.

Property concepts changed relatively little under Northwest Coast influence. The extended family, equivalent to the Athabascan band hunted over a common territory and shared the proceeds. It appears, however, that the crest group, which as we have seen was an honorific society cutting across family lines, also had hunting and fishing rights in common. But this particular development was probably the result of the transformation of a northern phratric concept under Bella Coola pressure.

Shamanism at Alkatcho also came under the influence of rank concepts. Shamans potlatched at the assumption of power. Shamans also used the wealth obtained through fees and in their magically increased economic powers to become nobles. Two versions of the same tradition of a famous shaman obtained at different Carrier villages, one in the east where potlatching was of minor significance, and one at Alkatcho, the two revealing clearly the different orientations. At Nazko the shaman gets a wife. At Alkatcho he becomes rich and then a great noble.

It is equally significant to observe the elements of Bella Coola culture that were not adopted. Northwest Coast culture is very rich in ceremonialism. The winter secret society performances were the high points of social life. It is true that the crest groups at Alkatcho are to be regarded as secret society analogues, and that a prerogative of housewrecking as a sign of displeasure with the hospitality of a potlatch donor is derivative from the Breaker Society at Bella Coola; but the religious content—seizure by the society supernatural, the return to the village in a frenzy, the ritual restoration to sanity, and the final restoration of the novice to normalcy—or the performance of dances symbolic of the society's myth was completely lacking at Alkatcho. If intermarriage could account for the adoption of a potlatch-rank complex, it ought to follow that secret society prerogatives which could be obtained in marriage should also have been adopted. But the Carrier accepted none of Bella Coola religious ideology. Their own religious practices and beliefs, part of the basic Athabascan culture, remained unchanged. This apparent religious conservatism may be attributed to a number of factors. In the first place, the Bella Coola were not anxious to reveal their secret society secrets to the Carrier, whom they were eager to impress and awe. Secondly, to the Carrier, whose religious outlook may be regarded as fundamentally pragmatic, the highly elaborated and pervasive religious ideology of the Bella Coola must have appeared as extraneous. Furthermore, it appears as though the Alkatcho Carrier accepted no more of Bella Coola culture than necessary to maintain proper marital relations. Finally, the fear engendered in the Carrier by the supernaturalistic aspects of secret society performances (any mis-step or breach of etiquette at these performances was severely punished by sorcery), apart from the great expense of conducting the long drawn out performances, must have acted as a deterrent against their adoption. Neither was the widespread Bella Coola sorcery taken over by the Alkatcho Carrier. And here again, the desperate fear of the Bella Coola "black box" might very easily have led to a scrupulous avoidance of any contact with these practices. If Bella Coola sorcerers were as much feared during the early days of contact as they are today, it is easy to understand how the Carrier would have avoided them like the plague. Such avoidance would obviate the possibility of learning the sorcerers' techniques.

In material culture, a crude counterpart of the Coast plank house was introduced. But apparently the Carrier never developed the appropriate skills to deal with the complicated art forms and wood working techniques of the Bella Coola. It would have been indeed an extraordinary industrial revolution for the Carrier, with their extremely rudimentary technology and art forms, to have reached in a short time the technological level of the Coast.

WHITE CONTACT AND THE DISSOLUTION OF THE POTLATCH-RANK SYSTEM

THE ABORIGINAL COMMUNITY

The present-day village of Alkatcho is an amalgam of a number of village populations combined as a result of a great population decline some seventy years ago. It is doubtful whether any of the villages in the vicinity of Alkatcho ever included more than 300 people. The village itself was primarily a winter settlement, and for the greater part of the year the Carrier lived as smaller family units scattered over a considerable area. Very often a good part of the winter was spent among the Bella Coola on the Coast. During the fall hunting season the families dispersed, each to its trap-line, where it lived in makeshift shelters in relative isolation. For a week or two late in the summer the village population again re-convened for potlatch festivities, and then scattered.

Carrier economic activity centered almost entirely about hunting and fishing. The women supplemented the resulting diet by gathering berries, digging wild roots, and scraping bark. In earlier times, before they were practically wiped out by improved hunting techniques, the caribou, beaver, and mountain-goat were the principal animals hunted. With the development of trade along the Coast, fur-bearing animals, otter, fox, marten, mink, lynx, fisher, and muskrat, became increasingly important. Fish ranked with mammals as the major source of food. The numerous lakes and streams were well stocked with salmon, trout, and suckers.

Before the introduction of guns, steel traps, and horses, the Carrier economic environment could barely sustain the population. Famines were not uncommon, and most winters were spent with the Bella Coola. At a later date, technological improvements made possible a higher living standard; but by and large, Carrier economy was little above the subsistence level.

The technological level was always relatively low. Animals were trapped in snares—spring traps utilizing the principle of the unequal balance, deadfalls, and surrounds. None of these techniques was very efficient. Even today, as much as 50 per cent of the animals spring the snares and escape. Game animals, like the caribou and deer, were hunted by large groups and driven into a surround made by attaching small sticks on a spruce root rope from tree to tree. Such a fence reputedly reached a perimeter of fifteen miles. At several openings in the fence a noose tied on a six-foot pole was set. When the deer or caribou got caught in the noose, the pole by catching in the trees delayed its progress until the hunters could catch up with it.

Hunting was done with spear and bow and arrow, the bow being sinew-backed, somewhat like the Eskimo type. The mountain-goat was run down with dogs and speared.

Fish were caught with nets in traps set at weirs or waterfalls, and were speared with the multiple pronged harpoon. The traps were of two types, the typical conical shaped basket set either in a narrow passage of a stream or behind a weir, and a basket type set below a waterfall to catch the salmon on the rebound. The bulk of fish were caught by such traps.

ECONOMIC CYCLE

Just before the heavy snowfalls late in December, the Carrier migrated *en masse* to Bella Coola where they wintered until February, returning to their own country to hunt the caribou. With the melting of the snows late in April they all moved to Long Lake for spring salmon fishing. This lasted about a month. Then they all scattered again into the mountains, hunting mountain-goats and ground-hogs until the end of the summer. The summer months were usually devoted to inter-village visiting and trading journeys. The fall months were devoted almost exclusively to hunting fur-bearing animals, particularly the beaver.

DIVISION OF LABOR

The sexual division of labor was never rigid. Women, if capable and willing, were permitted to participate in the same economic activities as men. Nevertheless, few women engaged actively in hunting and trapping. They coöperated with the men in fishing and in the large-scale coöperative beaver hunts, but devoted most of their time to food gathering and to the usual domestic activities. Men did women's work far less frequently than the latter did conventional men's work. Social status was little reflected in the division of labor. Carrier society recognized no leisure class; although nobles were exempted from most portage work.

TRADE

Though not as well organized, or conducted on a scale comparable with that of the tribes on the Coast, trade was of signal importance in Carrier economy as a means of acquiring a surplus for potlatching, and in earlier days as a means of survival. In this earlier period, probably prior to the development of the potlatch system at Alkatcho, caribou-hides, nettles, fur pelts, and baskets were traded at Bella Coola for dried salmon. Trade expanded with the coming of Whites to the Coast, and soon fur pelts were exchanged for firearms, tobacco, tea, manufactured clothing, utensils, dentalia, foodstuffs, etc. Many of the Alkatcho Carrier became active traders, trading ability practically becoming a prerequisite for social distinction. One of the most illustrious of the nobles remembered by contemporaries was Inkakuti; who died over forty years ago.

Men still living say:

> Only Inkakuti traded. He was a smart man. He traded all the time. That's why he was a big *meotih* [chief]. Other fellows are too lazy. They don't want to go to far places. Inkakuti even went to Fort Fraser, before the Hudson's Bay store was opened there, to trade skins. He even went to the Tsaten. He hired two or three men to pack for him.

When horses were first introduced, about 1870, they were immediately taken up as a trade commodity, and traded as far north as Hazelton.

WARFARE

Wars were reputedly waged against the Kitlope and Kitimat, Kwakiutl-speaking peoples, north of the Bella Coola, for plunder and slaves. There are no traditions of wars with the Bella Coola, though the Chilcotins had many bloody engagements with them. Wars, however, were extremely infrequent, and of little significance in Alkatcho social life.

GAMBLING

From the Carrier point of view, gambling was distinctly an economic mechanism. Individuals with the proper supernatural power never lost at gambling and soon became chiefs. Such persons made the circuit of the villages and came back loaded down with wealth.

In general, economic activity was stimulated by the drive for potlatch surpluses.

SOCIAL ORGANIZATION

The basic sociological constellation was the *sadeku,* the extended family unit of siblings and their descendants. Under conditions of stress, individual family groups could leave the *sadeku;* but for the most part its members were held together by bonds of common economic and social interest. *Sadeku* members forming an exogamic group defended one another's interests in feuds, hunted together over the same hunting territory, utilized common fishing sites, coöperated in potlatches, respected the limited authority of the eldest of the line, and frequently constituted a house group. The term *sadeku,* though its etymology is still in doubt, appears to mean "group of my house." The *sadeku* comprised all individuals descended through the line of grandfather, while beyond that was the *sadekuka,* "distant relatives," descendants through the line of great-grandfather. In theory the *sadekuka* was also an incest group; but in practice marriage of third cousins was condoned. The closeness of *sadeku* ties is reflected in the relationship terminology, a man referring to all individuals of his own generation as male or female, older and younger siblings.

Inheritance of non-material property, names, honorific prerogatives, songs, dances, crests, etc., was bilateral; and in that sense the individual belonged to the *sadeku* of his father and of his mother. But because residence was predominantly patrilocal, membership in an economic unit was in practice patrilineal. The relationship terminology, however, expressed no distinction between maternal and paternal lines. Functionally, nevertheless, the individual was much more a part of his paternal than of his maternal line, particularly if his mother came from some distant village. But if the mother's line were the more distinguished, that not infrequently influenced his kinship behavior.

The individual family—man, wife, unmarried daughters, sons —was by no means submerged as a functional unit within the *sadeku.* This group often lived in isolation during the fall trapping season, so that children learned very quickly the distinction between own and social sibling. Children also inherited names and social position from their own parents as well as from other *sadeku* members.

A fundamental characteristic of Alkatcho Carrier kinship structure is the cleavage between the *sadeku* and the line of affinals. A man's relations with his wife's family were formalized under the rules of bride-service and gift exchange; but relations were immediately disrupted either at divorce or death. In the latter event the essential solidarity of blood kin over affinal outsiders was demonstrated most vividly in the hostility already described with which the surviving spouse was treated.

SOCIAL STRATIFICATION

Three social classes were recognized—the *meotih,* "chiefs"; the *telen,* "poor men"; and the *Elna,* "slaves." The distinctions drawn between *detsa,* "first one," the *sadeku* headman, and *meotih,* and between the latter and *tcuindEn,* "rich men," are undoubtedly reflections of the pre-Coast culture period. Social stratification was based, not upon any fundamental differences in relationship to the means of production, but in theory at least upon genealogical distinction as on the Coast. Theoretically, the handing down of noble titles through the line of primogeniture, younger children and descendants of their lines thus being deprived of titles of nobility, was the backbone of the class system. But inasmuch as in practice no individual wealthy enough to potlatch was deprived of noble prerogatives, social stratification was effectively based upon wealth distinctions. The internal structure of the *sadeku* tended, however, to foster social inequalities. Only a first-born son received "legal" title to a trap-line, younger siblings remaining economically dependent upon him and obligated to assist him economically in property distributions. Each noble, though, attempted to elevate as many of his children as possible to nobility, those closest to the line of firstborn of first-born, etc., having the greatest success in that endeavor. The discussion of property relations will make this clear.

Slaves, taken in war or purchased from the Coast, formed a most insignificant part of the population; but attitudes toward the few slaves they had were modeled precisely upon those prevailing at Bella Coola. A slave who had been freed by his master and had acquired enough wealth could potlatch and become a noble. At least some individuals of slave status were escaped slaves who had taken refuge at Alkatcho from the Coast. The Carrier claim that nobles used slaves as workers and as trade commodities. The slave could not hold property and could not marry out of his class; but freed slaves apparently could acquire trap-line property.

There were a number of individuals, *alkoh,* heralds, or chief's speakers, who not forming a social class, occupied a rather ambiguous social position. Among the Kwakiutl, the position of *alkoh* (derived from *Kwakiutlalk^w,* "chief's speaker") was a socially distinguished one. But at Alkatcho, as at Bella Coola, the herald had to endure the insults of the potlatch guests, and was frequently the butt of general ridicule. A visiting chief enjoyed forcing the *alkoh* to consume candlefish oil until he vomited, or until the latter's chief came to his rescue with a distribution of property. The position of *alkoh* had its compensations, though. An *alkoh* was privileged to demand property from visiting chiefs, who were subjected to ridicule if they refused; but he could demand only property that was visibly present. This prerogative was hardly a cherished one, and in general the *alkoh* was viewed with no little contempt. Only children of poor men ever volunteered their services as *alkohs.* Yet when the *alkoh* by his begging prerogative accumulated enough wealth to potlatch and become a noble, he threw off the stigma of his former position. A faint aroma of disrepute, however, still clung to an ex-*alkoh.*

All nobles belonged either to one or a number of crest groups, the analogues of the Northwest Coast secret societies, stripped clean of religious content, and relatively bare of ritual. The most prominent crest groups, (*nEtsi*), were Tsayu, "Beaver Medicine," Datsan, "Raven," and Cas, "Grizzly Bear." Membership was either hereditary or purchased. In any event, membership had to be validated by a property distribution.

A novitiate into the Tsayu was offered a beaver tail by the

chief and was expected to pay heavily for it, the amount he offered to pay determining his social standing within the group. The property, in the form of skins, dentalia shells, items of clothing, guns, etc., was distributed to all the *nEtsi* members, and no return payment was expected. The Tsayu people at one village, Salmon House, had the following prerogative: if one of the Tsayu was walking outside and a gust of wind blew off his hat, another Tsayu member would dash to pick it up, and be privileged to purchase it at an excessive price. If the hat was worth five dollars, for example, as much as fifteen dollars would be offered for it.

The Ravens had this prerogative: a member of the group climbed up on the roof of the house and cried out, "kaw kaw," imitating the sound of the raven. It was then said that the raven crest mounted on the roof made the cry because it wanted to smoke. The cry was the signal for all to assemble at the house of the *nEtsi* chief for a small feast. The chief cut up tobacco and distributed it to those assembled. He also put some tobacco in a pipe with a number of stems radiating from it like the spokes from a wheel hub, from which the guests smoked.

The prerogatives belonging to the Grizzly Bear *nEtsi* included the right to construct a circular door opening in the potlatch house. This type of door seems to have had a special significance apart from its representation of a bear's den. In order to enter the house it was necessary to climb in, the threshold being raised about four feet from the ground. The men gathered at the door within the house to laugh at the women as they awkwardly tried to enter. In those days women wore only a large blanket. To avoid exposure some women tried to jump through feet first with their legs held tightly together. Others scrambled in head first. Still others were so embarrassed that they never ventured into the house. Noble women, however, were supposed to have walked boldly in disregarding the men. These women were respected for their boldness, fortified of course by their social position and ability to potlatch. The missionaries later forced the Carrier to cut away the threshold.

In a somewhat different category from the Carrier point of view was the *DzEgwanli* prerogative, derivative from the Bella

Coola Breaker Society. It is not entirely clear whether this was a society; but at any rate a number of nobles were said to have had *DzEgwanli*. The *DzEgwanli* was the prerogative of destroying property of the host at a potlatch, and of distributing property, but not as direct payment for the destroyed property. With the *DzEgwanli*, as with the *nEtsi* went a song and dance. The last *DzEgwanli* dancer was a woman. Guests at a potlatch had the right to demand small gifts from her, tobacco, some article of her personal clothing, etc. At the conclusion of her dance she always distributed tobacco. Host chiefs feared the *DzEgwanli* because of the damage done to the house when they were through. According to one informant, the *DzEgwanli* was a police force to maintain a high order of hospitality among chiefs. At least upon one occasion, the Alkatcho Carrier wrecked the house and dumped all the food into the fire of a chief of a neighboring Carrier village because he had not supplied enough food for his guests. When the *DzEgwanli* dancer was a woman her colleagues had the right to grasp her vulva in the dance. They had no other sexual rights over her.

PATTERNS OF SOCIAL DOMINANCE

Social status depended upon factors of kinship, age and rank. Because of a relatively strong stress upon sex equality the sex factor was of little significance.

KINSHIP

Even apart from social rank considerations, the first-born of a line of siblings, male or female, was the "boss," the person looked to for advice, the regulator of economic activities, the chairman in inter-familial discussions—in short, the family center. The authority and prestige of the "boss" became even more defined when associated with social rank, and was at a relative minimum in a family of poor people. In general, in intra-familial relations the generation and relative age factors were of significance in conditioning dominance behavior. The sibling classification distinguished linguistically between older and younger sibling, and in function younger siblings were expected to exhibit respect attitudes toward their seniors. The generation principle operated upon the same basis. The behavior of a man towards his parents-in-law was very clearly expressive of dominance relations. For at least the first two years of matrilocal residence the groom was a complete subordinate in the home of his father-in-law. He assisted him in every way, yielding up his entire fishing and hunting catch. In inter-familial disputes, or disputes between individuals of different families, the ultimate solution was frequently decided by force. In such disputes the individual belonging to the numerically stronger family had the advantage. Some men were known to be violent and quick tempered. That too gave their families an edge in a dispute.

AGE

The Alkatcho Carrier recognized a number of age classes, and in general the older people, excluding the very old men, were looked up to by the younger as superior persons. Young boys, not yet pubescent, constantly tagged along after the post-pubescents, who formed a sort of big-brother class for them. The older boys inducted the younger into sex. Age dominance was continuous from very early childhood. Within the household each child was responsible for the care of the next younger sibling, and undoubtedly the attitudes of dependence upon an older sibling reflected itself generally in age-status relations.

RANK

All dominance relations and rivalries found formal expression in the potlatch-rank system. The precise extent to which motives of social prestige and rivalry permeated all strata of Carrier society is difficult to determine. The poor people did not potlatch and were relegated to the side lines. But when we consider that as a rule potlatches occurred no more frequently than once in every two years, and that social status did not imply political power, it is evident that rank distinctions were for the most part of no extraordinary social significance. But social distinctions that tended to lapse during potlatch interims suddenly leaped into prominence as soon as a potlatch approached.

The formal occasions for potlatches were birth, marriage, death, elevation of a child or kin, and the assumption of full shamanistic power. A year or two after the death of some important person, the *sadeku,* led by the heir, coöperated in a potlatch to mark the cessation of mourning and the assumption of titles by the heir. The funeral potlatch was the most common form, and very often all other festivities such as naming and elevating children, payment of affinal exchanges, the assumption of new names and crest prerogatives, the giving of property to a rival, the construction of a potlatch house, etc., took place at that time. Very great chiefs potlatched on a number of separate occasions, but most nobles waited for a funeral potlatch in their village.

THE BUILDING OF RANK

As compared with the Kwakiutl, Alkatcho society was relatively democratic. The formal vestments of nobility could be obtained easily enough if a man had enough wealth, and in a number of cases individuals from poor families seem to have become nobles. On the whole, though, the structure of the family tended to further class distinctions.

It was assumed that all individuals desired to become a *meotih,* "chief." Most *meotih's* were created by their families, and relatively few individuals in practice became nobles through their own unaided efforts. An important noble at the birth of a child distributed property to the members of his own village and so validated the child's first name. At this time, too, a song-maker was employed to make a song for the child. About eight or ten years later, a second and larger potlatch was given in the name of the child, either by the parents, by an uncle or a grandfather. Again the child assumed a new name and acquired a new song. Over a period of years, the times depending upon the affluence of the family, two more such potlatches were given in the name of the child. At the conclusion of the fourth potlatch the individual became a full-fledged noble.

At the second or third of these elevating potlatches the child was directed to give some property to one of his age group from another village of the same social status as himself. This began a potlatching rivalry that continued for years.

Social rank was not static. Under conditions of status rivalry the noble who attempted to rest upon the record of his past achievements would soon be forgotten. It was necessary for a noble to seek every opportunity for public notice. Thus they became very sensitive to insult and by wiping out that insult with a property distribution achieved still greater prominence. At every potlatch the nobles displayed their songs and dances and validated the display with the distribution of small gifts to the assembly. Nobles systematically paid for the food they had eaten at potlatches. The greatest of the potlatch chiefs made a point of slighting a host by coming late.

The type of rivalry so fully developed on the Coast—the crushing of a rival with property—was not as prominent a feature of Carrier potlatching, at least in effect. Yet the greatest *meotihs* were those "whom nobody could beat." So long as the rival, really a "friend," did not "talk too high tone" the exchange of property with return of some increment continued on a fairly amicable level. But as soon as an individual became too boastful and arrogant his rival gave him property, which was as thrown into the fire. It could not be returned, and the potlatch relationship was terminated.

A Carrier Indian would say:

That *meotih* with whom I potlatch all the time is like my friend. Now that fellow talks bad talk to me. He talks high tone. Now I get mad. If I say *tsaxmeduts* (meaning unknown) then that fellow can't pay me. I beat him. He can't potlatch with me. He can potlatch with someone else. It is as though I had thrown away my friend.

If I see a *meotih* who talks too much high tone talk but doesn't potlatch good I go to beat him. Suppose he had given me two blankets, now I give him ten blankets. It is like I shoot him. I say, "Put this in the fire." Now he is ashamed.

When a noble has been unable to repay with increment a potlatch present and still continues to talk boastfully, he is rebuked sharply by his rival, who says, "You slave! How dare you talk to me like that. Have I not given you much property which you have not yet returned?"

Nothing resembling the fierce rivalries and the great destruction of property that take place on the Coast appeared at Alkatcho. A defeat in a potlatch meant only a temporary humiliation, the loser having every opportunity of recouping his lost prestige. For the most part Carrier nobles desired not so much to crush a rival, as to stand out above the rest.

Rank status was objectified in a number of ways. Both the invitation to a potlatch and seating in the potlatch house followed a definite hierarchial order. To mistake a noble's proper place or to invite improperly was to insult the guest and incidentally give him an opportunity for "throwing into the fire" property. The usual seating arrangement within the rectangular potlatch house was as follows: the most prominent guests sat at the rear behind the fire-place, lesser nobles sat along the side walls, and the common people crowded into the space along the front walls. Spouses sat together with their children (those that had not yet been elevated to nobility) before them. After the fourth elevation potlatch the child was permitted to sit between its parents. Thus the more children a family had potlatched the more room it occupied, and the amount of spread of a family was a concrete symbol of its prominence. The status of a great potlatch chief was marked by his possession of a large potlatch house, decorated with his crests, which had been dedicated at a large potlatch. The construction of such a house was the high point in any noble's life and entailed considerable expense. Once built, the house was the center of the village and the scene of all potlatches.

Rather striking personality differences among women seemed to have been correlated with social status. Two examples have already been cited, the behavior of women in climbing over the threshold into the Grizzly Bear potlatch house, and the woman *DzEgwanli* dancer who permitted male dancers to stroke her vulva. This behavior must be understood against the prevailing sex mores, and the strong emphasis upon sexual shame, particularly at indecent exposure. One other case can be cited. One woman *meotih* accumulated most of her wealth through gambling. She traveled about from village to village playing the stick game with men. Her technique was simple. When playing with a man she sat opposite him with legs spread. The man could not attend properly to the game, which involved some skill in recognizing cues from facial expression, and invariably lost. Informants were emphatic in their claims that an ordinary woman would not do this because of shame. But a noble woman was all the more respected for her dominant behavior. Women as a rule never gambled with men.

POLITICAL ORGANIZATION

Formal political authority was at a minimum. Within the *sadeku* the headman regulated economic activity and attempted to settle disputes. His success as a leader depended largely upon his personal prestige, but his authority grew when matters of potlatching were at stake. At that time, as the spear-head of the potlatch he received the willing economic coöperation of the family group, for the potlatching success of any chief reflected upon his family. Furthermore, since no single person of the family could potlatch alone, coöperation was essential. Where the headman was the leading noble and his siblings lesser nobles, they all had the opportunity of participating in the joint potlatch in their own right. Each could distribute property and increase his own status. The potlatch in this case involved reciprocal benefits.

When a number of *sadekus* occupied a village, the family chief recognized as the greatest noble was a village chief. And here again, the authority vested in him was only by virtue of his position as the potlatch spear-head in the inter-village potlatches. And the sanctions supporting his authority rested in the reciprocal benefits between the village chief and the supporting nobles. The authority of the village chief did not usurp that of the family chiefs. Outside of the potlatch realm, chiefs had relatively few special privileges. Still, these few were of some importance economically. In portage, before the coming of the horse, the family chief made but one trip with a load, while the others made three or four, or as many as necessary.

Disputes between individuals of different *sadekus* over property and over women were settled, if necessary, by force, the *sadeku* usually supporting its own member. There are no case histories of disputes within a *sadeku* that were not settled upon the advice of the headman. Yet, in spite of this lack of centralized authority with definite coercive sanctions, feuds were not common.

Of course, factors of status operated definitely as social sanctions and reinforced the authority of a chief. An individual incurring the displeasure of a family chief would receive no cooperation from the latter in the struggle for status.

No cases are known of individuals having been deprived of trapping and fishing rights, although men have been known to leave the family after a quarrel. By this action they almost automatically renounced claims to rank.

Perhaps the clue to the mechanism of social control lies in the early conditioning process. Even today, children obey the commands of their parents instantly and without demur. From earliest infancy no child is given the opportunity to evade a command.

SUPERNATURALISM

As far as could be determined, the Carrier have no general term for the supernatural, nor do they conceive of any generalized non-animatized force as *wakan, mana,* or *Manitou.* All supernatural concepts tend to be concretized. The world was conceived as populated by a number of spirits, mostly animal, who if appealed to in the proper way revealed themselves and directed the individual, giving him good luck. When the same spirit appeared recurrently in a dream, the individual knew that he was going to get shamanistic power. Dreams in general were prognostic. To dream of coitus was a sign of good luck. Most spirits were helpful; but the beaver and otter lodged in the body and caused illness. Each individual was supposed to have a ghost and a soul, the distinction between the two being only vaguely drawn. The soul, *bEtsen,* sometimes left the body temporarily, causing loss of consciousness, and could be restored only by the shaman to whom the *bEtsen* was visible. At death the *bEtsen* left the body through the top of the head, hovered about for a while and then disappeared. The ghost, *nautnił,* left the body also through the top of the head at death and hovered about the grave. Some individuals have accepted the Bella Coola tradition which conceives of the ghost as going to a land of the dead.

Cosmogonic theory was very weakly developed, and at present individuals show no interest in the problem. As one informant put it, "My father never talked to me about such things. He talked to me only about potlatching." And that is probably the best characterization of Carrier relations with the supernatural.

A fuller account was obtained of shamanistic concepts. The general term for illness is *nEdeta'*; but to be afflicted with an illness which may make one a shaman is called *nełtcEn*. The shamanistic cure for such an illness is *nełtcan*. The shaman himself is called *nełtcEn*, "causing to sing." The general characteristic of a *nełtcEn* illness was a dream in which some spirit appeared and gave the subject a song. Unless shamanistic aid was brought, the patient died. The illness was marked by the gushing of blood from the mouth and a comatose state. The shaman, whose guardian spirit resided in the palm of his hand, was enabled to draw out the foreign spirit from the patient's body. First the shaman determined the source of the "infection." He therefore projected himself to "bad places" where beaver or otter have played, and "cleaned them up." Through his spirit songs he utilized the power of his spirits, or rather the shaman acted as the corporeal agent of the spirits.

Shamanistic power was acquired voluntarily in more or less the same way as a guardian spirit came upon one involuntarily, or was inherited. Shamans sought constantly to increase their powers through more visions.

At Alkatcho where rank concepts were more highly developed than in the eastern Carrier villages, shamanistic practice was geared to the potlatch-rank system. Not only did the shaman make use of his special powers for greater success in trapping, gambling, and in general for the accumulation of wealth, but he signalized the completion of his novitiate by giving a potlatch. In fact, a shaman who had not been cured by other shamans and had not yet completed the potlatch was only half a shaman, who could cure only at his own risk. For example, one old man, an incompleted shaman, lost his life in a cure. His grandson, while whittling a stick, accidentally plunged the knife into his abdomen. The wound festered and the young man was close to death. The old shaman well aware of the consequences, cured the boy and died shortly thereafter. His body had not yet been made strong enough for his utilization of supernatural power. Had he been "made strong" by other shamans, which necessitated a potlatch, he would not have died.

For the Alkatcho Carrier supernaturalistic practices had one main function, the arming of the individual with another tool for acquiring wealth. It was entirely to this end that the guardian spirit quest at puberty was conducted, that men sought to make themselves pure by continence and by fasting, that people sought shamanistic power. Attitudes toward menstruants, and toward mothers at parturition were also conditioned by the fact that women at this period represented a source of danger to the food supply of the community. Of course problems of health were also concerned in supernaturalistic practices. The pubescent girl, by not adhering to the rigid dietary regulations, was liable to injure her health permanently. One practice at birth offered the mother two alternatives, if she hung the navel stump of her child from a tree he would always be successful as a hunter; if she threw it into the water her next delivery would be easier. This was always a difficult choice for any mother.

MORES—PROPERTY ATTITUDES

Property on the Northwest Coast, as we have seen, was given a high valuation; its possession gave the individual tremendous prestige, and its destruction testified to the strength of character of a noble. Property was wielded as a potent weapon in individual rivalries. To a large extent Alkatcho Carrier property attitudes conformed to the Coast pattern, although the destruction of property on the lavish scale of the rich maritime peoples was regarded as utterly absurd by the Carrier.

Each village embraced a none too sharply defined area of territory within which any village member could hunt, and from which trespassers were excluded. This village territory was roughly divided into a number of sadeku-held trapping grounds, over which village members could hunt but could not trap unless they were members of the *sadeku,* or were given permission by the *sadeku* headman. The *sadeku* trap-line was collective property to the extent that it was not further subdivided into a series of individual trap-lines. Although within the *sadeku* each individual family head set his own traps over the *sadeku* trap-line, and was for the most part entitled to the full proceeds of his fur catch, his line was not permanent and was determined for him by the *detsa.* As a rule, a group of brothers operated a trap-line jointly, sharing in the proceeds. Ownership meant use. If for any reason a *sadeku* discontinued the use of a trap-line some other family by developing it—setting traps—established a sanctioned claim over it. In other words, land was not valued for its own sake, but for its usufruct.

The distinction between hunting and trapping is certainly significant of the wealth competition between family lines. For the most part all the valuable fur-bearing animals were trapped, while the large food game were hunted. Under the rules of hospitality all food had to be shared within the village.

Inheritance of trap-line rights was in practice patrilineal, and followed the line of primogeniture. The eldest son inherited as a rule the titles and prerogatives of his father as well as his trap-line rights. The younger siblings then centered about him as a family head. The Carrier are explicit on this point. Younger siblings worked with and were dependent upon the elder. In the absence of children, trap-line rights descended to a next brother or a nephew.

The exercise and inheritance of fishing rights were similar to the trap-line forms. Streams and lakes were village property. But *sadekus,* by constructing weirs and fish traps, assumed exclusive rights over a particular section of the stream. Such weirs and traps were as a rule coöperatively built by the entire *sadeku,* and each member had rights to the fish caught, the headman frequently taking the apportionment of fish upon himself. If he was preparing for a potlatch he could take a larger share of the fish for himself. When a number of members of a *sadeku* constructed individual fish traps they were required to share the fish. Thus each morning the men inspected their traps and apportioned the fish. Because a number of families used the same stream, weirs had to include an opening for fish to pass upstream. Failure to do so was a frequent cause of trouble. Fish traps also descended in the line of primogeniture or along the collateral line. A series of basket traps suspended from a waterfall represented different forms of ownership. One trap belonged to a crest group, one to an individual, two to the village, and one had no claimant and fish could be taken from it by anyone. The bridge over the waterfall that made the traps accessible was built by the entire village.

Berry-picking grounds did not form property.

Certain animals, as the beaver and otter—for a long time the most important fur-bearing animals—were hunted and trapped as a collective *sadeku* enterprise. Each *sadeku* had its traditional beaver route that stretched for miles along the waterways. The natives refused to speak of this as "owned" property; but each fall when the beaver and otter hunts began, a family line announced that it was going on a particular route. Outsiders were often invited to accompany the party. If a *sadeku* in any particular season did not go beaver hunting, some other family used the route. These beaver hunts lasted for months, until the freezing of the streams made further canoe travel impossible. All members of the party contributed some useful labor. The women helped smash the beaver dams, the men speared the beaver, the children, depending upon their age assisted around the camp or helped in the actual killing of the beaver. At certain points where a stream made a hairpin bend, deadfalls were set to trap the beaver crossing over to the next bend. At the conclusion of the trip all the beaver were divided in the following fashion: children were given a small beaver each; all married men received an equal share. However, the "equal" division was not standardized according to our own legal concepts. As one informant put it, "Suppose I catch lots of beaver and the other fellow has only a few, then I give him some of mine." Efforts to elicit a more precise statement of the division merely met with a condescending smile.

Food was shared not only within the *sadeku* but within the village. A hunter, having killed a caribou, announced the fact to the village and invited people to return with him, and to assist in bringing in the meat. Often when a chief brought in a caribou he feasted the village. Food hospitality was freely extended, and no man desired to have the reputation of a "miser." Caribou and mountain-goat, the chief sources of meat supply, were most frequently hunted by a group. In some of the huge caribou surrounds the entire village coöperated, all sharing the food. Mountain-goats were hunted by a *sadeku* group, the distribution of meat being equal regardless of the extent of an individual's contribution to the actual killing of the animal. Within any pattern of food sharing, allowance was made for individuals who were planning to potlatch, these being almost invariably older siblings, and they were permitted to keep a larger share.

SEX ATTITUDES

It is rather difficult to disentangle present sex mores from the past, particularly with respect to the unformalized attitudes. Case histories give some clues to these. In a rather curious way two sets of contradictory sex attitudes run parallel to one another. On the one hand, particularly among noble families, pre-marital chastity seems to have been desired. At least strict watch was kept upon girls, and their sleeping quarters were so arranged as to keep them under parental surveillance. On the other hand coitus was thought to be required by all just pre-pubescent children to promote physical growth. Young boys were told by their older age-group, "you had better catch a woman pretty soon or you won't grow." It was also believed that defloration was necessary to bring on the first menses in girls. Women who were virgins up to their marriage (this the Carrier say was due to Catholic influence) were supposed to remain barren and to suffer from menstrual disorders. The Carrier always arranged for a mature man to induct a virgin while an older woman provided the boy with his first sex experience.

Although this was not actually verified in the field, it seems that this apparent contradiction in sex mores reflected class differences. On the Northwest Coast, the chastity of princesses was carefully guarded. This practice was adopted by the Carrier. Perhaps the compromise between the two practices was the basis for a strong insistence that all premarital sex relations were to be clandestinely conducted. Boasting of sexual exploits was decidedly in bad taste. Yet, as they must in a small community, sex affairs quickly became open secrets. Furthermore, the belief that lucky in love meant lucky in gambling put a high premium on seduction.

No conflict existed in theory with respect to post-marital sexual fidelity. Adulterers caught *in flagrante* were liable to be killed, although each case was considered on its merits, the culprits sometimes escaping with little more than a severe drubbing. Some men merely sent their wives away when they suspected them of adultery.

At present, attitudes of sexual shame are very strongly developed, particularly shame about bodily exposure. How much of this was aboriginal is difficult to determine. That present shame responses are derivative from an aboriginal base is evidenced by the differences in sex behavior permitted high caste women.

FOCI OF INTEREST IN CULTURE-VALUE SYSTEM

For the upper class at least all interest centered around the potlatch-rank complex. The most respected individuals were those who could accumulate most wealth and elevate their social status. The father of one informant spoke to his son only about potlatching. Supernatural experiences were sought almost entirely for the assistance supernatural power gave in accumulating wealth and in becoming a noble. Religious experience for its own sake had no appeal for the Carrier. The ideal person was one who was not lazy, who was up early, hunted all the time and was enterprising in trade. Even children, barely able to walk steadily were openly criticized for "playing too much." Children at the age of six were already setting traps for small game and were expected to become adults quickly. Everyone, from the youngest to the oldest, had to participate to the full extent of his capabilities in the household economy. The emphasis upon useful work was even reflected in the Carrier attitudes toward their dogs. Pups were looked upon scornfully as "playdogs." Old dogs, no longer able to hunt effectively, were driven out of the house.

INFLUENCES FROM OTHER ABORIGINAL GROUPS

The consequences of culture contact with other aboriginal groups have already been discussed. At present the Chilcotins appear to be usurping the position of the Bella Coola with respect to Carrier inter-tribal relations. Although considerable intermarriage between the two Athabascan groups has taken place, present-day Carrier have no little scorn for their southern neighbors. The Chilcotins are regarded as "wild" and uncouth in their manners, and not as respectable. In relation to the Chilcotins, the Carrier form a sort of bourgeoisie. The former seem to have much less interest in accumulating wealth. They are reckless gamblers, drinkers, spend-thrifts, are quick tempered, and warlike in Carrier eyes. Chilcotin women, though taken often as wives, are not as dependable as Carrier women. My principal informant claimed that his Chilcotin wife was more or less exceptional, but all other Chilcotin women were "crazy." When a Chilcotin son-in-law proves to be lazy, it is because he is a Chilcotin. The Chilcotins are respected for one trait—they ride like demons and win prizes in the rodeos. It is perhaps significant to note that the Carrier young men are very fond of the Chilcotins and their "wild ways."

Some contact is still maintained with the Upper Carrier. When a potlatch is given at Alkatcho it is invariably compared with potlatches at Hazelton or Fraser Lake to the detriment of the Alkatcho.

THE CONTACT CONTINUUM—NATURE OF INITIAL CONTACT

The lack of recorded accounts permits of only the sketchiest description of the initial culture contact with the Whites. The Carrier claim to have seen their first White man at Bella Coola, at the time that the potlatch system was still going strong. From time to time, after White fur-traders had come into the country in the early nineteenth century, there were occasional contacts. But the Carrier met with the traders more or less on equal terms and rarely came in contact with the White population. The initial contact was definitely not traumatic. There seems to have been not the slightest physical conflict with the Whites. The Chilcotins, for example, met the full brunt of an expanding, money-mad White population. Settled in good ranching country, and almost in the heart of the caribou gold fields the Chilcotins were soon overwhelmed by the Whites. Smallpox, venereal disease, and wars with the Whites quickly decimated the population. The Carrier villages along the Fraser River, in the direct line of the advancing traders and gold prospectors, never recovered from the first brutal impact of the Whites. Today, at least on the surface, the Fraser River Carrier are little different from poor White settlers.

The Catholic missionaries of the Oblate of Mary the Immaculate, a French Catholic order, followed closely upon the furtraders. From the Alkatcho Carrier account, the first Catholic priest they met some sixty years ago converted them quickly and easily to Catholicism. They had already heard of the missionaries from their Kluskus neighbors, whose conversion had preceded their own. An account of this first meeting was obtained from only one informant (about fifty-six years of age):

Father Morice came when I was a small boy. He came with an interpreter and three horses. He showed this Catholic business. He made camp some little way off. Some old men went over to see the White man. The old men came back and said, "It's a priest, he got big talk." We had heard from a long way about a priest. Now he came. An interpreter came and told us to go on the other side just a little way. Everyone came to the tent and sat outside. The White man sat inside. Then he came out and talked. "This people will all be Catholic by and by," he said. Then he talked a little bit and showed that Catholic business and then he went back. He told everybody to go to Kluskus next June. We did that. The priest was there. It was not Father Morice. He made me a Catholic. He put that water on my head, and gave me the name Charlie. I was too young to know then.

When they next met the priest at Kluskus, he appointed a village chief, a captain, two watchmen for the church, and two policemen. The Carrier approved of these appointments and apparently accepted the authority of these men.

The Alkatcho Carrier country is at present suitable only for trapping, and never has attracted White settlers. To this day, very few White men have visited Alkatcho. Within recent years the fertile Bella Coola Valley has been settled by Scandinavian farmers, and occasionally the Carrier work for the farmers during the summer. Cattle ranchers settled mostly in Chilcotin country, fairly remote from Alkatcho.

We can summarize the nature of White contact for the Alkatcho Carrier over the past fifty years as follows: With the early fur-traders contact was brief, intermittent, and experienced by the adult men for the most part. None of the early traders settled closer than seventy miles from Alkatcho. Within the past decade, an independent trading-post operated by a Russian and a Scotchman, and for some period by a German and his wife, has been in existence at Alkatcho. But the post is not occupied more than a few months during the year. The independent trading activities of the Carrier have brought them in touch with some of the larger White settlements, mainly at Bella Coola. None of the White traders was consciously concerned with changing the native forms of life, beyond attempting to develop in them a taste for the trade commodities in which they dealt. The Indians have thus been induced to purchase victrolas, accordions, and violins as well as the necessities, clothing, arms, tobacco, flour, tea, sugar, canned milk, etc. To an increasing extent the Carrier have become more and more dependent upon the Whites for these commodities. In fact the only item of dress still made by the Carrier are moccasins, which are the standard foot-gear even for the Whites in the country. They depend upon the Whites for all food except for meat and fish. Aside from snares, the Indians manufacture no other implements, or household utensils. Even lumber for houses is purchased from the Whites. Were they to lose touch with the traders, the Carrier would suffer real privation.

With the Church, relations have been and still are highly tenuous. The missionary attempts to make at least one trip to Alkatcho a year, but some years pass without his visit. When he does come, he stays a week or two. More than any other agency the Catholics have worked hard to transform Carrier culture. A battle has been waged against the potlatch, against all supernaturalistic practices. The Church has attempted to institute a political system, and a native formal court. But the Church had few means for enforcing its precepts, beyond the fact that some of the Carrier, especially the women, took the confessional seriously. The Catholic Church was, however, effective in preventing Alkatcho children from attending the only accessible schools in Bella Coola.

The Indian agent responsible for the Alkatcho Carrier lives at Bella Coola, and though he visits Alkatcho infrequently his authority appears to be well respected. When the Carrier visit the Bella Coola during the summer they bring their problems, complaints, disputes etc., to the agent. The present system of trap-line ownership is regulated by the Indian agent. One of the Indians remarked that his people had more respect for a jail than for the hell of the missionary. The Canadian government attempted to outlaw the potlatch; but again, because of the isolated position of the village, its enforcement depended primarily upon the willingness of the Indians to forsake these forms.

The life of the neighboring White settlers, farmers and ranchers differs little in outward respects from that of the Indians. Poverty has reduced the entire country to much the same level of material comforts. The Alkatcho Indians have little contact with them. Very few of the Alkatcho women have been known to enter into sex relations with the Whites. It is the boast of the Alkatcho Carrier—but difficult to check—that there are no half-breeds in the village.

NON-CULTURAL RESULTS OF CONTACT

At the time of early missionary contact the population of Alkatcho was 135. Today it is little over 100. One informant, however, claimed that before the coming of the Whites there were fewer people than today. Whatever the quantitative changes in Carrier population, the coming of the Whites did not decimate it. The Alkatcho Carrier have no record of epidemics, although about seventy years ago a smallpox epidemic swept through most of the Carrier villages. The use of the horse, however, and new economic opportunities offered by work on White ranches, to gether with the spread of cattle-raising caused some shift of population eastward toward the Fraser. But on the whole the population has tended to remain relatively stable. Both the Indians and the White traders claim that fur-bearing game is getting scarcer, and indirectly, the Whites by having created an expanding market for furs, and introduced efficient hunting techniques and implements have caused a sharper exploitation of natural resources. The economic crisis of the last few years, and the resulting fall in fur prices has proved an even greater impetus. Fortunately for the Indians very few White trappers have found their way into their country. A half-breed trapper at Tetachuck Lake some forty miles north of Alkatcho, has lately been setting a quick pace for the Indians. His fur catch almost doubles that of any other individual. Only in 1936 did the Indians learn a more efficient method of snare-setting that will increase production, but will further deplete the game resources. To date, however, the depletion of natural resources has had no marked effect upon the living standard. Lately the caribou have become practically extinct; but their place has been taken by the moose.

THE ACCULTURATION PROCESS—ACCEPTANCE OF NEW CULTURE ELEMENTS

Carrier material culture, never highly developed, changed almost immediately in response to the new techniques and commodities introduced by the Whites. As has already been noted, it was to the interest of the fur-traders to have the Indians accept White manufactured products. Of course, the wealthier persons among the Carrier were the first to accept these material culture elements. Members of the old nobility, far from being conservative, purchased expensive phonographs, one man even buying a radio that never worked. In a short time White goods became symbols of social prestige. For example only one Indian at Alkatcho sleeps in a spring bed; but the possession of a spring bed as a display item is a *sine qua non* of social status. Phonographs, chairs, tables, and milled lumber serve the same purpose.

Catholicism, in its surface ritual, was also accepted quickly and without friction. At least one reason for this ready acceptance of a new religious faith is the fact that as presented to the Carrier, Catholicism could be easily fitted into the rank system. The first missionary wisely selected the most prominent nobles and gave them positions within the church as chief, captain, policeman, watchman, bell-ringer, choir leader, etc. Thus these positions became analogous to the old honorific prerogatives. How much of a hold the religious and emotional elements of Catholicism took upon the Carrier is hard to say. The men seem to have accepted the Catholic Church as another "business" of the Whites. Many of the women though have become fairly devout, attending the church services and obeying the Friday meat tabu. But perhaps the women have reason to welcome the Church, for it released them of their menstrual tabus.

Economic life has remained fundamentally unchanged. Nevertheless a tendency can be observed for the gradual acceptance of cattle-herding as a sideline to trapping. Only three families at present keep cattle, and they still continue trapping and some trading. Others feel that if the village could be moved to good grazing ground they would give up hunting and concentrate upon cattle-herding. Yet the integration of the "cattle complex" is still extremely weak. Families neglect their cattle herds to go off on trapping expeditions, and many of the cattle simply die of neglect. Offhand it appears that cattle-herding involves some social prestige factors, the Indians who keep cattle being regarded as closer to the Whites, and in that sense somewhat superior. Cattle can hardly be regarded as a source of wealth, for the simple reason that it is almost impossible to bring cattle to market. Nor does beef form any significant part of the diet. Upon festive occasions, it is true, the diet is enlivened with some beef.

To some extent Carrier income is supplemented by outside work, either at the canneries at Bella Coola, or at the surrounding farms and ranches. But earnings are small.

Although economic forms have barely been changed, certain significant changes in economic relations have occurred that are eventually certain to affect the culture markedly. Under the potlatch-rank system, society was stratified on the basis of the economic validation of honorific titles and prerogatives. Today such rank distinctions are no longer acknowledged, and in form at least, Carrier society is less stratified than formerly. A more significant economic stratification is developing as a consequence of the introduction of the horse and the steel trap. The Carrier who had the cash and the foresight to invest in horses and in steel traps are now at a decided economic advantage. The lack of horses prevents the purchase of supplies at Bella Coola at cheaper prices. And even when some supplies can be brought in from Bella Coola the family running short must buy from the trader—sometimes an Indian—at high prices. The lack of steel traps (which cost about four dollars each on the average) cuts production at the expense of those not equipped with such traps. It is obvious that given a limited number of animals moving about over many trap-lines, the best-equipped trap-line will get most of the game. Thus once the cycle of technological inequality is begun it continues until eventually a few become very wealthy at the expense of the many. Nothing so drastic has yet taken place because the situation has developed relatively recently. The Indians, those who are poor, are very conscious of this new development, though they do nothing about it.

Trading, always important, has continued to blossom; but with diminishing success. Spurred on by an awareness of their exploitation at the hands of the White trader (actually the White trader is sometimes more exploited by the fur-purchasing monopolies than the Indians), and responding to a well-established form, the Carrier have organized a number of trading companies of their own in competition with the White trader. But only one man, who practised some purloining on the side had any success in trade. Yet every family has at one time or another organized a trading company and failed. No sooner does one company fail than another starts up immediately. The handicaps the Indians must face as trade competitors of the Whites are considerable. For the most part illiterate, they have no information about the state of the fur market. They must sell as a rule to a fur monopoly. They can never get the same wholesale price on tradegoods as the Whites. Nor does an Indian trading-company have any particular advantage over the Whites in relations with the native villages. The White fur-trader has but to cut prices ever so slightly, and pay just a trifle more for skins, and he can cut out his Indian competitor. The Carrier show no national solidarity.

The Indian trading-companies or partnerships are often set up across kinship lines, men combining because of their possession of some capital, or on the basis of friendship ties. The extended family as a coöperative economic unit has been generally fragmented into smaller family units.

Constant trading failures, curiously, have not developed any defeatist attitudes. Rather, the Carrier, though expressing some animosity toward the Whites for what they regard as a raw deal, are concerned with beating the Whites at their own game. If they could only learn to read and write, they feel they could compete with the Whites. They have conducted some ineffectual agitation for a school at Alkatcho. A school accessible to them at Bella Coola is Protestant controlled, and therefore the Catholic missionary, the Indians say, forbids their children to attend it. The Catholic mission school at Williams Lake is too far away.

The economic change which has affected social relations most strikingly has been the transfer of trap-line ownership from the extended family, the *sadeku,* to the individual family. Each family head is permitted to register his own trap-line. Even women may register a trap-line. Not only has the Canadian government established individual family trap-lines, but in the form of inheritance a relatively equal distribution of trap-lines among the children, with a share also going to the widow, has displaced the emphasis upon primogeniture. As a consequence of this land policy the economic interdependence of the *sadeku* has been broken down and social cohesiveness seriously weakened. Today no *sadeku* has a headman, and few family lines engage in any kind of economic coöperation. Only the memorial potlatch brings the *sadeku* together.

CHANGES IN SOCIAL RELATIONS

The most apparent social change among the Alkatcho Carrier has been the elimination of rivalrous potlatching and social rank distinctions. Potlatches are still held in commemoration of the dead, after the completion of the grave box, and to a large extent these feasts follow the old forms. But potlatches for rising in rank are completely gone. The funeral potlatch itself bestows no rank distinction upon the family, and is no longer the occasion for the assumption of names and prerogatives by the heir.

Two principal factors may be cited as forming the causal nexus for the breakdown of the potlatch-rank complex. First, the contact with the Whites and the gradual acceptance of Western evaluations upon property have tended to make the Indians rather reluctant to give up property. The Whites, they observe, either spend their money on luxuries or put it in the bank. Finally, the changes in trap-line ownership and their effects upon the structure of the extended family, the coöperative potlatch unit, removed the essential props from the body of the potlatch-rank system. Direct pressure for the elimination of potlatching was applied by the government and by the Church. But inasmuch as neither agency could effectively enforce a potlatch prohibition it is obvious that external sanctions alone could not have disrupted the system. The concurrence, however, of this direct pressure along with a changing valuation of property and the weakened sanctions maintaining the unity of the extended family was a blow that the potlatch-rank complex could not long withstand. The operation of the latter factor was probably decisive.

Today the basic social group is the individual family, each economically and politically independent. A younger brother who at one time was economically dependent upon the senior sibling now has his own trap-line and need not coöperate in any way. Furthermore, just as the breakup of the coöperative unit would hinder potlatching, any tendencies effective in invalidating the potlatch structure would in turn weaken the family structure which had achieved its initial unity through the potlatch system. The reciprocal interaction of these two forces was then instrumental in effectuating the gradual disintegration of the potlatch system. The individualization of families in terms of land ownership must also have led to individualization of behavior. *Sadeku* members no longer live together, and individual families are separated for long periods during the hunting season.

The absence of even weakly exercised centralized authority because of the elimination of the *sadeku* headman has permitted individuals to defy social forms with relative impunity. For example, some years ago, when the potlatch system was beginning to buckle, one man potlatched another some horses. The recipient refused to repay. Nothing was done about it. Once a break is made in the potlatch cycle the breach is inevitably widened. Occasionally, today, some individual remembering his past status attempts a revival of the rivalrous potlatch, but is only laughed at.

With the passing of the aboriginal property attitudes, the utilization of property in building social status, a new attitude toward wealth adopted from the Whites appears to be attaining dominance. Wealth is now hoarded. Thus, the two men in the village, who at one time would undoubtedly have been nobles by virtue of their industriousness, enterprise and shrewdness are now hoarders of wealth. One of these men is reputed to have 14,000 dollars in the bank at Vancouver. However, this new attitude toward wealth has not yet achieved universal acceptance, and these men are regarded scornfully by many as misers. The most socially acceptable use of wealth today is its expenditure upon luxuries such as glass windows, phonographs, radios, spring beds, etc. The young men particularly have adopted the philosophy of spend your money while you may. Yet one young man who was most vociferous in proclaiming this philosophy donated at a church collection fifty cents more than the village chief and shouted, "Now I am the biggest man in the world." This little incident is perhaps most revealing of present-day attitudes. They are changing undoubtedly, but the transformation is yet far from complete.

Although the *sadeku* has become individualized—a return to the earlier Athabascan pattern—the closeness of relations with affinals is still emphasized through the continuance of bride-service and informal gift exchanges. At present, and probably also in the past, bride-service and economic obligations to the father-in-law lead to some friction. To take one case as an example, the son of my principal informant having married the adopted daughter of his father's uncle, who lived in the same village, not only lived with his father-in-law but for some years gave the latter almost the entire proceeds of his hunting and trapping. At one time the young man gave some money to his own father, and his father-in-law resented it.

Affinal ties are also utilized as an escape from parental tyranny. In one case a young man married a woman unacceptable to his father. For a time he and his wife lived with his parents. Finally, unable to stand the nagging of his father, he left the house and moved in with his father-in-law. He has not yet claimed his own trap-line, but assists his father-in-law.

The new property regulations permitting a woman to inherit property from a deceased husband, or to operate her own trap-line, has freed women from dependence upon their own *sadeku*. This, too, must be regarded as a factor in the disintegration of the extended family. The effectual elimination of primogeniture had the same effect.

CHANGES IN POLITICAL STRUCTURE

Whatever political organization the Carrier ever possessed derived its authority from the sanctions inherent in the extended family structure. The potlatch chief was never more than the spear-head for the inter-village potlatches and had no real political authority. Today the village of Alkatcho has a chief (non-resident), a captain, and a council composed of the church officials, bell-ringer, church watchman and song-leader. The court, though, has no police arm and must rely for the enforcement of its decisions either upon the good graces of the litigants or upon the threat of a report to the Indian agent at Bella Coola. The court, however, is reluctant to press charges against any individual at Bella Coola. In effect then the court is such in name only. When this political arrangement was first instituted by the Church some fifty years ago all the important nobles became officials and enjoyed the prerogatives. At that time the court had a policeman who arrested drinkers, violators of the sabbath and of church regulations. Today no one wishes to accept the onus of "making trouble for somebody." Though lacking in authority, the court still offers its officers a certain amount of prestige. The present incumbents, however, do not take their office too seriously and are content to let well enough alone.

CHANGES IN RELATIONS WITH THE SUPERNATURAL

The Church is still feared and for that reason a check on present attitudes toward Catholicism is difficult. On the basis of church attendance, and from the statements of one informant there is reason to believe that the church is no longer in favor. Attendance at Church is confined for the most part to the women and younger girls. Very few of the older men, and practically none of the younger men attend church. On one Christmas Eve, no one attended the church. Informants claim that once they were all good Catholics, but now they are falling off. This religious lapse within a relatively short time might be accounted for by a number of factors. Amongst the complaints against the Church are the inconsistency of the priest, skepticism about the existence of heaven and hell, and what the Carrier considers extortion of money through fines and collections. Secondly, the absence of a resident missionary would in itself account for a falling off of interest in the Church. Yet, it seems, that the weakening of rank distinctions that in the period of first contact with the missionaries became associated with church offices, must also be considered as a contributing factor.

The loss of interest in Catholicism has been accompanied by a corresponding lapse in aboriginal religious beliefs and practices. As early as forty or fifty years ago puberty practices were already on the down grade. Old men questioned about their vision quests at puberty all replied that for some reason or another they had not observed the puberty rituals, although everyone else did. But an incomplete census of old men revealed that practically none of them had actually sought a guardian spirit. This might signify either an unaccountable discrepancy between theory and practice, or more probably, an actual change in religious practices. The Church may have had a strong effect upon the elimination of supernaturalistic practices. But again, as with potlatching, the Church was in no position to enforce its injunctions. A more plausible explanation for the decline in religious practices associated with the obtaining of economic success was offered by one Indian. According to him, in the old days when hunting and trapping were difficult and success uncertain because of their poorly developed technology, the people needed the assistance of the supernatural. Now that they have guns, and steel traps, hunting and trapping are rather easy, and supernatural assistance is no longer required. From this theory it would appear that the campaign of the Church against heathen religious practices was directed against a straw man. On the other hand, shamanistic practices and beliefs still flourish. If the Indian's theory is valid, it would necessarily follow that as long as the Carrier had no access to modern medical practice they would still require shamans. In fact all the Indians invariably try store medicines such as Pain Killer or Absorbine Jr. before appealing to the shaman. Of course a financial consideration is involved here; the shaman's fee is ten dollars. It is not at all unlikely that were medical facilities made available to the Carrier they would forego the services of the shaman entirely. The aboriginal theories of illness are still prevalent.

THE MODERN INDIVIDUAL—APPROVED PERSONALITY TYPES

In stories about great nobles in the old days, the Carrier consistently stressed their industriousness. The great chiefs were up early, hunted and trapped all the time, or organized trading expeditions to distant places. If one were asked to name the one personality trait most valued by the Carrier there would be no difficulty in identifying it as industriousness. Everyone, from the youngest toddler to the old men and women, was expected to work. To say even today that a child is playful is to express a grave criticism of his character. Fathers constantly enjoined their children to be up early, to sleep lightly, not to while away their time in play. The story is told of one father who, while his sons were asleep, left the house and then rushed into it again with a sudden whoop. When his sons awoke with alarm he emphasized the lesson. They should have slept lightly. Suppose it were a real enemy. No one was allowed to play string figure games in the quiet winter months because that would induce laziness. The basic interest in puberty rites for boys and girls was the promotion of habits of industriousness. There is simply no place for a lazy person in Carrier society.

Generosity is also admired, but more so formerly than today. People grumble at the ungenerous person who is wealthy, and in the next breath admit how smart he is.

Apart from an insistence upon the above two characteristics the Carrier have a rather catholic approach to personality. All people are supposed to be "smart." But smartness is not a general factor. The ability to do anything well makes one smart. The Chilcotins were smart because they rode well; the writer was smart because he could flip flapjacks. However, none who was lazy could possibly be smart, although a miser could. On the other hand, the Carrier regarded a young boy, a microcephalic with the definite stigmata of feeblemindedness, as "smart" in contrast to many of the other boys of his age group, who according to Western standards would have been regarded as smart. The microcephalic is up early and works until dark, bringing firewood, water, setting snares for small game, and in general doing many chores about the house. The other boys, who are more proficient in hunting but take time off either to lounge around or to play, are not so smart. As a result of the continued emphasis upon practical activity the play of children centers about some form of work. Children play at drawing water from the lake, at picking berries in the woods, at bringing firewood, etc.

Smartness also means proficiency in making money, as it did in the past. Thus, one of the big chiefs at Alkatcho had an honorific title that meant, "proficiency in accumulating wealth." One man at Alkatcho within relatively recent years made a lot of money by swindling the White traders. He was also smart. The miser who got rich was hated but acknowledged as being smart. It was smart for a woman to be prostitute for the Whites so long as she was well paid. One Indian, for example, boasted to me about the smartness of his wife. He used to pimp for her at Bella Coola, and she made a lot of money. However, very few women are reputed to have worked as prostitutes.

PERSONALITY

It was not possible in the field, due both to the briefness of the study and the high mobility of the Carrier, to determine any but the most general and rather vague personality pictures of Carrier individuals. There was no doubt, however, that personality differences were well marked so that we have no basis for the establishment of a personality "type." The socially approved personality traits, previously discussed, were possessed in some measure at least by all but one of the Carrier. Whether the aberrancy of this one individual can be regarded as a maladjustment resulting from the acculturation process is by no means certain. Yet the social behavior of this individual is so reminiscent of the maladjustment personality in a broken down culture that it deserves notice here.

If one were to ask any Carrier who the most disliked person in the village is, all fingers would unerringly turn to X. Now well past forty, X has never been married, and it is quite unlikely that he ever will be. It is one of the current jokes in the village that not even A, the old and very homely widow, would marry him. X wears a tailored, though ragged suit. He can read and write English (this makes him extremely useful to the Carrier in their trading enterprises, and they do make use of this ability, yet so great is their dislike of his character that this does not redeem him). Because of his slavish devotion to the ways of the White man, he is contemptuously called "mister."

X's great vice is laziness. For a month after the fall hunting season had started, X procrastinated about setting out for his trap-line. Day after day with one excuse after another he postponed the trapping trip. One day he had a cold—a running nose was sufficient to put X to bed. When his food ran out he hunted rabbits, and when unsuccessful he spent the day in bed. The men are very bitter against X and show him no sympathy. But the women have been known to bring him food secretly.

What X did not lack, though, was pride. No matter how many days he had gone without food he never complained or asked for charity. He maintained, in fact, a pretense that he was very well off and much superior to the "wild coyotes" as he called the

Indians. Somewhat, perhaps, as a gesture of defiance, X once spent his last sixty-five cents on a pound of bacon, a luxury in which none of the other natives ever indulged. He loves to display his possessions—a spring bed in which he actually sleeps (the only other spring bed in the village, owned by the "captain," being used as a display piece, and not slept in), china dishes kept clean, oilcloth-covered shelves, and a fiddle.

Not many years ago X was very well off, and had a number of good trapping seasons. Then he seems to have lost interest in life, and he developed a violent distaste for the company of his fellow tribesmen. He regarded himself as vastly superior to them intellectually and aesthetically, and even refused to drink in their company. Now he has lost most of his possessions, even having pawned his rifle. X's only response to his ever-worsening predicament is to withdraw into himself.

BIBLIOGRAPHY

Bancroft, Hubert H., *History of the Northwest Coast, Volumes 1 and 2,* A. L. Bancroft, San Francisco, Calif., 1884.

Boas, Franz, "Report on the Northwestern Indians of Canada," *Reports of the British Association for the Advancement of Science,* 1891, pp. 408–447.

Goldman, Irving, *The Alkatcho Carrier: Historical Background of Crest Prerogatives* (manuscript), Columbia University.

Jenness, Diamond, *The Bulkley Carrier* (manuscript [17]).

———— *The Sekani Indians of British Columbia* (manuscript [17]).

Mason, J. A., *The Northwestern Athabascans* (manuscript [17]).

McIlwraith, T. F., *The Bella Coola* (manuscript [17]).

Morice, Adrian G., *History of the Northern Interior of British Columbia,* Briggs, Toronto, Canada, 1905.

Osgood, Cornelius, *The Ethnography of the Great Bear Lake Indians, National Museum of Canada, Annual Report 1931, Bulletin 70,* pp. 31–99, Canada Department of Mines, Acland, Ottawa, Canada, 1932.

Smith, Harlan I., *Field Notes on the Alkatcho Carrier Material Culture* (manuscript [17]).

Teit, J., *The Tahltan* (manuscript [17]).

[17] The manuscripts referred to are in the possession of the National Museum of Canada, Ottawa, Ontario. Grateful acknowledgment for permission to use these manuscripts is offered to Mr. Diamond Jenness, Dr. T. F. McIlwraith, and to Dr. Harlan I. Smith.

EDITOR'S SUMMARY

CARRIER ACCULTURATION

The culture changes which have taken place in this group under first Bella Coola and later White contact are of particular interest since they have not been complicated by certain of the factors present in several of the other cases described. The Carrier have occupied their present territory since prehistoric times and even the arrival of the Whites seems to have produced no marked change in the local ecology. It is true that the moose has replaced the caribou as the principal game animal and that the supply of fur is decreasing, but neither of these changes has made the old subsistence techniques unworkable. Moreover, there has been no direct domination of the Carrier by any other group. The Bella Coola never penetrated their territory, and the White control has been of a rather incidental sort, with no direct competition between settlers and natives and no obvious exploitation. The changes which have taken place have, therefore, been voluntary and not dictated by necessity. Even the individual ownership and registration of trap-lines, perhaps the most revolutionary change which has taken place during the period of White contact, was not compulsory.

The first series of culture changes, those which resulted from contact with the Bella Coola, seem to have been motivated primarily by considerations of prestige. Dr. Goldman has pointed out the rôle of economic factors in initiating the practice of Bella Coola and Carrier intermarriage, and it is easy to see how Carriers who had contracted such alliances might assume with them the full series of Bella Coola marriage obligations, including certain forms of potlatching. However, this in itself would not be enough to explain the spread to the whole Carrier group of crest organization and those forms of potlatching not connected with marriage. This was made possible by the Carrier's admiration of the Bella Coola and their desire to be like them.

The same explanation would probably hold for the Carrier's acceptance of the plank house, which was not superior to the aboriginal semi-subterranean dwelling for practical purposes. This type of house seems to have found its main function among the Carrier in connection with the potlatching ceremonies and may be considered as a trait linked with them in diffusion.

If economic factors figured at all in the dissemination of crests and potlatching it was because certain changes in the economic situation of the Carrier made the acceptance of these patterns possible. With the opening up of markets for the furs in which the Carrier territory abounded, individuals and groups could accumulate the wealth without which there could have been no potlatching. The influence of economic factors is more clearly apparent in the changes which took place in these patterns after their acceptance. Thus the smallness of the gift exchanges, the absence of destruction of property and the development of techniques for terminating a potlatch competition without serious loss of prestige, all reflect the poverty of the Carrier.

It must have been difficult for the Carrier to equate the borrowed Bella Coola patterns of wealth competition and a flexible grading of social prestige based upon it with their own patterns of lineage organization in which leadership and the administration of lineage-owned resources was based on male primogeniture. Actually, it would seem that the borrowed social patterns were superimposed upon the aboriginal ones without really becoming integrated with them. Crest groups and wealth stratification existed side by side with the older lineage organization and the functions of the crest groups, outside potlatching, remained rather vague. Lack of integration on the part of the borrowed patterns is also indicated by the ease with which the Carrier abandoned them when they came under White influence. Their initial acceptance by the Carrier is the more remarkable since the Bella Coola could only influence Carrier culture by their own example. They exercised no political control. The whole situation illustrates the importance of the factor of prestige in certain cases of acculturation.

The second phase of Carrier acculturation, that resulting from their contact with Europeans, presents a somewhat different picture. The factor of prestige was still operative, for the Carrier seem to have accepted the superiority of the Whites as unquestioningly as they had that of the Bella Coola, but factors of utility and practical advantage now came to the fore. The first results of White contact were profound changes in the native technology, trade goods replacing most of the native manufacturies. The earlier trade goods were unquestionably superior to the things which they replaced, but as trade continued, the prestige factor increasingly asserted itself. With the aid of a little high-pressure salesmanship, the Carrier came to attach prestige value to a whole series of manufactured articles which they did not need. On the social side the effect of White contact seems to have been rather negative. It resulted in a sloughing off of the crest and potlatch patterns and a reversion to the older and simpler forms of organization. These forms were enough like those of the Whites to be compatible with the new contact situation. Except for losses, no profound change in the social organization occurred until it became possible to register trap-lines as individual property. This spelled the doom of the native lineages and left as the basic social and economic unit simple families organized on very much the European pattern. It is especially interesting that the recognition by the Catholic missionaries of the native system of rank and its incorporation into the organization of congregations they established seems to have had little effect on the perpetuation of rank concepts. As the tribe reverted to its older form of organization, these offices lost significance and power.

At the present time the Carrier seem to have reached a successful accommodation to the current conditions. The decrease in fur-bearing animals will probably produce economic stresses in the near future, but an economic substitute in the form of herding has already been introduced and they will probably be able to accommodate themselves. In spite of the presence of White settlers in parts of their territory and of traders, there seems to have been little race mixture. Their final assimilation into the White population is still far off.

7

THE SAN ILDEFONSO OF NEW MEXICO
by William Whitman *

INTRODUCTION [1]—EARLY HISTORY

The present Tewa pueblo of San Ildefonso or Powhoge, "Where the Water Cuts Down Through," [2] a small pueblo numbering 128 souls, lies twenty-two miles by road northwest of Santa Fé, New Mexico.

There is a tradition among the people that their original ancestors came from the north near Mesa Verde, and that from there they moved steadily south. In time they came to occupy the villages of Potsuwi and Sankewi and Otowi among the high mesas of the Pajarito plateau. Hewett, in his *Antiquities,*[3] writes:

The traditions of Otowi are fairly well preserved. It was the oldest village of Powhoge (San Ildefonso) clans of which they have definite traditions at San Ildefonso. They hold in an indefinite way that prior

---

* Dr. William Whitman died on September 3, 1939. In addition to the fieldwork of which results are recorded in this chapter, he had done extensive ethnological research in other Rio Grande Pueblos and among the southern Siouan tribes. Because of his death, Dr. Whitman was unable to read proof of these pages, and any errors in fact which they may contain, cannot be placed against him.

[1] The following study is a part of the material gathered at San Ildefonso during the summer of 1936 and the winter and spring of 1937, when I was in residence at the pueblo. I wish to acknowledge my indebtedness to the Council for Research in the Social Sciences of Columbia University, whose generosity made this work possible, and to Professor Ruth Benedict of Columbia University, whose insight and understanding of the Southwest have done much to influence the approach with which this work was carried out. I also wish to thank Mr. Kenneth M. Chapman of the Laboratory of Anthropology, Santa Fé, New Mexico, and my wife, for their assistance in the preparation of this paper.

[2] J. P. Harrington, *Ethnogeography,* p. 303.
[3] E. L. Hewett, *Antiquities,* p. 20.

to the building of this village they occupied scattered 'small house' ruins on the adjacent mesas, and they claim that when the mesa life grew unbearable from lack of water, and removal to the valley became a necessity, a detachment from Otowi founded the village of Perage in the valley on the west side of the Rio Grande about a mile west of their present village site.

There is also a tradition quoted by Harrington: [4] "The San Ildefonso Indians state very definitely that their ancestors and not the ancestors of the other Tewa villages lived at Tshirege." "Tshirege," Hewett [5] writes, "was the largest pueblo in the Pajarito district, and with the extensive cliff-village clustered about it, the largest aboriginal settlement, ancient or modern in the Pueblo region of which the writer has personal knowledge, with the exception of Zuni. . . . Tshirege is said to have been the last of all the villages of Pajarito Park to have been abandoned."

Just when San Ildefonso was first visited by the Spanish is not definitely established, but in 1593 Leyva de Bouilla and Antonio Gutierrez de Humana [6] are said to have made it their headquarters in an ill-starred expedition into New Mexico which ended in the murder of one and death at the hands of the Indians of the other. In 1598 [7] Onate stopped at San Ildefonso to which he referred by the name of Bove. At this time the pueblo stood on the east bank of the Rio Grande about a mile from its present location. A mission was built there in 1617 and from then until 1680 Santa Clara and San Juan were *visitas*. The population was estimated to be 800. During this period the Catholic Church made every effort to force its religion upon the reluctant natives. There were trials for sorcery and idolatry culminating in severe floggings.

In 1680 the villagers joined the Pueblo revolt, killed the two resident missionaries, Fray Antonio Sanchez de Pro and Fray Luis de Morales, and declared themselves independent of their Spanish conquerors and the Roman Catholic Church. When De Vargas descended on them in 1694, the whole village retired to

4 *Op. cit.,* p. 283.

5 *Op. cit.,* pp. 23–25.

6 G. P. Hammond, *Don Juan de Onate and the Founding of New Mexico,* Historical Society of New Mexico, El Palacio Press, Santa Fé, October, 1927.

7 E. R. Forrest, *Missions and Pueblos of the Old Southwest,* p. 67.

the top of the Black Mesa where they defended themselves successfully against the Spaniards.

Bandelier [8] writes:

It was on this cliff that the Tehuas held out so long in 1694 against Diego de Vargas. No documentary proof of this is needed. Vargas made four expeditions against the mesa, three of which proved unsuccessful. The first was on the 28th of January, 1694, and as the Tehuas made proposals of surrender, Vargas returned to Santa Fe without making an attack on them. But as the Indians soon after resumed hostilities, he invested the mesa from the 27th of February to the 19th of March, making an ineffectual assault on the 4th of March. A third attempt was made on the 30th of June, without results; and finally, on the 4th of September, after a siege of five days the Tehuas surrendered. Previously they had made several desperate descents from the rock, and experienced some loss of men and supplies. The mesa is so steep that there was hardly any possibility of a successful assault. The ruins on its summit are those of the temporary abodes constructed at that time by the Indians.

But the revolt was not entirely quelled. Pinched by crop failure [9] and continued Spanish oppression, the village made a last desperate bid for independence. In June, 1696,[10] "Two priests, Father Francisco Corbera and Father Antonio Moreno, were murdered by the Indians, who during the night closed all the openings of both church and convent and then set fire to the edifice. Several other Spaniards also perished." The uprising was short-lived. Most of the village fled, leaving only seventeen men and thirty-six women and children in the pueblo.[11] In 1702 [12] a number of Indians from Santa Clara were moved to San Ildefonso and lands, formerly the property of rebels, were assigned to them. In 1717 a new church was built almost in front of the site of the older one. Meanwhile the village had moved a short distance north of its former location. In 1760 the population was reported to be 484 with thirty Spaniards living in the pueblo. Between 1760 and 1780 [13] the population was so ravaged by smallpox that in 1782 the village was reduced to being a *visita* of Santa Clara. In 1793 the population was reported as 240.

[8] A. F. Bandelier, *Final Report, Pt. II*, p. 82.
[9] H. H. Bancroft, *History of Arizona and New Mexico*, pp. 214–215.
[10] A. F. Bandelier, *Final Report, Pt. II*, p. 82, note.
[11] H. H. Bancroft, *op. cit.*, p. 217.
[12] *Ibid.*, p. 225.
[13] *Ibid.*, p. 274.

Since the revolt the pueblo has been at peace with the outside world, and few references to it appear in the literature of the period. The village accepted Spanish, Mexican and American overlordship, each in turn, without formal protest. Such complaints as have found their way into state documents relate in general to land disputes and the encroachment of White settlers on pueblo grants. Concerning San Ildefonso the *Thirty-Second Annual Report of the Board of Indian Commissioners,* 1900, makes note of "systematic attempts to disregard their rights to land and water." And in 1919, after reporting a shortage of wood and water, the board states that "the San Ildefonso Indians have suffered great losses through squatters on their land, possibly more than any other of the pueblos."

There are no detailed accounts to suggest how the pueblo of San Ildefonso and its people lived or on what basis life was organized. Following the first impacts of Spanish domination, which the Indians resented but later were forced to accept, the people of San Ildefonso have accommodated themselves to the conquest with what grace they might. Since there are no records to compare, we cannot be certain of just what changes the Spaniards brought about in social and political organization and in religion, nor exactly how much they altered the general economy of the group. But there is no question that during this early period, pueblo life was modified by the Spanish culture which was pressed upon them by government and church, or which was absorbed from the Spaniards who came to live among them as simple agriculturists. For the purpose of this study, therefore, I shall arbitrarily treat as the aboriginal community, the community as it existed from the first Spanish contacts to the beginning of the present century, and as the modern community, the pueblo from the turn of the present century to 1937. During this latter period, due to the increasing activity of the Office of Indian Affairs, and perhaps even more due to the mobility of modern life, the mail-order house, and the tourist, San Ildefonso, and indeed all the pueblos, have been undergoing a rapid change in their way of life.

This division has obvious drawbacks, but is, I think, essential if we are to attempt to compare the earlier community which was primarily influenced by Spain with the modern community which is reacting to modern life in the United States.

SAN ILDEFONSO ATTITUDES

Before describing earlier economic forms and political and social organization, certain fundamental pueblo attitudes should be outlined. These attitudes, I feel, were probably as characteristic of San Ildefonso before the conquest as they are today.

Anyone who has attempted to carry on ethnological research among the Pueblo Indians will appreciate the difficulties of the task. For the Pueblo Indian is profoundly secretive about his life, especially his religious life. This is true even among those Pueblo groups whose culture seems to have been most broken by White contacts. Neither cajolery nor bribery will persuade the ordinary Pueblo Indian to talk about his religion. And those who are not too scrupulous are afraid to tell the truth.

On the whole, the Pueblo Indians, particularly the Tewa, have guarded their secrets amazingly well. This trait of secretiveness, I think, is probably pre-Spanish, though White contacts have unquestionably stimulated it. At San Ildefonso the Indian is secretive in all his relationships. The religious leaders guard their esoteric knowledge almost as closely from their own people as from the Spaniard or the American. Living in the pueblo the ethnologist discovers a feeling for concealment that extends far beyond the boundaries of religion into all other activity. Men's fears and hopes are secret. Children are taught to be secretive just as they are taught not to be curious. The apparent placidity of pueblo life is deceptive. It is a world where crisis is unwelcome, where passion is muted, where all men are ostensibly equal, but a world which despite its surface friendliness is full of hostility, where even the mildest curiosity is regarded with suspicion, and over which hangs the dread of witchcraft.

San Ildefonso culture was predominantly masculine, and women, theoretically at least, played only minor rôles in pueblo life. Men hunted, dressed the skins of the animals they killed, made their own bows and arrows, cut and sewed moccasins for themselves and their women, wove baskets, and wove and created their own dance costumes. Men also did all the "outside" work. They tilled the fields and the gardens, planted and reaped, and cut and hauled firewood. Within the village itself men built the houses, cared for the kivas, and swept [14] the plaza.

Women worked "inside." They cared for the household, ground the grain, cooked for their families and tended their children. They made the pottery. Women also built the fireplaces and plastered their houses and the kivas.

In the ceremonial life of the people the men were paramount. They controlled the various religious societies and directed the religious dances. A wife was not supposed to ask her husband where he was going when he left the house to attend to his ceremonial duties. When a woman was wanted at the kiva she was notified by the kossa. A woman was not supposed to venture an opinion on ceremonial matters.[15] She might belong to important societies, but her duties were auxiliary. Women had societies of their own which were to some extent counterparts of the male societies, but it appears that even these were more or less under the control of the male cacique.

Women were equally excluded from pueblo political life. They were not consulted, at least in theory, by their husbands on political questions, and had no part in the meetings of the pueblo officers and the council.

The one sphere in which women might compete with men was in curing. They were not shamans, but rather doctors who depended for recognition solely on their reputation to effect cures.

San Ildefonso's politico-religious as well as social organization was conceptually paternalistic. The cacique [16] was, in a very real sense, the father of the village. His devotional duties insured their prosperity and set in motion those forces which produced fertility and good health and a large crop. He exhorted them and taught them how to conduct themselves. His word was absolute in all phases of activity. No disputes could be brought before him. His

[14] Men sweep the plaza before fiestas and dances.

[15] Before or to men. As one woman informant said: "even if we know we are right we say nothing." Undoubtedly many women do not practise this restraint.

[16] Formerly there were two town chiefs in San Ildefonso. Today there is but one.

appointment was for life. He was addressed ceremonially as "father," and referred to in ordinary conversation as "father old man." The heads of societies, though less important, were also regarded as being in a father relationship to the people, while the senior officers were commonly addressed as "older brother."

Life at San Ildefonso was coöperative rather than competitive, especially among men. Men who were too frankly competitive were suspected of witchcraft, and signs of personal ambition were viewed with distrust. Religion, particularly in its ceremonial aspects, was expressed in coöperative terms. Everyone had to take part in religious exercises, attend dance practice and assist in some phase of the ceremonial life. All owed duties to the kiva. Such civil duties as sweeping the plaza were performed coöperatively by the men. Men worked together on the irrigation ditches in the spring; they helped to plough and plant and reap one another's fields. The labor of housebuilding was also, to a large extent, coöperative.

Less was expected of women than of men, though women would also coöperate. They would plaster a kiva or a house [17] together. The women of a family frequently baked bread together before a feast. Children were also taught to help anyone who asked them for help, with the understanding that they in turn might some day need the help of others.

Another point that should be borne in mind is the emphasis placed on the present. During the many hours I spent in the company of the Indians of San Ildefonso I seldom heard them voluntarily mention the past or speculate on the future. This attitude appears to have affected all their relationships. The dead were soon forgotten. Men and women frequently did not know the names of their grandparents, and though they were not forbidden to mention deceased relatives they seldom spoke of them. History, as they knew it, was represented by mythological legends preserved by the priests.[18] Indifference to the past not only extended to the dead but also to the living. A man or woman's

[17] Plastering a house was usually a family affair.
[18] Officers of the various societies.

past was seldom held against him or her. It was the immediate relationship between men and the community that counted.

The future had as little interest for the San Ildefonso Indian as the past. Today in nearly all the societies the necessary rituals to insure fertility and blessing are carried on by a few old men. But the ranks of these societies that are still thought to be vital to the welfare of the pueblo are not recruited to insure priestly succession. Tomorrow will take care of itself. This point of view is responsible in part for the gradual disappearance of much ancient lore. It is not that the young lack faith and are unwilling to carry on the traditions, but rather that the present alone is their concern, and that to thrust themselves forward would suggest that they entertained unlawful ambitions. The daily duty is faithfully performed. The next ceremony is a matter of conscientious activity. But, characteristically, the present factional quarrels which threaten the village are discussed without arriving at solutions that involve the future. Life in the pueblo is lived almost exclusively in the here and now.

SAN ILDEFONSO

In 1907 Harrington [19] wrote:

The plaza of San Ildefonso was formerly (previous to the uprising of 1696, according to Bandelier) just south of its present location, so that the row of houses south of the present plaza was then the row of houses north of the plaza. The south estufa was in the center of the former plaza. The house rows surrounding the former plaza were two or three stories high; most of those of the present pueblo are only one story high, while a few have two stories. According to San Ildefonso tradition, when the plaza occupied its former southern location San Ildefonso was a populous and prosperous village. It was big and several-storied. All went well until certain sorcerers advocated moving the pueblo to the north. . . . It was arranged at last that the good people and the bad sorcerers should hold a gaming contest. . . . The bad sorcerers won the game by witchcraft and according to their wish, the pueblo was shifted northward. Since that time the San Ildefonso people have decreased in number, have had pestilence, famines, persecutions.

[19] J. P. Harrington, *op. cit.*, pp. 305–306.

Since Harrington wrote, a large number of the inhabitants of the pueblo have moved south, and have built their houses around what is now known as the South Plaza. Today this geographical division of the present pueblo into South and North Plazas represents the two factions which divide the village.

The village house usually contains from three to four rooms. Each occupied house usually shelters a household consisting of a man, his wife and his unmarried children. Occasionally a man, his wife and, perhaps, a married son or son-in-law and his family will occupy a house. Certain families own more than one house within the village. In such cases the unoccupied house is left untended, for the people would rather build a new house than rent or buy an empty one. Within the last few years the government has turned over houses and land to the Indians which were formerly in the possession of Mexicans. A few Indians live in these houses, which are outside the village, during the summer or rent them to Whites, but in general the people live the year round within the village.

To the west of the village along the Rio Grande, and to the north between the Pojoaque road and the Pojoaque River, lie the village fields. A few families cultivate fields across the Rio Grande, most of which were recently in the possession of Mexicans. According to Hewett,[20] in the old days there was no individual ownership of land. Nominally it was re-allotted by the officers of the village each year.

Beyond the fields, many of which are no longer cultivated for lack of water to irrigate them, the grant is a wilderness of arroyos, dry washes and mesas dotted with cedar and piñon. A few cattle and still fewer horses belonging to the Indians graze there, but its chief value to the community is the firewood which can be gleaned from its slopes.

In 1933, according to the *Annual Report of the Division of Extension and Industry,* Washington, the grant totaled some 19,305 acres, of which 305 acres were in farms. Of this acreage, in 1933, crops were harvested from 150 acres. The number of farms was twenty-two; the number of households in the village, twenty-eight.

[20] E. L. Hewett, *Ancient Life in the American Southwest,* p. 71.

During the spring, summer and fall, though the men work in the fields by day, the life and heart of the people is within the village which they seldom leave except for occasional journeys to Santa Fé or to attend dances and fiestas at neighboring pueblos.

Since the early days of Spanish occupation, when at one time the pueblo was said to number 800 souls, there has been a steady decrease in population. Within modern times the number has maintained itself at about the present figure of 128.[21]

SAN ILDEFONSO ECONOMICS

Agriculture, centered about corn, was the basis of all pueblo economy. The old attitude toward corn is illustrated by the following: "The pueblo [22] of San Ildefonso is swept before the corn is brought home, 'because corn is just the same as people and must have the plaza clean, so that the corn will be glad when we bring it in.'" Agriculture was almost exclusively the work of men. As one old man said: "There are two livings, agriculture and religion." But religion was not so much a living distinct from agriculture as it was a necessary corollary to agriculture, as important in providing flourishing crops as tilling the soil, planting the seed and reaping the harvest. What little is known of the ancient religion shows it to have been largely concerned with agriculture in all its phases.

At the time of the Spanish discovery [writes Freire-Marreco],[23] the Tewa were cultivating, it would seem, maize, beans, pumpkins and other gourds, cotton and tobacco. The Spaniards added to the native resources by introducing wheat, oats, barley, chili, onions, other kinds of beans, peas, watermelons, muskmelons, peaches, apricots, and apples. The English-speaking Americans have introduced no food plant of importance.

No doubt the Spaniards' importations into New Mexico were not accepted without a struggle, but at the present day most of these plants constitute an indispensable factor of native life: they are regarded as

---

[21] *Indian Population in the United States and Alaska*, Bureau of Census, 1910, p. 104. The population of San Ildefonso is given as 1860, 154; 1871, 156; 1881, 139; 1890, 151; 1900, 137; 1910, 123.

[22] W. W. Robbins, J. P. Harrington, B. Freire-Marreco, Ethnobotany of the Tewa Indians, *Bureau of American Ethnology, Bulletin 55*, Washington, D.C., 1915, p. 83.

[23] W. W. Robbins, etc., *op. cit.*, p. 76.

"Indian Food" which may be eaten in the estufa, and they are named in the ritual formulas and prayers. Thus, a Tewa at San Ildefonso described the people as praying in the estufa for all the things they want to have —corn, wheat, melons, watermelons, onions, chiles, apples, peaches, all the things they have to eat—and clothes, shoes; and a long life, to live to be old men.

Once the people's own idea of a good diet embraced cultivated plants in addition to wild plants in season in considerable variety, drawing on the greatest possible number of different food plants, since the available quantity of any single plant was limited. Now the people draw on the unlimited but unvaried supplies of the American store, or on what they can afford to buy of them—white flour, coffee, and sugar. To buy what the store offers is less trouble than to hunt for plants in the open; further, an ideal of women's work and behaviour is growing up which rather discourages the old activities. The women are not to help to provide food (except by earning money), but to keep a clean house, cook, and serve hot meals.

In pre-Spanish days the people of San Ildefonso cultivated small fields and gardens among the high mesas of the Pajarito plateau. Later a change in climate and lack of water with which to irrigate their crops drove them into the Rio Grande Valley. Here fields were cultivated close to the river and irrigated by ditches, and certain foods, such as melons, were planted on the flat lands by the river which were at certain seasons of the year enriched by floods.

Agriculture was originally carried on by means of hoes and planting-sticks. Corn was planted in hills. But it appears from what records we possess that the people of San Ildefonso, since the conquest, have suffered numerous difficulties in raising crops, the most important being lack of water. With a rainfall of from eight to ten inches a year, the pueblo agriculturist was forced to rely in large part on his irrigation ditches. Changes in the river channel and floods made these difficult to maintain, and following the settling of the Spaniards in the neighborhood, sufficient water was diverted by non-Indians to impair seriously the productivity of their fields.

The agricultural year began in late March or early April when the community cleaned out the irrigation ditches. Corn and other crops were planted in April. Nearly all the able-bodied males then worked in the fields until the harvest was gathered late in September or early in October, depending on the crop and the season.

Grain was stored by nearly all families during the winter for the spring planting, enough being kept on hand in the pueblo to tide the people over in case of famine. For it was felt that in the case of certain crops like corn, only seed raised by the pueblo would flourish in their fields.

The people of San Ildefonso practised a limited animal husbandry. Turkeys were raised for their feathers, which are still used in village ceremonies. Nearly all families had and have dogs. Turkeys and dogs were possessed by the people before the conquest. Since the Spanish introduction of domesticated animals, the horse has been an indispensable factor in pueblo economy, although the pueblo appears never to have bred them to any extent. Only the poorest families today are without a team, but most of the horses in the pueblo have either been furnished by the government or have been purchased outside the pueblo. There are few saddle horses, and on the whole the people are not skillful horsemen. A few milk cows, beef cattle, hogs and hens are also casually raised. Today no sheep, goats or burros are owned within the pueblo.[24]

Hunting was formerly an important part of pueblo economy, and there are still references to former hunting traits in modern hunting techniques and in religious ceremonial. Like agriculture, but to a minor degree, hunting was worked into the religious complex. There was a hunt chief or Samaiyo, whose present duties consist in ushering the game animals into the pueblo during the January buffalo and animal dance. He was formerly in charge of the communal rabbit hunt in which men, women and children surrounded a large area and drove the rabbits and other small game into a gradually constricting circle where they killed them with sticks, bows and arrows, and, following Spanish occupation, with guns.

[24] The *Annual Report of the Division of Extension and Industry,* 1933, lists as follows: Horses, 44; cattle beef, 42; cattle dairy, 10; hogs, 16; fowls, 104; sheep, 4. Today (1937) two families own all the beef cattle and two families possess all but one of the dairy cows. No milk is sold in the pueblo except by Mexicans. There are only three hogs.

I was told that hunting ceremonies were held only before deer and buffalo hunts, but since hunting and religion are intimately related it is extremely difficult to get any information at all on this subject. The following practices are still remembered, and no doubt a few of them continue to be carried on. I was told that for four nights before a hunt the hunter "prayed to his gods for luck." During this time he smoked Indian tobacco to confuse the game. He had to remain continent; he had to wash and purify himself; he particularly had to avoid menstruating women. During the hunt the hunter sang and prayed. He prayed "to his gods and to his forefathers, and offered meal to them."

When an animal was slain, it was addressed ceremonially and then pointed head first toward the hunter's home. Offerings of meal were made again, and tobacco was smoked. The blood of the quarry was drunk. It was said that the animal was later taken to the town chief [25] who passed his hands over it and then breathed on them. Prayer feathers were offered. In the case of deer the bones were later taken back to the forest.

I was also told that following a kill there might be a dance in the pueblo itself in which the villagers took part, wearing deer masks. This, however, I was unable to confirm.

No one living remembers the buffalo hunt or anything connected with it. There appears to be no question, however, that parties of men would travel east to the plains in search of buffalo. These trips were hazardous and of long duration. The buffalo dance is usually held in January, though a form of buffalo dance may be danced later in the season. Certain rights connected with the January dance are said to be hereditary; for instance, the right to dance Buffalo Woman.[26]

Elk, big horn sheep, the puma and the bear are well known to the people of the pueblo, but for some time, with the exception of the bear, they have been driven from the mountains which border the Rio Grande, and so have played no part in the ceremony of the village.

[25] I could find only one man in the village who would mention the ceremonial aspects of hunting, and such information as he was willing to give me in secret he would not elaborate.

[26] See page 405. Buffalo meat was said to be sacred, i. e., to have been used in the kiva during ceremonies.

Jack rabbits, coney rabbits and pack rats were a source of meat. These were hunted by men and boys without ceremony. There were, however, ceremonies in which rabbits were hunted by the war chief and his officers and brought to the kiva.

In the old days the favorite method of hunting was the surround or drive in which men and boys took part. The men hunted with bows and arrows and used the throwing-stick. With the introduction of the gun there was an increasing tendency for individuals to hunt alone. Trapping was also practised. Just what types of traps were set before the day of the steel trap is not known, but there are the remains of pre-Spanish pit traps in the neighborhood. These were dug in well-worn game trails.

The following animals were considered not fit to be eaten (I was told that there was no religious prejudice against their flesh, but merely that they were not thought to be good meat): the bear, mountain-lion, wildcat, wolf, coyote, eagle, hawk and turkey-vulture.

Fish were caught in basket-like traps, and nets were dragged through the shallows of the Rio Grande. Occasionally trout were caught in this manner, but for the most part the fish were suckers or catfish since below the confluence of the Chama River and the Rio Grande, the water is too filled with silt to harbor trout. Fish did not play an important rôle in pueblo economy.

The techniques that were practised by the people of San Ildefonso up to about the turn of the century have in many cases been forgotten. Very few are still carried on, and these with changed emphasis. Each man, it was said, usually made his own bows and arrows. Men knew the art of tanning hides. Men made their own moccasins and they also made the long white moccasin boots that are still worn by nearly all married women. A few men were more skillful at this than others, but there does not appear to have been any specialization in techniques by individual families. Weaving of cotton was formerly practised by the men, who wove their own ceremonial costumes and the mantles worn by women. Basket-weaving and bead-work were done by men.

Women's techniques were primarily concerned with pottery

and preparing food. The clays that went into pottery making were gathered by the men, also the manure used in firing the pots, but the grinding of the clays and the making of the pots were done by women. Men, however, decorated the pots used for ceremonies in the kiva. Pots were not only used as household utensils, but large pots were used to store grain, meal and occasionally water. Women ground grain and dried the produce of the fields for future use in the homes. After the crops were gathered they were responsible for their use and preservation.

Though there is no evidence that "markets" were held for the exchange of commodities, barter was practised within and without the pueblo to provide an exchange for surplus goods. If a family raised a surplus of corn or fruit, they would exchange with another family who had raised or produced some other article which the first family lacked. Trade was, if possible, carried on within the pueblo and was not solely in goods since a man might exchange his labor for some desirable commodity.[27] There do not seem to have been any fixed values in the sense that a quantity of one product was valued as being the equivalent of a fixed quantity of some other product. Nor apparently was there one product, such as the blanket of the Plains Indian, which did duty as a fixed standard in relation to which all exchanges were made.

Trade or exchange was not only carried on within the pueblo, but it was also carried on with outside groups. Though the Indians of San Ildefonso were not wandering traders, the Santo Domingan traders visited the pueblo, and the Navajo and other groups occasionally came and brought with them silver and turquoise and rugs and baskets and other articles. The trade routes of the Pueblo Indians and their trading formulas are not known. But trade did take place and to such an extent that by the turn of the century certain native crafts, such as weaving and basketry, had at San Ildefonso more or less fallen into disuse.[28] Even those groups which were considered to be the natural enemies of the Pueblo peoples appear to have traded with them long before the White man put an end to Indian raids and wars.

[27] This is done today, and two informants said that it had been practised in the past.

[28] One man was said to know how to weave baskets; another man was said to know how to weave on a loom.

SOCIAL ORGANIZATION—THE FAMILY

The family, father, mother and children, was the basic social unit in San Ildefonso. It was predominantly patrilineal, the wife frequently taking the moiety and clan of her husband at marriage, the children taking the moiety and clan of their father. To this practice there were exceptions, but in general this was done throughout the pueblo.

Family control was exercised ideally by a gentle paternalism. A wife was supposed to obey her husband in all matters, and children were brought up to be quiet and submissive. Paternal authority was said to extend only until a child married and set up a household for himself or herself, but actually paternal influence lasted over a far longer period.

If a man died, leaving a wife and children, there was a tendency for the wife and her offspring to accept the guidance and help of her father-in-law and brother-in-law while actually maintaining a household independent of either. However, in such a situation the children might accept the mother as head of the family, and even after marriage take up residence with her, bringing their spouses to live in her home. This was likely to be the case if the spouse, as so often happened, had neither father nor mother living, and the members of the household were girls. Boys usually set up independent households within the pueblo if their parents were living, unless they were obliged to care for an aged mother or father, in which case they, too, took up residence in the family home.

Inheritance was through either family line, though land and house ownership usually were on the masculine side, but even here theory favored the even division of property among children regardless of sex. There was no inheritance of religious privilege, excluding moiety and clan affiliations, except for the following two cases: one where a man was said to "inherit" leadership of the Tseoke, the War Society no longer extant, and one where a girl was said to "inherit" the right to dance Buffalo Woman. Both of these cases are open to doubt, for a woman formerly privileged to dance Buffalo Woman is no relation to the present dancer. And the man who inherited Tseoke privileges is said not to be "head" of the order of which he is sole member, but merely the inheritor, and so guardian, of its paraphernalia.

KINSHIP TERMINOLOGY

In general, kinship terminology at San Ildefonso is essentially the same as reported by Harrington, Freire-Marreco, and Parsons for the Tewa pueblos. "Kinship nomenclature," writes Parsons,[29] "is variable among the pueblos, not only from town to town speaking the same language, but within the same town." The differences in kinship terminology, as I found it, and that previously reported, are no doubt due to this confusion not only among the villagers themselves, but also to their use of kinship terminology to express attitudes toward individuals. If first cousins, for instance, are fond of one another, they express this by using the brother-sister terms; then if coolness sets in, they will express their relationship by the uncle-aunt terms. I have known this to happen within the pueblo in less than six months' time. This is true not only of relatives bound by blood or marriage, but kinship terms are also applied freely to individuals who are not relatives at all. Another factor that must be taken into consideration is the tendency to bring distant relatives, either of the grandparent generation or second, third and fourth cousins into a close relationship by using terms such as uncle-aunt and their reciprocals. And at San Ildefonso we must take one other factor into account—the general discontinuance of the terms tunu and kii. These terms, as reported by Harrington and Parsons, signify in general uncle and aunt older than father or mother. In San Ildefonso these terms are generally used to express the concept of uncle or aunt and their children younger than father and mother. But the villagers themselves, as I have said before, are not logical, and the practice in the pueblo of referring to a man by his Mexican patronymic has helped to confuse matters.

Interesting points in this bilateral system are the distinctions

[29] E. C. Parsons, *Social Organization of the Tewa of New Mexico*, p. 69. See also J. P. Harrington, "Tewa Relationship Terms," *American Anthropologist*, N.S., 14, 472-498, and B. Freire-Marreco, "Tewa Kinship Terms from the Pueblo of Hano, Arizona," *American Anthropologist, N.S.*, 16, 269-287.

made between older and younger, the use of reciprocals, and the frequent lack of distinction between sexes.

KINSHIP TERMS

pebe: great-grandfather.

kugu: great-grandmother.

tete: grandfather.

saiya: grandmother.

papa: papatete, papasaiya. When *papa* is prefixed to the term for grandparent it signifies generation. Great-grandfather, etc.

tete.e: grandson.

saiya.e: granddaughter. The addition of *e,* meaning child, is the reciprocal.

ta: ⎧ father. *Ta sendo,* father old man, is sometimes used for the winter
tara: ⎨ cacique; *kwiyo sendo,* mother old man, is used for the summer
⎩ cacique.

dyiya: mother.

mema: uncle. This term covers a multitude of relationships not only of kin, but kin by courtesy. Besides father's and mother's brother, it may include grandfather's brother, father-in-law's brother, father's sister's husband, etc.

ko.o: aunt. Wife of *mema.* Besides father's and mother's sister it also may include father's brother's wife, grandfather's brother's wife, and mother's sister, and first cousin older than speaker.

mema.e: ⎧ nephew. These reciprocals for *mema* and *ko.o* may also in-
ko.o.e: ⎨ clude first cousins younger than speaker. Or in fact anyone
⎩ who addresses the speaker as *mema,* etc.

tunu: first cousin (male). This is the reverse of Harrington's identification. In San Ildefonso the term is seldom used and when used frequently indicates a relationship more usually expressed by *mema.* By a few it was said to indicate father's or mother's younger brother.

ki.i: first cousin (female). Wife of *tunu,* etc.

tunu.e: first cousin once removed. Child of *tunu* or *kii.*

kii.e: first cousin once removed. Child of *tunu* or *kii.*

na: self.

pare: older brother or sister. Used also for senior pueblo officers.

tiu: younger brother or sister. This and *pare* may be used for anyone who may be a brother by courtesy.

e: son or daughter. Child.

yasendo: father-in-law.

yakwiyo: mother-in-law.

t'owa: spouse.

ya.a: brother- or sister-in-law.

soyinge: son-in-law. Also sister's husband.
sa.i: daughter-in-law. Also brother's wife.
kwatara: step-father.
kwadyiya: step-mother.
popota: godfather.
popodyida: godmother.

MOIETY AND CLAN

The pueblo of San Ildefonso was divided into two groups, or moieties, the Summer People and the Winter People. These groups, though they were under separate religious leaders, united in coöperative enterprises for the pueblo as a whole, but otherwise they were conscious of their individual identities. In general, a man or woman followed the moiety of the father, but a shift in moiety was permissible. Women on marriage might change their moiety or not as they saw fit, and there are also cases where men changed their moieties.

Each moiety was under the spiritual guidance of a town chief.[30] These two priests were responsible for the general welfare, and indirectly exercised complete control over the pueblo. Winter Chief was in charge during the fall and winter, Summer Chief during the spring, summer and early fall. In matters of supreme importance, Summer Chief, I was told, took precedence over Winter Chief, but as there is no Winter Chief in San Ildefonso at the moment, this statement was impossible to check in the light of present practice. The moiety was a religious division, but as we shall see later, its influence extended further than religion.

Within the moiety was the clan. These clans appear to have exerted no direct influence over the moiety or the individual, and today many of the Indians confuse clan with moiety. In 1936 there were said to be only three clans—Sun, Red Stone and Turquoise. Other clans reported by Hodge [31] and Parsons [32] no longer exist, and I could get no information about them. Just what function the clan played in the pueblo it is now impossible

[30] Cacique.

[31] F. W. Hodge, "Pueblo Indian Clans," *American Anthropologist, Volume 9, 1896,* pp. 345-352.

[32] E. C. Parsons, *Social Organization of the Tewa of New Mexico,* pp. 91-94. Parsons gives (1927) Sun, Red Stone, Turquoise and Grass (p. 53). Grass I was unable to identify.

to say. There are no religious or social duties connected with the clan, and the figures of membership are so disproportionate, since the great majority of people are Sun, that no valid conclusions can be drawn in relation to possible dwelling or marriage choice. Turquoise clan is associated with Winter moiety; Sun and Red Stone with Summer. Many of the people today consider these clans merely alternate titles of the moiety groups. Clan, however, may possibly have affected dwelling choice, since the three Red Stone families live side by side in the North Plaza, and three Turquoise families (Winter) also live adjacent to one another.

In San Ildefonso, however, the division between Summer and Winter is no longer of any deep significance, since there are only three Winter families within the pueblo. Instead of the moiety division the pueblo has been split into two factions, and we find one plaza at odds with the other. The history of this split I shall describe later, but in any discussion of San Ildefonso social organization we must take this present schism into account.

THE CACIQUE SOCIETIES

Each moiety, Summer and Winter, had as its presiding priest a town chief. A town chief had to be a member of the society [33] in his moiety from which town chiefs were appointed. He was appointed for life, and he was chosen for his knowledge of sacred rituals, prayers, chants and ceremonial procedure.[34] In character he had to be benevolent, honest and temperate. He was in a sense father to the whole pueblo, and so was responsible to the omnipresent deities for the welfare of his people. No dissensions could be brought before him. His word was absolute and irrevocable. As assistants the cacique had a right- and left-hand man. These officers were also members of the cacique society, and it was said that the right-hand man succeeded on the death of the town chief. These officers, also, served for life. Whether the town chief was appointed in fact by the society or whether

---

[33] The name of the Summer society was Paioke, of the Winter, Oyike.

[34] I was told by two informants that knowledge, ability to learn, and character affected the choice of a town chief by his society.

he was appointed to the office of left-hand man with the understanding that eventually he would automatically become town chief if he lived long enough, I could not discover. The identity [35] of town chief's lieutenants was kept a secret from the world outside the pueblo. Aiding these three religious priests to carry out their duties were the other members of the society, men, women and children.

Today at San Ildefonso there is no Winter cacique and no Winter cacique society. If the Winter families wish to elect a Winter cacique, they will have to go to some neighboring pueblo possessed of a Winter cacique society for assistance.

A town chief or member of the society might also be a member of the other village societies not based on moiety.

The cacique society was recruited by self-dedication or by dedication during childhood or even before birth. Dedication during childhood was most common, and a child was frequently "given" to the society following some death or disaster in its family. Not many children, however, were so offered, because town chief duties were said to be onerous; the responsibilities were heavy and the tangible rewards negligible. Membership in the society was not inheritable, nor did membership run in families.

THE KOSSA

The duties of the kossa were manifold, and today they are the most important of the existing societies that do not make moiety a basis for membership. They were associated with the water serpent and the "rain sending and crop bringing kachina." They were said to have the power to bring rain. They brought water to the kiva from the sacred cardinal springs. They summoned the dancers for the dances, and called the women to the kiva for ceremonies. During certain ceremonies they guarded the dancers from possible evil. When "asked" [36] to appear at dances, they were privileged to act as clowns and to behave in a way which would have been considered profoundly improper if indulged in by other members of the pueblo.

35 In San Ildefonso the identity of the town chief is not a secret.
36 I was told that the kossa had to be "asked" before they could appear.

In general the clowns have a punitive and policing function in ceremonial matters, [writes Parsons,[37]] and through their license in speech
and song a somewhat similar function in domestic matters, ridicule being a strong weapon among the pueblos.

The flood-sending water serpent in the Rio Grande Valley has a punitive character. So it is quite consistent that the clowns should be associated with the water serpent and with the rain sending and crop
bringing kachina. But the clown groups have direct weather control and
fertility functions, they themselves impersonate kachina or other supernaturals who live in springs or lakes. As scouts or war dance assistants
the clowns have war functions. In short, through their police power,
their magical power and their license in conduct, all fear inspiring characters, social regulation is an outstanding function of the clown groups.

The male kossa, headed by the kossa sendo, had women helpers. The female kossa seldom came out to dance in their capacity
as kossa. Their duties appear to have been auxiliary. It was said:
"They did not know much."

The kossa of San Ildefonso generally speak of their order by
the Keresan term "koshare." This society recruited its members
irrespective of moiety. Children were dedicated during childhood, or adults might give themselves later in life, or be trapped.
If a man dreamt that he should become a kossa, or if he was ill
and believed that to join the kossa would cure him, he would go
to the head of the society and ask to join. If this was granted
him, he was initiated. Another method of recruiting members
was to trap them. If a man or woman entered the round kiva,
sometimes known as the "outside" or "south" kiva, and hesitated
on the ladder while descending inside, or failed to circle the
inside of the kiva properly (counter-clockwise), he could be
trapped and forced to join the society. Membership was not inherited. A kossa might belong to all the village societies proper
to his moiety.

THE MEDICINE SOCIETIES

There were two pufona or medicine societies, the Tewa ke and
the Tema ke, each having its own chief or leader.

Unusual and unpleasant events and most illnesses were thought
to be the result of witchcraft either within the pueblo or in some

[37] E. C. Parsons and R. Beals, "The Sacred Clowns of the Pueblo and Mayo-
yaqui Indians," *American Anthropologist*, N.S., 36, No. 4, pp. 499 *et seq.*

neighboring pueblo. Exorcising witchcraft was the medicine-man's chief duty. And since illness was the major product of witchcraft, medicine-men were believed to be able to cure all illnesses; just as they knew, but were unable to tell, who were witches. The medicine-men worked together as a society, or singly, depending on the emergency. Formerly they were a very powerful group, not above the suspicion of sorcery themselves. I was told they were not "paid," though occasionally they might be given presents from grateful patients. I was also told that they had to cure or else they would do themselves injury. The ceremony appointing them members of the society, which was held once a year in January, gave them at once the necessary knowledge and power to cure.

Membership was by dedication in childhood or infancy or by voluntary joining. Dreams and illness frequently compelled men and women to seek membership. Inheritance was not a factor.

In addition to the medicine societies there were doctors, men and women, who practised curing independently. They usually inherited this knowledge from their parents, or learned it from someone who had power to cure. Each of these practitioners had his own technique which usually applied to specific ailments. A doctor's popularity lay solely in his ability to cure. There are no longer any such men or women in San Ildefonso. If a man wishes to be cured, he must go to another pueblo.

Mexican men and women practised medicine [38] at San Ildefonso. Certain of them were popular and highly esteemed. Midwives frequently were Mexican.

SOCIETIES THAT NO LONGER EXIST—THE KWIRANA

Along with the kossa, there was a somewhat similar society, the members of which were known as Kwirana. This society still exists in some of the Tewa pueblos, but not in San Ildefonso.[39]

[38] Today Mexican doctors are used by those members of the pueblo who lack confidence in White doctors. One old man went to the government White doctor and a Mexican "doctor" as well to whom he paid fifteen dollars.

[39] E. C. Parsons, *The Social Organization of the Tewa of New Mexico*, p. 130. Dr. Parsons was given the names of two men in San Ildefonso (1927) as

THE TSEOKE

The Tseoke or war society no longer exists, though one man in the village is said to have inherited the paraphernalia.

THE BLUE CORN GIRLS

There were formerly two women's societies known as the Summer Blue Corn Girls and the Winter Blue Corn Girls.[40] The division was by moiety. Each of these groups had a leader. The societies had their own ceremonies which I was told were chiefly for rain. They never had fertility ceremonies for "children or anything of that sort," nor to make crops ripen and be fruitful. I was also told that the only work the societies did was to take care of sick children.[41] A girl decided for herself when she was about thirteen whether she wished to be a Blue Corn Girl or not. They had no voice, as has been suggested, in electing or proposing village officers. The society ceased to exist at San Ildefonso many years ago.

SOCIAL DOMINANCE

Theoretically San Ildefonso society was based on the concept of universal equality. The village officers, when not acting in their official capacities, enjoyed the same status as the rest of the village. Men had equal rights to land and equal standing in the village. In a small pueblo like San Ildefonso all men acted in some official capacity during the greater part of their lives.

Any man or woman who thrust himself or herself into a position of authority was likely to be suspected of witchcraft. Anyone who talked too aggressively or too freely was also suspected.

Such social dominance as may be said to have existed depended on success in agriculture and possibly success in hunting, though this was certainly of secondary importance. The successful agriculturist was thought to possess the favor of the gods.[42] He was,

---

belonging to the Kurena (Keresan) or Kwirana. Careful inquiries suggest that she was misinformed.

[40] E. C. Parsons, *op. cit.*, p. 139.

[41] I regret to say this seems unlikely.

[42] I was told this by two informants, but my feeling was rather that such a man was considered more to be lucky than blessed by a deity or deities.

therefore, by his industry and piety subject to be called upon to fill some public office in the village. Recognition was never ostensibly sought, and was even avoided. Such modesty had village approval. Responsibility was a duty rather than a goal.

No one village society was considered to be more important than any other. No one, except from distress, either joined or dedicated children to any of them.

Accounts from other pueblos [43] suggest that the two most important groups were the cacique societies and the medicine societies. Frequently these groups were at odds in matters of public policy—the medicine societies being referred to as sorcerers. Today the two medicine societies have little influence in the village, and there is only one cacique society.

Men, however, actually did take considerable satisfaction in their prominence in the affairs of the village. And success was recognized, if not officially, at least unofficially. People of means were flattered, and their opinions were respected.

Men and women were judged on their ability to conform to pueblo standards. Men ideally were hard workers, pious, and cooperative. They were not aggressive and minded their own business. They were successful, but not at the expense of others. Women equally were hard workers, and pious. They were good housekeepers. The children of such parents were, ideally, quiet and submissive.

POLITICAL ORGANIZATION—THE WAR CAPTAIN AND HIS WARRIORS

Midway between the religious and civil functionaries was the war captain, or outside chief, and his warriors. Theoretically these six men were appointed for only one year, but under certain conditions, chiefly failure to agree on new candidates, they might stay in office indefinitely.[44] The war captain sometimes acted under the authority of the cacique; sometimes under the authority of the governor. Among other duties, chiefly of a religious nature, he had to decide what dances [45] were to be per-

---

[43] Notably Acoma.
[44] This is true at San Ildefonso today.
[45] I could not discover whether he decided all dances or not.

formed. He had to guard the dancers during dances or the kiva when a dance was held within it. He had to fetch and guard sacred objects during ceremonies, and he had to help maintain discipline, though this was seldom needed, within the village. The war captain and his warriors might be members of either moiety.

THE GOVERNOR AND HIS OFFICERS

The governor, next to the cacique, was the most important figure in the pueblo. The office, symbolized by a silver-headed cane, is said to have been of Spanish origin. A new governor was supposed to be appointed every year. He was assisted by a right-hand man and a left-hand man and by an aguacil or police officer. He was selected irrespective of moiety. While it was said that the governor was elected by the principales, in reality he was selected by the cacique and his appointment was later confirmed by the principales.

The duties of the governor were many and his authority was seldom questioned. He settled village disputes, gave orders for such community work as sweeping the plaza before a dance, and was in charge of the spring cleaning of the ditches. He was also the man in direct contact with the outside world. In council with his assistants and the principales he settled land disputes, and fees, and in general acted as intermediary between the village and the United States government.

THE PRINCIPALES AND THE COUNCIL

The principales were a body of elders who at one time or another had acted as governors. They sat as a body to settle civil disputes in conjunction with the governor. The principales and the governor [46] settled minor matters of village policy within the

[46] I was told that the cacique really was the one to decide all matters of policy within the village, and that he made known his wishes to the governor who acted in accordance. I was also told that the head of the principales, usually the man who had been governor most frequently, decided matters of policy for this group. There was unquestionably a tendency toward paternalism in all matters, the oldest in the group dictating policy, the others concurring. Failure to follow this practice helped to split the village up into factions.

pueblo; major difficulties were treated by a council which consisted of practically all able-bodied and adult males.

THE PIKA (FISCALES)

These were usually four in number. They were in charge of burying the dead.

LAW AND ORDER

The governor and the pueblo executive officers were empowered to apportion land, settle land disputes and questions of water rights, and to collect and disburse tribal funds. Their decisions were seldom if ever questioned.

On the whole, there was little need of law in San Ildefonso. Disputes were usually avoided, and if they took place, were settled between the individuals without calling on the pueblo to take action. Such disputes, however, as might arise in the pueblo that could not be settled individually usually came before the governor, or in more serious cases, the governor, the war captain, their officers, and the principales.

Within the last fifteen years such a court tried a case of witchcraft, but I was told that no other case had been brought before it. Although the woman was found guilty, nothing was done, and the whole affair was kept a close secret even from her family. Murder and witchcraft, the telling of pueblo secrets to outsiders, failure to observe ceremonial obligations and duties to the pueblo, and marital difficulties might be brought before the council, or before the governor, depending on the seriousness of the case.

It was said that many years ago the death penalty was imposed in cases of murder and witchcraft, the sentence being carried out by garroting. In less serious cases a man or woman might be punished by imprisonment. The war captain in such cases was responsible for the prisoner.

The following are typical instances of pueblo disputes:

A young man who came from a neighboring pueblo, on declaring his wish to live in San Ildefonso for life, was given fields. Later he failed to attend to his communal duties. When I left the pueblo the officers were about to ask him to leave the village and intended to confiscate his fields, which he was not cultivating.

A man entered a woman's house and stole twenty dollars. He was discovered drunk, with part of the money in his possession. Nothing was done by the pueblo or by the woman. The money was eventually repaid.

A man and his wife separated. The man asked his wife to return. The affair was brought before the governor with the two godfathers appearing for the man and his wife. The wife was persuaded to return, though since that time they have separated again.

In general, the people are anxious to avoid disputes that may lead to quarrels. One woman accused a man of stealing her cow. The case was not brought before the governor. The woman seemed to derive sufficient satisfaction from repeating the story to her friends.

Two men quarreled about water rights, one accusing the other of taking water not his by right. The men had words, but no action was taken by either.

Another man told me that a member of the opposite faction had built a house on his land. Nothing was done about it.

When injured, the people frequently found sufficient satisfaction in complaints. Action, they said, might lead to a fight.

Actually there is little need of any law enforcement agency, though there is a police officer in the village.[47] The people on the whole are submissive to the paternal authority of their officers, and the officers themselves follow a tradition of non-aggression. When violence does occur, and tradition is no longer effective, the whole village becomes hysterical since there is no force organized or individual trained to direct the pueblo in such emergencies.

WITCHCRAFT

In comparison with the orderly cycle of ceremonial activity to insure the welfare of the pueblo, the practice of witchcraft was nebulous and secret. Undoubtedly certain San Ildefonso con-

[47] This is an honorary post probably of Spanish origin.

cepts of witch practice were borrowed from the Spanish, but it is impossible to say what was Spanish and what was native. Belief in witches appears to have antedated the conquest, and in the earliest reports we find trials and accusations by Spaniards of witchcraft. Witch practice was one of the pueblo cardinal sins and was punished by death.

Witchcraft on the whole was a suspicion rather than a fact. Strange lights at night, peculiar behavior on the part of animals, unexpected misfortune, sickness and death were all thought to be due to witchcraft.

A witch was an individual who worked evil out of revenge or jealousy or the wanton satisfaction of doing injury. Witches had the power to strike their victims with either a sudden or a lingering illness; they could steal the hearts of the unsuspecting or drive them insane; they could kill livestock and wither crops. They had the ability to turn themselves into animals, domestic or wild; they could assume the shape of birds, especially the ill-omened owl; or they could appear as disembodied lights. Their deadly malice might be directed at an individual or the pueblo as a whole.

Witches were said to learn their techniques either from a member of their own family or from some friend who was a witch. And they were said to become witches through choice.

Against witchcraft, the bewitched was defenseless. Violence was out of the question. The witch was seldom known. Only the medicine-men were able to combat it for they had the power to exorcise this type of evil and to detect the witch. But even this powerful group was not free from suspicion, and it was said that sorcery and sorcery techniques were a part of their cult.

Certain types of individuals were more likely to be suspected of witchcraft than others. Men or women who were aggressive, who spoke out in public, who expressed jealousy or resentment were frequently thought to be dealing in witchcraft.[48] But on the whole all men were liable to suspicion, even the cacique himself.

Though suspicion of witchcraft was universal, it is doubtful that rites or secrets pertaining to it were practised or taught to

[48] Any individual who did not conform to pueblo ideals.

any great extent. The notion of its prevalence was, I think, the expression of hostility and insecurity in a society in which aggression and violence were tabu. Each man and woman thought of his neighbor as a potential enemy. This feeling of insecurity was expressed by one woman who said that her grandmother had said to her, "Never have a friend. You can never know whether she is a witch. And never, never say 'yes' to a friend, if she should ask you to do something, for she might be trying to get you in her power."

In ancient times no one, it was said, would openly accuse another of witch practice. If an individual found another engaged in sorcery, he had to keep this fatal knowledge to himself. If he told, he would die, but if he kept his knowledge secret, the witch would die. This rationalization explained to the credulous pueblo why there were so few direct accusations when there appeared to be so many evidences of sorcery.

And yet the pueblo need for ceremonial unity exceeded their fears of witch practice. One man,[49] who was said to have killed another through witchcraft, this story being believed by all, was invited to return to the pueblo in order to take part in an important ceremonial dance. The man returned without protest from any villager or even from the family of the dead man. Nor was this thought to be in any way unusual.

SUPERNATURALISM—RELIGION

The people of San Ildefonso, as stated earlier, are extraordinarily secretive concerning all aspects of their religious life, so that very little can be discovered about it. The universe of the Pueblo Indian was peopled by various supernaturals who were on the whole kindly and beneficial, the Sun, the Moon, the Water Serpent as well as the Okuwah or Cloud Beings and others. For offenses against them, chiefly the telling of religious secrets, men were stricken with blindness and misfortune.

The welfare of the people was in the hands of the village priests, principally the caciques, who were in charge of nearly all

---

[49] This man's mother was said to have been a witch. No reason was given for this "murder," nor was any thought necessary.

important ceremonial activity. They interceded for the pueblo
with the supernaturals and they directed the necessary observances to insure rain, rich crops and other blessings. They and
they alone knew the meaning of the esoteric traditions and
rituals.

All men and women were required to take part in the ceremonies under the leadership of the priests, for ecstasy and individual religious experience had no part in the religious complex.
Success depended on the unity of the group asking blessing.
Power resided in ceremony, ritual and prayer, and not in the
individual. Even the cacique had power only in his capacity as
priest.

But apart from maintaining an orderly universe, the ceremonies and the dances that followed them had a very important
social function. In the kiva all men and women came together
for a common purpose, recognized as essentially beneficial to all,
without fear or suspicion.[50] Here they could enjoy themselves
socially in a way that was otherwise impossible. And it was in
the kiva that the village officers lectured the people on civic
virtue. "They teach us how we should act to one another and
how we should act to people from other pueblos. The teachings
are, don't quarrel. And give visitors enough to eat, even if you
have hardly anything to eat yourself."

THE MORES—PROPERTY

There were three classes of tangible property in San Ildefonso
—personal property which an individual might dispose of as he
pleased, joint property which one or more individuals might
possess together, and communal property which belonged to the
pueblo as a whole.

All adults possessed personal property, and children also were
said to own property. But unlike the child of the Plains, the
child at San Ildefonso had limited rights of disposal. If a child

[50] I was told that people were happy in the kiva. All San Ildefonso Indians
love to dance and sing. Small children learn dance steps and songs at a very
early age. In this they are encouraged by their parents, friends and other
siblings.

owned a ring or a bracelet or moccasins and wished to sell them, he had first to get the consent of his parents or of the relatives looking after him. This control ceased at marriage.

A man's personal property consisted of his houses and fields,[51] his personal effects, clothes, tools and weapons; his horses and livestock; his harnesses and wagons and agricultural implements; his trucks and automobiles; and the fruits of his handicraft and labor. These he might dispose of during his lifetime as he saw fit.

A woman in addition to her personal effects also owned houses, land and livestock. She was said to own the house furniture, but since there is no divorce in the pueblo, such property is never disputed.[52] She, too, owned the fruits of her labor either as a washerwoman or as a potter.

Joint ownership [53] was not uncommon within the family, and might also include near relatives outside the household. Father and son, father-in-law and son-in-law or brothers could share a plough, mowing-machine or team of horses. In such cases mutual consent was necessary for the disposal of such property. Land might also be owned jointly, and the produce divided.

The plazas and the land within the grant lying outside of individually "owned" fields were, and still are, the property of the pueblo as a whole; also, the four irrigation ditches, the wells and pipe lines installed by the government, tribal funds, and the community thresher.[54]

Sacred property consisting of masks and other objects of worship belonged to the various societies. Such objects could not be bought, sold or given away. They were entrusted to various families to be cared for.

There was little intangible property in San Ildefonso; rights, rituals, songs, etc., were not individually owned and were not

[51] Fields are now individual property.

[52] It was thought appropriate for girls to inherit furniture and for boys to inherit livestock, etc.

[53] Whether the produce of the fields when harvested was considered to be joint property I could not determine, but there were never any disputes as to its disposal.

[54] Kivas were considered to be the property of the moiety using them.

handed down within families. The one exception to this was individual curing techniques which might be sold.

Property was acquired through gift. Many couples, depending on their ability to give, presented a house or fields to their sons [55] and daughters at the time of their marriage. Property was also inherited. When a man or woman died, all his or her possessions were divided among the surviving spouse and children and in some cases grandchildren. It was also said that nieces and nephews might inherit. Theoretically no distinctions were made between boys and girls, although on the whole men received more than their sisters. The reason given for this was that while a man was supposed to provide for his wife and children, a woman could rely on her husband for support.

Houses, lands, livestock and farming implements were the really valuable items of property distributed after death. Of these, houses and land were the most important.[56] When a man or woman died, the house went to the surviving spouse and their children. If the surviving spouse married again, he or she might live on in the house, the survivor of the marriage being considered the owner. Following the death of this survivor the house then reverted to the children of the first marriage. If there were no children living by this first marriage, the house would become the property of the second husband or wife and then the children of the second marriage.

When a house was inherited by children, the vigas in the roof were counted and the number of vigas were divided among the children. The children might then arrange a supplementary division of the property.

Division of land followed the same principle, with the exception that while a woman might own land she had to have someone to work it for her, usually on a share basis. This also applied to inheritance of livestock and farm machinery.

[55] A woman stated the boys were paid by their fathers in cattle for their help in the fields, and that in this way they could acquire property before marriage. She said that school prevented this exchange, and that this was a reason some of the older people objected to boarding-schools.

[56] Houses were owned. Whether a son had rights to his father's fields, when these fields were nominally owned by the village, I could not find out. Today fields are owned, and ordinarily do not revert to the pueblo.

Any disputes or claims following the division of property among heirs would be decided by the governor.[57]

Adopted children shared equally with the other children in any distribution of property. Illegitimate children, if their paternity was known, also shared in their father's or mother's estate. Step-children, however, did not necessarily share with their step-brothers and sisters. Whether they did or not depended on the surviving step-parent.

If a child died without issue and unmarried, that child's property reverted to its father or mother. If both of these relatives were dead, it would go to the next of kin.

In cases where a family or an individual left the pueblo, his or her land or house was rented or sold within the pueblo. Land was sometimes let on a half-share basis, the man who worked the land paying the owner half the produce of the land. Formerly unused land reverted to the pueblo and was re-distributed to anyone in need of it.

As a result of gift and inheritance, men and women owned lands and houses in different parts of the pueblo. Occasionally they exchanged them with fellow townsmen, but in general ownership of scattered holdings appears to have caused no inconvenience.

SEX AND MARRIAGE

In comparison with neighboring Tewa pueblos,[58] the people of San Ildefonso are not greatly interested in sex. Children do not joke about sex or play sexual games. About the age of nine the sexes tend to separate. Little boys play together, and girls, also, form into small groups. As they grow older their interests become increasingly divergent.

All normal young men and women marry, and yet there is little evidence of courtship. Young men and women are almost never seen together within the pueblo. During the day they are

[57] There were no disputes that I could discover over inheritance. I rather suspect that if a child or spouse took more than his proper share, nothing would be done about it. Quarrels were avoided whenever possible.

[58] This statement is based on the opinions of Indians from other pueblos and on unpublished material.

busy at work, and in the evening they stay at home.[59] Whatever social life there is in the village takes place within the kiva. On the whole there is a tendency to marry outside the pueblo,[60] partly, I suspect, because there are few young people, and partly because those few have been brought up together in a small community in which cousins do not marry.[61]

When marriage does take place, it is usually successful. There are very few unhappy marriages in the pueblo, and no divorce. This inability to divorce is Catholic in origin, since it is said that in the "old" days divorce was possible by mutual consent.

Though the villagers are reticent about sex, with the exception of the licensed kossa, there is very little feeling against illegitimacy or pre-marital relations. Many of the girls have had relations with men before marriage, and this is not held against them. One woman who has borne several illegitimate children is well spoken of in the village; and though they do not approve of her conduct, she does not appear to be discriminated against. Moreover, the few women who are known to be run-arounds do not interest the men of the pueblo, but appeal rather to men from other pueblos or to neighborhood Mexicans.

Men and women following marriage are expected to be chaste and circumspect in their behavior, and post-marital affairs are rare.[62] People, I was told, do not have time to run around after marriage.

In matters of sex men are the initiators and women are permissive. Rape is unknown, for violence of any sort is distasteful. No abortificants or contraceptives were said to be known or used. There is no prostitution, nor is there any homosexuality.

Love-charms or medicines are not used in the pueblo.

[59] There was apparently no house-to-house visiting except in the case of relatives—and even this was rare.

[60] Boys and girls can associate today at boarding-school with a freedom not possible in a small pueblo. Many mothers do not approve of this.

[61] The incest group included close blood relatives on either side. No one individual was prepared to say just what degree of relationship prohibited marriage.

[62] Only two marriages in the village may be said to be failures. Neither of these couples is divorced, though they have separated. One of the men was a Navajo. He has left for good.

RESPECT

There are no formal respect relationships among the villagers of San Ildefonso, such as we find among the Plains Indians. There is no mother- or father-in-law tabu; no licensed joking relationships between selected kin. On the whole, all relationships are respect with the exception of age-mates of the same sex or young boys and girls. All ages tease, joke and play with the very young. The village elders and priests are respected by all.

Joking in general is distrusted, since the people do not clearly distinguish a personal joke from an insult. Where men and women vaguely suspect their neighbors of hostility, joking, except at oneself, is very liable to be misconstrued.

THE FOCI OF INTEREST

In the old days all men's interests were centered in agriculture. Crops of all sorts, and corn in particular, were the basis of pueblo economy. Moreover, nearly all religious activity, the many prayers, songs, dances and rituals which were so vital to pueblo existence, was largely concerned with a rich yield from the soil and sought to accomplish this through the exercise of proper supernatural techniques.

INTEGRATION AND CONTEMPORARY RATE OF CULTURE CHANGE

The early Spanish contacts do not appear to have greatly disturbed the pueblo way of life. Naturally secretive and naturally tenacious the people first resisted, and then, since violence was foreign to them, submitted. The two cultures were not at heart opposed. The Spaniards who came to farm the neighboring fields introduced new crops and new techniques, but, after all, they too were agriculturists and on much the same economic level. When the Catholic Church sought to wean them from their old religion and attempted to introduce new ideals, the Indians made a compromise. They accepted many of the Catholic tenets while maintaining in secret their own religious beliefs and practices. Today the Indians within the village see nothing incongruous in attending mass and ceremonies in the kiva on the same day. Whatever adjustments had to be made were made without affecting the integrity of the pueblo as a whole.

But within the last twenty years there has been a second period of change which is affecting the pueblo much more profoundly and rapidly. The mobility of modern life, the presence of wealthy tourists, the mail-order house, credit, and the subsidies of a paternalistic government are undermining the fundamental integrity of the pueblos as a group, and San Ildefonso is suffering accordingly. Because the pueblo is vulnerable and its economy will not support modern luxuries, the rate of change is rapid. The dollar is taking the place of exchange. Coöperation is giving way to competition. Pottery is upsetting agricultural values, and so women potters are beginning to dominate pueblo policies. Government schools and colleges are unsettling the young. Already the pueblo has split into two hostile factions,[63] and the schism is widening rather than healing. White ways are crowding out the Indian way, and from this change the whole village is suffering.

INFLUENCES FROM OTHER ABORIGINAL GROUPS

Although San Ildefonso was in frequent contact with other Indian groups, the people were slow to acquire new traits, and there is comparatively little in their culture today that appears to have been borrowed from non-pueblo peoples. Many of the non-ceremonial dances have been adopted from the Comanche and the Kiowa.

In dress [64] a few of the men wear their hair long and braided after the fashion of the Plains Indians. The men like to be photographed in Plains eagle-feathered war bonnets and in beaded Plains moccasins; on gala occasions both men and women adorn themselves copiously with Navajo silver concho belts, turquoise-set silver necklaces, rings and bracelets.

[63] See p. 409 and p. 431.
[64] See note 70, page 429.

THE CONTACT CONTINUUM

When the Spaniards conquered New Mexico they established themselves as overlords in many of the pueblos. The first groups to live in and about San Ildefonso were soldiers and priests who were soon followed by settlers.

The priests immediately set about converting the people to Catholicism and sternly tried to imbue them with Catholic and European ethics. The settlers introduced new crops, new methods of agriculture, and with their flocks, their horses and their cattle, rudimentary concepts of animal husbandry.

On the whole the Spaniards broadened the pueblo horizon without disrupting the culture to any great extent. Except for the Pueblo Revolt of 1680 in which San Ildefonso joined, the people submitted to their conquerors, and military pressure was not necessary in order to keep them at least acquiescent to the new régime. By training and by their sedentary way of life they were unfitted for war. They demanded only to be let alone and allowed to till their fields and harvest their crops in peace.

Pressure to eliminate the native religious activities, however, was brought to bear by the Church, and pueblo ceremonies and dances were fulminated against as heathen and obscene. There were trials for witchcraft and floggings. The pueblo withdrew into itself and carried on its old practices in secret.

In the meantime as the valley of the Rio Grande became increasingly settled, the people of San Ildefonso gradually accepted those aspects of the new culture which appealed to their sense of economy and did not violate their sense of propriety. White foods, new fruits and vegetables, as well as sugar, white flour and such commodities, began to find a place in the native diet. White textiles replaced skins and the ancient cotton fabrics. The gun took the place of the bow and arrow and the throwing-stick. Hoes, shovels, axes and ploughs, the horse and wagon, changed the character of farming. The pail took the place of pots and baskets.

As time passed, the people accepted the aggressive invasion of Catholicism and fitted it into their universe. Where the old religious ideas were incompatible with the new, they tended to practise both. The people attended mass and worshiped in the kiva. To their old marriage forms, for instance, was added a Catholic ceremony. Divorce became impossible.

And as a buffer between themselves and the invaders a governor [65] was appointed to deal with the alien world outside the pueblo.

Within the last half-century the mail-order house, credit buying, an awakened interest in Indian affairs as reflected by the Indian Service, Indian schools, and tourists, in addition to the mobility of modern life, have immeasurably accelerated the processes of acculturation. The marketable aspects of White culture have been brought to the Indian's door.

In the present confusion there are no leaders,[66] for the idea of dominating guidance is foreign to the people. And there are few external checks to culture borrowing. The people of San Ildefonso are not poor,[67] as many Indians are; and they live close enough to Santa Fé to visit the shops and the moving-pictures whenever they have either the money or the inclination. On the whole such checks to culture borrowing as exist are within the culture itself.

THE NON-CULTURAL RESULTS OF CONTACT

On the whole there have been very few non-cultural results of contact. The most striking perhaps has been the decrease in population due to smallpox and more recently to influenza.[68] Personal mobility has not been affected, since the people were village folk and their livelihood was centered in the fields about the village. Nor has contact vitally altered the economic resources, though Mexicans encroaching on pueblo land have threatened the pueblo water supply and in some cases have man-

[65] The office of governor is, perhaps, pre-Spanish. Since the conquest, however, the office has been one of increasing importance and responsibility.

[66] There are outstanding personalities in the pueblo who affect its destiny, but such individuals are not leaders in the European sense.

[67] Although poverty and lack of opportunity to borrow are less than in many other groups, they do to some extent affect San Ildefonso.

[68] Between 1760 and 1793 the population was reduced by smallpox from 484 to 240. In 1918 influenza killed off many of the old people and practically wiped out the Winter moiety.

aged to alienate valuable fields.[69] Finally the White man's canned goods, white flour, and so on have changed their type of food and methods of preparing it. The fact that a meal can now be prepared so quickly has given the women time for making pottery which would formerly have been used in grinding grain, etc. In other respects there has been but little change in the natural environment due to contact.

THE ACCULTURATION PROCESS—THE GENERAL ORDER OF THE ACCEPTANCE OF NEW CULTURE TRAITS

New elements were adopted which were economically productive or useful to the village. For instance, the pueblo was not slow to recognize the value of Spanish crops and Spanish methods of agriculture, and it was equally quick to see the value of Spanish textiles,[70] the horse, the gun and other importations. In the same way, as new American products were offered to them they were quick to respond to modernized houses and house furnishings. The stove, beds, bath-tubs,[71] hardwood and linoleum floors appealed to them not only as practical, but as articles which added to their prestige.

Moreover, as the children were sent to the Indian school there was a tendency common to all groups among them to take up American dress and to become familiar with other aspects of American culture.

On the whole there were no particular groups which affected White ways. Those people who could afford luxuries bought them, and those families who were poorer or less industrious were forced to do without.

The pueblo was much slower to adopt Spanish religious concepts and Spanish ethics, but Catholicism was eventually nomi-

[69] The Government is returning these lands to the Indians. Additional forest lands have also been made available to the Indians for gathering firewood, vigas, etc.

[70] The people of San Ildefonso use the Navajo and "Rio Grande" blankets (Chimayo, etc.). They also use Jicarilla Apache baskets in the basket dance and for domestic use. Mr. K. M. Chapman refers in a letter to the later use of sateens and silks and the change from the "Indian design" store-blanket and shawl to those with stripes.

[71] A few families have running water in their houses.

nally accepted and Catholic morals [72] were adapted to meet fundamental pueblo attitudes and prejudices. Last of all, modern concepts of medicine and sanitation have been accepted, albeit half-heartedly.

The traits that have been lost since the conquest are chiefly those that have been displaced by the acceptance of new ones. Old agricultural methods have given way to new; the household economy has been altered by the introduction of new White commodities. The hold of native religion has been weakened to some extent by White contacts, education, and Catholicism. Cult practices favored by the medicine societies, native curing, ceremonial techniques to assist hunting, and the like, have begun to disappear through lack of faith on the part of the community as a whole. Finally, such fundamental attitudes as coöperation in relation to competition are much affected. The world of the pueblo is becoming increasingly competitive. This is due to the economic change brought about by the sale of pottery to tourists, and by government work.

There is no organized opposition to the adoption of White ways, nor are there any nativistic movements. Men will occasionally complain that the government is interfering with the running of the pueblo, but these are usually the first to demand government assistance when difficulties arise. A few of the older people deprecate the sending of their children away to school because they feel that a child soon forgets its Indian ways, its native speech, its songs and dances.[73] A few mothers disapprove of the Indian school because boys and girls are allowed to meet socially, and they are afraid that their daughters may become "run-arounds." A few of the older men disapprove of having the young men leave the grant to go to college, for they say that they become discontented with village life and learn to have a taste for driving automobiles, visiting Santa Fé and drinking alcohol. Moreover, those young men who have attended col-

[72] The Catholic prohibition of divorce is accepted, but fornication is not very seriously regarded. Lying is almost a virtue.

[73] The Indians in San Ildefonso are extremely fond of dancing, and frequently dance for no good reason except sheer fun. They are very proud of doing the steps well and of having beautiful costumes.

lege profit little by their experience from the pueblo point of view. The fact that at school and college boys learn useful trades, such as plumbing or carpentry, means little, since there is no possibility of practising them at San Ildefonso. Many of these fears, while based on observation and experience, are the expression of the villagers' profound distrust for the world outside the pueblo.

SOCIAL ORGANIZATION—THE FACTIONS

No description of San Ildefonso today can avoid mention of the dispute which has separated the pueblo into two factions, Pimpieinai t'owa, North people, and the Agompieinai t'owa, South people. As to what caused the quarrel no two villagers will agree, even if they answer the question. The reply is usually, "I don't know," or "No one has told me," or "I was away at the time." Though they are reluctant to talk about the cause of the trouble, they are voluble in describing the iniquities of the opposing faction. On the whole, the people think of the quarrel in religious terms, completely ignoring its economic significance and its social implications.

I have already quoted from Harrington the tradition that many years ago the pueblo was tricked into moving north. As one old man told me, "People have always lived in the South Plaza. There was formerly a quarrel among the people when they moved north. It was said that they would break what was growing. And it has been that way."

Hewett in *Ancient Life in the American Southwest* [74] cites this tradition. He continues:

Then began the decline of Po hwo ge. Epidemics, famines, persecutions wore the population down until the wise men and women of the community saw that they were facing extinction.

With the coming into office of the present cacique, Ignacio Aguilar, supported by the wise and forceful governor, Juan Gonzales, the problem was seriously taken up. From then on I was in council with them. They stated that as things were going, their children and young people dying much faster than replacements came by birth, San Ildefonso would in twenty years be like dead Pojoaque. They believed that the calamity

---

[74] E. L. Hewett, *Ancient Life in the American Southwest*, p. 82, Bobbs-Merrill Co., Indianapolis, 1930.

could be averted by abandoning their plaza of misfortune and moving back to the south. I heartily concurred. They began the building of the new houses to the south, forming a new plaza around the ancient kiva that was now restored. Another large kiva was built to take the place of the one in the plaza that was being abandoned. In time the greater part of the community was shifted to the new south plaza and all ceremonials transferred to the new precinct. The results were up to the most fervent expectations. They point with pride to the large number of healthy children free from epidemics, and the slowing down of tuberculosis. My hopes were based largely upon improvement and morale and sanitation, and theirs upon the efficacy of a tradition. Between us we struck the remedy. Perhaps the visiting nurse deserves part of the credit.

The outcome of the move, however, has been far less successful than Dr. Hewett anticipated.

When the cacique, Ignacio Aguilar, and the then presiding governor, Juan Gonzales, suggested that the pueblo abandon the North Plaza and move south, by far the greater part of the land in the present South Plaza belonged to them. Ignacio and Juan moved and built themselves houses, and, according to Juan, offered building sites to any villagers who would follow them. The relatives of the two leaders went over as well as a few other families who were ceremonially allied to them. But not all of the villagers wished to leave their houses in the North Plaza. Numerically this group was in the majority, and they decided to stay where they were. Moreover, it included the most successful women potters, and the three remaining Winter families.[75]

For some time pottery had been bringing the pueblo wealth and recognition. N. and her two sisters as well as C. S. (all belonging to the North Plaza group) had grown increasingly wealthy and increasingly powerful in village affairs. N. in particular was well qualified by determination and character to influence not only the women of the village, but also the men. The N. sisters and their husbands formed a powerful group. They were famous and they were wealthy and they resented the authority of the cacique. From temporal affairs their influence spread into religion.[76] T., husband of N., and head of one medi-

[75] The Winter families were nearly exterminated by the influenza epidemic of 1918.

[76] E. C. Parsons in *Social Organization of the Tewa of New Mexico*, p. 162,

cine society and also Samaiyo, undoubtedly felt that he could act with some degree of religious authority.

When the cacique arbitrarily decided to move south the disaffection between the pottery group and the cacique group became more clearly defined. The Winter families headed by the kossa sendo decided to remain with the North.

At this time there were, according to one man, many long discussions in which the people who had moved tried to show those that stayed that life was not being ordered in the right way, and that proper ceremonies were not being held. The people who had stayed, however, remained unconvinced and personal animosities grew. In the meantime N. distributed favors among the women of her group; and she and T. opened a store at which North Plaza folk could get credit.

Exactly what caused the final split in the spring of 1930, I was never able to determine, but more or less what happened is admitted by both sides. Tension between the two groups had been increasing rapidly. Formerly much of the sacred paraphernalia belonging to the pueblo had been kept in the round kiva, but the South Plaza and the cacique became worried lest it should be stolen. Accordingly, it was removed to the house of the cacique for safe keeping. One account of the fight is as follows (North Plaza):

Once when the North people wanted to do their Buffalo Dance, they went to the cacique to get the necessary apparel, but he said that they should not have it. Then T. went to the door and said, "All you have to do is to open this." But the cacique would not. Then a woman pulled T.'s hair and was sent home. Then they got the paraphernalia. Juan Gonzales who was governor at the time said that he would call out the soldiers, but they never came.

It was said that there was considerable fighting during the seizure of the ceremonial objects and that the old cacique was beaten. At any rate certain sacred objects were taken, among them the buffalo heads, and have never been returned. The South Plaza suspects T. of having them in his possession.

---

refers to a quarrel in 1926 in the pueblo as to whether the young men had to dance Okuwah.

This seizure of sacred objects is very unusual. In discussing the matter with an Indian friend, I asked him why the people of the South Plaza, since they knew where the objects were and felt that they had a right to them, did not take them back again. He replied, "Oh that would cause a fight. We would never do that. Some time they may realize that they have done wrong."

Later when the time came for the election of a new governor, Atilano Montoya who was then governor, failed to turn his cane of office over to the cacique and principales. Instead he turned it over to a new governor elected by the North Plaza. Thereupon the South Plaza took the attitude that any governor elected by the North Plaza did not represent the whole village. From then on time, as it were, stopped for the South Plaza, and those who had held office during Atilano's governorship, including Atilano himself, still hold the same offices today, though many of them were originally only yearly appointments.

The North Plaza has continued to elect its own governors which are officially recognized as such by the Indian Service; the South Plaza has continued to ignore them. Though the North Plaza recognizes Ignacio Aguilar as Summer cacique, it will have nothing to do with him, preferring to carry on its own religious ceremonies in its own way. The South Plaza has not attempted to replace their civil officers, as they say that they lack the cane of office. All decisions are now made by the principales, headed by old Juan Gonzales. Since he is an old man and no longer in active health, the son of the cacique frequently acts for him. He, I was told, is the only member of the South Plaza to attend North Plaza meetings and in this sense he acts as go-between for the two factions.

In 1936 occurred other events which further strained the relations between the two groups. A motion-picture company came to the pueblo to film a Western picture, employing the villagers as extras and paying for the use of the site. All the pictures were taken in the North Plaza, but a great amount of the technical equipment made use of the South Plaza. At the conclusion of the picture, the film company paid the governor the sum agreed upon. This man divided the money between the members of the North Plaza, but none of it went to the South.

The South was outraged, but there was nothing that they could do except to express their feelings in talk. In the meantime not all of the people in the North Plaza were in agreement about the distribution of the money. At this time practically complete control of the North was vested in the three husbands of the·N. sisters. A minority of Winter families, headed by the chief kossa, and the brother of one of the North Plaza principales, said that part of the money should go to the South Plaza, and that until this was done they would refuse to take their own share. The quarrel spread, but the money had already been divided. When the South Plaza men went and reproachfully asked the governor why he had not informed them when the money was to have been divided, he is said to have replied that he had been unable to withstand the pressure of the principales to divide up the money immediately.

Another source of irritation was the division of land turned back to the Indians by the government. This land had been worked by Mexicans who claimed title to it. When the titles were settled, the lands were turned over to the North Plaza for division, as this fell within the duties of the governor and the council. Each head of a family was given so many acres. In this division the South Plaza complained that, although they got their share of land, nevertheless, the land that had houses on it went to the members of the North Plaza.

These major irritations were also augmented by minor ones. The South Plaza claimed that the North Plaza had burnt down their old kiva [77] in the North Plaza and had attempted to burn their new kiva in the South Plaza. They said they knew who had done it. There was a complaint by the North Plaza that the South Plaza was using water which belonged to the North. And when a new house was laid out by a member of the South Plaza, the North Plaza complained that it was being built across the passage between the North and South Plaza which the North Plaza corn dancers had to take when they came from the round kiva into the North Plaza to dance the corn dance. Then the North Plaza claimed that the South Plaza had deliberately built

[77] The South Plaza religious leaders felt that as they represented the more important members of the Summer moiety the kiva "belonged" to them.

a privy so that the door opened onto the North Plaza and that when the corn dance was taking place, the South Plaza people could use the privy, and so embarrass them. "Why," said one woman, "they might be seen coming out by the White people!"

Meanwhile there was disaffection in the North Plaza. The Winter families had little or no control in the direction of North Plaza affairs, and their stand for equal division of the moving-picture money was in part an expression of this. The brother of one of the North Plaza principales, who had also taken this stand, was equally disaffected, but as he was inclined to be assertive and arrogant, he was feared and disliked by both plazas, and his stand as the champion of justice did little to appeal to either side. In the winter of 1936–37 this dissatisfaction led to the withdrawal of the kossa sendo and the two other Winter families to the South faction.

In the meantime it has occurred to some of the acute villagers that the quarrel may be due in part to N. and her sisters, aided by C. S., who is next to N. in fame as a potter. In the South Plaza there is no consolidated group of women. Instead it is the familiar man's world. Women may labor at their pottery, but on the whole they are subservient to their men. But in the North Plaza, the potters set the economic level.

A North Plaza man, now gone over to the South Plaza, said: "The women of the North have got their men in a hole and they cannot get themselves out." He went on to say that the women were far "worse" than the men. A South Plaza man added: "T. is strong-minded but his wife is very strong-minded. E. M. is a good man at heart, but easily influenced by his wife and E. E. is said to be the worst of all because he is strong-minded and his wife is too. Many people are saying that it is the fault of the three sisters that there is so much trouble."

It is true that the women of the North Plaza are becoming increasingly conscious of their power. One young woman even went so far as to advocate that the women have a voice in the council meetings at which affairs affecting the whole pueblo are discussed by the men. This scandalous idea, however, found no support among the other women. But I was told that N., when she learned that the Winter families were going over to the

South Plaza, told one of the men that he could get no more credit at her store. As this was in the nature of a serious economic threat, the man hesitated, but eventually made the move.

And one North Plaza woman, when asked if there were to be any more defections to the South from the North Plaza ranks replied, "No. We must stay with the governor (N.'s husband) because N. is so good to us."

In spite of the efforts of the government and others who would like to see the breach between the two plazas healed, the split is widening. The South Plaza insists on its ceremonial prerogatives, and evidently the North Plaza feels capable of maintaining its own religious independence without the help of the South. They are building their own kiva and it is said that they are planning to elect their own cacique. This could be done if the candidate for cacique were installed with the help of a cacique society in some neighboring Tewa pueblo, but whether any North Plaza man would be willing to take on this serious responsibility remains to be seen. The only young male (a boy of ten) who is now a member of the Summer cacique society, however, belongs to the North Plaza. When this lad grows up, supreme religious authority may pass to the North.

In 1937, the religious and civil divisions by plazas were as follows: the South Plaza had the Summer cacique and his right- and left-hand man; they had the three male kossa; and the head of the Temake medicine society; in the civil list they had the war captain, who was war captain at the time of the split, and the man who was left-hand man to the governor, and two former governors as principales. To this group younger men have been elected to fill the positions of warriors.[78] Due to the fact that there are not so many men in the South Plaza as in the North a few of the men hold several offices, but a man can hold office and belong to several societies at the same time with perfect propriety. What is an innovation in the South Plaza is that offices which were formerly yearly appointments are so no longer.

The women, however, of the South Plaza are not members of societies with the exception of one small girl who is a member of the Summer cacique society. The wife of the present cacique acts

[78] Assistants to the war captain.

as head of the women. In general, however, there is no cohesive woman's group in the South Plaza.

In the North Plaza in 1937 there were few ceremonial officers. They had the Samaiyo who was also head of the Tewa medicine society; they had the man entitled to keep the scalps for the Tseoke society; and a boy who belonged to the Summer cacique society. In the civil list, they had a newly appointed governor and his right-hand man, several principales, a war captain and warrior, and an aguacil. Unlike the South, not all the men in the North Plaza were officers.

But if the North Plaza lacks ceremonial officers among the men, it is quite the other way round as far as the women are concerned. All the women kossa are North Plaza, as are all the women belonging to the medicine societies. L. B. is head of the women, but it is to N. that the women turn for counsel and help. A North Plaza woman has the inherited right, I was told, to dance Buffalo Woman in the January buffalo-deer dance. Among the women of the North are also the most famous of the potters. And there is a far greater group sense among them than in the South Plaza. They hold occasional meetings at the home of N. It was said they could all get credit at N.'s store.

It has been suggested that factional disputes are natural to the pueblos, and that possibly the division of the pueblos into moieties is an expression of this tendency to split into groups. Those who have lived among the pueblos sooner or later report factional feuds and bitternesses. Santa Clara, perhaps the most Americanized of the Northern pueblos, is split into many factions; Taos has a progressive and a conservative group disputing the use of peyote. In some cases the split occurs among those who favor government schools and those who do not; in others the schism may be purely religious.

In the case of San Ildefonso the split undoubtedly sprang from numerous causes; [79] among them the desire of one group to be independent of the established religious authority of the other. This was aggravated by economic pressure and the rise of the woman potter into power.

[79] No two members of the pueblo agree on the causes which underlie the present factional dispute.

No one can prophesy the outcome of this factional split, but without N. and the North Plaza women, it would seem that the differences between the two Plazas probably would have proceeded less disastrously. The present impasse is insoluble at the moment, and it is probable that the pueblo would split into independent villages if this were possible. It may be that disputes of a like nature in prehistoric times formed the independent villages of the Tewa. But the White man now occupies the land, and the Indian is confined to his grants which are laid out for him by law. Separation is scarcely possible, for there is no place to which the disaffected can go.

THE PRESENT COMMUNITY—POPULATION

In 1937 there were 126 individuals living in the pueblo.[80] Eight men and eight women have married out, and gone to live in neighboring pueblos, chiefly Cochiti and Jemez. A few have gone to live in California. Six men and six women from outside have come to live in the pueblo. Of this group three men have married women in San Ildefonso, while six men in the pueblo have taken wives from San Juan, Nambe, Taos and Picuris.

There were twenty-eight families living in the pueblo and twenty-five households. The household consists in adults and children sharing the same domicile. With very few exceptions all normal young men and women marry before the age of thirty, and barrenness is almost unknown.

The average number of living children to each couple was three, while the rate of mortality among children was, as nearly as I could discover, about 30 per cent.[81] Three children have been adopted, two from other pueblo groups, by families in some way related to them.

Within the last decade or so, due to the efforts of the govern-

[80] This figure does not include the Mexican families living in the pueblo. The government is gradually buying out all the Mexicans on the grant and turning their lands and houses over to the Indians.

[81] Government figures were not made available to me in this and other matters. It appeared from checking families that the average loss of children per family was a little less than two. This is probably conservative, and does not include miscarriages.

ment in furnishing medical care, providing good water, and encouraging sanitation, the population of the village has been slowly increasing.

ECONOMICS—AGRICULTURE

Agriculture is still nominally the basis of pueblo economy, but within the last twenty-five years it has slowly dwindled in importance. This is due to several factors—the returns from agriculture are small in comparison with working for the government; and the sale of pottery and paintings [82] has become increasingly remunerative. Moreover, the difficulties of irrigation and the lack of water have done much to discourage farming. Most of the older men are still energetic and dutiful farmers,[83] but many of the younger men prefer less arduous labor, and devote most of their time to government labor and to decorating pottery.

However, agriculture still tends to follow earlier patterns and is still the basis of pueblo religious life. In March the seed to be planted is brought to the cacique for blessing; late in March the sacred shinny game of punabe is played through the village and through the fields to insure fertility; the fields are then ploughed and planting begins in April. From then on nearly all ceremonies are for growing and ripening and harvest, and for rain to make this possible.

Today, even with the village divided against itself, many of the old practices are carried out. Neighbors belonging to the same faction still help one another to plough and harvest in return for like assistance.

Due sometimes to disinclination on the part of the owner, and sometimes to lack of water, not all the fields are worked. A few men who have no fields will work the fields of their neighbors on the basis of a half-share of the produce, and this is also

[82] E. L. Hewett, *Ancient Life in the American Southwest*, p. 148. "In a single village a man and wife, one modeling and the other decorating, make more money from their art than the whole community makes by farming."

[83] There are only six farmers in the pueblo who raise enough produce to support themselves and their families.

done for the women who are unable to work their own fields. Such work is usually done by a relative.

A few of the Indians share their fields with Mexican neighbors.

In addition to their fields many men raise gardens in which they grow vegetables.[84] These are seldom large and the vegetables are not very varied and are used almost entirely by the family of the farmer himself.

The following figures are taken from the *Annual Report of the Division of Extension and Industry for 1933:* [85]

Wheat	23 acres	259.80
Corn	60	833.28
Alfalfa hay	25	750.00
Other hay	30	200.00
Chili	2	30.00
Gardens *	8	475.00

* Nineteen families had gardens

A little fruit is raised in the pueblo, but it is inferior in quality and few families [86] bother to plant trees. At present there are apple-trees and a few peach-trees in the pueblo.

ANIMAL HUSBANDRY

On the whole stock does not flourish [87] in the pueblo and little interest is taken in animal husbandry. Nearly every man has a team. Three families have cattle [88] and a few milk cows. Two families own a pig apiece. There are no goats, sheep or burros belonging to the pueblo. Four families raise turkeys, and ten families raise hens. Nearly every family has an ill-fed dog in its possession.

[84] These are usually carrots, onions, beets, etc.

[85] In spite of the fact that the government has recently turned over to the pueblo lands taken from the Mexicans, it is doubtful whether this will increase the village cash revenue from agriculture to any great extent.

[86] Only four families possess fruit-trees.

[87] Several years ago cattle were turned over to the Indians by the government, but as no Indian feels it necessary to feed his animals properly, most of these died within a year. Sheep were also raised, but as they proved a liability rather than an asset they were disposed of.

[88] The following list is suggestive rather than accurate: out of 28 families 19 own 56 horses; 3 own 31 beef cattle; 3 own 5 milk cows, 2 own 2 pigs.

HUNTING

Nearly all the game, with the exception of rabbits, has been taken from the pueblo grant, and hunting [89] is indulged in today more as a sport than as a serious pursuit. Apparently the hunt chief or Samaiyo's only duty nowadays is to lead the January buffalo-deer dance into the village. Since the North and South factional dispute has split the pueblo the annual rabbit surround is no longer held. During the fall hunting season small groups of men go up onto the mesas armed with rifles, and usually several deer are shot each season, but from what I could learn, few of the young men observe the ceremonial restrictions that were formerly imposed on all hunters.

Rabbits are still occasionally hunted for ceremonial purposes by the war captain and others, but they are not hunted enough to affect the diet of the average family.

A few men set steel traps in the hills, but none makes it a regular practice.

Fish traps are no longer set in the river nor are fish netted. Today the only fishing is done by small boys in the ditches along the Rio Grande.

THE GOVERNMENT

Few of the men in San Ildefonso look for work outside of the pueblo. Occasionally a man will join a group of Indians in an attempt to capitalize his knowledge of Indian songs and dances; and sometimes a man will look for work outside as a common laborer. But the number is small, and their success is slender.

In recent years, however, the government payroll has come to play an increasingly important part in the economy of the village. During 1936–37 while fences were being built around the grant, nearly every able-bodied man was employed at some time or other on the project. How much the men earned it is impossible to say, since the Indians keep no record and the government files are not available.

Government employ, which is eagerly sought and a matter for jealousy on the part of the unemployed, is helping to break down

[89] Deer hides for moccasins are bought from traders.

the old coöperative structure, for today the men of the village think in terms of a daily wage, rather than the exchange of a day's work for a day's work. Moreover, there is a growing tendency to rely on government assistance. This is particularly true of the more improvident men in the pueblo, and of those who prefer a government cheque to the delayed and uncertain rewards of the harvest.[90]

POTTERY

Today pottery is of the greatest economic importance to the village. It supplies families not only with a livelihood, but with a surplus over and above the necessities of life. It buys automobiles, furniture, radios, and sends young men to college. Moreover, pottery is creating a leisure group within the pueblo, and the sale of pottery is helping to focus the attention of the people on the value of the American dollar.

Because the making of pottery is primarily women's work, it is giving women an economic and social importance that they never had before. Men have taken advantage of this situation, in that many of them decorate the pottery and help to fire it, and so have a share in the rewards, but men are not essential to its production or sale.

The history of the pottery renaissance at San Ildefonso is well known throughout the Southwest. Interested enthusiasts have seen fit to tell the story in terms of romance; in terms of the rehabilitation of the Indian. Extravagant praise and extravagant hopes for Indian and White relations and for Indian economic independence have been based on this unique and shining example of a craft renaissance.

In 1879 Stevenson first mentioned San Ildefonso pottery in his survey of pueblo pottery. And toward the close of the nineteenth century Edgar L. Hewett had bought pottery through Juan Gonzales. Early pottery designs were black, and later, black and red on cream ware, or black on red ware. But due to the introduction of the pail [91] and the fact that the potter had no

[90] In a few cases men no longer cultivate the fields, because they prefer government employ and are willing to take the risk of not getting it.

[91] K. M. Chapman in a personal communication writes: "The galvanized

ready market for her wares, the art of pottery tended to decline, or at least remain static. A few of the older women made pots but they were crudely made and fired and crudely decorated.

Carl E. Guthe writes: [92]

In 1907 Dr. E. L. Hewett of the School of American Research began a series of excavations in the ancient ruins of the Pajarito Plateau. The diggers were all Tewa Indians from San Ildefonso. They proved to be excellent shovelmen, who took a keen interest in everything they found. . . . The women of the Pueblo,[93] when visiting camp, often held animated discussions as to the vessels from the ruins, and it was suggested to some who were known to be good potters, that they attempt to revive their art, and try to emulate the excellence of the ancient wares. While the response was not immediate, there was observable, during the next few years, a distinct improvement in the pottery of San Ildefonso. Realizing the importance of this, the authorities of the Museum of New Mexico and the School of American Research threw themselves heartily into the task of stimulating the industry. They urged the women to do better and better work, and in particular induced them to return to the sound canons of native art. Some old pieces remained in the Pueblo, many others were in the Museum, of still others photographs were obtained. These were all brought to the attention of the potters.

When the Museum of New Mexico was organized at Santa Fé in 1909, Dr. Hewett had several of the women come in from San Ildefonso to the governor's palace to demonstrate the art of pottery. Among these were Ramona Gonzales, Maria, Maximiliana and Desideria Montoya, and Tonita Roybal. During this period Julian Martinez, husband of Maria Montoya, who was employed as janitor in the museum, took a keen interest in pottery design.

In 1915 Dr. Hewett [94] was appointed to take charge of the

---

bucket replaced to some extent the tinaja for carrying water, but the tinaja was superior as a container, both indoors and out because of its evaporation."

[92] Carl E. Guthe, *Pueblo Pottery Making—A Study at the Village of San Ildefonso,* Introduction by A. V. Kidder, p. 13, Yale University Press, New Haven, 1925.

[93] K. M. Chapman writes, "The women visiting the excavations were interested principally in the old symbolism and decorative schemes. They made a few attempts to use it, but it did not prove attractive to those who did not know its significance and was not particularly saleable so the movement soon collapsed."

[94] Dr. Hewett directed the entire section of anthropology at the San Diego exposition. Indian crafts were only a part of this section.

Indian exhibits at the Panama-California Exposition. Here an Indian pueblo was built on the grounds and Indian crafts were exhibited. Two or three of the women from San Ildefonso, during the period of the exposition, worked at their pottery before large crowds. Among them was Maria, who, accompanied by her husband Julian, discovered that it was possible to get better prices for their pots than they had believed possible.

But while this stimulated the potters, it did not of itself solve the problem of encouraging the Indians to make better pots than they had been making.

The undertaking was not an easy one, however, for it was difficult to get most of the women to go to the trouble of making good pieces when the tourists, who were still the principal purchasers, were equally or even better pleased with imitations of china water-pitchers, ill-made rain gods and candlesticks. The problem thus resolved itself into one of supplying a market. The Museum bought many good pieces, and Mr. Chapman, who from the beginning had been a leading spirit in the attempt at rehabilitating the art, himself purchased large amounts of pottery, never refusing a creditable piece, never accepting a bad one.[95]

In 1920 Madame Von Blumenthal, a Russian living in California, came out to Santa Fé with Miss Rose Dougan. Madame von Blumenthal had worked in Russia trying to encourage the production of lace by paying better prices and so stimulating an interest in better craft work. A crafts school was started on the mesa across the river from San Ildefonso, but it was not destined to be a success and the project was abandoned in 1922. The chief difficulty in carrying out the experiment was the fact that no two families brought to the school from San Ildefonso could agree, and within one or two days were on bad terms with one another.

Although the school failed in its purpose, the underlying philosophy behind it was pursued by Mr. Kenneth M. Chapman and Mr. Wesley Bradfield who were aided by the funds that Madame Von Blumenthal had provided. Better prices were paid than those asked in order to get better products.

This new stimulus, added to past encouragement, helped im-

[95] Carl E. Guthe, *op. cit.*, p. 14. From the introduction by A. V. Kidder.

measurably. Already a few of the women had shown great improvement technically and artistically.

Maria especially shone. By 1915 she had far surpassed all the others, her pots were in great demand, and at the present time she has a ready market, at prices which ten years ago would have seemed fantastic, for everything she can find time to make. Her income is probably not less than $2000.00 a year, and following her example, many other women are now doing fine work and are earning substantial amounts.[96]

Maria set the prevailing style. Though early in her career as a potter she had worked in polychrome, and though she still occasionally makes vessels of this type, she began to experiment in polished black ware. This was very successful. In 1921 she began innovations by decorating her polished black ware with dull black figures and designs. There was a great demand for this.

Meanwhile Julian,[97] who had experimented in design, began in 1920 to decorate Marie's pots as a source of income. In 1925 other men followed suit. Today nearly all the men decorate their wives' pots or the pots of close female relatives.

Today (1937) all the women make pottery or work at some process in the making of pottery.[98] Maria Montoya Martinez and Antonita Roybal still lead the women potters in reputation, but a few of the younger women are beginning to challenge their supremacy.

With the exception of ceremonial bowls, San Ildefonso pottery is made solely for sale to tourists. The polished black and red ware is made for decorative purposes and not for utility. Moreover, to one familiar with the pueblo and the women potters, each woman's handiwork is in some measure a gauge of her personal originality and skill.

Maria's skill as a potter and her originality in creating new forms is reflected not only in her pottery but in her relation to the industry of pottery. Maria has turned the front room of her

[96] Carl E. Guthe, *op. cit.*, p. 14. From the introduction by A. V. Kidder.

[97] Julian began to decorate Maria's pottery earlier than 1920. About 1920, however, he began to work practically full time at decorating, especially after the invention of the matte black on polished black.

[98] Women work almost compulsively at pottery. Many of them neglect their children because "they are too busy."

house into a store where she and Julian sell their pottery, and where Julian sells his paintings to the tourists who are brought there in buses. Realizing that she can command better prices from the tourists themselves than through traders who in turn sell the ware to tourists, Maria does not trade. But she has gone further than this, for her unmarried sister and her daughter-in-law assist her in her pottery making while her husband and son help with the decorating, since this is now a masculine occupation. To these pots she puts her own name and that of Julian. Moreover, in order to be able to spend more time at pottery making, Maria employs Mexican women to help her in her housework.

This boldness of purpose causes considerable jealousy in the pueblo which is muted by the fact that Maria, as leader, extends credit to her poorer and less successful rivals in the North Plaza faction. In the South Plaza her supremacy is not as yet challenged. There are five other women potters in the North Plaza faction who make and sell pottery independently of Maria. But the tourist buses do not stop regularly at their doors, and certain of them dispose of their pottery almost entirely to traders, either the traders who come and trade from door to door or the traders in Santa Fé.

With Maria and her two sisters, Desideria and Maximiliana, and Tonita Roybal dominating the production of pottery in the North Plaza there is less of a feeling of rivalry in this plaza than in the South. Isabel Martinez and her daughters, Petronella and Teracita, make pottery and sell it in their home, but their wares are made for the tourist trade and in times of need they dispose of it to the wandering trader. And while the other women make pottery, they either help Maria or dispose of their wares in Santa Fé. In the North Plaza there is little criticism to be heard of Maria and her forceful sales methods. They say instead, "Maria, she is so good to us."

In the South Plaza the situation is different. The women are not organized, and each works independently of the others. Only one woman, Rose Gonzales, the boldest and best potter in the plaza, and one of the best in the pueblo, sells her wares solely to the tourist and does not trade. The others sell a little pottery to the tourist, but in general dispose of their wares to the wandering trader or to the trading stores in Santa Fé.

I was told that formerly the women potters used to help one another, but today pottery has grown to be a competitive industry. One woman told me that she had said to another, "You must have lots of pottery. You help people and they help you." The husband of the amiable woman denied this. "It would be better if she did not help others," he said. "They don't help her. She had better do her own work."

Feeling has grown to such a pitch that women will not visit other women lest they be suspected of trying to spy on the number of pots their village rivals may have, or be accused of stealing designs. Women say jealously of one another, "She works night and day on her pottery." And the undercurrent of suspicion has reached a point where the women are not capable of forming a coöperative group in order to market their pottery to advantage.

Next in importance to the making and polishing of pottery, which is woman's work, is the decoration. This is usually done by the husband of the potter or some close relative, though there are cases where a man will decorate the pottery of a neighbor. Men unquestionably decorated the ceremonial bowls and still do this important work, but such decorations are traditional and are made by the ceremonial officers of the village, just as the bowls themselves are only made by the head women.

While men usually do the decorating of the pots, women may do it and a number of the women do so. Most of these women are widows, or women whose husbands do not know the art of decorating pottery. Such women prefer to work out their own designs rather than to share the profits of their industry with some man outside of their immediate family.

In general there are two styles of pottery in San Ildefonso which the women potters adapt to their own use. Maria is the innovator of one style, a dull black on a polished black surface; and Rose Gonzales [99] is the most successful potter working in the other technique, that of carving out the design. Both methods are popular among tourists and traders. Rose, who is a younger woman than Maria, came to San Ildefonso from San

[99] Rose is a widow and does all the decorating on her pots.

Juan. She learned pottery from her mother-in-law and after nine years of patient labor has developed her skill to such an extent that in conception and execution she is now the leader of the younger group of potters. She is a bold, careful worker and takes a great deal of personal pride in her ability to carve, polish and fire her pottery. The women of the pueblo divide their allegiance between Maria and Rose, that is to say, they copy the techniques of both.

Pottery in San Ildefonso is seasonal, though a little money is made from it during the entire year. In the winter the women have great difficulty in drying out their pots before firing them, and much of this drying has to be done before an open fire inside the house. Moreover, there is less tourist traffic during the cold weather. Yet in spite of this seasonal falling off in demand, the popularity of the San Ildefonso ware is such that even during the winter the women occupy much of their time with pot making.

In the economic scheme of the pueblo it is impossible to chart the part played by the potter, since if any woman or man knows what his income is from the sale of pottery, he keeps this information to himself. No one keeps a record either of the pots made or the pots sold or the prices received for the ware. Nevertheless, it is more than probable that the total income to the village is many thousands of dollars, and that certain individuals make over a thousand dollars apiece each year through their industry. This has unquestionably had a profound effect on the pueblo as a whole, particularly in determining the position of women. Where once women patiently worked in the house and managed the children and the household, they are now economically in a position of dominance. This is especially true in the North Plaza where the dominant women potters indirectly [100] control the village through their husbands; it is less true in the South Plaza where women are less group conscious and where the men are still dominant in social and ceremonial activities.

[100] This notion shocks all but the most realistic of the villagers.

PAINTING

Interest in design, stimulated by government school-teachers, the Museum at Santa Fé and tourists, soon found itself reflected in another medium, that of water colors. In the years shortly following the war Crescencio Martinez began to paint pictures in water color. The initial interest which this created stimulated other members of the pueblo. Crescencio [101] was followed by Alfredo Montoya. The painting of these men found a ready market, and stimulated others. Here was a craft that was pleasant, remunerative and which commanded praise and attention. Men had decorated pottery; it was logical that they should paint. The rise of painting was rapid. Alfonso Roybal (Awa tsireh), a young man at the time, showed considerable talent in this new field of expression. His pictures commanded good prices, and enthusiasts provided him with extravagant publicity. Men who had formerly confined themselves to the decorating of pottery now began to paint. With the exception of a few of the older men, all the men in the pueblo turned to this new art.

The effect on the pueblo was almost immediate. Men who before had decorated pottery for the women were now able to command an income from their own pictures. One man, it was said, made 900 dollars in one year. A few of the Indians left the pueblo to attend exhibitions of their work in large cities and to talk on Indian art. They swam in a sea of encouragement. A few of the men went so far as to build studios in their own houses.

And yet in spite of this, painting in the pueblo has suffered a decline. The boys paint in school; for that matter, so do the girls, and show remarkable proficiency. But interest in painting has declined among the men so that while nearly all of them lay claim to being artists, comparatively few of them exercise their abilities, and none of them devotes himself entirely to painting.

Moreover, those of them who showed the most promise have

---

[101] Crescencio's work first came to notice about 1910. Alfredo Montoya was doing single figures before 1915.

proved their inability to go beyond their early art forms which seemed at the time so fresh and so full of promise. But this does not explain why the men seldom paint, for there is always a market for their work, especially among the visitors of Santa Fé. Various explanations are offered by the men themselves; one of the most successful of the present-day painters has given up painting to return to agriculture because agriculture is the proper pursuit for a man and he has grown tired of painting, though he still paints a few pictures for sale. Another successful painter does little work now because he finds that decorating pottery is on the whole easier and by inference more remunerative. Another painter prefers to work for the government which pays better. Still another has failed to carry out the promise of his youth, he paints seldom and is often away from the pueblo.

Until recently, painting was man's work. The only woman painter was Tonita Pena who married out of the pueblo and went to live at Cochiti. But in 1937 two women from San Ildefonso exhibited paintings at Gallup and won prizes for them. Whether other women will also take up painting remains to be seen. Both of these women made pottery, but they were not among the most successful; both of these women's husbands are recognized artists.

From the economic point of view, painting, while it undoubtedly plays a part in pueblo economy, is now rather an auxiliary source of income than a fundamental one, in comparison with agriculture, working for the government and pottery. Only one man, Julian Martinez, the present governor (1937), makes his livelihood solely by painting and by decorating his wife's pottery.

THE CRAFTS

With the exception of pottery and painting, all the other native crafts in San Ildefonso have declined in importance to a point where they no longer affect the village economy. Only a very few men know the art of working leather and can still make the high white buckskin boots that the married women wear. Cloth is no longer woven even for the women's ceremonial mantles. Instead, these and the broad sashes which are also worn by married women are bought from the Hopi, or, if the necessity occurs, borrowed from friends in neighboring pueblos. Today men and women buy the greater part of their clothing in Espanola and Santa Fé. Many of the women make up their own dresses at home. While nearly all the married women wear the traditional married woman's dress, sash and moccasins, the young unmarried girls dress in the modern styles of Santa Fé.

Two or three men still do bead-work occasionally, but this practice is not pueblo and is usually done only at the request of White friends. In much the same way silver is worked by two men who learned this craft in the Indian school.

Baskets are no longer woven, but are bought from the Apache.

The decline in the arts is not so much due to indolence, for very few of the villagers are indolent, but from the fact that native crafts do not offer a sufficient return to interest the men. During the winter when much of this work was done, they can now work for the government at a higher wage than they could possibly hope to realize from pursuing a craft. Moreover, there is no market for native crafts within the pueblo, and in competition with other Indian groups little market without.

TRADE

Trade is still occasionally carried on with Santo Domingan traders, and wandering Navajos, but most of the women trade their pottery with White traders who visit the pueblos in trucks, or take their wares to Santa Fé where they trade at the trading-posts. Quite a successful cash trade is carried on by the women in their own houses where they sell pots and postcards to summer tourists.

There is one little Mexican store within the village which is chiefly patronized by the neighborhood Mexicans. Several years ago N. and T. opened a small store for the pueblo. Many of the Indians, particularly members of the opposing faction, resent this innovation, especially since they claim that the credit which is allowed the North faction does much to influence intra-village politics.

THE FAMILY

There have been no recent changes in the family or in the structure of kin groups.

Children four days after birth receive Indian names from their "Wash Mother," usually a female relative or neighbor. Later on at a Catholic christening the child receives its "Mexican" name. Neighbors are invited to act as godfathers and godmothers. These may be, and frequently are, Mexicans. When the child grows up and marries, if it has any marital troubles the godparents are supposed to be consulted in an effort to straighten out the difficulty.

The use of kinship terminology is declining, due to the use of the Spanish Christian name in address and reference. Also the native terms *tunu* and *kii* appear to be falling into disuse.

MOIETIES, CLANS AND SOCIETIES

Since there are only three Winter families in the pueblo, the moiety division plays little functional part in village life. There is neither a Winter cacique nor any Winter cacique society (Oyike), and it seems only a question of time before the Winter people [102] will cease to exist. Clan consciousness is also dying out. Many of the people today confuse clan with moiety, declaring that Sun is an alternative term for Summer just as Turquoise is the alternative for Winter. Red Stone or Coral people cannot or will not give any explanation of clan. Clans have no function in the pueblo. The Summer cacique society (Paioke) continues to exist, but much of the old lore has been forgotten. The factional dispute weakened the society which is largely in the hands of three old men. If these men should suddenly die, there is no one in the society who knows or could carry on the old traditions. This does not appear to worry the members. When such a break occurs, the lost ritual can be recovered from the Summer cacique societies of neighboring Tewa pueblos.

[102] The Winter families have a "head" who can direct them if necessary. Today they join with the Summer people in religious ceremonies. Recently one man who was Winter joined the Summer moiety.

Today there are only three male members of the kossa,[103] and all these are now members of the South Plaza. When the North Plaza need a male kossa, they have to invite one from a neighboring pueblo. No new members have been initiated into the society for some time.

While there are two medicine societies (Tewake and Temake pufona), they do little if any curing or exorcising, and only exist in skeleton form. Not much confidence is felt in the curative powers of either. There is only one male member in each society, and no new members have joined for many years.[104] When the villagers do not have confidence in the government doctor or visiting nurse, they usually go to some Mexican who knows how to cure.

Within the last few years there has been a slight shift of emphasis in patterns of social dominance. All individuals were said to possess equal status, but an increasing respect is being shown to the wealthy at the expense of the religious or cult leaders. Again, differences in wealth tend to increase intra-village resentment and jealousy.

POLITICAL ORGANIZATION

I have described the present political situation in the pueblo in the pages dealing with the factions. The following is, therefore, merely a summary of the present situation. The village is split into two political groups. The North Plaza has a governor, recognized by the government, and a right-hand man (Koingii). They have elected a war captain (Akogeip′o), warriors (Akogei) and an aguacil. There are two principales, and one pika (fiscales).

There has been an effort recently on the part of the government to give the governor greater powers in pueblo affairs. This is acceptable to the pueblo as a whole, provided the governor does not attempt to meddle in religion.[105]

---

[103] The kossa sendo is "head" of the Winter people and head of the Temake pufona; the cacique is also a kossa.

[104] The head of the Temake pufona is also Samaiyo. There are no young boys growing up in either society.

[105] This from a South Plaza man.

In the South Plaza there are the war captain, six warriors, three principales, and two pika. This group serves the wishes of the cacique who, while he is not, strictly speaking, a political officer, nevertheless is the most powerful political figure of the group.

There has been no recent change in the techniques for the control of the individual. Children are brought up from earliest childhood to be quiet and submissive to parental authority. And it must be said for most of the children that they conform willingly. As they grow older their submission to paternal authority is transferred to the authority of their religious and civil officers. Moreover, as quarreling is regarded with universal disfavor, few situations arise that demand energetic control on the part of society.

Individuals conform to the demands of the culture to a surprising degree. When an individual does not conform he is admonished by the village officers. If he still persists, the village does its best to ignore the trouble. If an individual should continue to behave in such a way that the village could not ignore it, the officers would probably call in the government to assist them. However, no such situation has as yet arisen as far as I could discover, although individuals out of jealousy or spite will inform on one another to the government.

What is true of the individual is not so true of the group. When groups become antagonistic within the pueblo there is no mechanism for resolving the conflict. In such cases the pueblo will voluntarily take its troubles to the government and ask them to assist. In serious splits, however, neither side will accept arbitration and the schism will continue indefinitely. Tests of strength are foreign to the culture, and each side relies on its conscious rectitude to bring it ultimate victory.

SUPERNATURALISM

Most of the men and women accept the religion of their ancestors. Whatever scepticisms may have been bred through White contacts and in government schools, all the people in the village [106] follow pueblo tradition and dutifully attend the cere-

[106] A San Ildefonso boy is studying for the priesthood.

monies in the kiva and in other ways fulfill their religious responsibilities. But as the old traditions are slowly becoming lost,
there has been a gradual curtailing of ceremony and ritual.

No men or women would dare mock or fail to take part in
the numerous rites that make up the pueblo ceremonial calendar,
but beyond attending to their individual duties there is little
religious curiosity or speculation. In religion they are not encouraged to think for themselves.[107]

A few of the older men and more of the older women regularly attend to their Catholic religious duties as well as their
native ones. But it would appear from observation that on the
whole there is little interest in Catholicism.

Everyone believes in witchcraft, and women and children in
particular are afraid to go out at night for fear of witches. Any
event that seems in any way peculiar is always attributed to a
witch or witches. The people are continually suspecting each
other,[108] particularly those whose conduct is not impeccably
pueblo, and will occasionally level specific charges of sorcery
against someone they fear or dislike. But on the whole the concept of witchcraft as it is supposed to be practised is vague, a
suspicion and threat to security.

Witchcraft is seldom discussed with acquaintances, because
they might be witches. But certain cases of sorcery are well
known to everyone. The last influenza epidemic was said to
be due to witchcraft, and in the past little children are supposed
to have been killed by witchcraft. There are many stories on
the subject, often of this type. A man shot an owl and discovered
that he had shot his father. An examination of all these stories
never discovers an actual witch. He or she is always just someone
in the village, the name of whom the teller of the tale does not
know.[109]

[107] Children are taught at home not to be curious. This lack of curiosity is
noticeable among school children. If a teacher tells her class that they will
not understand the answer to a certain question, the class is quite satisfied
and does not raise the question again.

[108] White people are not witches, but Mexicans are sometimes said to be.

[109] In many stories of witchcraft the evil is aimless. But on the whole children, the village, crops and livestock are said to be bewitched on account of
jealousy.

There was recently, however, an authentic case of suspected witchcraft. A man went to his neighbor's for a drink, and was found dead next morning. The pueblo is convinced that this was witchcraft in spite of government assurances to the contrary. And believing as they do, nothing has been done to the witch either by the dead man's family or by any member of the village. And when he left the village he was invited to return because he was needed in a dance.

PROPERTY ATTITUDES

There undoubtedly has been a change in the attitude toward land ownership during the present century. What was formerly communal property is now considered to be the property of individuals, who are said to have rights of disposal and transmission. I doubt very much whether today the pueblo officers could take land from an individual because he was not working it or prevent his heirs from taking it. It was said that in some cases involving the sale or transfer of property, deeds were being made out following White practice.

I was also told that wills are now occasionally drawn with regard to the disposal of property after death.

SEX ATTITUDES

In the old days men selected their wives for their industry and ability to keep house. Today White concepts of love affect the marriage choice. As a result, said the woman who told me this, marriage is not generally as successful as it used to be.

THE FOCI OF INTEREST

Where before the chief focus of interest was in agriculture, in the pueblo of today there has been a gradual shift in values. Agriculture is still the center of interest for a few men, but this is no longer true of the others.

As far as the women are concerned, life is almost completely centered in the making and sale of pottery.

The men's adjustment to new values, many of them certainly

introduced by the successful sale of pottery, has been less complete. A few have turned entirely to the arts for their livelihood. They paint pictures and decorate pottery for the money that there is in it. Others prefer to do government work for a daily wage. Where before men struggled to raise good crops, they now struggle to earn money. The desire to earn money, however, is not so strong that it has driven men to seek a livelihood outside the pueblo, but it has tended to be reflected in a decreasing interest in agriculture.

THE SUCCESS OF CULTURAL INTEGRATION

On the whole San Ildefonso must still be considered a well-integrated community in spite of the dispute between the two factions. Men owe allegiance to one party or the other, but within that party there is a high degree of solidarity and unanimity of opinion.

Though individuals within the pueblo are less coöperative and more competitive; though the practice of agriculture is giving ground to pottery and day labor; though there is a slow change from a predominantly masculine culture to one in which women have increased stakes and authority; and though native practices are gradually being displaced by the "White way," nevertheless the community is still integrated and shows few symptoms of immediate disintegration. In San Ildefonso the impact of White culture has been oblique in the sense that there have been no territorial removals, no change from one type of economy to another radically different, and no behavior patterns in one group that are intolerable to the other [110] so that adjustment has been possible without violence. But within the last thirty years the rate of change has been greatly accelerated by a change in basic economy. Whether the culture can remain integrated under this new pressure remains to be seen.

THE MODERN INDIVIDUAL

In San Ildefonso men tend to conform to one pattern. Men should be hard-working, self-effacing, temperate and faithful to

[110] I refer to the last century.

their religious duties. The modern man has these traits to a surprising degree. There are no outstanding leaders, though this does not imply that there are not great personality differences.

While the older men are well integrated and at harmony with the culture, maladjustments do occur, particularly among the young men who have been away from the pueblo to school or college and who find difficulty in settling down to the slow pace of pueblo life. Moodiness, intemperance and cultivating White people and White ways are, on the whole, the symptoms of their maladjustment.

The same standards that apply to men apply equally to women. Above all, they should be industrious. Since women seldom leave the pueblo and since the culture offers them fewer choices, their horizon is more limited than that of men and they are more conservative. They do not smoke or drink or gad about. On the whole, women appear to be better adjusted [111] to the demands of their culture, than men.

BIBLIOGRAPHY

The following bibliography contains only a list of those authors cited or those whose contributions have some immediate bearing on the report.

Bancroft, Hubert H., *The History of Arizona and New Mexico, 1530–1888*, The History Company, San Francisco, Calif., 1889.

Bandelier, Adolph Francis, Final Report of Investigations among the Indians of the Southwestern United States, *Papers of the Archaeological Institute of America, American Series, Volume 4, Part 11*, J. Wilson and Sons, Cambridge, Mass., 1890.

Benedict, Ruth, "Configuration of Culture in North America," *American Anthropologist, New Series, Volume 34, No. 1*, pp. 1–27, 1932.

——— *Patterns of Culture*, Houghton Mifflin Company, Boston, Mass., 1934.

Bunzel, Ruth L., *The Pueblo Potter*, Columbia University Press, New York, N.Y., 1929.

Burton, Henrietta K., The Re-establishment of the Indians in Their Pueblo Life through the Revival of Their Traditional Crafts, *Colum-*

[111] Only two women are unhappily married. These are two young women who are very progressive and modern, drive motor cars, and have worked outside the pueblo. Maria, who has introduced so many innovations into the pueblo, is one of the finest types of pueblo women. She is intelligent and industrious. While she conforms to traditional behavior, her natural force of character commands others.

bia University Contributions to Education, No. 673, Teachers College, Columbia University Press, New York, 1936.

Forrest, Earle R., *Missions and Pueblos of the Old Southwest,* The Arthur H. Clark Company, Cleveland, Ohio, 1929.

Freire-Marreco, Barbara, "Tewa Kinship Terms from the Pueblo of Hano, Arizona," *American Anthropologist, New Series, Volume 16, No. 2,* pp. 269–287, 1914.

Guthe, Carl E., Pueblo Pottery Making—A Study at the Village of San Ildefonso, Introduction by A. V. Kidder, *Publications of the Department of Anthropology, Phillips Andover Academy,* Yale University Press, New Haven, Conn., 1925.

Hammond, George P., Don Juan de Onate and the Founding of New Mexico, *Publications in History, Volume 2, Historical Society of New Mexico,* El Palicio Press, Santa Fé, New Mexico, 1927.

Harrington, John P., The Ethnogeography of the Tewa Indians, *Bureau of American Ethnology, Annual Report 29,* Smithsonian Institution, Washington, D.C., 1916.

—— "The Tewa Indian Game of Canute," *American Anthropologist, New Series, Volume 14, No. 2,* pp. 243–286, 1912.

—— "Tewa Relationship Terms," *American Anthropologist, New Series, Volume 14,* No. 3, pp. 472–498, 1912.

Harrington, John P., and Henderson, J., Ethnozoölogy, of the Tewa Indians, *Bureau of American Ethnology, Bulletin 56,* Smithsonian Institution, Washington, D.C., 1914.

Hewett, Edgar Lee, *Ancient Life in the American Southwest,* Bobbs-Merrill Company, Indianapolis, Indiana, 1930.

—— Antiquities of the Jemez Plateau, New Mexico, *Bureau of American Ethnology, Bulletin 32,* Smithsonian Institution, Washington, D.C., 1906.

Hodge, Frederick W., "Pueblo Indian Clans," *American Anthropologist, Volume 9,* pp. 345–352, 1896.

Indian Population in the United States and Alaska, *Bureau of Census,* 1910.

Parsons, Elsie C., Social Organization of the Tewa of New Mexico, *Memoirs of the American Anthropological Association, No. 36,* George Banta Publishing Company, Menasha, Wis., 1929.

Parsons, Elsie C. and Beals, Ralph, "The Sacred Clowns of the Pueblo and Mayo-Yaqui Indians," *American Anthropologist, New Series, Volume 36, No. 4,* pp. 491–514, 1934.

Robbins, Wilfred and Harrington, John H., and Freire-Marreco, B., Ethnobotany of the Tewa Indians, *Bureau of American Ethnology, Bulletin 55,* Smithsonian Institution, Washington, D.C., 1916.

EDITOR'S SUMMARY

SAN ILDEFONSO ACCULTURATION

The San Ildefonso and Carrier are the only groups described in this report in which the arrival of the Whites did not produce important changes in the natural environment through the destruction of the natural resources or the removal of the group to a new locality. Although there has been a destruction of game in the case of the San Ildefonso, their main subsistence technique, agriculture, is still effective when carried on by aboriginal methods. Moreover, the destruction of game is a recent phenomenon and was not a factor in the first phase of their White contact, that with the Spaniards.

The Spanish contact offers a situation in which the results of directed acculturation backed by force can be perceived with few complicating factors. The Spaniards attempted to introduce Christianity and a new type of village governmental organization and to eliminate the native religion. They succeeded in both introductions as far as the outward forms were concerned, but in both cases these forms were reinterpreted in the light of the previous culture and were adjusted to it. This integration was successful enough so that the forms survived even when all external pressure had been removed. The attempt to eliminate the native religion failed completely. It was met by the development of techniques of reticence and concealment which have also survived long after the necessity for them has disappeared. Although we have no direct information on this point, it seems probable that the Spanish attacks on the native religion actually heightened the group's attachment to it, giving it new symbolic values. The whole program of directed acculturation seems to have had much less effect upon native life than has the destruction of natural resources or elimination of aboriginal activities which we have observed in other groups.

The White contact of recent years also shows a very curious

case of the direction of culture development by the dominant group. The encouragement of native pottery making and painting is an almost unique phenomenon. It has set a premium upon individual initiative and inventive ability which was altogether lacking in the aboriginal culture. A woman who invents a new style of pottery or a man who develops a new type of painting is immediately given an economic advantage. It has also destroyed the effectiveness of the old sexual division of labor. The woman potter is now the mainstay of the family and the man finds it more profitable to work on the land. With this economic dominance goes an increasing social dominance which has not yet had time to reflect itself in new formal patterns. The women more and more rule but in theory are still subservient. The result is increasing stress. It seems possible that this altered position of men may also be linked with the diminishing interest in religious activities, which are predominantly masculine. Although the old ceremonies are still going on with full apparent vigor, it is noted that no young people are being trained to take the place of the old ones. It seems probable that the next few years will see a collapse of the esoteric aspects of the culture and a rapid acculturation of the society.

8

ACCULTURATION AND THE PROCESSES OF CULTURE CHANGE

by Ralph Linton

Like a number of other terms employed in the social sciences, the word acculturation came into general use without benefit of a formal definition. In his recent study of the subject Dr. M. J. Herskovits has traced its use as far back as 1880 and has shown the wide variety of meanings attached to it by various authors.[1]

It is evident that the students of culture change who have employed the term acculturation have seldom sought to define it, or to assess its implications before using it. . . . For some the word seems to imply the meaning inherent in its earlier uses—the result of somewhat close contact between peoples resulting in a give and take of their cultures; for others it appears to hold the significance implicit in Powell's usage of 1900—the process whereby a specific trait is ingested by a recipient culture; while still others apparently accept it as the means whereby an individual "becomes acculturated" to the patterns of his own society, a usage which makes the term acculturation a synonym for "education." Since all these are but phases of culture change, and in their psychological aspects equally involve the learning process, it is not strange that in the minds of some students all these meanings seem to be held simultaneously, with the result that sometimes this concept of culture contact appears to have one meaning for them and at other times the word is employed in a quite different sense.

In view of such confusion, it will be understood why the subcommittee on Acculturation appointed by the Social Science Research Council in 1935 felt that its first task was to define the term. "Acculturation comprehends those phenomena which result when groups of individuals having different cultures come into continuous first hand contact, with subsequent changes in

[1] M. J. Herskovits, *Acculturation*, p. 6, J. J. Augustin, New York, 1938.

the original culture patterns of either or both groups." To this definition the committee appended a note which must be regarded as an integral part of the definition. "Under this definition acculturation is to be distinguished from *culture change,* of which it is but one aspect, and *assimilation,* which is at times a phase of acculturation. It is also to be differentiated from *diffusion,* which, while occurring in all instances of acculturation, is not only a phenomena which frequently takes place without the occurrence of the types of contact between peoples specified in the definition above, but also constitutes only one aspect of the process of acculturation." [2]

As one who participated in the drawing up of this definition, I am both keenly conscious of its shortcomings and at a loss how to improve upon it. It must be remembered that the term acculturation has been in use for over fifty years and has accumulated a wealth of associations. To the average worker in the social sciences it seems to convey little more than a sense of a heterogeneous, unanalysed collection of processes any or all of which may be set in train by contacts between representatives of different societies and cultures. In the present stage of our knowledge regarding these processes and the causal factors involved, any definition more precise than the one given would introduce as many difficulties as it removed.

The crux of the definition lies in the phrase "those phenomena which result when groups of individuals having different cultures come into continuous first hand contact." "With subsequent changes in the original culture patterns of either or both groups" is really redundant, for it would be impossible to find any case of such contact which has not resulted in changes in the cultures involved. It can be seen that the definition makes no attempt to specify the *nature* of the phenomena which are to be treated as a part of acculturation. The determinants are (a) the particular situation under which the phenomena are present, and (b) a suggested rather than clearly indicated limitation of the field to those phenomena which seem to be results of the particular situation. The application of each of these determi-

[2] R. Redfield, R. Linton, M. J. Herskovits, "A Memorandum for the Study of Acculturation," *American Anthropologist, Volume XXXVIII,* pp. 149-152.

nants presents serious difficulties. The frame of reference established by the phrase "continuous first hand contact" cannot be delimited with any exactness. However, the general implications are clear enough. We can say that the situation of a group of European immigrants settled in an American city provides a valid basis for acculturation studies, while that of a group of Polynesian islanders, visited once a year by a trading schooner, does not. At the same time, the observed cases of contact between various groups show all degrees of closeness and continuity. They form a series within which there are no obvious lines of demarcation and the limits of acculturation on this basis must be left vague.

The second determinant is equally hard to apply. The only phenomena which could be considered results of the acculturation situation *per se* would be those which were always present under conditions of "continuous first hand contact" and under no others. If such phenomena exist, their presence has not been revealed by any of the investigations made to date. There are, however, certain phenomena which can occur only under conditions of continuous first hand contact, although they are not a constant accompaniment of such conditions. Thus the assimilation of one group by another has contact of this sort as a prerequisite but does not always occur when the contact exists. The European gypsies have remained unassimilated after many centuries. Whether such phenomena are to be considered "results" of the acculturation situation is an open question.

The only certain criterion for establishing a frame of reference for acculturation studies is thus a condition of "continuous first hand contact." In spite of the doubtful cases already mentioned, plenty of such situations are recognizable. However, to delimit a field for research on this basis is very much like delimiting one on the basis of a particular repetitive time interval, say the hours of four to six P. M. The phenomena observable during this period may differ somewhat from those observable at any other time of day, the differences being most marked in communities where the cocktail hour flourishes. Everything that happens between four and six on a series of days chosen at random can be observed and described. The data can then be compared and a composite picture developed on the basis of which it can be predicted with a fairly high degree of probability that certain things will happen on any day during this time interval. Nevertheless, as long as observations are restricted to this single frame of reference it will be impossible to understand the causes of many of the phenomena present. Similarly, the frame established by the acculturation concept helps to focus descriptive and comparative studies, but as long as we keep strictly within it we will learn little about process and be unable to understand many of the phenomena involved. The acculturation situation is the most complex of all contact situations and the key to an understanding of what may happen in it lies in the study of what happens in simpler situations where the relations of cause and effect are more obvious.

The proper starting point for any dynamic study of acculturation is an analysis of the processes of culture change in general. However, before beginning this, a word should be said regarding the culture concept itself.

A culture may be defined as the sum total of the knowledge, attitudes and habitual behavior patterns shared and transmitted by the members of a particular society. Its content and organization must be deduced from observations of the behavior of the society's members with the establishment of what appear to be the norms for this behavior under various circumstances. This at once raises the question as to whether cultures can be considered as anything more than constructs developed by the investigator. However, the problem of their ultimate reality is not important to the present study. The culture concept meets the acid test of all scientific formulations by making it possible to predict certain events with a high degree of probability. When the culture of any society is known, one can forecast the behavior of most of the society's members under most circumstances. Moreover, this concept is the best tool so far devised for describing the uniformities in the attitudes and behavior of a society's members in terms of a coherent functional whole, and for studying the changes in these which may occur under various conditions. Its justification lies in its proved utility.

Cultures are adaptive mechanisms and as such represent a

response to the needs of our species. These needs are psychological as well as physical. For satisfactory existence all normal persons require not only food, shelter and sexual satisfaction but also a sense of security, escapes from boredom and favorable responses from their fellows. The function of culture is to provide technique for the satisfaction of these needs and the effectiveness with which it accomplishes this will be determined partly by the environment, partly by the personalities of the individuals involved. The variables which the latter introduce into the situation are largely taken care of by a conditioning process through which the individual's crude needs are refined into concrete desires of sorts which the culture can meet under normal conditions. Thus all persons need food, but they desire only those sorts of food with which their culture has familiarized them. Again everyone needs sexual satisfaction, but the desire for a soul mate on the romantic American pattern will not be present unless the individual has been taught to expect that he will find one.

Under normal conditions every culture insures the survival of the society which bears it and also the contentment of most of the society's members. However, the adaptations which it provides are never so perfect that they cannot be improved upon nor are they ever completely satisfactory to all the society's members. Imperfections of cultural adaptations result in individual discomforts and dissatisfactions and these, in turn, provide the motives for culture change. The more widespread such states are within the society, the greater the willingness of its members to change their ways. Such states are immediately produced by any change in the environment which renders some of the current cultural adaptations unworkable with consequent deprivations for the group. For example, the disappearance of a form of game which has been the group's economic mainstay will immediately produce discomfort and cultural changes to meet the new conditions. However, individuals may suffer from dissatisfaction with the *status quo* even when there have been no changes in the environment. In spite of the influences of cultural conditioning, the members of a society remain individuals with capacities for individual thought, feeling and action. Once an individual realizes the existence of some shortcoming in the culture and changes his behavior with satisfactory results, the other members of the group who have observed this may also realize the disadvantage of the old way and copy the new.

Cultures are infinitely perfectable and everything indicates that all cultures are in a constant state of change. The rate of this change will, of course, differ from one culture to another and even at different points in the same culture continuum, but some modifications are always under way. This condition is evident even in the so-called primitive cultures, wherever we have observations over any prolonged time interval. This fact disposes once for all of the old theory that human beings are innately and irrationally conservative. Culture change is, at bottom, a matter of change in the knowledge, attitudes and habits of the individuals who compose a society. All of these things have been learned and can be modified by the familiar psychological processes of learning and forgetting. The individual can alter them whenever it is to his obvious advantage to do so. However, such changes always involve an effort and before he will exert himself he must be persuaded that the possible results are worth the trouble. Whether the individual has consciously thought the matter through or not, most cases of conservatism prove on analysis to have a rational basis. Either the advantages to be derived from the new thing do not seem great enough to compensate for the inconvenience involved in changing established habits, or the new thing threatens current advantages which the individual enjoys.

Let us turn now to the processes of culture change. As has been said above, the fundamental processes of culture change are concerned with modification in the knowledge, attitudes and behavior of individuals. What happens at this level will never be exactly the same for any two persons, but where whole societies are concerned the individual differences apparently tend to cancel out, making possible certain valid generalizations. The things which the individual has to learn and unlearn as a participant in culture change are current or potential parts of the culture of his society. We will refer to them, therefore, as culture elements, without attempting to define that term too strictly. The nature and qualities of different culture elements are, of course, almost infinitely diverse, but in connection with the processes of culture change they all seem to behave in very much the same ways.

It is obvious that a new idea or habit or appliance must originate and exist for a time before it becomes a part of culture. The origination of such elements might therefore be considered one of the phenomena of culture change. It is so with relation to culture as a whole, but in the present case we are dealing with what happens to particular cultures, the only workable basis for studies of change. In such cases the new culture element may originate either within the cultural-social configuration, through the processes of discovery or invention by members of the society, or it may originate in some other social-cultural configuration and be introduced in developed form. This spread of culture elements from one configuration to another is referred to as *diffusion* when the element is taken as the point of reference, as *culture borrowing* when the receiving society is taken as the point of reference. Such borrowing has been of the utmost importance to the growth of most cultures, making contributions which far exceed those of discovery and invention combined. However, the important thing for our present purposes is that the source of the element has only incidental effects on what happens to it after it has been brought to the attention of the society's members. An invention which has been made within the frame of a particular culture is likely to be more compatible with the preëxisting configuration and therefore somewhat more easily assimilated than an element which comes to the culture from without, but the actual processes of assimilation will be the same in both cases.

Culture change normally involves not only the addition of a new element or elements to the culture but also the elimination of certain previously existing elements and the modification and reorganization of others. Thus when the iron axe comes in the stone axe goes out, the techniques for making it are forgotten, methods of wood working are modified with reference to the potentialities of the new tool and the returns in prestige and profit which went to stone axe makers are eliminated. It is much easier to follow through what happens to the new element itself in such situations than it is to trace the widely ramifying results of its introduction. Partly for this reason and partly because of interest in the historic aspects of contacts between peoples, studies of culture transfer and culture change have been focused mainly on what happens to new elements. This is only one half of the picture, but since it is the part for which most information is available we may take it as our starting point.

The processes involved in the introduction of a new culture element may be divided into those connected with (1) its initial acceptance by innovators, (2) its dissemination to other members of the society, and (3) the modifications by which it is finally adjusted to the preëxisting culture matrix. The introduction of any new element into a culture begins with its acceptance by some individual or at most by a small group of individuals. We may call these agents of initial acceptance the *innovators*. The reasons why particular innovators accept particular new things are certainly highly diverse, including even factors of individual personality. However, we can observe certain general motives at work which can be classed under the heads of curiosity and desire for novelty and of the expectation of advantage. As in so many other social and individual phenomena it is impossible to say that one of these sets of motives is constantly dominant. Because of the value system of our own culture, European investigators are prone to think of the acceptance of new culture elements as conditioned primarily by considerations of immediate utility, yet we know that this does not hold even within the narrow frame of our own culture and society. The cigarette lighter was not more efficient than the match at the time it was introduced and it is an open question whether it is so even now. In spite of this, it has achieved a very wide acceptance. It must also be remembered that the practical advantages of new forms of behavior, or even of new tools, may not be obvious to groups unaccustomed to them. Until the native has learned the new set of muscular habits necessary to its effective use, the iron axe is not a more efficient implement than the stone adze nor the rifle a deadlier weapon than the bow. Actually, we know that many of the things which natives usually take over from Europeans on first contact are objects which excite their curiosity or which are, at most, useful for purposes of personal adornment.

Expectation of advantage is a broad term which must be understood to include not only the expectation of practical advantage through greater comfort or added efficiency but also the expectation of returns in the form of prestige. These returns may be intangible, but they are none the less important. The desire for prestige motivates a great deal of behavior in all societies and to be the first or one of the first persons to have or do a new thing always attracts attention. If it is something that other people would like to have or do themselves, the result is an admiration tinged with envy which is highly satisfying to the innovator's ego. Of course not all new things will evoke this favorable response and the knowledge of this acts as a check on the innovator's activities. There are certain new things which are, so to speak, out from the start because they are too much at variance with the established patterns of the group. Thus even the best high pressure salesmanship would find it difficult to popularize the wearing of nose rings among ourselves and one of the greatest difficulties would be to find anyone willing to start the fashion. At the other end of the scale, there are certain novelties which can be recognized at once as both advantageous and compatible with the preëxisting culture, but most new elements fall between these two extremes. They have enough advantage and are compatible enough to make their acceptance a possibility but not a certainty. It seems that innovators can always be found for elements of this sort but whether the community will accept them depends upon a number of factors, some of which bear no relation to the intrinsic qualities of the elements themselves.

This brings us at once to the second group of processes involved in the introduction of a new element of culture; those by which it is disseminated from the innovator to other members of the society. To understand these processes we must recognize first of all that a new culture element is rarely disseminated to all of a society's members and that it can be successfully incorporated into the culture without this. No single individual is ever familiar with the total content of the culture in which he participates and the part of it which he knows and employs will be determined primarily by his place in his society's system of organization. All societies have their members divided into categories such as those of men and women, nobles and commoners, initiated and uninitiated, etc. Although in any society a few things will be known to or done by all normal individuals above the age of infancy, most things will be known to or done by the members of some one of these categories and not the members of the others. New culture elements are rarely of a sort which would be useful to the members of all the existing categories or compatible with all the constellations of functionally inter-related culture elements associated with the various categories. This means that the dissemination of most elements is selective. Thus in a society in which sewing is strictly women's work a new appliance connected with sewing, say a superior type of needle, may spread rapidly among the women and achieve full acceptance by the members of this category without the men accepting it. The men would, of course, be conscious of its existence but it would not be a part of their sector of the total culture. Conversely, in a society in which men controlled all relations with the supernatural a new ritual or form of magic might disseminate to all the adult males while affecting the women only indirectly. Due to this differential participation in culture, the initial acceptance of a new element may even be considerably wider than the knowledge and employment of it after it has come to be taken for granted. Thus a new game may be played by everyone for a time and then relegated to children, or a new occupation, say weaving or pottery, practised by both sexes for a few years, then preëmpted by one or the other.

Side by side with this universal pattern of differentiation within the society and culture there runs a pattern of rating the various categories within the society in order of prestige. This rating usually extends to their differentiated activities. Those assigned to members of high groups are considered honorable, those assigned to members of low groups undesirable if not degrading. The significance of this in the dissemination of new culture elements is considerable.

If we turn now to the actual processes of dissemination we

find that they are simple enough. Other individuals learn the new thing from the innovator and pass it on to still others until it becomes known to all the members of the society or of a particular category or series of categories within the society. The real problem is what makes these individuals willing to receive the new thing and to change their habits accordingly. The same factors of utility and compatibility which influence the acceptance of the novelty by the innovator are clearly at work but the factor of prestige takes on a new aspect. With respect to prestige, the relation between the innovator and his innovation is a reciprocal one. The fact that he introduced it reflects some glory on him, but the new thing becomes associated with him in the minds of the group and gains or loses its potentialities for conferring prestige upon those who accept it later according to what his social status may be. To cite a concrete example, a waitress would scarcely be asked to endorse a new brand of cigarettes. Again, no one would try to launch a new fashion in woman's wear through the stores that handle cheap, ready-made stock. In such a case the innovators, in the sense of those who first wore the new models in public, would be persons of low prestige in our society and the new model would immediately become associated in the popular mind with low economic status. As a result, no one would accept it willingly. If, on the other hand, the new fashion appears first among millionaires and movie stars everyone will want to copy it. This phenomenon is by no means limited to our own society. There is no group in the world where the general acceptance or rejection of a new thing will not be strongly influenced by the auspices under which it is introduced to the group and the associations which are attached to it in consequence. The prestige level at which the new element enters the society very largely delimits the group of individuals to whom it may spread. New elements readily filter down to persons of lower prestige rating than the innovators, but they have to present great and obvious advantages to be accepted by those of higher rating. Since in many cases the advantages of new culture elements over those which are already present and providing for the same needs is not obvious, the factor of prestige often becomes the determinant of acceptance or rejection. In the case of borrowed elements the prestige associations which they derive from having originated in a particular group may have as much or more influence than those which they derive from a particular innovator. The importance of this fact for the understanding of what happens in contact situations will be discussed later.

To sum up, the factors which influence the dissemination of culture elements most strongly are the utility and compatibility with the preëxisting culture of the elements themselves and the desire of members of the receiving group for prestige and for novelty of experience. During the early stages of dissemination the prestige and novelty factors are extremely important. As time passes they tend to lose their force, i. e., the new thing becomes common, and the borrowed element must increasingly stand or fall on the basis of its own merits. It is not uncommon for a novelty to be accepted by large numbers of a society's members, even by whole categories, and then abandoned. In such cases we say that the new thing was a fad. First acceptance is always succeeded by sober second thought and if the element is to be retained it must prove its worth. This worth is, of course, a relative matter. The simplest condition is that in which the new thing is given up because it does not meet certain needs as effectively as do the older culture elements with which it is competing. The experience of the Comanche with firearms provides a case in point. According to old informants they were for a time very eager to get muskets. Then, as these weapons lost their novelty, they began to be weighed against the bow and were recognized as inferior to it for hunting and even in war. The muskets had greater range but had a much slower rate of fire, were difficult to load on horseback, and required ammunition which was hard to get. As a result, the tribe began to revert to the bow and were on the way to abandoning the musket except for a few special purposes when the introduction of the repeating rifle turned the tide again toward firearms.

The causes which lead to the abandonment of a novelty are rarely as simple and obvious as in the case just cited. New elements may be given up even when they are more effective than the old ones for reasons which we may lump under the rather vague term incompatibility with the preëxisting culture patterns. It is safe to say that no group, when it accepts a novelty, is able to foresee the full extent of the consequences. For example, who in 1900 could have predicted the full effects of the introduction of the automobile? As time passes, the effects of the new thing on the life of the group begin to be apparent. These effects may be abstractly phrased in terms of culture derangement, but concretely they produce discomfort and bewilderment for the society's members. It then becomes a question of whether the advantages to be derived from the novelty outweigh the trouble it causes. The group may conclude that they do not and go back to the old ways. An excellent example of this is the abandonment by some of the Tanala gentes in Madagascar of irrigated rice culture after they had practised it for some years. The new method produced more abundant crops than their original dry rice cultivation, but the opportunity for individual ownership of natural resources which it provided was subtly undermining many of their institutions. This case has been discussed at length in another publication.[3] Suffice it to say that among the gentes which did not abandon it, the final result was a breakdown of the extended family patterns which were basic to the whole original structure of Tanala society. Even when, for many members of the society, the gains from the new culture element outweigh its disadvantages, it will still be abandoned if it proves a threat to the advantage or privilege of the members of one of the dominant categories. Here also the total effects of the new thing do not become evident at once, and it may take some time for the opposition of the threatened group to become organized and effective. Thus, in a society in which the power of family heads is reinforced by ancestor worship, even these may be favorable to Christianity of first contact, recognizing the advantages of the gifts, medical aid, etc., given by the missionary. They will exert their influence against the acceptance of Christianity only when they begin to realize its potentialities for undermining their authority.

Let us turn now to the third group of processes involved in

[3] R. Linton, *The Study of Man*, D. Appleton-Century Company, Inc., New York, 1936, pp. 348–353.

the successful introduction of a new culture element; those by which it is brought into conformity with the preëxisting culture patterns. To understand these we must realize that all culture elements have form, i. e., directly observable qualities, and also meaning, i. e., a series of associations in the minds of the group. Thus the form of a dance would consist of those features of it which could be recorded by motion-picture and phonograph, its meaning of the attitudes and associations which the group have toward it. This meaning would include whether it was sacred or secular in import, whether the opportunity to perform in it was a privilege or an undesired obligation, ideas as to the general circumstances under which it should or should not be performed, etc. At the time of its introduction any new element will have tangible form and the changes in this aspect of it are designed to make it more compatible with the preëxisting experience or habits of the group's members. Such changes are largely conscious, improving inventions on the part of the individuals who employ it. Thus the original hafting of an axe as it is received in trade may be exchanged for one similar to that already in use with stone axes, thus making it possible to employ the same movements with the new tool as with the old one. Again, the native artist who borrows a European design will alter it in subtle ways to make it "look right" or the arrangement of borrowed music will be changed to conform to the preëxisting musical patterns. For example, the ways in which Tahitians have transformed Protestant hymns into lively dance tunes is somewhat startling to the European, while the way in which our own composers have adapted Indian melodies would surprise Indians.

The attachment of meaning to new culture elements is, on the other hand, largely unconscious, coming about as a result of the situations in which the new things are employed or the auspices under which they are presented to the group. The only associations which the new thing has at the start are those deriving from its connection with particular innovators, its origin, if this is known, and its superficial resemblance to elements already present. The last results in the immediate transfer to it of some of the group's associations with such culture elements. As the novelty achieves more general acceptance, these initial associations may change, and in any case new associations will be added until the new thing has been brought into agreement with preëxisting conceptual patterns of the culture. Thus new objects of utility may accumulate associations of prestige and become symbols of wealth or rank. When visiting one of the small tribes on the southeast coast of Madagascar I was struck by the number of iron cooking pots owned by most families. I discovered that these utensils had come into use only about twenty years before, the first ones having been brought back by men who had left the tribe to work as contract laborers. To do this was something which conferred prestige in itself, while to make enough money at it to purchase one or especially two pots conferred still more. It had become the custom for each returning laborer to bring back some of these utensils with him and to have a long row of them on display had become a symbol of the social importance of the household. In this culture, then, iron cooking pots had acquired a particular meaning which bore little relation to their practical utility. Again, when Catholic missionaries first began to work in Madagascar the natives were much puzzled by the phenomenon of saints. Supernatural associations were at once established, partly by the missionaries' observed attitudes and behavior toward the saintly images, partly because the Malagasy themselves had images which were associated with their ancestor worship. However, the Christian concept of the nature and function of saints had no native parallel. The Malagasy finally concluded that the new figures represented the ancestors of the Europeans. These ancestors were, of course, primarily interested in the well-being of their descendants, but would help non-relatives in return for a suitable fee. Having thus been rationalized and brought within the scope of native concepts of the supernatural, their worship was taken up with considerable enthusiasm.

Such modifications in form and meaning are a constant accompaniment of the process of integrating a new culture element into the preëxisting culture matrix. The possible changes in form under such circumstances are limited somewhat by the intrinsic qualities of the new thing, but the possibilities for change in meaning are almost unlimited. The conditions which give a new thing certain associations for the group on first appearance are often chance determined, while later associations always involve the ideological patterns already present in the particular culture.

The problem of the time required for the complete acceptance and integration of new culture elements offers an almost unexplored field for investigation. By integration is meant the completion of the series of modifications both in the new culture element and in the preëxisting culture which are necessary to eliminate conflicts and direct duplication of function. It would seem a priori that there should be a direct connection between the time required and the extent of the modifications which the introduction of the new thing entails. Thus an element of minor importance, such as a new game, would be integrated more rapidly than a new technique which had potentialities for revolutionizing the economic life of the group. However, we know that a number of the changes necessary to the integration of the new element may be carried on simultaneously and until we have more data on what has actually happened in a number of cases any generalization on this point is a pure guess.

In any case, it seems that under favorable conditions new elements can be integrated with considerable rapidity. The great advantage of culture over other adaptive mechanisms lies in its flexibility and the ease with which it can change to meet changing conditions. The integration of new culture elements depends upon the ability of individuals to learn and to change their preëxisting habits and we know that they can do both very rapidly when the incentive is strong enough. In our own society even middle-aged individuals have witnessed the acceptance and successful integration of many new culture elements within their own lifetimes. It may be protested that this is not a test case, since our own situation is complicated by cultural factors of high pressure salesmanship, etc., which do not exist in most societies. However, we have at least one example of almost equally rapid acceptance of a whole new complex of culture elements by a series of "primitive" groups. This case is that of the horse among the Plains Indians. The speed with which this novelty was taken over is the more surprising in view of its revolutionary effects on many aspects of the native life.

Let us turn now to what happens to preëxisting culture elements when new ones are introduced. This aspect of culture change has, unfortunately, received little attention and it is difficult to make many valid generalizations about it at present. It seems that, under normal conditions, every culture is adequate to meet the needs of the society with which it is associated. Its performance with respect to some of these may be poor but must be good enough at least to insure survival. Culture change thus becomes primarily a process of substituting new elements for old, but this involves much more than simple addition and subtraction.

To understand the phenomena involved in replacement we must digress briefly to consider the relation between culture elements and group needs. Although any culture can be dissected into literally thousands of different elements, the living culture operates as a whole. It satisfies the total needs of the society in somewhat the way that the whole body operates to keep the individual alive. Within the entire culture configuration it is possible to distinguish certain constellations of functionally related elements, trait complexes, which stand in somewhat the same relation to the needs of the group as the relation of the various organs to the needs of the body. These trait complexes are the smallest units of culture which can be said to operate for the satisfaction of particular needs. However, each of them includes numerous culture elements and their contents are not mutually exclusive. A single culture element may function in two or more complexes simultaneously, as when a knife is used in work, in war and for sacrifice. Moreover, these functional units seem to be of minor importance in culture change and even in the transfer of culture from one group to another. The modification of such complexes is accomplished by successive changes in their component parts, while in culture borrowing single elements, if they can be fitted into preëxisting complexes, seem to be taken over more readily than whole complexes.

When we attempt to link particular trait complexes with particular needs, the full complexity of the situation becomes apparent. Each complex is so organized that it can contribute to the satisfaction of several different needs. Conversely, each need can be met by any one of several different complexes. The most that we can say of any given complex is that its primary function seems to be in connection with such and such a need and its functions with respect to other needs secondary. However, the whole arrangement is highly flexible. If something interferes with the operation of one complex, the load of meeting the need will be shifted to the other complexes which already have secondary functions with respect to it. Thus in a culture in which the food need is taken care of primarily by agriculture, while hunting and fishing are primarily amusements, a crop failure will shift the emphasis of hunting and fishing from sport to food getting.

In order for a new culture element completely to replace an old one, it must be possible to substitute it for the old one in all the trait complexes toward whose functioning the old trait contributed. Such complete substitutions are not uncommon and in these cases the elimination of the old culture element seems to follow much the same course as does the introduction of a new element except that it follows it in reverse. When the innovator accepts the competing novelty, the old element becomes a latent part of his culture equipment, then, if it remains latent long enough, is forgotten. As the new element achieves increasing acceptance, the old one becomes latent for more and more individuals and in time a new generation appears to whom it is known only by hearsay. It finally drops out of the culture with the passing of the last die-hard conservative. Even the factor of prestige may play an important rôle in this elimination process. Retention of the old element may be injurious to prestige, an attitude reflected in our own derogatory use of the term "old-fashioned." Conversely, old ways may become symbols of high social position and continue to be followed by some group within the society long after the rest of the society has given them up.

An amusing example of the latter was told me by a Spanish friend. It seems that in pre-revolutionary Spain, where automobiles were rare and expensive, all car license plates were numbered in a continuous series and a new car always received a new number even if it was a replacement for one previously owned. To have an old car with a low license number became a symbol of long established wealth and social position with the result that, at least for town use, cars were kept running as long as possible. Parvenues would even pay exorbitant prices for cars which would be consigned to the scrap heap in America because of the prestige which their low license numbers would confer.

The substitution of a new culture element by no means always results in the complete elimination of the old one. There are many cases of partial as well as complete replacement. The novelty may be incorporated into certain of the complexes in which the analogous old element functioned and not into others. Thus, because of the associations which have been established with them, stone knives may continue to be used for ritual purposes long after metal ones have superseded them elsewhere, or the bow continue in use for sport long after it has gone out in war. In certain cases the old element may even take on new meanings and become integrated into new complexes, as when the practice or products of crafts which have been superseded for ordinary purposes acquire luxury connotations. Hand weaving in our own culture would be a case in point. Unfortunately, so little work has been done on this aspect of culture change that we do not even know whether partial replacements of this sort are, in general, more or less frequent than complete replacements. However, it seems safe to say that in the normal processes of culture change no element will be eliminated until the substitute has proved itself better, or at least as good, in all the complexes in which the original element functioned. Cultures seem to be almost infinitely tolerant of duplications in function. In fact at least temporary duplication is an inseparable accompaniment of culture change. However, they are highly intolerant of modifications which leave any of the group's needs even temporarily unprovided for. Old elements may be pushed aside to make place for new ones, but they will not be given up voluntarily until all their functions have been successfully transferred. As we shall see later, there may be situations in which an unreplaced culture element or complex is discarded as a result of outside pressure, but the results of this are frequently disastrous.

The general phenomena of culture change may be summarized as follows: The basic processes of culture change are the individual psychological ones of learning and forgetting. Its basic stimuli lie in the discomfort or discontent of a society's members which make them willing to change their ways. Culture change always involves not only the adoption of new culture elements but their modification in form or meaning or both, and also modifications in the preëxisting culture. The latter may include the elimination of certain elements but need not necessarily do so. In the acceptance of a new element certain stages are recognizable irrespective of whether the new thing originated within the social-cultural configuration or was borrowed from another group. It is taken up first by a single individual or small group of individuals; the innovators, who are for some reason dissatisfied with the *status quo*. These innovators anticipate advantage from the new thing, but this advantage may be in terms of practical utility, or prestige or both. From the innovators the new element may or may not spread to other members of the society, their acceptance or rejection of it being determined by considerations of advantage similar to those operative in the case of the innovators. Dissemination of the new thing to the total society is not necessary for its successful incorporation into the culture and its spread is, in practice, normally limited to the members of certain socially established categories of persons as adult men, nobles, etc. Dissemination of the new element may be followed either by rejection, if it fails to show superiority to the old element or elements which it might replace, or by acceptance, with progressive modifications both in it and in the culture matrix. These processes of modification run concurrently with those of dissemination, and their success is of the greatest importance for the final and complete acceptance of the new thing. Under normal conditions culture change involves duplication of function but no interruption in the satisfaction of the group's needs. It can, therefore, be accomplished without disorganization and with no more discomfort to the individual than is involved in changing preëxisting habits.

9

THE PROCESSES OF CULTURE TRANSFER

by Ralph Linton

In the previous chapter we discussed the phenomena of culture change in terms of the factors and processes which seem to be operative in all change situations and which may, therefore, be considered basic. We will now turn to the additional factors and processes which are present in a particular aspect of culture change, i. e., that of culture transfer as a result of contact between groups. There appear to be certain phenomena which are universally associated with this situation and which provide a background without which the variations observable in specific cases cannot be understood.

It seems best at the very outset to dispose of one factor frequently present in situations of contact and culture transfer. This is the factor of racial differences between the groups involved. The associations which the groups themselves come to attach to these differences may be of considerable importance in determining their behavior and attitudes toward each other, but it seems to be the associations rather than the differences which are significant. Racial differences are no bar to the amalgamation of two groups through intermarriage. In fact, open or illicit interbreeding is one of the commonest of contact phenomena and the offspring of such unions have never proved to be inferior in any respect to the parent stocks. As regards the transfer of culture from one group to another, all our present information seems to indicate that any race can assume any type of culture given a full opportunity to do so. It is possible that there are some exceptions to this due to physiological conditions. For example, a group with a strong hereditary susceptibility to tuberculosis, such as certain of the Polynesians have, might find it fatal to try to assume the method of life of a community of factory laborers. At the same time, all races

seem to be so much alike psychologically that behavior and attitudes which could be acquired by the members of one group could
presumably be acquired by those of any other. Actually, we know
that in the past culture elements of the most heterogeneous sort
have been diffused over great areas and accepted and assimilated
by groups of widely different race.

In our general discussion of culture change it was pointed out
that factors other than those of practical utility or even of compatibility with the preëxisting culture configuration may be of
great importance in determining whether a new thing will be accepted. The auspices under which novelties are presented to the
group and the associations which come to be attached to them in
consequence have a profound effect on their potentialities for
conferring prestige upon those who accept them, and this in turn
strongly influences willingness to accept them. It is at this point
that the origin of new culture elements becomes significant for
understanding subsequent developments. If the novelty originates
within the group, its associations will derive primarily from the
prestige status of the inventor and innovators. If it originates outside the group, its associations will derive not only from the innovators but also from the donor society. In other words, the attitudes
of the receiving group toward the donor group will attach themselves, at least initially, to the elements of culture which contact
between the two groups makes available for borrowing. Since it is
a demonstrable fact that most cultures owe a large part of their
content to borrowing, these attitudes are a factor in many situations of culture change. They are operative, without exception,
in what we have defined as acculturation situations.

It seems certain that anything beyond the most momentary and
superficial contact between groups of different culture will result
in some borrowing. Either discrete elements of culture or total
functional complexes of elements can be transferred from one
group to another. Thus a group can borrow either the entire horse
complex, including techniques for the care of the animal, appliances for its effective use, etc., or a single item such as a new
type of saddle. Obviously they will not borrow the saddle unless
they have horses or, to put it in more formal terms, culture elements will not be borrowed unless some function can be found

for them relative to the preëxisting culture. Enough cases of culture transfer have been observed to make it clear that the borrowing of elements is much more frequent than that of trait complexes, but the reason for this is still uncertain. The number of elements in any culture is vastly greater than the number of functional complexes, making their transfer much more probable on a purely chance basis. The adoption of single elements and their integration into preëxisting complexes also involves less modification in the culture of the borrowers than does the taking over of whole new complexes. Lastly, in many contact situations it may be easier for members of the borrowing group to perceive and imitate certain items in the culture of the donors than for them to apprehend the total complexes of which these items are a part. The problem offers an interesting field for further research.

It seems that, other things being equal, certain sorts of culture elements are more readily transferable than others. Tangible objects such as tools, utensils or ornaments are taken over with great ease, in fact they are usually the first things transferred in contact situations. They can even be passed from one culture to another in the absence of face to face contact between the groups involved, as when a laden derelict drifts ashore on an undiscovered island or goods are left for the members of a shy tribe to find in the hope that they will be lured to the explorer's camp. The transfer of patterns of behavior is more difficult. It requires at least face to face contact over a period long enough to enable one group to observe the activities of the other and does not always result even then. The transfer of elements which lack the concreteness and ready observability of objects and overt behavior is the most difficult of all. It requires not only face to face contact but also the presence of some means of communication adequate for the conveyance of abstractions. In general, the more abstract the element the more difficult the transfer. Thus we know that such things as folklore stories can be transmitted from one culture to another even when the means of communication are quite defective, say sign language or a trade jargon, while philosophical concepts are difficult to transmit even when the language barrier is of the slightest. The common element in this range of variation seems to be that of the relative ease with which the foreign element of culture can be perceived by members of the borrowing group. Objects can be perceived most easily, culture elements of other sorts with progressive difficulty.

The perception of culture elements by the borrowers is, obviously, the first step in their transfer. However, the most easily perceived aspect of a culture element, even such an abstract one as a story, is its form. Its meaning to members of the donor society can only be conveyed by elaborate explanations and not always then, for the most important meanings attached to many acts and objects are often imperfectly formulated and poorly verbalized. Thus a borrowing group can readily perceive a flag or the acts gone through in a religious ceremony but they cannot perceive the ideological context of these culture elements. At most they can observe that the members of the donor group seem to manifest certain emotional responses in connection with such objects or acts. The result is that most culture elements are transferred in terms of objective form stripped of the meaning which is an integral part of them in their original context. At most they may carry over vague associations of sacredness or importance derived from the observed behavior and attitudes of the donor group in connection with them. Their primary meaning, as far as the receiving group is concerned, will be that which they derive from the single fact of their original association with the donor group. In other words, the attitude of the borrowers toward the donor group will attach itself, at least initially, to the borrowed elements of culture, influencing the response to these elements and also to the innovators who are seeking to introduce them.

An example may make this clear. A group of Europeans coming into contact with a native tribe might notice the prevalence of face paintings; also that the patterns worn by different individuals varied. Unless the visitors were ethnologists on the lookout for such things, it would not be until months later that they would discover that the various designs had different significances, expressing, say, different sorts of war honors or the fact of being in mourning for a particular relative. Even when the visitors did learn this, it would remain a bit of disassociated information which would not influence their attitude toward the custom of face painting. The latter would be associated in their minds only with the primitive group and the lower prestige status which they ascribed to that group. For one of their own members to imitate the custom would certainly attract attention, but this would be of a sort that could only be satisfying if the innovator's previous prestige was so low that he felt any attention was better than none. The natives, on the other hand, might observe that the White men shook hands whenever they met after a separation of a few days. They could not understand the significance of this gesture to the Whites, but they would associate it with the White group and their superior prestige. The first natives to adopt the custom would not only attract the attention of their fellows, but would also derive a certain amount of prestige from being the first and a personal satisfaction from feeling that they were thus identifying themselves with the superior group. Perhaps, to go a step further, the adult males would then arrogate the custom to themselves, sternly discouraging hand shaking by women or boys. A generation later its origin might be forgotten, but by then it would be firmly intrenched as a symbol of membership in a particular social category.

The culture of an alien group presents itself to the potential borrowers as an aggregation of forms stripped of most of their meaning and of all but the most obvious and elementary of their functional relationships. Natives can see, for example, why guns and ammunition go together and understand that if they take over one they should also take over the other. However, they frequently do not see the connection between bright-colored, interesting suspenders, and drab and uncomfortable trousers and are likely to accept the former while firmly declining the latter. This brings us at once to another aspect of culture transfer, namely the factor of selection by the receiving group. It is safe to say that no society, so long as it exists as a distinct entity, will take over even the purely objective aspects of an alien culture *in toto*. It will pick out certain things from the range of those made available for borrowing and accept these while remaining indifferent or even actively opposed to others. In the presence of long contact, indifference and opposition may be progressively broken down, and under such circumstances the selective factor expresses itself in terms of sequence of adoption, certain things being taken over before others.

Aside from the factor of relative ease of perception of culture elements of different orders, the considerations involved in their selection and adoption seem to be fundamentally the same as those involved in the dissemination of culture elements within the group. New things are borrowed on the basis of their utility, compatibility with preëxisting culture patterns and prestige associations. All three of these are, of course, variables and the outcome of exposure to a new culture element will depend upon a very intricate combination of them. The possible ranges of variation in utility and compatibility are fairly obvious, but the importance of prestige is frequently overlooked. Although elements in foreign cultures are perceived objectively, certain more or less irrational associations with them are present from the start. The most important of these are the associations derived from their identification with the donor group. These are qualified, in some cases, by the donor group's attitudes toward these elements of their culture, in so far as these can be perceived by the borrowers. Thus if a respected foreign group apparently attaches great importance to some custom, say wearing clothes or sitting on chairs, the borrowing group will feel that this custom must have some advantages which are not obvious and be that much more eager to take it over. The prestige potentialities of borrowed culture elements will depend primarily upon the attitude of the borrowers toward the donors. Thus if the borrowers despise the donors, the prestige factor may be an active minus quantity. Individuals who take over habits from them will feel that by doing so they lose caste and the factors of utility and compatibility with the preëxisting culture must be very high to make the transfer worthwhile. Conversely, if the borrowing group admire the donors, elements from their culture acquire a positive prestige value and will often be accepted on this account even when they are not intrinsically superior to analogous elements in the receiving culture or when their acceptance entails considerable cultural readjustment. In other words, if one group admires another, they will go to a good deal of trouble and inconvenience to be like them, while if they despise them they will put up with a good deal of trouble and inconvenience not to be like them. The tropical native who begins to wear clothes and replaces his cool thatched roof with corrugated iron because he sees Europeans do these things, and the European in the tropics who keeps his stiff collars in spite of the temperature are cases in point.

To what degree these prestige factors influence the order of selection of culture elements under conditions of long continued contact and successive borrowings is a question which we are quite unable to answer. We do know that after initial contact and the consequent establishment of inter-group attitudes there is often a tendency to attach symbolic value to particular culture elements, thus influencing both the ease of their transfer from the higher to individuals in the lower group and the tenacity with which individuals cling to them. Trousers have acquired a value of this sort in most of the tropical regions where Europeans are dominant. While a native gains prestige by wearing them, a White man who appears in public in a native nether garment, no matter how voluminous or comfortable, loses caste. However, the attachment of such values seems to be largely chance determined. Other things being equal, the order of selection of borrowed elements is probably controlled primarily by considerations of utility and of compatibility with the preëxisting culture of the borrowers.

The acceptance and successful integration of certain culture elements may facilitate the acceptance of others which have been functionally related to them in the donor's culture. Thus the acceptance of agricultural machinery would obviously be made easier by a previous acceptance of agriculture. In fact it would be impossible without it. At the same time, we have seen that trait complexes may be borrowed as wholes, and we have no proof that the acceptance of certain elements is constantly or even usually followed by the acceptance of others which were originally related to them. Borrowed elements, even when they retain their original form with little modification, may be put to quite new uses by the borrowers and may acquire associations very different from those which they had in their original context. In such cases it is an open question whether their presence has any influence on the borrowing of originally related elements. The number of factors which affect borrowing is so large and the variation in the factors themselves so great that it seems probable that no significant generalizations can be made on this particular point.

Another interesting aspect of culture borrowing is the problem of the minimum time required for the full acceptance and integration of new elements. We know that this process requires time and it seems certain that some new things require more time than others. One might suspect that this time factor would be correlated in some way with the extent of the modifications in both the new element and the preëxisting culture necessary to its successful integration. However, we know that modifications of several sorts may go on simultaneously. All we can say is that under optimum conditions the transfer of a culture element can be accomplished with surprising speed, as when an entire group becomes conscious of the advantages of writing and practically all its members learn to read and write within a few months. This happened among the Cherokee after the invention of Sequoia's syllabary, and in certain of the Polynesian Islands under missionary encouragement. It is interesting to note in this connection the speed with which new societies and cultures can be synthesized from diverse elements once these have been brought together. Thus the life of cattlemen in the old West presented all the phenomena of a distinct culture, yet its development, flowering and final dissolution took place within a period of about sixty years.

In spite of the numerous studies which have been made on various aspects of culture transfer, there is not a single study now extant which tells us exactly what happened when one society borrowed elements of culture from another society. The ideal description should include:

1. What elements were selected by the borrowers and in what order.
2. Who were the innovators and what were their motives.
3. What categories of persons within the society were receptive or resistant to the new things.
4. What modifications were made in the form and meaning of the borrowed element in the process of its integration.
5. Time at which these modifications were made, relative both to each other and to the total time required for full integration.
6. What changes in the preëxisting culture matrix resulted from acceptance of the new element and how these changes were accomplished.

A study of this sort would entail little more than plenty of time and persistence on the part of the investigator. Culture borrowing is going on all over the world at such a rapid rate that in many communities all these questions could be answered by consulting the memories of persons still living. At the cost of no more effort and certainly of no more expense than has gone into collecting data on many problems in the physical and natural sciences, the investigation of culture transfer could be given a factual foundation which is now largely lacking.

Even in the absence of such exact data, enough situations of contact and borrowing have been observed to make two points clear. First, borrowing is normally a reciprocal process, and second, its logical, although by no means always its actual, end product is the amalgamation of the two cultures involved, resulting in a new culture differing in certain respects from either of its parent cultures.

Evidence for the reciprocal nature of borrowing is afforded by all cases in which two groups of diverse culture have been in contact for any length of time. However, the extent of borrowing by each of the two groups involved will usually be different, one taking over more than the other. At least two factors are operative in determining the differential in culture transfer. One of these is the relative effectiveness of the techniques for adaptation to the local environment which each culture provides. To cite a concrete example, Europeans in the Arctic have borrowed very heavily from the Eskimo, copying their clothing, housing, hunting methods and even, to a considerable degree, their food habits. These elements of culture represent successful adaptations to a type of environment alien to normal European experience and with which the established patterns of European culture cannot cope successfully. The tragic experiences of early explorers who did not adopt these elements of Eskimo culture illustrate the point sufficiently. The Arctic represents an extreme case, yet it seems that other things being equal, immigrant groups will borrow more heavily from those already on the ground with cultural adaptations to the local conditions worked out than the local groups will borrow from them.

The other factor is that of relative prestige. Other things being equal, a group which recognizes its social inferiority will borrow more extensively from its superiors than the superiors will borrow from it. However, considerations of superiority and inferiority are never strong enough to pevent some transfer upward. This process is facilitated by the tendency, already mentioned, for groups of different status in contact situations to single out certain elements of culture as focal points for prestige associations. The superior group will cling to these even in the face of considerable discomfort and may even forcibly exclude the inferior group from participating in them. At the same time, elements of the superior culture to which no such associations have become attached may be eliminated and replaced by new elements borrowed from the inferior group. Thus the European in West Africa clings to the full clothing which his ancestors developed in a sub-Arctic environment, but has changed his food habits in the native direction, adopting such delectable dishes as palm oil chop without any sense of losing caste. What actually happens under such conditions of mutual transfer will, therefore, depend upon the interaction of utility and prestige factors.

That the logical end product of reciprocal culture borrowing is the fusion of the two cultures involved to produce a new culture is obvious. Under such conditions one would expect the resulting culture to include those techniques for coping with the particular environment which had proved most efficacious, irrespective of their origin, and for the rest those elements of culture to which the highest prestige values had been attached. The new culture would, therefore, presumably draw more of its content from that of the group recognized as superior in the contact situation. However, these generalizations are purely speculative. To date, no hybrid culture has been completely analysed in terms of the original cultures involved, their relations in the original contact situation, their respective contribution and, lastly, the new elements of culture developed in the course of their amalgamation.

Perhaps one reason for this is that in the current interchanges of culture between European and non-European groups, the process of culture exchange is never carried through to its logical conclusion. The complete amalgamation of two cultures has as its inseparable accompaniment the complete amalgamation of the two societies involved. As long as these retain their separate identity their cultures will retain certain differences. Each society, even that represented by the population of an American village, has its own culture differing in certain respects from that of all other societies. In most cases the process of culture exchange results not in the production of a new, homogeneous culture but in the synthesis of two new cultures with mutual adaptations which permit the societies which bear them to live together in a symbiotic relationship.

All culture transfer has as its prerequisite contact between the groups involved, and the nature of this contact is one of the factors influencing the whole process. However, before going into this, something should be said of the influence of contact on culture change in general. The fact of contact in itself increases the force of the external and internal stimuli toward culture change which are constantly present. From the moment of its appearance the contacting group introduces a new factor into the general environment. In all but a few extreme cases of isolation, the environment of a given society includes not only natural phenomena but also other societies. Even sporadic contacts with a new group influence relations with the groups previously present. If desirable articles are obtained from the newcomers, trade with groups which did not have similar contact will be stimulated, or the added possibilities of loot will increase the contacting group's danger from attack. If the newcomers are hostile, their presence will be a strong stimulus to alliance with groups already known. If they are friendly, the possibility of obtaining help from them will increase the contacting group's truculence toward its neighbors. In brief, the appearance of a new group always leads to realignments and changes in the relations of those already present, with a consequent need for cultural adaptations.

Such contacts also lead almost inevitably to alterations in the natural environment or at least to changes in its potentialities for the resident group. Even if the newcomers are only transient traders, they will be in search of and exchange valuable objects for certain products and not others. These products may previously have played only an unimportant rôle in the native economy. Contrast the importance of rubber to a native tribe who used it only for the mouth-pieces of blow guns with the importance the same material assumed when it was discovered that it could be exchanged for tools, beads and cloth. Again, the small fur-bearing animals which played a minor rôle in the economy of the Canadian Indians before White contact rose to major importance immediately thereafter. Under such conditions new and more intensive methods of exploitation will be developed with an ultimate reduction of the supply and an upset in the natural ecology which may have far reaching consequences. If the newcomers actually settle in the region, their presence will result in a diminution of resources for the groups already there or even, in extreme cases, in the complete elimination of resources of a certain sort. The destruction of the buffalo by White hide hunters cut the very foundation from under the cultures of the Plains tribes and contributed more to their subjugation than all the White soldiers.

The society must modify its culture to meet these new environmental conditions if it is to survive. At the same time, the fact of contact has profound psychological effects upon the society's members. It goes without saying that any marked maladjustment of the group to its environment will be reflected in individual discomforts and consequent discontent, but the effects of contact are of a more direct sort. Under ordinary circumstances the average individual is no more conscious of the culture in which he participates than he is of the air he breathes. The discomforts and thwartings which its particular patterns impose upon him are accepted as inevitable, much as we accept the fact of a hot summer or a rainy day. The presence of another group with a different set of habits and values makes him culture conscious, and it is a short step from this to a critical attitude toward the institutions of his own society. He may disapprove of much of the newcomers' behavior, but at the same time he will envy them some of their liberties. Thus the European who goes to Polynesia immediately notices what seems to him an extraordinary laxity in sex mores and thinks of these people as enjoying a freedom vastly greater than that of members of his own society. It is only after close contact that he begins to realize the extent and intricacy of the tabus which hem them in at various points where the members of his own society are free. Conversely, the Polynesian notices first of all that the European breaks tabus which the native has been reared to believe were highly dangerous and that apparently nothing happens to him in consequence. Such observations give the individual something to think about.

The presence of newcomers also arouses the curiosity of individuals and provides opportunities for novel experience. All explorers can testify to the extreme interest that most natives take in everything that the visitors have and do. If the new experiences prove pleasurable, the members of the group develop new desires whose satisfaction calls for changes in the familiar routine. A man may have to hunt twice as hard as he did before or indulge in some new form of labor in order to get whiskey for the occasional sprees which, once experienced, become the high point of existence. To sum up, contact even without the transfer of culture elements, if such a thing is possible, is a strong stimulus to culture change. It not only modifies the environment but also makes the individual critical of the *status quo* and more receptive to novelties.

The range of possible forms of contact between groups is enormous. In fact, no two cases of contact are identical in all their aspects. Contacts may vary in duration, in closeness and in continuity, all three of these variables operating independently, but it is an open question how significant any or all of these factors are in influencing the processes of culture change. It seems that, at most, they impose certain limits upon the possibility of culture borrowing. Thus obviously there will be more chance for culture exchange under conditions of long, close and continuous contact than under conditions of brief and distant contact. However, in the matter of culture transfer the old adage that you can lead a horse to water but you can't make him drink is very much to the point. Some of the small religious communities in the eastern United States, for example certain Pennsylvania German sects, have been in close and continuous contact with other Americans since the eighteenth century, yet their cultural borrowings have been highly selective and the number of elements taken over relatively small. On the other hand, the Japanese, whose contact with Europeans has been much briefer and immeasurably less close in terms of space, have borrowed much more extensively and, apparently, with much less discrimination. Again, how are we to evaluate the rather frequent cases of discontinuous contacts which are close while they last? For example, whalers making seasonal visits to the Arctic often live on terms of the closest intimacy with Eskimo groups during the few months they are there. The Eskimos have the run of the ship and the Whites take temporary Eskimo wives. Are the chances for culture transfer better or worse in such a case than they are in that of a small colony of European administrators living year in and year out among natives whom they keep at arm's length?

Apparently the really significant features of contact as influencing culture transfer are not duration, closeness and continuity, but the effects of the contact on the preëxisting environment, the elements of culture which it makes available for borrowing and the attitudes which it engenders between the two groups involved.

The possible effects of contact situations on environment have already been discussed. In many of the cases recorded in this volume these effects were so far reaching as to become the dominant factor in changing the native life. They rendered many of the aboriginal economic techniques unworkable, and destroyed both the economic security and morale of the group. What happened to some of these tribes can only be interpreted as a desperate attempt to adapt themselves to new environmental conditions with the aid of any patterns which could be derived from either native or White culture.

The elements of culture which are available for borrowing represent a variable which is obviously of great importance in determining the culture transfers which may take place in contact situations. It has already been pointed out that no one individual is ever familiar with the total culture of his society and that the knowledge and activities included in that culture are divided among the society's members according to its patterns of organization. Thus men are expected to know and do certain things, women to know and do other things, etc. In the more complex cultures this division is often carried to great lengths. In contact situations it seems to be rather exceptional for the contacting groups to be fully representative of their respective societies. Thus even in the case of European immigrants to the United States there tends to be an initial selection along economic lines and also along sex lines. Many more men come than women, and more individuals from the lower economic levels than from the higher ones. In the case of contact between Europeans and natives, selective processes are also operative for the European group. The Whites who go to the tropics are predominantly men and most of them fall into one or another of three categories—traders, prospectors, etc.; missionaries and administrators. The members of the first group tend to represent more of a cross section of European male society than do those of the other two groups, but all three groups combined do not make the whole of European culture available to the native for borrowing. Even a band of settlers normally brings with it only a part of the total culture of the society from which its members were recruited. Thus a pioneer group settling in the territory of an Indian tribe would make certain elements of White culture available for borrowing by their aboriginal neighbors; these might be techniques for mending boots and certain tunes popular in folk music. They would not make available techniques for laundering dress shirts or the scores of grand operas. Such variations in the cultural equipment of the donor group can only be established by observations on the spot. As a factor in culture transfer their influence is negative, i. e., they limit the range of elements available for transfer but have little if any effect on the selection of elements by the borrowers.

The attitudes between the groups involved in contact situations are, on the other hand, positive factors in culture transfer. We have already discussed the way in which associations may attach to culture elements simply because of their connection with a particular group, and how these associations influence the willingness of a receiving group to accept them Behind all questions of the utility or apparent compatibility of the culture elements available for borrowing there lies the deeper question of whether the borrowers want to be like the donors or not. If they do, elements will be borrowed eagerly; if they do not, the elements will be borrowed reluctantly or not at all. The attitudes which may exist between groups which are in contact are as complex as those which may exist between individuals and as difficult to classify under such simple terms as hostility or friendship, admiration or contempt. There are all sorts of ambivalences and also differential attitudes toward the other group's abilities along various lines. Thus one tribe may despise another for the freedom of behavior it allows its women while admiring it for the courage of its men. Again, two groups may live for generations under alternating conditions of hostility and alliance against a common enemy.

It is particularly important in this connection to note that overt hostility, i. e., actual warfare, seems to impose very little bar to culture borrowing. Each of the hostile groups may recognize in the other a foeman worthy of its steel and one from whom elements of culture can be taken with a gain rather than a loss in prestige. Conditions of warfare may even be more favorable to culture transfer than those of peace. Objects from the enemy group are obtained as loot and subsequently imitated in native manufacture, war practices are observed and copied, while the taking of captives with their subsequent incorporation into their captors' society through slavery, concubinage or adoption establishes optimum conditions for culture transfer.

Again, the fact that one group has conquered another by force of arms does not necessarily imply that the conquerors will despise the conquered. They may even recognize their superiority in everything but warfare and be eager to borrow from them, clinging only to those elements of their original culture which have become symbolic of their dominant position. Thus in barbarian conquests of civilized communities there seems to be a strong tendency for the barbarians to be absorbed after a few generations and for the resulting culture to lean heavily toward the original culture of the conquered.

Lastly, there is the factor of the attitude of the dominant group toward cultural borrowing on the part of the dominated one. If they see in such borrowing a threat to their own social position or actual power, they will do their best to prevent it and, if their domination is strong enough, may be successful with respect to certain elements. Thus there are many parts of the world in which the Whites have successfully prevented the diffusion of modern firearms to the native population, others in which they have successfully discouraged the diffusion of White clothing or furniture. In the first case, the practical considerations involved are obvious. The worse armed the natives, the poorer their chances of revolt. In the second case the consideration is purely one of prestige. It is felt that when the native assumes European costume he narrows the social gap which the dominant group wishes to retain intact.

If one can generalize at all about the results of attitudes in contact situations, it would seem that the conditions least favorable for culture transfer were those which arise when a conquered group remains hostile and unreconciled but without hope of successful revolt. Under such circumstances the hostility expresses itself in terms of passive resistance and uncoöperativeness. The old culture of the conquered becomes, for them, a symbol of their lost independence and its maintenance a technique for perpetuating their individuality. This condition results in a sort of blanket opposition to the acceptance of any new elements of culture beyond those necessary to continued existence. Examples of such attitudes are to be found in some of the Mexican and Central American Indian communities which have succeeded in remaining un-Europeanized after centuries of White domination. Such communities will often develop elaborate techniques for preventing the introduction of new things, going to the extent of formally disciplining any of their members who try to introduce innovations.

There are two other factors present in contact situations which may be of some importance in determining their outcome. These are the relative size of the groups involved and the relative complexity of the cultures involved. Unfortunately, we have not sufficient information on the results of either of these factors to make any generalizations safe. The assumption that, when a large and a small group are brought into contact, the small group will borrow more extensively than the large one cannot be either proved or disproved at present. However, there seems to be no intrinsic reason why such should be the case. A hundred individuals can learn a new thing as readily as one. That this assumption has been made so frequently is probably due to an unconscious confusion between physical and cultural factors. When a large and a small group fuse biologically, the physical type of the larger group will tend to be dominant in the resultant mixed group, but it does not follow that its culture type will tend to be dominant in the resultant mixed culture.

The problem of the relative complexity of the cultures involved as affecting the outcome of culture contacts is an extremely complicated one involving first of all a clearer understanding of what constitutes culture complexity than we have at present. All cultures are complex in certain of their aspects, simple in others. Thus White technology is complex, White family organization extraordinarily simple, by contrast with the corresponding complexes in most other societies. It is safe to say that in culture transfer complex elements do not uniformly tend to replace simple ones; in fact any very high degree of complexity probably increases the difficulty of individual learning and thus makes the transfer harder. The most that we can say at present is that more complex technologies, if they provide a better control of the environment, will tend to supersede simple ones. However, the significant thing in such cases is not the greater complexity but the greater efficiency. The modern Indian prefers the auto to the horse not because it is more complicated but because it covers more ground in less time.

Lastly, there is a factor which has been deliberately excluded from our consideration of contact and culture transfer because it is not universally present in contact situations. This is the factor of active, purposeful interference of the dominant group with the culture of the dominated one and with the normal processes of culture transfer. The results of such activities are most apparent under the particular type of contact which we have chosen to call acculturation and they will be discussed in the next chapter.

In conclusion, it may be said that the basic processes of culture change, those discussed in Chapter VIII, operate in the same way irrespective of whether there is contact with other groups or not. The importance of contact lies primarily in the stimulus to culture change given by the resulting modifications in the group's environment, awakened consciousness of its own culture and presence of new elements waiting to be taken over. These factors are operative in all cases of contact, but their influence is modified by the sort of elements which the particular contact makes available for borrowing and the attitudes toward each other, and consequently toward each other's cultures, which the groups develop as a result of their contact. Although other features of contact, such as the relative size of the two groups, the relative complexity of their cultures and the duration and closeness of the contact probably exert some influence on the outcome, our present information is too scanty to permit us to generalize on these points.

10

THE DISTINCTIVE ASPECTS OF ACCULTURATION

by Ralph Linton

Some readers will no doubt feel that we have come a long way around to get to acculturation but we have really been dealing with it throughout. "Acculturation comprehends those phenomena which result when groups of individuals having different cultures come into continuous first hand contact, with subsequent changes in the original culture patterns of either or both groups." Under this definition acculturation must include the general processes operative in all cases of group contact and culture change. The specific processes and factors which may be associated with situations of "continuous first hand contact" are superimposed upon this broad foundation and are comprehensible only when seen in relation to it.

Although the descriptive studies of acculturation now available are incomplete and unsatisfactory in certain respects, they indicate that there is no phenomenon present in *all* continuous first hand contact situations which is not also present, at least sporadically, in other sorts of contact. However, there are some phenomena which can occur only under conditions of continuous first hand contact and others which are much more frequent under these conditions than under any others. These are the things which the term acculturation ordinarily brings to mind. Most of the phenomena which have continuous first hand contact as a prerequisite can be grouped under one or the other of two heads: (1) those associated with directed culture change, and (2) those associated with social-cultural fusion. Among the phenomena which are very much more frequent under acculturation conditions than under any others, the most obvious are those associated with what ethnologists usually term nativistic movements.

The term "directed culture change" is not altogether satisfactory, but its alternative, "enforced culture change" is still less so. There is enforced culture change whenever modifications in a society's environment make modifications in its culture necessary to survival. Directed culture change will be taken to refer to those situations in which one of the groups in contact interferes actively and purposefully with the culture of the other. This interference may take the form of stimulating the acceptance of new culture elements, inhibiting the exercise of preëxisting culture patterns or, as seems to be most frequently the case, doing both simultaneously. Thus the Spaniards in Mexico compelled the Indians both to attend Christian rites and to give up their own pagan rites.

The term "social-cultural fusion" will be taken to refer to those situations in which two originally distinct cultures and societies fuse to produce a single homogeneous culture and society. The blending of Norman and Saxon elements to produce the later English would be a case in point. Genuine fusion always involves not only the disappearance of the two original cultures but also the amalgamation of the two original societies through the biological process of interbreeding. Practically all cases of the so-called assimilation of one group by another group could be more accurately classed as examples of fusion, since the culture of the assimilating group is usually modified by the introduction of elements from that of the assimilated.

The term nativistic movements has been used with almost as wide a variety of meanings as has acculturation. However, to the ethnologist it carries fairly definite connotations. He uses it to refer to cases in which a society not only glorifies past or passing phases of its culture but also makes a conscious attempt to reestablish them. Thus the ghost dance of the Plains Indians would be classed as a nativistic movement.

The processes of directed culture change can only operate in those contact situations in which there is dominance and submission. Nativistic movements also appear to be rather closely correlated with this condition. The processes of fusion, on the other hand, may operate under conditions of either dominance and submission or equality. The processes of directed culture change seem to be most active and their results most obvious during the early period of a continuous first hand contact. Nativistic movements apparently tend to appear somewhat later; at least we have no examples in which they have developed at the beginning of a contact period. In contrast, the processes of fusion usually begin at the moment of contact and continue over a long period, in some cases for many generations. Directed culture change may take place either when there is little or no tendency toward fusion or during the early stages of fusion. Conversely, fusion may take place with or without directed culture change. On the whole, there appears to be no constant or intrinsic relationship between the phenomena of these three orders, and it seems legitimate to discuss them separately.

Attitudes of dominance and submission are a very frequent, although not necessarily constant, accompaniment of continuous first hand contacts. Even when there are no factors of conquest or forceful domination, one of the contacting groups will usually recognize the superiority of the other, with a consequent eagerness to be socially and culturally identified with it. The attitudes of the Carrier toward their Bella Coola neighbors, described in one of the accompanying papers, would be a case in point. Needless to say, the admired group usually concurs in the judgment of its admirers. It would be difficult to find a contact situation in which each group considered the other superior, but those in which each group considers the other inferior are not uncommon. Such attitudes make it possible for the dominant group to interfere in the normal processes of culture transfer. Even when they cannot force the inferior group to accept elements from their own culture, they can exercise what might be termed high pressure salesmanship with respect to certain things. Conversely, elements of the inferior culture of which the superior group openly disapproves will lose their value in the eyes of the inferior group and will tend to be abandoned more readily. Thus European immigrants in this country will abandon their national costumes, or practices which are ridiculed by their American neighbors, long before they will give up other elements of culture toward which Americans are indifferent. However, as long as the pressures exerted by the dominant group are purely psychological there seems to be no serious interference with the normal processes of culture change. What would otherwise be the normal order of acceptance of borrowed elements may be interfered with, certain adoptions being given precedence over others because of the added prestige factors, but no element of culture will be eliminated until a satisfactory substitute has been found. In other words, there will be no point in the process of culture transfer where techniques for satisfying all the group's needs are not present.

All attempts to direct culture change are really efforts on the part of the dominant group to modify and control its own environment. The subject group is always an important part of this environment, with potentialities for furthering or impeding the aims of the dominators. Thus it is to the practical advantage of the dominant group to make the members of the inferior one perform certain services for it, or buy its goods, or stop making war on it or on other groups with which it wants to trade. It will also contribute to the peace of mind of members of the dominant group if the inferior one gives up practices which the dominant group finds repugnant. Thus the average European is genuinely shocked and made uncomfortable by the knowledge that the natives with whom he has to deal are cannibals, or practise human sacrifice, or allow their women complete sexual freedom before marriage. Sixteenth to nineteenth century Europeans were even profoundly disturbed by the fact that native groups did not enjoy the advantages of Christianity.

How far the dominant group will be able to change the culture of the subject one, and the methods which it can employ for the purpose will, of course, depend upon the conditions surrounding the contact. If the dominance is of a purely social and psychological sort, not backed by force of arms, the only method available is that of persuasion backed by prestige. This may often be fairly effective. If, on the other hand, the dominance is of a practical sort, the inferior group being subjects, cultural changes can be enforced by active punitive measures.

The degree to which culture change can be enforced by punitive measures offers an interesting problem for investigation. It is obvious that certain forms of behavior can be inhibited and others enforced. For example, human sacrifices or war can be stopped by punishing members of the subject group who participate in them. Similarly, men of the subject group can be compelled to wear a loin cloth or women of the subject group to cover their breasts in public. In time such culture changes will become integrated with the older patterns and will be accepted by the subject group as matters of course, arousing no emotional response. However, all elements of culture which do not correspond directly to behavior lie beyond the reach of punitive measures. An individual can be punished for what he does or does not do, but he cannot be punished for what he thinks or believes. A native group can be compelled to attend church regularly but not to accept Christian doctrine. The use of force naturally arouses resentment and an added consciousness of cultural differences with, in most cases, attachment of symbolic values to many elements of the old culture. While punitive measures can unquestionably accelerate the transfer of certain culture elements, they probably delay the acceptance of many others. An excellent example of forced acculturation and its limits is given by the results of the Spanish-San Ildefonso contact.

In all cases of directed culture change the dominant group singles out certain elements of the subject group's culture for attack and also selects certain elements of its own for imposition. This selection is, naturally, in line with the dominant group's interest and advantage. As long as the subject group is allowed to exercise judgment in acceptance, i. e., in the absence of punitive measures, the program is not likely to be put over as a whole but the changes will be accomplished without too severe derangements in the life of the receiving group. If, however, the dominant group is in a position to enforce its will, the results for the subjects are often catastrophic.

In a previous chapter we discussed the phenomenon of multiple functions of culture elements and complexes. We also pointed out that, under normal processes of culture change, no old element is discarded until a satisfactory substitute has been found for it in all its functional relationships. The ramifications of such relationships are often very wide and are not obvious to the people themselves, still less to even the best meaning administrator or missionary. Under culture change which is both directed and enforced, the normal process of retention of old elements until satisfactory substitutes have been found is inhibited. The result is a series of losses without adequate replacements. This leaves certain of the group's needs unsatisfied, produces derangements in all sorts of social and economic relationships and results in profound discomfort for the individuals involved.

In the contacts of Europeans with natives, the first steps in the enforcement of culture change are usually negative, i. e., certain patterns in the native culture are inhibited. War is normally the first point of attack, since it interferes with the security advantageous to trade and the exploitation of local resources. The dominant Whites ordinarily feel that if they can protect the subject group from attack they have rendered war unnecessary. However, it would be difficult to find a culture in which the functions of the war complex did not extend far beyond defense and aggression. Thus, to cite an extreme case, Mr. Alonzo Pond, who has worked with the Tuareg in the Sahara, told me that the elimination of warfare was leading to the extinction of that group. Marriage requires the payment of a heavy bride-price, its size being a matter of pride. In the old days the necessary wealth was acquired through raiding. Even then, few men could afford to marry before middle age, and until that time contented themselves with Negro slave concubines. Free women have numerous affairs but all children born out of wedlock are killed. With the end of raiding it has become almost impossible for men to acquire the wealth necessary for marriage and since the infanticide rule is still in full force the number of free Tuareg is rapidly dwindling. Again, war honors may be the basis of a society's whole system of rank and social control. This situation was present among the Comanche. While warfare was still going on, the exactions of individuals who stood at the top of the scale were kept in check by fear of reprisals when some man of lower rank rose above them. The end of warfare froze the system, depriving able young men of all chance of social advancement and making the old men arrogant.

Such unfortunate results follow the suppression of almost any trait complex. In Madagascar the European authorities have refused to recognize the existence of witchcraft and punish the killing of witches as murder. At the same time, they have not altered the native belief in witchcraft. The consequence has been to give the wizards carte blanche for extortion and to raise them to a dominant position in certain tribes. The general population feels helpless in the face of the new conditions. Again, the discouragement of polygyny in a society organized along those lines produces all sorts of maladjustments. In the first place, a certain number of women are prevented from getting husbands. Quite aside from personal difficulties of the sort dear to psychoanalysts, such women will be at a serious economic disadvantage. There will be no place for them in the existing economic system. Prostitution is almost certain to result with disturbing effects to the whole society. In the second place, even the women who do find husbands will suffer from the change. They will have been reared to expect companionship in the household and assistance in domestic and field labor. The necessary adaptive changes in the rest of the culture will work themselves out in time but meanwhile there will be confusion and discomfort for everyone.

Examples of this sort are familiar to all students of acculturation. The only point which needs to be emphasized is that the bad results of enforced culture change probably derive as much if not more from the blocking of preëxisting culture patterns as from the introduction of new ones. Since the processes of forceful introduction and inhibition usually go on simultaneously, it is often hard to evaluate their specific results in particular cases, but a reference to the processes of culture change in general will make the point clear. The only elements of culture which can be forced upon another society are certain forms of behavior. The attitudes and values of the dominant group cannot be transferred in this way. The receiving group can usually modify and re-interpret the new enforced behavior in terms of its own value system and finally assimilate it successfully. However, if there is no inhibition of preëxisting patterns, this process will not differ fundamentally from that which goes on in any situation of culture transfer. The assumption of the new element will merely result in a temporary duplication of function, a condition to which all cultures are highly tolerant. The inhibition of preëxisting patterns, on the other hand, inevitably leaves some of the society's needs unsatisfied, with resulting hardship.

For some unknown reason students of acculturation seem to have been prone to overlook the inhibitory processes connected with group contact and to interpret the difficulties which arise as due to the introduction of new elements. Thus many studies of acculturation in Africa stress the disastrous results of the introduction of a money economy. The use of a somewhat broader frame of reference would have shown that this, in itself, cannot be a primary cause of social disruption. Many African tribes at nearly the same level of cultural complexity as those described had a money economy long before Europeans arrived. The fact that they used ingots, hoes and cowries instead of pound notes and pennies does not alter the basic situation. The real cause of social disruption is probably to be sought in the inhibition of war, the culture technique by which men could formerly achieve prestige and economic independence, the inhibition of the old techniques of family control, due to the opportunities provided for young men to escape from parental authority by leaving the tribe, and the creation of new wants which can be met only by the possession of money. That the introduction of money is not, in itself, destructive to native social systems can be proved by the case of Madagascar. There money was first introduced in the late seventeenth century, fully accepted and integrated with the preëxisting culture with, apparently, no more derangement of the native social and economic system than resulted from the introduction of beads or soap.

This brings us at once to the fact that the inhibition of preexisting culture patterns, with resulting lack of satisfaction for certain of the society's needs, is not a phenomenon limited to situations of directed culture change. The changes in the group's environment which are an inevitable result of the appearance of a new group or of movement into new territory have very much the same effects. Thus in the case of many of the American Indian tribes the destruction of game which resulted from the presence of Whites and the curtailment of tribal range made many of the previous techniques for obtaining food and raw materials unworkable. Conversely, a group of European peasants who settle in an American city find themselves in a new environment in which many of the techniques they brought with them are no longer effective. The problems of cleanliness and sanitation, for example, assume quite new aspects in the absence of brooks and barnyards. Such situations have in common with those of directed culture change failure of the culture to meet the needs of the group with consequent discomfort and disorganization which will continue until new techniques for meeting these needs have been developed.

Cultures are the most flexible of adaptive mechanisms. No need of a society will go unsatisfied for long. If two societies which have been brought into contact survive the shock of the initial impact, the cultures of both will soon be altered in such a way as to make it possible for them to get along together. Directed culture change is simply an effort on the part of the dominant group to make the subject group do most of the adapting to the new conditions. However, there is always a point beyond which it is harder to make the subject group change its habits than it is for the members of the dominant group to change theirs. To take a concrete case. Europeans in the tropics have repeatedly tried to instill into natives habits of punctuality, since these would greatly expedite dealings with them. However, the Europeans have uniformly failed and have finally given it up as a bad job. Irritations resulting from the native lack of a time sense have been eliminated by the unconscious loss of this sense among the Whites who habitually work with them. This change in the local variants of European culture is obvious to all newcomers to the tropics and arouses irritation in them at first. However, after a few months under the palms they find themselves adopting the same attitude and wondering why they ever made such a fuss about a few hours' delay.

When two groups have achieved a working adjustment to each other and to their common natural environment, the external stimuli to further culture change are largely removed. The internal stimuli, those deriving from the discontents of individuals and their belief that conditions can be bettered, will, of course, continue in force. These will be strong enough to prevent cultural stagnation in either group and new elements developed in one will frequently be transferred to the other by the normal processes of borrowing. However, after successful mutual adaptation has been achieved, any extensive changes in the culture of either group will necessitate compensating changes in that of the other. For this reason the dominant group is usually content to let well enough alone, although it may still interfere in the culture of the subject one under certain circumstances. Its members may, for example, have altruistic feelings toward those they dominate and set about bettering their condition. Such directed culture change is usually carried on like any other, i. e., with a bland indifference to what the victims really want, and has the same results of derangement and discontent. Again the dominant group may perceive advantages to be enjoyed from some change in their subjects' habits—if, for example, they could be persuaded to wear hats or to work in factories. Lastly, the dominant group may feel that the existence of the subject group constitutes a threat to it and, if it cannot eliminate it, may make a conscious effort to assimilate it. To the last category belong the various attempts to Americanize immigrant groups and the violent attempts which have been made from time to time in Europe to destroy the distinctive cultures and languages of national minorities. However, all such cases are comparatively rare. Directed culture change is essentially a phenomenon of initial contact, becoming less strongly operative as the duration of the contact lengthens.

Let us turn now to the second group of phenomena which can be present only under conditions of continuous first hand contact; those of social-cultural fusion. It must be stressed at the outset that fusion is not a constant or necessary accompaniment of such contacts. It is merely impossible in their absence. It seems that when two societies and cultures have reached a working adaptation to each other, they may exist side by side for many generations without any discernible tendency to fuse. This condition was observable in many parts of Europe before the recent rise of militant nationalism. For example, in Russia there were Swedish and German groups which had been there since the early eighteenth century living on amicable terms with their Russian neighbors but preserving their own language and customs. Such conditions may also exist among uncivilized peoples. In Madagascar the Southern Sakalava are really a confederacy of three tribes all of whom recognize the same king. One of these tribes, to use the picturesque native phrase, attends to the affairs of the sea, another to the affairs of the fields and the third to the affairs of the forest. The three groups exchange products and services and members of different tribes may even live in the same village. At the same time, each tribe has its own distinctive customs. The members of other tribes know these and even regulate their behavior by them when it is courteous to do so. For example, when visiting the village of another tribe they will keep its tabus. However, they have no desire to take over such customs. Intermarriage, although not formally prohibited, is extremely rare in practice. Even when it does happen it does not break down the tribal lines, since wife and child automatically follow the customs of the husband's group.

In the cases just cited the only bars to fusion seem to be psychological ones. We know that in individuals there are fundamental attitudes of security or insecurity which are deeply rooted in the personality and which influence behavior under a wide variety of circumstances. Similarly, there seem to be societies which are psychologically secure. Each of the groups involved in the long established contact situations just mentioned is so firmly convinced of its own superiority that it does not even need to reinforce this attitude by arrogant behavior. It simply never occurs to the members of such a group to envy the members of other groups or to want to be like them. It might be questioned whether such cases are not excluded from the field of acculturation study by the second half of our definition: "contact . . . with consequent changes in the original culture patterns of either or both groups." However, there is always some exchange of culture going on under these conditions, minor elements passing from one group to the other. For example, in the Madagascar tribes just mentioned, the sea group has taken over the custom of ear-marking cattle from the agricultural group so recently that its origin is still clearly remembered. Quite characteristically, they have borrowed the technique, not the patterns, of ear-marking, developing an entirely new set of patterns based on various shapes of fish tails. Such transfers do no more to bring about the fusion of the two groups than does our own custom of copying French styles in women's wear. The borrowed elements are modified and re-interpreted to fit their new context, while new elements appear from time to time within the cultures themselves, maintaining the distinction.

Although the circumstances under which fusion may take place are quite diverse, the actual processes of fusion are simple enough and exhibit considerable uniformity in all cases. Culture fusion begins with an exchange of elements. The factors of utility, compatibility and prestige involved in such transfers are the same as those operative in all cases of culture borrowing. So are the processes of integration into the receiving culture. The only difference is that the exchange of elements is continued long after a working adaptation of the cultures and societies involved has been reached. The stimulus to such continued borrowing seems to be primarily the desire of the group which feels itself socially inferior to become completely identified with the superior one.

It is extremely rare to find a case of fusion in which both sides have borrowed equally. The differential seems to be controlled primarily by two sets of factors, those of prestige and those of the degree of adaptation to the local environment of the two cultures involved. These factors are, of course, in constant interaction. It seems safe to say that, when both cultures represent successful adaptations to the environment, borrowing will be heavier on the side of the socially inferior group. This is in line with their greater desire for identification with the other group. However, when the culture of the socially superior group is not well adapted to environmental conditions, its members may do the bulk of the borrowing. What happens when a group of fighting nomads conquers and settles among a civilized urban people would be a case in point. This situation has occurred repeatedly in the Old World and has always resulted in the originally nomadic aristocracy taking over most of the culture of the conquered, reserving only those elements of their own culture which had become symbols of status. When the socially superior group also has the culture which is best adapted to the local conditions, the one-sidedness of the borrowing reaches a maximum. This condition is well illustrated by European immigrant groups in America. Most of these groups have, in the process of their absorption, taken over the preëxisting American culture almost as a whole, giving only a few minor elements of culture in return.

In most cases of fusion the culture exchange has not been so one-sided or the resulting culture so readily traceable to a single source. Due to the modification of borrowed elements and the adjustment of other parts of each culture to them, the end product of culture fusion resembles a chemical rather than a mechanical mixture. The resulting culture will not be a simple aggregation of elements all of which can be traced to one or the other of the parent cultures, but a new thing many of whose patterns cannot be directly referred to either.

The processes of social fusion also seem to follow a course which is basically uniform. Neither society absorbs the other as a unit. Instead, the fusion is accomplished by the progressive transfer of individuals from one group to the other. Under conditions of social inferiority and superiority, which seem to be accompaniments of nearly all cases of fusion, this transfer will be primarily from the inferior to the superior group. Persons in the inferior society assume the culture patterns of the superior one, associate with its members to the degree which these will permit, and, if all goes well, are finally accepted into it. This process is especially clear in the case of immigrant groups in America. It can be somewhat accelerated or retarded by the facility of spacial movements which the current conditions afford. Thus as long as an individual has to live with members of his original society his connection with it is not likely to be forgotten by either side. If he can move away and settle in a community composed of members of the superior group who do not know of his original association with the inferior one, his passage from one side of the line to the other will be greatly facilitated. An excellent example of this can be seen in the Negro phenomenon of "passing." A person with Negro blood, no matter how Caucasic in appearance or how perfectly familiar with White culture patterns, will not be accepted socially by Whites as long as he lives with a Negro community. However, he probably will be accepted in communities where his origin is not known.

Where there is a strong desire on the part of members of an inferior group to become fused with those of a superior one, this individual by individual transfer is, in itself, a factor which accelerates the process of absorption. The more energetic and able members of the inferior group, those who might become leaders in its separate life, devote their efforts not to attaining status within it but to getting out of it. The fact that repudiation of the inferior group's culture becomes a technique for the achievement of individual success changes the attitude of the whole group toward it and hastens its elimination. In this connection it might be mentioned that certain individuals in the socially inferior group may not desire to be assimilated and may emphasize the distinctive features of their own culture on that account. These are, with few exceptions, persons who enjoy a degree of prestige or privilege in their original society which they would find it hard to equal in the new society. For example, in some of the Middle Western Scandinavian communities there are certain families which have fought Americanization. These families were drawn from the Scandinavian nobility, and as a consequence received a degree of respect from their un-Americanized neighbors which they could not expect from Americans.

It was pointed out in a previous chapter that factors of racial difference appear to be of little importance relative to the normal processes of culture transfer. However, they become of great importance in connection with fusion. If we consider this as a biological phenomenon race is still unimportant. Any two groups can hybridize successfully and we know that such mixture takes place whenever two groups are brought into contact. Even the most elaborate social regulations have never been able to prevent this. The importance of race in fusion situations lies in the fact that obvious physical differences between groups can be used as criteria for the assignment of social status. Most contact situations entail attitudes of superiority and inferiority between the groups involved. Even in the absence of practical advantages from membership in the superior group there are prestige advantages which its members rarely desire to share. The desire of members of the inferior group to get into the superior one is usually met by an equally strong desire on the part of those already there to keep them out. As long as the differences between the two groups are purely cultural this presents practical difficulties. Members of the inferior group cannot be distinguished from members of the superior one once they have assumed its language and habits. The ease with which, here in the United States, persons of north European ancestry can transfer from immigrant to American society is a case in point. Attitudes of superiority and inferiority are present, as anyone who has lived in the northwestern United States can testify, but there is no way of telling the children of Scandinavian immigrants from old Americans. It is interesting to conjecture whether the more equalitarian attitudes of Americans toward these particular immigrants may not be a rationalization after the fact.

Where there are well-marked differences in physical type between the superior and inferior groups, it becomes easy to exclude members of the inferior group from the superior society. In spite of differences in the theoretical attitudes of various European groups toward natives, the color line is a fact in most contact situations. Easily recognizable racial differences delay fusion although it is highly questionable whether they are, in themselves, sufficient to prevent it. If the inferior group desires to be absorbed and holds to its wish, it probably is impossible to prevent fusion from taking place sooner or later. Even if the women of the superior group repulse all advances from men of the inferior one, a situation commoner in theory than in practice, the men of the superior group will rarely abstain from taking willing concubines. There is thus a steady transfer of blood from one group to the other with a consequent blurring of the original racial lines. When the two groups can no longer be distinguished physically, no amount of artificial regulation can prevent their social fusion.

Fusion may be either a slow or a rapid process, but it seems to be the ultimate outcome of any contact situation in which one or both groups wish to fuse. As we have already seen, there may be situations in which this attitude is not present. Both of the groups involved may be convinced of their own superiority so that the resistance to fusion is mutual and therefore more than doubly effective. Under such conditions the offspring of mixed unions will be looked down upon by both and, instead of bringing the groups closer together, will form a new caste at the bottom of the social order. The place of Eurasians in certain Far Eastern communities is a good illustration of this. It might be mentioned that such attitudes do not necessarily reflect the actual current situation of dominance and submission. A conquered group may still hold itself superior to its conquerors and refuse to cross with them legitimately or to take over more of their culture than the minimum required for successful adaptation to the new conditions. The Fox Indians, described in one of the accompanying papers, provide a good example of this attitude. Although actually dominated by the surrounding Whites and at present unable to exist without economic assistance from them, they still consider themselves superior, borrow White culture selectively and have not the slightest desire to be absorbed into White society.

There may also be changes in the attitudes of both groups toward fusion at different points in the contact continuum. Social lines may be drawn more or less rigidly as time goes on. Thus the eighteenth century Europeans seem to have been more receptive to elements of Oriental culture and more willing to accord social equality to members of Oriental groups than their descendants are today. Conversely, the general American attitude toward Indians has become more receptive during the same period. Interest in Indian arts and crafts has developed, and it has become easy for any Indian with outstanding abilities to achieve social acceptance in the average White urban community. The factors contributing to these changes in attitudes seem to be highly complex and are probably never exactly the same in any two cases.

There is one series of attitude changes which has repeated itself in so many contact situations that it might be said to constitute a recognizable pattern. This series begins with attitudes of respect and admiration on the part of the dominated group, coupled with a sincere desire to acquire the culture of the dominant one and an expectation of finally being fused with it. As the contact continues, these initial attitudes change to a more critical appraisal of the culture of the dominant group and increasing hostility toward it. In practically all cases this change in attitude is associated with individual disappointments and irritations resulting from rebuffs by members of the dominant group. It is significant to note that critical and hostile attitudes are rarely assumed by any large proportion of the inferior group as long as fusion is recognizably in progress. If the members of the inferior group know that there is a genuine possibility for the ultimate removal of their social disabilities, they will put up with all sorts of hardships and even injustices, considering them transitory phenomena. They may lose some of their respect for the dominant group but none of their eagerness to become a part of it. It is only with loss of the hope of fusion, which presents itself to the individual in terms of full social acceptance and equal opportunity, that the difficulties imposed upon the inferior group by the contact situation come strongly to the fore.

Such states of disappointment and of disillusionment with the new order may very well be the starting points for nativistic movements. We have defined such movements as a glorification of past or passing phases of culture with a conscious attempt to reëstablish them. Nativistic movements are thus characterized by two sets of phenomena which really are of different orders. The glorification of past or passing phases of culture is an almost universal accompaniment of situations of culture change. It is in no way related to culture contact *per se*. Even in the most progressive and forward-looking community, changes in culture produce some individual discomforts. At least some members of the group will develop nostalgic attitudes toward a past which appears rosy in the light of present difficulties. The more intense and widespread the discomfort due to change, the more widespread these attitudes are likely to be. When culture change is complicated by the presence of another group and by feelings of inferiority toward it, glorification of the old culture provides a convenient compensatory mechanism. A society which can find nothing to plume itself on in the present can bolster its self-respect by contemplating the real or imaginary glories of its past. It may even attempt to revive certain aspects of its past culture as a way of emphasizing these attitudes. Such revivals are rigidly circumscribed by the nature of the existing culture. They are never of a far reaching sort and they do not have to be. A revival of native literature or peasant art is as effective as a symbol and a reminder of the past as a reversion to an earlier economic system would be and at the same time vastly more convenient.

An interesting variant of this tendency is observable in many American groups of immigrant origin. Even after such groups have accepted American culture practically *in toto* and achieved a satisfactory economic status within the American community they may feel and be made to feel socially inferior because of their origin. As long as they continue as a distinct community this origin will not be forgotten by their neighbors. Their response to the attitudes of the Old Americans is in line with the familiar advertising slogan to play up the weakest point of your product. They glorify what they cannot conceal, collecting national antiques, celebrating national holidays with a revival of costumes and dances for the occasion, etc. Needless to say, such revivals are always of a very superficial sort. When the celebration is over the participants put on their store clothes and drive home in their Fords.

The phenomena just discussed can be legitimately termed nativistic movements under our definition but it is obvious that they differ considerably from such a phenomenon as the Ghost Dance. They lack the vigor of the latter and include a much larger element of realism. Nativistic movements of the first sort may arise in any kind of contact situation. It even seems safe to assume, although I have been unable to find an example, that they might arise in a dominant group which felt its existence threatened by the processes of fusion. On the other hand, violent and explosive nativistic movements seem to require a special combination of circumstances—subjection to another group, economic hardship, and loss of hope of bettering conditions by practical means. Apparently no one of these conditions is enough to produce such movements in the absence of the others nor does the whole series always produce them.

All the violent nativistic movements which have been studied include a large element of supernaturalism. How strong the stimuli have to be before such movements take shape is probably correlated to a considerable extent with the group's attitudes toward the supernatural and the strength of their belief in its ability to alter conditions in the material world. In such movements the revival of past phases of culture is not an end in itself but a magical technique. In other words, the group does not attempt to return to its earlier culture because it feels that culture to be superior under current conditions. It does so in the hope of enlisting supernatural aid to change the current conditions. At the basis of all such movements lies a quite irrational system of associations. Since the people were happy and contented in the old days when they had a particular culture in a particular environment, it is felt that a return to the culture will, in some way, reëstablish the total original configuration. At the same time, it is significant that such movements always retain enough touch with reality not to imply a complete return to the earlier conditions. Those elements of the current culture which are obviously superior to their earlier equivalents will be miraculously preserved. Thus in the Ghost Dance the millennium was to leave the Indians still in possession of rifles and metal cooking pots and, in some versions, of the White men's houses and stock.

No group has ever attempted to revive its total culture as it existed at any given point in the past. The revivals are selective and constitute symbols which are manipulated to produce certain results. In violent nativistic movements this manipulation is along magical lines and is foredoomed to failure. In the quieter and more normal type of nativistic movement the manipulations rely for their effect upon psychological factors which are operative in all groups. As a result, such movements very often succeed not in their avowed purpose of revivifying a dead culture but in their actual purpose of bolstering the ego of the group in the face of conditions of inferiority.

In conclusion it may be said that the only constant phenomenon in situations of continuous first hand contact, i. e., acculturation under our definition, is the establishment, in the two cultures involved, of mutual modifications and adaptations which will enable the two groups to live together. Even this is not absolutely constant, for one of the groups may not succeed in making such adaptations and become extinct in consequence. However, if both groups survive, the adaptations will be made. It also seems that the more stable the conditions of contact and environment which the two groups have to adapt to, the more readily the adaptations can be made. One of the most tragic features of our own dealings with the American Indians has been the constant changes in policy which, together with tribal removals, have rendered the adaptations which they successively developed successively unworkable. Lastly, everything indicates that the ultimate end of situations of close and continuous first hand contact is the amalgamation of the societies and cultures involved, although this conclusion may be postponed almost indefinitely if there is opposition to it on both sides.

Whether acculturation offers a legitimate field for independent study the reader must judge for himself. At least it should have been made clear that the phenomena associated with culture change, culture transfer and group contact are present here in their most complex form and with the largest possible number of variables operative. These phenomena are so poorly understood at present and there is such a lack of actual factual material by which conclusions can be checked that any statements made about them must be considered tentative and valid only in the light of our present very limited information. The most that can be said is that the conclusions which have been presented appear to check with the facts presented in the accompanying papers and also in other studies of contact situations.

INDEX

(1)